MIGHTY MARVEL VALUE STAMPS NO.'s 33 THRU 40

MIGHTY MARVEL VALUE STAMPS NO.'s 4

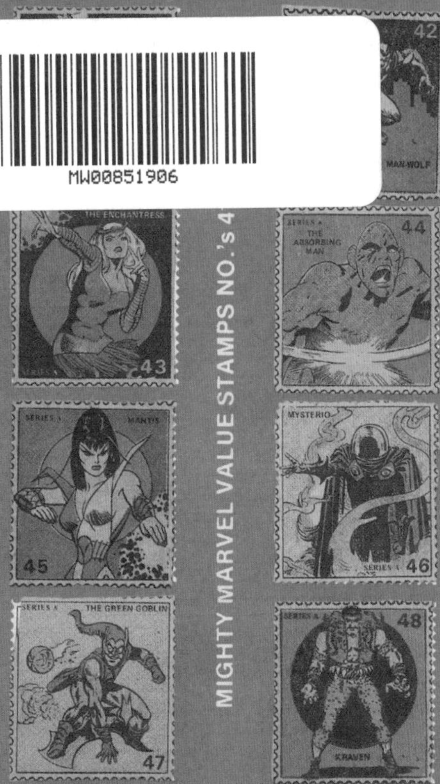

MIGHTY MARVEL VALUE STAMPS NO.'s 49 THRU 56

MIGHTY MARVEL VALUE STAMPS NO.'s 57 THRU 64

MIGHTY MARVEL VALUE STAMPS NO.'s 65 THRU 72

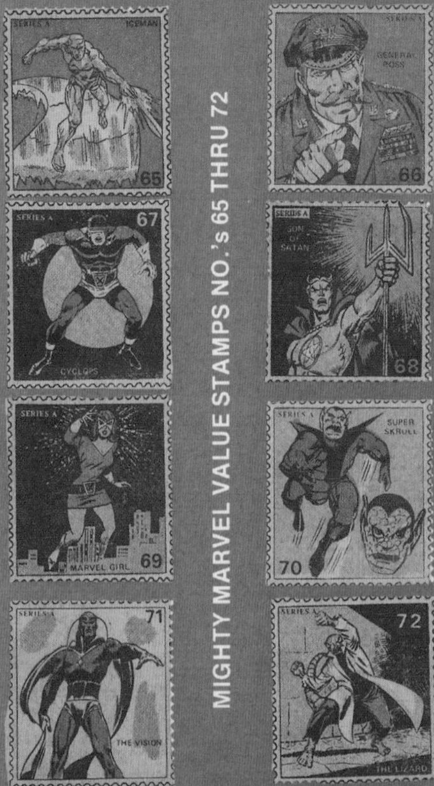

MIGHTY MARVEL VALUE STAMPS NO.'s 73 THRU 80

MIGHTY MARVEL VALUE STAMPS NO.'s 81 THRU 88

MIGHTY MARVEL VALUE STAMPS NO.'s 89 THRU 96

MARVEL

VALUE STAMPS

A VISUAL HISTORY

BY ROY THOMAS

ABRAMS COMICARTS • NEW YORK

THIS IS IT, TRUE BELIEVER!

YOUR MIGHTY

MARVEL VALUE STAMP

BOOK

THIS IS
STAMPBOOK
----------120697

THIS IS IT,
TRUE BELIEVER!

SERIES B

DEDICATED TO THE MEMORY OF STAN LEE—WHO STAMPED HIS AND MARVEL'S LIKENESS ON TWO HEMISPHERES.
—ROY THOMAS

Editor: Charles Kochman
Assistant Editor: Jessica Gotz
Designers: Kay Petronio and John Passineau
Managing Editors: Marie Oishi and Mary O'Mara
Production Manager: Alison Gervais

Library of Congress Control Number: 2020931621
ISBN 978-1-4197-4344-3

Text by Roy Thomas

Captions copiously compiled by Charles Kochman

Cover art by Alex Ross (July 2019)

Marvel Value Stamps Series A (#120697) and Series B booklets (including front and back endpaper images) from the collection of Charles Kochman.

The Mighty World of Marvel and *Spider-Man Comics Weekly* British coupon campaigns courtesy of Robert Menzies and Gerry Turnbull.

Spider-Man photo poster and mailing envelope and *The Mighty World of Marvel* promotional poster courtesy of Tellshiar.

Mighty Marvel Comic Convention program and photo courtesy of Roy Thomas.

All other images provided by Marvel.

Art for the MVS was primarily selected by John Romita Sr., Marie Severin, and Tony Mortellaro, with Severin doing the lion's share of the production work.

Initial research compiled by Don Rosa in *Amazing Heroes* no. 113 (March 15, 1987).

Special thanks to: Joseph Hochstein, Sven Larson, John Nee, Brian Overton, Sarah Singer, Jeremy West, and Jeff Youngquist at Marvel Comics.

Additional thanks to John Cimino for his help on this project; Andrew Smith for persistence, percipience, and patience; Josh Johnson for design assistance; Fredrik Malmberg and Jay Zetterberg at Cabinet Entertainment and Nick Barrucci for additional permissions; Robert Menzies for information and scans of *The Mighty World of Marvel* and *Spider-Man Comics Weekly* British coupon campaigns, and Gerry Turnbull for scans of issue no. 6; Mark Evanier for double-checking the captions and for his ongoing support; Alex Ross for creating a striking cover design and new artwork for the central image of Spider-Man; Michael Kochman, whose comics were unknowingly defaced by his brother so he could complete his stamp collection and one day write these captions and edit this book; and to Jackie and Jimmy DeFillippo, who were there at the beginning.

Printed and bound in China

10 9 8 7 6 5 4 3 2 1

ABRAMS The Art of Books
195 Broadway, New York, NY 10007
abramsbooks.com

YOUR MIGHTY

MARVEL VALUE STAMPS BOOK

INCLUDES

INTRODUCTION

Putting the Pieces Together by Roy Thomas

***THE MIGHTY WORLD OF MARVEL* BRITISH COUPON CAMPAIGN** (1972)

MARVEL VALUE STAMP BOOK SERIES A (1974)

Stamp Book

Marvel Value Stamps 1–100

Artwork Sources

MARVEL VALUE STAMP BOOK SERIES B (1975)

Stamp Book

Marvel Value Stamps 1–100 (10 puzzle pages)

Artwork Sources

PLAUDITS, PRONOUNCEMENTS, AND JUST PLAIN PLUGS – PONTIFICALLY PRESENTED!

STAN LEE'S SOAPBOX

This one's for you older Marvelites, for the True Believers who've been with us lo these many years. Remember how we used to rap about the fact that so many people thought comic-books were just for kids? And remember how I'd clue you in to Marvel's greatest crusade — to your Bullpen's vow to change that image — to give the comic-book its rightful place within the media — to have it fully accepted as one of the most powerful, most viable forms of communication the world has ever known? Remember how we'd pledge never to rest till the intellectual community bestowed upon the comic-book all the attention and the recognition it has so rightfully earned?

Well, I guess you know what I'm leading up to. We may not yet be all the way home, but we're mighty close. Never before have so many newspapermen, disc jockeys, college students, musicians, sports figures, and other assorted full-grown adult types been so fanatically tuned-in to the wondrous world of Marvel! Never before have we received such massive mountains of mail from so many campuses throughout the free world! In fact, within the past few months alone, yours truly just finished a whirlwind college lecture tour, speaking at Iowa State, Bennington College, Allegheny, Montana State, the University of Delaware, and Northwestern U., just to name a few. Never have I seen more enthusiasm, more excitement, or more ebullient interest — interest in the stories, the illustrations, the conception — everything in fact that has to do with the production and the philosophy of your friendly neighborhood Marvel mags!

So, on behalf of your breathless, blushin' Bullpen, let me thank each and every one of you for helping us make a dream come true. Yea verily, you and we together have transformed yesterday's feckless little "funny books" into one of today's most widely-hailed art forms — and Marvel loves ya for it!

Excelsior!

Stan

P.S. Please spare our poor little overworked secretary. If there's any campus I may have bypassed, send your lecture request directly to American Program Bureau, 850 Boylston St., Chestnut Hill, Boston, Mass. 02167. They just love to open mail!

S.L.

ITEM! All right, sahib — it's *teaser time!* See if you can guess just *what* this thing is, smack dab in the middle of our bombastic Bulletin Page (besides a picture of the ever-incredible *Hulk*, that is) — and *why* we stuck it there, anyhow!

Sorry, we can't let the cat (or ol' Greenskin) out of the bag till *next issue* — but at that time, we promise you a zingier bargain than you ever saw on "Let's Make a Deal"! And while you're waiting, why not send us your guesses as to what it is! Who knows? Even if you don't figure out quite what we're planning to lay on you come Christmastime, you're just liable to give us some far-out new ideas we never thought of!

ITEM! Oh, and lest we forget: Here's this month's immortal message about an upcoming epochal event in one of our mags. It's in our very own *Spider-Man Code*, and it goes like this:

RQF ILFBSHFXY UJDTUF
EFIRQ SO LIGXSVW — VSHDJP
BSSJ DJ RQF QUXW!

By the way, in case you're wondering why we've been using Spidey Code for the past few months, it's because that's the only one revealed to date in the pages of our special FOOM Magazine, which is sent out as an extra bonus to everybody who joins the wildest, way-outest fan club in comics history. But, more codes are coming up fast, 'cause even as we speak, jaunty JIM STERANKO is putting the finishing touches on our *fourth* fabulous issue.

If you're not yet a member of FOOM — why fool yourself? You're gonna join up sooner or later anyway, once the word gets back to you on what you're missing! Why not make it *sooner* — 'cause the way our ranks are filling up, there sure aren't gonna be any back issues of FOOM Magazine available for long! A word to the wise . . . !

ITEM! Starting next month: A *full page* of Bullpen Bulletins — *plus* a brand-new Bullpen Bonus Page, with nutty items about our giant 75¢ titles, eye-catching new FOOM ads and items — and just about anything else that catches our fancy! 'Nuff said!

MIGHTY MARVEL CHECKLIST
Now On Sale!

MONSTERS UNLEASHED #4: The Frankenstein Monster! Warrior of Mars! Plus — the Demon That Stalked Slaughter Mansion! Only 75¢!

VAMPIRE TALES #3: Morbius lives again! Satana, the Devil's Daughter, by Conway and Maroto! Just 75¢!

Plus these full-color classics:

FANTASTIC FOUR #143 (You demanded it — we did it! Dr. Doom strikes again!) — **SPIDER-MAN #129** (Meet the Jackal — and the deadly Punisher!) — **THOR #220** — **AVENGERS #120** (The return of Zodiac—the Sinister Team Supreme!) — **TOMB OF DRACULA #17** — **INCREDIBLE HULK #172** (And Canst Thou Slay — the Juggernaut?) — **CAPTAIN AMERICA & THE FALCON #170** — **POWER MAN #17** (Luke Cage — superhero for hire!) — **MAN-THING #2** — **IRON MAN #66** (Guest-starring the mighty Thor!) — **CONAN THE BARBARIAN #35** — **WEREWOLF BY NIGHT #14** — **MARVEL TEAM-UP #18** (Spidey and — wouldja believe — Mr. Fantastic!) — **SPECIAL MARVEL EDITION #17** (Shang-Chi, Master of Kung Fu! Marvel's newest sensation!) — **GHOST RIDER #4** ("Death Stalks the Demolition Derby!") — **THE DEFENDERS #12**—**MARVEL SPOTLIGHT #14** (The Son of Satan, as you've never seen him before!) — **STRANGE TALES #172** — **ASTONISHING TALES #22** ("It — the Colossus Lives Again!").

INTRODUCTION
BY ROY THOMAS

PUTTING THE PIECES TOGETHER

When I was growing up, and even when I was a young adult, business firms were always trying to get people to pull out a sharp pair of scissors and *cut up* things. Sometimes we were supposed to clip out a coupon or a picture and bring it into a store for a "fabulous free gift" (which may have been free, but was never fabulous) . . . mostly it was just a shill, of course, to lure us onto premises where we'd be tempted to spend money that otherwise we'd probably never have *considered* spending in that particular establishment.

In the 1940s, while I was enjoying my first decade on this planet, kids were always being tempted with premiums ballyhooed by excited-sounding announcers on the radio who told us that if we mailed in several box tops cut or torn from such-and-such breakfast cereal, plus maybe a dime for "postage and handling" (whatever that meant), we would soon be the proud owners of the latest Captain Midnight Decoder Ring (which wasn't a *real* ring, but a circular code chart). Or maybe the prize *was* an actual ring: I sent away for one once that was supposed to change colors to reveal what the weather was going to be, but all it ever did was turn green and stay that way, as if predicting that it was going to rain forever. Or maybe the proffered goodie was a whistle, or one or more little wooden or (later on) plastic figurines, or a little tin badge, or something made of cardboard that you folded and it was supposed to fly, or a reduced-size comic book, or . . . hell, it might've been just about anything.

And we kids bought them—or, to be more precise, we badgered our harassed parents into cutting the tops off those cereal boxes and mailing them in and then explaining to us every day why the promised prize hadn't come in the mail yet.

Adults weren't immune, either—not even to lures aimed specifically at them rather than at their offspring. The most famous ploy intended for them was the "S&H Green Stamps," which were very popular in the United States starting in the 1930s and for roughly the next half century. People would receive the tinted stamps along with their change when they bought something at a supermarket or gas station; when you'd collected enough of them to give Seabiscuit a hernia, plus pasted them in a little book, they could be "redeemed" (their term) for products in an approved S&H Green Stamp Catalog. The Green Stamps spawned a lot of imitators, just like Captain Midnight's Decoder Ring did.

Naturally, it was only a matter of time before comic books got into the act.

The first company to do so, at least that a guy like me born in 1940 could notice, was

OPPOSITE The unnumbered Hulk stamp appeared on Marvel Bullpen Bulletin pages in comics dated February 1974 and differs from the subsequently released Hulk stamp no. 2. The illustration is by John Buscema and Frank Giacoia, adapted from a four-page glossy insert included with copies of *Fantastic Four* no. 128 (November 1972).

Fawcett Publications. Back in 1942 (before I could read, of course), they briefly printed two "Comix Cards" on the back cover of each issue of their bestselling title *Captain Marvel Adventures,* depicting characters such as the "Shazam!"-spouting Captain and his family (Mary Marvel and Captain Marvel Jr.), fellow heroes Spy Smasher and Bulletman, and bad guys Doctor Sivana and Captain Nazi. But that bonus feature didn't last long. Comix Cards reappeared in 1947 and '48 inside various Fawcett comics, spouting images of the still-popular Captain Marvel, deceased movie cowboy Tom Mix, Nyoka the Jungle Girl, and sappy teenagers Ozzie and Babs, each figure rendered with dotted lines bordering the art—a clear invitation for a kid to cut the picture out and stick it to a notebook or wall or whatever. But there wasn't anything you could "redeem" with them if and when you'd collected a whole set, so I was never tempted to mutilate any of my Fawcett comics. I just considered the artwork mini-pinups.

Besides, these Comix Cards weren't called "stamps," and weren't designed to resemble them either.

Fast-forward two and a half decades to 1973, when I was pushing thirty-three . . . along came Marvel Value Stamps, courtesy of my boss and mentor, Stan Lee (until the previous year the main editor and writer of Marvel Comics and now its publisher). Those stamps were his baby from start to finish—and he wasn't about to let anyone stand in the way of their becoming the Next Big Thing inside the cover of a Marvel mag.

Only—that said—I now have to back up nearly a year, because what I don't recall knowing that day in 1973 when he called me into his office was that Marvel Value Stamps were an idea he had already tried out—in another country!

You see, in the autumn of 1972, Stan had decreed that henceforth Marvel was going to publish its own special *weekly* comics for the British market and would produce the (mostly reprint, black-and-white) titles in our New York City offices, beginning with a comic called *The Mighty World of Marvel*. As his new editor-in-chief, I already had my hands full with the several dozen magazines we were putting together each month for the US audience, so we were both happy for me to stay as uninvolved with the new "Marvel UK" line as possible. Instead they were produced by a new division of the company, set off in its own little office down the hall, under one-time Marvel production manager Sol Brodsky, who had recently returned to Marvel after a solo venture hadn't quite panned out. Sol and I got along great—but we were always careful not to tread on each other's spider-webbed toes.

As a result, I'm not sure I ever even *heard* of this predecessor of Marvel Value Stamps—for the record, they were referred to as "coupons" in the UK periodicals themselves—until fairly recently, when a regular correspondent of mine, Robert Menzies of Glasgow, Scotland, brought them to my attention.

So, before we return to the story of the Marvel Value Stamps proper, let's have Robert relate the story of their United Kingdom precursors in his own words:

With the launch of *The Mighty World of Marvel* no. 1 (cover-dated October 7, 1972), Marvel attempted to gain a foothold in the crowded British comics marketplace. It was a concerted effort: Not only did they offer free gifts of T-shirt transfers and stickers with the first three issues, they combined this with a poster reward scheme that required the collection of eight coupons (i.e., stamps), out of a possible ten. In order, here are the ten coupons:

Unlike the Marvel Value Stamps that came out in the US two years later, these stamps were given dedicated pages, usually a double-page spread. The prize was initially a mystery (note that the characters on the cover of *MWoM* no. 1 promote a "mystery surprise"), with clues given until issue no. 6, when it was revealed to be a poster. Then, in issue no. 7, readers were asked to unscramble three nonsense words to discover a clue about the poster's content: "ISX EURSP EEHSOR," which readers discovered in issue no. 8 meant "SIX SUPER HEROES!"

At this point, *The Mighty World of Marvel* was only a reprint title, and it had just three strips—*Hulk*, *Spider-Man*, and the *Fantastic Four*, which were all being reprinted from their first appearances in the early 1960s—therefore the stamp images were severely restricted in number and subject (they avoided villains). So the coupons also featured alter egos, something the Marvel Value Stamps never needed to.

These promo pages were created in the New York offices, and Stan took a close interest in the British experiment, writing exclusive content in the form of a "Special Message from Stan Lee" column. Sometimes Stan directly referenced the giveaway reward, calling the poster a "sensational MYSTERY SURPRISE" in issue no. 1, "a merry Mystery Gift" in no. 5 (November 4, 1972), and a "glitzy gift" in no. 9 (December 2, 1972). The poster, like the cover to issue no. 1, was penciled by John Buscema and is now quite rare (occasionally they show up for sale or at auction and cause some animated bidding). At the time, this poster was identified as the work of John Buscema and inked by Joe Sinnott and Mike Esposito. But several authorities on Marvel comics art believe Sinnott wasn't involved and Buscema's work on this poster was finished by the team of Frank Giacoia and Mike Esposito, who inked many Marvel comics and covers during this time period.

The first published reader letter appeared in *MWoM* no. 5 (November 4, 1972), and the writer, Christopher Thompson, of Middlesex, commented that he and his friends had "decided to collect all the numbered coupons in the hope that we can soon receive one of your surprise gifts." A high proportion of *MWoM* back issues sold on eBay are missing the stamps, similar to Marvel comics in the US. (There isn't much on the letters pages about the coupon campaign, except just about everyone who did mention it was cutting them out.)

MWoM's coupon campaign must have been popular, as it was repeated early the next year when Spider-Man was given his own weekly comic in

Britain. The third issue of *Spider-Man Comics Weekly* (March 3, 1973) launched another eight-coupon cut-and-paste "surprise gift" campaign, culminating in an 18" x 26" mail order photo poster of Spider-Man swinging over New York City that was revealed in *SMCW* no. 11 (April 28, 1973). This is the exact same poster that the US issued the following year with Series A of their Marvel Value Stamps, so US fans can wonder no more the reason that particular premium was included. Why make a new poster when there were already copies available in England from H. P. Dorey & Company Limited?

What I've never said out loud, and no one has commented on before to my knowledge, is that not only were we the first to run a Marvel stamp campaign, nearly two years before it debuted in the States, but the huge success of that initiative here may have caused Stan to repeat the same idea on a larger scale in the US! In other words, we may be at least partly to blame for Marvel Value Stamps!

Probably so, Robert . . . but I forgive you.

As for the Marvel Value Stamps that appeared in Marvel's comics a bit later:

Sometime in mid-1973 or thereabouts, Stan Lee called me into his spacious office to hear his latest brainstorm. Having divested himself recently of the troublesome title of "president" so he could avoid all those dull business and bottom-line meetings, Stan was spending every minute trying to come up with ways to increase the company's sales, which were the highest in the field but had nonetheless stalled a bit. Quite simply put, comic book companies were hemorrhaging locations to actually *sell* our product, even though we knew there were still plenty of people out there eager to *buy* it. Five-and-dime stores no longer existed (what could you buy for a nickel or ten cents, anyway?) . . . most drugstores didn't consider comics worth the trouble to display anymore, with their mere twenty-cent price tag (even if they were poised to soon go up to a whole quarter) . . . and the so-called "mom-and-pop" stores that had once dotted many city corners were giving way to big chains that had little interest in comics, for the same economic reasons.

Besides, Stan and I were painfully aware that—shocking as it might've been to us—not *every* Marvel fan bought *every* Marvel comic book title. Some might purchase *The Amazing Spider-Man* but not *Fantastic Four,* or even *Marvel Team-Up* (in which Spidey usually costarred), let alone *Iron Man.* Others might buy *The Avengers* but not pick up the thematically similar *The Defenders.* Others followed *The Incredible Hulk* but none of our burgeoning lineup of monster-hero titles like *The Tomb of Dracula, Man-Thing,* or *Werewolf by Night.* Still others might purchase *Captain America* one month but skip it the next in favor of another series. Many super hero fans wouldn't take a flyer to learn if *Conan the Barbarian* or *Sgt. Fury* or *Amazing Adventures* (with its new "War of the Worlds" series) was worth following . . . let alone *Worlds Unknown,* with its no-continuing-character science-fiction adaptations. And, horror of horrors, there were even a wayward few who might buy *Thor* one month and *Superman* the next!

What Marvel needed, Stan had decided, was a gimmick that would make *every* reader—or at least, every reader with access to a reasonable amount of money—latch onto *every* Marvel comic, if possible. Or at least as many as we could convince them to take a look at.

By and large, we felt, Marvel's comics contained good stories and good art. But we needed that little something extra—a "grabber"—to give folks that slight additional incentive to acquire one or two or maybe even a dozen more of our titles. And if that meant that *Batman* or *Archie* or *Richie Rich* lost a sale or three . . . well, that's what competition is all about, right? We figured that DC Comics publisher Carmine Infantino and his staff were staying up late trying to figure out some way to do the same thing to *us.*

As it happened, the "coupon" and "surprise gift" gimmicks in the recent Marvel UK weeklies—which had, of course, likewise been Stan's idea—had suggested to him a gimmick that might increase our sales. Thus, on that day, he looked at me and paused for dramatic effect. Then he said: "Marvel Value Stamps!"

I don't know if my heart sank the instant I heard those words, or if it took a few moments and a bit of elaboration on his part for their impact to sink in and for me to understand what he was talking about. But it didn't take long. After all, I had those Fawcett Comix Cards in the back of my consciousness, even if I hadn't paid much if any attention to the Marvel UK "coupons."

Stan already had the whole thing basically mapped out in his mind. His ultimate model, whether he stated it overtly or not, was surely the S&H Green Stamps and their ilk.

He envisioned there would be a Marvel Value Stamp in every issue (not including reprints or our black-and-white magazines). The MVS would consist of a numbered image of one of our heroes—the Hulk in one comic, Daredevil in another, Ka-Zar or Ghost Rider or the Son of Satan in still another, etc., right across the line. Either Stan already had in mind that there was going to be an even one hundred of them, or else that total came a (very) little later. But the idea was pretty much fully formed by the time he shared it with me.

We would also make available to readers "virtually at cost" (as Stan would soon scribe for a Bullpen Bulletins page, the gossip-and-plugs column that appeared in every comic) a "Marvel Value Stamp Album" into which the reader could paste their Marvel Value Stamps—which, unlike true postage stamps, wouldn't come with their own stickum on the backside, ready for either licking or a soggy sponge. And once all the stamps were secured into the album (with tape or glue), there'd be all sorts of goodies to which the happy completist would be entitled.

All the lucky reader had to do was (gasp! shudder! sob!)—*cut the stamps out of their Marvel comics!*

That's the moment I decided I really hated the idea of Marvel Value Stamps.

I recall bringing up to my esteemed mentor the mentality of the true comics *collector.* I had that mentality—always had, since age four. We didn't cut up our comics! (Well, I had, at age six or so, but only to make up my own adventures with the cutouts. And that phase had soon passed.)

But comic books as we know them hadn't really existed until Stan had entered his teen years in the last half of the 1930s; thus, he hadn't really grown up reading comics and had never really collected or even read them avidly, so he didn't think of them as something to be treasured and *preserved*. At least, not when weighed in the balance against prizes and premiums that were the rapturous reward for nothing but a bit of facility with scissors and mucilage. Keep in mind, this was also before photocopy machines, especially color ones, were readily available.

My argument didn't move Stan, however. To him, getting readers to separate the Marvel Value Stamps from the original comic book pages and paste them into their Marvel Value Stamp Albums was the whole point of the exercise! The object was to get readers to buy more comics—and assembling all hundred Marvel Value Stamps in the album would somehow entitle the collector to discounts on some of the madcap Marvel merchandise that would be advertised in our mags, including the just-begun *FOOM* (*Friends of Ol' Marvel*) magazine, Marvel's own official, self-published fan magazine. In the past, during the Merry Marvel Marching Society fan club days, Marvel had produced T-shirts and posters and Mephisto-knows-what-else. All those things would be offered again, and the list would no doubt expand once this MVS campaign was underway. As Stan described his plans to me, it was clear he was really on a roll with this thing.

"But they'll have to cut up their comic books," I recall muttering one last time.

Stan's response: "Well, then they can buy *another* copy!"

I couldn't argue with that kind of logic . . . so I didn't try. My job—should I decide to keep it, and trust me, I wanted to keep my job—was to carry out Stan's directives as best I could; so I decided then and there that if Stan wanted our readers to cut Marvel Value Stamps out of their comics, then we were going to try to make it worth their while to do exactly that! In for a penny, in for a POW!

Actually, I got a bit lucky after this close encounter of the commercial kind. I was able to unload nearly all the day-to-day work on creating the actual Marvel Value Stamps to others so I could concentrate on overseeing the covers and editing the stories, working with the artists and writers on our monthly comics.

You see, over the past year, despite the general slowdown in the comics market, Marvel had bypassed DC to become the bestselling comics company in the country, if not in the world. In addition, Stan had succeeded, by working with our conglomerate owners Cadence Industries (née Perfect Film & Chemical Company), to get Marvel Comics a no-fault divorce from Magazine Management Co., of which it had long been a part (purveyor of men's adventure, romance, movie gossip, and crossword puzzle mags) and had enlarged our in-house staff accordingly to handle whatever needed handling. When I came to work for Stan at Marvel eight years earlier, in 1965, I had become only the sixth comic book person on staff (i.e., editorial or production)—and that included Stan. Now, there must've been something like a couple dozen additional staffers, including production people who handled layouts, lettering, coloring, pasteups, Photostats, photocopying, and the like. Sure, they (we) were being stretched to their (our) limits, especially since it seemed as if Stan was, almost daily, adding new publications to the schedule, including a line of extra-thick, mostly comics, black-and-white magazines such as *Dracula Lives!* and *Savage Tales* and the *MAD* magazine wannabe *Crazy* . . . but hey, this was the company whose flagship title, *Fantastic Four,* boasted a hero who could stretch to nigh-infinite lengths, right? What more aspirational model could a beleaguered bullpen have?

Now, from this point on in my narrative, I'll admit that I must rely upon a combination of personal memories (vague), deductive reasoning (tricky), the evidence within the comics themselves, and the research of others—particularly online resources and an article written by (sheer coincidence here, honest!) my good friend and manager, John Cimino, for

Back Issue! magazine no. 76 (TwoMorrows Publishing, October 2014). In addition, Don Rosa, artist of Donald Duck comics for Disney, compiled a near-complete checklist for the appearance of each MVS from Series A for issue no. 113 of the *Amazing Heroes* fan magazine (March 15, 1987). Heartfelt thanks for their sensational spadework.

With Stan as our off-and-on taskmaster, Marvel started gearing up to produce what was destined to be Series A of the Marvel Value Stamps—an even *one hundred* images, each of which was to appear in several different comics issues, in order to give readers a better shot at collecting all of them, even if they did miss a mag or two along the way. Hey, we wanted their coins, sure—but we didn't want to be unreasonable about it. After all, "Value" was the Stamps' middle name, and we wanted to give fans all the value we could for their money and effort. This was supposed to be *fun,* people!

Now, it's totally beyond my powers of recollection or divination to say *who* decided precisely *which* one hundred Marvel characters—heroes, villains, and supporting characters—would be pictured in the first series. Though it's doubtful, it's not beyond the realm of possibility that Stan personally made up the list, just to make certain it was Done Right. Or I may have done it myself and simply forgotten about it, given all my other editorial duties plus my freelance writing at the time. At the very least, I probably had to check over and metaphorically sign off on the work of whoever *did* compose the list. After all, what if the whole "century" of images was printed, all those precious stamp albums filled—and we suddenly realized we'd left out some major hero, like the Vision or Power Man (Luke Cage's new moniker)? Given the madcap seat-of-the-pants way Marvel operated in those days, such an occurrence was scarcely impossible—and even likely.

Whoever compiled the list, at least we have Stan himself to thank for making sure, in the April '74 comics, that Marvel's readers (and we ourselves, pushing half a century later) knew who was responsible for picking out and assembling all the artwork for these stamps: namely "Jazzy Johnny Romita, Mirthful Marie Severin, and Titanic Tony Mortellaro."

John, of course, was the master artist who, beginning in 1966, had helped turn *The Amazing Spider-Man* from Marvel's second-bestselling title into its top one, and who was, by 1973, acting, at least unofficially, as the company's art director.

Marie, after a spell drawing Doctor Strange, the Hulk, and the humor mag *Not Brand Echh,* had elected to concentrate instead on coloring and cover layouts; her background in production made her ideal for this assignment.

Production man Tony had been a comic book artist since the early 1950s; indeed, he'd drawn one of the most infamous panels reproduced in Dr. Fredric Wertham's 1954 screed *Seduction of the Innocent*, though at this time Tony mostly moonlighted as John's inking assistant on *Spider-Man* (plastering his name onto billboards or the sides of delivery trucks in every comics panel he could).

This talented trio probably had some additional help in the bullpen with the actual pasting up and the like, but it was their six eyes that chose the particular figures that—with all distracting background art removed by scissors, X-Acto blades, and Wite-out—would comprise the one hundred stamps.

Stan, who by then had mostly turned over the non-Stan's Soapbox writing of the Bullpen Bulletins pages each month to me and others, did the entire honors himself in the comics with the cover date of February 1974 (appearing on stands in late 1973). The only art on that Bullpen Bulletins page was an image of the Hulk, framed against an orange background inside a square stamp shape. No text, no number—just the drawing.

Announcing that it was "teaser time," Stan challenged readers to guess why that picture was there and promised to reveal its secret in the very next issue. I suspect we got a mountain of mail speculating as to what Marvel had on its mixed-up little mind.

Just thirty days later, a "Blockbustin' Bullpen Bonus Page" in all the monthly Marvel titles (proclaiming "Marvel's Merry Christmas Present to You")—again written by Stan—revealed that the Hulk item in the previous issue had been . . . a *stamp.*

Ah, but (as Stan put it) "not just *any* run-of-the-mill, lick-it-and-stick-it-on-a-postcard stamp, but the fabulous forerunner of a whole herd of—are you ready for this?"—and then, below that paragraph, in big boxed letters against a Daredevil-red background—

"MARVEL VALUE STAMPS!"

Stan decided not to let all the four-color cats out of the bag right away, though. This time around, he invited Marvelites to try and reason out what "those nutty *numbers* . . . in the upper corner of each stamp," now included in the sample image, meant—"or *why* you ought to keep them safe and secure, like the family jewels." But he assured readers it'd be "worth your while—and a heaping handful of *fun,* besides!"

Stan the Man continued: "From our earliest mail-samples, it seems that just about everybody on the planet guessed that our perforated-edged portrait was meant to be a stamp of some kind." This was pure flimflammery on Stan's part, of course, because those March-dated issues had only gone to press weeks before the February ones had gone on sale, let alone before any letters about their contents could be written to us. Still, I'd bet he was right. I mean, the Hulk thingy *did* look like a stamp. It had been *designed* to look like a stamp.

But, because this was Marvel in 1974, there had to be a foul-up as well. Stan went on to write that the readers should page through the issue they were holding to see if the sample

NEW! NEW! NEW! BLOCKBUSTIN' BULLPEN BONUS PAGE NEW! NEW! NEW!

MARVEL'S MERRY CHRISTMAS PRESENT TO YOU!

You *know* it, neighbor! In our regular Bulletins section, elsewhere in this issue, we promised you a *whole 'nother page* of Marvel madness and munificence. And here it is!

From now on, we'll be using this space to herald the latest developments (both personal and professional) in our giant-sized 75¢ line, which is taking comicdom by storm—in our cockeyed CRAZY Magazine, which is gonna give the Humor Establishment a run for its money—in our far-out FOOM Club, which is already one of our biggest smashes ever (but you ain't seen *nuthin'* yet, folks)—in short, in just about *every* field of Marvel endeavor that we think would move and shake you!

Meanwhile, for our very *first* Bullpen Bonus Page:

Remember how, last month, we promised to reveal unto you the Senses-Shattering Secret behind the pic of the Incredible Hulk that appears below? Well, Marvel always keeps its word—when we remember what we said, anyhow.

What it *is*, friends, is a *stamp*.

And not just *any* run-of-the-mill, lick-it-and-stick-it-on-a-postcard stamp, but the fabulous forerunner of a whole herd of—are you ready for this?—

MARVEL VALUE STAMPS!

That's right! From now on, one of these glitzy mini-posters—each featuring a different Marvel star or starlet—will appear in virtually every one of our mixed-up original-material mags—and in many of our collectors'-item reprints, to boot!

Now, we don't want to reveal *everything* about these way-out stamps right off the bat.

For instance, we'll keep you on pins and needles a few weeks longer about what those nutty *numbers* mean in the upper corner of each stamp—or *why* you ought to keep 'em safe and secure, like the family jewels. Just rest assured that it'll be worth your while—and a heaping handful of *fun*, besides!

Oh, and before you ask — from our earliest mail-samples, it seems that just about everybody on the planet guessed that our perforated-edged portrait was meant to be a stamp of some kind. Inscrutable we'll never be!

Anyway, to see if the mag you're now reading contains a stamp to match the one on this page, why not flip over to the letters section! If the mag doesn't *have* a letters section, then maybe it'll be squirreled away somewhere else in the issue — or maybe this is one of very few mags we haven't got around to yet! (But by *next* month, just watch our smoke, O frantic follower of foolishness and frivolity!)

Right now, here's our irrepressible, irreplaceable, irremedial checklist — — !

In March 1974, stamps began appearing on the letters pages of Marvel's comics. This is Stan's "very first" Blockbustin' Bullpen Bonus Page, which once again includes the Hulk stamp on the opposite page (numbered this time, but still different than the one that was later released).

Hulk stamp—with a number 5 in its upper right-hand corner—appeared somewhere in it, maybe in the letters section. Unfortunately, his crack staff had seen to it that the Hulk stamp was printed on that selfsame Bonus Page, making us all look as if we were a bit uncoordinated. Which we were. Surely somebody—including myself as editor-in-chief, of course—should have spotted this anomaly and rewritten Stan's copy to reflect the reality. But, in the fuss and flurry that was the bullpen in those days, nobody noticed the mistake until copies were on sale across the nation. Well, it didn't matter much. Our readers expected goofs like that from us. And we rarely disappointed them.

Meanwhile, we were balancing the other things that Stan (and Cadence Industries) wanted done to take advantage of Marvel's new number one position in the field: the nascent FOOM fan club and its official publication; various "secret codes" through which Stan would deliver cryptic messages to the cognoscenti in both *FOOM* magazine and in the comics' letters columns (only the Spider-Man code was up and running so far); and, oh yeah, also processing dozens of color and black-and-white comics every month, including launching and promoting new heroes such as Iron Fist (a notion I'd come up with one night after seeing my first kung fu movie).

The April-dated issues, out around January 1974 or so, were the ones whose Bonus Page finally revealed in full what Marvel Value Stamps were going to be like, under a heading

proclaiming "Value, Value—Who's Got the Value?" (Stan and I didn't see a whole lot of, er, *value* in being subtle about these matters.)

This was the first time readers learned that the stamps would appear on each issue's letters page, as opposed to elsewhere in the comic . . . and that there would be "an even *hundred* of them in 'Series A,' which covers calendar year 1974," with the web-masked likeness of Spider-Man (who else?) destined to decorate MVS no. 1. As to whose mug would appear on Stamp no. 100—well, Stan wasn't telling just yet. To underscore that point, the only art on that half of the Bonus Page was a MVS shape numbered "100" with a big red question mark inside.

Stan informed readers that Stamp no. 100, "positively the *rarest* one of 'em all," would be "popping up in only *one* Marvel title during the whole blamed year!" But he hastily assured them it wouldn't be buried in "one of our western re-runs or *any* of our rhapsodic reprints," but would appear in one of our "awesome *all-original* epics over the next few months." If someone missed it—well, there was always "*swapping* and *trading* with your fellow Marvel madmen who might've been luckier, right?"

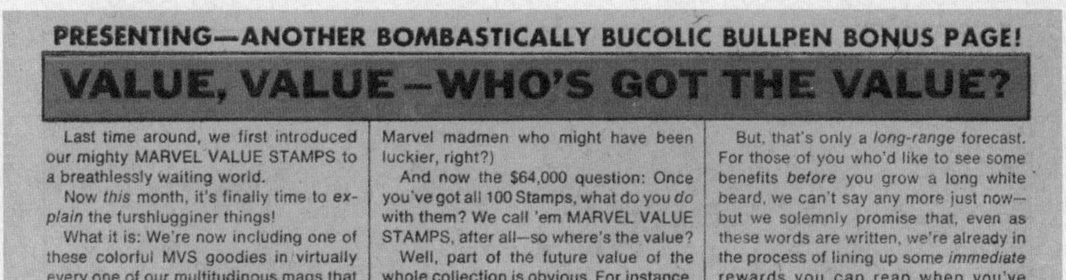

PRESENTING—ANOTHER BOMBASTICALLY BUCOLIC BULLPEN BONUS PAGE!

VALUE, VALUE—WHO'S GOT THE VALUE?

Last time around, we first introduced our mighty MARVEL VALUE STAMPS to a breathlessly waiting world.

Now *this* month, it's finally time to *explain* the furshlugginer things!

What it is: We're now including one of these colorful MVS goodies in virtually every one of our multitudinous mags that has a *letters page*. There'll be an even *hundred* of them in Series "A," which covers calendar year 1974, starting with #1 (your friendly neighborhood Spider-Man, who else?) and winding up with #100, which sports a dynamic likeness of none other than—well, we'll let you guess till *next* time just *whose* mug will replace that mystery-shrouded *question mark* when the coveted #100 Stamp finally appears!

All we can tell you about it right now is that, although some of our Stamps will appear much more often than others, MVS #100 will be absolutely, positively the *rarest* one of 'em all, popping up in only *one* Marvel title during the whole blamed year!

(No, no, Suspicious One—it won't be sneaked into one of our western re-runs or *any* of our rhapsodic reprints, but will be featured prominently in one of our awesome *all-original* epics over the next few months. If you miss it, or one of the others which you need to complete your collecton—you can always do a bit of *swapping* and *trading* with your fellow Marvel madmen who might have been luckier, right?)

And now the $64,000 question: Once you've got all 100 Stamps, what do you *do* with them? We call 'em MARVEL VALUE STAMPS, after all—so where's the value?

Well, part of the future value of the whole collection is obvious. For instance, in the next month or three, we'll be offering you an *MVS Stamp Album* virtually at cost, so that you can paste in all of them and have a complete set—which is bound to become a real collector's item in the years to come. (After all, didja know that FANTASTIC FOUR #1 is now selling for up to $50 in many back-issue comic-book stores across the nation, and that SPIDEY #1 isn't far behind?)

But, that's only a *long-range* forecast. For those of you who'd like to see some benefits *before* you grow a long white beard, we can't say any more just now—but we solemnly promise that, even as these words are written, we're already in the process of lining up some *immediate* rewards you can reap when you've amassed a complete set. So, you'll not only have the frolic and fun of collecting the full 100 MVS mini-masterpieces, but—at least for many of you—it'll mean money in your pocket, to boot!

How's *that* for a grabber?

We also pledge a *fuller* explanation of this all-important point over the next few issues—verily, we swear and affirm it by the mile-long Adam's-apple of Reed Richards!

So keep on clippin' and collectin', pilgrim!

By the time summer rolls around, virtually all *100* MARVEL VALUE STAMPS will have appeared in our liltin' letters pages, or in some other designated spot—

—And that's when the fun *really* begins!

P.S.: Special thanks to Jazzy Johnny Romita, Mirthful Marie Severin, and Titanic Tony Mortellaro for digging up the spiffiest bunch of superhero drawings since George Washington first said "Cheese!"

A teaser stamp for MVS no. 100 appeared on this "Bombastically Bucolic" Bullpen Bonus Page in issues dated April 1974.

Next, Stan asked what he termed "the $64,000 question" (after the popular 1950s TV show—though if he'd thought about the fact that the big quiz shows of that era had turned out to be *fixed,* he'd probably have used a different phrase): "After you've got all 100 stamps, what do you *do* with them? We call 'em MARVEL VALUE STAMPS, after all—so where's the value?"

Stan's first gambit was to reveal that, "in the next month or three," we'd be offering an "*MVS Stamp Album,* virtually at cost, so that you can paste in all of them and have a complete set—which is bound to become a real collector's item in the years to come." Stan pointed out that a good-condition copy of *Fantastic Four* no. 1, which ten years earlier sold for ten cents back in 1961, was then selling for up to fifty dollars in back-issue comics stores. (He was right: although cutting the stamps from these comics drastically reduced the value of those issues, a complete Marvel Value Stamp Album is indeed a collector's item, selling for over a thousand dollars. That is, if you can find one for sale.)

Stan also vowed that Marvel was "already in the process of lining up some *immediate* rewards you can reap when you've amassed a complete set." Just stay tuned, he advised, and all would be made known unto ye.

Likewise, he promised that "virtually all *100* MARVEL VALUE STAMPS" would have appeared "by the time summer rolls around"—"and that's when the fun really begins!"

(Then, in a postscript, he credited John, Marie, and Tony for "digging up," picking out, and pasting up "the spiffiest bunch of super hero drawings since George Washington said 'Cheese!'")

The actual stamps began to appear in the issues of Marvel's comics cover-dated May 1974—a month in which, for the first time in a long while, there was no "Stan's Soapbox" (wherein Our Fearless Leader preached to the faithful, promoting peace and goodwill and plugging product). Instead, I was forced to fill in with a column I christened "Roy's Rostrum"—and yes, I was aware that it might sound vaguely *dirty* to some eyes and ears whose owners had no clear idea of what, precisely, a "rostrum" was, but I figured that was their problem, not mine. A "rostrum" is roughly equivalent to a "soapbox"—i.e., a podium from which one might give a speech—so I simply informed readers that Stan was busy "leapfroggin' all over Europe," and proceeded with my own brand of gossip about the Marvel gang.

Only thing is, since I wasn't privy to the details of what Stan had in mind for the Marvel Value Stamps program, all I said about them on that Bullpen Bulletins page was that we had received a "Brobdingnagian batch of mail" on it—and that, next month, we'd tell them about "the first (but not the last) of several Bonus Benefits you can obtain once you've amassed a full collection of the first hundred stamps!" (I somehow neglected to mention that one of the first actual stamps could be found elsewhere in that very mag—on the letters page, just where Smilin' Stan had decreed.) *Fantastic Four* no. 146, for instance, featured a stamp marked "Series A" and "91" at the bottom, and "Hela, the Goddess of Death" at the top, above a picture of that *Thor* cast member. Said art image had been lifted from the cover of issue no. 186 of the thunder god's eponymous title (dated March 1971), as penciled by John Buscema and inked by John Verpoorten. None of the information in the preceding sentence was mentioned in conjunction with the stamp, though; it's all been ferreted out over the intervening years by dedicated comics fans and collectors and compiled in the very book you are now reading.

In the June-dated issues, Stan was back from Italy (he'd been at the world-famous annual Lucca comics convention) and was so eager to sing its praises, and to relate how "adults . . . far outnumbered the youngsters in attendance," including "professors, businessmen, scientists, filmmakers, lawyers, and literally hundreds of other mature, serious fans" interested in the "comic strip" art form, that he wound up having to end that Bullpen Bulletins page by delaying till the *next* month all the news he'd promised to reveal about Marvel Value Stamps.

I suspect that, by this point, at least a few fans out there were beginning to feel like Stan was stalling, playing for time—that maybe there weren't going to be any real goodies to be gained by collecting and pasting up all those stamps after all—but in the July 1974 comics, he was as good as his word. Maybe better. The "Bombshell Bullpen Bonus Page" was back, nearly all of it devoted, directly or indirectly, to Marvel Value Stamps!

First off, Stan announced the availability of the promised Marvel Value Stamp Book, available for just fifty cents with the filling out and sending in of a coupon printed on that same page. Of course, the coupon was designed (with broken lines, etc.) to be, you guessed it, *cut out* . . . and surely more than one distressed reader must have wondered if it was okay to simply photocopy that coupon, or even just to write their name and address in a *letter* and send it off to "MARVEL VALUE STAMPBOOK, c/o Marvel Comics Group." (I have no recollection of how we handled those orders.)

> **You win! These cockamamey MVS Stamps are fillin' up my whole house—and I've gotta have someplace to put 'em! Please rush me my MARVEL VALUE STAMPBOOK! I enclosed 50¢ in coin, to cover postage and handling, whatever that means! (And don't forget my FULL-COLOR BONUS POSTER, okay?)**
>
> **Name____________________**
> **Address____________________**
> **City__________State_____Zip______**
> **(Please Print Clearly)**
>
> **Send to:**
> **MARVEL VALUE STAMPBOOK**
> **c/o Marvel Comics Group**
> **575 Madison Ave.**
> **N.Y.C., N.Y. 10022**

Each stamp book, Stan announced, would have "its own special number—which'll be of ever-increasing importance as the weeks go by! Why? Don't ask—not yet, anyway. After all, we've gotta keep a few secrets for a while, don't we?"

But that, he informed our readers, wasn't all. Marvel was tossing in a "SPECIAL BONUS POSTER, in full color," with each and every stamp book order. "We can't tell you just what Marvel super-star it features, but take it from us—this is an offer you can't refuse!"

(That poster, I'm informed—I don't recall actually seeing one at the time—measured eighteen inches by twenty-six inches and featured a photographically realistic depiction of Spider-Man high above a cityscape, shooting out a webline. A notation in its lower left-hand corner reads: "Printed in England by H. P. Dorey & Company Limited." And, in the lower right-hand corner: "TM and © 1973 Magazine Management (London) Ltd. All Rights Reserved." Whatever its origins, it couldn't have been a bad deal in 1974 to mail off half a buck and receive in return both a Marvel Value Stamp Book and a bonus Spidey poster.)

Once you'd properly pasted up the stamp book, Stan went on, two of the largest comics conventions in the US "have cheerfully volunteered to give *special discounts* on admission to every person who shows up with a completely-filled *MVS Stampbook!*" He assured readers they wouldn't have to part with their precious stamp books—only get them duly stamped in a certain "pre-marked place . . . so that you can use it another day, another way."

One of the cooperating cons was Phil Seuling's annual New York Comic Art Convention, held the weekend of July 4, and still at that time the largest in the country. Stan specifically mentioned that "Rascally ROY THOMAS and Jazzy JOHNNY ROMITA" would be in attendance.

The other con on board was the up-and-coming San Diego Comic Convention (only in its fifth year and not yet officially called Comic-Con), held each summer in that Southern California city. Stan informed readers that West Coast–based Marvel folks like "Stainless STEVE ENGLEHART, Mischievous MIKE FRIEDRICH, and Far-Out FRANK BRUNNER" would be on hand at that one—and that *I* was scheduled to be the con's "Special Guest" that year. (More on what Stan and SDCC cofounder Shel Dorf turned out to have up their sleeves for Yours Truly a bit later.)

However, if an MVS collector was unable to attend "any comic-book conventions, either on the coasts or in between," all was not lost. The very *next* Bullpen Bonus Page, Stan informed readers, would clue them in on "still *another* amazing extra that'll be yours when that spectacular stamp book is full to overflowing." In fact, he even invited Marvel fans to mail in their own suggestions about "things that Marvel could offer you without making you send in your treasured Stampbooks themselves." They were urged to scribble their comments when they filled out the coupon at the bottom of that page.

Stan closed with what he called a "deathless thought":

"MARVEL VALUE STAMPS! Now, more than ever, 'Value' is our middle name! End of plug!"

Well, of *that* one, anyway.

I suspect Stan greatly enjoyed this byplay with readers, even if it was pretty much one-sided at this point. He really meant it, I'm sure, when he indicated that Marvel would be eager to add offers that the readers themselves suggested. He figured the people who read Marvel's comics would think of a zillion things that he, as a card-carrying adult and non-comics-reader, would never come up with.

August's books must've been a bit of a disappointment to readers, because they contained no Bonus Page, only the letters sections (with their second offerings of Series A stamps) and the usual Bullpen Bulletins Pages, in which Stan vowed to soon offer "several more blockbustin' bargains" they could get when they had collected all one hundred Marvel Value Stamps.

In the September issues, he proudly announced that this was "the month when the awesome, ultimate MARVEL VALUE STAMP will appear somewhere—sometime—in one (count 'em, one) of our colorful classics." He couldn't say which one it would be, but he reminded Marvelites that it would be featured "once and once only all this year," while the next month's issues would feature a long list of "comic-book stores" across the land where presenting your filled stamp book would "get you a galvanizin' FREE GIFT!" (Stan was pretty liberal with words in all capital letters during this period.)

Okay, we won't keep *you* in suspense the way Stan did Marvel's readers in 1974. The "ultimate" Marvel Value Stamp, no. 100, depicted the world-devouring Galactus, and it was to appear solely in *Sub-Mariner* no. 72 (cover-dated September 1974) . . . which, perhaps by coincidence, perhaps not, became the final issue of that particular series. However, by sheer accident, while I was recently paging through *Fantastic Four* no. 154 (January 1975), that no. 100 stamp was on the letters page of *that* issue as well! I'm not just succumbing to "Marvelspeak" when I say that my first thought on spotting the duplication was: "Well, leave it to us at Marvel to mess up our 'ultimate' Value Stamp!" Whether or not we got a deluge of mail on that point, I have no recollection. Hell, for all I know, it appeared in a *third* comic to boot! [Editor's note: It does—in *The Amazing Spider-Man* no. 145, cover-dated June 1975.]

As for the list of comics stores mentioned above—that *didn't* appear in the October issues as promised. In fact, as far as I can tell, there was no real mention of the stamps anywhere in the October-dated Marvel mags, unless it was a throwaway reference in one of the letters pages that I missed in research for this volume. For the first time, something—though I've no memory of what—had temporarily derailed the thundering locomotive that was Stan's Marvel Value Stamps express. Whether there was a problem coordinating Stan's plans with the growing number of comics stores across the nation, or perhaps an examination proved that arranging for these retail outlets to give away free items to patrons would have been unproductively expensive, I know not (the current phenomenon of Free Comic Book Day was still years away at this point).

The November 1974–dated Marvels contained a reference that reads today as if we were desperately treading water. Along with a hint that a *second* series of Marvel Value Stamps would begin "not many moons from now," Stan again pushed ordering the stamp books, and said that Marvel was even then in "the final stages of preparing a list of *dozens* of comic book stores and conventions all over the US and Canada where you can use your filled-up stamp book to get *free Marvel mags* at a special *MVS Discount*." That must've raised heartbeats and pulses all across North America. At last—cutting up one hundred comics was actually going to prove to be *worth it*!

And then—unaccountably—nothing.

Nothing for four fantastically long months. Not a Bonus Page, not a word on any of the Bullpen Bulletins Pages (though the stamps themselves continued to appear on the letters pages through the December 1975–dated issues). Series A was now complete—and already Series B was quietly being readied.

I'm not sure what John Romita and I may have done or said at Phil Seuling's New York con to appease the holders of their completely filled stamp books . . . although "Stan Lee's Soapbox" for the January 1975 issues (on sale in fall of '74) said that he wished Marveldom Assembled (i.e., the readers) "could have all been here to toast our own Roy Thomas as he was co-guest of honor at a special, luminary-packed luncheon," as well as applauding John, Marie, Gil Kane, and other Marvel stars who were on panels and the like. There's no mention of any special MVS event at that con—and indeed, the luncheon guests, all interviewed by Phil, were Joe Simon, Frank Robbins, my then-wife Jean Thomas, and myself. As far as I can tell, there was no connection with Marvel Value Stamps at all—not even a mention of them—and a transcript of that luncheon interview has since been published. But maybe there was some special MVS event at another time and place during the con that I've forgotten.

A few weeks later, however, when I was likewise a guest of honor at the fifth San Diego Comic Convention, cohost Shel Dorf and his West Coast wunderkinder did manage to stage a special gathering off in a room somewhere for what was referred to as "the Marvel 100 Club." I remember this primarily because, a few months later, the program book for our own Mighty Marvel Comic Convention, held in March 1975 at the Hotel Commodore in New York City, dedicated two of its pages to Marvel-related events at "San Diego 1974." Included was a photo of fourteen or so lads and lasses, described in the cutline as "A portion of the hardy souls who managed to clip and paste all 100 Marvel Value Stamps!" Showing their filled stamp books had covered the "price of admission" to that cataclysmic conclave. They're shown sitting on chairs—supposedly listening raptly as I hold forth about something or other Marvel-related, since this little assemblage with me as its center had been heralded by Stan back on the June 1974 Bonus Page as one of the special treats stamp completists could receive.

Rascally ROY THOMAS

I'm glad to say I wasn't the only attraction at that confab. Also on hand were artist Frank Brunner, writer Mike

Friedrich, and Jim Harmon, then the editor of Marvel's black-and-white *Monsters of the Movies* magazine. (Ironically, only a couple of weeks after this con, I would step down as editor-in-chief and opt for a contractual writer/editor situation that would last for the rest of the decade. Rumors that I resigned my post just so I could avoid being involved with Marvel Value Stamps Series B are, however, untrue.)

The program for the Mighty Marvel Comic Convention held at the Hotel Commodore in New York City on March 22, 23, and 24, 1975, included a photo of MVS collectors at the 1974 San Diego Comic Convention. Images courtesy of Roy Thomas.

Happily, albeit belatedly, Stan got around to giving readers extra value for their Value Stamps. In the April 1975–dated issues, he preens: "Looks like just about the hottest thing in town is still our mighty MARVEL VALUE STAMPS!" He goes on to mention that "your batty Bullpen is constantly being deluged with letters wondering just what sort'a goodies you can get by being the proud possessor of a completely-filled Stamp Book." (He doesn't mention that not all of those letters were quite that politely worded. A few collectors out there felt Marvel had lured them into cutting up their comics and to date hadn't given them much of anything in return, especially if they didn't live near New York City or San Diego.)

Stan delivered the goods, though. He announced that a full MVS book "will entitle you to a whoppin' *ten percent discount* on any of the matchless merchandise being offered to you by your big-hearted House of Ideas." All you had to do to collect was to send "your completed stamp book, along with a large-sized, stamped, self-addressed envelope" to Marvel in Manhattan, and the MVS book would be mailed back to you with a "dazzling discount coupon, faster than you can say 'Quicksilver'!" And every time the fan bought something, they would receive *another* coupon, granting them a discount on the next item Marvel offered. Holders of completed MVS books would be eligible for a "*perpetual* ten percent discount—besides having your name inscribed on our great, golden Honor Roll here in the hallowed halls of Marvel." Stan also promised to keep printing the stamps to give those who hadn't yet filled their stamp books a chance to catch up—although, as far as I could see, paging through my bound collection of mid-1970s Marvels, stamps only appeared on letters pages for another two months or so. Still, Marvel continued to publish dozens of comics containing all-new material each month, so that extension surely helped a few folks complete their collections.

It must've been difficult for some completists to send off their filled stamp books and count on getting them back—but I'm not aware of an uproar around that time due to lost stamp books and thus loss of discounts, so perhaps everything (or at least just about everything) went smoothly. That's all we can ever hope for in this world, isn't it?

Marvel wasn't done yet, though. In the issues dated December 1975, Stan—or someone hosting his style in an "Item" on the Bullpen Bulletins Page—heralded the *second* series of Marvel Value Stamps, now just about ready to be unleashed.

In the April 1976 issues, it was announced that the second series (officially Series B) was already appearing in Marvel's comics. And then came the whole spiel again, in modified form: send fifty cents for a stamp book, clip, paste, mail, etc., etc. This time, however, the stamps were a bit different. Instead of one hundred stamps each containing a different Marvel character, there would be ten drawings, one to a stamp book page, each composed of ten horizontal stamp pieces that needed to be cut out from letters pages and then assembled to make a final image. This was a whole lot trickier than Series A, since not only did one have to clip and paste the pieces, one also had to, as phrased on the inside cover of the stamp book, "figure out what each group of ten stamps forms a picture of." (In all fairness, the character name at the top did provide a clue.) It was like stamp collecting and assembling a series of small jigsaw puzzles put together! The idea for this, it would be revealed in the July 1976 issues, came from one of the bullpen's most enthusiastic and fan-oriented members, Paty Greer, soon to be Paty Cockrum when she married *X-Men* artist Dave Cockrum.

Nine of the images (composed of ten pieces each) were of Marvel super heroes: Spider-Man, the Fantastic Four, the Hulk, the Silver Surfer, Conan the Barbarian (a licensed character), Dracula, Thor, Doctor Strange, and Captain America.

As for the tenth image, when completed, the caption promised to reveal "*the most powerful of all beings in the Merry Marvel Universe. He holds the life and death of every capricious character in his hands . . . There's but one way to find out, Faithful One! So get out your scissors and glue and start pasting this pin-up into position—how else can you discover the true maniacal mind behind the Mighty Marvel Madness?*"

Who could this possibly be, readers speculated? The Watcher? Galactus? Thanos?

Before long, this ultimate MVS puzzle image was revealed to be none other than Stan Lee himself, taken from an earlier Marvel house ad illustrated by Marie Severin.

It wasn't until the May 1976 issues that Stan announced that there would be a "special, super-secret stamp number 100" in this series, too. That turned out to be the upper-right corner piece of the "Stan (the man) Lee" stamp puzzle, which identified him as the character on the puzzle page.

In addition, Marvel made slightly better use of the stamp books themselves this time around. Included were two pages of actual *ads* for the FOOM fan club, comics subscriptions, and posters. There was also, on the back cover, a bunch of "specially-reserved space[s] for some Marvel-boosting comic-art conventions to do their thing," like maybe offering discounts or the like. There were spaces labeled "New York Comic Art Convention," "San Diego Comic Book Convention," and "Convention (Other)" . . . plus six more spaces for MVS Discounts labeled A through F. I trust the conventions came through.

This second series of stamps appeared in comics with cover dates of December 1975 through August 1976, and most of the stamps appeared only once or twice, and thus involved a much smaller number of comics than Series A had.

As far as I can see, that's pretty much the last reference in any Bullpen Bulletins to Marvel Value Stamps. Presumably, stamp books were filled and sent in so that their proud owners could receive coupons to jump-start their "permanent ten percent discounts," but following the ins and outs of things from here on is frankly beyond my purview. Or capability.

For us—for this *book*—the *stamps* of Series A and Series B are the thing. And each and every one is reproduced here for the first time, alongside their letters pages and image sources, preserved in all their late Marvel Age splendor!

Oh, there were attempts to *revisit* or even *revive* the Marvel Value Stamps from time to time. After all, a decade or so later, the people running the bullpen were some of the same folks who had collected one or both of the earlier series, so the idea was all but inevitable.

In 2006, there appeared Stamp no. 101, a continuation of Series A, in a publication called *Marvel Legacy: 1970s Handbook.* The hero pictured was none other than Forbush-Man, the secret identity of onetime Marvel mascot Irving Forbush, the Alfred E. Neuman of 1960s and '70s Marvel Comics. Forbush-Man had appeared in several issues of the company's late-'60s spoof comic, *Not Brand Echh.* Stamp no. 101 was apparently designed and assembled by Mike Fichera, one of the writers of the *Handbook* . . . but the artwork was that of none other than the great Marie Severin.

Also in 2006, the release of *Marvel Spotlight: Warren Ellis/Jim Cheung* startled readers by announcing on the inside back cover that "Marvel Value Stamps Are Back!" Eight stamps appeared therein, and a total of twenty-eight stamps appeared over the course of nearly a dozen subsequent issues, featuring both new and old heroes (Sgt. Fury and the Hulk among the latter, Arana and the faux-pre-Marvel Age character the Sentry among the former.)

In 2007, for a publication titled *Marvel Legacy: The 1960s–1990s Handbook,* Stamp no. 102 was assembled, again by Mike Fichera. It depicted none other than Willie Lumpkin, the mailman who, in *Fantastic Four* no. 11 (February 1963) and occasionally in subsequent issues, had delivered mail to the FF in the Baxter Building. Actually, Lumpkin's first name hadn't been revealed in that early story; it was simply assumed to be Willie because, in the early 1960s, Stan Lee had briefly written a newspaper comic strip about a quite different-looking mailman named . . . *Willie Lumpkin.* (In the 2005 film *Fantastic Four,* Stan Lee would portray

such a mailman—whom longtime fans assumed to be Willie Lumpkin—in one of his multitudinous film cameos!)

Sometimes an idea is just too good—just plain too much *fun*—to let go of.

Such an idea may be abandoned, even forgotten for a while—even for years—but sooner or later, somebody who liked that notion, who grew up on the idea, will find a way to bring it back (which, I'm told, was my editor's impetus for this very book you are reading).

MARVEL VALUE STAMP 01
ARANA
MARVEL VALUE STAMP 02
SGT. FURY
MARVEL VALUE STAMPS ARE BACK!!!
MARVEL VALUE STAMP 03
SENTRY
MARVEL VALUE STAMP 04
HULK
MARVEL VALUE STAMP 05
SPIDER-WOMAN
MARVEL VALUE STAMP 06
SPIDER-MAN
MARVEL VALUE STAMP 07
MS. MARVEL
MARVEL VALUE STAMP 08
DR. DOOM

And such, clearly, was the honest, unabashed, unbridled enthusiasm (as well as, admittedly, the canny commercialism) of Stan Lee that his Marvel Value Stamps concept has become part of his legacy. Not up there with Spider-Man and the Hulk and the Silver Surfer, perhaps, but still a part of at least the tail end of what he christened the Marvel Age of Comics.

ROY THOMAS has been a comics writer and an editor (for Marvel far more often than not) since the day Stan Lee hired him, roughly fifteen minutes after they met. Roy regards that Friday, July 9, 1965, as one of the most important in his eighty-plus years of life—along with Wednesday, June 8, 1977, the night he met Danette Couto, the future Dann Thomas. Roy has written for movies, television, and especially comic books, with notable runs on *The Avengers, Conan the Barbarian, The Incredible Hulk, Star Wars,* and *X-Men.* Roy was Stan Lee's first successor as editor-in-chief from 1972–74, and left Marvel in 1980. In 1981, he became a writer for DC Comics, soon working on self-generated titles such as *All-Star Squadron, Arak/Son of Thunder,* and *Infinity, Inc.* Since 1986, he has been a freelance writer for Marvel and occasionally other comics companies. In 1999, Roy Thomas was voted no. 5 among favorite comic book writers of the twentieth century, and no. 4 among favorite editors, in a *Comics Buyer's Guide* poll of comics professionals and fans. In 2011, he was inducted into the Will Eisner Comic Book Hall of Fame at the San Diego Comic-Con. He currently edits *Alter Ego* magazine, writes online *Tarzan* and *John Carter of Mars* comic strips, and pens the occasional comic book. Roy Thomas is also the author of two definitive histories for Taschen—*75 Years of Marvel: From the Golden Age to the Silver Screen* (2014) and *The Stan Lee Story* (2019). He lives not far from St. Matthews, South Carolina.

The Mighty World of Marvel no. 1 (October 7, 1972).

The Mighty World of Marvel no. 2 (October 14, 1972), no. 3 (October 21, 1972), no. 4 (October 28, 1972), and no. 5 (November 4, 1972).

INSIDE: A CLUE TO YOUR FREE POSTER!
THE MIGHTY WORLD OF
MARVEL
5P
No.7 WEEK ENDING NOV 18 1972
THE INCREDIBLE HULK BATTLES FOR HIS LIFE!
ONLY ONE CAN BE THE VICTOR- THE MONSTER OR THE MACHINE?
Also in this issue: The AMAZING SPIDERMAN and the FANTASTIC FOUR

The Mighty World of Marvel no. 6 (November 11, 1972), no. 7 (November 18, 1972), no. 8 (November 25, 1972), and no. 9 (December 2, 1972).

The Mighty World of Marvel no. 10 (December 9, 1972).

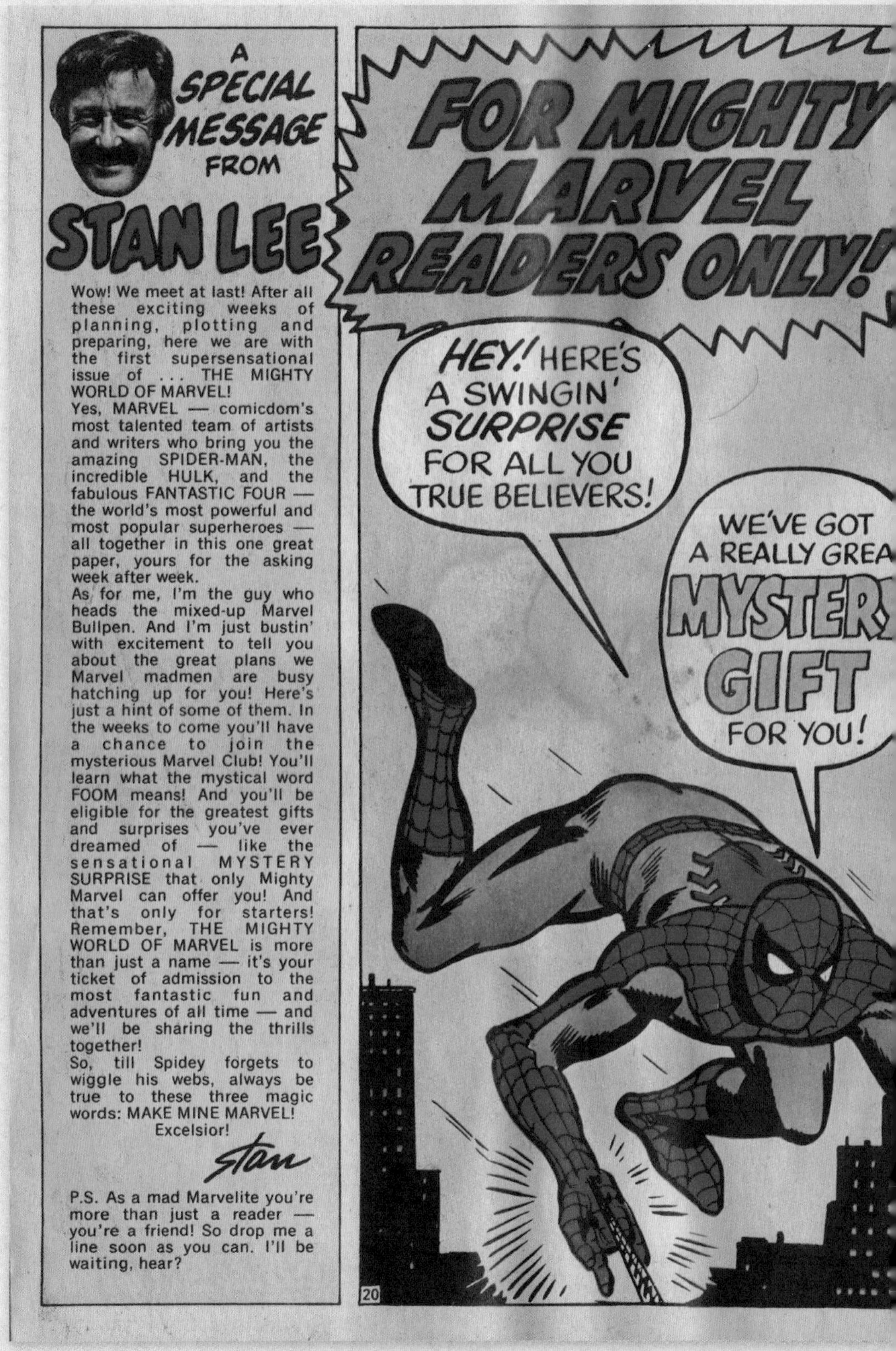

A SPECIAL MESSAGE FROM STAN LEE

Wow! We meet at last! After all these exciting weeks of planning, plotting and preparing, here we are with the first supersensational issue of . . . THE MIGHTY WORLD OF MARVEL!
Yes, MARVEL — comicdom's most talented team of artists and writers who bring you the amazing SPIDER-MAN, the incredible HULK, and the fabulous FANTASTIC FOUR — the world's most powerful and most popular superheroes — all together in this one great paper, yours for the asking week after week.
As for me, I'm the guy who heads the mixed-up Marvel Bullpen. And I'm just bustin' with excitement to tell you about the great plans we Marvel madmen are busy hatching up for you! Here's just a hint of some of them. In the weeks to come you'll have a chance to join the mysterious Marvel Club! You'll learn what the mystical word FOOM means! And you'll be eligible for the greatest gifts and surprises you've ever dreamed of — like the sensational MYSTERY SURPRISE that only Mighty Marvel can offer you! And that's only for starters! Remember, THE MIGHTY WORLD OF MARVEL is more than just a name — it's your ticket of admission to the most fantastic fun and adventures of all time — and we'll be sharing the thrills together!
So, till Spidey forgets to wiggle his webs, always be true to these three magic words: MAKE MINE MARVEL!

Excelsior!

Stan

P.S. As a mad Marvelite you're more than just a reader — you're a friend! So drop me a line soon as you can. I'll be waiting, hear?

FOR MIGHTY MARVEL READERS ONLY!
HEY! HERE'S A SWINGIN' SURPRISE FOR ALL YOU TRUE BELIEVERS!
WE'VE GOT A REALLY GREA MYSTER GIFT FOR YOU!
20

ABOVE AND OPPOSITE *The Mighty World of Marvel* no. 1 (October 7, 1972).

THE WORLD'S GREATEST FREE GIFT OFFER!
EVERY WEEK (FOR THE NEXT TEN WEEKS) YOU WILL FIND A NUMBERED COUPON ON THIS PAGE! AND HERE'S YOUR FIRST ONE!
HOW GOOD ARE YOU AT FIGURING OUT CLUES? WE WON'T TELL YOU WHAT YOUR MYSTERY GIFT IS YET 'CAUSE TRYING TO GUESS IT WILL BE HALF THE FUN! BUT BESIDES YOUR SPECIAL COUPON, WE'LL GIVE YOU A NEW CLUE EVERY WEEK! READY? HERE'S YOUR FIRST CLUE...
COUPON NO.1
IT'S BIGGER THAN A BREADBOX!
WHEN YOU'VE COLLECTED ANY EIGHT DIFFERENT COUPONS, MAIL YOUR SET TO THE MIGHTY WORLD OF MARVEL MAGAZINE MANAGEMENT (LONDON) LTD, 120 NEWGATE ST. LONDON EC1 A7AA
CONGRATULATIONS! YOU'VE ENTERED THE MIGHTY MARVEL AGE OF COMICS AND THE EXCITEMENT IS JUST BEGINNING!
21

ABOVE AND OPPOSITE *The Mighty World of Marvel* no. 2 (October 14, 1972).

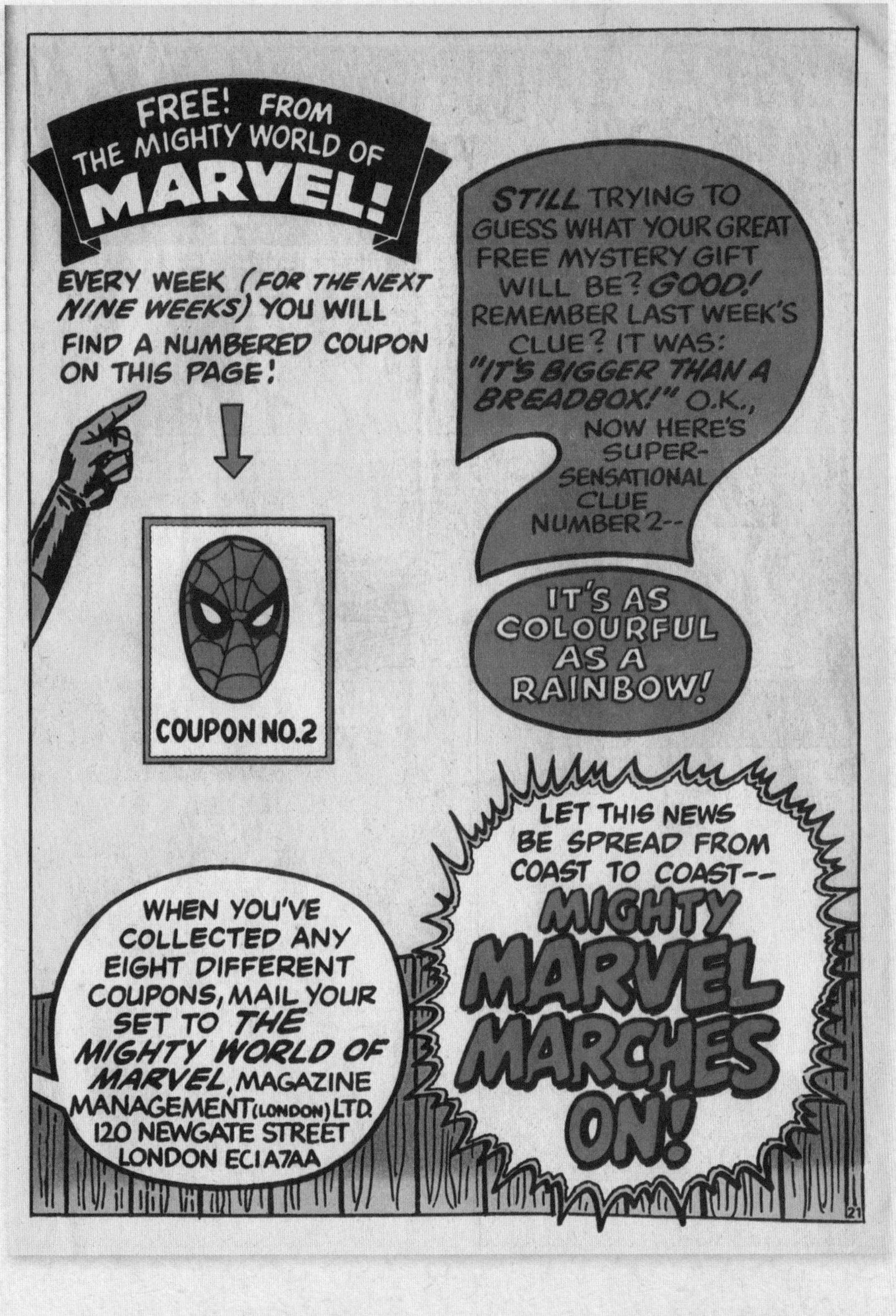
FREE! FROM THE MIGHTY WORLD OF MARVEL!
EVERY WEEK (FOR THE NEXT NINE WEEKS) YOU WILL FIND A NUMBERED COUPON ON THIS PAGE!
COUPON NO.2
STILL TRYING TO GUESS WHAT YOUR GREAT FREE MYSTERY GIFT WILL BE? GOOD! REMEMBER LAST WEEK'S CLUE? IT WAS: "IT'S BIGGER THAN A BREADBOX!" O.K., NOW HERE'S SUPER-SENSATIONAL CLUE NUMBER 2--
IT'S AS COLOURFUL AS A RAINBOW!
LET THIS NEWS BE SPREAD FROM COAST TO COAST-- MIGHTY MARVEL MARCHES ON!
WHEN YOU'VE COLLECTED ANY EIGHT DIFFERENT COUPONS, MAIL YOUR SET TO THE MIGHTY WORLD OF MARVEL, MAGAZINE MANAGEMENT (LONDON) LTD. 120 NEWGATE STREET LONDON EC1A7AA
21

ABOVE AND OPPOSITE *The Mighty World of Marvel* no. 3 (October 21, 1972).

THE WORLD'S GREATEST FREE GIFT OFFER!
EVERY WEEK (FOR THE NEXT EIGHT WEEKS) YOU WILL FIND A NUMBERED COUPON ON THIS PAGE!
COUPON NO.3
HAVE YOU GUESSED IT YET? NO? WELL, DON'T WORRY--WE'VE STILL GOT A LOT MORE CLUES FOR YOU! REMEMBER THE FIRST TWO? No.1 "IT'S BIGGER THAN A BREADBOX!" No.2 "IT'S AS COLOURFUL AS A RAINBOW!" WELL, HERE'S EARTH-SHATTERING CLUE NUMBER 3:
YOU CAN FOLD IT, ROLL IT, OR HIDE BEHIND IT!
YOU COLLECT ANY EIGHT DIFFERENT COUPONS--THEN MAIL YOUR SET TO THE MIGHTY WORLD OF MARVEL
MAGAZINE MANAGEMENT (London) LTD., 120 Newgate Street, LONDON EC1A7AA
--OR HULK WILL BE ANGRY!!
LET THIS NEWS BE SPREAD FROM COAST TO COAST--
MIGHTY MARVEL MARCHES ON!
21

ABOVE AND OPPOSITE *The Mighty World of Marvel* no. 4 (October 28, 1972).

FREE! FROM THE MIGHTY WORLD OF MARVEL!
EVERY WEEK (FOR THE NEXT SEVEN WEEKS) YOU WILL FIND A NUMBERED COUPON ON THIS PAGE!
COUPON NO.4
WOW! JUDGING FROM THE MOUNTAIN OF MAIL YOU'VE BEEN SENDING US, IT SEEMS THAT EVERYBODY'S TRYING TO GUESS WHAT THIS MARVEL MYSTERY GIFT WILL BE-- EVEN STAN "THE MAN" LEE HIMSELF! (OL' STAN MUST HAVE FORGOTTEN THAT HE'S THE ONE WHO CHOSE YOUR GARGANTUAN GOODIE!) ANYWAY, REMEMBER THE LAST 3 CLUES WE GAVE YOU? (1) IT'S BIGGER THAN A BREADBOX. (2) IT'S AS COLOURFUL AS A RAINBOW. (3) YOU CAN FOLD IT, ROLL IT, OR HIDE BEHIND IT. AND NOW-- (TA TA TA TAAAAAA TA TA!)
CLUE #4: "CAREFUL! IT MIGHT LOOK DOWN ON YOU!"
WHEN YOU'VE COLLECTED ANY EIGHT DIFFERENT COUPONS, MAIL YOUR SET TO THE MIGHTY WORLD OF MARVEL, Magazine Management London Ltd., 120 NEWGATE STRFET, LONDON, EC1A7AA
LET THIS NEWS BE SPREAD FROM COAST TO COAST-- MIGHTY MARVEL MARCHES ON!

A SPECIAL MESSAGE FROM STAN LEE

Gosh! Can you really believe that a whole month has gone by since our wild first issue of THE MIGHTY WORLD OF MARVEL exploded on the scene like a sky-rocket!

It's been a fantastic, exciting month—a month in which MARVEL has become a household word the length and breadth of Britain! But, even more important, it's been a month in which your flood of letters has made me feel like we've been pals for years! And, starting this issue, I'll print as many of your masterful missives as possible, so that we can share the fun together on our brand-new Letters Page!

And don't forget—in another few weeks you'll discover the secret of your merry Mystery Gift—you'll learn how to join our mixed-up Marvel Club—and you might even guess what the mystical word FOOM means!

Yep, there's a whole kaboodle of thrills and surprises in store for you as you follow the adventures of the world's greatest superheroes on these phantasmagoric pages each and every week! So keep those wonderful letters and postcards pouring in, and don't dare miss an issue—you know how *angry* the Hulk can get!

Excelsior!

Stan

HERE IT IS AGAIN!
(SO YOU'VE NO EXCUSE FOR MISSING OUT, HEAR?)

THE WORLD'S WILDEST FREE GIFT OFFER!

IT'LL BE ALL YOURS IN A FEW SHORT WEEKS! WHILE YOU'RE WAITING, CAN YOU GUESS WHAT IT IS? REMEMBER YOUR FIRST FOUR CLUES--

1. "IT'S BIGGER THAN A BREAD-BOX!"
2. "IT'S AS COLORFUL AS A RAINBOW!"
3. "YOU CAN FOLD IT, ROLL IT, OR HIDE BEHIND IT!"
4. "CAREFUL! IT MIGHT LOOK DOWN ON YOU!"

HERE ARE THE RULES TO FOLLOW: EVERY WEEK (FOR THE NEXT SIX WEEKS) YOU WILL FIND A NUMBERED COUPON ON THIS PAGE...

COUPON NO.5

YOU COLLECT ANY EIGHT DIFFERENT COUPONS.. THEN MAIL YOUR SET TO THE MIGHTY WORLD of MARVEL
MAGAZINE MANAGEMENT (London) LTD., 120 NEWGATE STREET, LONDON EC1A 7AA
OR HULK WILL SMASH YOU!!!

ABOVE AND OPPOSITE *The Mighty World of Marvel* no. 5 (November 4, 1972).

AND NOW, HERE IS THE 5TH CLUE!
AH HA! STAN SEZ THE CLUE FOR THIS ISSUE IS... "IT RHYMES WITH TOASTER!" CHEE! I SURE WISH I WUZ A POET!
IMPORTANT NOTICE:
Even if you were injudicious enough to have missed any of our exciting earlier issues, don't despair. You can STILL qualify for your free Marvel Mystery Gift!
Just let us know which copies you lack, and we'll knock ourselves out to find them and send them to you, so that you can complete your collection of Marvel coupons and catch up on all our Marvel madness!
Simply drop us a note, enclosing 8p (includes postage and handling) for each copy desired. Address your rollicking requests to: THE MIGHTY WORLD OF MARVEL,
MAGAZINE MANAGEMENT (London) LTD.,
120 NEWGATE STREET, LONDON, EC1A 7AA

ABOVE AND OPPOSITE *The Mighty World of Marvel* no. 6 (November 11, 1972).

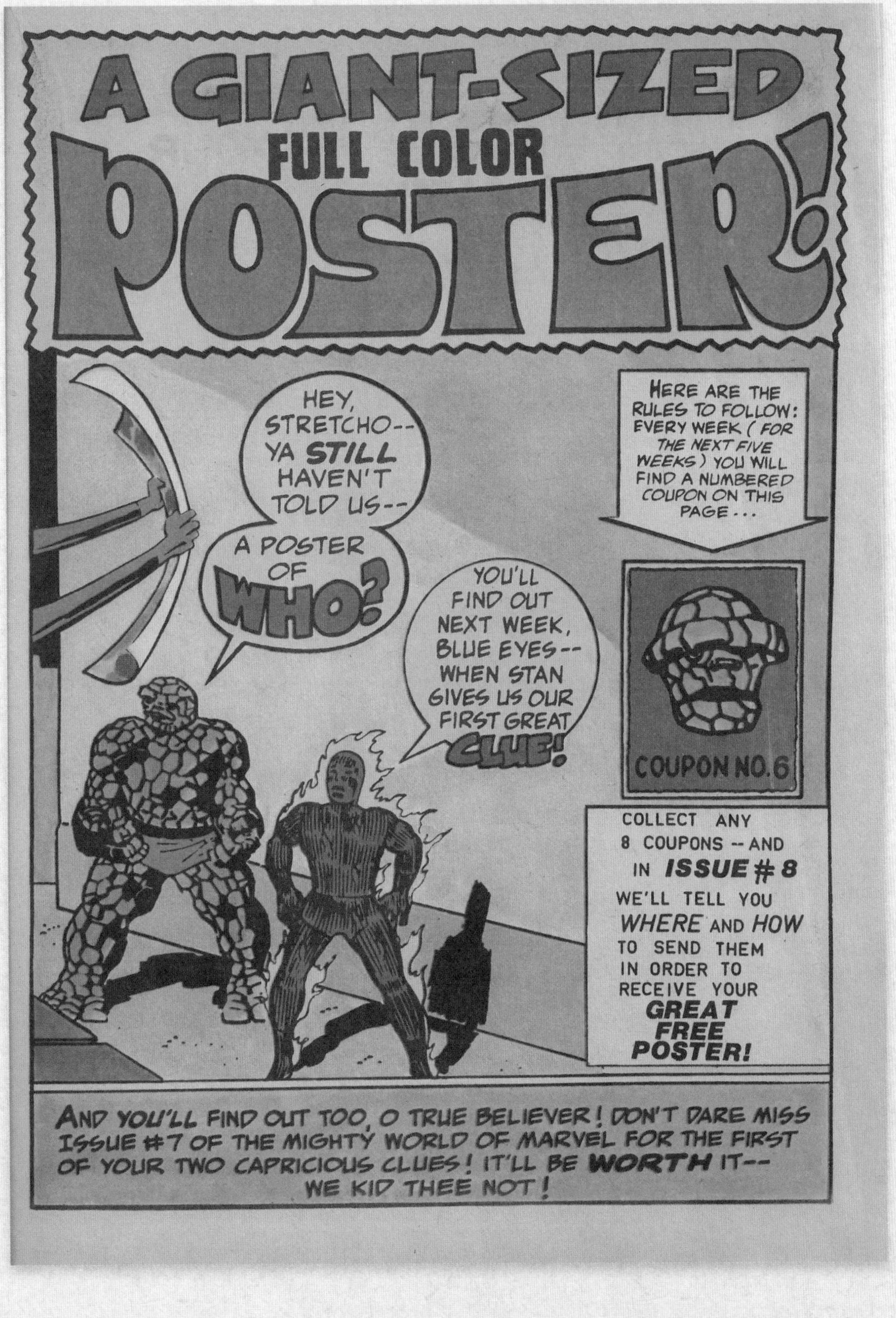
A GIANT-SIZED
FULL COLOR
POSTER!
HEY, STRETCHO-- YA STILL HAVEN'T TOLD US--
A POSTER OF WHO?
YOU'LL FIND OUT NEXT WEEK, BLUE EYES-- WHEN STAN GIVES US OUR FIRST GREAT CLUE!
HERE ARE THE RULES TO FOLLOW: EVERY WEEK (FOR THE NEXT FIVE WEEKS) YOU WILL FIND A NUMBERED COUPON ON THIS PAGE...
COUPON NO.6
COLLECT ANY 8 COUPONS -- AND IN ISSUE # 8 WE'LL TELL YOU WHERE AND HOW TO SEND THEM IN ORDER TO RECEIVE YOUR GREAT FREE POSTER!
AND YOU'LL FIND OUT TOO, O TRUE BELIEVER! DON'T DARE MISS ISSUE #7 OF THE MIGHTY WORLD OF MARVEL FOR THE FIRST OF YOUR TWO CAPRICIOUS CLUES! IT'LL BE WORTH IT-- WE KID THEE NOT!

ABOVE AND OPPOSITE *The Mighty World of Marvel* no. 7 (November 18, 1972).

ISX EURSP EEHSOR! *
IN ORDER TO FIND OUT WHAT THIS CLUE IS, JUST UNSCRAMBLE THE LETTERS AND PUT THEM IN THEIR PROPER ORDER!
EVERY WEEK (FOR THE NEXT FOUR WEEKS) YOU WILL FIND A NUMBERED COUPON ON THIS PAGE!
COUPON NO.7
COLLECT ANY 8 COUPONS -- AND IN ISSUE # 10 WE'LL TELL YOU WHERE AND HOW TO SEND THEM IN ORDER TO GET YOUR GREAT FREE POSTER!
*SEE THE ANSWER TO ISX EURSP EEHSOR! IN OUR NEXT GREAT ISSUE!

ABOVE AND OPPOSITE *The Mighty World of Marvel* no. 8 (November 25, 1972).

YOUR GREAT GIFT POSTER WILL PRESENT--
SIX SUPER-HEROES!
HERE ARE THE RULES TO FOLLOW: EVERY WEEK (FOR THE NEXT THREE WEEKS) YOU WILL FIND A NUMBERED COUPON ON THIS PAGE...
COUPON NO 8
COLLECT ANY 8 COUPONS -- AND IN ISSUE # 10 WE'LL TELL YOU WHERE AND HOW TO SEND THEM IN ORDER TO RECEIVE YOUR GREAT FREE POSTER!
NEXT ISSUE YOU'LL LEARN THE IDENTITIES OF ALL SIX OF MARVEL'S MOST POPULAR POSTER PIN-UP!
IF YOU'VE COLLECTED ALL YOUR COUPONS, DON'T DARE LOSE THEM! YOU'LL BE GETTING FINAL INSTRUCTIONS IN ISSUE NO. 10!

A SPECIAL MESSAGE FROM STAN LEE

Hi, True Believers! We've got a lot to tell you this issue, so let's not waste a minute!

First of all, if your letters keep pouring in at the rate they've been swamping us, they'll have to build a couple of new post offices here in London just for our merry Marvel mail! So don't stop writing, hear? The more letters we receive, the happier it makes pretty Pippa, our glamorous gal editor — who just happens to be a stamp collector! And, if you promise to behave yourselves, and not reveal Spidey's secret identity, we'll print a practically perfect photo of precociously precious Pippa (whew!) for you some day!

Next, we thought you'd like to know that Marvel has become the biggest thing in Britian since the Stones! (Sam and Sybil Stone, a couple of friends of ours!) In fact, next to Foom, we're the most talked-about—whoops! Sorry! We're not supposed to mention Foom so soon. It's our biggest, newest secret, and we'll tell you about it in the weeks to come!

But, now that it's about time for all you happy heroes to claim your glitzy gift poster, don't think we're about to stop the surprises! Oh no! The fun and excitement are just beginning. As soon as we can catch our breath we'll give you the low-down on the sensational Club we're forming, and tell you how to join it! We'll also dream up some generous gifts, goofy gizmos, and gargantuan gimmicks—just for you! In time, you'll learn how to earn your very own exclusive No-Prize, and more, more, more!

So stay with us, stalwart one — we may not know where we're going, but Marvel marches on!

Excelsior!

Stan

(The man behind the Foom!)

20

IMPORTANT NOTICE:

Even if you were injudicious enougn to have missed any of our exciting earlier issues, don't despair. You can STILL qualify for your free Marvel Mystery Gift!

Just let us know which copies you lack, and we'll knock ourselves out to find them and send them to you, so that you can complete your collection of Marvel coupons — and catch up on all our Marvel madness!

Simply drop us a note, enclosing 8p (includes postage and handling) for each copy desired. Address your rollicking requests to:

THE MIGHTY WORLD OF MARVEL
MAGAZINE MANAGEMENT LONDON LTD.
120 NEWGATE ST.. LONDON EC1 A7AA

ABOVE AND OPPOSITE *The Mighty World of Marvel* no. 9 (December 2, 1972).

--WE'RE ALL ON THE POSTER! THE HULK! SPIDER-MAN! MR. FANTASTIC! THE THING! INVISIBLE GIRL and THE HUMAN TORCH!
YES, WE'RE ALL ON IT! A FULL COLOR LARGE SIZE 20"x25" POSTER-- AND NEXT ISH, WE'LL SHOW YOU WHAT IT LOOKS LIKE!
EVERY WEEK FOR THE PAST EIGHT WEEKS, YOU'VE FOUND A NUMBERED COUPON ON THIS PAGE...
MARVEL COMICS GROUP
EXTRA BONUS COUPON
IF YOU'VE COLLECTED YOUR EIGHT DIFFERENT COUPONS (AS EVERY TRUE BELIEVER SHOULD HAVE DONE!) DON'T DARE MISS OUR NEXT GREAT ISSUE-- THE LONG-AWAITED #10! THERE YOU'LL LEARN EXACTLY HOW TO RECEIVE YOUR GREAT FREE POSTER!
NEXT WEEK! THE END OF THE CONTEST! BUT THE BEGINNING OF MANY MORE SURPRISES!

The Mighty World of Marvel no. 10 (December 9, 1972).

The Mighty World of Marvel promotional poster (1972). Art by John Buscema, Frank Giacoia, and Mike Esposito.

The Mighty World of Marvel no. 10 (December 9, 1972).

Spider-Man Comics Weekly no. 3 (March 3, 1973).

Spider-Man Comics Weekly no. 11 (April 28, 1973).

For fifty cents ("to cover postage and manhandling"), readers in the US in 1974 could order a Series A stamp book, which came with this "Special Bonus Poster" featuring Spider-Man. Measuring 18" x 26", the poster was printed in England by H. P. Dorey & Company Limited and marked ™ and © 1973 Magazine Management (London) Ltd. All Rights Reserved. Stamp books and posters were mailed in plain manila envelopes, a copy of which can be seen on the last page of this book.

THIS IS IT,
TRUE BELIEVER!

YOUR MIGHTY

MARVEL VALUE STAMP

BOOK

THIS IS
STAMPBOOK
________120607

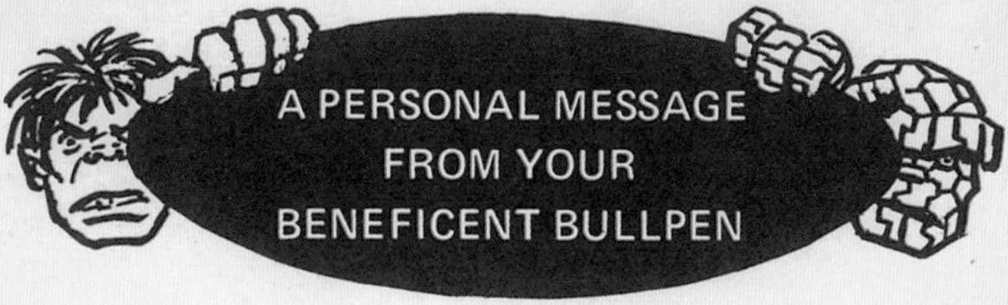

We promised it to you—and here it is!

By the time you receive this colorful Marvel Value Stampbook in the mail, chances are you've either amassed a complete series of 100 Marvel Value Stamps—or else you're within web-spinning distance of it, right?

So now, here's what you do, effendi:

Simply clip the stamps out of the comic mags themselves, paste each one into its proper, numbered slot in this catalog—and, when all 100 spaces are properly filled, take this treasured tome around to any of the star-studded Comic Book Conventions, comic art dealers, or other centers of contemporary culture which you've seen enumerated in recent issues of Marvel mags. There you'll collect your MVS discount, free gift, or other goodies. The conventioneer, dealer, or whoever will then mark this book in the proper place on the back page—so that you can hang on to the Stampbook itself, which is sure to increase in value as years, months, even weeks go by!

Don't lose it, hear? 'Cause we've got other plans for it as well—which concern the special number on the cover of this Stampbook!

Oh yes—and if you want to get set for the next lettered series of MVS mini-posters to paste and ponder over, just send 50¢ to cover postage and manhandling to:

MARVEL VALUE STAMPBOOK
c/o Marvel Comics Group
575 Madison Ave.
New York, N.Y. 10022

We've got a million of 'em—and you know how the Thing's dear Aunt Petunia hates those cluttered-up old warehouses!

MIGHTY MARVEL VALUE STAMPS NO.'s 1 THRU 8
SPIDER-MAN
1
2
HULK
SERIES A
3
CONAN
THE
BARBARIAN
SERIES A
THING
4
5
DRACULA
SERIES A
THOR
6
WEREWOLF
7
8
SERIES A
CAPTAIN AMERICA

MIGHTY MARVEL VALUE STAMPS NO.'s 9 THRU 16

MIGHTY MARVEL VALUE STAMPS NO.'s 17 THRU 24

MIGHTY MARVEL VALUE STAMPS NO.'s 25 THRU 32

MIGHTY MARVEL VALUE STAMPS NO.'s 33 THRU 40

MIGHTY MARVEL VALUE STAMPS NO.'s 41 THRU 48

MIGHTY MARVEL VALUE STAMPS NO.'s 48 THRU 56

MIGHTY MARVEL VALUE STAMPS NO.'s 57 THRU 64

MIGHTY MARVEL VALUE STAMPS NO.'s 65 THRU 72

MIGHTY MARVEL VALUE STAMPS NO.'s 73 THRU 80

MIGHTY MARVEL VALUE STAMPS NO.'s 81 THRU 88

MIGHTY MARVEL VALUE STAMPS NO.'s 89 THRU 96

STAMPS NO.'s 97 THRU 100

O.K, that takes care of the first 99 . . .

This space reserved for the rarest
Marvel Value Stamp of all!

Who'd you **think** we were gonna feature? **Millie The Model?**

Now, here's a specially-reserved space for some Marvel-boosting comic-art conventions to do their thing--!

NEW YORK COMIC ART CONVENTION	SAN DIEGO COMIC BOOK CONVENTION	CONVENTION (OTHER)

MVS BARGAINS OTHER THAN CONVENTIONS:

MVS DISCOUNT "A"	MVS DISCOUNT "B"	MVS DISCOUNT "C"

MVS DISCOUNT "D"	MVS DISCOUNT "E"	MVS DISCOUNT "F"

Time to start saving the **NEXT** nifty series of **MV** Stamps? To get another stampbook, send 50c to: MARVEL VALUE STAMPBOOK, c/o MARVEL COMICS, 575 Madison Avenue, NYC, 10022. 'Nuff Said!

ARTWORK SOURCES

THE HAMMER STRIKES

c/o MARVEL COMICS GROUP, 575 MADISON AVE. N.Y.C. 10022

Dear Gerry and John,

You guys really had me going for a while! In fact, I honestly thought I saw Irving Forbush somewhere on page one!

It was SOME homecoming... THOR #218, that is. The last THOR I had laid my eyes upon was #161, just a bit over fifty issues and four years ago. Thor (and Asgard) had just escaped Mangog's attempts at invoking Ragnarok and had humbled the mighty Galactus. I still believe these stories with their assortment of characters (including Ego, the Recorder, Rigel, and the Wanderers) and fine artwork reign supreme.

I don't know what made me buy this THOR. The title, perhaps--it was catchy ("Thor Fights Alone!"), or my curiosity. But whatever the reason, I'm glad I have it now!

Seems as though I'd never left. The plots are just as spectacular and the artwork, magnificent. I'm glad Thor is still spacebound, as I always felt you guys wrote your best stories away from Earth's inhibiting presence, out where your imaginations could run wild.

The Black Stars are indeed a formidable foe, and once again I see a good story grabbing out at me from the pages. It's a pleasure to know Marvel still has a decent fantasy line to go along with those (ugh!) monster books!

I'm not saying THOR #218 was perfect. But any mistakes I found were not in any way detracting from the theme.

I'm eagerly awaiting #219. And wondering why I ever left.

Humbly yours,
Larry Ross
126 Parkledge Drive
Snyder, N.Y. 14226

Yeesh, Larry—we're wondering why you ever left, too! If the urge to do so again ever hits you, please write and tell us first, huh? Maybe we can correct whatever it is that's gone awry!

Anyway, by now, you should be comfortably hooked again, and curious as all get-out about the characters introduced since last you visited these hallowed pages—personages like Hildegarde, Silas Grant, Krista, and others.

Oh, by the way—Honest Irv was on page one of THOR #218. But he was hidden behind Volstagg, and thus couldn't be seen. And a good thing, too! We hear he was dancing a double jig with a crazed troll at that moment!

Dear Roy, Gerry, John, and Jim,

Tell me, whose idea was it to turn THOR into a one-man "Star Trek" series? I ask because I want to know whom to vote for in the fandom polls next year. The past few issues of THOR have been some of the best in the history of this fine mag. I implore you, keep Thor and Company in the starship Starjammer as much as possible. Odin could appoint Thor as a travelling ambassador for Asgard, so that Thor could visit all sorts of strange worlds to spread his culture and learn of others. I am sure you could find a way for him to slip away occasionally to take part in Avengers business.

Special recognition should go to John and Jim for some fine artwork. Jim's inking is just right for the sci-fi atmosphere of late. Try to make his stay on THOR a bit longer than his "permanent" one-issue stands on MARVEL TEAM-UP and SPIDER-MAN.

You've got a good thing going in the pages of THOR. Don't blow it, please.

Bob Margolis
215 Ritchie Ave.
Cincinnati, Ohio 45215

Believe us, Bob, we don't intend to blow it. (Of course, nobody ever exactly intends to! But we don't even intend to do it accidentally! Got that?) True, Goldilocks won't always be soaring through the spaceways in the Starjammer, but we do plan to keep the great majority of his adventures in other-than-earth settings for quite a while to come.

As for Jim Mooney... well, his stay on THOR was a bit longer, though not as permanent as we'd hoped. Seems his pencilling chores on GHOST RIDER and SON OF SATAN demanded too much of his time. But we think you'll agree we've found one heckuva replacement in ever-lovin' Mike Esposito! Mike's even been surprising us with the super-ultra-fine work he's been turning out lately—and we knew he was good!

Digressing...

A few issues ago, we questioned, half-seriously, what the gods of Asgard might talk about at cocktail parties, since politics as such doesn't exist in the Realm Eternal. Well, our offhanded bit of wondering-aloud-in-print inspired the following correspondent to these heights of poetic prose:

Dear Sirs,

Cocktail parties in Asgard?! It is easy enough to imagine the Asgardians feasting and drinking wine, ale, or mead, but not having cocktail parties. As for what to talk about—of that there is no lack. The deeds of warriors and heroes, of battles fought and monsters slain, of adventures in lands wondrous and strange. Who has been to the kingdom of the trolls? Who knows the feeling of a fine blade as it slices through a troll's skull? Who has been to the realm of Mephisto and lived to tell of it? How Thor journeyed to the Golden Star to free his father Odin and all Asgard from the slavers' dungeons. How he entered the Dark Nebula to search for his lady Sif.

Perhaps, like the Vikings, the Asgardians would listen to the skald (poet) tell of deeds done in olden days. Or make up riddles for one another to answer. Or just do some boasting about their own prowess.

Leonard Phillip Zinna
271 Etna St.
Brooklyn, N.Y. 11208

Y'know, all of a sudden this topic fascinates us! Anybody else out there have ideas on what day-to-day life in Asgard might be like? (You know where to send 'em.)

Oh, and by the way, Mr. Zinna—you've earned yourself a no-prize for your little bit of speculation. Now let's see if your fellow Marvelites can help flesh out the picture and give us a notion of what a typical Asgardian day is like.

Dear Marvel,

Whatever happened to the "God Squad" that Ego-Prime (as Odin's instrument) created so many issues ago?

Also, here's a clipping from a recent NEWSWEEK that seems pertinent and might interest you.

G. Andrew Maness
44 Romney Rd.
Wheeling, W. Va. 26003

Gerry has promised that we will be seeing more of Asgard's young gods at some indefinite time in the future, Andy. But when—we just can't say.

And thanks for the clipping, Mr. Maness. This, too, rates a no-prize. It's from the August 20th issue of NEWSWEEK—and it tells of a small cult in Iceland that has actually revived religious worship of Thor, Odin, Loki, and the other gods of Asgard!! (No. We are not putting you on.)

Ah, well... just remember, up there in Iceland, these gods are currently under contract to Marvel and are forbidden from performing miracles without first obtaining Stan's written permission.

Excelsior!

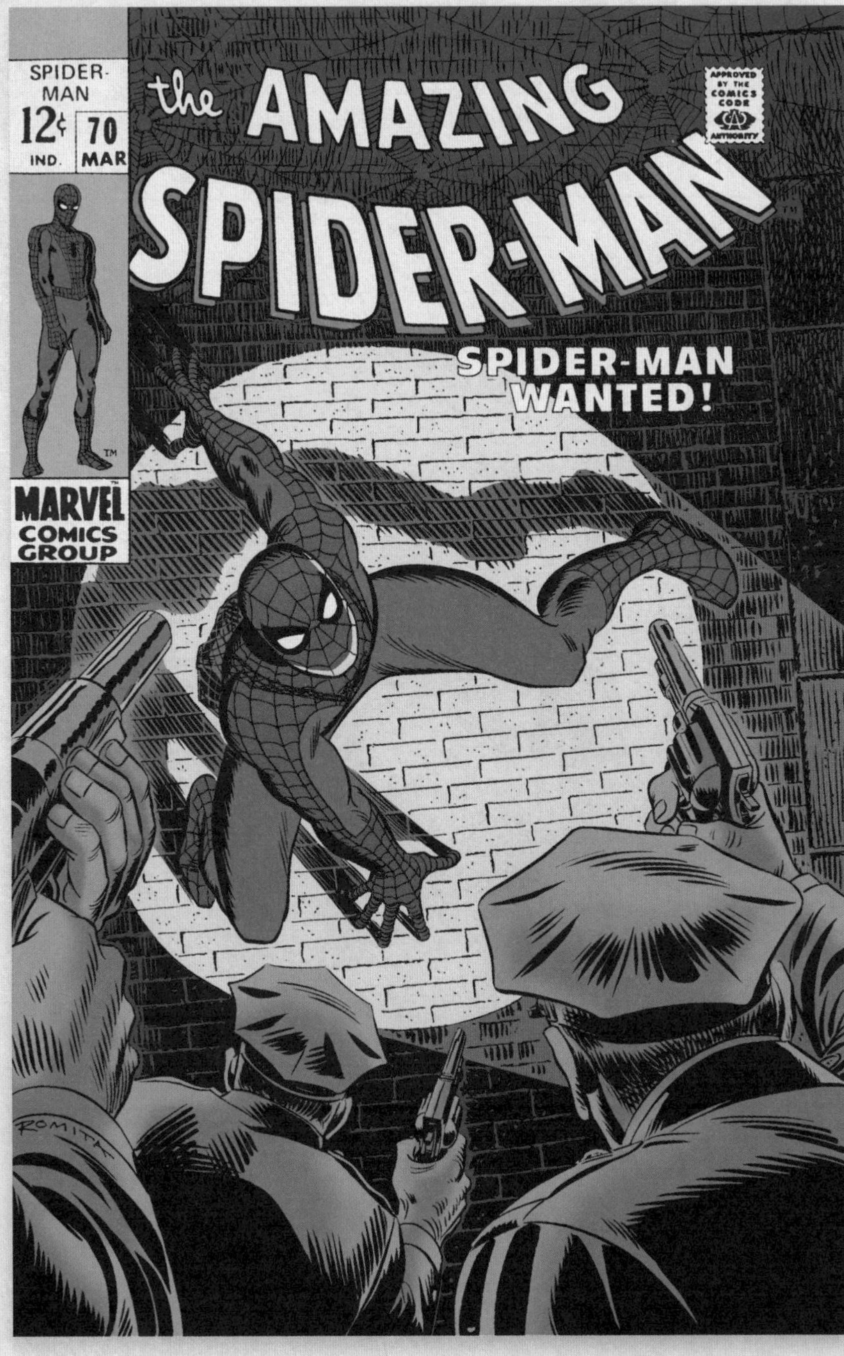

OPPOSITE 1: **SPIDER-MAN** from *Thor* no. 221 (March 1974). Stamp also appears in *Power Man* no. 20 (August 1974) and *Captain Marvel* no. 35 (November 1974).

ABOVE *The Amazing Spider-Man* no. 70 (March 1969), art by John Romita Sr. The image was retouched by Romita and also appears in *Marvelmania Catalog* no. 2 (1969), on the back cover of the mini comic book reprint of *The Amazing Spider-Man* no. 42 that was included with copies of *Eye* magazine (February 1969), the cover of *The Monster Times* no. 13 (July 19, 1972), and in many other promotional pieces from the time.

Your name, Steve Gerber,

You're under arrest. Never mind your rights. Just tell us where ya got all dem extra ration coupons! What do ya mean, "what ration coupons?" For the weekly allotments of inspiration, ya dirty little punk. Who do ya think ya are, anyway, walking around all inspired all the time?

Ya want evidence, huh? Alright, then chew on this, buster. First, ya risk your neck talking sense. Heaven help us talking sense about our nation's crimes against the Vietnamese, that's your first offense, Stevie boy—courage. Then, ya go and start this political stew to boiling, with intra-Asian power struggles, ideological disputes, psychological ploys, plus the always entertaining forces of greed and ego. So it's easy enough to name your second mistake—intellect. Last, but certainly not least, little man, ya go and dredge up all this long-neglected stuff, like the pain inherent in wearing a mask or the sometimes gothic, sometimes cosmic nuances of the human-machine relationship, or even the intense struggle one must make in order to see the world other than as a nationalist. Now we know your third blunder, Gerber—perception.

Why, if there's any justice at all, the judge'll give ya five to ten years. Writing Iron Man.

Love,

Billie Klie,
East Lansing, Michigan

We hope we got your name right, Ms. It was a bit hard to read. Sorry if we've made an error.

All of us here in the Bullpen (and out in California's Bullpen-West) know about Steve Gerber's courage, intellect and perception. However, all of the specifics you "charge" him with in the IRON MAN series are more correctly credited to its regular scripter, Mike Friedrich.

And now while we're scraping up Mike's grossly punctured ego off the floor and are attempting to pump it back up again, we'll move on to our next letter....

Dear Mike, George, & Roy,

IRON MAN #68 was a fantastic issue. I like the idea of Iron Man being able to use his weapons by mental telepathy. Now that the Mandarin is back in his own body, the show-down is going to be exciting.

Now I am trying for my first no-prize. On page 26 of IRON MAN #68, when Sunfire is teleported away from the battle by the Mandarin, Iron Man said that the last time he had seen anyone teleported away, it was himself (see TALES OF SUSPENSE #76). But, in CAPTAIN MARVEL #31, Moon Dragon, Captain Marvel, The Destroyer, and Iron Man were teleported by Thanos. You can't say that the events in #68 happened before Captain Marvel #31, because Iron Man's new mask had not yet been invented at the time of Mar—Vell's mag.

Do I get the no-prize?

Scott Jackson
1208 Sherman Street
Ypsilanti, Mi. 48197

As we explained to Bob Roman above IM is now working his weapons by "mental telepathy" (a redundant term, you'll also note...since "telepathy" is defined as "mental"). However, Scott, if you've been following the AVENGERS letters pages recently, you'll note that you've tripped up what Steve Englehart, Jim Starlin and Mike Friedrich considered a fairly tight chronology — and so, yessir, you DO receive that no-prize. No-mail has already arrived at your home announcing the no-fact.

Dear Builpen,

I want to congratulate you guys on bringing back Iron Man to his former greatness. I think some of the reasons for this are Friedrich's writing, Tuska's drawings and Esposito's inking: not to mention that lately Iron Man's been fighting Oldies-But-Goodies. By this I mean the Masked Marauder, Firebrand, Doctor Spectrum, etc., etc. Plus Iron Man has gone back to continued stories. I'm big on continued storeis, because you get much more depth and action. I don't see why you guys don't bring this mag back to a monthly basis. Right now, he's one of the best mags you've got.

Now on to issue 68. This is one of the greatest buildups in a long time. I mean how can you go wrong with the Mandarin and the Unicorn? Add Sunfire and the story is great. Then Yellow Claw and the story is a classic. Don't blow it, you've got all the ingredients for a classic series. Don't hurry it; if it takes three, four or five issues, let it.

And now two wishes, don't let the Unicorn die! You've saved people in worse conditions. He's one of my favorites! And bring back the X-Men in their own mag!

Arturo Tijada,
Phoenix, Arizona

We've already alluded to one of your last two wishes in a previous answer, Arturo, but since we're supposed to keep quiet about it, we shan't say any more!

And next issue will tie up the first phase of Marvel's greatest epic story...so we'd like to see how you feel it's turned out, okay? That goes for all of you folks...all of your letters are carefully read and all reasonable suggestions you make are considered. So write us, already!

Till next issue...

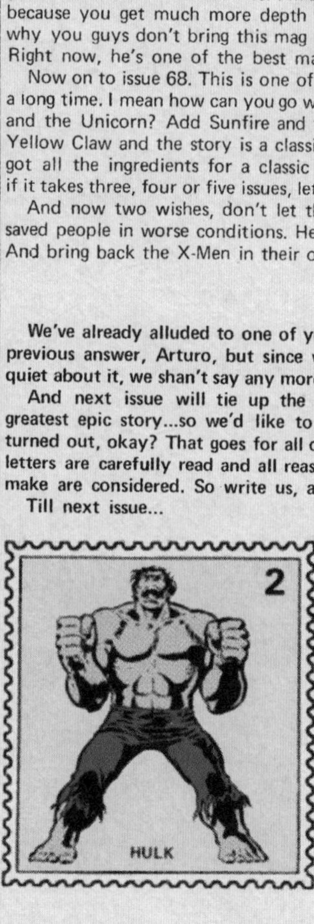

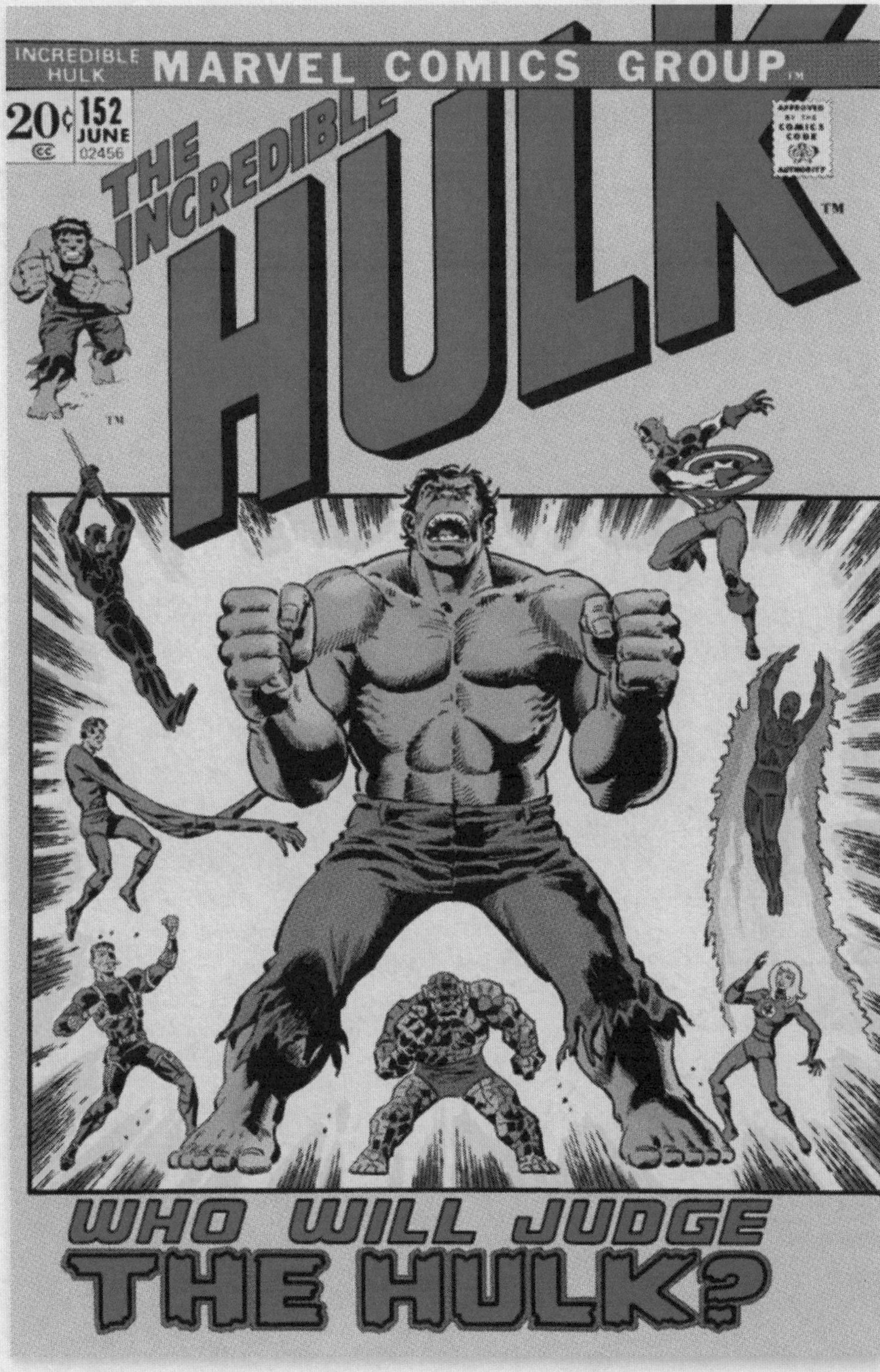

OPPOSITE **2: HULK** from *Iron Man* no. 70 (September 1974). Stamp also appears in *The Amazing Spider-Man* no. 130 (March 1974), *Giant-Size Fantastic Four* no. 4 (February 1975), and *Captain Marvel* no. 41 (November 1975).

ABOVE *The Incredible Hulk* no. 152 (June 1972), art by Herb Trimpe and John Severin.

COMMENTS TO CAGE

c/o MARVEL COMICS GROUP, 575 MADISON AVE. N.Y.C. 10022

Dear Roy, Tony, Billy, and Frank,

In HERO FOR HIRE #16, Tony Isabella and Billy Graham have done an epic ending for the mix-up left in the previous issue.

Characterizations were what Tony did best in "Shake Hands With Stiletto." The amoral, almost noble Comanche and Shades, who refuse to fink on Cage at the end the greedy Flea, who also has his good points Mrs. Jenks, who dies a heroine; and Rackham, the out-and-out villain, were all well-done.

The only characterizations I didn't care for were those of Phil Fox and Luke Cage. The alcoholic journalist is an old stereotyped cliche. And Cage shouldn't be having second thoughts about being a mercenary. What else is he going to do—join a circus?

Cage's scrap with Stiletto was a real knock-down, drag-out fight. It's too bad it was unresolved. I guess with two deaths in one issue, something has to be saved for the future.

The preview illustration was a little disappointing. POWER MAN is a very commercial-sounding name, while HERO FOR HIRE conjures up all sorts of images of hard-boiled detectivism. Who has been waiting for a fight between Cage and Iron Man? Captain America and Doc Savage are the characters Luke is ideally suited to battle and adventure with. But you people did a good job on the Luke Cage/Spider-Man crossover, so maybe the Iron Man crossover will work, too.

Bob Hobart
7741 Dahlia Drive
Mentor, Ohio 44060

Don't forget, Bob, that in the eyes of the general public, Iron Man, too, is a "hero for hire", though exclusively in the employ of one man—Tony Stark. While, in reality, Tony is Iron Man, and the superhero bit is not the way he makes his living, as it is with Luke, but more a way of helping mankind in his leisure time. We figured that two such divergent personalities—the wealthy playboy versus the nitty-gritty ghetto-born mercenary—would make for an interesting clash. Hope you agreed, now that you've seen POWER MAN #17.

Dear Marvel,

HERO FOR HIRE #14-16 featured Billy Graham on pencils, and those issues contain some of the finest artwork around today. I hope that after having seen just how fine Billy is, you won't consign him to the relative obscurity of inker. Billy has everything required for a penciller—he has an excellent story-telling style; he conveys mood and emotions superbly. His depiction of the hid-out Shades and Comanche had an aura of authenticity that I don't think any other artist would have acheived. He has a colorful way with costumes. And above all these standard "requirements", Billy has a fresh, exciting approach that offers relief from the too-familiar styles of your other, busy artists.

"Retribution" was one of the best CAGE stories I've read, and about one of the best comics stories ever written. What made it so good was the simple fact that the story offered no simple solution: The only real disappointment was that you didn't spin out the complications for another couple of issues.

I'm not happy with the upcoming changes in CAGE. For one thing, the present title HERO FOR HIRE is one of those perfect titles that come along maybe once in a decade, like "Superman" or "The Avengers". The other changes sound like efforts to make Cage like other superheroes, only in blackface. If you're going to have a black superhero, you might as well make him as black as possible. There's no middle ground.

Brian Earl Brown
Mishawaka, Ind.

Yes, there is, Brian. There has to be. Because, as linguistic experiments over the past few years have shown, a "black-as-possible" superhero mag would be utterly incomprehensible to a white audience. The ghettos have spawned their own styles of speech, their own idioms, combinations of words that whites are utterly unfamiliar with. (Check it out. Tests were administered to white college students, containing a one-paragraph story written in the language of the ghetto. Less than half of the students had any idea what the story was about!) So, since we're not producing POWER MAN—which, incidentally, was the original title for this series, "Hero For Hire" being a later inspiration—for an exclusively black audience, we have to walk a tightrope between true authenticity and seemingly authentic dialogue and situations.

That doesn't mean we're turning this magazine into a minstrel show, however. Our readers would despise us for that—and we wouldn't feel too thrilled with ourselves, either. Just give the changes a little time to grow on you, Brian. If they have the effect we hope for—putting POWER MAN near the top of the Marvel line-up—everybody will be happy in the end.

Now, for our next sermonette...!

Dear Bullpen,

About the controversy over violence and killing: I cast my vote with those against it. Not that all characters should be immortal, but I think it's being overdone. I don't mind the stories of Luke Cage, because they are set so vividly in a tough part of New York, and Luke faces guys who are all bad. These all-bad baddies are different from the type of villains Stan Lee once talked about in his Soapbox...the misguided ones, the psychotics, the emotionally-deranged I'll-save-the-world-by-conquering-it types

It may be that I'm used to the superhero saving the life of whomever the villain is threatening, but I still think the Bullpen writers (I'm not sure Conway and Englehart are the only ones) should go easy.

Please keep Billy Graham as artist on LUKE CAGE. I hope we'll see more of D.W.

Ken Melarned
494 Victoria Ave.
Montreal 217 P.Q.
Canada

Billy Graham will definitely be pencilling an upcoming issue or two—or three, or four, or eight hundred and ninety, if Don McGregor gets his way—of the new BLACK PANTHER series in JUNGLE ACTION. We hear this is some of his most exciting work yet, by the way, so don't miss it. (Besides, ol' T'Challa is rapidly achieving superstar status just on the merits of McGregor's bizarre villains and plots. Pick up on it. You may never put it down.)

And writer Len Wein does, we're sure, plan to keep D.W. around as a regular character in POWER MAN, so never fear, Mr. Melarned. (Hope we've got your name right, Ken. Your writing was just a tad difficult to decipher in spots.) We hope we don't have to ask for your—and the rest of Marveldom Altogether's—reactions to Len's scripting, by the way. He wants to know if you dig it, and so do we.

All of which brings us—finally!—to the main body of your letter. We, too, feel that killing is being overdone. But we tend to think there's a lot more of it being done, over- or otherwise, by people on streets and in battle zones than by people on our peaceful little staff. Sometimes, Ken, we can't help thinking, if we can prevent one murder/war/mugging by showing the basic ugliness of it all, then whatever violence appears in our magazines is justified. We've never portrayed the taking of life as a fun thing to do on a Saturday night, as all too many movies and television programs have done. We think it's a wrong, unhuman, sick sort of activity. And that's the way we try to show it.

Further comments, people?

THIS IS IT! YOUR
MARVEL VALUE STAMP
FOR THIS ISSUE!

CLIP 'EM AND COLLECT 'EM!

OPPOSITE **3: CONAN THE BARBARIAN** from *Power Man* no. 18 (April 1974). Stamp also appears in *The Amazing Spider-Man* no. 134 (July 1974) and *Power Man* no. 23 (February 1975).

ABOVE *Conan the Barbarian* no. 32 (November 1973), art by John Buscema and Ernie Chua.

Bruce Banner? All too often, Banner is merely a plot device to get the Hulk into some difficult situation. In #179, however, we caught a real glimpse of Banner as an individual a man whose very existence is so fragmented that he has begun to grab, Hulk fashion, for any shreds of peace. It was lovely to see him fishing with Linc, to see him smiling at the children's games. Then came the dawning horror of his realization of Linc's problem and finally, the inevitable emergence of the Hulk to do what had to be done. The dualism of Hulk/Banner played a real part in the story. #179 was beautifully done and a welcome cog in the humanism/destruction cycle.

Finally a word on Betty's body. The question is not, "Should there be naked bodies in Marvel Comics?" but, "Was Betty wearing clothes when she became the Harpy?" Answer: no. Betty was tastefully nude in #168. Therefore, she should have been tastefully nude in #170, in the opening panels at least. If comic fans want realism, they can get it aplenty on the 7 o'clock news. But credibility? Now, that's different. And since we all know we can't get that on the 7:00 o'clock news...Make Mine Marvel!

Jean Hardie
(no address given)

Interesting comments, Jean. We suspect a lot of other readers will have a lot to say in reply to them, too. We'll see.

For our part, as we mentioned in our answer to Bob Rodi's letter, we tend to agree. Bruce Banner is a necessary component of the Hulk's character. Without the spark of humanity which dwells within him, and which occasionally emerges, we believe he'd be a far less interesting character.

As for the credibility of comics versus the credibility of television news...don't be so hard on those scoop-hunters, Jean. Half the time, they probably can't believe the stuff they've had to report lately!

Dear Marvel,

When I first picked up the new HULK I was utterly disgusted and disappointed. As usual it had a great story line, and another ending where a new villain pops up out of nowhere. But when I read the part about Hulk being the strongest thing to walk the earth, I got so mad I ripped the comic in two. I had a good reason for it, because for many years I have been arguing with my friends saying that Hulk is strong but not the strongest. Did you forget Galactus, Watcher, Odin, Mangog, Absorbing Man, Silver Surfer, Juggernaut, Ego-Prime, Zeus, The Demolisher, The Destroyer, Pluto—etc., etc.? Remember "whoever you are, there is always someone stronger." If Hulk is made too invincible, no one will buy his comic any more, because they knew no one could hurt him.

Eric Keitz
2425 William's Bridge Road
New York City, 10469

Hold on a second, Eric! You've done us a grievous wrong! Allow us to explain...

In terms of sheer strength, the Hulk probably is more powerful than the Absorbing Man, the Juggernaut, Ego-Prime, the Destroyer, and so on. But each of those characters has some power other than his brute strength to rely on, in addition. Sure, Hulk might be able to best them in a purely hand-to-hand combat situation— but any encounter would likely not be so simple.

As for Odin, Galactus, Mangog, and Pluto, they are not truly earthly beings. Galactus is a creature of space; Odin and Pluto inhabit the Asgardian/Olympian dimension (wherever that is); and Mangog, too, exists not on earth, but in Asgard and the surrounding vicinity.

The Watcher? The Silver Surfer? Here again, Hulk is probably more powerful than either one in terms of muscle power. But he lacks the intellect and space-time-related abilities of the Watcher and the awesome Power Cosmic of the Surfer...not to mention the Surfer's near-light speed, his ability to live without air in the trackless void of space, and like that.

In short, then, though Hulk may be the strongest being to be born on earth, he is likely not the mightiest.

Are we forgiven?

THIS IS IT! YOUR
MARVEL VALUE STAMP
FOR THIS ISSUE!
CLIP 'EM AND COLLECT 'EM!

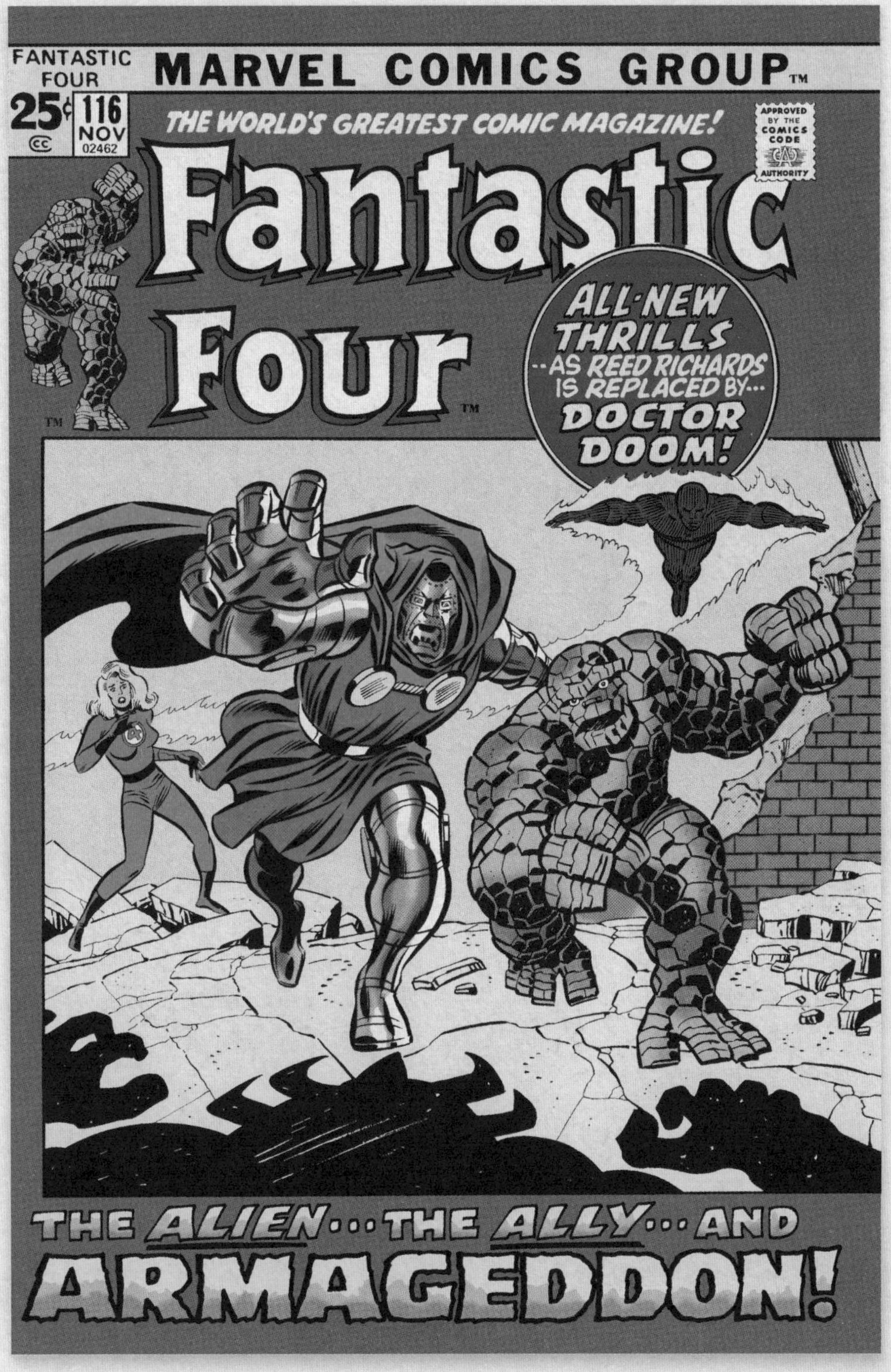

OPPOSITE **4: THING** from *The Incredible Hulk* no. 183 (January 1975). Stamp also appears in *The Avengers* no. 123 (May 1974) and *The Amazing Spider-Man* no. 135 (August 1974).

ABOVE *Fantastic Four* no. 116 (November 1971), art by John Buscema and Joe Sinnott.

Short interludes to the story could be taken. Thus, while Stephen is having a conversation with Eternity in some distant part of the omniverse, Wong could be contemplating troubles of his own personal life (assuming his personal life goes beyond his service to Dr. Strange.)

Meanwhile, I suggest that you don't move Clea's studies in mastering the mystic arts too rapidly. Let her grow into them as they become part of her. Let her express and discuss her feelings with Stephen, not hide them as she did for so long in STRANGE TALES. Allow this period in Clea's life to be a period of discovery and growing self-awareness of her identity as a woman – not to mention her ability as a sorceress.

There it is, Steve and Frank. Do with it what you will. Who knows? Some day, Stan, you may be publishing "Marvel Premiere featuring: DR. STRANGE, MASTER OF THE MYSTIC ARTS and CLEA, SORCERESS SUPERNATURAL."

May the Winds of Watoomb be ever at your back, and may the Eye of Agamotto look upon you with favor.

Byron Brewer
729 Benson Ave.
Frankfort, Ky. 40601

DOC #1 should have satisfied many of your yearnings, Bryon. It is our firm intention to feature Clea ever more prominently in the series as she grows and develops her skills. But as for Wong...well, it seems to us that his life was summed up on page 16, panel 1, of our premiere ish (not to be confused with our PREMIERE ishes!). In addition, and unfortunately, as inflation has eaten away at the length of our tales, it's become more and more difficult to find space for the examination of subordinate characters. We wish it were otherwise...but that's a longing for unreality, etc., etc.

Dear Co-Creators,

I just finished #13 and it was great, as usual. The art, of course, was great, but, mainly I wish to speculate on the future stories. Now, if Sise-Neg says that there is a finite amount of mystical energy that exists, then when Clea finishes all her studying (she'll be almost as powerful as Doc Strange himself), the energy in that time period will be divided even more and the good Doctor's powers will be weakened, right? Now that can't happen to him, can it? So, he'll either have to knock off Mordo to restore his powers or, someone will kill good ol' Clea. I, personally, would prefer the latter, because he's rather young to be worrying about a disciple, and, as the years of his mag go along and Clea becomes more and more powerful, he'll be taken out of the spotlight and stuck with a sidekick. Oh, there might be a third possibility; you could have her become evil and have Dr. Strange knock her off.

A closing thought! Take Doc out of the Defenders! He's being ruined with mediocre art and ridiculous plots. And do not team him up in one of your mags, like MARVEL TEAM-UP and TWO-IN-ONE.

Steven Dong
14627 River Forest
Houston, Texas 77024

Let us explain, Steve! What we meant was this: there is a finite amount of magic—but that amount is incredibly large. Only a god like Sise-neg could ever control it all. Dr. Strange, even as the sorcerer supreme, will still control only a fraction of the total, and Clea, Mordo, and a hundred others will not lessen Doc's power one iota. Okay?

Gentlemen:

I wish to add my appreciatory comments to those of the readers in the last three issues of DR. STRANGE. It is obvious that, from the rather feeble intellectual background of the average "funny book," you have evolved and synthesized an entirely new art form, unlike any I have previously experienced. In my views, it is a profound success.

It is obvious, however, that many of the basic concepts of ancient and nameless evils find their roots in the Cthulhu mythos of the late H. P. Lovecraft. Virtually all of these ideas and characters have passed into public domain, so why not incorporate some of them in toto? I, for one, would love to see how your talented artists would handle dread Cthulhu, or, perhaps, "the mad, faceless god, Nyalarthotep, (who) howls blindly in the darkness to the piping of his two amorphous, idiot fluteplayers".

Regardless of your decision in this regard, please be assured of my admiration of your efforts. Please also try to make your subscription service a little more available to those of us in "the boonies"; I, at least, have had some trouble in this area.

Sincerely,

David S. Grauman, M.D.
Box 1207
Soldotna, Alaska

Thanks for your letter to DOC, Doc. Evidently, you must have missed some of the earlier issues of PREMIERE because in them, Editor Roy Thomas did ask his writers to incorporate elements of the Cthulhu mythos, albeit the elements involved in the writings of Robert E. Howard. Unfortunately, the combination of the two didn't come off too well, and when Steve and Frank took over, they moved away from such things. But maybe some day, again....

NEXT: Doc faces Death— and wait till you see what Death *is*! And wait till you see what happens....afterwards! Rest assured, this one's another mind-boggler, so send your astral body down to the store NEXT MONTH for DR. STRANGE #3 (but don't pay for it with an astral quarter!).

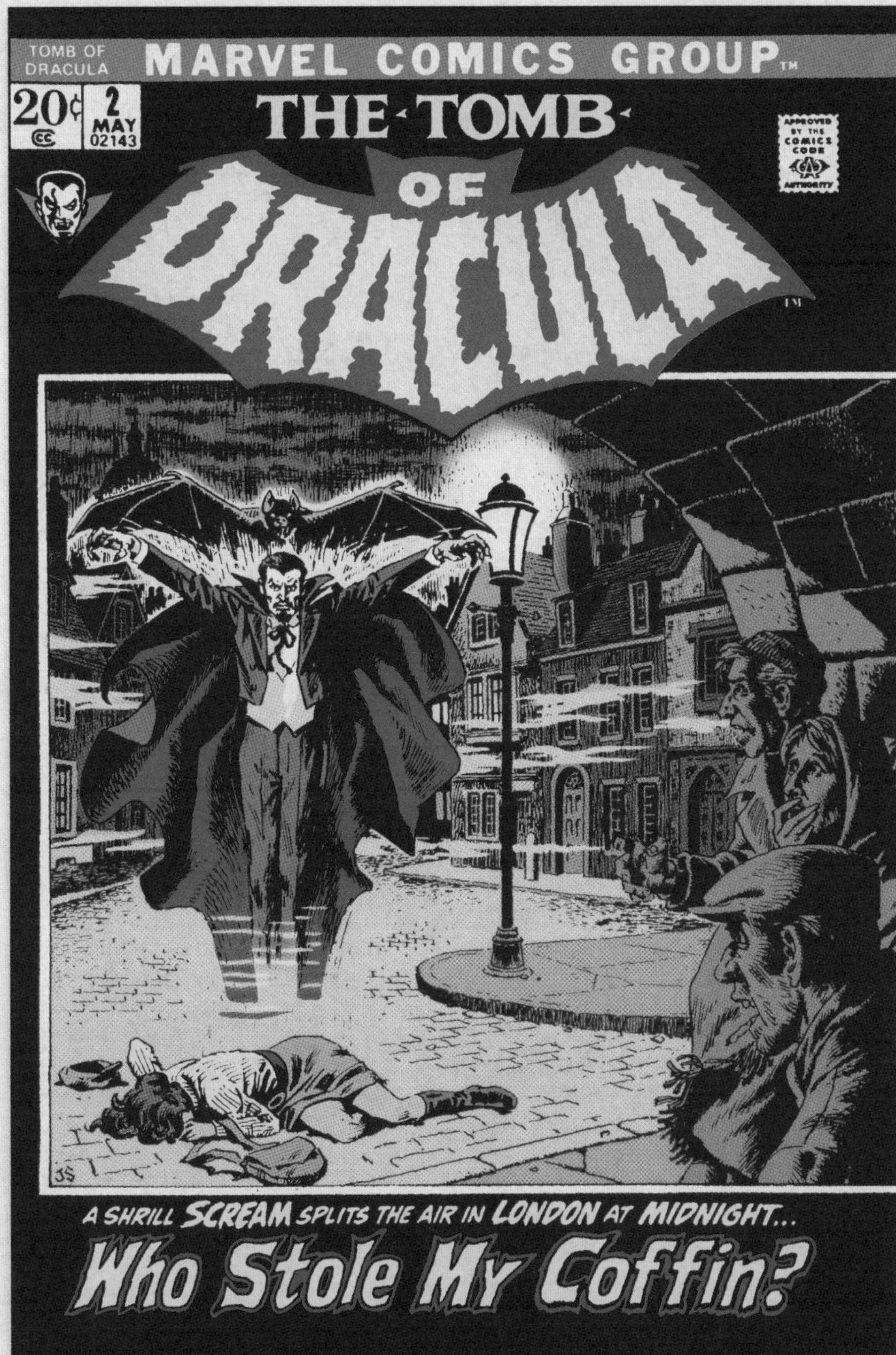

OPPOSITE **5: DRACULA** from *Doctor Strange* no. 2 (August 1974). Stamp also appears in *Marvel Spotlight* no. 14 (March 1974) and *War Is Hell* no. 11 (February 1975).

ABOVE *The Tomb of Dracula* no. 2 (May 1972), art by John Severin.

I hope IRON FIST makes it, because I enjoy it very much.

Demetrios Frangos
Berkeley, Calif.

If you've read this issue's tale, Demetrios, you're already aware of the bizarre twist that played havoc with Iron Fist's plans and desires for revenge. (We won't elaborate any further on that here, just in case you haven't read the mag yet, but...!)

As for Iron Fist's relationships with women— you're right. It's going to be an interesting element in the strip in issues to come, as I.F. goes about establihsing a life for himself in the Big Apple. But will it be a weakness? Difficult to say. For despite his lack of experience with the opposite sex, Daniel Rand has been trained to "read" people's intents and emotions in their bodily movements. So if he can anticipate a person's reactions...well, let's just wait and see.

Dear Marvel,

I've just finished reading the first two issues of IRON FIST, which I thought were pretty good. But I see in the feature certain trends that, if continued, could lessen its quality.

For example, if every story is going to have I.F.'s right hand "light up" at the critical moment and then smash through steel, bone, or whatever, a rather dull and predictable pattern is going to emerge.

Also, I was disappointed in the "it only appears once every ten years" gimmick you applied to K'un-Lun. It seems that all those potentially great supporting characters may never come back, ten years being a frightfully long time in terms of comics.

Lastly, I would appreciate it if, in the future, you were a little less graphic in the blood-flowing sequences. I know this sounds a bit strange in these days of violent excesses, and in the kung fu genre especially, but I feel you can get the message across without using a bucketful of red ink.

Edward B. Via
1648 Dean Road
Roanoke, Va. 24018

Point by point, Ed...

Iron Fist's power isn't quite in the same category as, say, Bruce Banner's transformations into the Hulk. I.F. has complete control over when his fist will "light up." He need only focus his concentration to bring the power to bear. And under those conditions, we don't think it's any more "predictable" a gimmick than Spider-Man's shooting of webs at the proper moment. Okay?

On the matter of K'un-Lun's decade-long disappearing act...I.F. may yet discover some way to pierce whatever barrier it is that separates that sacred city from our own reality. (An Iron Fist/Dr. Strange team-up? Hmmm. Weird. But an intriguing thought, no?)

Finally, on the matter of any overabundance of blood: we try not to be too graphic most of the time, but there are occasional instances in which the red ink is necessary. Once, for example, I.F. delivered a blow to a villain's forehead, and our usual black blotch in that case would have looked more like an accidental smearing of the artwork than the result of a kung fu smash. So we used the crimson, more for clarity's sake than out of a desire to be overly graphic.

Dear Marvel,

In your "Iron Fistfuls" column in PREMIERE #16, I saw the word "nunchaka" in reference to a kung fu weapon. The correct spelling is "nunchak*u*," and that weapon is not a chain with weighted ends. That latter weapon is called "manri kigusari."

Larry Grossman
Miami, Fla.

Having neither nunchaku nor manri kigusari handy, we gave Tony Isabella, who wrote that column, a thousand lashes with a wet chow mein noodle for making such a mistake. He'll never live it down.

THIS IS IT! YOUR
MARVEL VALUE STAMP
FOR THIS ISSUE!
CLIP 'EM AND
COLLECT 'EM!

OPPOSITE **6: THOR** from *Marvel Premiere* no. 19 (November 1974). Stamp also appears in *The Amazing Spider-Man* no. 132 (May 1974), *Captain Marvel* no. 33 (July 1974), and *Marvel Premiere* no. 25 (October 1975).

ABOVE *Thor* no. 219 (January 1974), art by John Buscema and Mike Esposito.

even harder when the book has as long and colorful a history as DAREDEVIL.

So I set all the wrong goals for myself. I was trying to do Gerry's D.D., or Roy's D.D., or Stan's D.D., and basically fighting my own instincts about where the strip should go.

That changed with D.D. #107, the finale of the Terrex series. Because, whether I liked it or not, I had inadvertantly steered Daredevil on a course toward a major break with the past. Several long, involved discussions with editor Roy Thomas helped clear my head about the characters, the villains, the interpersonal relationships in the strip...and I was on my way. After that, I relied on you, the readers, for guidance. And, incredibly, with a more than slight assist from Bob Brown and Gene Colan, it all seems to be coming together in such a way as to please all of us. Meaning you folks out there, and we folks on the allegedly creative end of the magazine.

We're all in there trying. Myself. Bob Brown. Vinnie Colletta. Roy. All of us. And while we'll never be content enough to think we've got the problem "licked" (no problem's ever licked when the next deadline is only thirty days away), we do know the mag has improved. And your mail bears us out.

One last note. About your mail. It's been a tremendous source of help and inspiration (and, occasionally, depression) for me. Reading all your varying views of what D.D. should be was a major factor, I'm sure, in how I went about coming up with my own conception of the character. You all contributed something— every one of you who took the time to write.

And there just aren't words to express our appreciation. Enough. Onward—!

Dear Marvel,

You can't imagine my joy when I found Gene Colan did DAREDEVIL #110. With Gene on TOMB OF DRACULA. I figured he'd have lost his touch at drawing superheroes. The result was yes and no. No, because D.D. was even better drawn than ever; yes, because the Thing wasn't.

But what the heck? The story was good, anyway. I mean really good! And you know what? For awhile, I thought Black Spectre and the Secret Empire were sort of connected! Then, D.D., Capt. America, and the Falcon, along with the X-Men and the other mutants would collide...thus beginning another senses-shattering epic for this year! Anyway, just try to have Gene Colan do D.D. for a few more issues and maybe,

just maybe, we'll be friends again. Happy Fooming!!

John Flagg
7 Park Vista, Apt. 805
Toronto, Ont.
Canada

And that's another thing that happens to writers, John: as with the Steves, Englehart and Gerber, this time, they sometimes hit on the same good idea at the same time. So the White House got hit twice in two months, once by the Secret Empire, once by Black Spectre. (And they shouldn't complain! Not after what the commentators do to them five nights a week!)

Anyway, even though Gene couldn't continue with D. D. as a regular feature, you'll have to admit, we think, that Bob Brown's been turning in one magnificent job after another these days. We think he's improving every issue— and who can ask more than that? Especially when a guy's work is as fine as Bob's has been these past several issues?

THIS IS IT! YOUR
MARVEL VALUE STAMP
FOR THIS ISSUE!
CLIP 'EM AND COLLECT 'EM!

OPPOSITE **7: WEREWOLF [BY NIGHT]** from *Daredevil* no. 114 (October 1974). Stamp also appears in *Tomb of Dracula* no. 18 (March 1974).

ABOVE *Werewolf by Night* no. 12 (December 1973), art by Gil Kane and Don Perlin.

THE HYBORIAN PAGE

c/o MARVEL COMICS GROUP, 575 MADISON AVE., NEW YORK, N.Y. 10022

A few words of explanation are in order-- both for this issue: and for the next.

First of all, the regular Conan reader may be wondering why this issue was drawn by Nefarious Neal Adams, instead of Big John Buscema. The answer is simple. Neal and Roy were hard at work on a 25-page Conan saga for our 75¢ SAVAGE TALES magazine when the decision to "wait and see" with that title was made. Thus, and because "The Curse of the Golden Skull" fits into a very definite niche in the Conan saga, they were forced to shorten the tale by several pages and sandwich it instead into the 20¢ title. (This latter is by way of explanation in case one or two points of "Skull" seem slightly less explored than the compleat Hyboriophile is used to. Sure, Roy and Neal would both have liked to show more of Juma, of the princess Yolinda, even of the wrathful Rotath himself-- but those half-dozen pages which of necessity were ripped untimely from the story force us to leave a few loose ends for our more creative Conan-lovers to tie together for themselves.)

Next issue, still another first-- as John Buscema both pencils and inks a full-length fantasy called "The Warrior and the Were-Woman," adapted freely from the Robert E. Howard thriller "The House of Arabu." Big John fell so in love with this tale as he was penciling it that he decided he just had to ink it himself-- so we're keeping enterprising Ernie Chua busy with a few other features for a month or twain.

Meanwhile, to get our Hyborian Pages up to date, here are a random sampling of comments on issues 32-33, the first two parts of our recent "Flame Winds" trilogy:

CONAN #32 was a joy to read. On the surface it was perhaps merely another stud-vs.-monster saga, but on second glance it became much more. The wench/atrocity offered Conan a sanctuary of sorts from the city guard; a deus ex machina solution for his problem. He accepted, and became ensnared in a series of tentacle/entanglements which when severed would continuously regenerate. Okay, let's substitute a couple of tags for the characters. Label Conan "the natural man" and the foxy creature "society," "the establishment," or whatever else angry young rebels are fighting this month. By accepting any mechanical solution at face value, the so-called authentic man negates the self and virtually surrenders his life-- as Conan almost did. . . .You probably never pitched for that, Roy, but to my mind it was there and I'm grateful.

Koala (Rich Arnold)
Berea, Ohio

What can I say? CONAN #32 is the start of yet another spectacle. How can someone argue, after reading it, that CONAN isn't the best sword-and-sorcery mag ever to be produced? I don't care what anybody else (including Paul Watson) says: Big John and Ernie Chua are great on CONAN. "Flame Winds of Lost Khitai" was great-- except that Khitai wasn't lost!

Don Jacobson
2243 Falcon Ave.
St. Paul, Minn. 55119

It was suggested in CONAN #33 letters-page that Roy's scripting has been faltering lately. Well, I strongly disagree. I feel that no one in the Bullpen-- not Gerry, Len, Steve E., Marv, Mike F., or even Steve G.-- could outdo Roy's scripts of late. In other words: keep Thomas on CONAN! P.S.: The rest of CONAN #33 was great, too.

Jeff Wills
Tallmadge, Ohio

That was a beautiful cover by Trimpe on CONAN #33, but what mis-bred son of a scum put those %*$# a !'!'! word balloons on it?? Is it too much for a Marvelite to beg that one of Marvel's titles be kept free of those stains? Aaarrgghhh!

K. J. Robbins
1314 Cooper St.
Missoula, Mt. 59801

[We interrupt this letters page to bring you a special announcement. Roy informs us, first of all, that the cover was actually a collaborative effort by Herb Trimpe and John Romita, who forgot to sign it-- and that 'twas he (Roy, that is) who was the M.S.O.A.S. who put the word balloons on that cover (and who has a better right?), because he felt it needed it. Sorry about that, friend, but after all, you have approximately thirty other CONAN covers, both earlier and later, to revel in.]

For a while I wasn't too interested in your CONAN book. After all, he wasn't a regular Marvel modern-day superhero. Thus, I missed many issues. I bought the current issue (#33), though, because the cover looked good. **[K. J. Robbins, take note! --RT.]** Great story inside, too! Now, I'll never miss buying an issue of CONAN THE BARBARIAN!

Ron Brown
P.O. Box 02105
Cleveland, Ohio 44102

Having just read CONAN #33, I noticed you said you won't be printing any Carter/de Camp stories. Personally, I think this is in your favor. I'm not a critic, but I've read all the Conan paperbacks out and I think Roy Thomas is consistently and considerably better than they. They conceive excellent plots, but they haven't captured Howard's Conan the way Roy does. For instance, in one recent story by Carter and deCamp entitled "The Black Sphinx of Nebthu," only one Conan fight is even referred to! What's the use of a peaceful barbarian?

Wayne Moss
189 Palm Ave.
Auburn, Calif. 95603

Thanks for that from Roy, Wayne-- though we've no wish to throw rocks at Conan stories from any other source, many of which we've rather enoyed ourselves. Incidentally, your letter is typical of many we've received, in that it applauds the fact that Conan has become even more of an action-oriented strip in recent months than it was before. Though we realize full well that action is not a substitute for other elements in a story, the decision to play up the "savage" side of Conan since John Buscema took over the strip has been deliberate, and has resulted in a CONAN comic which is, in many ways, even more popular than before!

One final note, lest someone mistakenly infer from the above paragraph that we're now maligning Barry Smith: Even now, despite the perhaps-temporary hiatus of SAVAGE TALES, there are plans afoot (if all goes well) for a regular, larger-sized Conan color comic-book in addition to the regular 20¢ title! In that forthcoming mag, which will probably come out four times a year, we plan to have no regular Conan artist, but rather to have various talented artists each try their hands at a Conan tale-- and that includes, hopefully, one Barry Smith (who has recently been spending his waking hours practicing on his electric guitar and who thus has not had time for any comics work anyway!)

How's that for an earth-shattering pronouncement to end a jam-packed Hyborian Page? We did it 'cause we love ya-- and because next issue's story is a page or two longer than "The Curse of the Golden Skull," and we may not have room for an LP! Till then, may Crom never notice you-- you're better off that way!

THIS IS IT! YOUR
MARVEL VALUE STAMP
FOR THIS ISSUE!

CLIP 'EM AND COLLECT 'EM!

OPPOSITE **8: CAPTAIN AMERICA** from *Conan the Barbarian* no. 37 (April 1974). Stamp also appears in *The Defenders* no. 15 (September 1974), *Werewolf by Night* no. 24 (December 1974), and *Frankenstein* no. 16 (May 1975).

ABOVE *The Avengers* no. 58 (November 1968), art by John Buscema and George Klein. This cover was also used as the source for MVS no. 15.

current story-line reflects. We aren't denying the existence of magic and sorcery in the Savage Land (that would also be inconsistent with Ka-Zar's past stories in the early ASTONISHING TALES), but they will not be in the foreground. We hope this is to your satisfaction.

Dear Marvel People,

I'm a jungle-story lover and thus I dig jungle comics. Yes indeed I do! So, when I stumbled on KA-ZAR #1, I was thrilled to say the least. But I do have one complaint and it comes from issue number two. Don Heck's art doesn't make it on Ka-Zar and he just murders Shanna. And Mike Royer only did a fair job in #1.

Maybe it's not that their art is that bad, but you have Marvel Madmen that could do much better on it. Gil Kane, would be tops, but Frank Brunner or Barry Smith could grace the pages so much better. The story-line is out-of-sight and the covers for issue #1 and#2 have both been fantastic.

Hey, how about a 35¢ Ka-Zar with more pages, and say 10 pages of Shanna in the back? No good, huh? Well, think about it, okay?

Keep on foom'ing'!

Sam Combs
Rt. 1 Box 25
Pinewood, Minn. 56664

You've given us a lot of things to say, Sam. First, believe it or not, the idea of a larger-size mag featuring Ka-Zar has crossed our minds and it just may come about if the 35¢ or 60¢ titles we've introduced with other features (like Spidey, the FF, Conan, Dracula) prove to be sales successes.

As you can see from the letters joining yours in this column, Don Heck's artwork has been well-received by a majority. Yet you've probably already noticed that Frank Brunner drew this ish's cover and may have the time (if he can get ahead on DR. STRANGE) to draw more covers for us in the future. What may be of even more interest is our announcement that beginning next issue, our artist will be none other than the illustrative John Buscema (!), whose bang-up cover for KA-ZAR #1 has had everyone raving!

Dear Ka-Zar Men,

In the issue of KA-ZAR number two, on page 15 panel 3 you have a common Triceratops. The dictionary defines the Triceratops as a plant-eating creature that feeds on shrubs and bushes. This brings up the contradiction, why would a herbiverous Dinosaur by nature, resort to carniverous activities such as eating "pet horses." Let's see you weasel out of this one.

Mark Sisson
2665 Balmoral Court
Ann Arbor, Michigan 48103

AH-HA! Have we got you, Mark!

The contradiction you pointed out was intentional! In fact, it was essential to the entire plot of the story! If you read later on in the story you'll see that this "meat-eating" (carnivorous) episode on the part of the Triceratops was precisely what tipped Shanna the She-Devil off to the fact that the dinosaur was a phony and that therefore the Red Wizard was also a fake.

You'll have to pardon our exuberance, Mark. It is not at all intended as a put-down. It's just that we get "caught" so many times with mistakes for which we have to cough up no-prizes out of our no-treasury, that we can't restrain ourselves when it's a Merry Marvelite that makes the mistake! Maybe you should send us a no-prize this time, okay?

THIS IS IT! YOUR
MARVEL VALUE STAMP
FOR THIS ISSUE!
CLIP 'EM AND COLLECT 'EM!

OPPOSITE **9: CAPTAIN MARVEL** from *Ka-Zar* no. 4 (July 1974). Stamp also appears in *Fantastic Four* no. 145 (April 1974), *Jungle Action* no. 12 (November 1974), and *Werewolf by Night* no. 27 (March 1975).

ABOVE *Captain Marvel* no. 29 (November 1973), art by Jim Starlin and Al Milgrom. John Romita Sr. redrew the face.

THE HYBORIAN PAGE

c/o MARVEL COMICS GROUP, 575 MADISON AVE., NEW YORK, N.Y. 10022

Dear Roy, John, and Ernie,

"I have a little shadow that goes in and out with me/And what can be the *harm* of him is--er--more than--uh..."

Seriously, though, "The Shadow in the Tomb" was as exceptionally good a tale as it was a marvel of economy: *two* tales in one, yet united by that shocker of a last panel. However, don't try this trick too often, or (as your CRAZY writers would put it) Conan might suffer from a severe case of flashback!

The characterization of Malthuz was carried off well, but, oh, those plot elements...! A search-and-destroy mission? Discontent among the enlisted men about the morality of the war? The domino theory as applied to Turan? "C'mon Roy, knock it off!" I gasped, as I rolled over, clutching quivering sides.

Artwise, Chua is finally getting a feel for Big John's pencils, and produced a very effective job (the best since his premiere). And finally, regarding your open question on continued stories, I can only say that I haven't seen enough continued stories to judge their merits against the one-shot type; therefore, I urge you to have more multi-issues epics, and *then* put the question to us again.

Mark A. Obert-Thorn
Huntingdon Valley, Pa. 19006

And that, Mark, is precisely the tone of the vast majority of letters which we've received to date, regarding the single-story-vs.-continued-story controversy. 'Twould seem that you Hyboriophiles want us to keep you off-guard for a while, bouncing from one to the other, till a clear pattern emerges. So be it--as a certain Thunder God from Asgard (not Aesgaard) would say.

By the way, Roy is under penalty of--well, we'd rather not say what dire deprivations he faces if he fails to mention in print that the major antagonist in issue # 31 was suggested to him by his lovely blonde wife, Jean. It seems that our author/editor was wracking his brain one evening trying to come up with just the right combatant for Conan to face in that far-northern crypt, when Jeanie suddenly turned to him languidly and said, "Why don't you have him fight his own shadow?" Presto--one of the most acclaimed CONAN original tales to date was born! (Personally, Roy considers it one of his most successful stories ever because our cute colorist, Glynis Wein, told him that its final panel caught her by surprise and made her shiver. Now that, friends, is rare praise indeed! Thanks, Glyn.)

Gentlemen,

While not exactly the usual person who would write a fan letter to your magazine, I find that I must tell someone how much I enjoy reading CONAN. I have been trying to keep up with his exploits, but often make it to the newsstand too late to find any trace of him.

I am a twenty-four-year-old former English teacher. I was introduced to CONAN by a barbarian friend who has since vanished from sight. When I was in a particularly up-tight situation and needed to relax, my friend told me that he read CONAN comics. As a former Army sergeant, he believed that only a hero like CONAN could live the life he himself longed for. He was a true barbarian and friend.

After reading my first CONAN, I found myself falling under his spell. Of all the methods of escape available to people today, I find my comic-book friend the safest and probably most enjoyable. I recommended it to several other friends and they, too, have fallen for him.

I want to praise all those who bring CONAN to me, from Robert E. Howard to Roy and the gang. My students all appreciated my further renditions of CONAN, made up at the spur of the moment when all else failed. They would like to thank all of you, too. And, if I may, I'd like to thank my lost friend for starting the whole thing.

Irene L. Coccato
217 Greene Ave.
Middlesex, N.J. 08846

You sure can, Irene. We just hope that, somewhere-or-other, your barbarian friend and benefactor is still reading and savoring CONAN the same way you are.

Roy especially enjoyed your heartfelt missive because he, too, was an English teacher of 24 when he opted for joining the Marvel Bullpen, a mere eight years ago. Crom! Where does all that time fly to, anyway? Seems like just the other day that the only other people who came into the office every day were Fabulous Flo Steinberg, Jolly Solly Brodsky, and Mirthful Marie Severin. Now Marie is assistant art director, in charge of coloring, corrections, and CRAZY-ness; Sol is Marvel's brand new administrative head (whatever that means--he's still not quite sure); and Fab Flo is a valued friend who stops by the office once in a while to kibitz and carouse.

And they say the Hyborian Age was a long time ago!

Dear Mr. Thomas:

I realize that Conan is about to go into his pirate era, but once you are done with that phase of his life I hope you will give consideration to the situation I am about to propose.

What would happen if Conan found himself in a time and a place completely alien to him...in all aspects of life. To be specific, imagine if you will a place where the system of life is completely geared to the orderly continuation of life...the human race. In this place we find machines in control because they make the logical desicion... however man and machine are becoming as one. The humans go about their daily tasks as robots... the emotion of love died long ago...as did hate, and fear, and every other feeling. What would the barbarian do in this situation. The system would of course try to eliminate him....he is not an orderly nor logical part of the system.

Would Conan try to save humanity...would it be worth saving? Here we have a society whose one function is to keep a race going long after the culture, the civilization of that race had died. Would the cultists still exist...if so would they see the barbarian as their champion or their enemy? Would Conan be more at home in the company of these wizards and devil-worshippers, or with the walking zombies of humanity? Also what effect would magic and scorcery have on the system? Of course Conan would have to return to his old stomping grounds...but it would be interesting to see what he would do in that situation. Thank you for your time.

Peter J. Mellen
92 Main St.
Milan, Ohio 44846

Afraid that's all you <u>will</u> thank us for, Pete--'cause the closest we ever plan to come to the kind of modern-day Conan tale you request is the story called "The Sword and the Sorcerer," which Roy and Bashful Barry Smith presented several years back, and which was later reprinted in CONAN # 16. Sorry about that--but we've got a hunch that a horde of Hyborian hellions would descend upon the hallowed halls of h'alliterative Marvel if we even hinted that we were planning such a tale. Are we right, friends? (Just this once, at least?)

Dear Roy and John,

CONAN # 31 was up to standards artwise, which is nothing less than sensational--but the flashback scene was *great!*

I haven't seen a bad CONAN yet!

By the way, John Romita's cover on # 31 was very good (that *was* by Romita, wasn't it?), but Kane is a better cover artist.

Steve Laffer (no address given)

Actually, Steve, the cover of CONAN #31 was penciled by Gil Kane; for various reasons, the looming shadow thereon was re-penciled by Jazzy Johnny, our peerless art director, who then inked the whole thing by special request of Roy himself (who remembered well that the Kane/Romita cover of CONAN # 18, "The Thing in the Temple," had made that earlier issue one of the best-selling CONANs ever).

Otherwise, of course, the many-sided Mr. Kane has penciled the covers for all the Buscema CONAN issues to date except # 26, which was done by Big John himself from a Romita layout -- and # 33, done by Romita and Trimpe. Of course Ernie Chua has inked most of these Kane covers.

This issue, though, because Gil and Roy are busy on the sensational new series heralded in this month's FOOM message on our bombastic Bullpen Page, Ernie both penciled and inked the cover over a layout by John R.!

As to why Buscema the Elder pencils so few covers these days, the answer is simple: He doesn't like doing 'em, not for any book. He prefers telling stories, not doing individual illustrations--even though he is easily one of the very best draftsmen in the whole kookie comic-book industry! So sue 'im!

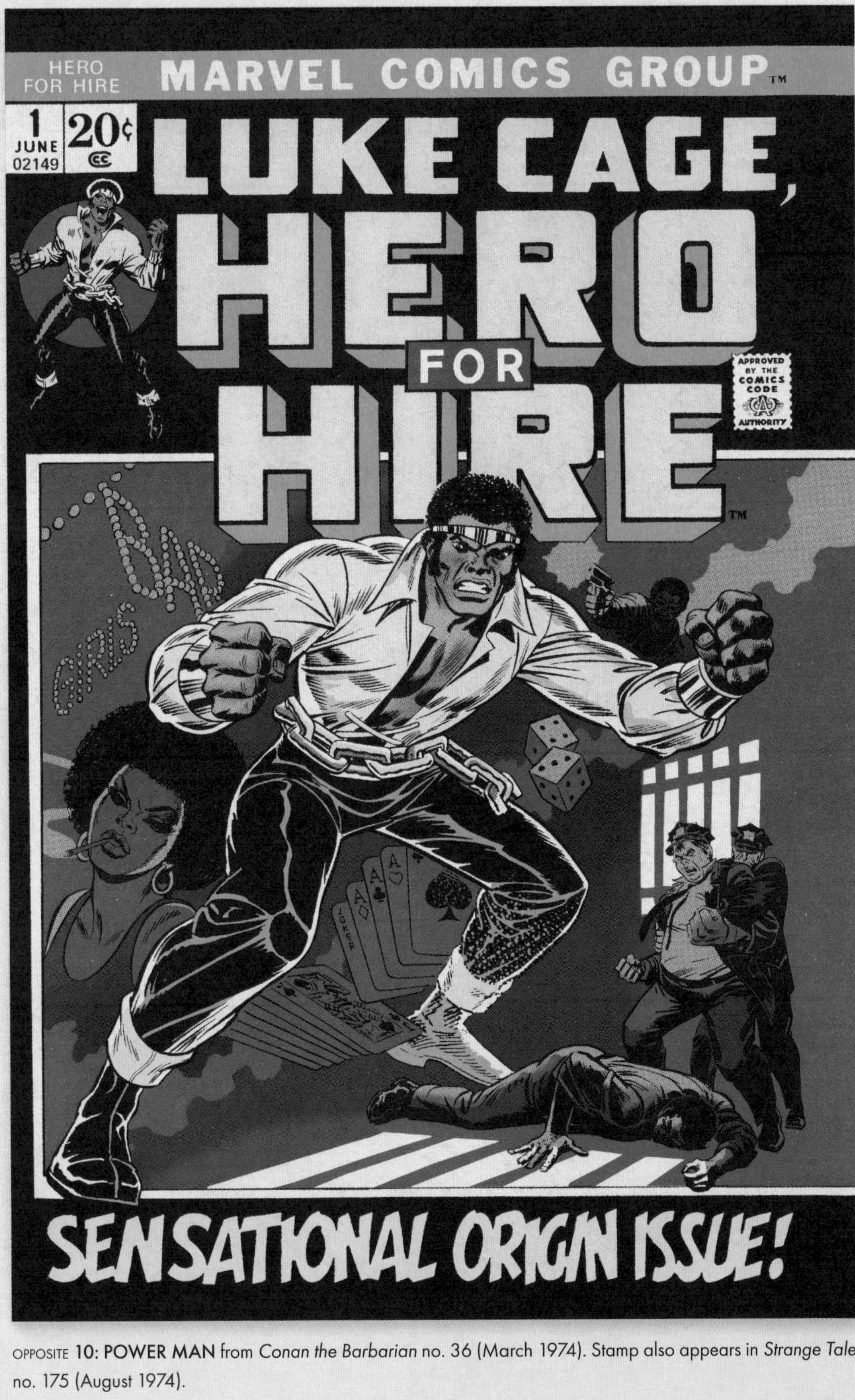

OPPOSITE **10: POWER MAN** from *Conan the Barbarian* no. 36 (March 1974). Stamp also appears in *Strange Tales* no. 175 (August 1974).

ABOVE *Hero for Hire* no. 1 (June 1972), art by John Romita Sr.

GREEN SKIN'S GRAB-BAG

c/o MARVEL COMICS GROUP, 575 MADISON AVE. N.Y.C. 10022

Dear Marvel,

As usual, you have raised an important point without, I guess meaning to. To wit: on page 15 of the January HULK, last panel: "His final thoughts are of the girl." Girl? The other two scientists are men, right? Not boys. Alexandria Knox is stated to be an equal partner in Soulstar, right?

OK—it's just a word and all that, but the point is that it is this type of (I shudder to use the word) sexist writing that cheapens the comix and can turn a possible piece of art into an offensive piece of dross. It makes the whole nudity controversy silly—if we are dealing with just girls (as you occasionally imply), well, we can't allow nekkid children—you can really get busted for that.

See my point? Words are just marks on paper, but they reflect the attitudes of the writer and of the society that the writer portrays. Thanx for listening.

J.P. Gordon
4709 Caritina Dr.
Tarzana, CA 19356.

And without those marks on paper, we'd just have a bunch of empty word balloons issuing from our characters' mouths. Could you imagine Spider-Man, in the heat of battle, turning to Doctor Octopus and shouting!"

Honestly, JPG we really didn't *mean* anything by that "girl" remark. Besides holding down the editorial reins around the Bullpen and spending his evenings putting those unintentionally sexist words into other people's mouths. Lively Len spends the rest of his time making a concerted effort to avoid being a Male Chauvinist Whachamacallit—and his glitzy mate Glynis is ever at his side to help him along.

There was nothing meant to be implied by the word "girl," JPG. It's simply that the Lively One tends to write his caption copy for the *meter* of the line sometimes, much like the lyric of a song. In this particular case, "girl" fits that meter far better than the two-syllabled "woman"—at least to Len's ear. That's all there was to it.

'Nuff said?

Dear Marvel,

WOW! I really got my money'zz worth when I bought HULK #183! Now I *know* Len and Herb are definitely the team for ol' Jade-Jawzz! Zzzzax izz one of the Hulk'zz better (if not hizz bezzt) foezz, zzo why don't you guyzz keep him around for at leazzt two issuezz?! There'zz only one thing I don't understand; both timezz Zzzax has been defeated by zzomeone other than the Hulk! Firzzt it wazz Hawkeye, and now it'zz Mark Revel who'zz defeated Zzzax! And can you dig thizz? Both timezz he waxx dizzentegrated, it wazz by uzze of an arrow (or zzpear) with a cable on it! Are you guyzz trying to tell uzz zzomething?

No-prizze time! In HULK #166, if Hawkeye defeated Zzzax by connecting Zzzax with water, why did the rain (in HULK #183) have little effect, if any, on him?

Thankzz for a great Hulk zztory! And thankzz for Zzzax!

Kirk Bath
11156 Pearl St.
Northglan, CO 80233

Why didn't the rain affect Zzzax, Kirk? We don't know. Maybe he wazz wearing nizz zzpecial rubber-zzoled Kedzz zzneakerzz, zzo he wazzn't grounded. Maybe he wazz wearing a big invizzible yellow raincoat. Maybe we made a big fat boo-boo.

In other wordzz, Kirk—we goofed! But, unfortunately, in keeping with our new policy of awarding thozze coveted little non-entitiezz zzolely for contributionzz of monumental import, we can't zzend you your no-prizze. Bezzidezz, you wouldn't really want it anyway. Our latezzt batch of no-goodiezz got water-logged in that zzame zztorm.

Dear Marvel,

Ho-hum, Zzzax again! And that's the only negative thing I can say about this issue, because it was, as usual, another great Hulk yarn.

I can't believe the way Herb's art just keeps getting better and better! It's astonishing!

Good story. Banner becoming a janitor was a superlative touch of irony. The three supporting characters were good, altho brief. I thought the idea of Zzzag taking off with the chick and playing King Kong, Chicago-style was a bit too funky. Why or how would a creature like that have any love for a human female?

What I loved best was Hulk's comments about water-from-sky. Delightful!

Chris Kanes
347 S. Westmoreland Ave.
Los Angeles, CA 90020

Why would Zzzax love a human female? The answer to that hangs on the same line that offended JPGordon, Chris. "His final thoughts are of the girl." Zzzax, as the story states, draws nourishment and knowledge from feeding on the electrical energies of the human brain. Stan Landers' final thoughts, those of his love for Alexandria Knox, were so strong that they overwhelmed any other thoughts in Zzzax's twisted mind and became his driving force.

Did you follow that? We didn't think so, folks.

NEXT ISSUE: We finally get right down to it, as the Hulkbusters (and a certain jade behemoth) invade the darkest reaches of Siberia to rescue the *real* Glenn Talbot? Or *is* he the real Glenn Talbot? Be here in thirty days, Faithful One. You know how we hate to start without you.

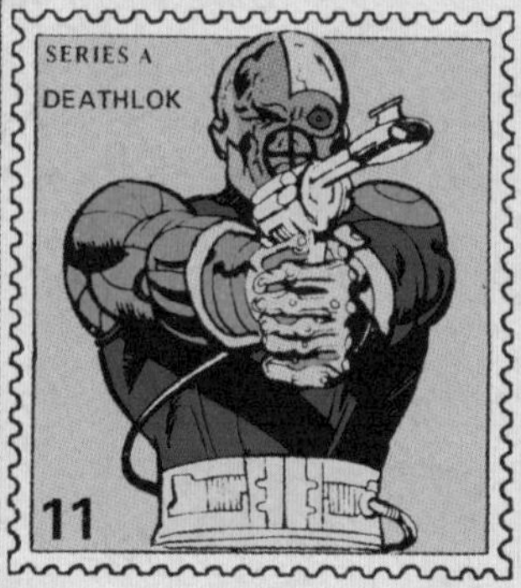

THIS IS IT! YOUR
MARVEL VALUE STAMP
FOR THIS ISSUE!
CLIP 'EM AND
COLLECT 'EM!

OPPOSITE **11: DEATHLOK** from *The Incredible Hulk* no. 186 (April 1975). Stamp also appears in *Master of Kung Fu* no. 19 (August 1974) and *Marvel Team-Up* no. 29 (January 1975).

ABOVE *Astonishing Tales* no. 25 (August 1974), art by Rich Buckler.

THE HAMMER STRIKES

c/o MARVEL COMICS GROUP, 575 MADISON AVE., NEW YORK, N.Y. 10022

Dear Gerry and John,

You're back in step again, I see, with THOR #219. "A Galaxy Consumed!" was one of the greatest interstellar THOR epics yet...or rather, the beginning of a great epic. Or maybe the middle? I don't know, but I liked it!

I've followed the adventures of the Thunder God since his debut in JOURNEY INTO MYSTERY more than ten years ago, so I guess I'm not what you'd call your "average" THOR reader. But for what it's worth, having seen the mag evolve from earthbound superheroism, through a mixture of earth-oriented stories and Asgardian mythological epics, into an all-Asgard period, and now, finally, into a strange combination of mythology and speculative fiction...I think the current period is the best. The concepts Gerry's been tossing at us lately have been very exciting. And the John Buscema art rivals anything of the old days. I guess I'm in a minority here, too, but to me, all of Kirby's work tended to look alike. After a few issues it would get tiresome. John is more versatile, more varied, though, I suppose, also less imaginative in certain areas. In any event, I prefer Buscema's work.

Just one last thing: please continue with the far-out science-fiction-oriented yarns. The mythical Asgardians deserve a rest; earth has too many heroes on it already; the best place for a Thunder God these days is outer space. Thanks.

Randy Enrolk
Boston, Mass.

Rest easy, Randy. Gerry does plan to have Thor & Company do a bit more trekking out among the stars before they return to earth or Asgard. It's his favorite kind of yarn, too—and most of Marveldom seems to agree with him and with you that it's perfect for Goldilocks.

All of which reminds us, in an out-to-left-field sort of way, that Gerry's latest science fiction novel, published by DAW Books, should be popping up on the Nation's bookstore shelves very shortly— this month, we believe. It's called Mindship, and if you can't find it at your local paperback dealer's, scream and yell a lot, and tell him to get you a copy. We hear it's terrific. That's Mindship, by Gerard F. (ahem!) Conway.

(Okay, Gerry...now you can stop looking over our shoulder and get to work on the plot for next issue!)

Dear Marvel,

Is Thor a two-timer? In THOR #216, we see the God of Thunder fondly embracing the lovely Sif. Yet, in MARVEL SPECTACULAR #2, we find him on the verge of renouncing his godhood so that he might wed a pretty little thing named Jane Foster. What gives?

Robert Hammack
Hialeah, Fla.

The stories in MARVEL SPECTACULAR are reprints, Robert. They originally appeared in Thor's own mag several years back and are now being rerun, so to speak, for the benefit of fans like yourself who may have missed their original publication. Unfortunately, until recently, all the confusion and general busy-ness around the Bullpen has made it impossible for us to look up the original issue-numbers and place them on the reprints, and, as a result, we've confused a lot of folks, yourself among them.

If you continue to follow the series in MARVEL SPECTACULAR, you'll see how Thor's relationship with Jane Foster was resolved and how he met Sif. (And if you've never read these stories before, don't miss 'em this time around. They're among the most memorable of all the early THOR sagas.) Okay?

We apologize for the confusion, by the way. And, as you've probably noticed, we've begun featuring the original-publication info on almost all our reprint mags. Are we forgiven?

Dear Marvel,

The answer to the all-important question of "how many trolls can dance on the beards of the three billy goats gruff?" can be arrived at simply and summarily with a series of pseudo-complex algebraic computations.

The problem would appear as follows:

Let T = the average weight per troll.

Let S = the average holding capacity per square inch of beard

$$\frac{T}{S(BB - MB - LB)}$$

If we arbitrarily assign the average weight per troll as 90 pounds and the holding capacity per square inch of beard at 53 pounds, and then calculate the area per beard at four square inches for the large beard (LB), three square inches for the medium beard (MB) and 1.5 square inches for the baby beard (BB), the problem can be solved quite easily

$$\frac{90 \text{ lbs.}}{53(4 - 3 - 1.5)} = 7.099$$

Answer: 7.099 trolls may dance on the beards of the three billy goats gruff. But only if they waltz. Goats are old-fashioned and do not appreciate modern dance.

One other point I would like to make. It seems to me that no-prizes should be awarded by the Bullpen whenever you are inclined to do so, and that readers should not ask for or expect them merely for detecting mistakes in a story. It would seem more of an honor to receive one without having to ask. Oh, well...!

Until Dr. Strange gives the Eternal Vishanti a box of Screaming Yellow Zonkers, Make Mine Marvel.

Bret B. Hamilton
2699 Westwood Dr.
Placerville, Ca. 95667

On your point about the no-prizes, Bret, we've got to agree. Somehow, it became custom over the past few years to dispense our much-hallowed little no-things for the spotting of mistakes, and, as a result, every little slip-up by a colorist or inker or letterer, whether it substantially affected the story or not, became just cause for the awarding of a no-prize. We've decided to call a halt to that.

In the future, we'll be giving out our awesome non-awards a bit more sparingly— and only for especially incisive comments or suggestions on our stories, the spotting of really dumb mistakes that would be important to story content, or good bits of creative thought, such as your own billy goats equation.

However, even though you get the no-prize, you're wrong, Wrong, WRONG! First of all, trolls weigh much more than ninety pounds, even though they're only four feet tall or so (on the average), because they're incredibly dense. Moreover, as we've mentioned in an earlier issue, they are also incredibly clumsy, and therefore cannot waltz— or do modern dance. They have their own ritual tribal dance called the Twitch. We dare not describe it in a family publication.

So the controversy rages on. How many trolls can dance on the beards of the three billy goats gruff? If you know, reader— don't let us die of suspense, okay? Write!

(And you might include a line or two about the THOR mag you hold in your hands, too. Gerry and John are as concerned about solving the goat/troll question as anyone, but they'd kinda like to think somebody's reading the stories, too!)

THIS IS IT! YOUR

MARVEL VALUE STAMP

FOR THIS ISSUE!

CLIP 'EM AND COLLECT 'EM!

STATEMENT OF OWNERSHIP, MANAGEMENT AND CIRCULATION
ACT OF AUGUST 12, 1970: SECTION 3685,
TITLE 39, UNITED STATES CODE

1. Title of Publication: THOR.

2. DATE OF FILING: September 25, 1973.

3. Frequency of Issue: Monthly.

4. Location of Known Office of Publication: 575 Madison Ave., New York, N.Y. 10022.

5. Location of the Headquarters or General Business Offices of the Publishers: Marvel Comics Group, 575 Madison Ave., New York, N.Y. 10022.

6. Names and addresses of the publisher, editor, and managing editor are: Publisher: Stan Lee, 575 Madison Ave., New York, N.Y. 10022; Editor: Roy Thomas, 575 Madison Ave., New York, N.Y. 10022; Managing Editor: John Verpoorten, 575 Madison Ave., New York, N.Y. 10022.

7. Owner (If owned by a corporation, its name and address must be stated and also immediately thereunder the names and addresses of stockholders owning or holding 1 percent or more of total amount of stock. If not owned by a corporation, the names and addresses of the individual owners must be given. If owned by a partnership or other unincorporated firm, its name and address, as well as that of each individual must be given.) Cadence Industries Corp., 21 Henderson Drive, West Caldwell, New Jersey; a public held company on the New York Stock Exchange.

8. Known bondholders, mortgagees, and other security holders owning or holding 1 percent or more of total amount of bonds, mortgages, or other securities (If there are none, so state) None.

9. For optional completion by publishers mailing at the regular rates (Section 132.121, Postal Service Manual) 39 U.S.C. 3626 provides in pertinent part: "No person who would have been entitled to mail matter under former section 4359 of this title shall mail such matter at the rates provided under this subsection unless he files annually with the Postal Service a written request for permission to mail matter at such rates."

In accordance with the provisions of this statute, I hereby request permission to mail the publication named in Item 1 at the reduced postage rates presently authorized by 39 U.S.C. 3626.

(signed) John S. Ryan, Vice President, Director of Circulation

10. For completion by nonprofit organizations authorized to mail at special rates. (Section 132.122, Postal Manual.) The purpose, function, and nonprofit status of this organization and the exempt status for Federal income tax purposes. (Check one.) [ ] Have not changed during preceding 12 months. [ ] Have changed during preceding 12 months. (If changed, publisher must submit explanation of change with this statement.)

11. EXTENT AND NATURE OF CIRCULATION.

A. Total No. Copies Printed (net press run): Average no. copies each issue during preceding 12 months: 405,894; single issue nearest to filing date: 425,000.

B. Paid Circulation: 1) Sales through dealers and carriers, street vendors and counter sales: Average no. copies each issue during preceding 12 months: 194,013; single issue nearest to filing date: 198,484. 2) Mail subscriptions. Average no. copies each issue during preceding 12 months: 1226; single issue nearest to filing date: 1205.

C. Total paid circulation: Average no. copies each issue during preceding 12 months: 195,239; single issue nearest to filing date: 199,749.

D. Free distribution by mail, carrier or other means. 1) Samples, complimentary, and other free copies: 150; single issue nearest to filing date: 150. 2) Copies distributed to news agents, but not sold: Average no. copies each issue during preceding 12 months: 210,344; single issue nearest to filing date: 225,000.

E. Total distribution (sum of C and D): Average no. copies each issue during preceding 12 months: 405,733; single issue nearest to filing date: 424,839.

F. Office use, left-over, unaccounted, spoiled after printing: Average no. copies each issue during preceding 12 months: 161; single issue nearest to filing date: 161.

G. Total (sum of E & F—should equal net press run shown in A): Average no. copies each issue during preceding 12 months: 405,894; single issue nearest to filing date: 425,000.

I certify that the statements made by me above are correct and complete.

(signed) John S. Ryan, Vice President, Director of Circulation

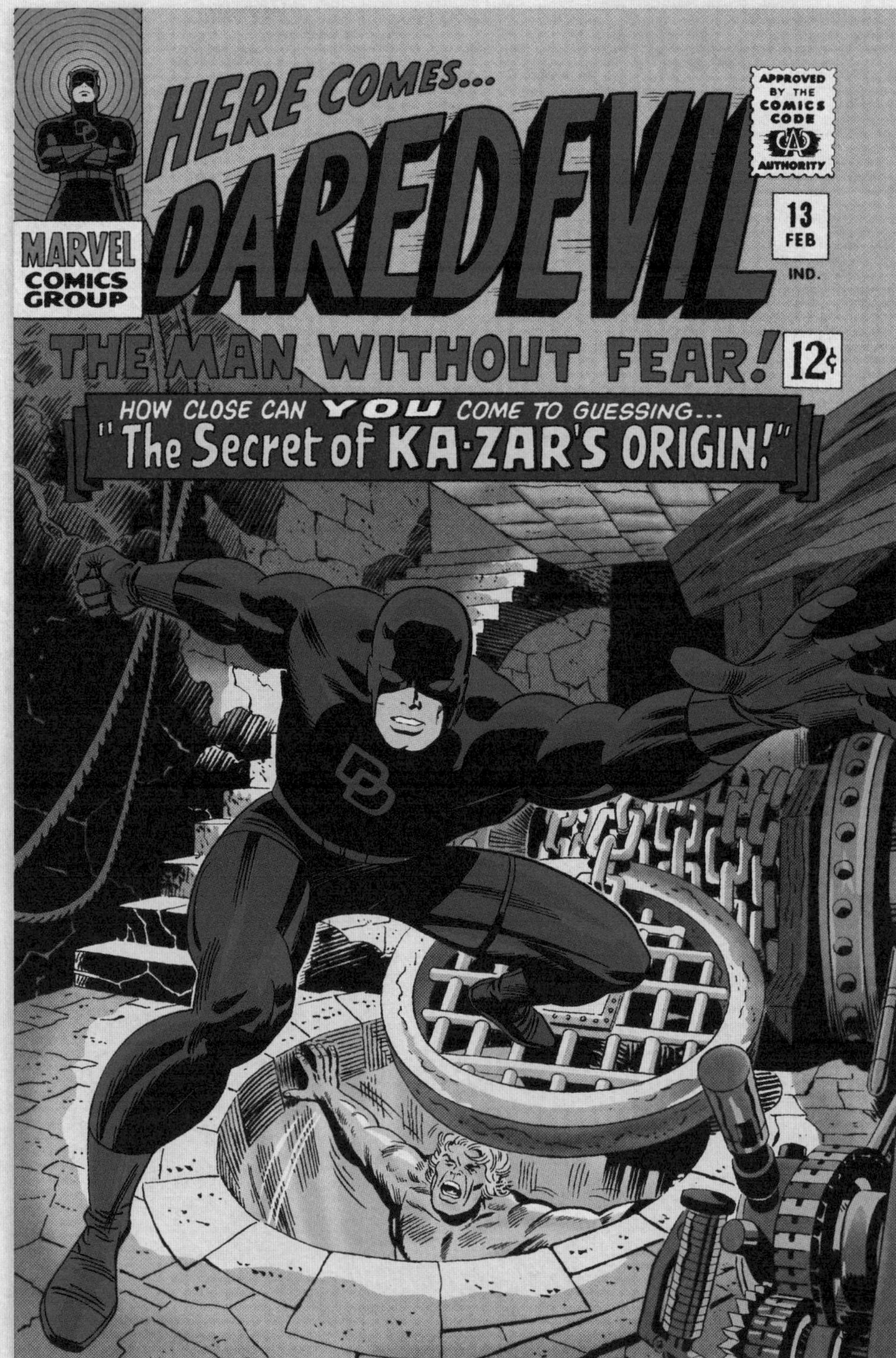

OPPOSITE **12: DAREDEVIL** from *Thor* no. 223 (May 1974). Stamp also appears in *Frankenstein* no. 11 (July 1974) and *Tomb of Dracula* no. 37 (October 1975).

ABOVE *Daredevil* no. 13 (February 1966), art by Jack Kirby and John Romita Sr.

AMAZING MAILS

c/o MARVEL COMICS GROUP, 575 MADISON AVE., NEW YORK, N.Y. 10022

Dear Marvel,

AMAZING ADVENTURES #21 successfully continues the epic-like story of WAR OF THE WORLDS. The pace is quick and the writing is often clever, although predictably it is the girl, Carmilla Frost, who frees the imprisoned Killraven. Much like James Bond, Killraven's abilities seem to lie principally in his brute strength and his power over women. Like Bond, Killraven is continually captured, continually tortured by the nasty villain, and continually escapes...usually with the help of a beautiful girl. Killraven even seems to be out of the same "male chauvinist" mold as Bond. Witness his remarks to Carmilla after she has freed him from the clutches of the Warlord and she suggests that they get out of there before the Warlord's troops arrive. "I don't know who you are, siren or vixen, but Killraven doesn't need any female to tell him his place," he shouts. "So that's why you're always lost!" She retorts in fine Women's Lib fashion.

The idea for WAR OF THE WORLDS is very clever, although I doubt that old H.G.W. would be too happy about it. It has the same scope and epic proportion that made the "Planet Of The Apes" series such a successful saga.

All in all an entertaining 'zine, and I'm looking forward to future stories.

Joel Uman
755 Montpellier
Montreal 379, Quebec, Canada

Your analogy of Killraven to Bond is fascinating, Joel, and it's surprising Don never thought of it since he began reading the Fleming novels (and enjoying them) long before Bond became a classic literary and cinematic hero. The WAR OF THE WORLDS saga, though, will soon move into other areas as we explore more of the characters that make up Killraven's band of Freemen. In just a short while, if most of them survive the Washington terrors, the Freemen will head toward the Indianapolis 500, and you can just bet things aren't going to be at all quiet for them there.

H.G.W. might not completely like the direction we're taking, but we are trying to make this one of the first science-fiction oriented comics to succeed! We'll need your help to do it, Marvelites, both at the newsstands and in the letter's pages; but you've come through for us before and we know you'll do it again. And believe us, Pilgrim, when we say that these letters are read and evaluated by the very people who work on these magnificent mags. They are.

So flip back through the pages of "The Legend Assassins", Gang, and then sit down with pen and paper and let us know what you liked and didn't like. We're open for critiques, in-depth analysis of characters and stories, including its themes, or just short notes saying you liked it or thought we missed the target. We know you're out there, we know you have reactions to these magazines you're reading, and we'd like to have you share them with us.

How's that for a straight forward, Marvel type sober answer? See you in the letter's pages, People.

Dear Guys,

Concerning AMAZING ADVENTURES #21. Yankee Stadium! Far out. The idea of seeing famous landmarks in New York such as Yankee Stadium all bombed out is totally fantastic. Don put the House That Babe Ruth Built (and the House The Martians Tore Down) to a very good use as a scene of gladiatorial battle. I can just picture it now: World Series, 2018. The Mars Globs versus the Cleveland Mutants. Such grandeur! Such spectacle!

However, leave us return to the business at tentacle. I have a slight (very slight) idea on this certain "affinity" between Carmilla Frost and Grok. Could it possibly be that Ms. Frost and the pre-cloned Grok were lovers? Could it be that Grok is the spawn of he who was done in by the Masters for some obscure reasons? That would also explain why Carmilla turned tail for no really apparent reason to help Killraven and Company against the Warlord. Does my educated guess earn a No-Prize, or am I doomed to wander the corridors of the no-No-Prized?

Herb was really smokin' this issue as was Don (BLACK PANTHER) McGregor. But who the heck is Yolande Pijcke? Whoever he was, he replaced Sal Trapani and John Severin as Herb's best inker.

I would forward one suggestion, if I may. Please don't have the Martians themselves pop up in picture every issue. The only time the Martians were visible in this issue was a meaningless appearance on the splash page. That was very good. It kind of takes away from the mystery, of the beasties, to see them every other panel. About the best thing in the Gene Barry "War Of The Worlds" movie was that we never really saw them, until the very end.

But I do want to see more of those bombed-out landmarks. Let's try the Empire State, Times Square, the U.N. and why not show a leveled 575 Madison Ave? The way you guys talk, things must always look like a bomb just hit anyhow.

Don Jacobson
2243 Falcon Ave.
St. Paul, Minn. 55119

It does, Don. It does. But so many of us are senses-shattered here already that we barely notice it.

We agree with many of the points you've brought up, though, which is one of the reasons that the High Overlord is introduced in this issue. We never actually see what type of malignant life form squirms about in that towering encasement and we won't see it for awhile. And when you and the rest of Marveldom finally do...well, let's just say the only senses shattered won't just be at 575.

One of the fascinating aspects to futuristic series is in seeing the changes time has wrought on various landmark symbols of our time, and that's why Don and Herb decided to have the Freemen move on toward Washington. You don't get many more landmarks than that in such a close area. Agreed?

Good guess at Grok's relationship or "affinity" to Carmilla, but we aren't going to give everything away yet. We're dropping you clues, and perhaps even a few misleading but fair-and-square clues, before we tell all about Grok and Carmilla. But we're glad to see that you're interested enough in the cast to start wondering about their origins. And you'll be seeing more of those origins in upcoming issues. (Which is a subtle way of saying, "Be here when it happens!")

Anyhow, on the less subtle side, Yolande says she thanks you for the compliments on her inking. The "she" and the "her" are the important words there, and just to show you how subtle we are (heck, we're almost so cool that subtle is an unsubtle word to us) we won't even make any comment on your glaring, eye-catching error. Boy, talk about subtle.

Dear Editor,

AMAZING ADVENTURES featuring WAR OF THE WORLDS is one of the best non-superhero comics around. When I first heard about it I figured that it would be just "another" adaptation. (Don't get me wrong! I like comics like SUPERNATURAL THRILLERS.) Anyway, when Killraven's book finally came out, I glanced through it and nothing in particular caught my eye, except for the unique cover. It was excellent. Well, I decided to pass on this one. (I spend so much money on comics as it is.) About 3 months later I bought a gob of back issues and among them found a copy of A.A.#18. The cover caught my eye again as I was about to pitch it in the "sell" pile. I read it and really enjoyed. Then I rushed down to a store which keeps comics on the racks for 3 or 4 weeks and frantically searched for A.A. #19. I finally found it! I read it and have become addicted to Marvel's WAR OF THE WORLDS!!! I'm glad that it's nothing like the Perry Rhodan books.

Issue #21 has come around and I'm happy to say that I think it's the best yet!!! I very much liked the introduction of Carmilla Frost. It's good to see some 20th Century names still used in some comics. I kind of get the impression that she was a traitor to the Martians. When they reached the arena, I thought she had led Killraven and crew into a trap: but I was happy that she didn't. I hope she'll become a permanent addition to K.R.'s ranks of Freemen.

Grok is also very interesting. Keep him around for awhile.

I liked Killraven's original costume, but I like his new one even better. The idea of getting it from a museum is excellent.

Scott Taylor
1202 Eastwood Dr.
Rockville, Indiana 47872

Okay, Scott. You had us hooked there for awhile. We weren't sure how this suspense letter was going to turn out, but we're glad you finally got exposed to Killraven's adventures. As you've no doubt noticed Carmilla and Grok are still with Killraven's band and next issue gives them a chance for more exposure than ever before. All of which leads us into the little yellow box below. As we said earlier, "See you in the letter's pages, People."

NEXT ISSUE: **"FOR HE'S A JOLLY DEAD REBEL!" The Washington Trilogy comes to a cataclysmic end (and we don't use the word cataclysmic loosely) as the action moves from The President's archives to the Lincoln Memorial. Abraxas, Sabre, Mint Julep and Killraven and his followers clash in one searing, final confrontation As if that isn't enough Rattack will be back...and just to keep things from becoming boring, a few cannibalistic bats will visit the scene. We said bats...not rats. Plus, a New Years Eve party celebrating the year 2019. You might want to join us just to see how we're going to work all of that into one story. We'll see you then.)**

THIS IS IT! YOUR

MARVEL VALUE STAMP

FOR THIS ISSUE!

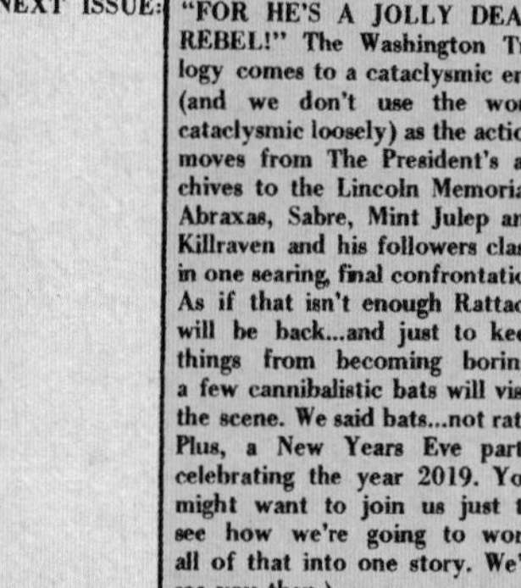

CLIP 'EM AND COLLECT 'EM!

OPPOSITE **13: DR. STRANGE** from *Amazing Adventures* no. 23 (March 1974). Stamp also appears in *The Avengers* no. 127 (September 1974) and *Son of Satan* no. 1 (December 1975).

ABOVE *Strange Tales* no. 127 (December 1964), art by Steve Ditko.

Upon examination, Roy Thomas notes that "the source for the Dr. Strange stamp is more or less panel 8 on page 7 of the Ditko-drawn in *Strange Tales* no. 127—only not *entirely*. Clearly some Marvel staff artist has redrawn the backing (the stand-up part of the cloak) to turn Doc's original cape into his later, better-known Cloak of Levitation . . . while the curved spell-ray originally overlapping part of his cape and left arm have been whited out. However, Doc's head in the 1964 art has been replaced by a new one, very Ditkoesque, but from an uncertain source (at least, I'm not certain of it), presumably to achieve a full-on frontal view, with none of his chin hidden by the cloak's folds. The part of the cloak above Doc's left shoulder has likewise been altered, removing a bit of texturing depicted in the earlier version. The resultant composite drawing was perfect for the type of Marvel Value Stamp that Stan wanted. I suspect the head was at least partly touched up by Marie Severin, since it has that kind of 'Wally Wood lighting' on the face which he used to chuckle about and was parodied in *Not Brand Echh*, making it look as if the hero was holding a flashlight up to his head to create that effect."

Dear Steve, Frank, Dick, and Roy,

Right now, I feel as if I must take time out from studying for finals to compliment you on the superlative story appearing in MARVEL PREMIERE (DR. STRANGE) #14.

"Sise-Neg Genesis" was a masterpiece! Brilliant! To think I went to Hebrew School two years and a comic answered all my theological questions.

Heck with the people who say the "Golden Age" was in the 30's and 40's. The Golden Age of Comics is happening all around us! Right now! Your "Sise-Neg—Genesis" proved it!

It was a rare comic in that it transcended the printed page. Mordo and Strange arguing over the good and bad in man, playing the roles of Satan and Christ in tempting god, who is a man! The coming to Sodom and Gomorrah! The reappearance of Shuma-Gorath! But the clincher, the absolute clincher was pages 30 and 31: Sise-Neg's final lines.

How wonderful it was. How beautiful. I thank you all.

Sheldon Gleisser
5005 So. Barton Rd.
Lyndhurst, Ohio 44124

Dear Steve, Frank, Dick, and Roy,

Allow me now to slightly rephrase and expand upon Genesis' final cosmic declaration in DR. STRANGE #14.

Steve and Frank are imperfect, but this dream-bred dimension of ethereal pageantry that they have created is the closest approximation of perfection throughout all of Comicdom. None could improve, much less even attempt to improve, upon what they have done already. We are all now privileged that these titans will continue to recreate this universe, with exactly the same superlative skill as before.

May the Vishanti reign over you.

Alan Rothman
151-12 24th Road
Whitestone, N.Y. 11357

Dear Mr. Lee,

The other evening at our church's Christmas social, a young member of my congregation showed me a comic book you present, called MARVEL PREMIERE (#14, March). He told me that it dealt with God.

I borrowed the comic from him, thinking that I would find another denigration of our Lord in the manner so fashionable these days. However, after reading this issue, I must commend you on the taste and perception you, your editor, and your writer showed in handling a very difficult subject. It is magazines such as yours which truly perform the Lord's work, and open new eyes to His majesty.

I have since recommended MARVEL PREMIERE to many of my congregation and friends. Thank you, Mr. Lee, for your fine work.

Rev. David Billingsley,
8794 East-West Highway
Denton, Texas

THIS IS IT! YOUR
MARVEL VALUE STAMP
FOR THIS ISSUE!
CLIP 'EM AND
COLLECT 'EM!

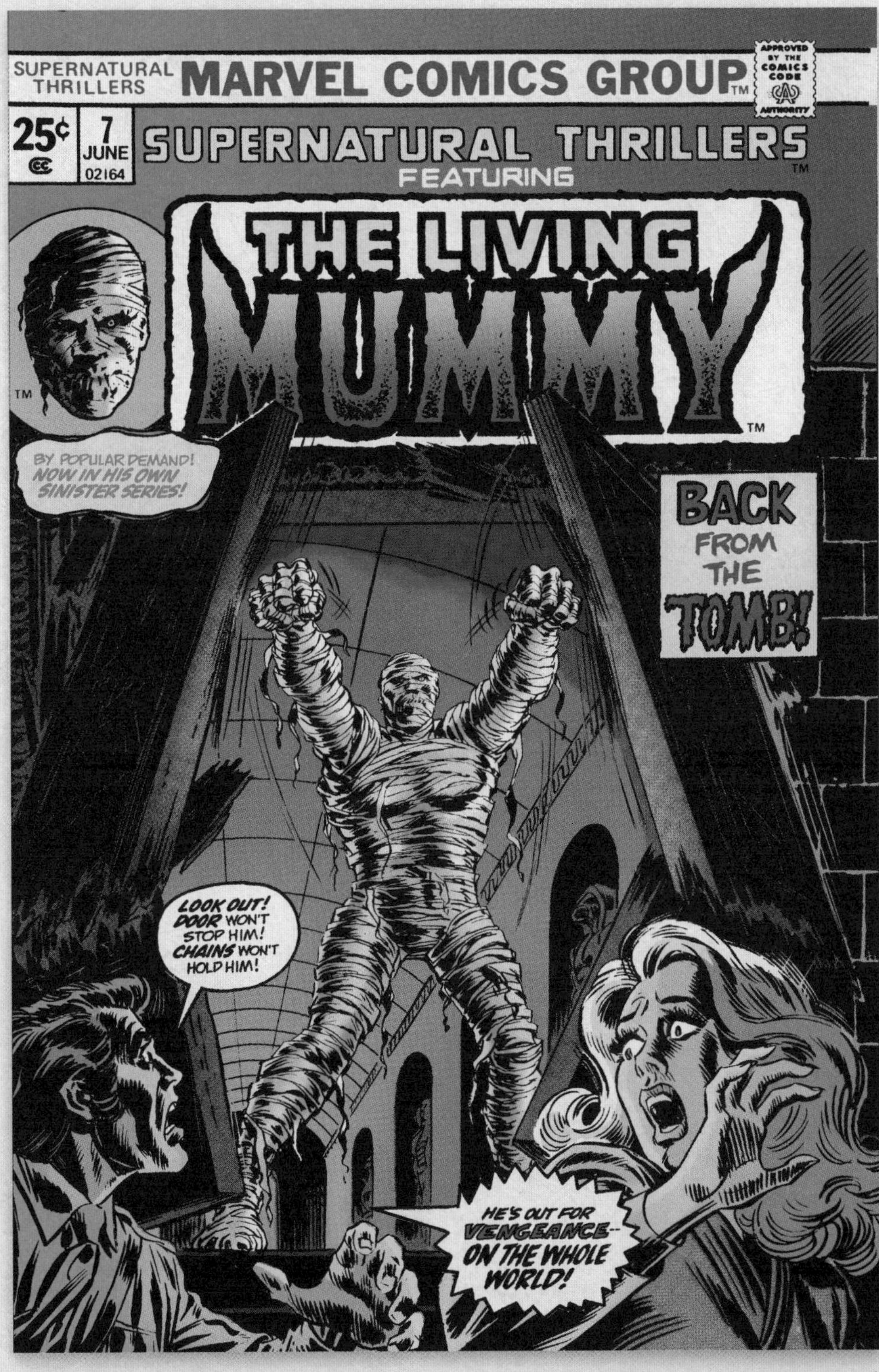

OPPOSITE **14: THE LIVING MUMMY** from *Doctor Strange* no. 3 (September 1974). Stamp also appears in *Marvel Spotlight* no. 19 (December 1974).

ABOVE *Supernatural Thrillers* no. 7 (June 1974), art by John Romita Sr.

precedent.

We've passed everyone's comments along to our coloring department, though, and made them promise to take them to heart. See what letter writing can do?

Dear Steve and Sal,

The latest CA&F was beautiful..... This Moonstone thing has been building quite nicely the last four issues, particularly since it didn't build this time. I mean, we've had a steady pressure on Cap right along, and it was well-planned to have a tangental story with an old-time super villain running (flying?) around, so we could just sit back and observe what the pressure has done to Cap. Everything he has believed in is crashing down on all sides of him.

At the same time, we see the Falcon getting his wings under control —but with the crazy touch of him climbing the light pole! Are we to assume that author Englehart is not going to stop at simply handing the Falcon a power, but is going to examine the effect of the change on our man?

I'd imagine so, with Steve's track record. From the day he first took charge of this strip, it shot from the most cardboard of all Marvel books to the most intricate and enjoyable. He's made me believe there could be a Captain America and a Falcon, and, brother, that's hard to do.

So, until Marvel publishes The Waltons, make mine...uh...

Tim Cross
8416 Cayuga Avenue
Bethesda, Md. 20034

Yeah, well, Cap and Falc say they DON'T believe in you, Tim Cross! (Just kidding, effendi. They didn't say any such thing.)

Dear Steve and Sal,

As an old X-Men fan, all I can say is thanks for bringing them back, even if only for a guest shot. I really liked the way two-year-old plot threads were brought into the picture to give us a picture of what our muties have been up to since their mag died and the Beast's strip ended. I'm hoping the series lasts a long time, just to see the X-Men back in action, but I'm also dying to find out what happens (hopefully the X-Men with their own book again! X-MEN FANS UNITE!).

I think it's about time I took a shot at a no-prize along with the rest of Marvel-dom. Page 10, panel 1: I'm willing to bet that in this scene from AVENGERS #110-111, Jeanie (Marvel Girl) was not wearing the costume shown. I liked the X-Men's third set of costumes best, but if you're going to change them back, at least be consistent about it.

Oh yeah, Cap was okay this issue, too.

Bill Wormstedt
5 Highland Hall
Bellingham, Wash. 98225

You ought to be willing to bet, Bill. It's a sure thing. But still, we have explained that those AVENGERS issues occurred at a point when we were changing our minds about which costumes the mutants would wear, and for that reason, they sported different threads on the inside and on the cover of AVENGERS #110. Well, all along we've assumed that the new uniforms inside were right and the old ones on the cover were wrong, but if it were the other way 'round...well, maybe that's why the two versions of the scene don't agree.

But how should we know?

NEXT: What will the world do without a Captain America? More importantly, what will Cap do? Whatever it is, you'll see it all in CA&F #177, along with the Falcon, Redwing's riotous return, and a pair of power-mad superbaddies, both of whom happen to be our old fiend, Lucifer! Sound intriguing? You bet your socks!

OPPOSITE **15: IRON MAN** from *Captain America* no. 176 (August 1974). Stamp also appears in *Creatures on the Loose* no. 28 (March 1974) and *Master of Kung Fu* no. 24 (January 1975).

ABOVE *The Avengers* no. 58 (November 1968), art by John Buscema and George Klein. This cover was also used as the source for MVS no. 8.

doesn't have the intellect to worry about the repercussions— the innocent people who might be hurt, the pain and suffering the guilty would feel (the guilty have feelings, too), and anyway, who is to say who's guilty and who isn't? I don't even know how to punctuate those questions, let alone answer them. Those questions wouldn't even bother the Hulk.

That is one reason why the Hulk is so appealing, so I agree with Robert Strothman who called for more devastation. But I also agree with Brian Earl Brown, who wanted less monsters and more humanistic stories. I've never been mad at a monster, so there's no catharsis for me when Hulk battles one.

Richard Nathan
2002 Fourth St., Apt. #208
Santa Monica, Ca.

We have a feeling this Devastation-versus-Humanism debate is going to be with us for quite a while, so we're keeping our collective mouth shut on the subject until we hear more from you people. But though our lips are sealed, our eyes are wide open, so— WRITE!! Let us know where you stand on this question or any other concerning the Hulk. What kinds of stories do you most want to see?

We will say this, though, so as not to pass the entire buck this time around: we've always thought of HULK more as superhero book than a monster book, which seems to dictate rather a different approach than that applied to MAN-THING or THE LIVING MUMMY, for example. MAN-THING in particular relies almost totally on mood, plot, and characterization (of supporting players) because the murk-dweller cannot leave his swamp, cannot think, cannot indulge in the kind of battle the Hulk can.

Ol' Greenskin, however, can make those tremendous leaps through the air, is remarkable quick for his size and weight, is able to reason...and on and on. The two monsters are worlds apart in almost every respect, which automatically dictates a different type of story for each.

'Nuff said. Let's hear your thoughts now.

Dear Roy and Herb,

Everybody knows that the Great Refuge is an ultra-modern city, and everybody knows that ultra-modern cities do not have garbage cans (as seen in HULK #175, page 16, panel one). Didn't Herb know that the Great Refuge uses that ultra-modern gizmo that turns garbage into smouldering dust? Be sure to send my no-prize by green mail?

David Jones
Inglewood, Ca.

Sorry, David, but instant incendiary garbage disposal is just one thing the Inhumans have never mastered— for a good reason. The garbage is collected from those trash cans and used as fuel to power the Great Refuge's dynamos.

Several cities in the United States are using similar systems now. It's a fantastic anti-pollution scheme, keeps the streets from filling up with smouldering dust.

Yep. The Great Refuge runs on its great refuse!

THIS IS IT! YOUR
MARVEL VALUE STAMP
FOR THIS ISSUE!
CLIP 'EM AND COLLECT 'EM!

OPPOSITE **16: SHANG-CHI, MASTER OF KUNG FU** from *The Incredible Hulk* no. 179 (September 1974). Stamp also appears in *Fantastic Four* no. 155 (February 1975).

ABOVE *Giant-Size Master of Kung Fu* no. 1 (September 1974), art by Ron Wilson and Mike Esposito.

Second place went to the elves, and third to an evil wizard. The trolls, as we all know, have very tiny toes, but only managed eight dancers to a beard.

Thus, twenty-four trolls can dance on the beards of the Three Billy Goats Gruff.

Jackie Biggers
153 Midland Avenue
Columbus, Ohio 43223

Aw, c'mon, Jackie! You don't really expect us to believe that?! A convention of creatures and beasties?!? Sheesh! Let's move on to the next letter!

Dear Marvel,

You are cordially invited to attend the 201st Annual Fantasy Creatures and Creepie Beasties Festival, to be held on the ninth of August in Columbus, Ohio. Events will include competitions in biting, flame-breathing, stomping to death, and goat dancing. B.Y.O.G.

Wakanda Con Enterprises
Bronx, N.Y.

Didja ever get the feeling these pages were running out of control? That you just couldn't stop them? Didja? Didja?

Jackie Biggers, if you're still with us, the no-prize is yours!! END OF GOAT CONTEST!! Okay?

Let's try a serious question. Really. Honest. Serious. Ahem—!

Gentlemen:

As an avid THOR fan, I have a question regarding his origin. I have read many of the old THOR comics and also the story in which Dr. Don Blake finds Thor's hammer. Who was the original Thor, and what became of him? Or does the soul of Thor possess the body of the person who holds the hammer?

One last query. When Don Blake was newly transformed into Thor, he didn't act or speak like an Asgardian. Is there an issue of the Thunder God's reception by Odin (after he returned in Blake's body)? If there was, it would make a good reprint.

You are doing a fine job on THOR.

Riley Foster
216 S. 9th, Apt. #2
Laramie, Wyo. 82070

Thanks, Riley. To answer your question...there's only been one Thor. What happened was this: Odin was annoyed that his son, for all his strength and power and nobility, lacked a quality essential in a god, that of humility. So, he arranged for Thor to be "reborn" on earth—fully matured, as a medical student named Donald Blake— where, living as a cripple, ministering to the needs of the sick and helpless, he would learn compassion for his fellow beings.

When Donald Blake came upon the hammer Mjolnir some years later...when he learned he could transform himself into a Norse god of thunder...he had no idea that that was indeed his true identity. Odin had erased all memory of Asgard from his consciousness. But as time went on, the personality of Thor began to dominate, that of Blake began to recede, until, finally, Thor took his rightful place among the gods of Asgard once again, his memory and mannerisms returned.

The story was told in full in THOR #158 & 159, some years back, by the way. And we'll get around to reprinting it sometime soon. (Keep an eye on MARVEL SPECTACULAR. All our classic THOR yarns are being rerun in that mag.)

And that, friends, is just about all our poor little systems can take— until next issue, of course. Stay well. Stay happy. And join us here again in thirty days, hear?

THIS IS IT! YOUR

MARVEL VALUE STAMP

FOR THIS ISSUE! CLIP 'EM AND COLLECT 'EM!

OPPOSITE **17: BLACK BOLT** from *Thor* no. 225 (July 1974). Stamp also appears in *Man-Thing* no. 4 (April 1974) and *Ka-Zar* no. 6 (November 1974).

ABOVE *Fantastic Four* no. 59 (February 1967), art by Jack Kirby and Joe Sinnott. This cover was also used as the source for MVS no. 34.

THE HAMMER STRIKES

c/o MARVEL COMICS GROUP, 575 MADISON AVE. N.Y.C. 10022

This was one of those months when, of all the mail received, two letters of slightly-longer-than-normal length captivated our interest to the extent that we're presenting them here for the rest of you Thor buffs to examine and comment upon—sans our usual editorial comments.

For those of you who may view this singular departure from established tradition askance, be assured that we'll return to the normal selection of shorter letters next month.

Until then, keep your wings dry—all of you!

Dear Len ang Gerry,

Loki/Thor battles are always interesting and this one, in THOR #234, was certainly no exception. The story was fast-paced (thanks to the unbelievable Buscema break-down), had lots of action, plenty of apprehension, and just tons of enjoyment. It was perhaps the finest THOR ish of the last two years.

The basic Thor/Loki stand-off was more interesting than usual, because not only did it involve an inter-Asgardian battle, but it also incorporated a gigantic Midgard force fighting to retain its freedom. Super-extravaganzas similar to this have been done before, but Loki portrayed enough arrogance, and enough newly-acquired powers to make it believable that he could succeed.

This concept was excellent, yet the finest element adding to the tale's effectiveness was its structure. The premises and battleground were established, and then each new development—Thor's capture. Firelord's coming to help, and Thor's eventual escape leading to his victory—was perfectly planned. The timing was so beautifully honed to perfection, each additional plot twist adding and adding to the excitement.

The final, hand-to-hand combat between Thor and Loki was the best I recall in this book since Thor and Herc took each other on in #125. There's something about straight knock-down, drag–'em–out fights that exudes such excite-ment, and can't be captured by any other means.

The interesting sub (future) plots of Odin's "humility" lesson, and Sif's and Herc's search for the Runestaff (Hawk-moon's?) nicely rounded out the ish.

The art work simply could not have been any better. John's pencils and breakdowns gave much strength, quick-ness, and tension; and I must give due credit also to the definite all-time best super-hero inker, Joe Sinnott. As much as I love John's work, Joe's, simple, clear, and distinct lines added so much that his influence was as great as John's! With, two such fantastic talents handling the art, we got superhero art as best as it could possibly be.

Gil's cover illo was another beauty, but it was totally destroyed by the horrendous red and pink coloring. Gad, what a disturbing effect.

Dean Mullaney
81 Delaware Street
Staten Island, NY 10304

Dear Marvel Armadillos:

THOR is usually a good but unexciting magazine: the Thor/Loki war story is something completely different. For one thing, there is the strong symbolic impact of the events we see being played out: Washington, D.C. with all its meaning in terms of our history and liberties, is being invaded. Perhaps the invasion would be comprehensible if it was conducted by a Soviet military force or even an army of aliens from another world with futuristic weaponry.

Instead, incredibly, the menace is a medieval-style army before which all of America's military might is helpless. It is as if the past were invading the present, or as if the appearance of powerful men resembling our ancestors re-duced us all to mere helpless children. Moreover, this invading force is from a place thought to be mythical, Asgard, and has the power of sorcery on its side. Our world of the known has been invaded by the powers of the unknown. Things we once thought unreal—magic, Asgard—prove to be all too dangerously real.

Indeed, if this story has a flaw, it is that you don't develop this theme. How does the general public react to their new knowledge that magic and Asgard are real? Indeed, how do they react to the idea of America being invaded? You let us see one man's reaction last issue, but that isn't enough. As for Judith, it's hard to believe anyone would be so stupid as to think it was all a put-on. If she is intended to be the spokeswoman for my generation that she pretends to be. I want to age fast.

But the best part of the issue was Sawyer's reaction to the idea of using nuclear weaponry. We are not told exactly why he feels the way he does. Is he thinking of the deaths of all the innocent citizens in the Washington area that the bomb would cause, or about the fallout's effects on the whole country?

Somehow I feel that Sawyer wasn't thinking primarily of deaths when he said our civilization was coming to an end. His main concern, I think, must have been the damage to America's moral spirit that using this most terrible of weapons on other intelligent beings would cause. Hiroshima is far away in space and time: Those who want to ignore it find it easy to do so. But no-one could shut his eyes to mass murder in our nation's capital. It's this idea which truly makes THOR #234 a memorable issue.

Peter Sanderson
27 Gov. Belcher Lane
Milton, MA 02186

OPPOSITE **18: VOLSTAGG** from *Thor* no. 237 (July 1975). Stamp also appears in *Astonishing Tales* no. 24 (June 1974), *Ka-Zar* no. 5 (September 1974), and *The Amazing Spider-Man* no. 144 (May 1975).

ABOVE Unpublished cover for *Thor* no. 170 (November 1969), art by Jack Kirby and Bill Everett.

MAIL IT TO MAR-VELL

c/o MARVEL COMICS GROUP, 575 MADISON AVE. N.Y.C. 10022

People:

It started with IRON MAN, developed and exploded with CAPTAIN MARVEL, and the shock waves are just beginning.

Better than Jack Kirby, better than Steranko. His name......is Jim Starlin.

Need I say more?

Joshua Orzeck, SUNY Brockport
Brockport, New York 14420

Nope—especially with seemingly everyone in the free world sending in his personal response to Jim's most popular issue to date. Strangely enough, #29 wasn't particularly controversial (the reaction we'd expected)—because everybody loved it! For example—

Dear Jim, Al, Tom, and Roy,

Stupendous! Metamorphosis has got to be the best of Captain Marvel since he was reborn. Jim, your supradimensional galactic backgrounds made this the best mag in the "cosmic" line of art I have ever seen (and, believe me, I have stacks!). And the coloring! It all gives one the feeling of being there — actually spanning the infinite vastness in milliseconds.

Starlin's style of exaggerating thins and thicknesses bothered me at first, but, as I see more and he becomes accustomed to the strip, the style now makes CAPTAIN MARVEL what it is. With this, the infinitesimal detail, and the well-planned lack of panel borders, well, Jim Starlin has got to be one of the best artists Marvel has ever had. The scripting aided the effect, making this story unique among nearly all of Marvel's titles. Only WARLOCK compares, because the situation was unique only to the particular character, and no other hero could ever fit into the same situation. Also, I liked the way Eon subtly changed without any mention at all in the script—it fit the mood exactly. All in all, Jim Starlin is made for Captain Marvel!

David Burica
RR#3 268AA
Paulding, Ohio 45879

Dear Bullpen,

In CAPTAIN MARVEL #29 the reader got a Daredevil's head running around with legs and a tail, an one-eyed, curly-topped plant monster, a sadly cruel resurrection, a quaint mythology that was nothing more than a scrambled up, diluted version of Greek mythology, a tree with faces, stone monsters, and a fight with the "Inner Self." To think that it took twenty pages and all that trouble just to get a new hair dye. The comic was a bit too complicated and abstract for any reader to completely understand. The story was blatantly bizarre and the artist has been trying again to shock the reader with another psychedelic mess that he has a great love for.

Although new confused and overly abstract, CAPTAIN MARVEL has changed for the better. Jim Starlin is the best new artist that Marvel has, and hopefully he will stay on for a long time to come. The comic also has a startling, new, great villain, a science fiction wonderland called Titan, and plenty of good plotlines like the search for the cosmic cube.

If only the writer could tone down on the pretty psychedelics and avoid cosmic operas and metamorphoses, CAPTAIN MARVEL could become one of Marvel's true greats.

Daniel Parker
(no address given)

MARVEL VALUE STAMP

CLIP 'EM AND COLLECT 'EM!

OPPOSITE **19: HOGUN, BALDER, and FANDRAL** from *Captain Marvel* no. 32 (May 1974). Stamp also appears in *Man-Thing* no. 7 (July 1974).

ABOVE *Thor* no. 169 (October 1969), art by Jack Kirby and Bill Everett.

left. Please don't bring him back. He belongs in his own mag and nowhere else. Next, the Hulk and Doc Strange must go! They, too, belong in their own mags. Neither has ever really been a "group" hero. They are too individual.

The Defenders line-up should be Valkyrie, Nighthawk, Hawkeye, Black Knight, and maybe one or two other reformed baddies. They would be unique in the fact that they were all once on the other side of the law. It really has fantastic possibilities.

Chad B. Goyette
4401 Clark Ave.
Long Beach, Calif. 90808

Maybe, Chad. But if we eliminate Dr. Strange and the Hulk, we're also cutting out, we think, two of the major reasons many readers purchase the book. And, too, now that Subby's own mag has been discontinued, we're hesitant to exclude him forever from the Defenders roster.

As a matter of fact, we're planning an early return for Sub-Mariner to the Defenders...and we predict that the circumstances surrounding that dramatic re-entry will completely and utterly blow your ever-lovin' mind!

Meanwhile, though, what's your reaction to Luke Cage's power-packed guest-appearance in this issue? How do you think he would fare as a regular member of our super-team? (It's interesting to note, incidentally, that both Subby and Cage have villainous backgrounds also, Namor having been a longtime foe of the Fantastic Four and Luke, an escaped convict.)

Dear Marvel,

Defenders I'd like to see: Red Wolf and Lobo: break up Daredevil and the Black Widow and put the Widow in the Defenders; also, Sting-Ray (Namor's buddy).

Tom Long
R.R. #3
Edwardsville, Ill. 62065

Dear Marvel,

I hope you will soon let the Hulk and Subby take a leave of absence and bring in a few replacements like Nighthawk. Another possibility is Venus, last featured in SUB-MARINER #57. After all, she's here on earth to stop war and destruction. Sting-Ray is another excellent possibility, as is Balder, who never does much in Thor's mag.

Robert Hewko
8309-134 Avenue
Edmonton, 31, Alberta
Canada

Dear Marvel,

Nighthawk should become a Defender! He is the find of the year. Make him a regular. Valkyrie is being underused, and the Hulk is being overused. Val and Nighthawk could take over the comic if you let them. I didn't mind having the big guns around for the initial issues, but now let the lesser characters take over. Dr. Strange is the group's organizer and should remain in it. I don't care one way or the other about Namor. The Surfer does not belong in the Defenders; he should get his own comic.

Steve Humphreys
2909 Grover Street
McKeesport, Pa. 15132

The Black Widow? Sting-Ray? Venus? Balder?

We won't say "no" on any of those highly intriguing—and weird!— possibilities. But we won't say "yes," either. Fact is, we're still wondering ourselves just which characters will eventually be permanent fixtures in the DEFENDERS mag. And for proof of that statement, check out this very issue, in which the Hulk quits (again!) and Valkyrie takes a leave of absence.

And we've got a whole slew of other characters— old and new— we want to try out for membership, as well as one character who's never appeared anywhere before!

But we're still wide-open to suggestions, folks. The address is at the top of the page. Let's hear from you!

OPPOSITE **20: BROTHER VOODOO** from *The Defenders* no. 17 (November 1974). Stamp also appears in *Sub-Mariner* no. 69 (March 1974) and *Ghost Rider* no. 7 (August 1974).

ABOVE *Strange Tales* no. 169 (September 1973), art by Gene Colan and Dan Adkins.

hundred issues ago?...Reed and Sue are getting a divorce?! ...oh...

Fellas, your books aren't fun to read anymore. Why call them the Fantastic Four? They're neither fantastic nor four. They were both several years ago. Y'see, you've gone too far. Back in 1963-5, you had what no one else had— real people who just happened to have super-powers; Joe Average in a skintight suit. Oh, he had his downs, sure, big ones. But lordy, every so often, his "innate goodness" (that used to pervade Marvel comics) would shine forth with the light of a thousand suns and all that, and he'd *win,* by dammy, and get the girl for a while. Okay, so we knew we couldn't *be* Mr. Fantastic or Spider-Man, but we could sure identify.

And what have we today? A stable of all-*too*-relevant manic depressives. Aren't we aware enough of the big, bad world without having it soaked into our escapist fantasy? Why did Superman and the Big Red Cheese make it so big when they appeared decades ago? Because they were heroes, and they could win the battles— because we wanted to feel good in a world that made us feel bad.

So people and the world have changed since then: things are more complex, and there is great disillusionment. Must it be everywhere? Must comic heroes not only never find victory or peace for themselves, but also deny it to us?

Folks, you have a good deal of power at your command, creative and otherwise. In a world that is sorely lacking them, please give us some Good Guys.

Richard A. Pini
(no address given)

Gosh, you mean the Sub-Mariner did all that,...just to? ...for Reed and Sue??...and they're together again, and a team, and...? Wow.

(In other words, the difference between the world of 1974 and the halcyon days of 1963 is that it takes a whole lot longer, Rich, for things to start straightening themselves out. Because the world has spent those past nine years working so hard against its own good...and still is. But occasionally, good will win out. Not like a thousand suns. Maybe just a pinpoint of flickering light, if that. But it happens.)

Dear Marvel,

Faan-TAS-tic!

When I picked up F.F. #147 and took a gander at the front cover, I thought to myself, "They wouldn't, would they?" Then I took it home and decided, "Yes, they would!"

My hearty congratulations on taking a good hard look at a nasty— and painful— subject: divorce. I started reading the F.F. in 1963 and was impressed by the subjects these four people (not superheroes— at that point in time, I did not think of superheroes as people) handled. Like, can a superhero have human feelings and human problems? Everything I saw in FANTASTIC FOUR indicated that a strong "yes" was your reply.

But divorce...! When I started writing my Master's Thesis proposals (fall, 1973), I mentioned the possibility of divorce entering into a superhero's life and was met with derisive cries of, "nobody's gonna do that!" The more I saw of Reed and Sue's relationship, especially Reed's decision (which was necessary, which made it all the nastier) to shut down his son's mind— the more I felt that divorce or at least legal separation, was the ultimate end of the Richardses' current relationship. (I have also noticed Medusa's compassion for Reed, which seems suspiciously like something more than compassion.)

I don't like the idea that two people whom I've grown to respect and admire and like would have to go through something as painful as divorce, but I am glad that you respect your readers and your characters enough that you aren't "copping out" of a bad situation by having them ignore a very real problem.

Samanda Jeude
1438 Eigenmann,
Bloomington, Ind. 47401

Our feeling precisely, Samanda. What we're doing today is an outgrowth— not a betrayal— of what we began in 1961. Closing our eyes to the ills of the world...*that* would be betrayal.

OPPOSITE **21: KULL** from *Fantastic Four* no. 151 (October 1974). Stamp also appears in *Marvel Spotlight* no. 15 (May 1974).

ABOVE *Kull the Destroyer* no. 11 (November 1973), art by Mike Ploog.

LET'S LEVEL WITH DAREDEVIL

SEND YOUR LETTERS TO:

THE MARVEL COMICS GROUP
SIXTH FLOOR
575 MADISON AV.
NEW YORK 10022
N. Y.

THE GERBER CURSE, OR..EVEN PARANOIDS HAVE REAL ENEMIES

Somewhere, in some demon-haunted castle perched upon some craggy promontory overlooking a swirling sea of boiling oil, a mad sorcerer peers deep into his crystal ball, cackles, and asks himself, "What can I do to screw up Steve Gerber's books *this* month?"

Or so it seems. For poor, innocent Steve has, in his first year of comics writing, encountered a decidedly unnatural number of unexplainble accidents (?) with the various magazines he has authored. So many, in fact, that we in the Bullpen have come to believe in the existence of a phenomenon we call "The Gerber Curse", engineered by the mad mage mentioned above.

Thus far, that admittedly very creative evil conjuror has come up with such abominations as: blue surface-men in "Tales of Atlantis": a chameleon-like Man-Thing who changes color virtually every issue; a linguistic innovation---"chow" meaning "goodbye"; and countless other major and minor catastrophes, culminating in his greatest, most horrifying achievement of all, "The DAREDEVIL Puzzle Page!"

What a triumph that was! Page seven of DAREDEVIL # 105, on which panels 1,2, 3, and 4 were printed in a wholly incomprehensible new arrangement--2, 1, 4, and 3--thereby convincing hundreds of thousands of readers that (a) something queer had happened to their water supply; (b) something queer had happened to our water supply; or (c) they had accidentally purchased the Hebrew edition of DD and/should have been reading from right to left:

Oh, sure...there's a perfectly natural explanation for how it came about. But we prefer to blame it on that faraway sorcerer in his faraway castle. And we've even convinced Steve that that evil magician is responsible for his many troubles. He'll never know about our Conspiracy to drive him berserk! Never! Never!

(Thunderclaps. Lightning flashes.)

---The Bullpen.

Gents,

Never in my life would I think of putting Don Heck to work on DAREDEVIL. Heck's bulkier style is fine when applied to broader, more muscular types like Iron Man and Subby. but DD needs a more fluid hand; the grace of a Romita or Colan or Adams: Don Heck just doesn't fit--or so I thought.

DD # 103 changed my mind completely! Heck handled Matt, the Widow, and Spidey (Spidey!) with such finesse that I was astounded. After the artistic mess of the past two issues (what happened to Rich Buckler, pray tell?), this Heck extravaganza was a delight! If this keeps up, I promise I'll forget the Hawkeye and Stilt-Man stinkers. OM!

Marc De Matteis
1100 Ocean Avenue
Brooklyn, N.Y. 11230

P.S.: Don't think I've forgotten you, Steve. You seem to really have the feel of the strip now, and your work has been, to say the least, impressive.

Dear Steve, Roy, Don, and Sal,

It is to be expected that the team of Conway, Colan, and Palmer would be a very tough act to follow, but your offerings thus far have been an outrage. DAREDEVIL # 103 sank to the ultimate depths of your neglected effort to maintain the precedent of quality and ingenuity which I have come to take for granted.

Quite simply, DAREDEVIL demands the finest of artists and writers to regain that once dearly-held standard. Don Heck recently did enough damage to the AVENGERS. Please don't allow him to drag this strip down, too. Similarly, Steve Gerber has not yet proven to any degree of satisfaction that he is capable of handling the writing chores. If all he intends to do is have DD and Natasha aimlessly fight every bug-eyed baddy that happens to be in the neighborhood, with painfully insipid dialogue in between, certainly he does not meet Marvel's standards by any means.

You need not ponder the situation long to realize the errors you have made, and take immediate action to correct them.

Thank you.

Alan Rothman
151-12 24th Road
Whitestone, N.Y. 11357

And that, folks, is the kind of polarization of opinion that DAREDEVIL # 103 created among Marveldom. Most readers either loved it or hated it, and there were precious few in-betweeners. What can we say?

More importantly, what will you say about the rather drastic alterations we've sprung on you this issue? We suspect you'll be favorably disposed toward Bob Brown's pencilling and Steve Gerber's script, per se. But what about the new storyline? And the move back to New York? And the return to the old cover logo? (Which reminds us: Natasha will continue to appear as a major character in DD, despite the absence of her name from the cover-banner. The change was instituted primarily because we felt the double logo actually de-emphasized both characters' names too much.)

We'll be waiting for your comments--with fingers and toes crossed.

Dear Guys,

DAREDEVIL # 103 was a pretty good comic, but on page 15, panel seven, you said that Ramrod's strength had increased tenfold--and that his bones were replaced with steel bands. Right, so far?

Now, if I remember correctly, bone marrow makes blood cells. Other parts of the body do this, too, but bone marrow makes the most. So how could Ramrod be ten times as strong without blood cells?

Try to get out of that one!

Sharon Kasmanoff
81 Winding Way
West Orange, N.J.

Several readers took us to task on this point, Sharon, and our defense is a very simple one:

Ramrod didn't keel over and die from lack of blood cells, so obviously Moon Dragon and Broderick must have installed within him some sort of device to compensate for his missing bone marrow. Granted, we didn't mention it in the story, but that doesn't mean it wasn't there!

Gentlemen,

I enjoyed Spider-Man's guest-starring role in DAREDEVIL # 103. However, there were several large gaps in the logic of the tale. To begin with, Spider-Man has known who DD is since DAREDEVIL # 16; he even wrote a letter to Murdock in DD # 24 telling him of this. Nevertheless, this fact is totally ignored in DARE DEVIL # 103.

On a similar track, when Daredevil first met Spider-Man in SPIDEY # 16, his radar sense did a very concise description of what Spidey looked like. Granted that Daredevil might not have recognized him when they first met for the interview, but he most certainly would have recognized the similarity in heartbeats between Parker and Spider-Man during or at least after the fight with Ramrod when Parker once again popped up on the scene.

Try and get out of that one.

William Alexius
21 Jen-Ho Road, Rei-Kang
Yunlin, Taiwan

Okay, here goes...!

In DAREDEVIL # 54, horn-head faked the death of Matt Murdock (for his own purposes) which prompted Spidey, on page 13 of that issue, to think, "Funny...I once thought DD was a blind lawyer! But Matt Murdock's dead now! So scratch one web-headed hunch!" Later, when the whole business about Matt's phony twin brother was made public, Spidey accepted the explanation that the Daredevil he had suspected to be Matt was actually "Mike" Murdock. And that was that.

As for DD not recognizing the similarity in heartbeats between Pete's and Spidey's....well, we'll award you a tentative no-prize, Mr. Alexius, on the grounds that we should've said something and just plain forgot! In other words, maybe--just maybe--DD does know Spidey's secret. But we'll have to wait for a future issue to find out. Okay?

OPPOSITE **22: MAN-THING** from *Daredevil* no. 108 (March 1974). Stamp also appears in *Iron Man* no. 69 (August 1974), *Amazing Adventures* no. 27 (November 1974), and *Astonishing Tales* no. 27 (December 1974).

ABOVE *Fear* no. 12 (February 1973), art by Jim Starlin and Rich Buckler.

THE HAMMER STRIKES

c/o MARVEL COMICS GROUP, 575 MADISON AVE. N.Y.C. 10022

Dear Gerry, John, and Dick,

THOR #232 was outstanding. To begin with the cover was one of the best I've seen on this mag in a long while. This was mostly due to a lack of cluttering word balloons and a good job of inking.

The only words I can find for the interior art are inspiring and excellent. John put a great deal of expression into each and every face, especially the Thunder God's.

I've always heard that the way a finished panel of Buscema art will look is very dependent upon the inker. In this, Dick Giordano has shown his great skill as an embellisher. He seems to bring out every line of John's pencils, without having to mute his own easily-recognizable style. Please, do your best to keep him on as inker for THOR.

Oh yeah, the story was pretty good, too.

David L. Simons
CCC Tomaroa
Governor's Island
New York, NY 10004

Dear Gerry,

I never expected to see it, but the longest-standing injustice of the Marvel Universe has been uncovered. You should get a no-prize.

That trial of Jane Foster's was jury-rigged; the judge wanted his grandchildren to be all-godchildren. And if not meeting with approval by the in-laws didn't crush her, Odin's going away gift was humiliation enough: *Another* blond doctor.

Oh, it was Odin's ultimate insult to we the people, that he could toss away Thor's friend from the beginning. She is an embarrassing link to a time when perhaps there has never even *been* a Thor. Jane had been in love with Don Blake first, her love for Thor was after that fact. Don the doctor wasn't the son Odin always wanted.

Well, whatever this reintroduction of Jane Foster means, it means she didn't get along with Odin's computer-date match.

Marilyn Sue Knapp
80 16 S. Harmon
Marion, IN 46952

What Ho, Marvelites—

The most unexpected character of all, you said. Surely, if I *ever* hear anyone calling Marvel a liar, I'll have a thing or two to tell them. But a question. Now that you have Jane Foster back, what are you going to do with her? A rhetorical question to say the least. Surely you would not bring her back just to kill her off two or three months later, and indeed, there would be mass revolt in Marveldom if Thor were to go back to her.

Wilf Campbell
1656 Lloyd George Cres
Verdun, Quebec, Canada

Hey, people—what's everybody talking about these days? We'll give ya *one* guess. Right the first time! The rapturous reappearance of Jane Foster, what else!

But we gotta admit, it's a pretty rare day (month...*year)* when someone Out There recommends someone Back Here for a no-prize. Sheesh! Gerry's so stun-boggled that he could only warble that old Ringo standby, "It Don't Come Easy," in response.

What, indeed, are we going to do with Jane Foster, Wilf? Why, that would be telling. And you know how we'd hate to ruin your fun (not to mention Gerry's disposition) by revealing that *here.* Heck, ya gotta wait and see—that's the fun of it.

Okay, Thor persons, it's time to boogaloo, stage left; otherwise we may run out of

THIS IS IT! YOUR

MARVEL VALUE STAMP

FOR THIS ISSUE! CLIP 'EM AND COLLECT 'EM!

STATEMENT OF OWNERSHIP, MANAGEMENT AND CIRCULATION ACT OF AUGUST 12, 1970: SECTION 3685, TITLE 39, UNITED STATES CODE

1. Title of Publication: THOR.

2. DATE OF FILING, September 18, 1974.

3. Frequency of Issue: Monthly.

4. Location of Known Office of Publication: 575 Madison Ave., New York, N.Y. 10022.

5. Location of the Headquarters or General Business Offices of the Publishers: Marvel Comics Group, 575 Madison Ave., New York, N.Y. 10022.

6. Names and addresses of the publisher, editor, and managing editor are: Publisher: Stan Lee—Marvel Comics Group, 575 Madison Ave., New York, N.Y. 10022; Editor: Len Wein—Marvel Comics Group, 575 Madison Ave., New York, N.Y. 10022; Managing Editor: John Verpoorten—Marvel Comics Group, 575 Madison Ave., New York, N.Y. 10022.

7. Owner (If owned by a corporation, its name and address must be stated and also immediately thereunder the names and addresses of stockholders owning or holding 1 percent or more of total amount of stock. If not owned by a corporation, the names and addresses of the individual owners must be given. If owned by a partnership or other unincorporated firm, its name and address, as well as that of each individual must be given.) Cadence Industries Corp., 21 Henderson Drive, West Caldwell, New Jersey.

8. Known bondholders, mortgagees, and other security holders owning or holding 1 percent or more of total amount of bonds, mortgages, or other securities (If there are none, so state) None.

9. For optional completion by publishers mailing at the regular rates (Section 132.121, Postal Service Manual) 39 U.S.C. 3626 provides in pertinent part: "No person who would have been entitled to mail matter under former section 4359 of this title shall mail such matter at the rates provided under this subsection unless he files annually with the Postal Service a written request for permission to mail matter at such rates."

In accordance with the provisions of this statute, I hereby request permission to mail the publication named in Item 1 at the reduced postage rates presently authorized by 39 U.S.C. 3626.

(signed) Ivan Snyder V.P. Operations Publishing Division

10. For completion by nonprofit organizations authorized to mail at special rates. (Section 132.122, Postal Manual.) The purpose, function, and nonprofit status of this organization and the exempt status for Federal income tax purposes. (Check one.) ☐ Have not changed during preceding 12 months. ☐ Have changed during preceding 12 months. (If changed, publisher must submit explanation of change with this statement.)

11. EXTENT AND NATURE OF CIRCULATION.

A. Total No. Copies Printed (net press run): Average no. copies each issue during preceding 12 months: 387,083; single issue nearest to filing date: 433,525.

B. Paid Circulation: 1) Sales through dealers and carriers, street vendors and counter sales: Average no. copies each issue during preceding 12 months: 204,723; single issue nearest to filing date: 229,286 est. 2) Mail subscriptions. Average no. copies each issue during preceding 12 months: 1,115; single issue nearest to filing date: 1,025.

C. Total paid circulation: Average no. copies each issue during preceding 12 months: 205,838; single issue nearest to filing date: 230,311 est.

D. Free distribution by mail, carrier or other means. 1) Samples, complimentary, and other free copies: ---; single issue nearest to filing date: ---. 2) Copies distributed to news agents, but not sold: Average no. copies each issue during preceding 12 months: 178,164; single issue nearest to filing date: 199,763 est.

E. Total distribution (sum of C and D): Average no. copies each issue during preceding 12 months: 384,002; single issue nearest to filing date: 430,074.

F. Office use, left-over, unaccounted, spoiled after printing: Average no. copies each issue during preceding 12 months: 3,081; single issue nearest to filing date: 3,451.

G. Total (sum of E & F—should equal net press run shown in A): Average no. copies each issue during preceding 12 months: 387,083; single issue nearest to filing date: 433,525.

I certify that the statements made by me above are correct and complete.

(signed) Ivan Snyder V.P. Operations Publishing Division

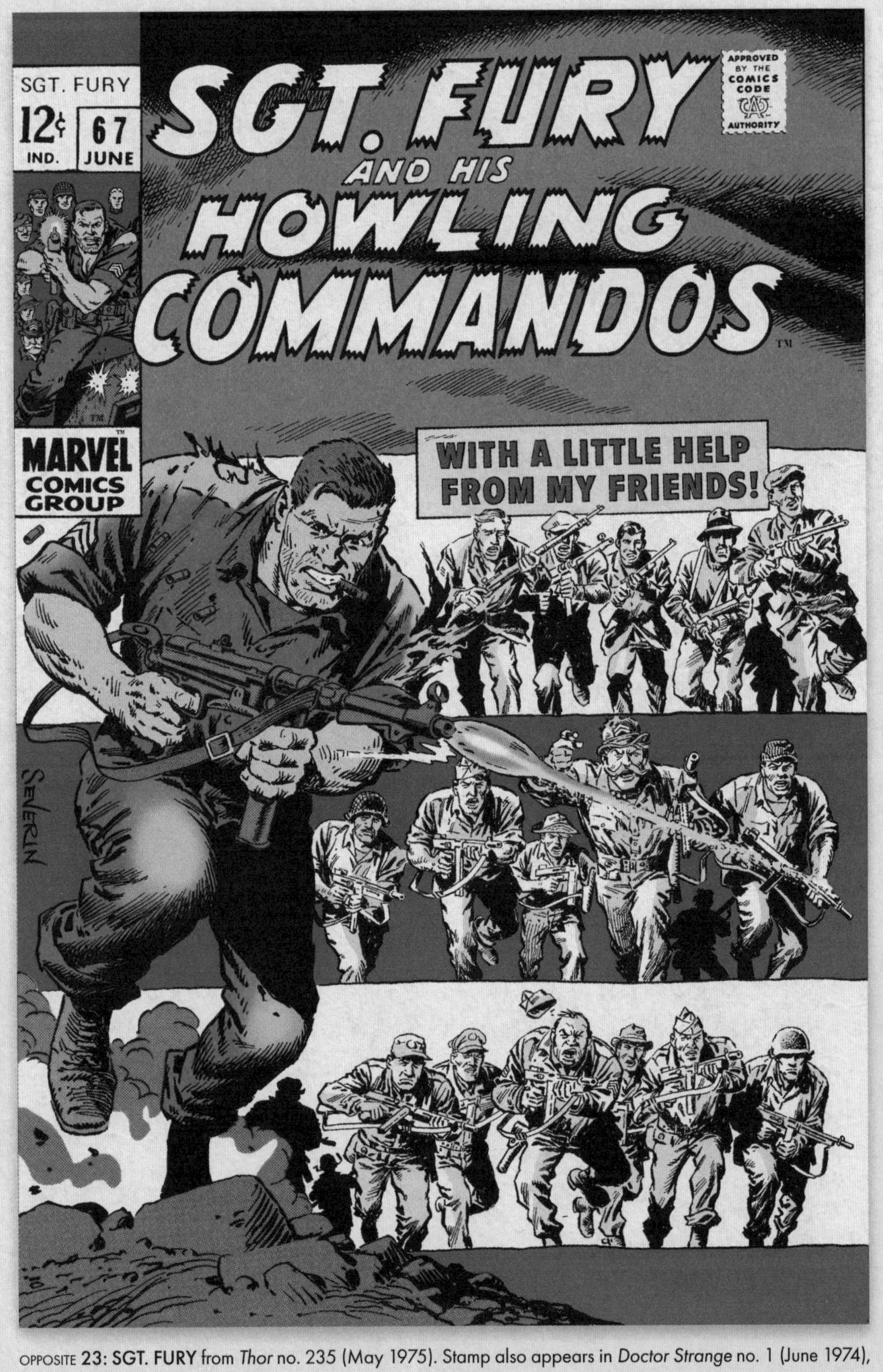

OPPOSITE **23: SGT. FURY** from *Thor* no. 235 (May 1975). Stamp also appears in *Doctor Strange* no. 1 (June 1974), *Fantastic Four* no. 152 (November 1974), *Tomb of Dracula* no. 30 (March 1975), and *War Is Hell* no. 13 (June 1975).

ABOVE *Sgt. Fury* no. 67 (June 1969), art by John Severin.

GHOST WRITERS!

c/o MARVEL COMICS GROUP, 575 MADISON AVE. N.Y.C. 10022

Dear Gary,

In general, GHOST RIDER is getting better every night. But he needs a new locale, now that his Indian girlfriend's free to leave. So...take him to India, especially Talbot Mundy's India of the book Om, The Secret of Ahbor Valley, where he can fight devil-spawned forces and meet H. Rider Haggard-type villainesses and explore lost worlds. He would stand out as much more unique in such a setting, rather than appearing just "another hot-rodding cyclist" in the Southwest.

Nags:

Linda can see Johnny's cycle of fire in G. R. #3, but claims she can't ride it, because she's lost her Satanic powers. Baloney! She has to be able to see and ride it. I can't picture your suddenly having a guy riding a non-visible cycle through the streets.

There are too many "race-to-the-death" scenes. This mag's about Ghost RIDER, not Ghost CYCLE.

At the end of G.R. #3, the Hell's Angel-type gets zapped by Johnny and hits an oil tanker. Unnecessary and crude, even to give Johnny self-reciminatory thoughts for future issues.

In the same vein, why did G.R. have to fall in the middle of the freeway on page sixteen, causing multiple crashes? So the cops can gun for him from now on? Too much SMASH for too little reason. He's already got the police after him.

On page six, Linda shows G.R. how to conjure up a cycle...right arm full extended, left arm cocked at the elbow. So why is G.R. doing the reverse? This is too obvious. (Next, he'll be praying to a Cross of David catty-cornered on an altar of vibranium.)

How come when Johnny Blaze awakes in the hospital, he doesn't tell someone about Linda's being stranded in the desert, as he promised her he would?

Thanks for a good mag, though.

Dennis Melvyn
3607 N.E. 14th St.
Amarillo, Texas 79107

Let's try to your answer your letter point-by-point, okay, Dennis? Here goes...!

First, we think it might be a little difficult to justify Johnny Blaze's suddenly departing for India. He's never been there before (that we know of). He's not inclined toward Eastern mysticism (since he's got his hands full with the Western devil). He didn't even perform at the Bangla Desh concert! But...we'll see. If not India, perhaps some other exotic land awaits up the highway.

Secondly, we never claimed Johnny's fire-cycle was invisible! Linda couldn't ride it simply because it was a magical creation and so could only be ridden by someone with magical powers, like Ghost Rider.

On the matter of too-abundant races-to-the-death: do the rest of you out there in Marvel-land agree?

Regarding all the auto smash-ups in GHOST RIDER #3, we may have to admit you're right. And yet, you have to admit they were fun to look at in a perverse sort of way. G.R. is, however you slice it, a menace to highway navigation. As such, whether he likes it or not, and he doesn't, he's going to get involved in crashes of that sort. You have to remember that GHOST RIDER is a sort of paper-and-ink demolition derby.

We didn't read any particular symbolism into the way Ghost Rider conjured up that cycle. Chances are, for that particular spell, it just didn't matter which arm was in which position. (Yeah, we know that's pretty lame, so how 'bout the Absolute Truth, Most Likely: Jim, we think wisely chose not to repeat the same pose in the next panel, so that the page would have a little more visual variety. But since the cycle still showed up, we gotta maintain that it really didn't matter, or the story wouldn't make any sense...!!)

Finally, Johnny didn't mention Linda's danger at the hospital because he was (a) in a state of semi-shock and (b) heavily sedated, thus delirious, on top of that.

We hope that answers your questions, Mr. Melvyn, 'cause we're outta breath, our typewriter ribbon is starting to fray, it's 3:20 A.M., and we're ready to collapse!!

Dear Roy,

I've been looking at the cover of GHOST RIDER #3, and something about it was bugging me. I just realized what it was.

G.R.'s fire-cycle doesn't emit exhaust fumes, but fire. Fire consumes oxygen, right?

So if everyone sells his (or her) soul to Satan, goes back on the deal as Johnny did, and learns how to control his/her powers—we'll be in a lot of trouble. Somehow, I just can't picture a fire-auto. That's something to think about.

Mark Brooks
20 Mayflower
Hallowell, Me. 04347

It's something to think about, all right, but not at 3:25 in the morning, Mark! Come on! Give us a break, willya!

SATAN SPEAKING: "It is my plan to rid the mortal world of air pollution, Mark Brooks! If all men traverse the byways of earth in fire-autos, thus consuming oxygen, there will eventually be no oxygen. No air...no air pollution! 'Tis simple as that! HaHaHaHaHaHaHa! Yuk, yuk, yuk, yuk!"

Dear Marvel,

GHOST RIDER is one of my favorite comics, and I hated seeing it go bi-monthly. The reason I'm writing is to try for my first no-prize. In MARVEL SPOTLIGHT #12, when Johnny and Linda were coming back to "the world" in the Son of Satan's chariot, Johnny was in his human form. But in GHOST RIDER #3, in the exact same scene, he is the Ghost Rider. How can you get out of this one?

Don Fleming
313 S. Forrest Ave.
Adel, Ga. 31620

Easy, D-Don...ZzZzZ...we just...ZzZzZ...award you a n-no-priZzZzZze....and go...to sleep...! See, it's 3:32 in the morning...ZzZzZ...and... ummm...g'night....!

THIS IS IT! YOUR
MARVEL VALUE STAMP
FOR THIS ISSUE!

CLIP 'EM AND COLLECT 'EM!

OPPOSITE **24: THE FALCON** from *Ghost Rider* no. 5 (April 1974). Stamp also appears in *Conan the Barbarian* no. 42 (September 1974) and *Creatures on the Loose* no. 33 (January 1975).

ABOVE *Captain America* no. 170 (February 1974), art by Sal Buscema and Vince Colletta.

against his former masters, then in #11, he became the servant of Zo, a "god" from deep space. In #16, he discovered that Zo was a put-up job engineered by rebellious Kree leaders, but in combating them, he received a massive dose of negative radiation. The Supreme Intelligence, ruler of the Kree, gave him his current red costume just before Marv was sucked into the Negative Zone...and later (in ish #17), his life was merged with that of Rick Jones. In his time, Marv has been through three complete metamorphoses, ten writers, nine artists, and two cancellations (along with, fortunately, two rebirths).

Whew! Any more questions?

Dear Jim and Mike,

You guys realize, of course, that if you keep up the present quality of CAPTAIN MARVEL you can never lower your standards. Foomers of the world will always expect high things from this mag! And if the level of the greatness lowers even one decimal of an iota on the mag, you will be the recipients of unimaginable amounts of cries of anguish and anger!

So you may be pleased to find this particular foomer has nothing but screams of praise for CM #32! Having Isaac, the world-wide computer of Titan, assume a functional humanoid form is a fanatistic idea! He is a great addition to Drax and Moon Dragon and the rest. Keep the humanoid Isaac roaming around; I've grown accustomed to him. This comic-book has acquired a rather unique cast of supporting characters. What are your plans for all of them once the Thanos saga is finished?

Brian W. Prescott
132 Bonair Ave.
W. Springfield, Ma. 01089

Most of the characters Jim's introduced over the past issues are being set aside for now, Brian, as he delves into a different sort of plot. But rest assured, the world won't be without them for long.

Dear Bullpenners,

This is getting pretty boring, you know. Just one great issue of CAPTAIN MARVEL after another. CM #31 has finally pooled all the elements together...it might as well be titled CAPTAIN MARVEL, THE AVENGERS, THE DESTROYER, MOON DRAGON, AND THE TITANS. C'mon now, remember whose mag this is; it must be Cap's hand that brings the final fall of Thanos (as we know he must so Captain Marvel may survive—or are you planning on renaming the book THANOS THE FIRST?).

Jim Starlin's artwork is beyond belief...beautiful! No words can truly describe the magnificence (or a reasonable facsimile thereof). By the way, why do we see the word "Gemini" in the lower right hand corner of the cover?

Various and sundry notes:

1) why did you decide to change Cap's hair from white to blonde?

2) That's some heavy chick Thanos has; who is she really?

3) When this is all over, what can you do for an encore?

David Kell
5702 W. Kell Road
Fairview, Pa. 16415

More by-the-numbers answers:

1) Marvel (Mighty, not Captain) felt he would look younger that way.

2) Jim's not telling any more than he already has in the stories. In fact, Steve wrote an explanation based on what Jim has told him for this issue, and Jim edited it out. We leave it for you to ponder.

3) You're seein' it!

NEXT ISH: Captain Marvel dying or dead on Earth! Rick Jones trapped in the Negative Zone! The Lunatic Legion (whoever they are) gearing up for a second assault on the Earth! Annihilus! Ant-Man! The Wasp! And (though we forgot to mention him in the final caption) The Living Laser!

What more do we have to say?

THIS IS IT! YOUR

MARVEL VALUE STAMP

FOR THIS ISSUE! CLIP 'EM AND COLLECT 'EM!

OPPOSITE **25: THE [HUMAN] TORCH** from *Captain Marvel* no. 34 (September 1974). Stamp also appears in *Marvel Team-Up* no. 20 (April 1974) and *Captain Marvel* no. 36 (January 1975).

ABOVE *Fantastic Four* no. 134 (May 1973), art by John Buscema and Joe Sinnott.

Steve, is it not healthy for Americans to question the motives of their "heroes"? Why is "crises of confidence" bad? Perhaps, had the American people timed their present crisis of confidence earlier, we wouldn't have a fugitive in the White House.

Steve paints a bleak picture of American media in these recent stories. Perhaps, television and radio executives may be as irresponsible as to allow the anti-Cap advertisements to be broadcast. However, there is a law which provides for equal time. Cap has that option open to him in this case, I think.

I'd like to add, sadly, that Steve portrayed validly the susceptibility of the American people to demagoguery and mass media saturation. American people often have very little depth of thought in these matters. In this headline society people rarely look between the lines; in short, believing everything they read. I really don't mean to sermonize, but the American people are too contented to sit back and listen to Pete Hamill OR William Buckley—but not to both. They too easily accept others' opinions instead of formulating their own. When the morality of our government is riddled with corruption and rotten at the core, this is a dangerous attitude to take.

Peter Cucich
55-20 103 St.
Corona, N.Y. 11368

Who says it's not healthy to question the motives of heroes? Who says crises of confidence are bad? Certainly not Stainless Steve, Pete. The way we read it, he said the exact opposite in his statement. Calling such things "commonplace" isn't calling them "bad," you know. Heck, the entire thrust of CA&F these days is to show that these things are good for America—not to mention Captain America. (Boy, #173 must have been even more confusing than we thought!)

We'll have to take issue with you on your second paragraph too, Pete. We don't consider the broadcasting of anti-Cap ads to be irresponsible. To the contrary, refusing to broadcast such ads would fly in the face of the Constitution and its "Free Speech" Amendment. The media in those stories was simply depicted as conducting "business as usual."

Dear Steve, Sal, Vin,

Just a word or two, to let you know an appreciative fan has recognized the improvement that CAPTAIN AMERICA is taking. Before the Falcon was given the means to fly, I really could not stand him! To me he was just another form of tokenism. But his personality seems to have undergone a subtle change along with his powers. If the trend continues it would not surprise me to see him in his own mag, say, six months from now.

Gregory Kelley
127 N. Chester, Apt. 3
Oildale, Ca. 93308

The Falcon continues to be caught up in forces that are modifying his personality, Greg, and when you see where all this is leading him in the months to come, you're guaranteed to be more than amazed. After all, though the focus of attention in recent months has been on Cap, leave us never forget that the Falc's a part of it all as well!

NEXT ISH: The two Lucifers get down to some serious business as they begin an all-out campaign to remove the flying half of our heroes from the scene—and if they succeed, you may yet be reading PEGGY CARTER COMICS. Don't miss #178, 'cause it's the craziest one yet!

THIS IS IT! YOUR

MARVEL VALUE STAMP

FOR THIS ISSUE! CLIP 'EM AND COLLECT 'EM!

OPPOSITE **26: MEPHISTO** from *Captain America* no. 177 (September 1974). Stamp also appears in *Tomb of Dracula* no. 19 (April 1974), *Iron Man* no. 71 (November 1974), and *Marvel Spotlight* no. 20 (February 1975).

ABOVE *Silver Surfer* no. 17 (June 1970), art by John Buscema and Chic Stone.

IRON FISTFULS

c/o MARVEL COMICS GROUP, 575 MADISON AVE. N.Y.C. 10022

Dear Marvel,

Marvel Premiere #21 was great, super, and fantastic. This issue is really great—I read it twice. How about forming a group of female Kung Fu fighters? They can call themselves the Kung Fu Queens—what a group they would make. Have Iron Fist join the Defenders, and also have Iron Fist meet The Mantis.

He is one of my favorite heroes.

Wilson Rivera
89 Maujer Street
Brooklyn, NY 11206

Dear Marvel,

I am a steady reader of Marvel Comics and Iron Fist is one of my favorites. The way the stories are written with this "you are" bit is really great.

There's a problem here that shouldn't be overlooked, though. In issue #16, he fought off four regular "nobodies," which took up half of that issue. In issue #15, for example, he fought and defeated four trained martial arts fighters in 60 seconds (which it stated in the story). Don't make Iron Fist too invincible.

Arvell Jones is not the right artist for this book; Gil Kane would do much better—he did a great job in #15. Now, it's no-prize time. In issue #19, when Professor Wing was telling Iron Fist of his experiences in his search for Kun Lun, on page 11, he said "I came upon a monk called Da Tempa. Yet, in issue #18, it was clearly stated that Da Tempa was the old man who took care of Meachum while he was recovering, not the Tibetan monk who visited the village. I think I've made a good point and this shouldn't go unnoticed.

Anyway, keep up the stories, you've gat a great character—and Make Mine Marvel!

Billy Siegler
67-00 192nd Street
Flushing, NY 11365

Well, Billy, ya caught us right red-handed! And what's more, ya caught us on a wearisome Wednesday, when our resistance is at its weakest. Therefore, Billy old pal, rather than attempt to wriggle out of that little boo-boo, we're going to unceremoniously present you with one of those nefariously-elusive No-Prizes. How do ya like *them* apples?

Dear Marvel,

You guys goofed!

I know that sounds kinda familiar, but it's true. In MARVEL PREMIERE #21, page 15, panel 4, the Sun Goddess says she is Shaya, the shade which she is *not,* evidenced by the rest of the story. I know this isn't the biggest mistake you've ever made, and you're really getting

stingy with those No-Prizes, but if you have one lying around, could ya send it to me?

Please?

Scott Scharfman
89 Bayview Avenue
Great Neck, NY 11021

Whaddaya mean, we goofed? What is this, a letters page or Mighty Marvel on trial?

(If it's the latter, by any chance, let us make it perfectly clear right out front that we plead guilty, okay, Scott. Fact of the situation is that there's not even any sense in our disputing whatever new boo-boo you caught us committing; we'll save the smart-aleck repartee for next ish, when we'll be back at the top of our form. Meanwhile, never let it be said that we're stingy—and to prove it, we'll send you a No-Prize! That makes two on one letters page, people—stew over that!)

Iron Fists and leaden feet, we'll be doing the old Kung Fu shuffle right here in one mighty short month (yeah, we're *monthly* for the summer, folks). See ya then!

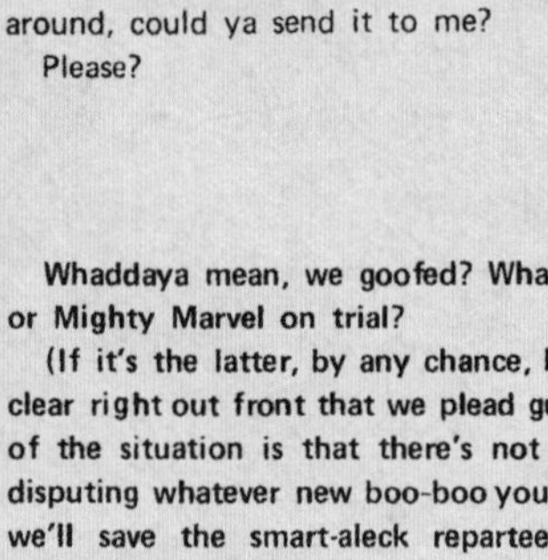

THIS IS IT! YOUR

MARVEL VALUE STAMP

FOR THIS ISSUE!
CLIP 'EM AND COLLECT 'EM!

OPPOSITE **27: THE BLACK WIDOW** from *Marvel Premiere* no. 23 (August 1975). Stamp also appears in *Tomb of Dracula* no. 22 (July 1974), *Fantastic Four* no. 150 (September 1974), and *Power Man* no. 24 (April 1975).

ABOVE *Daredevil* no. 99 (May 1973), art by John Romita Sr.

LET'S LEVEL WITH DAREDEVIL

SEND YOUR LETTERS TO: THE MARVEL COMICS GROUP SIXTH FLOOR 575 MADISON AV. NEW YORK 10022 N. Y.

Gerber, you're weird, dude:

I think you're the only comics writer who's ever made me so angry that I turned your name into a foul curse, yet, who's also made me wriggle in ecstatic joy, in fear that I'll finally have to finish the story.

I gotta be honest—that Terrex story was about as interesting as "Let's Make a Deal." But, man, oh man...this Death-Stalker deal... hey, Steve, what kind of childhood did you have, huh?

There were a few stereotype realities–like when Rory never woke up to see DD... when Foggy used a certain bit of knowledge to inform Matt, even as Candace calls him a coward... but they were necessary to give us this drama–so I don't mind.

The art is beauty incarnate. Never have I seen Bob Brown produce work like this. His style is unique, too, going well with Gerber's writing. Colletta's delicate inks enhance each page—every panel—and the art comes out as the best since the Colan-Palmer days. And even they have only a slight edge.

By the way, Steve, out of sheer curiosity–what magazine do you enjoy scripting the most? (My favorite of yours is MAN-THING).

Allen Bradford
Box 3, Lago Tr. Park
Winterville, GA 30683

Steve G. tells us, Allen, that MAN-THING is probably his favorite of the mags he writes, too— but not the one he enjoys scripting most. Too much agony goes into that book's writing to term it "enjoyable," he says.

He finds the actual process of scripting most enjoyable on MARVEL TWO-IN-ONE, Benjy Grimm's team-up mag, where he gets more of a chance to turn loose his warped sense of humor.

The reason we mention this, by the way, even though Steve is no longer writing DAREDEVIL (having moved on to THE DEFENDERS, starting this month), is that we've never really delved much into writers' feelings about their various strips before— and we're curious to know if you're interested. Each writer does approach each strip differently, you know, with a whole different set of aspirations and expectations. And if you'd really enjoy getting a peek inside their heads on the matter, we'll see what we can do. Let us know, huh?

Which reminds us...we reported erroneously that Tony Isabella would be assuming the scripting of DAREDEVIL with this issue, and as you're aware by now, this particular ish was written by DD veteran Gerry Conway. The explanation: this tale was originally prepared for a fill-in issue some time ago, but for reasons we can't recall, was never inserted into the schedule. Since Tony wanted to reread his DD collection in preparation for taking the scripting reins, we figured now was the time to spring the Ringmaster on ya, to give the Tigerish One time to do his research.

Dear Marvel,

There was a period directly after Stan left to become publisher when Marvel began falling apart. Oh, I can't really pinpoint what it was that was so bad: it was just a feeling as if no one cared anymore. It was evident in the plots of your major titles: AVENGERS, DAREDEVIL,, F.F., CAP, THOR, and SPIDER-MAN; they were all using stale ideas or plain dull ones. Nothing seemed to be happening.

Then slowly things began to shape up. First it was Cap, followed by Spider-Man (the last four issues being the very best of Spidey ever produced);and the F.F. bordered from great to ho-hum. The months ticked by; then came what I call the New Age of Marvel. Daredevil went bi-monthly, and with its first bi-monthly issue it became fantastic!!! Realistic dialog, stories and plots that just really gave you a sense of people caring what happened to the books. In that one issue we had: D.D. back in New York, Foggy back in the picture and a beginning of a mystery (what D.D. and Spidey need). And even more great, like times of old, Marvel wanted OUR ideas, OUR brain storms; and the book USED them. And too, you really wanted to know in each issue of what we thought of each adventure. What did we think of the writer, the artist, plot, setting, villains, if Marvel should do this-or-that, next issue. It really made the reader feel as if he was a part of Daredevil, that everyone at Marvel REALLY CARED that we CARED about what was happening to our heroes.

Thanks, one and all, for bringing me back to the joy of comics, just when I was beginning to feel I had grown too old to enjoy them anymore.

Mike Iacampo
2522 Walnut Ave.
Altoona, PA 16601

And we're only beginning, Mike! This month heralds two more far-out, phantasmagorical events in the Second Marvel Age of Comics: the return of WARLOCK in STRANGE TALES #178 and the start of Howard the Duck's own series in GIANT-SIZE MAN-THING #3. What other company could offer you a mind-bending messiah and a maniacal mallard within the space of thirty days?!?

And, in all seriousness...many thanks, Mr. Iacampo. We're pleased and proud that the excitement we're feeling over our magazines is contagious.

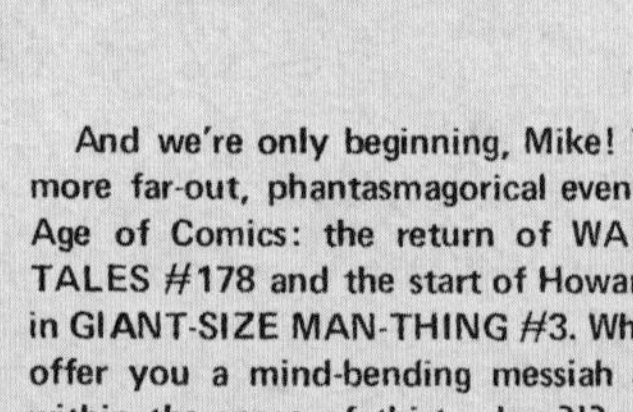

THIS IS IT! YOUR

MARVEL VALUE STAMP

FOR THIS ISSUE! CLIP 'EM AND COLLECT 'EM!

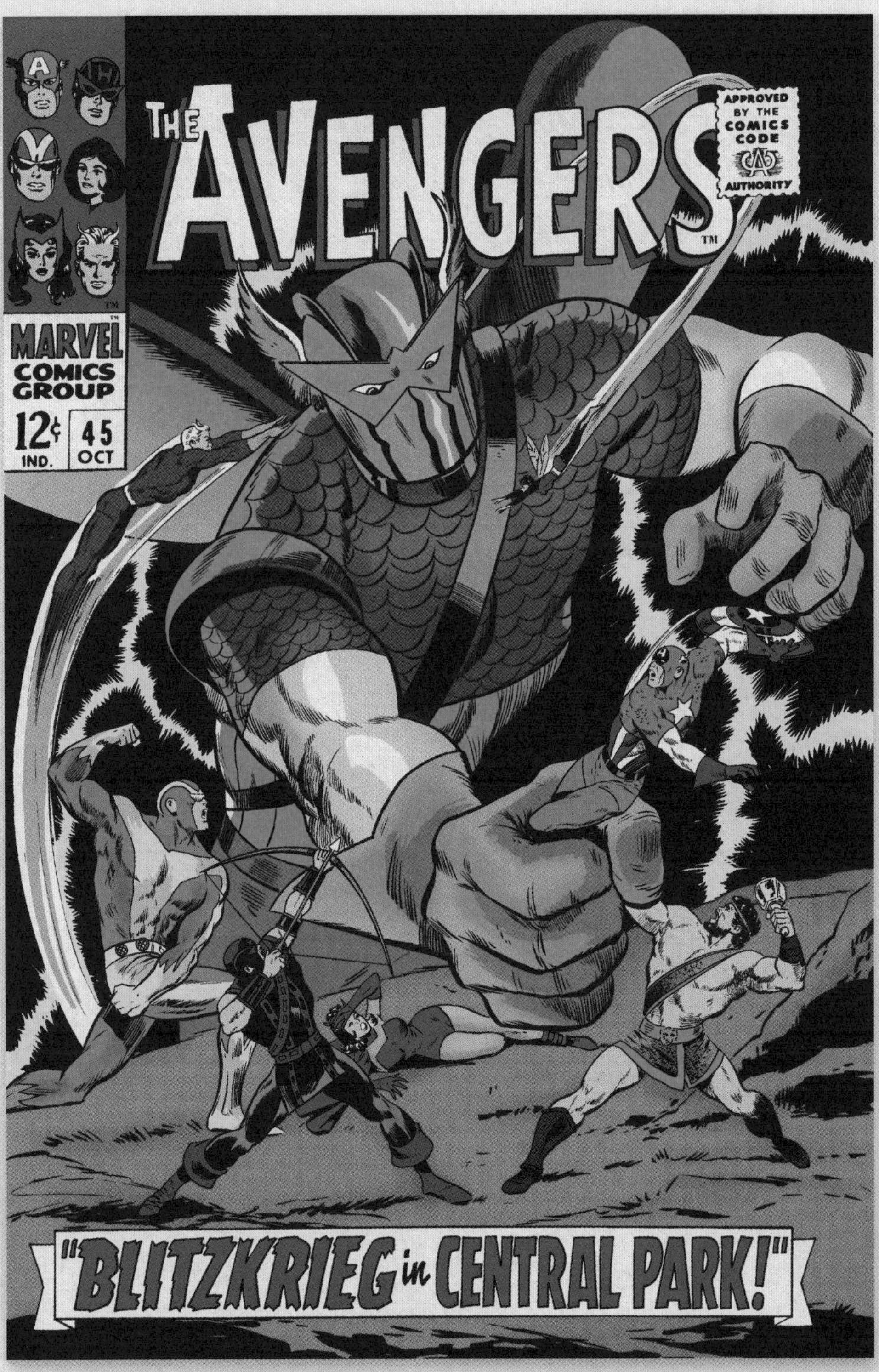

OPPOSITE **28: HAWKEYE** from *Daredevil* no. 118 (February 1975). Stamp also appears in *Ka-Zar* no. 2 (March 1974), *Marvel Team-Up* no. 23 (July 1974), *Man-Thing* no. 11 (November 1974), and *Werewolf by Night* no. 26 (February 1975).

ABOVE *The Avengers* no. 45 (October 1967), art by John Buscema and Vince Colletta.

SOCK IT TO SHELL-HEAD

c/o MARVEL COMICS GROUP, 575 MADISON AVE. N.Y.C. 10022

A SPECIAL ANNOUNCEMENT FROM STAN, ROY, AND MARVEL COMICS

By the time this message appears in any of our mags, you'll already have noticed that all of our 36-page comic magazines are now 25¢— a nickel more than they were a few short weeks ago.

Maybe your first reaction to the price hike was the same as ours might be if we were in your shoes: "What's Marvel trying to do to us, anyway? Don't they know we've got enough troubles, what with inflation, shortages, and an energy crisis on our hands, without trying to clip us for 5¢ more every time we want a little fantasy-filled escape from it all? What is this— some kind of rip-off, so that Stan and Roy can vacation on the Riviera this year?"

If that was your reaction, it's an understandable one— and we'd just like to ask you to listen to our side of it for a minute before you decide:

This year, the widely-publicized paper shortage(in addition to various labor settlements among the companies that print, sell, and distribute Marvel Comics) caused additional expenses to Marvel of several hundred thousand dollars. That means that we had to make that much extra money just to stay even, despite the fact that our sales in 1973 were the best in the business.

So, we had no choice, really, but to increase the cover price of our magazines, the same way that just about everybody else has to.

And, just in case you think we're now getting rich off that new-found nickel: Believe it or not, that extra copper only covers about half the cost of the paper strike and other shortages.

What're we doing about the whole situation?

We think the answer's obvious, if you take a look at some of the titles we're now publishing besides our 36-pagers. There's our increasingly popular 75¢ line of full-scale magazines, first of all. Already, our four flagship 75-centers are being joined by THE DEADLY HANDS OF KUNG FU and the return (on March 26) of SAVAGE TALES— with two or three more much-requested types of mags already in the works.

Likewise, there's our spanking new, sensational 35¢ giant-size comics— a full 52 pages of colorful cavorting, and now a bigger bargain than ever!

Not only that, but the next few weeks will herald the coming of a brand new Marvel phenomenon: our swingin' SUPER-GIANTS, featuring one hundred big pages for just 60¢ including a feature-length new tale each and every issue. The Bullpen Bulletins Pages will give you the full scam, next time around— but rest assured that you're gonna be getting your money's worth!

Not only that— but we've got other plans we can't even hint at yet!

Well, that's about it. We've had our say.

About the only other thing we can do is to affirm once more that, just as we've been doing for over a decade now, every artist and writer in the Bullpen will be striving night and day, even harder than ever (if that's possible), to see to it that you consider— each precious coin spent on a Marvel mag to be one of the wisest investments you ever made.

Let's lick this thing together, okay?

Thanks for listening.

Dear Bullpen,

No-prize application: Iron Man issue #65. On page 18, panel 6, and again on page 23, panel 4, reference is made to the "GAMES-master" from Avengers #69.

This is, of course, a mistaken reference to the GRANDmaster.

Application approved? No-prize granted? I'll be watching my no-mail for it.

David Williams
1117 St. Christopher
Columbia, Missouri 65201

It was no-sent, Dave. Last no-week. Or is that too much no-sense for you?

Dear Bullpen:

Issue #65 was good! Mike Friedrich, George Tuska, and Mike Esposito make a great team. On page 30, panel 4, the prism merges with Iron Man, but I suspect this Iron Man is none other than Eddie March, ex-boxer. If I'm right, you can have Irv drop my no-prize off on his way to the tavern.

Jerry Ordway
533 S. 5th St.
Milwaukee, Wis. 53204

Your no-prize was sent in the same no-batch with Dave Williams, Jerry...with a no-gold seal, because you were the reader to write in with a correct guess as to the injured "Iron Man's true identity!

THIS IS IT! YOUR

MARVEL VALUE STAMP

FOR THIS ISSUE!
CLIP 'EM AND
COLLECT 'EM!

OPPOSITE **29: BARON MORDO** from *Iron Man* no. 68 (June 1974). Stamp also appears in *Supernatural Thrillers* no. 9 (October 1974).

ABOVE *Marvel Premiere* no. 13 (January 1974), art by Frank Brunner and Crusty Bunkers.

THE HYBORIAN PAGE

c/o MARVEL COMICS GROUP, 575 MADISON AVE., NEW YORK, N.Y. 10022

SPECIAL NOTE: In ish #32 we mentioned that one good source of CONAN back-issues (in addition to the various dealers who have ads in each of our mags) was the Supersnipe Comic Art Emporium. Unfortunately we accidentally caused its friendly bearded proprietor, Ed Summer, a mound of trouble by getting the address wrong! It's 1617 Second Avenue, New York, N.Y., not Third as we said

Close— but no cigar.

Dear Folks at Marvel,

I thought CONAN was thru when Barry Smith left, and John Buscema took over the art. But I for one have to say John's doing a helluva job, most likely his best in years. Not one single panel looks rushed.

Still, at the present time CONAN is headed toward certain doom around issue #90 or so. Why? Well, people, if you read any of the Conan paperbacks, he must be about 28 years old now and will very soon become a pirate, Roy. you're following the R.E. Howard outline too closely. Make up new stories, longer adventures, or else before you know it Conan will be 60 and be sailin' off to Mexico!

Eric Greenspan
2811 S. Oakhurst
Los Angeles, Ca.

Ulp! All those nice words about our award-winning CONAN mag, Eric— and now we've gotta blow the whistle on you 'cause you haven't done your homework. As a cursory reading of Conan's life history, (reprinted in SAVAGE TALES #2 a few months back) will plainly show our blade-wielding barbarian is a mere 21 or 22 years old at this point in time; if he seems a bit older, it must be remembered that the average lifespan in the Hyborian Age was probably under 50, as it was in ancient times and the Middle Ages. And, since the CONAN comic-book will be four years old in just a few short months, it seems to us that the sullen Cimmerian has been aging at almost exactly his natural rate— which is what Roy planned all along, of course. The Rascally One's not sure if he'll continue that type of natural aging when Conan meets Bêlit in a year or so, however; we'll just have to wait and see on that one!

So cheer up, Eric, old buddy. You've still got nearly four decades till Conan discovers—America!

Dear Stan, Roy, and John,

I think I have an answer to your problem (voiced in CONAN #33) whether Roy should write CONAN or one of the mags he used to script. My answer is a question: Why can't he script both? After all, he's recently taken up scripting the KULL magazine. Personally, though, I'd much rather see him working wonders for either the F.F. or THE AVENGERS.

Lane Renfro
160 Garden Spring Rd.
Columbia, S.C. 29209

And Roy'd be the last one to mind trying to work those wonders, Lane, though he feels that Gerry Conway and Steve Englehart are doing quite well by them right now. At any rate, you'll notice that (after scripting a couple of issues of THE HULK, which had some of its most popular moments under his typewriter's aegis a couple of years back), he's gone back to writing little more than CONAN and the new Thomas/Giordano adaptation of Bram Stoker's novel Dracula now appearing in DRACULA LIVES.

An aside: On sale any day now will be the first issue of a new 35¢, 52-page title called GIANT-SIZE SUPER-STARS. Sure, it's kind-of a nutty title, but it'll be coming your way every month— featuring rotating heroes ã la Colombo, McCloud, and MacMillan & Wife. The three stars? The Fantastic Four— Spider-Man— and Conan the Barbarian— three of the most important, influential comics features since the invention of the four-color press! As we stated here last issue, that title will give various artists a chance to show how they'd do Conan— and believe us, there are few adventure-artists in the field who wouldn't give their right elbow to do the strip, at least once!

Already Roy is hard at work with Rich (Swash) Buckler on a Conan story, plus an Esteban Maroto tale of Red Sonja for the same issue— and at the same time Roy and Barry Smith are working on a two-issue adaptation of "A Witch Shall Be Born," one of REH's greatest Conan sagas. The first 35¢ Conan-starrer will be on sale in late-April, Crom and the paper mills willing— and we think GIANT-SIZE SUPER-STARS (and a companion-mag we'll be telling you about real soon now) are gonna take comicdom by storm!

Dear Marvel,

Since issue #26, CONAN has lost its magic. Roy's scripts now tend to rely too much, I feel, upon fast, raw action and half-concealed sex. John's art is his worst, due, for the most part, to Ernesto Chua, whose sloppy, thick strokes make each page a line-strewn mess. Now, instead of a panoramic world of fantasy and sorcery, I see a monotonous stretch of unimaginative yecch. Instead of a lithe, savage Conan, I am forced to accept an ugly, bearlike brute.

Michael Phillip Capurso
Rochester, N.Y.

Your letter, Mike, is one of many we received when we asked for comments on whether CONAN in general, and Roy's scripts in particular, were going downhill. Predictably, the vast majority of letter-writers felt that, due as much to Roy's verbal skill as anything else, the mag is still one of Marvel's (and the comic industry's) very best— which is fitting enough, since in the past year or so CONAN has skyrocketed to being one of the most popular Marvel titles of all. Certainly nobody's buying up all those issues just to keep Roy smiling!

However, we wanted to present a balanced picture— so we printed your letter in part, as typical of the strong feelings, both pro and con, which both artwork and script can arouse in the compleat Conan-lover.

We could, of course, argue with your facts: for instance, Robert E. Howard described Conan in his first chronological appearance as having a "powerful frame... broad heavy shoulders... massive chest, lean waist, and heavy arms." The two authors of the "Informal History of Conan," reprinted in a recent issue of SAVAGE TALES, theorized that as a teenager (and still short of his maturity) Conan stood six feet tall and weighed over 200 pounds. And, as an occasional fan-letter used to remind us when someone thought Conan's first artist, Barry Smith, was drawing the Cimmerian too short and thin, Conan was often referred to as both a brute and a veritable giant. (Perhaps you're confusing the barbarian's vaunted suppleness, or litheness, with leanness?)

Truth to tell, though, REH himself wasn't entirely consistent either in visualization or in characterization of his Hyborian-Age hero. His constant use of "wolf" and "panther" imagery sometimes seemed to conflict with an overlapping "tiger" imagery which suggested greater size and power.

Besides, the first "modern" Conan is the one painted on so many paperback covers by one Frank Frazetta— and, as we recall, Frazetta's Conan doesn't exactly have a lean hungry look.

Still, when all is said and done and re-said, we're gratified that CONAN arouses such fierce loyalty— and we mean it when we say that, just this once, we wish it really were possible to please all of the people all of the time. Maybe, though, with GIANT-SIZE SUPER-STARS about to get into full swing with four extra, non-sequential Conan epics a year...!

Naaah. Why fool ourselves? We could publish a hundred Conan tales a year, drawn by dozens over different artists and scripted by an equal number of writers, and there'd still be some intrepid soul in Upper Osh Kosh who'd voice a complaint— quite possibly a valid one, since perfection has never been one of our most noticeable achievements.

Anyway, keep those cards and letters cascading in, folks. It's never dull either in the Hyborian Age— or in the Marvel Age of Comics!

Dear Roy and Friends,

I thought you might be pleased to know that at least one professor at ISU (Indiana State University) won't be "horrified" to learn that one of your letter writers took time off "to write a comic book, of all things." Quite the contrary, Professor Steve Connelly c/o ISU's English Department, will probably be happy. He devotes time in his Introduction to Literature class to comic books. And though he talks about a great number of comics, try and guess which one is the required text. You guessed it! Conan! Conan one week, James Joyce the next, can you beat that? Maybe some day they'll wise up and create a whole course in comic books at State. Or better yet, a course in Conan! Meanwhile at least we have Connelly and his few days to keep us going. This place isn't a complete desert.

Raymond Stopper Russ
ISU Grad

Roy— who hails from the Show-Me state of Missouri himself— never said that the Midwest was a desert, Ray. And please extend his personal thanks to Professor Connelly for spreading the word! Roy hasn't been so close to a classroom since he gave up being a high school English teacher back in '65. Now, ahem, about that honorary degree...!

THIS IS IT! YOUR

MARVEL VALUE STAMP

FOR THIS ISSUE!

CLIP 'EM AND COLLECT 'EM!

OPPOSITE **30: THE GREY GARGOYLE** from *Conan the Barbarian* no. 38 (May 1974). Stamp also appears in *Creatures on the Loose* no. 31 (September 1974).

ABOVE *Journey into Mystery* no. 113 (February 1965), art by Jack Kirby and Chic Stone.

guest-shots by Dracula.

(Isn't it great the way we can drop a dumb joke like that without even giggling, keeping a perfectly straight face and all. It is a joke, isn't it, Steve? Steve??)

Oh, well...while we send the Bullpen Brain Police out to grab our mad scripter, let's get a look at some slightly saner suggestions for the Defenders roster.

Dear Marvel,

The Defenders are on their way to becoming the second best super-group in the field. Some things have to be remedied though. Create a super-villain group that they can call their own. The Squadron Sinister was an old Avengers staple and the Wrecking Crew, if my memory serves me correctly, also appeared in a long past Avengers saga. C'mon guys, there's gotta be some new menaces to pit the Defenders against.

As for the membership question, my choices would be Subby, Hulk, and Doc (for sales purposes) and Nighthawk, Valkyrie, Sting-Ray, and Shanna, the She-Devil (for personal reasons). Don't ever consider Spidey, DD or Captain Marvel (simply because they're just about the only ones left not part of some team). Forget Black Widow and Hawkeye, Ant-Man and Wasp (for the simple reason that they are, were, and will always be Avengers). Shang-Chi is getting over-exposed while Luke Cage is not quite the team type. Iron Fist might be a good idea, but Daimon Hellstrom is not, Ghost Rider is a "maybe" also. Thanx for listening to and, most of all, entertaining me with your special brand of heaven.

Jim Canepa
1732 Blake St.
El Cerrito, Calif. 94530

Just stick around, Jim. We do have an idea for a very new, very villainous super-combo to pit against the dynamic ones, and you'll be seeing it in the near future.

In the meantime, they'll be coming up against the Squadron Sinister again in GIANT-SIZE DEFENDERS #4 (under extremely weird circumstances), so keep your eyes peeled for that spectacular, zapping your way in sixty days or so.

Spidey, Daredevil, and Mar-Vell are all likely prospects for DEFENDERS guest-shots, but, you'll be pleased to learn, not for membership. Web-head already is holding forth in a trio (a quartet if you count SPIDEY SUPER-STORIES) of mags of his own: D.D. is too much the loner type: and our Kree captain has blasted off for new adventures beyond earth.

As for others you mentioned— you'll be seeing Hank Pym in that fourth giant-size book. But not as Ant-Man. Black Widow is still an integral part of the DAREDEVIL strip. Shang-Chi, like Spidey, is getting enough exposure already.

Ghost Rider? Iron Fist? Son of Satan? All possible. As are Sting-Ray and Shanna. But...well, let's just wait and see.

Dear Marvel,

You asked to hear from readers regarding regular members for the Defenders, so here goes. First, I'd like to say that I'm just recently a Defenders fan and that, being new to this particular mag, I've found the characters quite stimulating and exciting. Whatever else you do, *don't* get rid of *Nighthawk or the Valkyrie.* Both of them are about the most colorful, exciting, and interesting characters that I think I've ever met in the Marvel mags. Especially Nighthawk. How about a quick review of his origin? Since I'm new to the mag, I don't know much about him and I'm curious.

I don't know much about Dr. Strange, but he seems to be a good leader for the group as well as adding a touch of mystery and magic to them. Definitely keep him. I don't really care about the Hulk. As for Namor, drop him back in the ocean and *forget him.* He's a *lousy group member.* So's the Black Widow. *Bring back the Black Knight.* I've never seen *Venus,* but she sounds like a *great* member possibility. Also, you should have more members, say, *at least four or five.* In #17, there's only *two* of them! I mean, *really,* you *can't* call that a group! Especially when the Avengers have four times that.

Well, until Nighthawk races Aragorn in the Triple Crown, make mine Marvel.

P.S. Love the new H.Q. Keep it!

Janice A. Meixner
5365 NE 1st Terrace
Ft. Lauderdale, Fla. 33308

You're ours forever, Janice! Aragon is a four-year-old.

And, speaking of fours, there are currently that many Defenders, even if they didn't all appear in #17. Valkyrie and the Hulk are still with the group.

Okay. Now some serious thoughts on this little debate: Steve says he wants to keep the membership at no more than six, and considering the limited space in each issue we think that's an altogether reasonable idea.

The present four Defenders will be staying on for the forseeable future. As should be evident from this issue, Steve is fascinated by the Valkyrie character; as will be evident from next issue, he is equally intrigued by Nighthawk.

So we've got room for two more. And Steve feels, as do many readers, that they should be characters who do not presently have their own magazines. Which opens up some interesting possibilities.

So here's what we're gonna do. Suppose each of you sends us your *two* ideal choices. Which *two* characters would you most like to see as new Defenders? We'll tabulate all the votes and report the results on this page.

And since Steve reads each and every letter personally... you can bet the results won't be ignored. Let's hear from you!

OPPOSITE **31: MODOK** from *The Defenders* no. 20 (February 1975). Stamp also appears in *Jungle Action* no. 9 (May 1974) and *Conan the Barbarian* no. 40 (July 1974).

ABOVE *The Incredible Hulk* no. 169 (November 1973), art by Herb Trimpe and Jack Abel.

Dear Marvel,

IRON FIST hit me from about six directions at once. It was well-paced and very dramatic, in the best sense of the word. But I was a bit displeased with your depiction of K'un-Lun, whose "silent music" seems to be the slamming of fist against man or machine. A paradise whose key is beating up the many or beating up the one seems rather shallow.

Kim Draheim
RD #2, Box 204
Seneca Falls, N.Y. 13148

And the issue had its share of dumb-dumb mighty Marvel mistakes, too. One in particular...

Dear Marvel,

I spotted a glaring mistake on page fourteen of PREMIERE #15, where you showed Harold Meachum gloating, after he has killed Wendell Rand Harold says, "Well, now there is no more Meachum & Rand...only RAND, INC." Well, he should have said "Meachum, Inc.", right? You bet.

So I want what's coming to me. Preferably, a lifetime subscription to IRON FIST. If you're really feeling generous, you can throw in subscriptions to CONAN, KULL, MAN-THING, DR. STRANGE, SON OF SATAN, GHOST RIDER, and all the back issues of the SILVER SURFER mag. Thanx. Love & kisses...

Kip Eichhorn
615 N. Jefferson
Moscow, Idaho 83843

The lifetime subs are yours, Kip.

Unfortunately, they were for Wendell Rand's lifetime and have thus already expired. (Nya-a-a-ah!) Will you settle for a no-prize?

Dear Marvel,

You have another winner on your hands with IRON FIST. I hope you will make I.F. more like a superhero and not like Shang-Chi, who is not a superhero in the ordinary sense of the word. I.F. should come to America.

I thought the artwork and writing were both great, by the way.

David Burch
San Diego, Ca.

Iron Fist will be slightly more in the superhero vein than Shang-Chi, David. We intended from the start that this book would be more action-oriented than the somewhat more philosophical MASTER OF KUNG FU.

We haven't decided yet on precisely the sort of villains we want for the mag yet, though, and we'd appreciate reader reaction on this matter. Super-villains? Other martial arts masters? Un-costumed criminals? Which do you prefer, and why?

THIS IS IT! YOUR
MARVEL VALUE STAMP
FOR THIS ISSUE!
CLIP 'EM AND COLLECT 'EM!

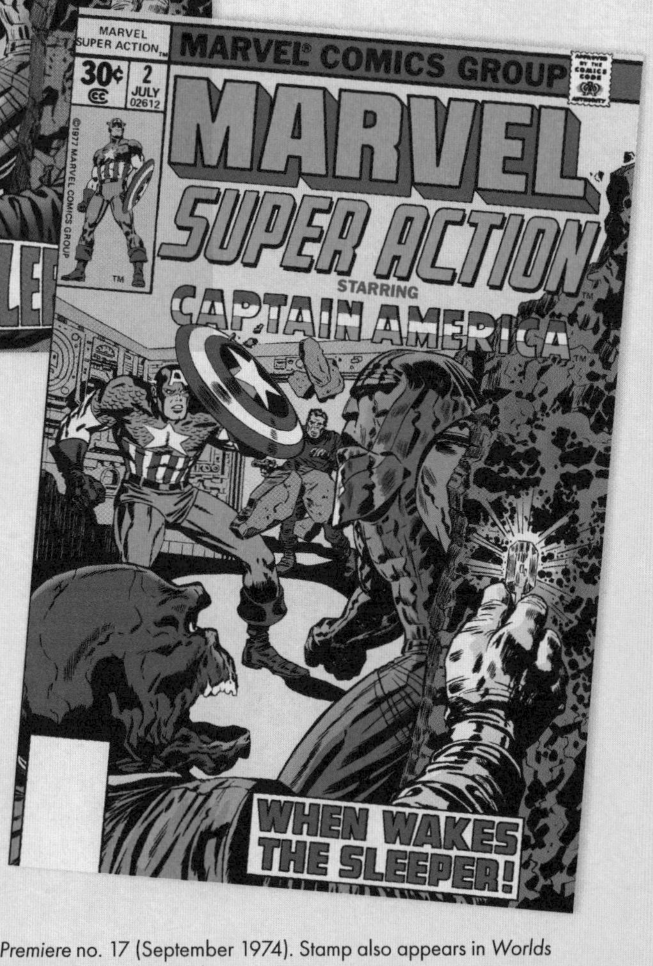

OPPOSITE **32: THE RED SKULL** from *Marvel Premiere* no. 17 (September 1974). Stamp also appears in *Worlds Unknown* no. 7 (June 1974) and *Fantastic Four* no. 160 (July 1975).

ABOVE *Captain America* no. 101 (May 1968), art by Jack Kirby and Syd Shores. John Romita Sr. redrew the face of the Red Skull on the cover, but the stamp uses the unaltered artwork, which also appears on the cover of *Marvel Super Action* no. 2 (July 1977).

we are fragmented, alone, striving for a unity which by rights should come most naturally. Today's myths speak no less deeply, no less meaningfully, but much less loudly. Today we have myths not of peoples, but of persons. Dr. Strange is just such a myth. There is a growing audience, and perhaps need, for his adventures.

MARVEL PREMIERE #10 was the herald, but DR. STRANGE #1 was the consumation. The art was Brunner at his best (which makes it greater than great), while the plot led Stephen Strange into realms of humanness. Now he is truly a man, and not just a mystic. With the death of the Ancient One, we feared that the flat personality of Dr. Strange was not capable of upholding the mantle of sorcerer supreme. With issue #1, however, our fears were laid to rest. Dr. Strange is no longer playing a role, but humanly fulfilling an archetype.

Richard Shapiro
256 Duke Street, Apt. 601
Hamilton, Ontario, Canada

Dear Steve and Frank,

I'm not going to rave over specfics of DR. STRANGE # 1 (although I easily could) simply because what blows my mind most is the whole series: starting with the death of the Ancient One, every mag has been superlative. After each issue, I think "They can't do it again," and every time you two guys follow up with another excellent mag. The only story I can say I didn't like as much as the others was the conclusion of the Sise-neg storyline, and that's only because I don't accept the concept of a created universe. And how often can a comics reader say she didn't care for a particular story because she doesn't agree with the metaphysical assumptions propounded therein? The best possible writer, the best possible artist, and a lot of weird ideas make the mag what it is. I don't know how you'll manage it, but I'm convinced you'll keep up the fantastic work.

Jana C. Hollingsworth
1415 East Second Street
Port Angeles, Washington 98362

Dear Marvel,

The caterpillar's philosophy on pages 30, 31 and 32 actually outlines the dangers of over-escapism, whether through drugs or anything. In the end, we have to face ourselves. A fine effort. I'm proud of you.

Tom Murray
#810-1340 Burnaby Street
Vancouver 5, British Columbia

Dear Steve & Frank & Dick & J. & G.,

Opening with the brooding, deep feeling is in line with the best possible use of the mysterious "strange" nature of the book. It was nice to see Clea being used intelligently for once, with Strange having a mature relationship with her... very artfully done...and since most Marvel characters would have stayed there with Clea, it had me thinking for a little while on how different Dr. Strange is from most of the Marvel Universe.

And the gong going "wong"! Really!

As usual, the story unfolded economically and logically. Each time I expected you people to take the easy way out, in story or art, you done me in. The rabbit, which at first I thought a usual battle-type scene, just plain jumped out the window. Silver Dagger dispatched Clea and Wong easily (very nice trip with the eye sending out them alarm bolts). And best of all, actually stabbing Strange himself. I kept expecting it to be a dummy or illusion. Ha! Not so!

Pages 22 and 23 were beautifully done...just fantastic. Better than anything Ditko, Colan, or the various others ever did (good as they are).

And then into the smoking caterpillar. Just the right combination of charm and menace, 'cause that's the Doc's world—one of illusion, where nothing is what it seems.

Victor Schwartzman
111 West 10 Avenue
Vancouver, British Columbia

THIS IS IT! YOUR
MARVEL VALUE STAMP
FOR THIS ISSUE!
CLIP 'EM AND COLLECT 'EM!

OPPOSITE **33: SUE RICHARDS, INVISIBLE GIRL** from *Doctor Strange* no. 4 (October 1974). Stamp also appears in *Marvel Team-Up* no. 21 (May 1974) and *Jungle Action* no. 13 (January 1975).

ABOVE *Fantastic Four* no. 56 (November 1966), art by Jack Kirby and Joe Sinnott.

THE SPIDER'S WEB

SEND YOUR LETTERS TO:
THE MARVEL COMICS GROUP, SIXTH FLOOR 575 MADISON AV., NEW YORK, N. Y. 10022

Dear Bullpen:

SPIDER-MAN #127 had the usual good cover by Romita and an exceptional interior art job by Ross Andru. Hope they both keep it up.

It looks as though you've got a few new subplots coming in. Harry Osborn as the Goblin should be good for an issue or two (any more would probably mean a fan revolt), and Spidey calling Mary Jane "Gwendy". I hope you don't just ignore this last item; it should start M.J. thinking (either Peter is Spidey, or Spidey was trying to hustle Gwen from Peter, or something else?).

No matter what you do, you've got me hooked for good.

Bill Wormstedt
Box 482
Westport, Wash. 98595

Dear Spidey-Writers,

"The Dark Wings of Death" in SPIDEY #127 was great, superb, fantastic, and etc.! A super-baddie whom I've always liked. Lots of mystery, surprises, and everyday problems. The laughing, carefree, loveable Mary Jane involved with murder! The Spider-Mobile (which I'm dying to see completed) and the Human Torch. Harry Osborn following in his father's footsteps and becoming Green Goblin, Jr., And, speaking of surprises, Mary Jane almost killed as Gwen was. And, finally, Spidey supposedly falls to his death! And, mysterious women whom we need to know about. All I can say is: see ya next issue!

Tim O'Conner
50 Dolly Drive
Parsippany, N.J. 07054

And that, happily, is how most of the mail went on SPIDEY #127. Most of Marveldom's response could be measured in degrees of ecstasy, wonderment, or plain ol' good vibrations.

Bill, Tim, and all the rest of you who wrote... we thank you.

This is not to say that there weren't those who didn't like the mag, of course. And the common complaint of this minority of readers centered upon Ross Andru's depiction of the Web-Slinger: they hated it. Cries of "Bring Back Gil Kane!" resounded through their letters. Which we think—in our deranged way—is sort of amusing, considering all the "Bring Back John Romita!" letters we received when Gil took over the strip and the "Bring Back Steve Ditko!" letters that poured in when John took over the strip!

So, we'll just answer all those letters with this one sentence: give Ross a chance. You'll probably be writing "Bring Back Ross Andru!" letters if we replace him with________________. (Fill in the blank.)

Dear Marvel,

Please allow a longtime Marvelite to reflect a bit on the past. I remember:

(1) When the letters pages used to be two pages long.

(2) When a full Marvel Checklist appeared in each mag each month.

But before you send the Kingpin after me...I also remember:

(1) When there were no letters pages or checklists.

(2) When Marvel published eight beautiful mags a month. Now it is more like four times that many.

(3) When the art was good, instead of too beautiful for words, as it is now.

(4) When Marvel introduced an unusual foursome and a friendly neighborhood whatchamacallit which have evolved into revolutionary comic-mag institutions.

(5) When you brought out a black-and-white SPIDEY SPECTACULAR (which I would like to see come back--hint, hint!).

(6) Most of all I remember a beautifully small, overworked Bullpen, which ground out those monthly masterpieces.

Now, it is a larger overworked Bullpen. But the beauty is still there. Thank you.

Jim Rodgers
1517 Locust
Eldorado, Ill. 62930

Believe it or not, Jim, we're working now on a means of bringing back the two-page LP and the complete monthly Checklist, keep your fingers, toes, and eyes crossed, and maybe we'll succeed. Honestly, we miss 'em, too.

And, by the way, thanks for pointing out so eloquently that although some things have changed around the Merry Marvel Bullpen over the years, most of the upheaval has been for the best. We feel that way. And we feel even better things are on the way, now that we're past most of our growing pains. Just wait and see—and above all, don't stop believing! We're not getting older—we're getting weirder. (Or something like that.)

Dear Marvel,

I feel that you took the right and necessary step in SPIDER-MAN #121 and 122. Issues since then have been...well, okay. Ish #127, though, was a high-caliber one, and I'm glad to see that Peter is finally getting over Gwen's death.

Although I really liked John Romita and Gil Kane, I'm more than happy with Ross Andru's work! I think it'd be interesting if you ran a couple of issues with different artists such as: Barry Smith, Neal Adams, or Rich Buckler. Steranko would be great if you could get him away from FOOM.

SPIDER-MAN is one of my favorite mags, trailing behind CONAN, which follows the now-faltering DAREDEVIL. The only place, besides our real world, that I could put up without SPIDEY is on Counter-Earth! Bring back WARLOCK!!! Bring him back with Gil, or maybe Ross, or Rich Buckler, or Gene Colan, or Neal Adams or etc. He was Number One on my list.

Oh, yeah...you spelled Harry's last name Osborne instead of Osborn on the cover of SPIDEY #127. Is this something new?

Until Hulk grows a moustache, Make Mine Marvel and keep on' FOOMIN'!

The singer Dionne Warwick changed her name to Dionne Warwicke, we understand, for reasons of numerology—that occult science which converts letters to numbers, totals 'em up, and tells you whether you're going to live or die or get indigestion or fly to Denver on wings of denim. Maybe Harry just wanted to fly to Denver—for that one cover only. (Or more likely, our proofreaders goofed. And, in so doing, earned you a no-prize.)

But never mind that! What we wanna know is—what's this stuff about DAREDEVIL faltering, Chuck? We'll just have to assume you haven't seen the incredible, fantastic, mind-stunning masterworks that Steve Gerber and Bob Brown are turning out for that mag! (Steve insists we have to assume that.) Pick up next month's ish in which horn-head takes on the menace of Black Spectre and see if "faltering" still applies, huh?

Which reminds us...Gerry Conway, who just happens to author SPIDER-MAN, as well as FANTASTIC FOUR and THOR, is now also handling the scripting chores on another of Marvel's longest-running, most popular mags: SGT. FURY AND HIS HOWLING COMMANDOS! This one's a real departure for Gerard, and we think you'll get off on it too. It's the old-style FURY guts 'n' glory, now with mind-boggling Conway captions! Don't miss it!

'Nuff plugged! Keep thy webs untangled, and we'll see you here next month.

CLIP 'EM AND COLLECT 'EM!

OPPOSITE **34: MR. FANTASTIC** from *The Amazing Spider-Man* no. 131 (April 1974). Stamp also appears in *Giant-Size Creatures* no. 1 (July 1974) and *Creatures on the Loose* no. 32 (November 1974).

ABOVE *Fantastic Four* no. 59 (February 1967), art by Jack Kirby and Joe Sinnott. This cover was also used as the source for MVS no. 17.

Steve does too, Bob. His very first assignment at Marvel was to write additional dialogue for Carole Seuling's SHANNA #1 script, and as you know, he scripted a couple of the later issues himself. He admits to having a special fondness for the character. (He thinks she's almost as pretty as Man-Thing.)

Regarding reader response to DAREDEVIL #111, we can only reiterate what we've been saying these past few months. in the space of only a few issues, your comments have done virtually a 180-degree turnabout. All of a sudden, and with no small effort on the parts of Steve G., Bob Brown, and Gene Colan, you people seem to be having a love affair with DAREDEVIL once again.

We made a prediction a few issues back that D.D. was going to be the surprise superhero mag of 1974. We still believe that. And if you've read the ending to this issue's tale (don't peek), you know we're not kidding around. We're taking, appropriately, a rather daring new direction with this magazine, exploring some ground that we don't believe any superhero mag has trod before.

Dear Marvel,

I enjoy the current series of stories with Black Spectre. However, I wish you would end it so that Tasha and Matt can get back together again. Their relationship is the most "adult" in any of your mags. They know they're in love and don't have to speak it every issue. If one is in danger, they act instinctively and without half-hour speeches of vengeance against the transgressor.

Keep up the good work.

Yours 'til Matt defends Nixon.

Brad Oseland
447 Dulaney Ave.
Wood River, Ill. 62095

Dear Marvel,

It seems that the Black Widow is retaining a small but important spot in DAREDEVIL. This is fine as long as she appears only when desperately needed. D.D. hardly needs a partner. As an owner of every D.D. issue, I seem to have this outrageous idea that the magazine belongs entirely to him. Am I wrong about this?

Bob Smith
Rm. 16 Highland Hall
Bellingham, Wash. 98225

The debate rages on. One month, your comments seem to favor a permanent parting of the ways for Matt and Natasha: next month, all of Marveldom Assembled wants them back together again.

In other words, be confident at least that whatever happens between Daredevil and the Widow will happen not by contrivance, but because it seems right. And incidentally, you can look forward to at least one major development in the very next issue— one we think that'll really catch you off-guard. Unless, of course, you've picked up on the clues we've dropped in the past couple of books.

THIS IS IT! YOUR
MARVEL
VALUE
STAMP
FOR THIS ISSUE!
CLIP 'EM AND
COLLECT 'EM!

OPPOSITE **35: KILLRAVEN** from *Daredevil* no. 115 (November 1974). Stamp also appears in *Worlds Unknown* no. 6 (April 1974) and *The Amazing Spider-Man* no. 141 (February 1975).

ABOVE *Amazing Adventures* no. 20 (September 1973), art by Herb Trimpe and Frank Giacoia.

often of the boy she knew in World War II..." Then, "What would he have said if I'd asked him..." Is your name Steve Rogers?"

Ah, I see the horrifying gleam in your eyes at having been caught in a mistake. You really need not worry, though, for not so way back, in AVENGERS #107, you yourself provided the answer to this perplexing puzzlement.

The answer was that the Space Phantom had erased the knowledge of Cap's identity from the minds of all people, including Peggy.

What's that you say? Why wasn't Sharon affected?

Ah, the simplest of questions shall yet be answered.

The reason is that in the self-same issue in which Cap revealed his identity to the world, he also had revealed it to Sharon a short time before that, and the Space Phantom only erased this knowledge from people who didn't know beforehand. Peggy, of course, was affected because during this period in time, her mind was suffering from a mental breakdown, so that she wasn't aware of anything, let alone Cap's identity.

I hope this little statement will save you from the onslaught of mail you will receive from other CAPTAIN AMERICA true believers pointing out the same mistake.

Till Redwing's feathers turn gray and moult...Make Mine Marvel!

James W. Drake
6613 W. Palo Verde
Glendale, Arizona 85302

Actually, Jim, there was only one other letter asking about that statement of Sharon's in TOS #75, but we thank you for springing to our defense anyway. However, as we think we explained in #179, the space Phantom did erase everybody's memory of Steve's secret ID—including Sharon's. It's because that portion of her memory was blanked out that she now has no inkling her sister knew the secret in 1945 (she doesn't remember Peggy telling her about it). Needless to say, neither does Peggy.

Whew! Now you can chalk up #178 as completely perfect, huh?

Dear Steve, Sal, and Vince:

After reading CAP #179 you've changed my opinion on a few items. Number one is the overall plot involving Steve's reevaluation of himself and his country. Although I felt issue #176 was a good one, I couldn't accept Cap's decision as believable. I thought he should have realized that just because certain high officials are bad the government itself is still a viable one, which he could represent. I still feel this way, but looking at the situation in a broader light I see that you made the right decision.

When evaluating a long continued plot such as this one it is hard to judge each segment by itself. The best way to do it justice is by looking at it as a whole, when the tale is completed. Therefore (although the story isn't finished yet) I can better see your intentions with the addition of these two latest chapters. The basic premise is the deep psychological trauma Steve/Cap is experiencing: in other words he is finally growing up to meet the times. Along with this growing up comes the questioning of one's purpose. Steve, as a man out of his time, has become a very troubled person trying to deal with this. But, as a man, he must face up to this question at one time or another. Oh yes, he's done this before, but never to the extent that he is now and he's one helluva confused person because of it. Since his revival Steve has tried to deal with the rest of the world aging and all that, but never before have his thoughts been so intense and inward as they are now.

The second opinion of mine that you shattered was my general dislike of the character of Hawkeye. I always felt him to be an unrealized personality, but in this one issue he has come to life. He showed an insight that until now he has not made us aware of. His correct evaluation of Cap's troubles was amazing and it was heartwarming to see him bury the hatchet and help Cap out in his time of need. It was more than the rest of Cap's friends did; where the others tried to help by talking, Hawkeye used a more unconventional (and perfectly in tune with his character) method—direct action. This plan was a well thought out one and Hawkeye has gained my respect because of it. When he was the young impetuous member of the Avengers, Hawkeye experienced his growing pains. The man responsible for bringing this near impossible task about was no one else but Cap. That old Hawkeye would never have admitted this fact, but the "new" grown up Hawkeye of this issue would, and did. He claims that his reason for helping was one of paying back a debt, but I see it as more of a friendship and respect growing for the man in red, white, and blue. He succeeded in his plan and made Steve think a lot more about himself and the role he plays in the world. Bravo and applause.

Other interesting items in the book go as follows: The Falcon's pushing around of Morgan was nice—he's finally seem to realize that he can make it on his own if he depends on himself and not someone else. His decison of non-involvement when Steve was chasing the Golden Archer was sad to see, though an understandable one. Because of the misunderstandings between them, Sam has completely turned away from Cap and has decided to go it alone. The newest CA imitator has gone down the proverbial drain as his predecessor likewise did. It's amusing to see these "tough guys" beat up while trying to do the easiest superhero maneuver. Lastly, Steve's words to Peggy were harsh indeed. I could feel her heart tearing apart as each syllable came out.

Dean Mullaney
81 Delaware St.
Staten Island, N.Y. 10304

SPECIAL NOTE: The other day, while Stainless Steve was idly calculating a few future plotlines for this book, he suddenly realized that CAPTAIN AMERICA #200 will hit the stands in July, 1976! How d'ya like them apples, kismet-fans?

NEXT ISSUE: The blurb at the end of this ish tells it all! Everything you've read here in the past months has been leading toward CA&F #183, so you know which end of the line to be at when that Cap-classic goes on sale! Just be sure you sit down before you read it! Bye!

THIS IS IT! YOUR
MARVEL VALUE STAMP
FOR THIS ISSUE!
CLIP 'EM AND
COLLECT 'EM!

OPPOSITE **36: ANCIENT ONE** from *Captain America* no. 182 (February 1975). Stamp also appears in *Supernatural Thrillers* no. 8 (August 1974) and *Giant-Size Man-Thing* no. 4 (May 1975).

ABOVE *Strange Tales* no. 115 (December 1963), art by Steve Ditko.

Dear Steve and Frank,

The mad tea party in DR. STRANGE #2 was wonderfully mad. The maddest touch of all, of course, was the fact that Nick Fury had his eye patch on the wrong eye. Fury also had the best line in the book ("Ya yellow-brickin' gold-bellied...")

And DR. STRANGE #4! I was crazy about it, as usual, but I object to two things, one major and one minor. The minor point: I don't like the ankh on the Doc's forehead. The symbolism is certainly appropriate, but I would just prefer that Doc look like a normal human being in all ways. One of the reasons I like Dr. Strange better than Marvel's other cosmic characters (the Silver Surfer, Warlock, Captain Marvel, the Watcher, etc.) is because, in spite of his power, he is a normal human being, just like you and me. He pays income tax, he has his laundry done, he reads about Watergate in the newspapers, he has a charge account at the local drug store: he does all kinds of perfectly ordinary things, and except for his weird outfit, he looks perfectly ordinary.

The major point I disliked was the intervention of the Ancient One. It is inconsistent with the concept of universalism expressed in MARVEL PREMIERE #10 that the Ancient One, in his new state, should have any interest in any individual, even Dr. Strange. I also consider it unworthy of a writer as good as Steve Englehart to set a premise in which Dr. Strange can be gotten into any impossible situation and then be gotten out of it by the Ancient One showing up and saying it was a test. Although it is an excellent notion that a sorcerer supreme must go on learning and advancing, Dr. Strange should be independent of the Ancient One by now.

But other then the ending, it was a superb mag, and was sometimes even magically correct as well. Even during his other "superb" periods (Lee/Ditko and Thomas/Colan/Palmer) Dr. Strange's magic was never particularly authentic. I only criticize you on some things, Englehart, because you seem to know what you're doing on the rest.

Jana C. Hollingsworth
1415 East Second Street
Port Angeles, Washington 98362

Jana (Jana, Jana Jana Jing Jing Jing!) you deserve some answers, and here they be:

Minor: lack of space prevented us from more fully explaining the purpose of the ankh until this ish; to wit, it only appears when a time of life and death is approaching the good doctor. During ordinary times, Doc will still look ordinary. (The ankh, by the way, was Steve and Frank's second choice for a memorial to Doc's becoming eternal. A previous plan, to turn his hair white with black streaks, was vetoed from above for the same reason Captain Mar-Vell is now blond: white-haired heroes are felt to appear old. Now, that would have been a permanently visible change; the ankh isn't.)

Major: you missed the point here, Ms. H. The Ancient One didn't pull Doc out of his jam. He just appeared to explain what it all meant after Doc had saved himself. The problem was a real one, as will be all future problems; when the Ancient One said there will be more tests, he meant only that fate is bound to place Doc in positions where he must grow and change, and it's up to him to respond correctly. Nobody set this situation up for him (well, nobody except Steve and Frank).

Madmen—

Hey, you may not have noticed it, but some of the best musicians around seem to be Marvelites, too! Al Stewart, for instance, on his PAST, PRESENT, AND FUTURE album, had a guy on the cover dressed up as Doc Strange, and through some trick photography, they had it appear as though he were passing through some dimensional gateway! Something else!

After listening to the album, I then decided that Doc and Mr. Stewart do indeed mix very well together!

Who knows? Maybe we'll find Spider-Man somewhere on the next Emerson, Lake and Palmer album!

Frank Brunner forever!!

Ron Snyder
3600 Ripple Creek
Austin, Texas 78746

NEXT ISSUE: Dr. Strange in the dark dimension, while Clea is trapped on Earth facing...well, if you haven't finished this ish yet, we won't spoil it for you. But if you see the theme of this new sequence already, you won't want to miss the developments next time. Come to think of it, even if you don't see where we're headed, you probably aren't planning to pass our seventh issue by. So we'll all meet right here in sixty days, right? Right! Bye!

OPPOSITE **37: THE WATCHER** from *Doctor Strange* no. 6 (February 1975). Stamp also appears in *Creatures on the Loose* no. 29 (May 1974), *Man-Thing* no. 8 (August 1974), and *The Invaders* no. 1 (August 1975).

ABOVE *Fantastic Four* no. 113 (August 1971), art by John Buscema and John Verpoorten.

For instance, on the 7th page of the story, a couple of captions had to be cut that read: "Karota does not protest as he leads her to the MODERN HOSPITAL in the middle of Central Wakanda, and although the electric lights are a phenomenon she has witnessed before, still she expresses a silent distrust—

—until he gently hands her over to the tribal herbalist, MENDINAO, who leads her past HIGHLY TRAINED SPECIALISTS who wield their surgical specialties in the elaborate waiting rooms, decorated in tribal ornaments that mask the technology in that building."

Okay, room dictated that be cut, but in future issues, as mentioned, we will explore many of those areas. Believe us. We've given it a lot of thought.

One thing's for sure. You're right. The Wakanda aren't the Waziris. No put down...just no way.

Hey, Marvelites, we don't want to say THE BLACK PANTHER has become the rage of the world, but he has made appearances in the comic fanzines not only here in America but even as far away as England.

So here, without further ado, is Richard Burton (that's what it says, don't blame us) reviewing our first BLACK PANTHER appearance in JUNGLE ACTION #6.

"At long last the Black Panther kicks off with his own series and a good start it is too with a new and excellent art team. Buckler is rapidly proving himself to be one of the leaders in the "new wave" of artists with his new art. With inker Klaus Janson, his work is even better. Don McGregor too seems to be becoming synonymous with Buckler, and these two could bear some watching in the future. However, as to this series: T'Challa returns to Wakanda to find that yet another big strong meanie is terrorizing the land in his absence. But, as this is an intro into the series, it shouldn't be judged to harshly. Don seems to be steering away from the super-scientific, prosperous Wakanda of Jack Kirby to show the more traditional African settlement, even to including two maps on the letters page; one of Central Wakanda and the other of the whole area of Wakanda. Thereby he has set himself limits to work in (there's even an 'uncharted area' called "Domain of the White Gorillas"!). A series to watch - it could be good."

* * * *

And we hope it turned out that way for you, Richard. This review originally appeared in Comic Media's companion review zine which is edited by Nick Landau. But just in case you think the Panther was shunned here in the U.S., here is Guy Lillian's review of JUNGLE ACTION #8 in the Menomonee Falls Gazette.

"PANTHER is obviously Don's best work; it shows a lot of effort, and his strong, sharp ability is well put to an interesting task. Rich Buckler's artwork is tremendous this time, even though the action segments aren't as powerful as last issue —dig that two-page splash the most! Fine work all around as Killmonger continues his attack on Wakanda, this time through a svelte villainess named Malice, another of KM's crummy crew. Her beauty is welcome, considering Baron Macabre, coming up next issue... Gil Kane takes over from Buckler in that issue, a fine artist indeed, but I hope a temporary replacement.

* * * *

Extremely temporary, Guy. Gil was able to do only one (excellent) issue.

Now Billy Graham is handling the pencils. But Klaus is still along for our ride into oblivion and with his ever increasing virtuosity as an inker, we think we'll retain quite a sense of continuity.

Thanks for the favorable reviews, Fellas! We're glad you like the end results of those months of effort on the BLACK PANTHER strip.

And now let's get back to our regular correspondents.

Dear Roy, Don, Rich and Klaus,

The latest JUNGLE ACTION (#8) shows signs of creativity (well, the first three pages anyway. From there on it looks like them old deadlines blues again.)

Keep up the good work, though. The idea of a combination primitive—scientific society that belongs to no time is fascinating.

My only real complaint is the length of the stories. C'mon! Can't you do something?

Fillers can be a rip-off on the consumer, forcing (sort of) him to buy 4 or 5 pages of reprints to get only 14 pages of the real thing. And besides, features like "Black Panther Artistry" are just gonna get you in trouble...it made me miss Barry Smith!

Rock on!

John Hayman
22 Copley Terr.
Pittsfield, Ma. 01201

Sorry you feel that way about the feature pages, John. We don't happen to think they're a rip-off. Actually, they are supplied compliments of several people (among them Danny Krespi, Jim Salicrup and Ed Hannigan) who have offered their time and efforts to Don so that reprint material can be held to a minimum.

If having the Panther remain at 15 pages means it will survive as a series, we can't be entirely against it. The series means that much to its creators.

Of course they'd all like to see it expand, including Stan and Roy, and hope that it will happen soon.

Meantime, we're issuing these feature pages to give you as visually interesting sidelight concepts as possible, exploring related facets of the series. Hopefully, because it will be impossible to keep these feature pages going forever, sales and reader response will warrant the Panther spreading through the entire book.

As for Rich, though he's sadly had to leave the Panther, he and Don will team again in AMAZING ADVENTURES #25, where Rich lends his dynamic style to Killraven and WAR OF THE WORLDS.

But let us know how you feel about the first appearance of our man, Billy Graham. We'll be waiting on your answer, Marvelites.

Hang in there!

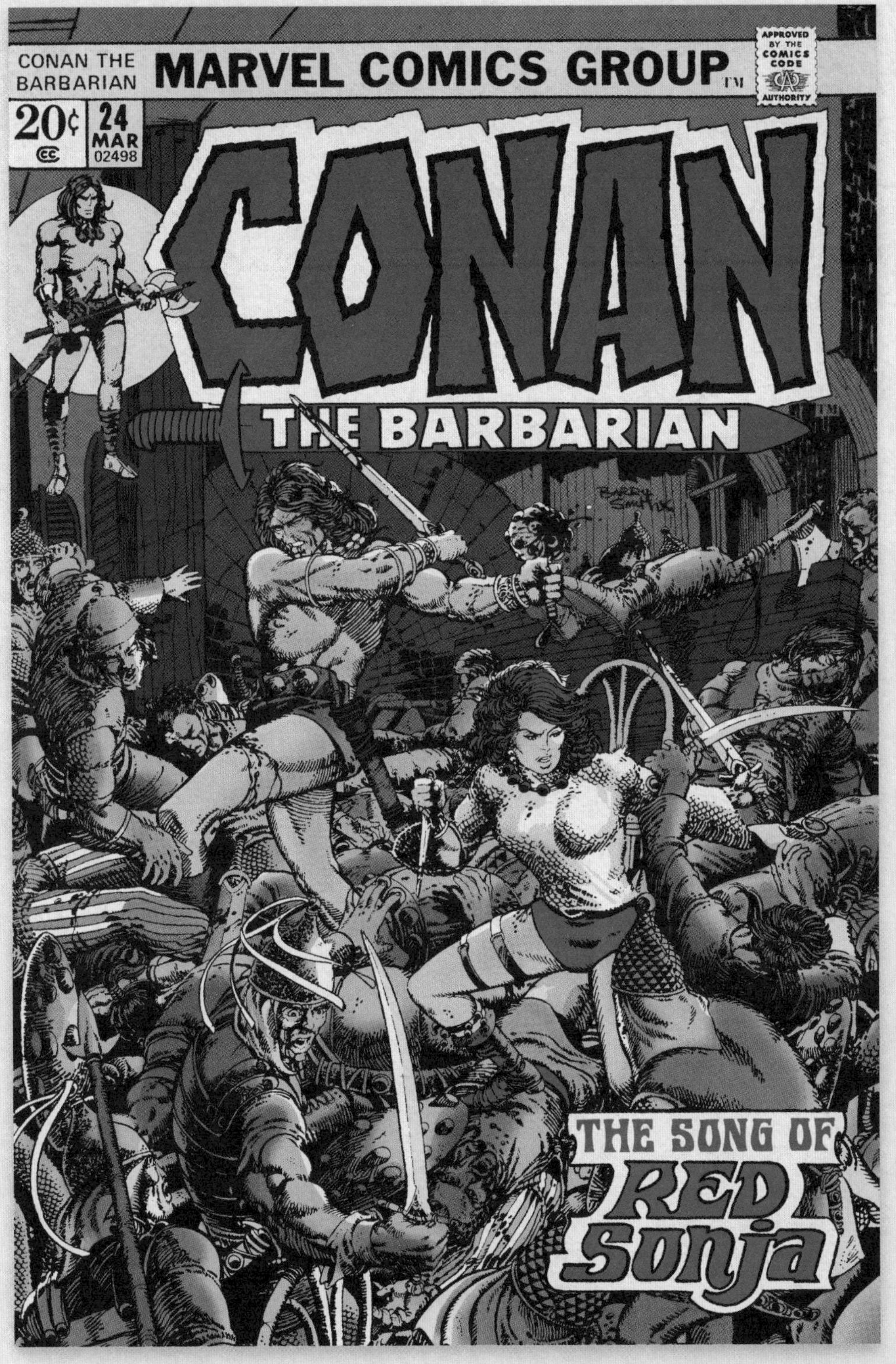

OPPOSITE **38: RED SONJA** (misspelled SONIA on the stamp) from *Jungle Action* no. 10 (July 1974). Stamp also appears in *Fear* no. 24 (October 1974) and *Ka-Zar* no. 8 (March 1975).

ABOVE *Conan the Barbarian* no. 24 (March 1973), art by Barry Windsor-Smith.

GREEN SKIN'S GRAB-BAG

c/o MARVEL COMICS GROUP, 575 MADISON AVE. N.Y.C. 10022

Dear Friends,

Re: HULK #173. Beautiful I admit it— I am a HULK freak. I have dozens upon dozens of the mags in which the HULK appeared. And some of my fondest memories are of the days not so long ago when the resident Hulksters were a couple of gents by the names of Roy Thomas and Herb Trimpe. And let me tell you, when I saw the same team reunited on #173— well, let's just say the neighbors mighta wondered about that sudden ecstatic scream of pure unbridled joy exploding from my house during the wee hours of the morning when I first read #173.

Anyway, you raised the question in the LP of that issue as to whether your readers preferred "usual" type super-villains (e.g.,the Leader) or the more weird variety (Dynamo, Capt. Omen, etc.) Well, personally, I feel comics are a medium with great, often unused potential, and one way not to exhaust said potential is to blindly try to stick to more "usual", cut-and-dried, previously tested material, while ignoring the "weirdness" which I think defines comics more than anything else. There are new frontiers out there— let's not forget 'em, huh?

Peace!

Donald H. T. Parker
42 Campbell Avenue
Williston Park, N.Y. 11596

Thanks, Don. The reaction to the return of Roy Thomas to the scripting of HULK was nothing less than wildly enthusiastic as evidenced by your letter and several of the others.

Unfortunately, that triumphal return was all too brief— in fact, if ya blinked, ya probably missed it!— but it seems to us that Gerry Conway has the writing situation well in hand, and of course, Herb's still pencillin' away like mad, so maybe all's right with the world after all. Or something like that.

On the matter of "weird" versus "usual" type villains, the vote seems to be running just about even at this point, which probably means that we'll be featuring both types in the months to come, weirdos like the Harpy and Capt. Omen, and nice, normal, ordinary joes like the Abomination.

THIS IS IT! YOUR

MARVEL VALUE STAMP

FOR THIS ISSUE! CLIP 'EM AND COLLECT 'EM!

MIGHTY MARVEL CHECKLIST

A Magnificent Mish-Mash Of Marvelous Mags Now On Sale!

First, our sizzling 75¢-centers:

DEADLY HANDS OF KUNG FU #2: Shang-Chi! The Sons of the Tiger! Plus everything you always wanted to know about the martial arts — but were afraid to ask!

MONSTERS OF THE MOVIES #1: Surprise! A magnificent new 75¢ spectacular, just bursting with the best in photos and features, all dealing with the movie-monsters you love to hate!

TALES OF THE ZOMBIE #6: Simon Garth, Boy Zombie, stalks again! Plus more photos and features on the Walking, Talking Dead!

MONSTERS UNLEASHED #6: The Frankenstein Monster — plus more of the most macabre tales ever!

CRAZY #5: "Worstworld" — where nothing can possibly go wRitE! And you'll forget that trip to Disneyworld once you've cast your eyes on — Nixonland! A 40¢ fun-fest!

Plus these full-color fantasies:

SUPER-GIANT SPIDER-MAN #1 (Like we said, Spidey meets Dracula — or does he?) — **GIANT-SIZE CREATURES #1** (Werewolf meets Were-Woman!) — **GIANT-SIZE SUPER-TEAMS #1** (The Defenders — from cover to cover!) — **SPIDER-MAN #134** (Never shake hands with a Tarantula!) — **FANTASTIC FOUR #148** (The Frightful Four — minus one!) — **THOR #225** (Exit the Destroyer, enter Firelord — *plus* one!) — **HULK #177** (The death of Warlock! No lie!) — **CAPTAIN AMERICA #175** — **AVENGERS #125** (Guest-starring Captain Marvel!) — **CONAN THE BARBARIAN #40** — **DAREDEVIL #111** (Would you believe — the Silver Samurai!) — **TOMB OF DRACULA #22** — **MAN-THING #7** (The deathless menace of — the Conquistadors!) — **MASTER OF KUNG FU #19** — **MARVEL TEAM-UP #24** (Fire vs. cold! The Human Torch vs. Iceman!) — **SUB-MARINER #71** — **MARVEL SPOTLIGHT #16** (The Son of Satan — exorcist extraordinaire!) — **KA-ZAR #4** — **DEFENDERS #14** (A Defender leaves the ranks — perhaps forever!) — **MARVEL PREMIERE #16** (The Origin of Iron Fist — part two!) — **JUNGLE ACTION #10** — **CREATURES ON THE LOOSE #30** (The Mark of the Man-Wolf! J. Jonah's star-cursed son — now in a series all his own!) — **MARVEL TWO-IN-ONE #4** (When the Thing teams up with Captain America — look out, world!) — **FRANKENSTEIN #11** — **CAPTAIN MARVEL #33** — **AMAZING ADVENTURES #25** (Killraven vs. the Devil's Marauder!) — **SGT. FURY #120** — and **KID COLT #184!** (Watch out for the Kid — he'll probably dance on all our graves!)

MARVEL BULLPEN BULLETINS • MARVEL BULLPEN BULLETINS • MARVEL BULLPEN BULLETINS

HOMILIES, HIJINX, AND HAPPY NEW YEAR —FROM THE HALLOWED HALLS OF MARVEL!

STAN LEE'S SOAPBOX

Well, here it is — the start of a brand new year for all of us! It's the perfect time to clue you in on some of the fabulous, far-out projects in store for you from mighty Marvel, where wonders never cease — and where the future has never looked more exciting!

We don't have to tell you what a smash sensation our Spider-Man medallion coins have been — you're probably wearing one right now! But that's only the beginning! Every other product manufacturer seems to be discovering Marvel at the same time. So, in the coming year you'll be seeing more of our swingin' super-hero gizmos than you can shake a spider-web at! But, that's just for starters — !

Even as I pen yon momentous monograph, Marvel's vast, world-wide network of legal experts (okay, so it's one over-worked lawyer with a scratchy pen) is in the process of signing a contract with one of America's largest and most famous book-publishing companies to do a series of hard-cover books about — you guessed it — your favorite Marvel masterworks! We'll tell you more in coming issues, and we hoodwink thee not — it'll herald a whole new world of reading excitement for all Marveldom Assembled — even for the few heretics who still may be at large!

Naturally, FOOM is still growing by leaps and bounds. Your batty Bullpen has just scheduled a special meeting to vote on all the new goodies and surprises in store for the Friends Of Ol' Marvel, may their luster never dim! And of course one of our zingiest new sensations is the Value Stamp project we've just begun — which Rascally Roy will discuss with you in living color — if I ever leave him enough space!

Since no mere mortal can bear too much mind-staggering munificence, I'll merely hint at some other dynamite developments to come. Wouldja believe a full-length feature film about some of our cataclysmic characters? And how about the two top TV producers who are making us an offer we can hardly refuse? And, we've gotta admit we're still sneakily working on plans for new, earth-shaking characters and concepts in our ever-growing line of Marvel comics and mags. So watch your newsstand, watch these pages, and watch out for enemy agents! We mustn't let a word of this reach the competition!

Excelsior!

Stan

ITEM! Sheesh! It's January again — and it seems like only yesterday that the whole batty Bullpen were auld-lang-syning each other at New Year's parties all over Manhattan, the Bronx, and Staten Island too. Anyhow, just for the heck of it, we thought you might wanna see some of the *New Year's Resolutions* dreamed up by our nutty artists and writers for 1974. So here goes — !

Merry GERRY CONWAY resolves he'll take the time to memorize the agreement of all Asgardian pronouns and verbs. (He's got no choice! Rascally Roy stamped 'em all over Mr. C's forehead!)

Macabre MIKE PLOOG vows to make his new project, the Man-Thing, as horribly hairy and hellishly heinous as his Werewolf, Ghost Rider, and Frankenstein Monster put together.

RICH (Swash) BUCKLER pledges to make the Fantastic Four even more popular than it already is. (And you know something? The lad just might make it!)

Jazzy JOHNNY ROMITA swears he'll sneak away from his post as art director long enough to actually draw a Spider-Man saga or two, just for old times' sake.

STEVE (Baby) GERBER and Battlin' BOB BROWN jointly avow that they will both figure out every one of the gimmicks in Daredevil's billy-club before 1975 rolls around — they hope!

Big JOHN BUSCEMA promises to remember that a right-handed Barbarian wears his sword on his *left* side, not on his right.

Sibling SAL B. claims he'll get a new compass to help him draw those difficult, painstaking stripes on Captain America's shield.

Marvelous MARV WOLFMAN and Gentleman GENE COLAN affirm that they'll invent at least *three* unique and previously untried ways for Count Dracula to die! (Lotsa luck, fellas!)

Rascally ROY THOMAS declares that this year Conan will definitely go thru one whole issue without once referring to his Cimmerian god Crom. Or, if not *this* year, then maybe the *next* — !

And Smilin' STAN LEE, our publishing potenate, swears that this'll be positively the *last* year he lets his ever-lovin' editor make up New Year's Resolutions for the whole blamed Bullpen!

But now, onward — !

ITEM! We need a *breather*, people — honest! So many of you have been sending in for your full-fledged FOOM kits and all the other Marvel-type merchandise we've been offering you, that we've got to discontinue our ads for 'em for the next few weeks, just long enough to get caught up on all the mountains of mail that're piling up! That's just by way of letting you know that, if you're one of the few Marvelites who haven't yet signed up for membership in our FOOM fan club, you'll get your chance an ish or two from now. A word to the wise . . . !

ITEM! And now, in closing, here's our mirthful message in SPIDER-MAN CODE for the merry month of January — to warm the cockles of your heart with news of a Marvel longtimer who'll be getting his very own series in the months to come. Like so:

NFVZM NZBDOFV GTDODVQO —
BY OFV, QMD BZV-KFWE!

Ponder over *that* little tidbit for a while, Straight Arrow!

MIGHTY MARVEL CHECKLIST
Now On Sale!

SPIDER-MAN #131 (Aunt May marries — Dr. Octopus?) — **FANTASTIC FOUR #145** — **THOR #222** (Thor and Hercules vs. Ares and Pluto!) — **HULK #174** — **MASTER OF KUNG FU #17** — **TOMB OF DRACULA #19** (Snowbound in Hell!) — **AVENGERS #122** — **CAPTAIN AMERICA #172** (The Howl of the Banshee!) — **WEREWOLF BY NIGHT #16** (Enter the Hunchback!) — **MAN-THING #4** — **CONAN THE BARBARIAN #37** (The Curse of the Golden Skull!) — **GHOST RIDER #5** — **POWER MAN #18** — **IRON MAN #67** (The Fury of the Freak!) — **FEAR #21** (Morbius the Living Vampire!) — **MARVEL TEAM-UP #20** (Spidey and Black Panther!) — **KULL THE DESTROYER #13** (The Fiend in the Flames!) — **STRANGE TALES #173** (Brother Voodoo!) — **ASTONISHING TALES #23** (*It* vs. Granitor — and Fin Fang Foom!) — **WORLDS UNKNOWN #6** ("Killdozer!" Theodore Sturgeon's greatest!) — Plus a Cornucopia of Colorful Comic-Book Classics!

THIS IS POWER!

THIS IS IRON FIST!
COMING IN FEBRUARY, IN **MARVEL PREMIERE!**

OPPOSITE **39: IRON FIST** from *The Incredible Hulk* no. 177 (July 1974). Stamp also appears in *Fantastic Four* no. 144 (March 1974).

ABOVE Marvel Bullpen Bulletin (April 1974), art by Gil Kane. According to Roy Thomas, "Hard to tell if Gil Kane penciled the Iron Fist figure or not . . . John Romita Sr. sometimes did those type of 'upper-left corner' drawings, but it may well be Gil."

created full-blown by Odin or not, seems to be a real human being, with a personality and a consciousness all his own. In short, he's unique among heroes' alter egos, and we're not sure, even after all these years, just what the full implications of that uniqueness may be. We'll just have to wait and see, as his story continues to unfold.

Dear Marvel,

Bring back the down-to-earth Thor of years ago. You have turned him into a super being with too much "super." Don't make his powers so unbelievable that he can shatter a planet, etc. I have to cast my vote with Joe Cerniglia and Fred Lee Cain in issue #224. The Destroyer story was fine thus far, and this is the type of foe I like to see Thor fight. Let's get away from those worn-out "end-of-the-universe-unless-Thor-wins" stories and bring back the more human Thor. Thanks for listenin'.

Charles Murphy
1524 Judis Lane
Lancaster, Pa. 17603

Dear Marvel,

I vote for dropping earth out of THOR entirely. If THOR belongs to a superior race of beings, if he comes from an astral plane above ours, then what is he doing on a planet already chock-full of superheroes when such vastly greater conflicts must rage above? What is "super-super" here must be only "super" at best in a realm of other beings such as Thor. Thus, his adventures would be entirely believable in such a setting— given that Gerry and Rich could give us a believable fantasy world, for that is what it would have to be. The God Jewel and Black Star episodes show something of what could be done without earth as a shackle. I hope the current indecisions of Thor/Donald Blake will end the incipient schizophrenia and liberate Thor to find his destiny far, far away from our green and blue sphere.

Rob Bier
910 S. State #1
Ann Arbor, Mich. 48104

Green and blue?? Maybe it's green and blue in Ann Arbor, Rob, but here in Fun City the skies are a kind of sickly blue-grey and the waters a sort of murkish brown. (And that's the drinking water! You should only see the beaches! But seriously, folks...) And in a way, we think that's why Thor needs to return to earth now and then. To provide a contrast. After months of viewing the unspoiled landscape of Asgard, there's something just a little sobering about seeing the magnificent thunder god outlined against our poison skies, soaring over our filth-ridden waters. Sobering for Thor; sobering for us.

Like, you can't escape all the time, Rob.

But, of course, the battle continues to rage over the locale for Thor's adventures, and right now the scales seem to be tipping back toward earth-centered tales. Let's hear from you, people! Which setting do you prefer— and why? Or do you like what we're doing now, mixing up the backgrounds against which our stories are played? We'd like to know that, too! But for Asgard's sake, don't sit silent!

We have spoken— now it's your turn! So be it!

THIS IS IT! YOUR
MARVEL VALUE STAMP
FOR THIS ISSUE! CLIP 'EM AND COLLECT 'EM!

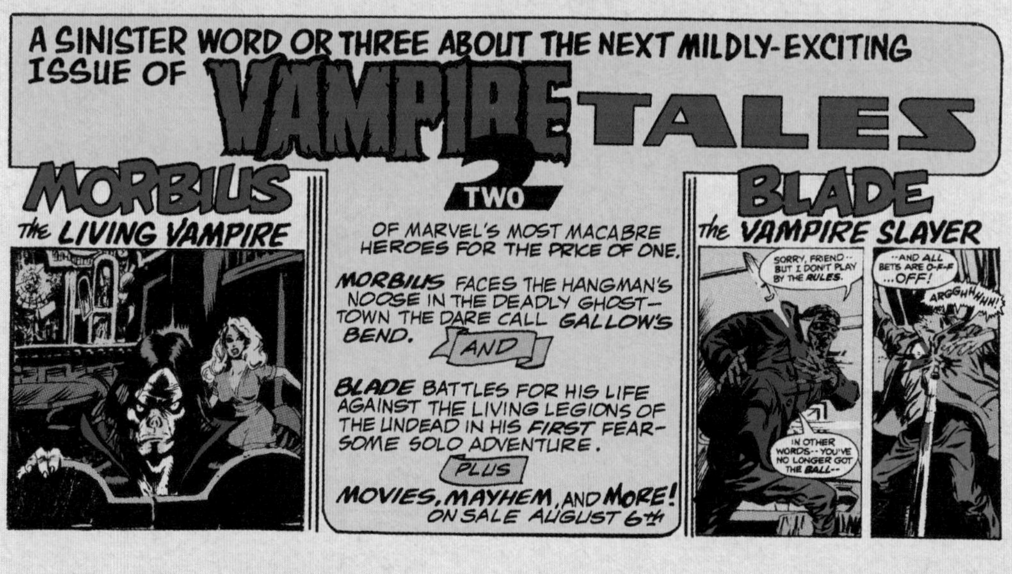

OPPOSITE **40: LOKI** from *Thor* no. 228 (October 1974). Stamp also appears in *Kull the Destroyer* no. 14 (June 1974).

ABOVE *Thor* no. 207 (January 1973), art by Gil Kane and Joe Sinnott.

THE HAMMER STRIKES

c/o MARVEL COMICS GROUP, 575 MADISON AVE. N.Y.C. 10022

SPECIAL BULLPEN NOTE:

Controversy and suggestions.

For some reason, this month's THOR mail was full to the brim of an Asgardian goblet with controversy and suggestions.

No, there's nothing here to shock you or stun you, nothing to outrage you or move you to righteous indignation (we hope). But we would like to ask that you consider the following letters— and our replies to same— with care and thought. And if you have something you'd like to add to the discussion— feel free. The address is: The Hammer Strikes, 575 Madison Avenue, New York, N.Y. 10022.

Now...ONWARD! For Odin and for Asgaaaaard—!

Howdy,

THOR #218 was excellent. I have some suggestions, though. Reinstate "Tales of Asgard". Feature Balder for a few issues, then Karnilla, expanding the Balder/Karnilla relationship. Explore Karnilla's witchcraft, and show it successful in winning Balder's attention. Then spotlight Fandral. I can see it now— Fandral walks into an Asgardian bar, spies a girl, and proceeds to join her. He tells her a tale of his dashing swordsmanship. Next issue features the brawl in the bar when the girl's boyfriend returns from the rest room. That brawl could be strung out for a two-parter. Ha! You can pick the next featured character. I hope I've got you started thinking on "Tales of Asgard" again.

By the way, John Buscema's art keeps getting better and better.

Thanks.

Del S.
(no surname or address given)

First of all, Mr. S., please sign your full name next time you write, and please include your full address on the letter as well as on the envelope. We'll be happy to withhold anyone's name or address if he or she so desires, but we dislike printing anonymous— or, in this case, semi-anonymous— letters. Okay?

As for bringing back "Tales of Asgard" ...well, we'd like to, one of these days. And if there were enough reader demand for a return of the series, we might move in that direction even more swiftly. The only problem is— where do we put it? We suspect that most THOR readers would not approve of our cutting the regular feature down by five or so pages a month to accommodate "Tales of Asgard". Agreed, people? Or have we made another mighty Marvel misjudgment?

Dear Bullpen,

I am writing this letter amid comic books ranging from 1967 to 1973. There is quite a vast difference in these magazines, and I feel the older ones are much better. I would like to point out my reasons why.

I think your "monster mags" have slowly begun to take away from your "superhero mags", the reason being that monsters are affecting the reality of your superhero mags. For instance, the Werewolf or other wolfmen appeared in WEREWOLF BY NIGHT, CAPT. AMERICA, SPIDER-MAN, and MARVEL TEAM-UP over a two-month period. Isn't that a bit ridiculous?

Also, because of the "monster mags", your regular mags are losing the best artists. Take, for example, Jim Steranko, Jack Kirby, Gene Colan, and John Buscema. Kirby has left; Colan does strictly monsters; Buscema does FRANKENSTEIN and THOR, having left FANTASTIC FOUR; and Steranko organizes FOOM while doing no artwork at all.

Third, great stories and artwork have been ruined by sketchy covers filled with word balloons. Speaking of stories, remember when Stan Lee

wrote almost everything? He is sorely missed.

In conclusion, I would like to say that I think you guys have too many mags, and, as a result, can't concentrate on each one as individually as a few years back. By the way, I wrote to THOR because it fills almost every category except covers. It's really a great mag. Thanks for listening.

Steve Jetta (a FOOM member)
R.D. #2
Malvern, Pa.

First of all, Steve, thanks for your extremely thoughtful letter. As we've mentioned before, we appreciate criticism of the constructive variety— especially when it's offered without shrill, strident cries predicting the end of Marvel, the death of comic books, and Ragnarok for the entire civilized world if we don't move this artist to such-and-such a strip.

However, we feel duty-bound to set you straight on a few points. Jack Kirby left Marvel for reasons which had absolutely nothing to do with our monster magazines. Steranko is overseeing FOOM because that's what Steranko wants to do. Likewise, John Buscema prefers drawing THOR, FRANKENSTEIN, and CONAN to working on the F.F. (and besides, we don't think our frolicsome foursome is exactly suffering under Rich Buckler's hand!). And Gene Colan, after six years of drawing horned masks and double-D's, just decided he wanted to make a change; that's why he's drawing TOMB OF DRACULA. In every case, it was the artist's choice, not that of some dictatorial powers-that-be. Okay?

Secondly, we've been rather proud of our covers of late. It's true, of course, that when a company publishes as many mags as we do, some clunkers are going to be created along with the masterpieces, but now that we've pared down the size of our line to something we think is reasonable, in terms of the talent and staff available, we're hoping the ratio of "thuds" to "huzzahs" will decrease dramatically.

Thirdly, we admit it: we've overdone the werewolf theme a bit. From now on, it'll crop up only occasionally in the superhero books—we promise! We're reserving it mostly for our black-and-white mags and, of course, WEREWOLF BY NIGHT.

Finally, every writer working at Marvel these days grew up on the early stories by Stan Lee, and not a soul among them would dream of disparaging those halcyon masterworks. But times have changed. Marvel has changed. Our readers— yourself included— have changed. And so, our stories have changed. Stan would be the first to admit that every word he wrote was not some imperishable gem. And he would be the last to admit that Marvel's current crop of wordsmiths are anything less than capable, talented, creative men and women who enjoy producing good comics.

Which brings us back to you folks out there. We're out of words. We're just about out of space, too. And we had a few dozen more letters we wanted to print on this page! But, since we can't, we'll close with a request:

Let us know what you're thinking about Marvel! And, particularly, what you're thinking about THOR. (The other mags have their own letters pages!) WRITE!!

'Nuff spake! So be it! And don't take any wooden hammers!

OPPOSITE **41: THE GLADIATOR** from *Thor* no. 222 (April 1974). Stamp also appears in *The Amazing Spider-Man* no. 138 (November 1974), *Giant-Size Avengers* no. 3 (February 1975), and *Master of Kung Fu* no. 25 (February 1975).

ABOVE *Daredevil* no. 18 (July 1966), art by John Romita Sr. and Frank Giacoia.

THE SPIDER'S WEB

SEND YOUR LETTERS TO:
THE MARVEL COMICS GROUP, SIXTH FLOOR 575 MADISON AV., NEW YORK, N. Y. 10022

Dear People:

Congratulations! SPIDER-MAN #143 was indeed one of the most thoroughly satisfying Spider-Man sagas I have ever thrilled to. I would like to congratulate everyone credited with this MARVELous issue. Ross Andru's art, which had dropped below peak excellence, is again at it's original best. This first part of Spidey's adventure with the Cyclone is one of the most dramatic and mindboggling stories ever introduced into the pages of SPIDER-MAN (I am of course referring to JJJ's kidnapping and Mary Jane's and Pete's sudden affection for each other. I have only one request. Let Pete graduate from college.

Ever since SPIDER-MAN #1, Pete has gone through school in close accordance to the time it took me to go through school. When first the awaiting public spied Pete, he was a senior at Midtown High School where he graduated in issue #28. He was then out of school for the summer vacation. Pete began attending college in issue #31 and he's been there for the last nine years. It's time for Peter Parker to graduate and move on in life.

In closing, I would just like to say two words: "FOOM Forever!"

Chip S. Lind
2342 10th Street
Rockford, IL 61108

Group!

I just finished reading SPIDER-MAN #143—for the third time. After the first reading, my reaction was WOW! Now I've changed my mind. CLASSIC!

Reasoning: Gerry Conway's story. While "...And the Wind Cries: CYCLONE" was not quite up to the level of the Xorr/God Jewel series in THOR, it should still be up there in his gallery of landmark stories. Sandwiched in between Robbie's proposal and the Paris sequence was the beginning of a new life for Mr. Parker. Mary Jane has been growing on me—and certainly on Pete—for some time now. Sooner or later, you had to do something with her. Although it was the more predictable choice, I'm glad you did this.

Congratulations, Mr. Conway. Pete and MJ have some rethinking to do, some changes to make, but with you at the helm (you WILL be at the helm, won't you?), I'm sure they'll do all right. And congratulations, Ross Andru. Len, He's GOOD, so don't get rid of him anytime soon. He's just about the best choice for doing SPIDER-MAN.

The letters page—first off, I should think it obvious what Peter Parker is doing in his ninth year of college: Flunking way too many classes. Also, I feel he should "but outta college," as you put it. What to do then? Don't ask me. However, the job he takes up (after quitting at the *Daily Bugle)* should give him plenty of flexibility. The guy's had enough hassles along the lines of "Where-were-you-while-Spider-Man-saved-the-city?" Give him a break.

Let me repeat: Group, with SPIDER-MAN #143, you did it again.

David R. Baldwin
(no address given)

Dear Gerry and Ross,

SPIDER-MAN #143 was a typical Conway story; the kind I would expect from you, Gerry. Sure to be a masterpiece, and that seems to be the category for the Mysterio stories in the last issue. Your dialogue reads like what real people would say in the same situation.

I'm glad you have strengthened the loose bond that held Peter and Mary Jane together. Mary Jane's personality had been unstable at best but this issue ended all that. The scene at airport showed that Peter is ready to accept a new girlfriend, and that he and Mary Jane do care very much for each other. This plot should be played up, Gerry.

It was a good idea to have Peter and Robbie go to Paris; it was a good change of pace from New York. Having JJJ get kidnapped was also a good idea. And I like your latest super-villain, Cyclone, because he is also a good change of pace from your other super-villains; but I didn't like the art, except on Spider-Man himself.

However, all-in-all, it was a great issue.

Billy Matheny
1006 Lane Avenue
Titusville, FL 32780

If you think #143 was great, Billy, then boy do we have an issue in store for *you*! Check out SPIDER-MAN #148, cause you ain't seen nothin'—but nothin'—yet. You doubt us, amigo? Then *be here,* in a scanty 30 days, for web-slingin' action as you like it!

And if you *don't* like it after that tremendous come on, we know we'll be hearing about it. Cause you Marvelites ain't about to let us rest on our roseate laurals, and that's a fact.

Dismissed.

THIS IS IT! YOUR
MARVEL VALUE STAMP
FOR THIS ISSUE!
CLIP 'EM AND COLLECT 'EM!

OPPOSITE **42: MAN-WOLF** from *The Amazing Spider-Man* no. 147 (August 1975). Stamp also appears in *Kull the Destroyer* no. 15 (August 1974) and *The Amazing Spider-Man* no. 139 (December 1974).

ABOVE *Giant-Size Super-Heroes* no. 1 (June 1974), art by Gil Kane and Mike Esposito.

LET'S RAP WITH CAP

SEND YOUR LETTERS TO:
THE MARVEL COMICS GROUP
SIXTH FLOOR
575 MADISON AV.
NEW YORK 10022
N.Y.

Dear Stan, Roy, and Steve,

I like the use of the Yellow Claw, even if he is just an imitation of Fu Manchu with more super-science and without Fu's deep philosophy. What I found interesting, though, was that one of the Claw's two-bit henchmen was named Chi-Foh. In Emperor Fu Manchu, this name was used by U.S. Agent Tony McKay while he was working undercover in China. Coincidence?

And speaking of the henchmen, isn't it a racial
Suwan might have yellow coloring from whatever immortality potion they used, but the Chinese really don't have skin coloring as yellow as the colorist gives them.

But I do like the Claw. He's an interesting change from the super-mechanized villains, for his "tools" are of the weird, unearthly variety--spiders, mummies, etc. I also like the Falcon fighting in Harlem. In fact, why can't he make his own super-enemy, and not just fight Cap's? Luke Cage does, all the time.

Harvey Phillips
10222 Kirkhill
Houston, Texas 77034

The problem with coloring comics, Harvey, is that the so-called "four-color" process we use allows only 32 possible color combinations--not nearly enough to make all the distinctions we'd like. We can get good approximations of Caucasian, Negroid, and American Indian flesh--but Oriental coloring is simply not available. The closest we can come is Caucasian.

However, in the early days of comics (when there were only 16 colors, by the way) the practice was to color Orientals solid yellow, and many people in the industry still automatically color that way. Even newer folks usually use a pale yellow out of respect for convention. That's not a good reason, but it's the truth.

Still, change is in the air. When Steve colored the premiere issue of MASTER OF KUNG FU himself, he used Caucasian for Shang-Chi's Oriental opponents (although Fu Manchu, the personification of the Yellow Peril myth and a man who always dressed in yellow, was given pale yellow skin as a motif--and Shang-Chi, he of mixed blood, was orange).

Naturally, Marvel isn't trying to slur anyone; we're just doing what we can within the limits of the medium. But we'd be more than interested in hearing Marveldom Assembled's opinions on this subject. Any takers?

Dear Steve,

Issue #167, page 23, top panel: "You see why I desired allies in my latest assault, Suwan! Their workings in terror have freed my mind for planning!"

What are you trying to pull? That's not the Yellow Claw. Just because you shave his beard and give him a yellow tint, you can't fool me. The "Master of Mystery" is really Smiley! I should have known ol' Stan Lee couldn't keep out of his comics.

M. Calam
84 Fairfield Road
Fairfield, N.J. 07006

But then, does that make Rascally Roy out to be Suwan? And are Steve and Sal the mummies or the spiders? Hoo boy!

Dear Steve and Sal,

Have just finished reading CA&F #166, and, having thoroughly enjoyed it, I felt compelled to write this letter. In this issue, I have found a fit of nostalgia for the Good Old Days of the '60's when Cap appeared in TALES OF SUSPENSE and Nick Fury in STRANGE TALES. I just loved the way you sneaked in so many characters from the past in this book. Nick Fury, boss of three-fourths of your characters, nearly losing his life to Cap was genius. Throwing in Val whom I hadn't seen since STRANGE TALES #167, was beautiful.

Now, before you think this is all praise, here come the complaints. I wish you would decide the status of the Falcon in CA. His presence in this issue seemed forced. Cap should have gone to the Avengers Mansion and slept there. Why not put him in MARVEL FEATURE and let Cap have the book to himself.

As for Peggy, she should go back where she came from. And he should take Cap's super strength with her. He doesn't need any more strength than he was given in 1941.

So, until the Falcon meets Dracula, I say Make Mine Marvel.

Stive
5575 Winchelsea Drive
Normandy, Missouri

You know, Stive (is that a first, last, or middle name by the way?), your last sentence gave us an idea for a nutty new title: WEIRD TEAM-UP. Think of it--Spidey in MARVEL TEAM-UP, Bashful Benjy in MARVEL TWO-IN-ONE, and now this! We can see it now, blasting out at you from your newsstand: AUNT MAY AND THE ZOMBIE, MASTERS OF OLD AGE!

....Sorry, got carried away for a moment. Getting back to reality, we hope Sam Wilson's new wings settle his status in your mind. As with Cap's strength, it'll be the trend of the letters we receive that determine whether the wings stay or go. (And for those of you who have been wondering, Cap's strength got THE nod from Marveldom Assembled. Sorry, Stive.)

MARVEL
IS ON THE MOVE AGAIN!

THIS IS IT! YOUR
MARVEL VALUE STAMP
FOR THIS ISSUE!

CLIP 'EM AND COLLECT 'EM!

OPPOSITE **43: THE ENCHANTRESS** from *Captain America* no. 172 (April 1974). Stamp also appears in *Jungle Action* no. 11 (September 1974) and *Marvel Team-Up* no. 28 (December 1974).

ABOVE *The Avengers* no. 7 (August 1964), art by Jack Kirby and Chic Stone.

teams. Get rid of the Hulk, and let him star in the DEFENDERS maybe twice a year.

Dave Stevens
316 S. Appleton
Amboy, Ill. 61310

Right off the bat, Dave, let us say that yours are some of the most unusual— and, in many ways, most interesting— suggestions we've received in quite some time.

How would the rest of you feel about Iron Fist as a Defender— or at least in a guest-shot with the dynamic ones? And what about some of the former X-Men? Or Black Bolt? (Though we think he's a bit unlikely, Mr. Stevens. True, Medusa left the Great Refuge to join the Fantastic Four, as did Crystal for a time before her. But neither of them was the monarch of that hidden land; Black Bolt is.) Ant-Man and the Wasp seem to be popping up more frequently in reader mail these days, so maybe we can persuade Len to feature them in an upcoming issue.

But the idea of yours that really grabbed us, Dave, was Professor X as interim leader of the Defenders if Doc Strange ever had to take a leave of absence. He has all the qualifications, up to and including the ability to mentally summon the group together. How do the rest of you feel about it? Would you enjoy it, just for an ish or two if Doc were occupied elsewhere or rendered unable to lead the Defenders?

Dear Marvel,

You've got a great mag in THE DEFENDERS, and I hope you keep it that way by rotating the members of the group. (You could also do this in THE AVENGERS.) Since they don't hang around together in their off-hours, they need someone who can get in contact with them quickly, like Dr. Strange. But how about giving the good doctor a leave of absence. You could then enlist the Cat; since she's due to make an appearance soon, you might as well get her circulated. With her telepathic abilities, she could make contact with everyone when they're needed.

You're probably wondering why I want the Cat in the group. Well, they need some more powerful members (maybe even Son of Satan). Think on it.

Tom Melchiorre
831 McDowell Ave.
Chester, Pa. 19013

As you probably know by now, Tom, the Cat is no longer the Cat, but Tigra the Were-Woman— which still doesn't rule her out as a potential part-time Defender. But even in her more human form, Greer Nelson's alter ego never had the kind of telepathic abilities you seem to be attributing to her. She was able to sense people's feelings at very close range and so anticipate in some cases what their next move might be, but that was the extent of it. It had more in common with, say, Spider-Man's spider-sense than with Doc Strange or Professor X's capacity for telepathic communication.

As for Son of Satan...well, he will be appearing in a near-future issue. (Perhaps even this issue. As we write this deathless prose, we're not quite sure.) But we can't quite agree that a team which boasts the membership of the Hulk and the Valkyrie is exactly hurting in the power department. As it is, they probably have as much raw strength on hand as the Avengers and more than the Fantastic Four!

Still, interesting suggestions, all! And we'll be looking forward to more of same in the next batch of mail. You folks are giving us more ideas than we know what to do with, but keep 'em coming! Who knows— we've already got teams that Avenge and Defend; maybe we'll have to start a new one, say, the OFFENDERS, who would start the fights themselves, just to accomodate all your outasite suggestions for new members!

Excelsior!

THIS IS IT! YOUR

MARVEL VALUE STAMP

FOR THIS ISSUE! CLIP 'EM AND COLLECT 'EM!

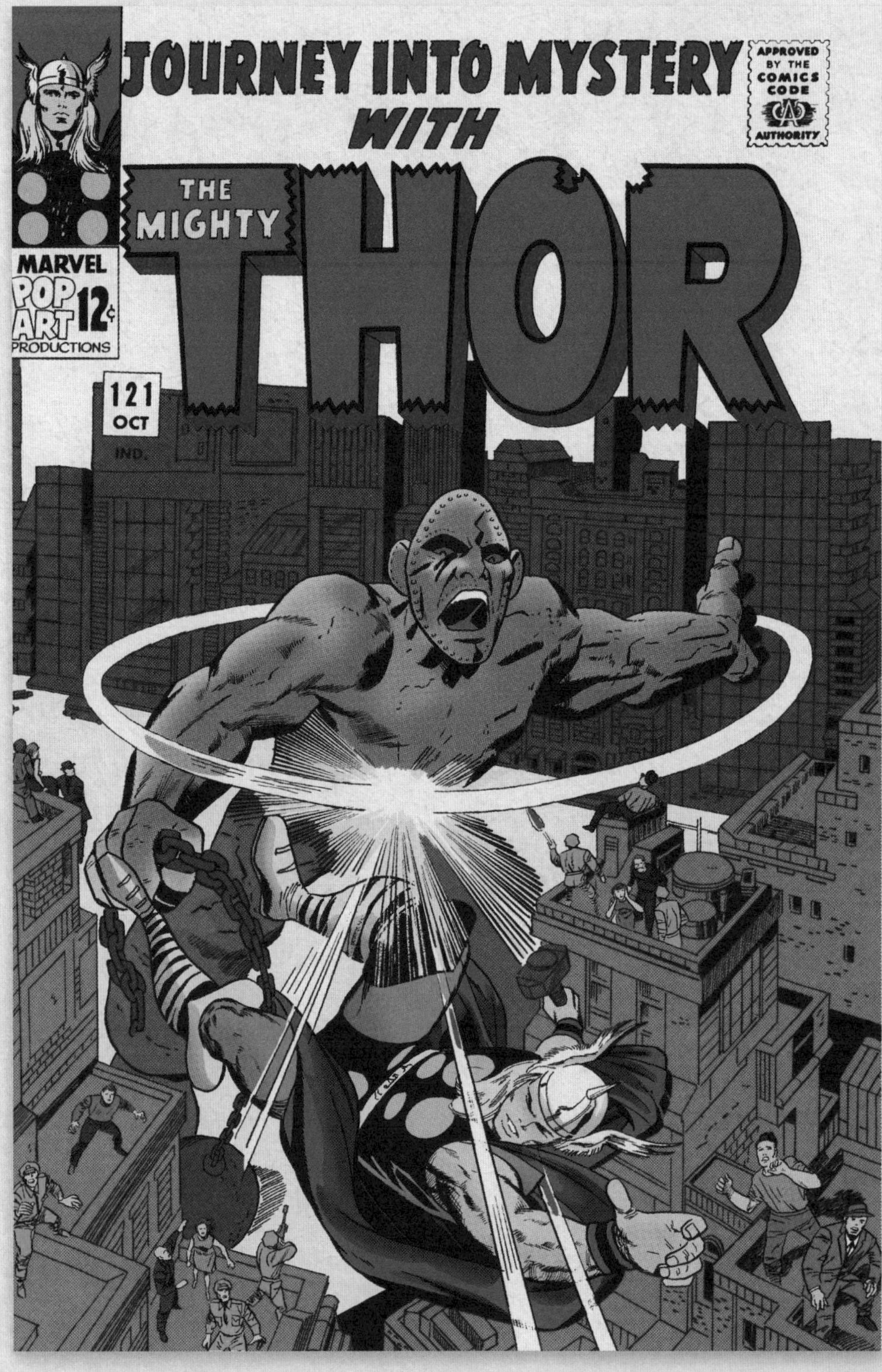

OPPOSITE **44: THE ABSORBING MAN** from *The Defenders* no. 16 (October 1974). Stamp also appears in *Strange Tales* no. 174 (June 1974).

ABOVE *Journey into Mystery* no. 121 (October 1965), art by Jack Kirby and Vince Colletta.

Which is also why we didn't explain that the human and human-descended populations of the Jupiter and Pluto colonies, whence came Charlie-27 and Martinex, were slain to a man when they attempted to revolt against the Badoon in the years between 3007, when the invasion occurred, and 3014, when the tale in MT-I-O #5 took place.

Others wondered why we added Vance Astro's psychokinesis power, when he had been merely a copper-sheathed human in MSH #18. The answer? Reread MSH #18, folks... we *didn't* add it. It was displayed in the original story.

Several readers also questioned the need for Charlie-27's mask. Upon reading their letters— so did we!! When the Guardians show up again, it'll be absent. We promise.

Still others wished we had explored the Guardians' personalities more deeply, delved into their personal agonies as outcasts. We only wish we'd had the room. That was one of Steve's greatest regrets about the story.

And then, there were two more queries which popped up regarding MT-I-O #5...

Dear Marvel,

At the end of the letters page in MT-I-O #5, you said, "The Thing and Thor— in MARVEL TWO-IN-ONE #6." But on the last page of the mag you said, "...next issue when Ben meets...Doctor Strange!" Why?

Also, Major Vance Astro states, "Any exposure of my skin to fresh air...and I crumble into dust." But he is human. He must eat and breathe. So how does he use the bathroom after his food is digested?

Paul Melletle
P.O. Box 1544
Daytona Beach, Fla. 32015

At the last moment, Paul, Steve and Roy realized that Thor had appeared only a few months earlier with the Human Torch in MARVEL TEAM-UP. Thus, as we try to keep our guest-stars from appearing at intervals of six months or less in MTU and MT-I-O, it was decided at the last moment that Doc would guest with Benjy in ish #6. There was time to catch the error on the last page, but not on the letters page.

As for Vance Astro's waste-elimination problem...he feeds intravenously. Martinex has invented a device by which the feed-tubes can be inserted utilizing a dimensional probe that passes through his metallic body-sheath without piercing it. His bladder is allieviated from stress in similar fashion. (Hoo Hah! And you thought we hadn't given it any thought, didn't ya!?!)

And now, on to two more, eh, pressing questions...!

Dear Marvel:

Why *not* a Thing/Howard the Duck team-up? Couldn't you see bashful Benjy, Howard, and Dr. Strange banding together in some alien dimension against a baddie like Nightmare? The interplay of two down-to-earth types like Ben and Howard against this background could be classic. It is difficult to imagine who would be more startled— Ben, at the sight of a cigar-smoking, talking duck; or Howard, at the sight of a wisecracking pile of flower pot fragments. Please consider this suggestion. After all, what could it hurt?

Robert F. Gillian
2538 Augustine Dr.
Parma, Ohio 44134

Not enough readers are acquainted with Howard yet, Bob, to make a Thing/Duck team-up feasible right now. But they'll get a chance to view him again in GIANT-SIZE MAN-THING # 3, on sale next month, in which Steve G. and Frank Brunner combine talents on Howard's first solo adventure, "Frog Death!" For those of you who missed our wild water fowl's first appearance, this is your chance to meet the character whose very name brought thunderous applause at comics conventions on two coasts.

THIS IS IT! YOUR
MARVEL VALUE STAMP
FOR THIS ISSUE!
CLIP 'EM AND COLLECT 'EM!

OPPOSITE **45: MANTIS** from *Marvel Two-in-One* no. 7 (January 1975). Stamp also appears in *Strange Tales* no. 173 (April 1974), *Marvel Spotlight* no. 17 (September 1974), *Tomb of Dracula* no. 31 (April 1975), and *Marvel Two-in-One* no. 12 (November 1975).

ABOVE *The Avengers* no. 114 (August 1973), art by John Romita Sr.

issue is undoubtedly *the best comic magazine ever printed!* The last page, in which Number One is revealed (we don't have to see his face; we all know who he was) and the closing comments concerning Cap's feelings toward the country of his birth are the most powerful statements I have ever seen in any literary form. The whole CAPTAIN AMERICA AND THE FALCON series, from the time they first joined forces up to CA&F #175, should be required reading for all philosophy majors, political science majors, English maj...heck, make it an entrance requirement for the whole student body.

In closing, let me thank you for putting out such excellent publications and elevating the comic book to its well-deserved position as a literary art form. Even at 25¢ (or even more), Marvel Comics are the best buy today.

MAKE MINE MARVEL!

Mike Luckenbill
26 South Mary Street
Lancaster, Pa. 17603

Dear Roy, Steve, and Sal,

You're no longer wasting time with trivialities in the CAPTAIN AMERICA style. That's for sure. This comic, while apparently not meeting with the wildest approval thruout fandom, is making me think more than any other on the stands, and of course that's good in itself.

It's also obvious that Steve has looked at the questions of the day, and came up with answers, and put them into the strip. He has treated them as opinions, and others have been presented as well. It certainly seems that Steve is using Cap himself to mouth his own (Steve E.'s) sentiments. It's a realist way to handle the strip. It is thought provoking. I don't happen to look at things like you do at *all,* but I certainly admire your having the guts to come out with straight-talk when a lot of folks are hedging. So congratulations on a very powerful script.

To dodge the point of the letter for a minute, before I forget, I liked the cover by JR very much. His layouts have been kind of shaky lately, but this was more like the old Romita magic. The interior art was a little less than Sal has come up with in the past, but another solid job.

Now, I've praised your initiative in facing up to the current political situation, and I've even said I like the *way* you did it. DESPITE ALL THIS—I wish we could all go back to the old Cap. Not because I disagree with your politics. Not because I think Captain America is special (I do, but that ain't my point). Because— I do not like relevancy in comics. It is great to see a character make a big decision, like Cap did this ish. But we all know that Cap has 'quit' before. He never was more sincere, or more determined to see it through. But he has done it before, and he will do it again, and again. This is why I object to relevancy in comics. The ideas are interesting, but they must eventually be dealt with in a superhero way. In other words— we have Cap giving up this month. Next month, or seen anyway, he will realize that the only way to clear up some situation, or save somebody, is to be Captain America again. And like I said last issue, the book wouldn't seem quite as interesting if it were titled, "Steve Rogers– Man in Doubt!"

I hope you see my point. Too much realism, too close approximation of realistic emotions and actions is impossible to achieve in comics. You just reach a point where you say, "where do we go from here?" The superhero is just not suitable for that much realism, 'cause the strip must end to be like the real thing. It doesn't end, and so the way out of situations appears to be phony, and contrived.

I wish you would just state some kind of policy statement. as I could see your point of view on this, and your aims in bringing in relevancy in the first place. I enjoyed this ish, but I know I will yawn when I see Cap go back into action. He is no longer the rock-ribbed symbol of a solid American ideal. And any further attempt to portray that image, without a pretty darn good explanation, will look empty to me. You can bring back Captain America. But if you feel the strip sells well enough, and means enough to the fans, maybe you should think about *why* Cap is popular. Some folks might say that he sells because he is just another colorful superhero. *I* say, there just aren't many of them around any more to say that. To have lasted this far, a character has to have more going for him than a fancy costume. People have to admire the man behind the mask. I think people do like Cap. And I see no reason at all to deny that the reason he is popular is because he represents America.

It still means something to a lot of us.

Bill Blyberg
6 Black Norse Drive,
Acton, Mass. 01720

Bill, your letter is well taken, and your analysis is correct. The Nomad will soon take up the cowl of Captain America again. As you say, we're not interested in retitling this book STEVE ROGERS, and reality dictates that this man return to his prime calling. But we bet you never expected to see the saga develop as it has, avoiding (we hope) the obvious—and we bet that when you see how the Nomad proceeds to his final decison, you'll be equally satisfied. We *have* done some thinking, amigo, and we don't think you'll find the coming months either phony or contrived—but we'd be very interested in hearing from you when it happens as to whether you yawned or not.

Our policy, as always, is to entertain, to provoke a little cogitation, and to be true to our characters' heads. In this case, Steve feels Captain America demands interaction with America, and we hope to make you agree,—effendi.

OPPOSITE **46: MYSTERIO** from *Captain America* no. 181 (January 1975). Stamp also appears in *Ka-Zar* no. 3 (May 1974) and *The Avengers* no. 126 (August 1974).

ABOVE *The Amazing Spider-Man* no. 13 (June 1964), art by Steve Ditko.

GREEN SKIN'S GRAB-BAG

c/o MARVEL COMICS GROUP, 575 MADISON AVE. N.Y.C. 10022

Dear Steve and Herb,

This HULK series with Modok was great. The idea of the Harpy was great. In fact, I can't think of one thing I disliked about any of three issues. However, there were a few things I didn't understand, such as howcum Betty didn't revert back to the almost human-vegetable she was before Modok transformed her into the Harpy?

And secondly, why did the Bi-Beast die when Modok shot him if he (the Bi-Beast) was able to survive the Harpy's blasts, which, according to Modok, were as powerful as atomic blasts. Modok's weapon couldn't have been that powerful.

Last but not least, how did the Harpy/Betty survive that avalanche of rock and steel?

I hope this letter or a similar one gets printed, as I think these are questions that should be answered. Thanks, and keep on truckin'!

Mike Hanly
Paris, Ky. 40361

Oh, well...nothing like a few gaping plot-holes to keep a trucker alert, right? Okay, Mike, here come the answers:

Betty didn't become a vegetable again because (we suppose) the cosmic ray bombardment cured her of her affliction. The Bi-Beast died because (are you ready?) the structure of his nervous system was such that it could withstand a single blast, like that from the Harpy, but not a series of blasts striking different parts of its body all at once. Betty survived the avalanche by sheer dumb luck—the rock and steel fell in such a way that it created a cozy little shelter for her.

And now that that ordeal is over, we're happy to say: thanks for the good words! We're glad you enjoyed the series. But next time, fer gosh sakes—mind your own business and don't ask so many questions!!! (Just kiddin', Mike.)

Dear Roy, Steve, and Chris,

You goofed! In HULK #170, page two, panel 2, you gave the wrong speed for the Hulk and Betty's fall.

Distance = ½ x Acceleration x Time^2

8 mi. = ½ x (32 ft.) x T^2 = 16 ft. x T^2

$\frac{8 \text{ mi.} \times 5280 \text{ ft/mi.}}{16 \text{ ft.}} = T^2 = 2640$

T = $\sqrt{2640}$ 51.5 = Time of Fall

Now:

Velocity = Acceleration x Time = 32 ft/sec^2 x 51.5 sec.
= 1648 ft./sec; 1648 x 60 sec/min x 60 min/hr
= 119,328 ft/hr

$\frac{11{,}932{,}800}{5280}$ Velocity in M.P.H. = 1,123.5 M.P.H.

The above shows your guess (?) to be off by a factor of 10. But this is only valid if you discount wind resistance. The maximum velocity attainable by a body in free-fall, unless it is very compact and heavy, is not much over 120 m.p.h., which is a reduction of my figures by a factor of 10.

Just thought I'd set you straight. Keep up the good work.

Stuart Brackman
885 S. 42nd
Springfield, Ore. 97477

Fascinating...!

Enjoy your no-prize, Mr. Brackman. It's hurling toward you at a velocity of—no, never mind.

Dear Stan and Roy,

I'm sorry to say I got mad with you today. The reason, you will probably say, is petty and moot. But behind it is seriousness. It concerns the "cliff-hanger" between HULK #169 and 170.

Basing this purely on the power of my eyeballs, I find no credible reason that Betty Talbot should be wearing any clothing when she returns to us from being the Harpy! Looking at the last four panels of #169, I find a head and arms reaching out from beneath a pile of debris. Then a pair of legs. And finally a pair of silhouettes. All of which strategically imply that Betty is nude. Then—BANG! On page one of #170, Betty's in a brown sack.

I do and I don't want X-Rated comics. I don't, because I started collecting comics when I was seven, and I don't want any seven-year-olds missing out on the treasure I found in comics. The [illegible]. Yet, I would like to see a good love scene (and a deserved one) between Daredevil and Natasha (which I would prefer to show to a seven-year old over a war comic; I'm sorry, that's how I feel).

Look, I'm babbling on and on, and what I want to say is: if you imply nudity, then carry it off, subtly or overtly. Don't cop out!

You at Marvel have thundered through the archaic barriers. You've got werewolves and vampires. People are dying in comic books again. You've shown us junkies, corrupt and foolish people in high places, and that good doesn't always win right off. You can't become fig-leafers now!

"Tin soldiers and Nixon's coming." What will Conan do?

Alexander Kaihn
27 Division St., 3-A
Somerville, N.J. 08876

Whatever he does, Alex, it won't have anything to do with Betty Talbot, so why worry? (Okay, okay! We just can't resist a joke!)

Actually, we've received a surprising number of letters that agree with you, Mr. Kaihn, and we can't help but be curious about the opinions of the rest of Marveldom Altogether. So we'll reserve comment until we hear more on the subject from you folks out there.

How 'bout it, people? Did you approve or disapprove of our cover-up conspiracy? And why? We'll be awaiting your letters with our naked eyes glued on the mailbox!

THIS IS IT! YOUR
MARVEL VALUE STAMP
FOR THIS ISSUE!

CLIP 'EM AND COLLECT 'EM!

SIMON GARTH--THE
ZOMBIE
VS. THE VOODOO LEGIONS
OF MR. SIX!!
ON SALE
DEC. 4TH!
TWO MORE
MONSTER
MASTERPIECES
FROM MACABRE MARVEL!
DRACULA
LIVES!
THE LORD OF
VAMPIRES
STRIKES--
IN THREE
SOUL-SEARING
THRILLERS!
ON SALE
DEC. 18
ONLY 75¢--FOR 76 BIG PAGES!

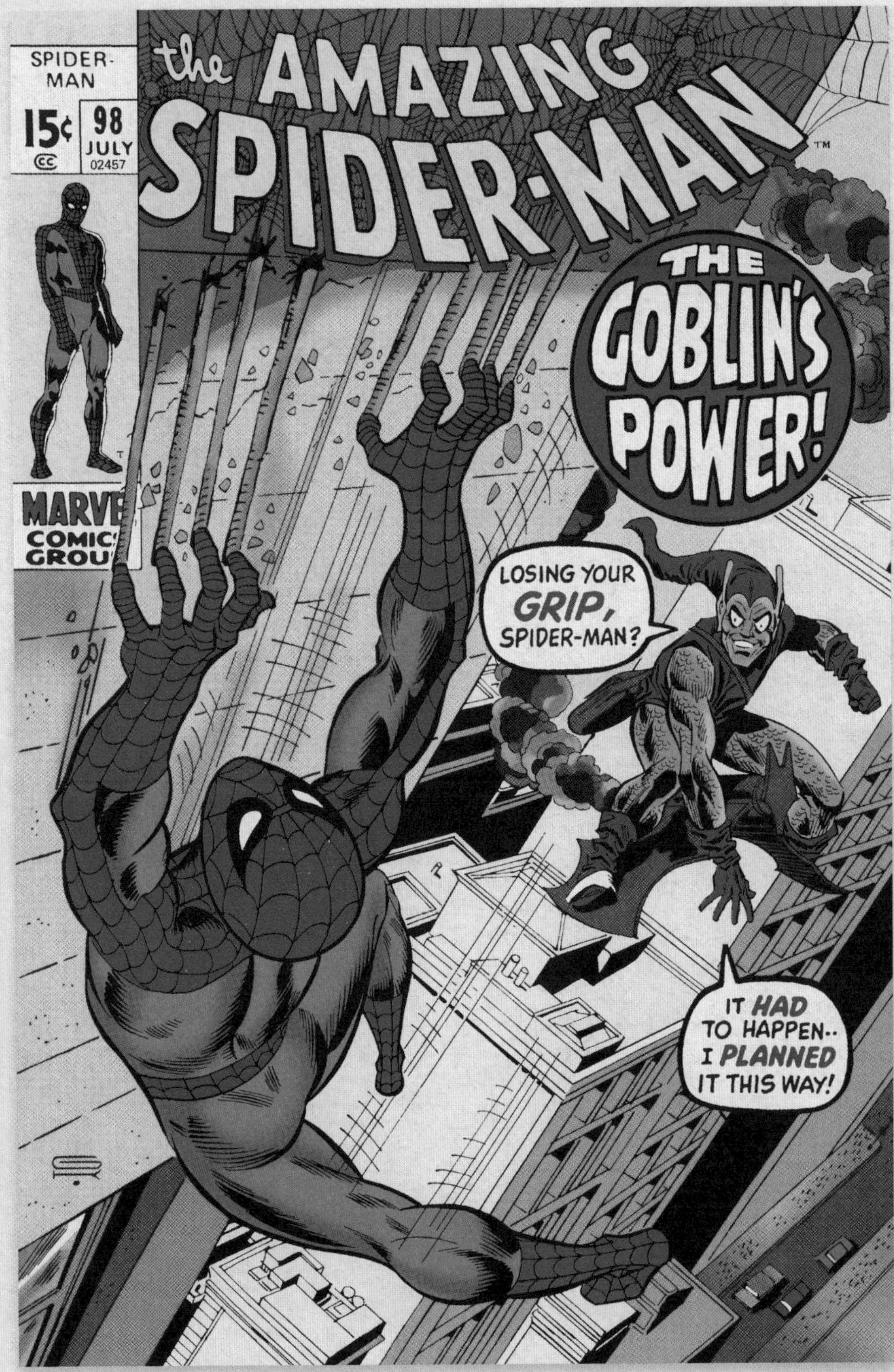

OPPOSITE **47: THE GREEN GOBLIN** from *The Incredible Hulk* no. 174 (April 1974). Stamp also appears in *Marvel Two-in-One* no. 6 (November 1974).

ABOVE *The Amazing Spider-Man* no. 98 (July 1971), art by Gil Kane and Frank Giacoia.

writer dream up a real plot? A plot that extends far back into the hero's past, while he's fighting all those other shallow villains, until he's come face-to-face with this monstrosity, and is REALLY helpless?"

Such is the dilemma of Captain America, and I am surprised at how frightening the thing can be. After reading CAPTAIN AMERICA almost religiously for the past year, I've seen mainly personal troubles and battles with regular villains (known as "one-issue-stands" out here in comicdom). The fact that The Committee To Regain America's Principles was up-and-coming seemed to slip my mind.

And while this fool-proof plot has been growing. Cap has been beating up Dr. Faustus, the Yellow Claw, and even a Falcon Werewolf...he's been kicked around as Steve Rogers, torn apart by the unknowing Peggy Carter, and feeling guilty about his love for Sharon. Now, EVERY Marvel hero has a list to match or even top that, but now, Cap's faced with the plot...yes, THE plot, and everything else is aside.

Cap's life is falling down around him. What can he do? Run? Punch somebody's face in? He doesn't even try. NOW I do know what a real hero would do when etc. etc. But I still don't have a single idea how he'll get out of it.

Best of luck in this fabulous new story-line!

Bob Rodi
34 Chatham Ln.
Oak Brook, Il

That story-line reaches its grand finale next month in our 175th ish, Bob— and we want to tell you right here and now that Cap does get to punch some of his foes and wreck a little machinery. But when your bulging eyeballs scan the real end of our little tale, you're gonna know the days of shallow stories are long gone around here. Next ish not only ends a tale, but also begins a new plot-line even more outrageous than this one! 'Nuff said?

Dear Bullpenners,

Don't, I repeat, don't let Cap leave that jail through other than due legal process.

Cap was (is?) himself a cop. If he has no faith in our judicial system, how can any of the rest of us? Perhaps you can attempt to justify this action (should it occur) by saying that this is not an ordinary person or circumstance, and that it was necessary for Cap to take a short-cut around the law. But if it works that way for Cap, would it not also be valid for President Nixon or ex-Vice-President Agnew to take the same course of action, reasoning that special persons should be exempt from the law and get special treatment? I am of the opinion that the law should work the same for all, regardless of race, creed, or socio-economic position.

Also this escape attempt might be the work of Quentin Harderman. Just one more trap to tarnish Cap's reputation.

I suggest that the Falcon return from Africa, post haste, and clear his partner's name. That would strengthen the partnership, and would keep Cap from having to break the law.

Speaking of the Falcon, his woman, Leila, ought to try out for the title role in "The Taming of the Shrew." Poor ole Sam Wilson has sure got his hands full with her.

R. E. Miller
VT-31, NAS
Corpus Christi, Texas

As you saw in #171, R.E., Cap decided not to break out with his so-called supporters, using exactly the same reasoning you did. No man is above the law— or should be. As Steve noted last time, this sequence was supposed to be only fantasy with philosophic overtones, but America caught up to CAPTAIN AMERICA... and the rest is literally history.

More on Leila (and Peggy, and Sharon— and Morgan) coming up shortly.

Next-to-finally, we'd like to make mention of a post card we received from Dr. Jazz, O.D., in Hollywood, Cal. Unfortunately, the card covers some matters we can't go into on the printed page (that ought to make the rest of you go crazy, but it can't be helped). In any event, your perspicacity is appreciated, doc.

And finally... if you didn't get the hint in our answer to Bob Rodi, don't fail to get CA&F #175. It's an issue Marveldom Assembled won't want to miss!

THIS IS IT! YOUR
MARVEL VALUE STAMP
FOR THIS ISSUE!
CLIP 'EM AND
COLLECT 'EM!

A GALLERY OF SPIDER-MAN'S MOST FAMOUS FOES!
KRAVEN THE HUNTER
FIRST APPEARED IN...
THE AMAZING SPIDER-MAN
15 AUG.
NOW HERE IS ONE CHARACTER WHO IS EVERY BIT AS DANGEROUS AS HE LOOKS! KRAVEN HAS HUNTED AND DEFEATED EVERY WILD BEAST KNOWN TO MAN, AND ACCOMPLISHED THAT FEAT ALONE AND UNARMED!
HIS SPEED RIVALS THAT OF A CHEETAH, AND HIS SAVAGERY AND STRENGTH ARE IN A CLASS BY THEMSELVES! THUS WE HAVE KRAVEN, THE HUNTER, WHOSE ONE BURNING DESIRE IS TO LURE SPIDER-MAN INTO THE JUNGLE AND ACHIEVE A FINAL VICTORY OVER HIS YOUTHFUL FOE!

OPPOSITE **48: KRAVEN** from *Captain America* no. 174 (June 1974). Stamp also appears in *Ghost Rider* no. 8 (October 1974) and *Giant-Size Defenders* no. 3 (January 1975).

ABOVE *The Amazing Spider-Man* Annual no. 1 (September 1964), art by Steve Ditko.

strength of any," declares Dracula. "be they living or Undead, rests only in themselves."

Thanks to Stan Lee for a truly Satanic publication.

L. Dale Seago
Priest of Mendes, Church of Satan
1440 23rd Street, #107
Santa Monica, Calif. 90404

Dear Marv, Gene, Tom, and Roy,

Plaguing this series from its very inception has been a nagging inconsistency in the quality of both its literary and graphic facets and constructions. Marv, Gene, and Tom can one month place poetry into motion, while allowing this feature to stumble over its own feet the next. Such was the case with the two-part Dr. Sun tale.

Dealing with the artwork first, it pains me to say this, but I now believe that Gene and Tom are not placing their full-fledged ability and effort into their work any more. Are they truly the two pencil and ink magicians who wove the legendary ethereal pageantry of the old Doc Strange series? Wasn't it they who also made Daredevil one of Marvel's proudest showcases? Judging by their current offering in T.O.D. #21, I almost dare to think not. Gene's pencils are unfortunately now scratchy, conservative and stiff. No longer does he attempt innovative panel layouts, deftly delineating even the most minute details. Similarly, Tom's inks have sorely lost their luster, cleanliness, and precision. Why have these masters slackened off?

Leveling my gripes with Marv, his grasp of the characters and unique plot inventiveness appears to have gotten away from him. Issues #'s 20 and 21 were far too incoherent, leaving scraggly edges all about. Dr. Sun's diabolical machinations had the potential for a classic in the making, but rushed production and unclear thinking towards his inevitable demise was a sad sight indeed.

I ask you to take a step back for a while and reassess what you have done and where you are going. Dracula is not exactly standing on his firmest legs right now. But surely you can revitalize this comic with talents such as yours combined. I still have faith in all of you.

Alan Rothman
151-12 24th Road
Whitestone, New York 11357

Al, obviously we have to disagree with your feeling of Marv, Gene and Tom losing sight of Dracula. And, if other reader reaction says anything at all, it is that they would also disagree.

We know it is virtually impossible to produce classic after classic without putting in an occasional clunker. Dracula has, undoubtedly, had some sore spots in the past where, due to deadline hassles or because someone was just not up to par that particular day, elements of a story did go awry, but, we believe sincerely that Dracula has maintained quite a high level of quality.

Marv has spent quite a few issues now brushing up on his work, trying to improve every story by giving it interesting characters, concepts and story ideas. Gene and Tom have also done some of their finest work ever on this series. The detail in figures and backgrounds is almost mind-staggering in concept.

We're not going to try to change your mind; for our part we'll simply continue to try harder and harder to improve Dracula, and we hope that you'll soon come around to our side. In the meantime, we hope that you'll begin by spending some time reviewing this issue and tell us what you think.

Dear Roy, Marv, Gene, and Tom,

Ahh, what the heck! I wasn't going to say this, but I might as well. It's my opinion, but a few others might agree. What EC did for short horror tales, Marvel has done for continued horror tales with your fine TOMB OF DRACULA book.

The art, by Colan and Palmer, was, as usual, flawless. There used to be a lot of penciller-inker combos who were dubbed the 'team-supreme' by fans. My offering is Gene and Tom. From Doc Strange's most memorable days to the current Dracula series, these two have never failed to turn out superior artwork. They are masters, because they can do the two basic art treatments perfectly: they can be as clear and sharp as anyone (Adams, Williamson, anyone); and they can suggest form and emotion thru the most subtle work, equal to Frazetta or Graham Ingels at their best. Colan was for a long time the most fluid artist in comics, and under tight inking by Giacoia and Sinnott, gave us some of the best super-hero work by Marvel. But Palmer, with his magnificent shading effects, has added more dimensions to Gene's work. Truly the masters of horror comics, they are probably the most beautiful art team in comics today.

Marv is doing a beautiful job plotting and scripting, and takes a back seat to no one. But I get carried away by artwork, so pardon me, Marv. Dracula is the most interesting character in comics today. And that takes a lot for an old Subby fan like me to say (I like your work on him too, Marv). Dracula carries a good deal of the script, and the actions and words of the other characters often add insights into his character. He is the most dominant lead character today. The book revolves totally around *him.* And yet, Marv keeps an aura of mystery, and terror built up around him. I would think that with familiarity comes an absence of fear, and certainly a knowledge of the individual. But there is neither. Marv has accomplished this while not overwriting, and he's also managed to keep the plot moving faster than any other comic. New people are being introduced (and quickly eliminated in many cases) at a rapid pace. But the ideas behind the story remain uncluttered. The pure force of Dracula keeps the book more 'together' than I would have thought possible. Needless to say, I think this is one of the best Marvel has ever produced. It's a really super job!

My one suggestion (can't resist, I guess) is to keep the Dracula hunters involved in the story. I'd like them to move in and out, not always dominating but having a few big showdowns a year. And one by one, they'll all get it. It's only natural. Dracula has a hero-villain feel, in a way. I'm not saying he's someone you can identify with (If you can, keep away from me!), but he's noble, and I found myself pulling for him to get away from that copter in this issue. The only other bad guy I ever sided with at all was Doc Doom, and he's been watered down a lot in the last few years. So, to get back to the Dracula hunters, I feel they should get killed eventually, but keep adding members, so they never really run out. Maybe keep Frank Drake around for good. Being Dracula's descendant, he should provide a lot of good plots.

That's all for this ish. Keep it going, folks!

Bill Blyberg
6 Black Horse Drive
Acton, Mass. 01720

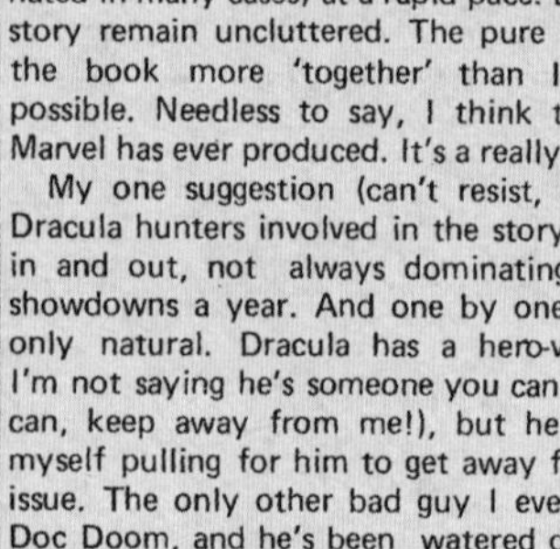

OPPOSITE **49: ODIN** from *Tomb of Dracula* no. 25 (October 1974). Stamp also appears in *Fear* no. 22 (June 1974) and *Supernatural Thrillers* no. 12 (April 1975).

ABOVE *Thor* no. 147 (December 1967), art by Jack Kirby and Vince Colletta.

LET'S RAP WITH CAP

SEND YOUR LETTERS TO:
THE MARVEL COMICS GROUP
SIXTH FLOOR
575 MADISON AV.
NEW YORK 10022
N. Y.

Dear Steve and Sal,

You've done it again. CAPTAIN AMERICA & THE FALCON # 167 was another S.Buscema/ S. Englehart masterpiece!

The story was a fitting ending to the Yellow Claw-vs.-Cap and Falcon saga. This past three-part epic was some of Cap's best adventures, Steve. Your characterization of the Yellow Claw has paid off. He is Cap and Falc's most dangerous enemy. Your work on the rest of the characters is going very well, too. Especially with the Falcon and Peggy Carter.

Sal, what can I say about your magnificent art that hasn't already been said? Your action scenes are superb and rarely matched by any artist in comicdom. You are also doing great work on THE DEFENDERS, Steve and Sal.

Sal, since your brother, John Buscema, will be leaving FANTASTIC FOUR soon, I sure wish you could draw the mag.

Frank Giacoia, you did a great inking job this issue. Just like Steve and Sal, you're getting better and better.

Thanks for a fine mag. See you next issue.

Jackie Frost
Rt. 3, Box 176-C
West Monroe, La. 71291

And thanks for a fine letter, Jackie!

As you no doubt have noticed, the Stainless Mr. Englehart is taking a brief respite from CA&F, leaving melancholy Mike Friedrich to chronicle the pair's adventures while he (Steve) relocates to sunny California. Let us know how you like Mike's handling of star-spangled shield-slinger and his fine feathered friend, huh?

Meanwhile, Sal just keeps plugging away, turning out hit after hit. And though he won't be drawing the FF mag, J.F., he is scheduled to take over the artistic chores on Bashful Benjy Grimm's own magazine-MARVEL TWO-IN-ONE-beginning with the third ish. Don't miss it, hear?

Dear Steve, Sal, Roy, and Stan,

CAPTAIN AMERICA # 167 was very good. So you killed off another longtime creation. But I never did like Suwan, anyway.

The art was good as always, but I feel the best inker for Sal's pencils is Frank McLaughlin. He and Sal produced the greatest artwork ever in #155, 156, 160, 165 and 166. Please, if it is possible, have Frank work on CAP & FALC more often.

Steve is a very good writer. Issues 153-167 were the best CAPs I have ever read---and I've read them all (from SUSPENSE # 59 to CA&F # 167). It's about time Cap was given the power he deserves. Please keep it, and make him stronger! Also, please keep the Falcon as Cap's partner. They go well together.

Ronald DeLong
15 Equator Ave.
So. Bound Brook, N.J. 08880

Don't worry, Ron. We're sure Cap and Falc will be together for many, many moons to come. And, too, we believe that Cap and his super-strength won't soon be parted. Now that he's become accustomed to smashing through steel doors, ripping walls apart, lifting Volkswagens, and pulverizing powerful do-badders with one potent punch, we don't think he'd give up his new magic muscles for anything...except maybe for a slice of pepperone pizza, which happens to be his very favorite. (Wha--?)

Incidentally, mucho thanks from Steve and Sal for the gift of good words.

Dear People,

CA&F is getting better and better! I especially like the change in Leila: since she stopped scowling all the time, she begins to seem like someone you'd like to know. Why don't you give us something on her background?

And still discussing the Falcon and Leila, when are you going to let the Falcon star in CA&F? Captain America has done it several times. Cap has always been and will always be one of my favorites, but I think the Falcon is good enough to stand on his own once in a while.

Gail Teague
P.O. Box 218
Riverdale, Ca. 93656

Actually, Gail, the Falcon does go it alone a good portion of the time, particularly when covering his own beat in Harlem. He teams up with Cap mostly against the major menaces that neither could handle alone. But as for an issue featuring the Falcon as The Big Star---well, let's leave that up to your fellow Marvelites. Yea or nay, folks? Wouldja enjoy it, or do you prefer the present arrangement with Cap and Falc sharing the spotlight equally most issues?

As for Leila's background, we're confident Steve and Sal will be delving into it from time to time, as aspects of her past become relevant in the storyline.

And that winds it up for this month, Capfans. Until we meet again, thirty days hence, remember what they say in the circular shield manufacturing plant: "I tossed my frisbee in the air; it came to earth I know not where? But I heard a horrible scream from around the corner and there was all this blood and yecch and...!"

THIS IS IT! YOUR
MARVEL VALUE STAMP
FOR THIS ISSUE!

CLIP 'EM AND COLLECT 'EM!

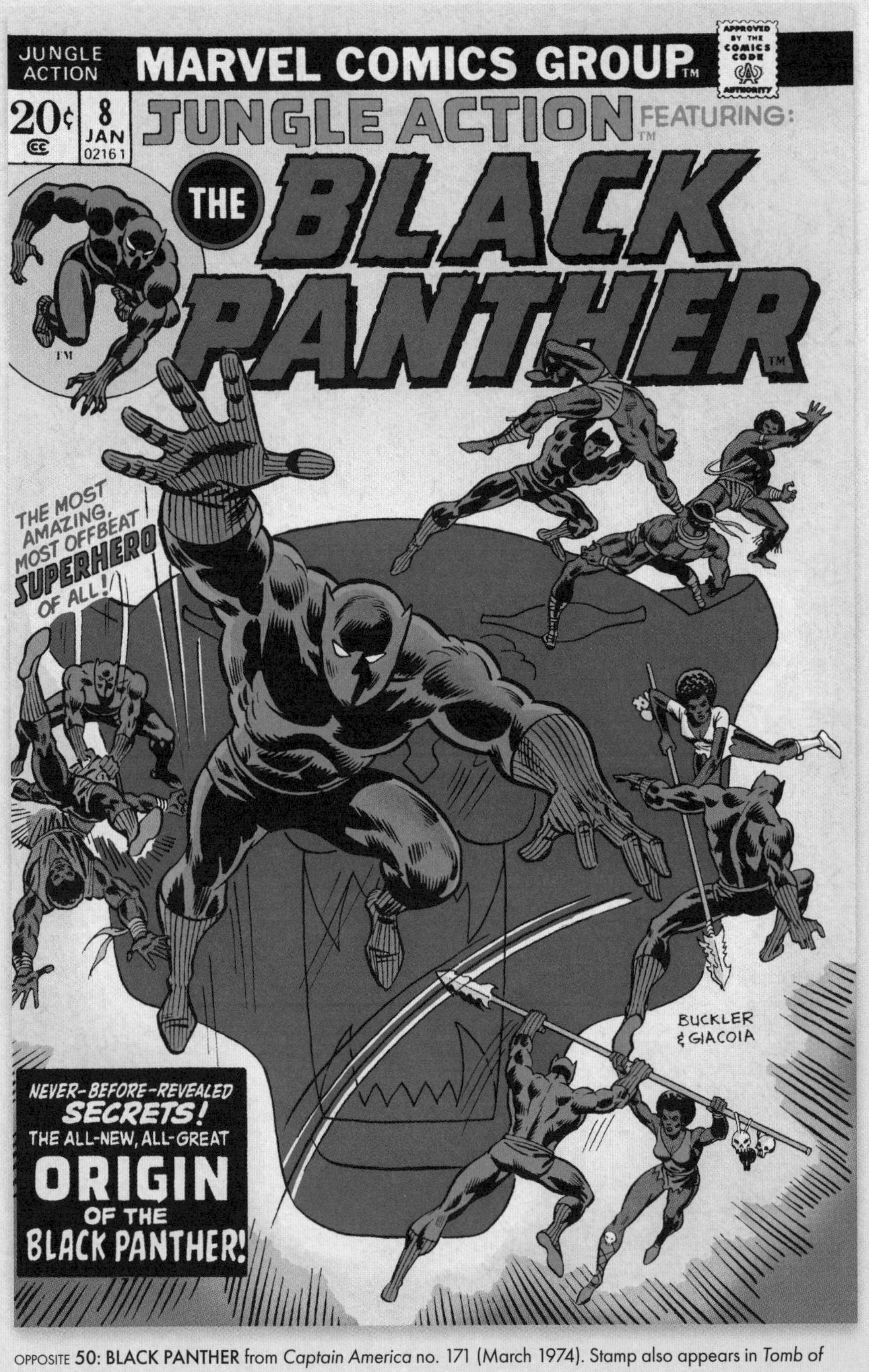

OPPOSITE **50: BLACK PANTHER** from *Captain America* no. 171 (March 1974). Stamp also appears in *Tomb of Dracula* no. 23 (August 1974).

ABOVE *Jungle Action* no. 8 (January 1974), art by Rich Buckler and Frank Giacoia.

Dear Bullpen,

After reading DAREDEVIL last night and being shocked by your bi-monthlly switch, I decided to write you in fulfillment of your request for an avalanche of mail. Here's my part of the avalanche.

Just to write and say, "I like DAREDEVIL. Please don't stop publishing it," would be a waste. What I can do, however, is tell you what I like and dislike about DD. Hopefully, if enough readers do the same, you will be able to alter the comic to fit the readers' desires.

Because I'm a regular buyer of DD, I obviously have little to complain about (otherwise I wouldn't buy it). I have only one complaint. I think it's not DD and the Widow who need changing, but the villains they fight. The villains all seem too far-fetched, too powerful, and all bent on the same goal: the destruction of San Francisco. Whatever happened to the old villain who only wanted money? What happened to the Beetle, (he's going to be in # 108, I see), the Ox, the Trapster, the Gladiator, and all those other villains DD fought? I think you need a return to less powerful and more credible villains.

On to what I like.

First of all, I like Matt. I like his sense of humor. I really like Natasha; she's beautiful (that costume is too much). I really like DD when he uses his radar senses in some special way (example; reading emotions from heartbeats). I also like it when villains are baffled by DD, not knowing how he does something with his radar sense that a sighted person couldn't do. I like DD's acrobatic skill and billy club. And lately, I like the interaction between Matt and Natasha.

DD is a unique character, and he has much potential, so I really hope he prospers both economically and literarily. Also, thanks for giving us readers a warning, a chance to make DAREDEVIL what it used to be.

Grey D. Dimemna
(no address given)

Dear Swingers,

Call off your gods! Between D. Dran, M. Jones, and T. Rex (sorry), we've had a surfeit. I'd much rather see DD and Natasha tackling either acrobatic felons such as the Jester, Nighthawk, or the Serpent Squad, or sharp operators like Champion, Faustus, and Starr Saxon (there is every reason to believe that Starr Saxon is still alive).

I think you should leave the supporting cast on the sidelines until you go back to monthly publication and have the two stars off by themselves with some really spectacular hand-to-hand fights to attend to.

Jonathan Burns
(address in flux)

Dear Bullpen,

Don't forget that this magazine should be about Daredevil, not about super-villains. Here's a mature adult who's had little that's intelligent to say lately, with a top-class law practice we've seen practically nothing of, and who has a partner (Black Widow) whose participation in the strip has been naught but the occasional launching of a widow's sting. We've lost, that office now, and Steve Gerber has yet to replace it with anything else.

What we need now is to get to know our characters again. Forget the incredible super-bad-guy-monsters, and let Tasha and Matt sit at home one issue; you can have a burglar break in or something, but leave it at that. Let DD and BW be people!

It's hard to say whether or not my suggestions/complaints– go along the right lines. I do know that DAREDEVIL has great potential, and it's a shame that it isn't realized. Bob Brown is a welcome change on the art. Here's hoping the sales figures have jolted you folks out of your rut. I look forward to having a revitalized DAREDEVIL as a monthly again real soon.

Rody Miller
710-206 S.W. 16th Ave.
Gainesville, Fla. 32601

Whew!

If it seems we've printed an unusual proportion of critical comments in this issue's letters section, the reason is ...we asked for it. Literally. We specifically requested that you people let us know what you thought was wrong— and right, of course— with the way we've been handling DAREDEVIL.

You responded. And we're grateful.

And, as you've probably noticed, we've taken your suggestions seriously enough to have put some of them to work– already. As regards the stories, we've moved the series back to New York— at least for the foreseeable future. We've brought back Foggy Nelson. We're picking our villains by a whole new set of criteria. And, too, we're introducing some new characters and some new subplots.

Most of all, Steve Gerber is paying extra-careful attention to re-establishing, reinforcing, and revitalizing Matt Murdock's character and DD's particular powers and talents— something he had intended to do from his start on the strip but/which somehow managed to slip away.

In the art department, we've installed Bob Brown as DAREDEVIL's permanent penciller. And Bob, like Steve, is deeply committed to making DD one of Marvel's top books again.

And you want to know something? We think they're well on their way already to succedding.

Now...what do you think? We're still wide open for comments, suggestions, criticisms, praise (!), and, of course, any general-type insights you may be able to provide about our stories, artwork, the characters themselves— anything concerning this magazine!

Please, people, Steve reads every letter personally. He discusses your mail regularly with Boby and with editor Roy Thomas. We're trying hard to please you, but we can't do it unless we know what you want.

So keep in touch. Okay?

A final note: we'd like to thank longtime DAREDEVIL artist Gene Colan for filling in this issue while Bob Brown was vacationing in Europe. (Bob will be back next issue, of course.) Hope you enjoyed Gene's brief reunion with the character he pencilled for more than six years as much as Gene himself and we did.

NEXT ISSUE: A startling new foe appears on the scene! The mystery of Black Spectre moves toward a fateful climax! Shanna goes into action at last! All this— and some new info on Candace Nelson, too! It's in DAREDEVIL #111, friends. Don't miss it!

OPPOSITE **51: BUCKY BARNES** from *Daredevil* no. 110 (June 1974). Stamp also appears in *Werewolf by Night* no. 22 (October 1974).

ABOVE *Tales of Suspense* no. 65 (May 1965), art by Jack Kirby and Chic Stone.

has gone sour in 1974, if there seems to be as much tyranny within bureaucratic confines as there is on foreign shores, then it's time for that much needed reappraisal Steve Rogers gave to his life this issue. The government scandals and the White House suicide are only the icing on a cake that's been baking for over ten years. Perhaps this renouncing of Steve's alter-ego was a foregone conclusion, and perhaps it was inevitable. Regardless, as a story it's going to long be remembered as a Cap classic and turning-point issue. I want to thank everyone concerned for having the courage to put it out.

Ralph Macchio
188 Wilson Drive
Cresskill, N.J. 07626

We got so much mail on #176, and so much of it was so reasoned and well-taken, that we'll be presenting the cream of the crop on both this month's and next month's LP. We'd have to honestly estimate that over 95% of the letters we read applauded the issue, but those who didn't dig it all raised a point we'd like to respond to. Viz:

Dear Roy and Steve,

I had hoped your editorial in CAP #173 would mean that the public would be spared the agonizing of Watergate in comic book form, at least as far as the CAPTAIN AMERICA AND THE FALCON mag was concerned. But reading issue #176, I was disappointed to see the magazine take such an obvious political role. Cap's superhero role has been perverted into a political role where Cap is merely the mouthpiece for a writer's political views. I hope Cap sheds this new characterization in the future.

Peter J. Sinnott
Fordham University
555 East 191 Street
Bronx, N.Y. 10458

Pete, it seems to us that Cap has always been a mouthpiece for his writers' political views. Far from being a new characterization, this is the thing that has always made him different from, say, the Falcon or Daredevil. But if, as we suspect, it's the *type* of views Cap holds that bother you...why then, we'd still have to say thee nay. We may be crazy, but we don't think Cap's changed his basic standards at all. Rather, it's America which has changed around him. That may land him in the anti-establishment camp, but only because the establishment has gone astray for a while—and we don't think Cap cares what camp people put him in, so long as he stays true to the precepts of freedom and justice he's always sworn alliegance to. 'Nuff said?

Dear Steves (Englehart and Rogers) and Sal,

Like Cap, I, too, have had all my beliefs shattered concerning something I formerly loved and worshipped. I *never* trusted the U.S. government; what I no longer believe in is Marvel.

Where once I was enthralled by the four-color adventures of my favorite super-doers, I am no longer as excited by them as I used to be. Even my former favorites, FANTASTIC FOUR and SPIDER-MAN, seem just plain dull. The reason for this, I think, is that I read so *many* comics, full of fantastic, super-spectacular, world-shattering occurences and battles, that I can't get interested much in any particular comic. CONAN is a refreshing change of scene from the super-hero stories. And then there's CAP.

I find it incredibly pleasing to sit back and revel in the current goings-on of Captain America, Falcon, and Sharon. Congrats on a job very well done, Steve and Sal.

John Weyler
6400 Montcrest Drive
Charlotte, N.C. 28210

THIS IS IT! YOUR
MARVEL VALUE STAMP
FOR THIS ISSUE!
CLIP 'EM AND COLLECT 'EM!

OPPOSITE **52: QUICKSILVER** from *Captain America* no. 179 (November 1974). Stamp also appears in *Daredevil* no. 109 (May 1974), *Sub-Mariner* no. 71 (July 1974), and *Amazing Adventures* no. 33 (November 1975).

ABOVE *The Avengers* no. 75 (April 1970), art by John Buscema and Tom Palmer.

MISSIVES TO THE MASTER!

c/o MARVEL COMICS GROUP, 575 MADISON AVE. N.Y.C. 10022

Dear Roy, Steve, and Jim,

When I first saw the ad for THE HANDS OF SHANG-CHI, MASTER OF KUNG FU (nice, simple title you've got there), I figured it was "Marvel Cashes In" time again. I would like to take this opportunity to extend a most humble and abject apology!

First, the artwork. Pages 2 & 3, top of 7, 14, 15, top of 17, 18 & 22...I give up! Every page was outstanding! Starlin strikes me as being a student of Steranko, Buscema, Smith, and not a little Ditko. I see these influences, but his art is undeniably his own, and is superb.

Next, the story. Ah, the story! A work of sheer beauty. This story is the most forceful display of intelligent control I have ever seen, How many times it could have descended into the maudlin! There is no mawkish sentiment about murder. In the proper situation, the assassin kills. Simple. Does Shang-Chi blindly accept the evidence of Smith? No, he checks out a second, and presumably ultimately reliable, source. Well done! But the best of all is page 31--he is willing to listen to the other side of the story. Intelligent, but never overdone.

The mood and the pacing rank among the best I have ever seen. I am awed, gentlemen.

Nick Francesco

Dear Steve and Jim,

I must admit I was apprehensive about a comic about kung fu. I didn't know what it would be like, but I knew it couldn't be as good as TV's "Kung Fu."

Well, to be frank, I was right. MASTER OF KUNG FU was good--very good, in fact--but Shang-Chi can't match Kwai Chang Caine in any way. Caine's humbleness, his sincerity, cannot be imitated. WARLOCK tried it, and blew it. Shang-Chi has shortcomings that can't be overlooked. Caine wouldn't have killed Petrie, father or no father. He wouldn't have killed the gorilla while it was still possible to disable it.

Don't get me wrong, though. I thoroughly enjoyed MASTER OF KUNG FU. I'm prejudiced, and it's obvious. I identify with Caine, while I only enjoy Shang-Chi.

Ron Bain
2345 Neeley
Batesville, Arkansas 72501

Ron, enjoyment is a fine response to our efforts, as far as we're concerned. However, we would like to make one thing perfectly clear: Shang-Chi is not Caine. Caine was raised to be a priest, and often had contact with the world outside his temple. Shang-Chi, on the other hand, was raised to be an instrument of Fu Manchu, and had no contact with the outside world. Though he was obviously instructed in philosophy, he must have been affected by the evil pall that always surrounds his father. Thus, while basically good, he most definitely has shortcomings--he is not as perfect as Caine, nor is he meant to be. It is "the rising and advancing of his spirit" that we are chronicling. So don't look for one-to-one similarity between TV's hero and ours, okay?

Don't get us wrong, though. We thoroughly grok the television show. We're just doin' our own thing.

Dear Steve, Jim, and Roy,

I just got done reading the first issue of MASTER OF KUNG FU and it was superb!

Steve Englehart's story was excellent. A regular character possessing simply the mastery of the martial arts probably would not have been able to stand up for more than a couple of issues. The blending of the world's most famous villain, Fu Manchu, into the storyline was both natural and a stroke of genius, and should insure MASTER OF KUNG FU a long run.

The artwork was astounding! Jim Starlin has moved up through the ranks of Marveldom to become a top-notch artist. His Steranko-ish style lent itself perfectly to the mood and theme of this landmark issue.

It will be interesting to see in coming issues how Shang-Chi, who has lived in isolation all his life, adapts to a world that can be just as insidiously evil as his father.

Rick Thoman
Palo Verde West
Tempe, Arizona 85281

Steve, Jim, Al, Tom, and Roy,

This morning at a quarter to eight. I went downtown to make sure I got my copy of SPECIAL MARVEL EDITION #15 and still made it to school on time. And it was worth it!

MASTER OF KUNG FU had, as I had hoped, more plot than action. I have nothing against action, but a minimum of it is what makes the television show about Kung Fu so good. Unlike the movie versions, which seem to emphasize the martial arts with little of the mental aspects, your new book is quite intelligent.

One question: why did Fu Manchu have almost no skin color, while his half-breed son looked more like a comic-book's idea of an oriental? (And why was the Japanese Tak white?)

Brett Bakker
4 Richmond Avenue
Cranford, N.J. 07016

Oddly enough, Brett, we explained the skin color problem in the letters page of CAPTAIN AMERICA AND THE FALCON this month--and rather than run through it again here (it was a pretty long and thorough answer), we refer you there. (Boy, what a sneaky way to sell books!)

Steve, Jim:

All right, you did it. You may very well have pulled Marvel out of the slump they were in, and put them so far ahead it'll take at least twenty years for another comics company to make it to second place.

The story was different, yet familiar. It was like reading a pulp, or watching a late '30's or early '40's movie. It has a quality about it that's only been touched in bits and pieces by other books. CONAN had it when it first started. DOC SAVAGE had it. The only word that describes it is "atmosphere."

Stephan Freidt
PO Box 1131
Yakima, Washington 98907

Glad you like our humble efforts, Stephan.. even though you can harldy expect us to agree with you when you say that Marvel's been in a slump. Seems to us you must have us mixed up with some Different Company's mags.

Dear Steve and Jim,

Unbelievable! With only one issue, MASTER OF KUNG FU has taken the number three spot on my comics Top Ten, right after CONAN and CAPTAIN MARVEL. I expect this book to match the records set by SPIDER-MAN, CONAN, and LUKE CAGE by going monthly with its fourth issue.

Chief quibble: Fu Manchu never had a moustache. Just ask Jack Gaughan in LOCUS #139. (Pause here for unabashed plug for SF fandom's favorite zine).

K. J. Robbins
1314 Cooper Street
Missoula, Montana 59801

The trouble with making MASTER OF KUNG FU monthly, K.J., is that it takes so long to produce. Jim has been able to do only layouts since the first issue, and Steve spends up to twice his normal amount of time on the scripting. Still, we managed to set some sort of new record, by changing the entire title of the book to MASTER OF KUNG FU, beginning with this third issue.

Now, we know that Fu never had a moustache, and, in fact, Jim's original pencils didn't give him one. But editor Roy Thomas felt that a hairless Fu just didn't make it visually. After all, a "Fu Manchu moustache" is a recognized thing, even if it is recognized from old Boris Karloff movies instead of the original Sax Rohmer books. So, Jim added the 'stache.

Steve and Jim,

I really enjoyed your latest issue of SPECIAL MARVEL EDITION, with MASTER OF KUNG FU. Steve's script was excellent, and should serve to win a large audience for this book. I'll be doing my best to get my friends to read it. And boy, Jim Starlin's done it again! His fight panels on pages 18 and 22 were great, and I think Steve made a wise choice not to use sound effects on those pages, because I could feel the impact of Shang-Chi's blows without the Pow's and Bwam's. Once again, Jim has shown his imaginative flair for layouts. I just loved page 17, panel 1, for instance. Keep thinking, Jim.

Well, I guess you'll be getting a ton of mail on your latest endeavor, and this ten-year Marvelite just wanted to tell you, Make Mine the House of Ideas!

Pete Crescenti
50 First Avenue
Bay Shore, N.Y.

NEXT ISSUE, Shang-Chi makes his first assault on the empire of evil run by Fu Manchu, and Sir Denis Nayland Smith makes a dramatic decision. But Fu Manchu hasn't survived and prospered by being a pushover, and when he retaliates with the horrors at his command... well, just don't miss our fourth issue (also known as MASTER OF KUNG FU #18)! It'll rock ya!

THIS IS IT! YOUR

MARVEL VALUE STAMP

FOR THIS ISSUE!

CLIP 'EM AND COLLECT 'EM!

OPPOSITE **53: THE GRIM REAPER** from *Master of Kung Fu* no. 17 (April 1974). Stamp also appears in *Man-Thing* no. 9 (September 1974).

ABOVE *The Avengers* no. 102 (August 1972), art by Rich Buckler and Joe Sinnott.

They were putting an end to an excellent magazine, you to an outstanding character, but such unoriginal, feeble death-rattles make the demises seem justified, even welcome.

Eighteen months ago, I was of the firm conviction that anything Gerry Conway wrote promised to be sensitive and creative. Now my faith has been brutally murdered. The "Last Supper" sequence on page eighteen was painful, and the crucifixion was worse. Herb Trimpe certainly didn't help. As for the rest of the issue...well, how many times can you use words like "weak" and "tasteless"?

I hope you've considered the implications of Warlock's death. Counter-Earth is finished. Only Adam's intervention kept the High Evolutionary from destroying it as soon as the Man-Beast interfered with his handiwork. It's cosmically messy to leave a second Earth floating around without an unresolved storyline.

However, there are still characters in the Warlock story who deserve to live. Astrella, any of Adam's followers who survived, and most important, Warlock himself. His magazine was always dangerously messianic, ultimately a limiting vehicle for one of Marvel's best ideas. Maybe it's best that he die. Each time he has returned to the cocoon, he has emerged more advanced. Let him rest, let your own ideas develop, and only if the time is ever right again, let his return mean something. Even if it's just one good story in someone else's mag.

As for the Hulk himself...old Greenskin is too strong and satisfying a comics character to do anything but let this one fiasco roll off his back. So, keep on truckin'!

Mary Jo Duffy
231 Stone Hall
Wellesley College
Wellesley, Mass.

Uh...Jeff, Derek, Mary Jo...
Are you sure you all three read the same comic book?

Now, friends, you really know why editors, writers, and artists go berserk in the mind.

Three readers. Three letters. Three totally different interpretations and reactions to the same story. Jeff sees it as a reverent retelling of the story of Christ. Derek sees it as a plea (we think) for revolution. And Mary Jo considers it tasteless, whatever it is.!

Okay. We won't cop out. We really were doing an allegory, in case there was any doubt left in anyone's mind after that story's conclusion in HULK #178. And yes, the tale did have political implications as well. (But we'd prefer you draw your own conclusions as to what those implications were. There were several different interpretations, all equally valid. Take your pick.)

We did not think the story was tasteless, or we would never have presented it. (Most readers, incidentally, agreed. The overwhelming majority of the mail praised the story as a giant leap forward for comics.) And we have not, Ms. Duffy, written off either Warlock or Counter-Earth. Several writers already have some unbelievably bizarre plot ideas in mind for Adam's future. And as soon as one of those sagacious scribes gets the nod from editor Roy, you will be seeing the gold-complected semi-savior again. Eventually. We do plan to wait quite some time before continuing his exploits, and for exactly the reason Mary Jo suggested— we want Warlock's return to be something very special and wholly unexpected.

We'll reserve further comment until next issue's letters section, which, of course, will deal with the concluding chapter of the Hulk/Warlock trilogy. In the meantime, our sincere thanks to all who wrote. We appreciated hearing all 4,789 different ideas on what the story was about, what its merits and demerits were.

THIS IS IT! YOUR
MARVEL VALUE STAMP
FOR THIS ISSUE!
CLIP 'EM AND COLLECT 'EM!

OPPOSITE 54: **SHANNA THE SHE-DEVIL** from *The Incredible Hulk* no. 181 (November 1974). Stamp also appears in *Astonishing Tales* no. 23 (April 1974) and *Man-Thing* no. 13 (January 1975).

ABOVE *Shanna the She-Devil* no. 3 (April 1973), art by Ross Andru and Vince Colletta.

Kane draw them, *not* as regular people, please!).

Pat Ford
1900 S. Lincoln A-26
Santa Maria, Ca. 93454

Funny you should mention that, Pat. For, even as we speak, Barry and Roy are working in tandem on a lyrical adaptation of one of REH's greatest weirdest tales— "The Worms of the Earth" — for a very early issue of THE SAVAGE SWORD OF CONAN. He and Roy talked things over and, since Barry didn't have the time to return to Conan on a permanent basis, they agreed that they ought to do a special project or two together instead. See future issues of SWORD for the full details— if, by the vagaries of comics publishing (in which this letters page is written before the full contents of SWORD #2 are fully determined), a full ad for Roy and Barry's Bran Mak Morn tale has not already actually appeared. Save your sheckels, Pat — when it comes to heroic fantasy in the months to come, Marvel is definitely gonna make you a bunch of offers you can't refuse.

Dear Stan and Roy:

I am once again deeply distressed that SAVAGE TALES hasn't been circulated widely (or at all) in Cincinnati. I've already spent a wad getting back issues of CONAN from magazine dealers, and I hoped I wouldn't have to go that route again. So please, mighty Marvel, give old Cincy a break!

Jim Bomhamp
7208 Longfield Dr.
Cincinnati, Ohio 45243

Jim, we're turning your heartful letters over to Honest John Ryan, our energetic new Circulation Director— just as we do <u>all</u> mentions of problems in getting hold of our comics, of whatever size. John naturally can't send personal replies to the various complaints and pleas we get each week— but a record is kept, and eventually they are acted upon. It's a long uphill fight— and thanks for bearing with us!

Incidentally, most of our 75¢ and $1 mags now contain ads for back issues of Marvel magazines, though at higher than list price because of the expense of storage and handling, as well as the laws of supply and demand. Check there to see if we've got the one you need— but don't expect to see some of our early issues, as (due to an error at the printing plant) these issues were once advertised for sale but were never shipped to us— so that it took us months to refund all the money sent for issues we couldn't supply, and we had to get out of the back-issue department for a while. You'll find SAVAGE TALES #2-4 advertised there right now— but don't expect to find #1 (which sells for as much as $10 or more now, on many dealers' lists), as even Rascally Roy himself has only a few dozen priceless copies salted away as a hedge against inflation.

Dear Roy,

Knowledge of a foreign language is necessary if one wishes to express his views in said language. When I began to read comic-books (after having been an addict of their French adaptations), I immediatley had a lot of things to say about them, but I could not. Well, that was two years ago, and now I feel I can say what I want to say.

What relation is there between this fact and CONAN, you may inquire. It is very simple: I can write this letter because of your comics, CONAN in particular. Comics are perfect as educational material, as some American teachers have already proven in your columns. Your scripts, Roy, are excellent, exciting, and entertaining, and probably the best in the business. (Did you know that you have received the *Best Foreign Writer Award* at the French Comic Convention this year?) and they have made the exploration of English an exciting adventure for me. For this, I thank you. You make a point, I think, of not writing more barbarian-hero-versus-evil-wizard-or-fearsome-monster type stories but, on the contrary, try to build a coherent universe, with all its different people, each with their different customs, behaviors, and speech-patterns. In the background of your stories, a whole new world is revealed to us, and this is why CONAN is one of the most realistic magazines: it does not reproduce reality, but creates it instead.

This was not a very intelligent and thoughtful letter, I fear, but your comics (CONAN, SPIDER-MAN, FANTASTIC FOUR, and CAPTAIN MARVEL in particular) provide me with great entertainment and I had to thank you.

Jean Daniel Breque
1 Rue Maurice Utrillo
33700 Merignac, France

<u>Au contraire</u>, Jean, it is we who should thank you— for brightening up our editorial day with your letter. It reminds us of one which Stan Lee received a few years back from Mario Puzo, author of <u>The Godfather</u>, which read: "Thanks to Marvel Comics for teaching my son to read when the public schools failed." And, as one who learned to read on comic-books himself back in the middle 1940's when he was four and five years old, so that he had a vocabulary of several hundred words by the time he entered the first grade just before his sixth birthday, Roy— who used to be an English teacher himself and doesn't want to put down the school system— probably appreciates such comments as yours at least as much as any other writer in the business. Since he's also acted in a goodly number of plays during his high school and college days, and made pin money for several years in the early 1960's as a rock singer in his native Missouri, it's safe to say that Roy's chief aim in writing and editing comics is to provide sheer entertainment, not education or political enlightenment. Still, it's great to be reminded of the other vast potentials of the graphic-story (comic-book) medium.

Like we said: thanks.

OPPOSITE **55: MEDUSA** from *Conan the Barbarian* no. 43 (October 1974). Stamp also appears in *Giant-Size Dracula* no. 5 (June 1975).

ABOVE *Fantastic Four* no. 144 (March 1974), art by Rich Buckler and Joe Sinnott.

LET'S RAP WITH CAP

SEND YOUR LETTERS TO:

THE MARVEL COMICS GROUP
SIXTH FLOOR
575 MADISON AV.
NEW YORK 10022
N. Y.

Ever since we announced Jack Kirby's return to this titanic title, myriad missives have been pouring in singing the praises of our once and future "King."

And we couldn't agree with them more.

So rather than fill this column with paeans of praise for past projects (as well as those carloads of criticism), we're informing you of an event you should not miss—the history-making return to the fold of the greatest comic book artist of all time—next issue!

Jack's back!

(And ain't life grand!)

Dear Stan,

I have been reading Marvel steadily since 1961. I was there when Iron Man had his first heart attack and Johnny Storm his first heartburn. I grew up on the art of Jack Kirby and wept when he left. Today, I learned that he is returning to the Bullpen. I rejoice. After far too long a wait, the King returns to usher in a welcome relief. Thank you.

Welcome home, Jack, we've missed you.

Dave Emmons
(address not given)

Dear Marvel,

One day I was just sitting around wondering, and I thought to myself (I often do that), "Jack Kirby has been away from Marvel for a long time."

Then seconds after that, I thought, "Will he ever return?"

Then sometime after that I picked up a copy of GIANT-SIZE DAREDEVIL, and as I often do, I looked upon the bullpen page first.

WONDER OF WONDERS! THE KING HAS RETURNED TO MARVEL WHERE HE BELONGS!

Gregory A. Maddux
13410 Hinchbrook Blvd.
Valley Station, KY 40272

Dear Fourth of July Firecracker Firers,

I'm sure gonna be glad when you're through fiddlin' around with Falc's life. It's getting a little tiresome watching Sam, Snap, or whoever he is walking around in a daze going, "Who am I?" See, I'm all set for the 12-part bicentennial special comin' up featuring the return of Captain America's creator and one of Marvel's founding fathers (trumpet's blaring!) JACK "KING" KIRBY!!! (Bombs bursting in air! Rockets' red glare!)

I'm so glad he's back at Marvel (hopefully to stay). His fling at the distinguished competition was super, but *this* is where he belongs!

Now, if you could get Stan the Smiler off his publishing duff...

Mark Dooley
105 Wehmeier St.
Columbus, IN 47201

Bullpen,

I want to thank you for bringing him back and for those of you who don't know what I'm talking about, it's the *King*—! And the crown fits just as well as it did years ago!

Thanks again Bullpen.

Alberto Panganiban
7320 E. 50th Street
S. Tulsa, OK 74145

To whoever is writing Captain America this month,

When I read Jack Kirby was taking over this book in the bullpen page, I was so overjoyed that the yell of glee I let out is still echoing through the blocks. It should reach your offices soon, and since I live in Colorado you can imagine how loud it was! Just to see Jack on the pages of a Marvel Comic again is too great a dream come true to explain. Thanks for getting him back. He belongs here.

Doug Zimmerman
11322 Lafayette Street
Northglenn, CO 80233

To all my heroes,

The King is Back!!!
The King is Back!!!
YAAA-HOOOO!!!

Kirk Winkler
23 Woodland Dr.
Nashua, NH 03060

Kirk, we couldn't have said it better ourselves if we wrote a novel!

See you next month— we'll be lookin' for ya!

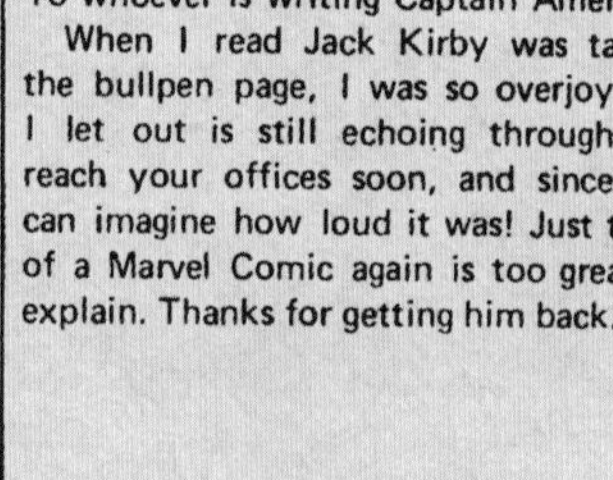

THIS IS IT! YOUR
MARVEL VALUE STAMP
FOR THIS ISSUE!
CLIP 'EM AND COLLECT 'EM!

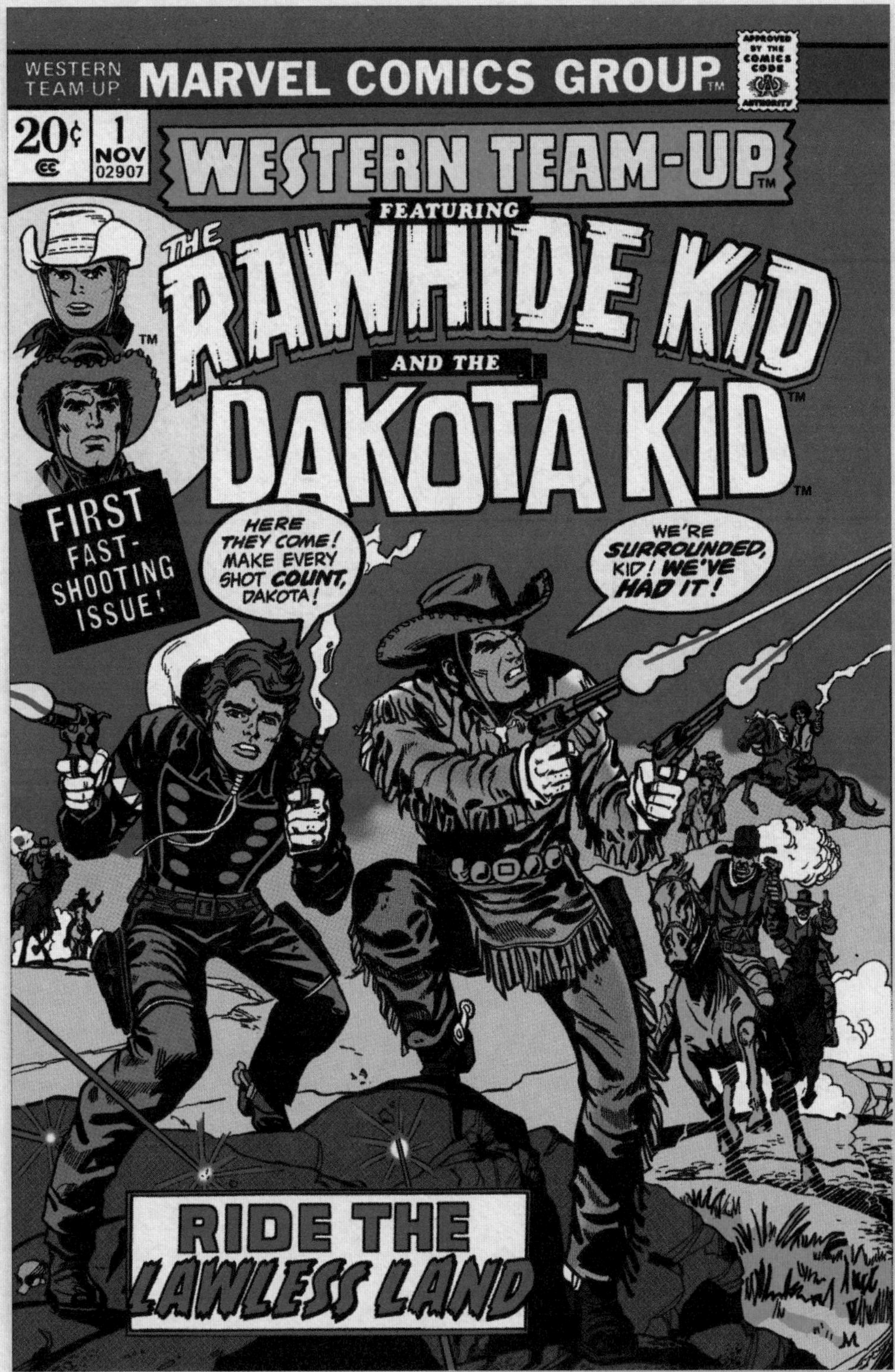

OPPOSITE **56: THE RAWHIDE KID** from *Captain America* no. 192 (December 1975). Stamp also appears in *The Incredible Hulk* no. 175 (May 1974) and *Marvel Team-Up* no. 26 (October 1974).

ABOVE *Western Team-Up* no. 1 (November 1973), art by Larry Lieber, Vince Colletta, and John Romita Sr.

Hannibal King. He is nothing short of fantastic. Never before have I come across a 'good' vampire. I was not surprised when you revealed his secret on p. 31. I realized King was a vampire back on p. 11. I was even more sure on p. 16 when Dracula says to King, "Your gun's bullets can not harm me—as you already know."

On the next page, Dracula lobs the hapless King out a second-story window and says he must leave "before the buffoon returns." Any normal person wouldn't have a chance of returning so soon. This is proven when King comes back and beats up on Drac's slave.

As a final clue, Dracula makes repeated claims to being Hannibal King's "Master." Mr. King is indeed the best vampire-fighter to come along since Blade. Although it would be interesting, refrain from teaming him up with Harker's crew. The shrewd pros would immediately suspect something when King only comes around in the evenings.

Before I sign off, I would like to apply for a nefarious No-prize. Reason one: the above clues. Reason two: the cover has Dracula saying "These two tracked us here as humans! But when they leave—they, too, will be vampires!" He is pointing to Hannibal King and Adrianne Walters. Either you guys goofed or Dracula had his fangs twisted.

That's it. Until Dracula starts renting out his coffin, Make Mine Marvel!

John Ward
2170 Lazor St.
Indiana, Pa. 15701

And so it continued...as far as we can tell, to date there have been *no negative comments* on #25, and to that, Marv, Gene, Tom, and John are overjoyed. We sort of feel these guys put even more effort than usual into that thriller, so there is no small amount of satisfaciton in seeing how well it was received.

Now, onto the clues, et al. We were surprised that so many of you outguessed Marv and Gene. We expected some of the more obvious clues to be spotted, but truth to tell, we never thought the time clue on page 15 would be spotted, and most of you did.

For a run-down on the clues as best we remember them:

1) p. 7. King says the "blasted vampire killed everyone inside." Since he was inside the factory, he had to be slain as well. And, yes, the white-haired vamp is the one who killed Blade's mother.

2) p. 11. The mirror. We placed it so early in the story hoping no one would be suspicious.

3) p. 11—last panel. King says he can "hear the barkeep's ticker a mile off." No easy thing unless you have incredibly acute hearing.

4) p. 14—the crowbar doesn't really hurt King. It would bash in most people's skulls.

5) p. 15—several on this page, gang—the 3 minute journey—impossible to make on foot.

6) panel 5 mentions there is a sign tacked to a wall saying "Welcome, come in." Vampires need to be welcomed into a private place, unlike the public bar.

7) last panel shows him on the second floor. The only staircase goes UP, not down. There is an open window, so obviously he came through that—the staircase to the first floor is probably on the other side of the hallway.

8) Dracula says he is King's Master. He ONLY uses that term with other vampires.

9) Dracula throws King from a second-story window and knows he will not die.

10) the wisp of smoke in page 17 is not Drac leaving, but King re-entering the building.

11) p. 27. It takes quite a bit of power to make the axe go totally through the vampire leaving only a wooden handle in the body.

That's it—those of you who found 9 of the 11 clues, consider yourself no-prized. For the rest of you, you'll have a chance to redeem yourself in an up-coming issue of VAMPIRE TALES when Live-It-Up Len Wein and Frightful Frank Thorne combine to present chapter one of "Night Of The Burmese Bat"—a brand new series starring ole Hannibal King himself.

Until then, seeya next ish!

THIS IS IT! YOUR
MARVEL VALUE STAMP
FOR THIS ISSUE! CLIP 'EM AND COLLECT 'EM!

OPPOSITE **57: THE VULTURE** from *Tomb of Dracula* no. 28 (January 1975). Stamp also appears in *Tomb of Dracula* no. 24 (September 1974).

ABOVE *The Amazing Spider-Man* no. 128 (January 1974), art by Ross Andru, Frank Giacoia, and Dave Hunt.

Third, we agree, too, that *fewer* mags doesn't equal *better* mags or covers. And it doesn't eliminate the occasional problem of a "misleading" cover, either. But by concentrating our efforts on a slightly smaller line, we can spend just a little more time on each cover, put in just a little more thought and consideration. And *that,* very often, does produce a better result.

Fourth, and finally, thanks for your encouragement on the direction our mags are taking. Much as every single writer in the Bullpen admires Stan's work— and still looks to it for inspiration— our expansion was bound to mean diversification in style, subject matter, and so on. We're convinced we're doing a good job, generally speaking. We can only hope that you and your fellow Marvelites agree. And, too, that you'll forgive us when we do blow an occasional issue. It happens. They can't all be gems. But if they're not, it isn't because we're not trying!

Dear Marvel,

I just finished THOR #222 and I enjoyed it very much. However, nothing is perfect, and good old Thor does have a fault. It is: wilt, thou, thee, verily, canst, and yon. A little of this is okay, but you make him sound like a 17th century Puritan.

Richard McCartney
Sherman Oaks, Ca.

Verily, Richard, dost thou sayest that Thor speaketh so elequently that thou canst not understandeth a word of it? If such be true, how manyeth of thy fellow Marvelites agree with thee? Shalt we asketh Thor to clammeth up on the thee's and thou's? Or do ye prefer it as 'tis? VOTETH, all ye who readeth these words! Let thy voice be heard! (And will somebody please send a translator over to tell us what we just said?!?)

Dear Marvel,

I have been reading your mags for years now, and I think they are great. BUT— whatever happened to: Mr. Hyde, the Cobra, the Tomorrow Man, the Grey Gargoyle, the Growing Man, the Enchantress, the Wrecker, the Destroyer, Mangog, Him (Warlock), the Thermal

Man, Surtur, the Demolisher, Ego-Prime, Mephisto, the Absorbing Man, Ulik, who made Thor's comic what it was?

And what happened to the Red Skull, Batroc, the Super-Adaptoid, the Exiles, Hydra, Baron Strucker, the Scorpion, the Eel, Viper, Porcupine, Plantman, Scarecrow, the Serpent Squad, and Modok and A.I.M. in CAPTAIN AMERICA?

The Lizard, Ka-Zar, the Prowler, the Sandman, Morbius, the Rhino, Kraven, the Gibbon, the Vulture in SPIDER-MAN? Diablo, Mole Man, the Frightful Four, Sub-Mariner, Blastaar, the Sentry, the Mad Thinker, the Puppet Master, the Silver Surfer, Maximus, the Skrulls, Galactus, Dragon Man in FANTASTIC FOUR?

Do you get what I'm driving at?

Daryl Jackson
420-46-4141
71st Aux. Co. (AH)
Box 198
A.P.O., N.Y. 09047

You want more romance in the books, right, Daryl?

Dear Marvel,

I have just finished reading THOR #222 and was compelled to write. In your letters section, you asked us to tell you what we thought of Marvel Comics. Because you asked for it, here it is:

Marvel Comics is number one in my book and always will be. I've been reading your mags since I was four years old. I'm sixteen now, and I'll be reading them until I'm ninety-six, if I live that long.

You fellas at Marvel have provided me with many, many hours and years of reading pleasure, and I'll never forget it. Maybe I'm getting too serious, but *I believe in comics.*

Before I close, I would like to put in two requests: (1) Ever since Doc Strange came out again, I hoped he would meet Dracula. (2) Bring back the Silver Surfer.

Thanks for listening.

Stephen Mac Donald
Stellarton, N.S.
Canada

There is simply no answer to a statement as clear and forthright as "I believe in comics", Stephen. So we won't even attempt one.

We'll just say thanks. And thanks again.

Till next ish, group, remember this old Asgardian saying: two berserk trolls in the bush are worth three on the open market.

MARVEL VALUE STAMP

FOR THIS ISSUE!

CLIP 'EM AND COLLECT 'EM!

OPPOSITE **58: THE MANDARIN** from *Thor* no. 226 (August 1974). Stamp also appears in *Amazing Adventures* no. 24 (May 1974) and *The Incredible Hulk* no. 184 (February 1975).

ABOVE *The Incredible Hulk* no. 107 (September 1968), art by Marie Severin and Frank Giacoia, redrawn by John Romita Sr. The artwork that appears on the stamp is the original cover art by Severin and Giacoia and would later appear on the cover of *Marvel Super-Heroes* no. 61 (November 1976).

children of today would realize that nudity is a natural state, not something to drool over as the children of yesterday do now as adults.

Mike Shonk
1621 S. Park
Gonzales, La. 76737

Nudity in comics has never appealed to me. I don't think I'd like the idea of having to show an I.D. before I buy a comic book. If things come to that point, I'll have to go five years without comics. So please keep nudity out of your books, not just for me, but for all your readers who are minors.

Lloyd Hemingway
3026 Exchange
Wichita, Kans. 67217

Our world and society of today have seen enough lies and fakery to last us a lifetime. A love scene between two of your characters, done with the taste and grace that I know Marvel can accomplish, would be beautiful.

Michael Arndt
412 E. Olive St.
Decatur, Ill. 62526

I have one reservation about nudity in comics. I realize that the controversy in HULK centers around a specific example, but still, the discussion seems to be about *female* nudity rather than nudity in general. The female body is beautiful, the male body is beautiful— the *human* body is beautiful: it isn't a matter of gender. If you have nudity applying only to women, if you draw a sharp distinction between male and female nudity, you may be reinforcing artificial distinctions which can be quite harmful.

Adrienne Fein
26 Oakwood Ave.
White Plains, N.Y. 10605

Before making any statements of our own on this question, we feel we do have to clear up one point in reference to Joel West's letter:

Absolutely none of our readers, Joel, have said they "want bareness" in our magazines. Rather, the tone of the mail has been simply that they don't wish for us to *avoid* nudity when it seems a natural part of a specific story. There's a tremendous distinction there, and we can only hope you understand it. If a hundred issues went by without a single instance in which nudity would be appropriate, we suspect that not one reader would object—whereas, it seems, many more than we suspected *would* be annoyed if we purposefully copped out on showing a nude figure when there was a logical reason to do so.

All of which forces us to conclude that a sizable portion of our "young" readership (as opposed to the "adult" readership of more conventional mags) may just hold a far more mature— or at least, more liberal— position on this question than does our society in general.

It's weird, folks. We expected to be swamped with piles of letters expressing utter outrage at our even raising the question for discussion. That didn't happen.

Nor did any of the pro-nudity letters we received seem to wish for its inclusion on a sensationalistic basis.

What most of you seemed to be saying was, in effect, that you just wanted us to be more honest and maybe a little more liberated.

And that gives us food for thought, friends.

No, we're not going to make any major policy changes just yet, because we strongly suspect that this batch of comments is going to elicit yet another storm of controversy, and we want to read those letters, too.

So if you haven't expressed your views yet— WRITE!! Now! No matter what some people may say, silence on the part of the people is the very antithesis of democracy.

See you next ish!

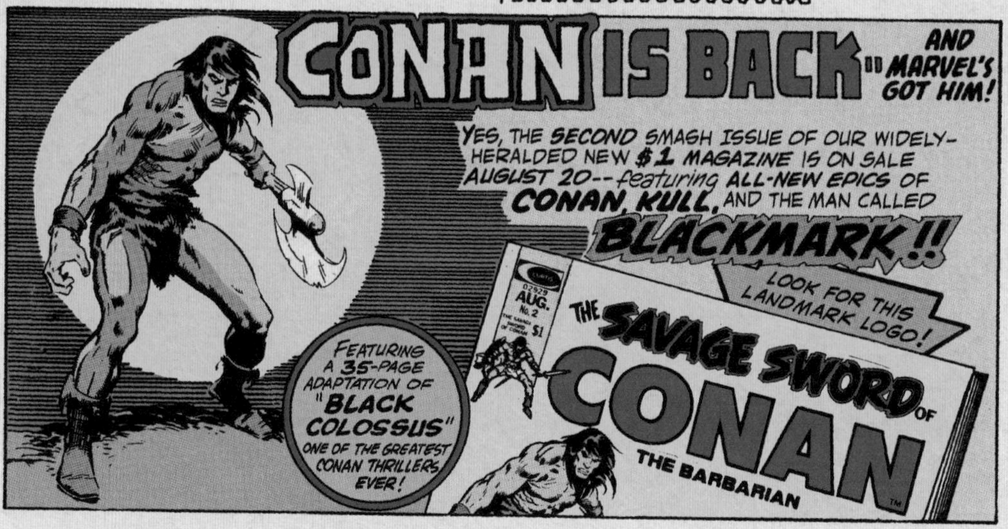

CONAN IS BACK AND MARVEL'S GOT HIM!
YES, THE SECOND SMASH ISSUE OF OUR WIDELY-HERALDED NEW $1 MAGAZINE IS ON SALE AUGUST 20-- featuring ALL-NEW EPICS OF CONAN, KULL, AND THE MAN CALLED BLACKMARK!!
LOOK FOR THIS LANDMARK LOGO!
AUG. No. 2
$1
THE SAVAGE SWORD OF CONAN THE BARBARIAN
FEATURING A 35-PAGE ADAPTATION OF "BLACK COLOSSUS" ONE OF THE GREATEST CONAN THRILLERS EVER!

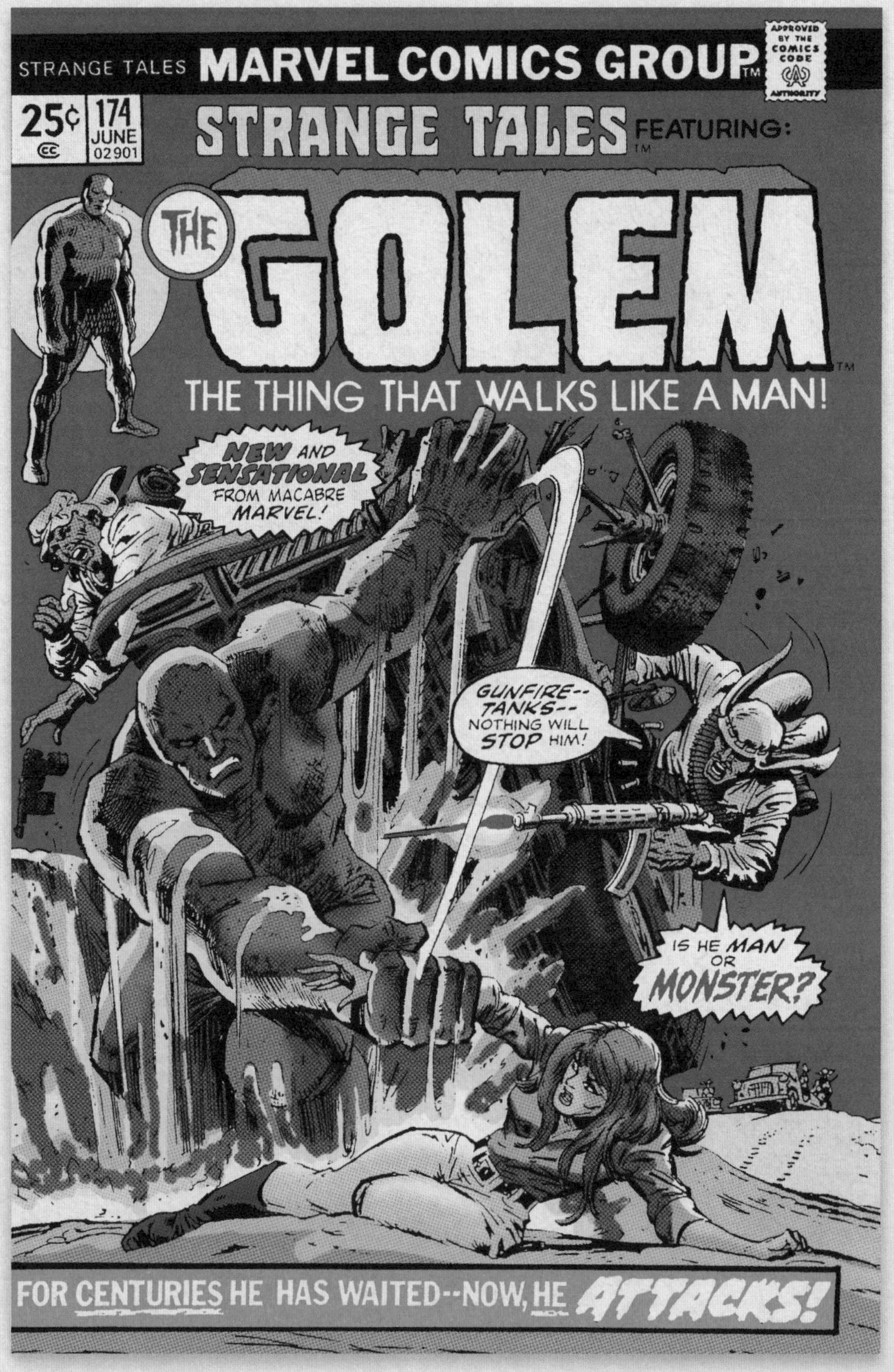

OPPOSITE **59: THE GOLEM** from *The Incredible Hulk* no. 182 (December 1974). Stamp also appears in *Frankenstein* no. 12 (September 1974).

ABOVE *Strange Tales* no. 174 (June 1974), by Gil Kane and unknown; upper-left corner art by unknown.

movie version. He makes the head square, and the face too smooth. It's just not ugly enough as we're used to from Ploog's and Buscema's versions. If Bob tries to make the face more like Ploog's, I'm sure he could handle the strip better.

Thanks for listening.

Fred Wienke
7 West Fairchild
Danville, Ill. 61832

Dear Marvel,

I am a Frankenstein fan from 'way back, and I would like to present some facts about the Monster. First, the Monster's name in Mary W. Shelley's novel was "Adam." And another thing I must point out is that the Monster's— or Adam's— skin is yellow and his hair black. I do not see why you have not gone strictly by the book. I know I would like to see him in his true colors.

By the way, Mr. Brown, your new ghoul in monster art, is a genius for making the Monster look more like Mr. William (Boris Karloff). Don't ever lose a good artist like Mr. Brown.

Edward Tarver
(no address given)

Dear Marvel,

Well, I've now seen Bob Brown's debut on FRANKENSTEIN in ish #11. I like Bob on DAREDEVIL. I liked what he did on THE AVENGERS. Unfortunately, I don't like him on FRANKIE. He still draws the Monster in the Buscema style. I almost thought it was another Buscema issue, until I looked at the credits.

Couldn't you come up with a totally new look on this magazine? Get someone with a different style and a fresh outlook on the Monster to draw the mag. Someone like Val Mayerik (who did the Monster in a recent MONSTERS UNLEASHED), Klaus Janson, Al Milgrom, or Dave Cockrum!

Keep your electrodes on straight, and don't grunt when people ask you a question!

Brian Wilkes Prescott
132 Bonair Avenue
W. Springfield, Mass. 01089

We hope all you folks at home were reading the previous four letters carefully, 'cause we're about to make one of those brilliant points, those masterpieces of insight, we're so famous for.

WE CAN'T PLEASE EVERYBODY!!

Here we have Greg Beeman who thinks the art is "good again" in T.F.M. #11, thanks to Bob Brown...followed by Fred Wienke, who dislikes Bob's version because it comes too close to the movie version...followed by Edward Tarver, who applauds Bob's work precisely because it was closer to the Karloff look...followed by Brian Prescott, who thinks Bob is great on DAREDEVIL but all wrong for FRANKENSTEIN.

If we weren't so cool, calm, collected and basically good-natured, we'd scream at all of you to go away and let us alone, while we jump out the window!!

Seriously, though (who was kidding?), for some reason we've been utterly unable to get any sort of consensus on who ought to draw FRANKENSTEIN, what style the artist should employ, whether we should have him appear more human or more monsterish, whether we should go for something closer to the movie version...and so on, *ad infinitum*. Nobody seems to agree on anything. It's enough to drive a Bullpen berserk in the mind!

Which is why we're settling back comfortably, stretching, and calmly, cooly, collectedly, and basically good-naturedly awaiting your response to this issue...to our updating of the saga of the Monster...to Val Mayerik's artwork...to Doug Moench's scripting.

We prefer to space our traumas at sixty-day intervals.

'Nuff said. Arrgh.

CONAN IS BACK
AND MARVEL'S GOT HIM!
YES, THE SECOND SMASH ISSUE OF OUR WIDELY-HERALDED NEW $1 MAGAZINE IS ON SALE AUGUST 20-- featuring ALL-NEW EPICS OF CONAN, KULL, AND THE MAN CALLED BLACKMARK!!
LOOK FOR THIS LANDMARK LOGO!
AUG.
No. 2
THE SAVAGE SWORD OF CONAN THE BARBARIAN
FEATURING A 35-PAGE ADAPTATION OF "BLACK COLOSSUS" ONE OF THE GREATEST CONAN THRILLERS EVER!

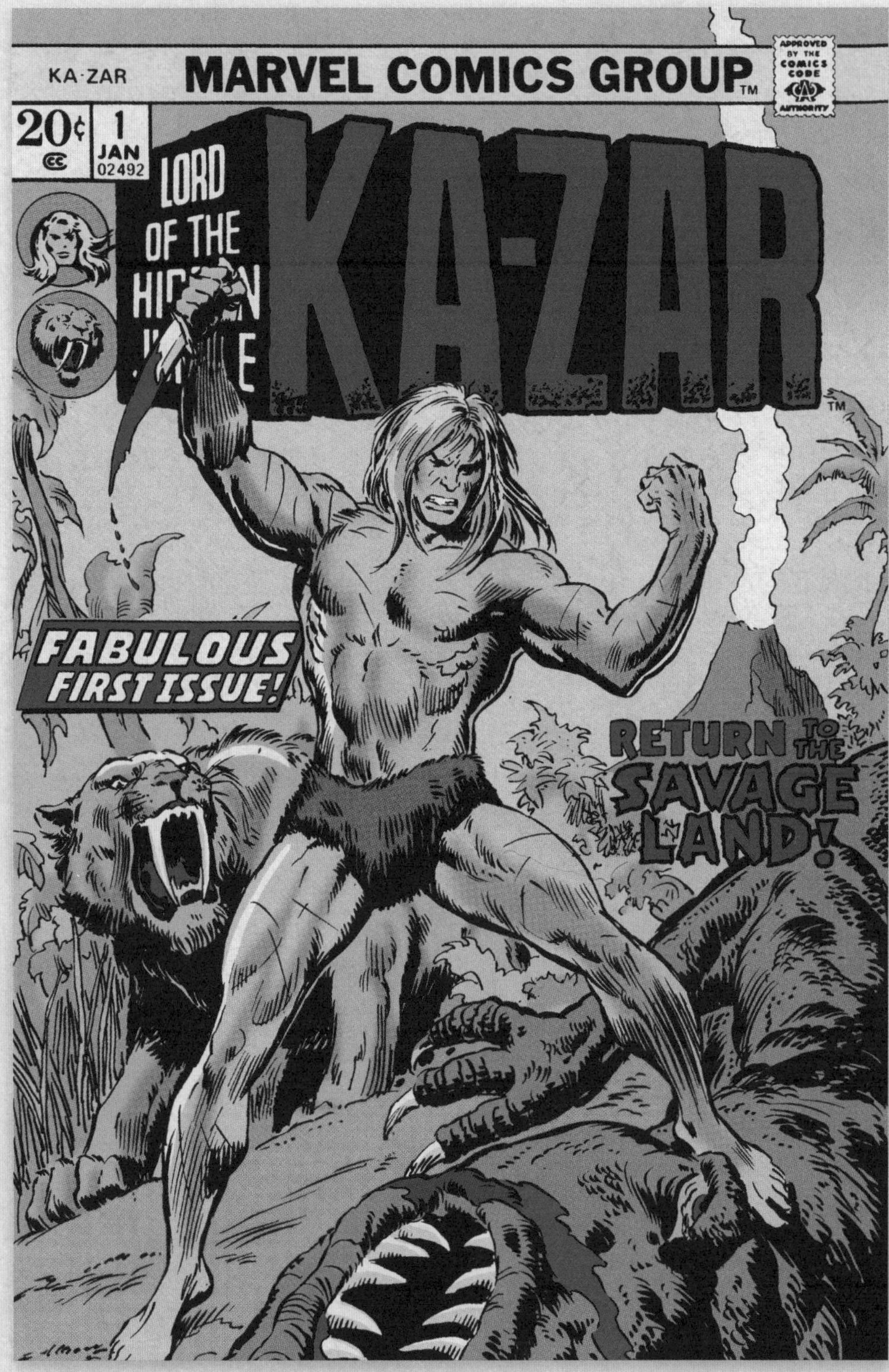

OPPOSITE **60: KA-ZAR** from *Frankenstein* no. 13 (November 1974). Stamp also appears in *Man-Thing* no. 3 (March 1974).

ABOVE *Ka-Zar* no. 1 (January 1974), art by John Buscema.

Dear Sal, Steve and Roy,

So after 76 issues of his own mag, CAPTAIN AMERICA is going to fold. It is very obvious that you guys would not drop a successful mag; and you know Captain America would not be quitting his secret identity if the mag was going well. Now, having Steve Rogers quit being Captain America is a subtle way of ending the magazine; very clever. I must say that it was one of my favorite comics, but I know economic reality, and if CA has to go, he has to go. We all know he said he was going to quit and we know Cap means it for real this time. We Marvelites know the BULLPEN would not rip us off by not having Cap really quit.

You can rename CAPTAIN AMERICA, THE FALCON. Still you can MAKE MINE MARVEL even without CAPTAIN AMERICA.

Thomas Graham
9380 Prichard Street
Bellflower, California 90706

Sorry, Tom, but this book is in no danger at all of cancellation. There have been times in the past when it was in trouble, but today it's one of Marvel's most healthy titles. So sit back and watch with the rest of us, Mr. G.—the best is yet to come!

Dear Steve, Sal, and Vinnie,

"Captain America Must Die!" is probably one of the most off-beat stories you'll ever publish, beating out even the HULK story published in 1971, in which the Green Goliath didn't appear. "Captain America Must Die!" had no real plot; it was just a recap of Cap's career. And that mini-recap on pp. 10 and 11 was almost as good as the whole story.

So, Captain America died.

My only plea is: don't cop out.

Don't all of a sudden decide that Cap was wrong, so he will once more take up his cowl. You showed us in this issue that Cap covered all the facets of the problem long and hard, that this was no spur-of-the-moment decision.

There are really only three things you can do with the mag from here on out that would be in any sort of good taste:

(1) discontinue it.
(2) retitle it THE FALCON.
(3) have someone other than Steve Rogers decide to become Captain America. It happened before; it can happen again.

As it is, I know that you guys have already decided what will happen to Cap. I hope you make the right decision.

Neal Meyer
Bickleton, Washington 99322

NEXT ISH: The 'Ncredible Nomad is joined by none other than the Avenging Son himself, Prince Namor, in a battle to the death with the sinister Serpent Squad smack dab in the middle of the wide, rolling seas—while Roscoe makes his debut as a Captain America back in New York. Does this spell the end for the Cap we used to know—or what? Find out next time, right here!

THIS IS IT! YOUR
MARVEL VALUE STAMP
FOR THIS ISSUE!
CLIP 'EM AND COLLECT 'EM!

WAR IS UGLIER THE SECOND TIME AROUND
--AS YOU'LL SEE FOR YOURSELF IN THE SECOND NERVE-NUMBING EPISODE OF THE MOST STARTLINGLY-DIFFERENT WAR SERIES OF ALL!
THE ACTION BURSTS UPON YOUR NEWS-STAND WHEN YOU SEE THIS CHILLING COVER-LOGO!
WAR IS HELL
MARVEL COMICS GROUP
25¢
10 DEC
WAR IS HELL
ON SALE SEPT. 24th

A GALLERY OF THE FANTASTIC FOUR'S MOST FAMOUS FOES!
THE RED GHOST AND HIS INDESCRIBABLE SUPER APES
FROM F.F. #13 APRIL
THE WARPED BRAIN OF THIS BROODING COMMUNIST SCIENTIST FIRST CONCEIVED THE IDEA OF MATCHING POWER FOR POWER WITH THE FANTASTIC FOUR BY SUBJECTING HIMSELF AND HIS TRIO OF TRAINED APES TO THE SAME COSMIC RAYS FROM WHICH THE FANTASTIC FOUR HAD DERIVED THEIR POWER! AND THEN, LOCKED IN MORTAL COMBAT, THERE WITHIN THE LOST CITY OF THE MOON, BOTH TEAMS OF SUPER-POWERFUL FOES HAD THEIR SHOWDOWN BATTLE... WITH THE FATE OF EARTH HANGING IN THE PRECARIOUS BALANCE!

OPPOSITE **61: THE RED GHOST** from *Captain America* no. 180 (December 1974). Stamp also appears in *Captain America* no. 173 (May 1974) and *Werewolf by Night* no. 19 (July 1974).

ABOVE *Fantastic Four Annual* no. 1 (September 1963), art by Jack Kirby and Sol Brodsky.

Since we've seen Steve's coloring skill, when do we see the penciling and inking we hear about two years ago? Fiawol!

K. J. Robbins
1314 Cooper Street
Missoula, MT 59801

Hard to say, K.J. It's been so long since Steve used a pencil for anything other than indicating where the balloons should go, he's gotten completely out of practice. Maybe someday...

The murder charge, now, is only a minor facet of this strip. You've probably noticed that it's faded into the background during the past two issues, and it's always been Steve's intention to have Sir Denis, who must have brought the charges after Petrie's death, use his influence to have them quashed. The future scripter will probably work that out for you.

(Incidentally, that scene in the construction pit that turned you on, K.J., is an actual place in lower Manhattan. The entire plot of our second story came into being one night last spring when Steve, Jim, Al Weiss and Al Milgrom were wandering through the city on an evening of revelry. When they stumbled upon the pit (after spending a few hours in lower Manhattan, which all looks like a '30's movie set of New York), the story just leapt into life.

Dear Marvel Editors,

The first issue of "Master of Kung-Fu" was well done and far, far better than the other current martial arts mag—Yang—which is a poor adaptation of TV's Kung-Fu. Just a few comments and suggestions.

1. Be careful of the racism that pervaded Rohmer's books. Making Shang-Chi the hero is a good start. Also making it clear that Fu Manch couldn't operate in the People's Republic was a good swipe at anti-communists who might well see Fu as the incarnation of the Red and Yellow Peril together.

2. You should also be able with this mag to get into the whole Chinese-American scene. If you do that seriously, in your own way, of course, this mag could have important social significance. For example, putting Fu Manchu among (but not behind) the Chinatown sweat shop businessmen who exploit recent women immigrants who can't speak English, etc. You can do this kind of thing well when you put your mind to it; ie, one of the SPIDER-MAN episodes gave a critical look at the conditions behind prison riots, and MAN-THING concerns ecology.

3. On the drawings of the fight scenes: have Starlin study the Kung-Fu literature so taht he draws Shang-Chi using real Kung-Fu styles and not something obviously different. Also, try to have fight sequences follow logically. For example, the last pic on p. 2 shows the position of the attacker as one from which he couldn't possibly get to his position in the first pic on p. 3, although Shang-Chi could have. Also, the fight scenes with Tak begin well but then have the same problem. Do it right and you will pick up the martial arts crowd as readers.

I am looking forward to the next issue of this mag. Good Luck.

Harry Cleaver
Professor of Economics
Universit'e De Sherbrooke
Sherbrooke, Que.

Prof, you touched on a good point in your letter. The epithets that issued from the mouths of Sir Denis and others in the early issues, such as "yellow devil" and so on, were used because they were part of the Fu Manchu mystique. Both Nayland Smith and the devil doctor stood four-square behind their particular ethnic backgrounds, having very little of a pleasant nature to say about each other's cultures, during their decades-long war, and it was decided to touch on that in the introductory episodes. But Sir Denis, at least, is getting his consciousness raised at a fast clip by the events he's experiencing these days.

Dear Marvel,

I must compliment you on your fine new series, "Master of Kung Fu." It was the finest first issue I have seen in ages. However, it is only a matter of time before Shang-Chi is destroyed. Surely Fu Manchu has figured out that the surest way to render a Karate expert helpless is to throw huge quantities of Jello at him. He might split the glob in two but it will hit him none-the-less, dulling his senses and messing up his clothes. You will then have to call the strip ' Fu Manchu, Master of Jello". I think there is a great future in food oriented comics. "The Agricultural Four," "Tales Of The Uncanned,""Sgt. Turnip And His Growing Vegetable," "The Chopped Liver Kid, Outlaw," "Conan The Vegetarian," and "Pot Roast By Night."

Gringo

We don't think you're taking this thing seriously, Gring.

Dear Steve, Jim, Al, Roy, Tom, & Linda,

This is my third letter to Marvel, all within the recent months. And considering the fact that I've been a Marvel freak ever since the dawn of super-hero mags under that banner, something pretty far-out must've gotten into my head to make this letter happen. The second Marvel Age of "Keep you on the edge of your seats" magic is here.

"Shang-Chi, Master of Kung-Fu" #2 in SPECIAL-MARVEL-EDITION #16 has recaptured that magic. I haven't felt such tense excitement since I hid from the Sandman with Spidey behind the garbage cans in some New York alley way back...well, way back there somewhere.

The character of Midnight was so fantastically complete for a one-issue introduction. And the battle sequences remind me of Steve Ditko's Spidey bouncing back and forth off of Doc Ock's men. I hope we see more detailed and carefully worked out scenes such as these in all the Marvel mags. This has been a true missing factor in the new Marvel Age, probably because of so many anti-violence crusades. An all-out battle issue between two equal opponents on the dark streets of New York! All I can say is thanks.

And even if the Thing teams up with Patsy and Hedy in MARVEL TWO-IN-ONE, I'll always "Make Mine Marvel!"

F. A. Yanero
F.O.O.M. Member
903 4th St. APT. 3
Fairmont, West Va. 26554

Dear Stan, Roy, Steve, Jim, Al & Tom,

"Missives to the Master" is going to be very boring indeed. I mean, a whole page of praise and nothing else?!...

Kim Thompson, president of the
Let's-See-How-Long-You'll-Keep-Steve-Jim-And Al-On
The-Mag-Hopefully-Forever Club
Gen Del Box250
APO NY NY 09184

P.S. Is Jim Starlin the reincarnation of Steranko? I hope not. 'Cause that would mean....

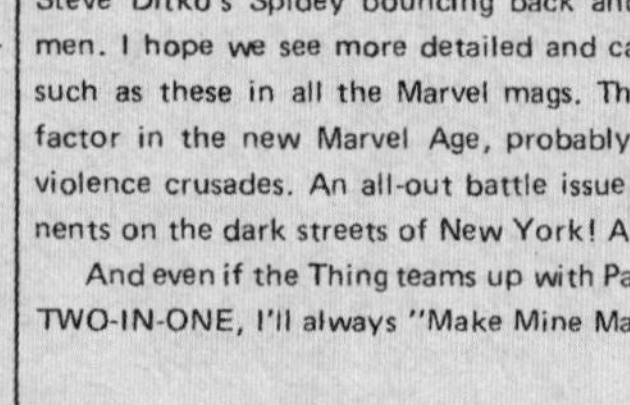

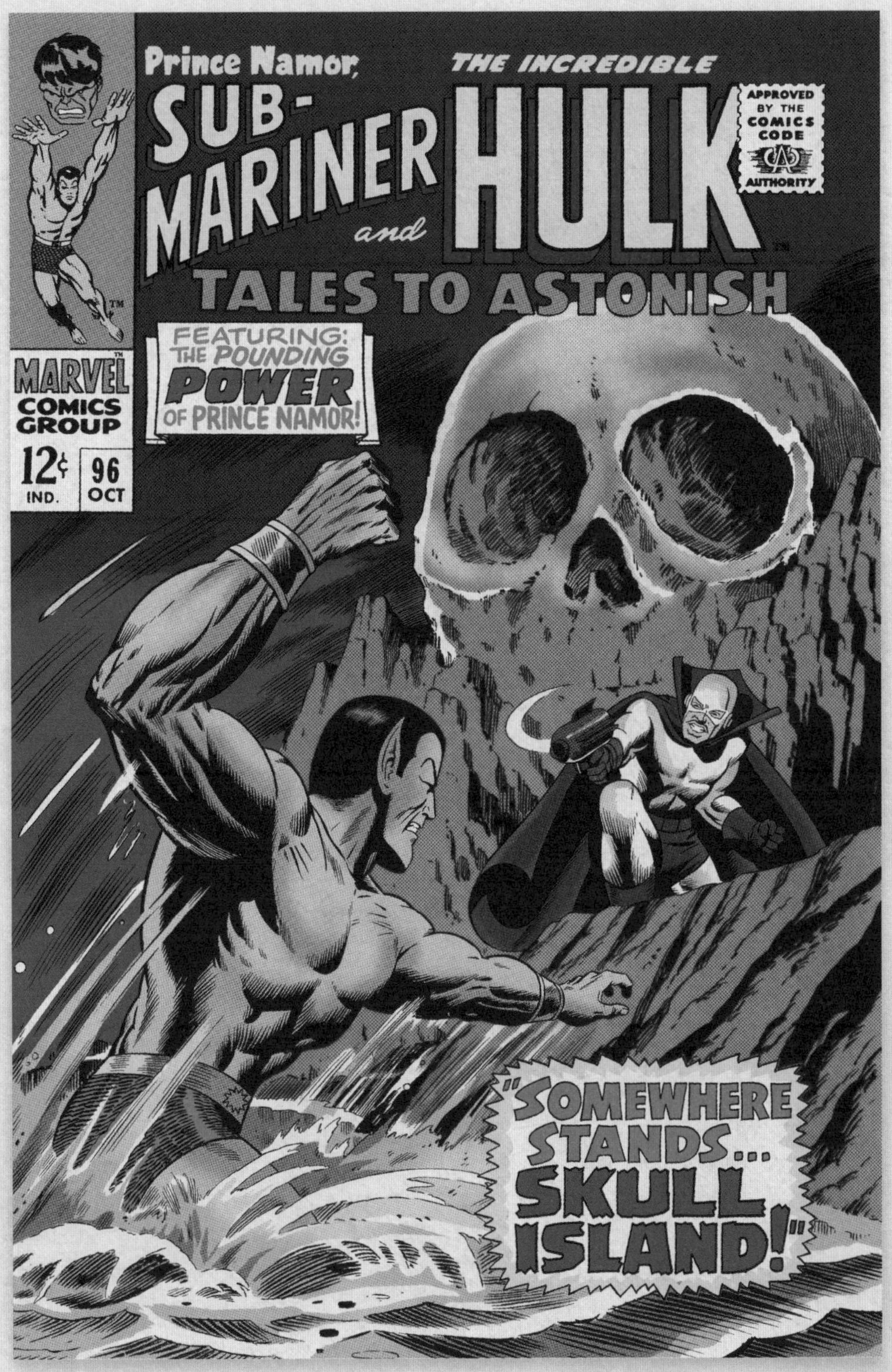

OPPOSITE **62: THE PLUNDERER** from *Master of Kung Fu* no. 18 (June 1974). Stamp also appears in *Master of Kung Fu* no. 21 (October 1974) and *Fantastic Four* no. 153 (December 1974).

ABOVE *Tales to Astonish* no. 96 (October 1967), art by Dan Adkins.

indeed his strengths and weaknesses as the protagonist of a comic book. And so many of Anne's ideas parallel the conclusions we've reached over the past few months...!

Re: Daredevil's character. Right on the button! A man who's seen more than most people, even more than most people, even more than most superheroes, despite his blindness— a crusader by nature, but one who realizes his human limitations— a man who'll tempt fate, laugh in the face of fear, risk anything for his cause— but who knows, deep in his heart, that eventually it's all gonna catch up to him!

Re: villains. Again, Anne, you score one hundred per cent! Weird types. Bizarre and haunting types. But not gods of the Terrex variety. Eerie more-than-humans like the Owl, Electro, the Purple Man, the Jester, the Gladiator— all of whom are slated for early reappearances.

Re: the tone of the magazine. Precisely! Over the last few issues, Steve has been working toward formulating a certain mood and feel for the book, something to set it apart from other superhero mags and give it a distinct flavor all its own. Wait'll you see next issue!

And we could go on and on. But we'll stop here, let you mull over our comments and Anne's, and say, simply, that we predict DAREDEVIL is going to be *the* surprise superhero mag of 1974. And it's mostly due to the incredible way you people have responded to our call for insights, criticism, and praise when you think we do well.

There's no sense getting mushy, gang, but we want to thank each and every one of you who took the time and trouble and thought to let us know what you were thinking. And Steve and Bob— not to mention Roy and Stan— hereby promise not to let you down in the months ahead. We know where we're headed now...but we're still depending on *you* to tell us where we hit and where we miss.

Whatever else you don't do— don't stop writing! We read each and every letter; we take all your ideas, even the wildest, weirdest ones, into consideration. So, please, group, don't fail us now!

'Nuff said! Onward to some more of your mail!

Dear Bullpen,

Mark Stevens in DAREDEVIL #109 suggests you get rid of Black Widow. You'd better not. She's the reason I read the mag again. I dropped DD years ago, but BW aroused my curiousity. I think DD is great with her. If she goes, I go. Also, Bob Brown is good for the artwork, but replace Don Heck as inker. Finally, if I'm going to pay 25¢ for a mag, I want *two* superheroes for the price of one.

Rether Denscott
219 Williams St.
Hammond, Ind. 46320

The DD/BW romance is still up in the air, Rether, There'll be some new developments in that regard next issue. And even though Natasha doesn't play a major role in DAREDEVIL # 113, we can guarantee you'll still be getting your money's worth: Daredevil. The return of an old villain. The introduction of a very bizarre new villain. And the last guest-star you ever expected to see in this mag!

And that's about all we have room for this time around Remember, though, join us again in thirty days for what we think is going to be one of the most unusual Daredevil sagas in some time.

Keep thy billy club polished! Tamam shud!

THIS IS IT! YOUR
MARVEL VALUE STAMP
FOR THIS ISSUE!
CLIP 'EM AND COLLECT 'EM!

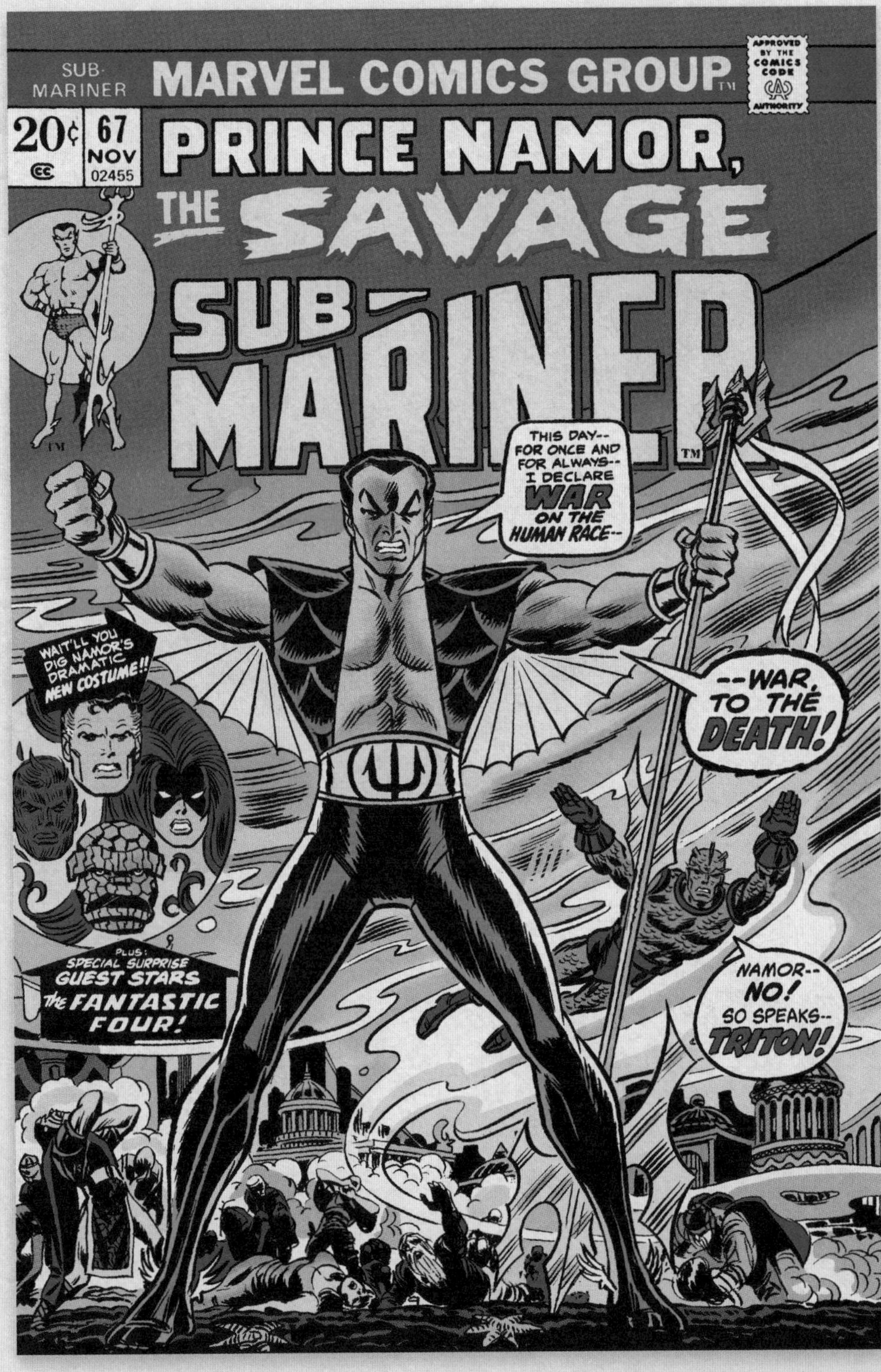

OPPOSITE **63: THE SUB-MARINER** from *Daredevil* no. 112 (August 1974). Stamp also appears in *Marvel Two-in-One* no. 2 (March 1974), *Werewolf by Night* no. 25 (January 1975), and *Iron Fist* no. 1 (November 1975).

ABOVE *Sub-Mariner* no. 67 (November 1973), art by John Romita Sr.

Dear Bullpen,

Luke Cage...Powerman! Englehart replaced by Wein! Ethnic dialogue to be played down! Billy Graham may leave art chores! Thus speak the new zines about future developments for LUKE CAGE, HERO FOR HIRE. If these items are indeed accurate, I can only say "Great!".

Mighty Marvel has done it again! HERO FOR HIRE always seemed like such an oddball title—such a strange unusual concept. POWERMAN—now there's a great, typical superhero title. It really sounds like a Marvel superhero—Spider-Man, Iron Man, Ant-Man, Iceman, and now...Powerman.

I hope that dull Hero for Hire concept goes, too. It's too offbeat. Maybe Dr. Burstein can be killed by crooks, and Cage can vow on his grave to devote his life to the bringing to justice of all those foul fiends that prey on an innocent society (lightning flashing). He can start off with the Mandarin, A.I.M., Dr. Doom (again), Ego, and Galactus.

Thank Goodness that jive dialogue is going! It made Cage too unique and individual. In the past, his atrocious language made you think he came from Watts or Harlem—I mean, who can identify with that? Englehart was the worst thing that ever happened to Cage, with his reliance on tight characterization, dialogue, plot, and pacing, rather than that old Marvel staple, Action.

As for Billy Graham leaving—I certainly hope so. But why stop there? Get rid of Tuska, too. They gave the strip too much personality.

(The letter goes on to suggest such things as a Powergirl and Sparky the Powerdog...but you get the idea).

Michael Gilbert
40 Pinewood Dr.
Commack, N.Y. 11725

To paraphrase Rascally Roy's comments on the letters bemoaning Barry Smith's first adieu to CONAN...if they make it look as if Marveldom Assembled is just a wee bit fond of HERO FOR HIRE—well, so be it!

But those letters were written in the heat of anger before the new team had a chance to strut its stuff on CONAN, and so it is here. If you picked up POWERMAN # 17, you saw that Luke hasn't really changed his job; and that Len Wein, certainly one of comics' most respected writers, is now behind the typewriter; and that Billy Graham remains intact. So, we trust, does Luke Cage—and we'll see what Marveldom Assembled had to say about the changes after they saw them in our next letters column.

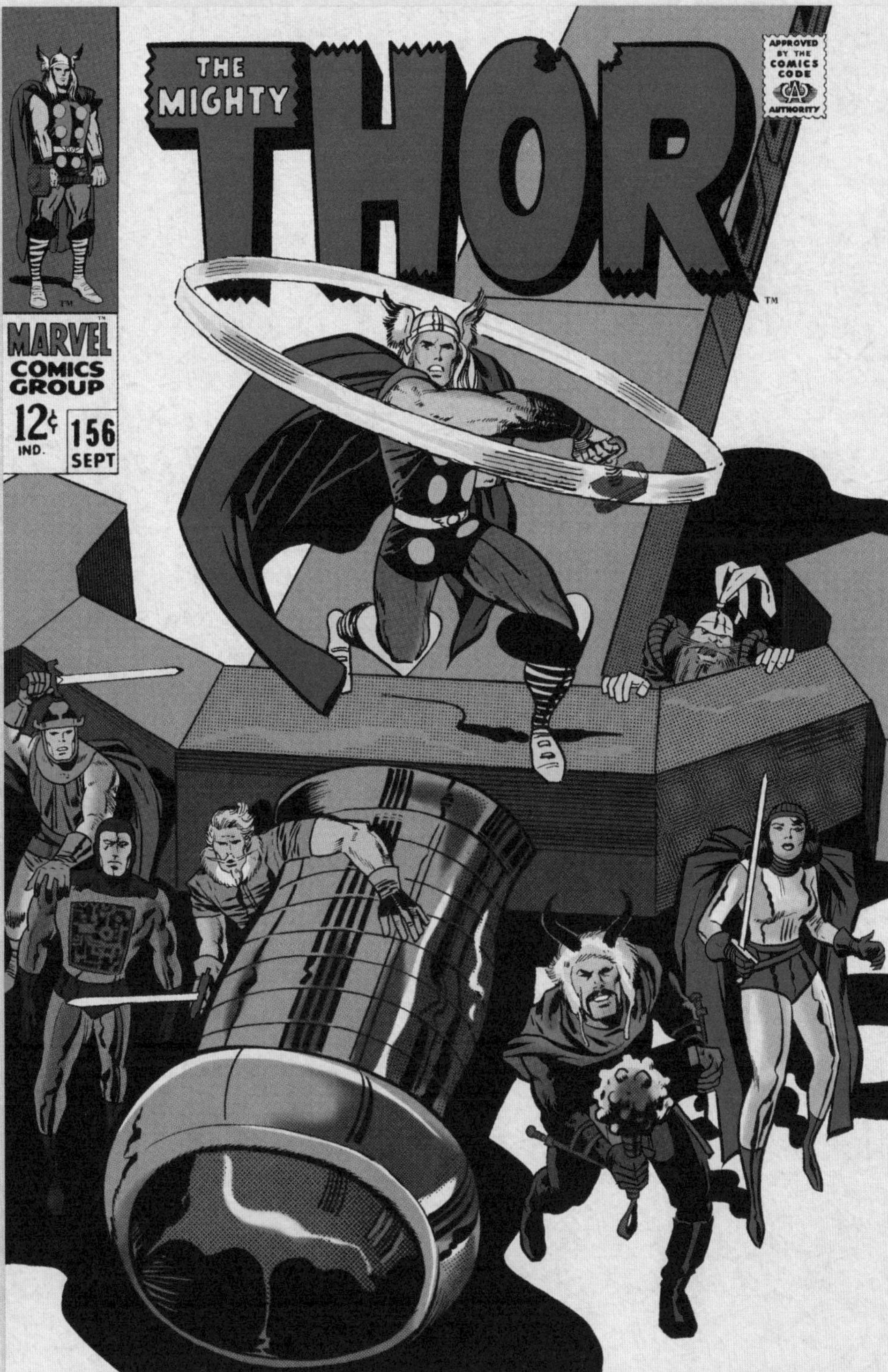

OPPOSITE **64: SIF** from *Power Man* no. 19 (June 1974). Stamp also appears in *Man-Thing* no. 14 (February 1975).

ABOVE *Thor* no. 156 (September 1968), art by Jack Kirby and Vince Colletta

WEREMAIL BY NIGHT

ADDRESS YOUR LETTERS TO:
THE MARVEL COMICS GROUP, SIXTH FLOOR
575 MADISON AVE.,
NEW YORK, N. Y. 10022

Friends of Ol' Marvel,

The time has come! I've been a Marvelite for over ten years, and I've only written to you once, about nine years ago. But the silent enjoyment of your books has come to an end.. I must express my joy!

WEREWOLF BY NIGHT #11 & 12 were two of your best issues yet in the WEREWOLF series.

Marv Wolfman is becoming one of your best scripters, and his "Hangman" two-parter was exciting and action-packed from cover to cover, And wow, did Gil Kane and Tom Sutton and Don Perlin do a fantastic job on the art. I thought Mike Ploog's great work on your early issues could never be matched, but Kane has brought that ghoulishly wolfish flair back to the strip. I wonder sometimes how I could not have liked Gil's early Marvel work. His WARLOCK was superb, also. Keep him under the full moon.

Beware, Marvel, my years of silence have ended. Your books give me too much enjoyment to contain. It must and will come out. When you please, I'll let you know. And when you aggravate, you'll know that, too. So, face front!

Peter Crescenti
Bay Shore, N.Y.

We never face any other way, Pete. Frankly, we're paranoid...we figure somebody's after us... but we're too chicken to look over our shoulder and see who (or what) it is. In any event, we applaud your decision to write us, and we hope other readers will be thus inspired by your example. You know, we really do read all these nutty letters!

Anyway, Marv, Gil, Tom, and Don wish to express their heartfelt thanks for the warm reception you gave the "Hangman" stories. They're among Marv's favorites of his Marvel work so far. (Now, if he'd just quit writing fan letters to himself and get to work on the next TOMB OF DRACULA...!)

Dear Marv, Gil, and Tom,

I have been waiting, and at last it's come to pass. Wolfman writing WEREWOLF has been my desire since I first glimpsed Marv's writing (which, unfortunately, has only been recently). Marv has become one of my four favorite writers in just a very short period.

WEREWOLF BY NIGHT #11 was controversial, to say the least. The characterization of Jack's stepfather were MARVelous. Gil is one of my favorite artists and Tom, one of my favorite inkers.

You must keep Gil on WEREWOLF BY NIGHT. He's perfect for the strip. You could take him off covers and have him do only WEREWOLF and SPIDER-MAN.

Speaking of SPIDER-MAN, Jack is more like Peter Parker now than ever.

Marv is the best supernatural writer you have, so he must stay on. And Sutton has the WEREWOLF style. I'd say you have yourselves a winning combination.

FOOMer, P.M.M. Earl Loudenslager
Hwy. 7 N.
Pelsor, Ark. 72856

Uh-oh.

As you've no doubt noticed by now, Earl, Marv has had to leave the WEREWOLF strip, since the love of his life, CRAZY Magazine, which he edits, has been stepped up to eight times a year. (Or is it seven? Oh, well...it's more than six! That much we know.)

But he's left the scripting in the capable hands of Iron Man's best friend, Mike Friedrich. And we think we've got an artist on W.B.N. this issue who more or less has the WEREWOLF style down pat. (Agreed?)

Let us know what you think of this new combination—though chances are, we''ll have changed it by the time we hear from ya! (No, that's not meant as sarcasm. It's just that sometimes we get confused ourselves by all the author/artist switches on our mags. In fact, now that we think about it, which letters page is this? Who are we? Where are we? What year is it? What planet...etc., etc.)

Dear Wolfpen,

Please keep Tom Sutton on this strip, if he's available for anything. 'Nuff said.

Again and again, I've had to admire the device of "the forest" in the Werewolf's thoughts. I've never seen a fusion of innocence and savagery so clearly put across in comics. And when it's illustrated by Tom, with those nostrils, gums, and teeth...egad! Exactly the shot in the arm that the moth-eaten image of werewolfery needs.

Keep snarling.

Jonathan Burns
23 Lee Man Park
Raub, Pahang, Maylaysia

Unfortunately, Jon, Tom isn't available right now. But you can rest assured that if you're gonna take the time and trouble to drop us a line all the way from Maylaysia, we're gonna go all out to make each ish of W.B.N. better than its predecessor— no matter who's drawing it!

Dear Marvel,

I have been recently reading WEREWOLF BY NIGHT. I am not going to make this a long letter, so I'll get right down to it. I think you should make one improvement. In every issue of W.B.N., you have Jack narrate the story. I think this is wrong, because when Werewolf is in a jam, we know in advance he's going to get out of it, because Jack is telling the story.

Richard Nonn
(no address given)

Interesting point, Rich. And though we've never received criticism on it before — and though we ourselves would like to maintain the first-person narration, if only for its uniqueness— we're open to comment and controversy on this question. Opinions, people?

OPPOSITE 65: ICEMAN from *Werewolf by Night* no. 16 (April 1974). Stamp also appears in *Creatures on the Loose* no. 30 (July 1974).

ABOVE *The Amazing Spider-Man* no. 92 (January 1971), art by John Romita Sr.

Jackie is actually much more sinister in some ways, and definitely far less noble than Gobby ever was.

Mike: If you liked Midnight Dancers, don't fail to pick up on Gerry's latest sci-fi novel, Mindship, which should be on sale now in paperback from DAW Books. And, yes, the Punisher will be back— and very possibly in a strip all his own. No definite word yet, though. Ross and Gerry thank you for the good words.

Amos: Don't leap to any hasty conclusions about what face is hidden behind the Jackal's mask. It could be Harry, true. Or it could be someone we've never met before. For that matter, it could be Howard the Duck! One thing we will tell you: when you do find out who Jackie really is, it'll be the shock of your comics-reading life.

Dear Marvel,

I have found that there is at least one Marvel character for each letter of the alphabet: Ant-Man, Black Widow, Captain America, Daredevil, Electro, Falcon, Goliath, Hulk, Iron Man, Jonah Jameson, Kraven the Hunter, Lizard, Mar-Vell, Namor, Otto Octavius, Prowler, Quicksilver, Rhino, Spider-Man, Thor, Ulik, Vision, Warlock, Xorr, Yildiz, Zzzax. I challenge any Marvelite to come up with a list of completely different names.

Jody Hall
Bellflower, Ca.

Hmmmm, Arkon, Betty Brant, Conan, Dr. Doom, Eon, Fandral, Giant-Man, Hawkeye, Invisible Girl, Jackal, Killraven, Luke Cage, Man-Thing, Norman Osborn, Odin, Pepper Hogan, Quincy Harker, Reed Richards, Son of Satan, Thanos, Umbu the Unliving (!), Victorius, Wundarr, X-Men, Yellowjacket, Zartra. (We can't resist a challenge.)

Gentlemen,

I think I like the way you are handling the SPIDER-MAN magazine. I say "think" because it's a rare occasion when I am able to find SPIDER-MAN in Bowling Green. If it weren't for the numerous explanatory notes throughout the magazine, I'd be completely at a loss as to what was going on. But suffice it to say I enjoyed #129 very much.

Mr. Conway wrote a very good story this issue. The Punisher character particularly impressed me, because he is not the usual cold-blooded, totally evil villain. Instead, he was a human being, with human emotions and human frailties. He was so caught up in self-righteous indignation against the evil which he thought Spider-Man committed, that he was unable to see the true evil in the Jackal. After reading this story, I thought about all the times I'd ever judged a person hastily, without knowing all the facts.

As for the regular characters, I almost feel that I know them from the real world. J. Jonah Jameson— so caught up in his work he has no time for anything or anyone else; Mary Jane— so intent on having a good time she doesn't care for anyone but herself; and of course, Peter Parker— torn between the rigors of being a superhero and those of being human.

This is what I consider to be very good writing. And coupled with Ross Andru's action-packed artwork, those are two big reasons why I liked SPIDER-MAN #129 and why I wish I could find the magazine more often.

Brian Schuck
Bowling Green, Ohio

Thanks much for the obviously heartfelt words of praise, Brian. We appreciate it.

But there's no need for you to wonder from month to month whether you'll be able to find the current SPIDER-MAN. If no store in your area carries the mag regularly, why not subscribe to SPIDEY— and your other favorite Marvel mags, too? All the information you need to get a subscription is contained in the small print beneath the title page of each magazine. Check it out. (And we'll do our part and check out the distribution situation in your area.)

And that's it for this month's Spider's Web, gang. We'll, be back again in thirty days— and we hope you will, too. Meanwhile, don't forget you can also enjoy Spidey, and a different guest-star each issue, every month in MARVEL TEAM-UP. And don't forget what they say around the water cooler at the Daily Bugle: the solution to the energy crisis is to harness that hot air that blasts from J.J.J.'s mouth.

OPPOSITE **66: GENERAL ROSS** from *The Amazing Spider-Man* no. 133 (June 1974). Stamp also appears in *Astonishing Tales* no. 26 (October 1974) and *Ghost Rider* no. 11 (April 1975).

ABOVE *The Incredible Hulk* no. 174 (April 1974), art by Herb Trimpe and Jack Abel.

The answer is: almost everybody! Jack Kirby drew the awesome origin tale as well as several issues after that. Steve Ditko was Jack's immediate successor. And Steve, in turn, was followed by such talents as Gil Kane, John Buscema, Bill Everett, Marie Severin, and a host of others. At one time or another, almost every artist in the Bullpen has drawn the HULK strip. Herb Trimpe's first outing on the book was #106, and he's been at it ever since.

Dear Stan, Roy, Tony, Jack, and Herb,

Roy Thomas' return to an already-excellent mag made it even more so. Roy's plot was terrific, and Tony Isabella wrote a fine script. Roy's method of bringing the Juggernaut back into our present world was a brain-thrush. Finally, we see the appearance of some of the X-Men.

Herb Trimpe is the artist for the Hulk. Your artwork is really getting better, Herb! Not only are you putting out brilliant artwork in HULK, but also in SON OF SATAN and WAR OF THE WORLDS. Pages 17, 18, 26, and 31 of HULK #172 were astounding. As for Jack Abel's inks, they are suited perfectly for the pencils of Trimpe. I hope Jack and Frank Chiaramonte continue as Herb's inkers. Keep up the great work. Foom seeing ya.

Jackie Frost
Rt. 3, Box 176-C
West Monroe, La. 71291

Not if you see FOOM first, Jackie— or something like that.

Anyway, there've been a few changes (as usual) since HULK #172. Roy Thomas, overwhelmed once more by his editorial duties has had to relinquish the scripting reins on HULK to Gerry Conway. And Herb Trimpe, by choice, has left SON OF SATAN to Jim Mooney and will shortly be handing over WAR OF THE WORLDS to Rich Buckler.

But Herb just keeps pluggin' away at our Jolly Green Giant, and shows no sign of letting up. So, no matter what else changes, no matter how the universe reshuffles itslef, there will always be a Hulk, and there will always be a Herb, and chances are they'll be together. (Gee. That was almost poetic.)

Gentlemen,

HULK #172 was a little better. Not much, but better. Mr. Trimpe was as good as always. But the Hulk's ever-changing writing staff was a little off. The Hulk's rather distinct speech style was there, for a change, but there was a lot else missing.

Like credibility (hah— everyone turns into a Hulk when hit by gamma rays). I've seen people go to lengths to dredge up villains, but you did a four-star job this time. And then, after you go through the far-fetched maneuver of bringing Juggernaut back, he's defeated in two simple panels, by half the X-Men, no less.

Nevertheless, with all its faults, this issue was some of that good old Hulk-fun I've always enjoyed.

Onward!

Verde
103 Beech Dr.
Franklin, Pa. 16323

P.S.: Where's the letters page?

Right here, Verde. Both of it.

But about HULK #172, it lacked credibility, you say. The villain was defeated too easily, you say. But it was the kind of issue you've always enjoyed??

We think we're confused...we think.

Anyway, let us know how you think Gerry Conway is doing, handling the Incredible One's plots and dialogue these days, huh? (And we also heartily recommend, to those of you who enjoyed this issue, all the other Marvel mags the ubiquitous Mr. Conway authors— SPIDER-MAN, FANTASTIC FOUR, THOR, and SGT. FURY. And, too, Gerry has a new science fiction paperback on the stands these days. It's called Mindship— and he's called Gerard F. Conway on the cover— and it's published by DAW Books. Look for it at your neighborhood bookstore. And tell 'em Marvel turned you on to it.)

Dear Marvel Madmen,

I know little about art except what I like, so I can't give you any advice on it, but the storyline is something I do believe I know about. I just looked over the last ten issues of our green-skinned gremlin and noticed they really didn't show much of the Hulk's other side, Dr. Bruce Banner. Thinking back, he hasn't done much in quite a while.

Considering what Banner's problem is, I've been thinking about the strain this must put on his mind. I realize the title of the magazine is not "The Incredible Dr. Banner", but it would help if he had his own sub-plot, such as possibly getting in touch with someone who can help cure him.

I've also been thinking that if I had Banner's pressures on my mind, I'd go stark raving bananas. The good doctor's brain has little to do with that of the Hulk, so why not try it?

This has been just another comment from

The Inner Dimension
(no address given)

The fact that Bruce Banner usually remembers little or nothing of what he experiences as the Hulk is probably what has saved his sanity, Inner. (Chee. Don't people have names anymore? Verde! Inner Dimension! What happened to simple, all-American names like John, Mary, Joe, or Yezdigerd?) But you've brought up an interesting point:

We've always put far greater emphasis on Greenie himself than on Bruce Banner, since we figured that the smashing, breaking, yelling, crushing, and other assorted mayhem that the Hulk commits is why you people read the mag. Have we been wrong— or maybe just a tad overenthusiastic? Should we put a bit more emphasis on Banner than we have in recent months? Or should we show him even less? Or do you like things the way they are in this regard? Let us know, people.

And speaking of the Hulk's alter ego...

Dear Stan,

One thing puzzles me concerning General Ross' search for the Hulk. Since he knows the Hulk's other identity, why doesn't Ross try to capture him when he becomes Bruce Banner?

Jim Barry
Box 275
Hector, Minn. 55342

He's tried, Jim, but something always seems to go awry. Don't forget, all it takes is a minor trauma to start Bruce's cockeyed metabolism churning, and once that happens— it's all over. And even powerful sedation— which Banner has used on himself to attempt to keep the Hulk buried within him— has failed.

Which is not to say that Ross or Armbruster won't come up with another alledgedly foolproof scheme one day in the future. But it ain't as if the ol' military mastermind ain't thought of it before.

Until next issue, thirty days from now— stay calm, stay cool. Or you're liable to find yourself turning, growing, metamorphosing into a green giant, too. And nobody likes a mammoth pepper. (Wha—?)

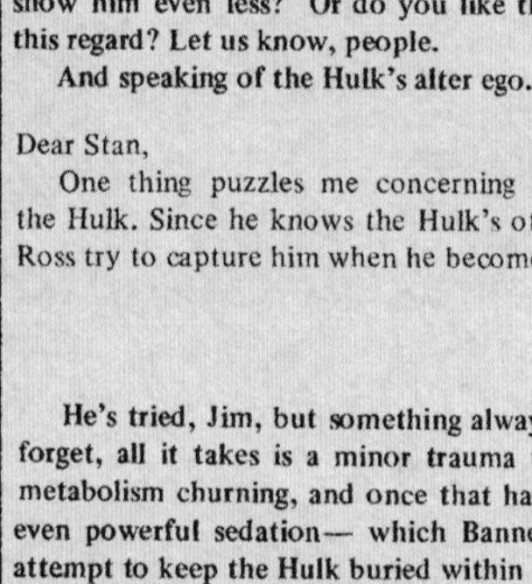

THIS IS IT! YOUR
MARVEL VALUE STAMP
FOR THIS ISSUE!
CLIP 'EM AND COLLECT 'EM!

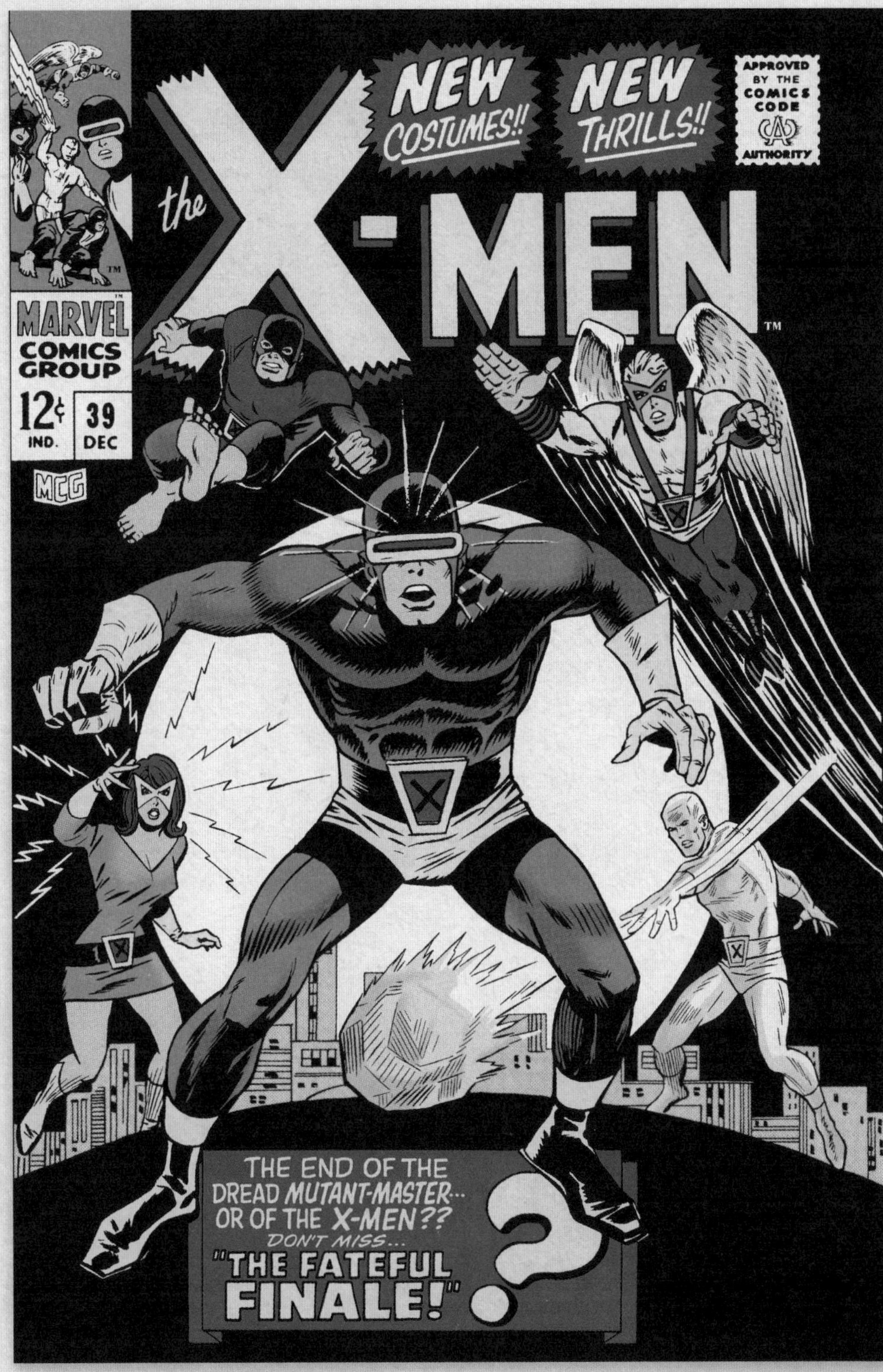

OPPOSITE **67: CYCLOPS** from *The Incredible Hulk* no. 176 (June 1974). Stamp also appears in *The Incredible Hulk* no. 180 (October 1974) and *The Amazing Spider-Man* no. 146 (July 1975).

ABOVE *The X-Men* no. 39 (December 1967), art by George Tuska. This cover was also used as the source for MVS no. 69.

ASTONISHING MAILS

c/o MARVEL COMICS GROUP, 575 MADISON AVE., NEW YORK, N.Y. 10022

SPECIAL BULLPEN NOTE:

This issue of ASTONISHING TALES features the debut appearance of the man-machine called DEATHLOK, as chronicled by Doug Moench and Rich Buckler. We'll be looking anxiously forward to your comments on this (we think) unique new series. Don't fail to write and let us know what *you* think of Rich's bizarre new creation.

Meanwhile, here are some of your reactions to DEATHLOK's predecessor in this magazine, the walking mass of stone known only as IT!

Dear Marvel,

I like your new IT, THE LIVING COLOSSUS series. Mostly because it's just plain fun. I don't want relevance all the time! Tony Isabella has come up with good scripts, and there's a lot going on in this book besides monsters! There's Bob O'Bryan's ability to transfer into the Colossus while he's stuck in a wheelchair. Many different characters populate the book: Diane Cummings, Grant Marshall, Magnor, and the "Star Lords" crew. A lot of thought and consideration went into this series' creation.

I've enjoyed Dick Ayers' artwork, also. He has the right feel for monsters.

Fin Fang Foom is a good choice for an adversary. I'd like to see Bruttu (remember him?) make a return appearance. He'd make a good hero-villain!

Brian Wilkes Prescott
132 Bonair Ave.
W. Springfield, Ma. 01089

Dear Marvel,

Thank you! Thanks for IT! Nostalgia was never so thick in the air. IT is something that should have come around five or six years ago.

Gil Johnson
833 Poplar St.
Wmspt., Pa. 17701

And our appreciation to you, Gil and Brian, for the good words on IT. We kind of enjoyed the series ourselves.

So why did we discontinue it, you ask?

The explanation, we're afraid, can be made all too briefly, all too simply. Nostalgia is fun, but it can only lead you back to where you started. Thus, despite our affection for Fin Fang Foom, Tim Boo Ba, Rama Lama Ding Dong, and all those other weird monsters of the fifties and early sixties, we've decided to leave the nostalgia to our reprint books and forge boldly ahead into the seventies and beyond. The old stories will still be around for anyone who wants a respite from the ongoing comics evolution/revolution, but, at least for now, you'll be seeing them only in their original form in JOURNEY INTO MYSTERY, WHERE MONSTERS DWELL, MONSTERS ON THE PROWL, and so on.

But despair not, creature-lover! Those beasties of the bygone days have their modern counterparts. And you can find them in TOMB OF DRACULA, WEREWOLF BY NIGHT, THE FRANKENSTEIN MONSTER, THE LIVING MUMMY, MAN-WOLF, MORBIUS, MAN-THING, and other all-new, all-great Marvel titles. And with all due respect... we've come a long way, Bruttu!

Makers of IT,

I feel you have what will gradually become a hit in the new IT series, despite the letters you receive telling you where to kick yourselves.

Mr. Ayers and Mr. Isabella make a great team, but I feel the "Darlin' One" needs a stronger inker. Question: is the letterer in A.T. #23 Dick Ayers?

No need to make this letter long. Just bring back WARLOCK, DOC SAVAGE, and the beauteous SHANNA THE SHE-DEVIL.

Tom Garland
7106 Dearborn
Houston, Texas 77055

You can catch Shanna in the current issue of DAREDEVIL (#112), Tom. It's still on sale— if you're lucky. No decision yet on a return of DOC SAVAGE. And we'll probably have wrapped up the WARLOCK series in an ish of the INCREDIBLE HULK's mag by the time you read this.

Yes, Dick Ayers did letter ASTONISHING TALES #23... and *all* the IT yarns, as a matter of fact.

Now that IT has passed on into that great rockpile in the sky, you'll be finding Dick's work in various other Marvel mags. Watch for it.

As for Tony Isabella, he's not exactly sitting around twiddling his thumbs, either. You'll find his scripting prowess displayed in GHOST RIDER, POWER MAN, and the new LIVING MUMMY series in SUPERNATURAL THRILLERS, as well as a couple of other books we can't quite remember offhand.

Which reminds us: the two titantic talents who have lent their efforts to this issue of ASTONISHING TALES are also highly visible elsewhere in the Marvel firmament.

Doug Moench is currently writing THE FRANKENSTEIN MONSTER, that same creature's series in MONSTERS UNLEASHED, the tales of Brother Voodoo which will appear regularly in TALES OF THE ZOMBIE, and he'll soon be assuming the writing chores on MASTER OF KUNG FU! Not since the days when Smilin' Stan batted out what seemed to be a zillion scripts a month has Marvel seen so prolific a personage as Doug.

As for Rich Buckler, we need only say two words: FANTASTIC and FOUR. That pretty much sums up the hurricane of enthusiasm he's generating in one of our longest-lived, most popular superhero mags.

And that's it for now, folks. As we mentioned, we'll be eagerly awaiting your comments on DEATHLOK. Drop us a line...or a hook or a sinker, for that matter...and let us know what you think.

Remember, in the words of IT, THE LIVING COLOSSUS: "leave no stone unturned." Rock on!

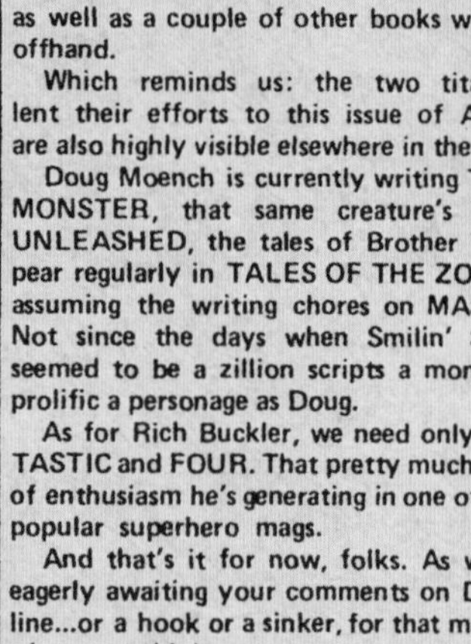

THIS IS IT! YOUR

MARVEL VALUE STAMP

FOR THIS ISSUE!
CLIP 'EM AND
COLLECT 'EM!

OPPOSITE **68: SON OF SATAN** from *Astonishing Tales* no. 25 (August 1974). Stamp also appears in *Frankenstein* no. 9 (March 1974) and *Marvel Team-Up* no. 27 (November 1974).

ABOVE *Marvel Spotlight* no. 13 (January 1974), art by John Romita Sr.

Heck. If you plan to keep Heck around at Marvel please have Vince Colletta ink his pencils. Please!

Vallard Eding
1435 14th Avenue
San Francisco, Cal. 94122

THE AVENGERS is a book which is usually late for the printers, because there's so much more to cover in it than in most comics that it takes everyone concerned longer to produce. Dashin' Donnie, like Mike Esposito before him, was often in the uncomfortable position of being the last man to work on each issue, and so carrying the weight of the Dreaded Deadline Doom down to the wire.

Still, we've gone through several art changes since then (haven't we always?). First, Dave Cockrum has come in to do finished pencils and inks over another artist's breakdowns. And second, the identity of that "other artist" has changed enough to warrant a complete answer in and of itself. You see, when Bob Brown left to do DAREDEVIL, we snagged Big John Buscema for the honors. But, after finishing this issue, Roy snagged him back to do more CONAN. So next ish, Blushin' Bob returns for a one-ish fill-in job, and after that...well, just wait and see.

(By the way, in the next ish, we'll see the Avengers lose one of their members, in the midst of one of the most outrageous plots you've ever encountered, so miss it not!)

(And even more by the way, Val, you won't want to miss Brown as embellished by Cockrum.)

Dear People,

Right now you've got the four most fascinating personalities you've ever had in the Avengers—the Scarlet Witch, the Vision, the Swordsman, and Mantis—and you're allowing one-dimensional guest-stars to dominate the book. They're guest-stars no matter what you say. The Big Four are not one-dimensional in their own strips, but THE AVENGERS is not their strip. Nothing important can happen to them in THE AVENGERS; their personalities can't be developed or even particularly well displayed; they can't be changed or influenced by anything; they can't do anything of significance; that sort of thing all has to occur in their own books. All they do is take up space that could be far better occupied by Wanda, Mantis, the Vision, and the Swordsman.

For years now the Avengers have worked as a large group, but I strongly believe the Avengers did some of their best issues with only four members—Cap, Hawkeye, Quicksilver, and the Scarlet Witch. Like the "regular" Avengers of today, that was a small group of low-power super-heroes, with distinct personalities. Interaction was the key to their success: they interacted well in battle (teamwork won most of their encounters) and not so smoothly personally (all those marvelous arguments and bickering). The four regular Avengers now are an even better set of personalities than were the four New Avengers.

Jana C. Hollingsworth
1415 East Second Street
Port Angeles, Washington —
98362

The controversy continues, Jana...and we're still listening.

Finally: several issues back we promised you the official chronology of the Thanos-war which has raged throughout the Marvel universe for over a year. Unfortunately, upon assembling it, we found the truth of the old adage, "Too many cooks spoil the goulash." In other words, with five writers, more artists, and the entire editorial staff at work on various parts of the series, discrepencies crept in. Now, with a little artistic license (such as changing Moon Dragon's stay at the Black Widow's abode from two months to two days), the blasted thing hangs together—so we invite anyone daring enough to peruse his or her back issues, form the chronology, make the necessary changes, and send it along. We'll print what we feel is the first correct answer in CAPTAIN MARVEL as soon as it's received. Deal?

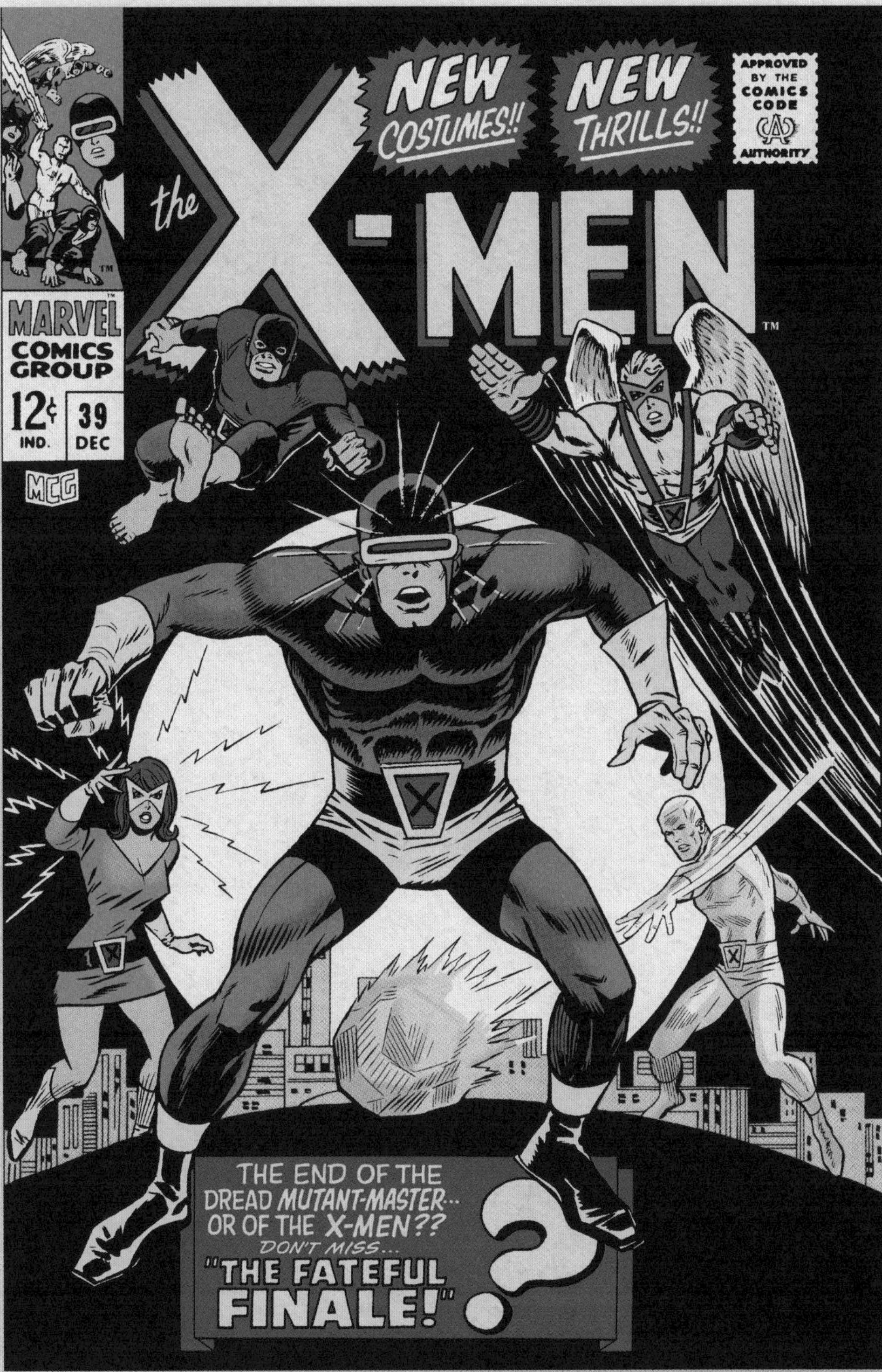

OPPOSITE **69: MARVEL GIRL** from *The Avengers* no. 125 (July 1974). Stamp also appears in *Frankenstein* no. 10 (May 1974) and *Tomb of Dracula* no. 27 (December 1974).

ABOVE *The X-Men* no. 39 (December 1967), art by George Tuska. This cover was also used as the source for MVS no. 67.

and that she was once a Russian agent, trained to kill. Obviously, as with any rigorous training that deals with the mind as well as the body, attitudes are bound to remain, despite her new lifestyle. Ms. Romanoff's occasional viciousness is the emotional release of that training. I hope this will be played up in the future, Steve, because this usually subdued trait serves to separate Natasha from the other Marvel lovelies who seem to be finally feeling their women's lib oats.

I can really see you guys are all taking a lot of time and thought with each issue. The least everybody can do out here is to buy a couple copies of DAREDEVIL, 'cause this book really should be monthly. Much luck for increased success.

Ralph Macchio
188 Wilson Drive
Cresskill, N.J. 07626

Dear Marvel,

Bob Brown! Yecch! All through DAREDEVIL #108 we are saddled with bad anatomy, stupid layouts, and **ridiculous** fight scenes! I realize Gene Colan is a hard act to follow, but he's not <u>that</u> hard! Let Bob draw BROTHER VOODOO and put Gene back on DAREDEVIL!

By the way, kudos to Alan Rothman for his letter in that issue. Everything he said was right on, although I think he was a little hard on Steve Gerber for his scripts. The problem isn't that they are as rotten as week-old fish left in the sun, but that they're just plain boring.

As long as you're changing your logo, why not change it back to the one on your letters page?

Also, who reads our letters? Does some editorial assistant read them, answer them, and throw them in the trash without their having been seen by people in a position to take into consideration what I have suggested?

Brad Rader
2901 Providence Drive
Anchorage, Alaska 99504

Now, before we move on, we'd like to answer one of Brad Rader's questions— the one about who reads your letters. Steve reads them...all of them...personally. And he discusses them in detail with Roy, the negative comments as well as the positive. Steve and Roy then discuss them with Bob. Because the idea of asking you people for letters is not, as some cynics assume, to fill the space on these pages, but rather to find out what you're thinking, so that we can create a magazine you'll want to read. 'Nuff said? Good. Then WRITE!! All of you! WRITE, WRITE, WRITE, WRITE, WRITE! And when you're done, write some more!

And, now, back to your comments...!

Folks,

I was going to write about Lucretia Jones being black in issues 105 and 106, and white in #108; and, this being more than a mere coloring mistake, how I deserved a no-prize. I then realized that this was but another example of The Gerber Curse at work. You may award me a no-prize anyway, however, as I don't have one yet.

Doug Elinson
9-05 166 St.
Whitestone, N.Y.

Okay.

Dear Marvel,

I spotted a mistake in DAREDEVIL #108. The little article in the left-hand column of the letters page came out printed backwards!!! Don't you all agree that I should get a no-prize for being so observant?

Kevin Williams,
16203 Oregon Avenue
Bellflower, California 90706

The no-prize is yours, Kevin.

(Aside to Marv Wolfman & Don McGregor: What did I tell you?— S.G.)

Dear DAREDEVIL People,

DAREDEVIL is better than ever. I love the move to New York, mostly because it isn't permanent, but that's not what's worrying me. When is Natasha's lease on the mansion in San Francisco gonna run out? It's been over two earth years, and I would think that it's at least two Marvel years since she rented it with her entire fortune. When and if she does get kicked out, what is she going to do?

The Black Spectre is good. I just hope (he, she, they, it) does not have anything to do with the Hate-Monger. If it does, I'll FOOM it to ya!

E.J.F.D.G.
2080 N. Techny
Northbrook, Ill. 60062

We're safe on the Black Spectre bit, as known by now, E.J.F.D.G., but as for Natasha and the mansion...like we said, there are some rather startling surprises in store in the months to come. For now, let's just say you've touched a nerve.

And speaking of nerves, ours are crackling in anticipation of your letters on his issue. Don't let us down, peopel. We could beg, we could plead, we could get down on our collective knee and sing three choruses of "Please Mr. Postman" in four-part harmony, but instead, we'll just threated:

WRITE— OR WE'LL JUMP!! (Hope we sounded pathetic enough. The lengths we won't go to to startle a few hundred thousand apathetic potential letter-writers...!)

NEXT ISH: The senses-shattering finale of the Black Spectre saga! The Mandrill in the White House! Shanna under the knife! The Black Widow in rebellion! And the Man Without Fear, in action, as you've never seen him before! Don't dare miss DAREDEVIL # 112!

THIS IS IT! YOUR
MARVEL VALUE STAMP
FOR THIS ISSUE! CLIP 'EM AND COLLECT 'EM!

OPPOSITE **70: SUPER SKRULL** from *Daredevil* no. 111 (July 1974). Stamp also appears in *The Avengers* no. 128 (October 1974) and *The Avengers* no. 131 (January 1975).

ABOVE *Thor* no. 142 (July 1967), art by Jack Kirby and Vince Colletta.

Marvel Comics itself is a good showcase for the growing Kung Fu movement. With our readers and writers alike clamoring for us to do some martial arts material, the summer of 1973 saw the first issue of MASTER OF KUNG FU— starring Shang-Chi, the son of Fu Manchu, in his battles against his father's evil empire. We followed this with a giant-sized 75¢ magazine called THE DEADLY HANDS OF KUNG FU and the comic mag you're now reading—IRON FIST.

Not being the sorts to overlook the humorous aspects of Kung Fu, we lampooned the TV show in CRAZY MAGAZINE #1. Since then, a number of other humor magazines have followed suit.

Meanwhile, the newest of the martial arts flicks has just opened here in Manhatten. It's called The Dragon's Vengeance and just may be the deadliest Kung Fu thriller of them all. It stars Barry Chan, already being called "the next Bruce Lee". While he doesn't yet have the mastery and poise shown by the late lamented Lee, there's no doubt in my mind that he'll be the undisputed best in a very short time.

The Dragon's Vengeance tells of a young fisherman who sets out to avenge the deaths of his wife and father at the hands of Japanese invaders. This is just prior to America's entry into the Second World War when Japan had conquered much of the Orient. He vows to track down and kill the three murderers and, in the process, manages to rack up an impressive body count against the Japanese Army. Soldiers are simply scattered to the four winds as Blastin' Barry rips, tears, and smashes his way to revenge. Just for good measure, he does a neat number with some bricks. No, he doesn't chop them in half. He rams them through a couple of his opponents. It's an exceptional flick, worth looking into. Not as well-made as Enter the Dragon, it makes up for any shortcomings with action that almost literally never stops. For more details pick up the second issue of THE DEADLY HANDS OF KUNG FU, on sale in March. We'll have a full-length review waiting for you there.

While we're on the subject, look for Barry Chan's next Kung Fu film, The Chinese Mechanic. As this article is being written the distributors plan to release it in mid-February.

From the same distributors, we have word of From China With Love, which should be hitting your neighborhood movie theater any day now. The folks who put together the television spot for this film confided to me that they thought it one of the best Kung Fu movies ever made. They stressed that, in addition to the high-flying action we've come to expect, the film boasts a strong plot and well developed characters. Watch for it.

Next issue, this section will feature your comments on IRON FIST's pulse-pounding premiere. But don't fret. THE DEADLY HANDS OF KUNG FU will keep you on top of what's happening in the martial arts movement. You'll find the latest scoops on Kung Fu in those pages.

So go in peace, valued one. And, yea, should you be set upon by uncouth brigands, just think of Bruce Lee...

...and drop-kick them across the street!

THIS IS IT! YOUR
MARVEL VALUE STAMP
FOR THIS ISSUE!
CLIP 'EM AND COLLECT 'EM!

OPPOSITE **71: THE VISION** from *Giant-Size Master of Kung Fu* no. 3 (March 1975). Stamp also appears in *The Avengers* no. 122 (April 1974), *Marvel Premiere* no. 16 (July 1974), and *Conan the Barbarian* no. 44 (November 1974).

ABOVE *The Avengers* no. 57 (October 1968), pencils by John Buscema.

THE HYBORIAN PAGE

c/o MARVEL COMICS GROUP, 575 MADISON AVE., NEW YORK, N.Y. 10022

A SPECIAL ANNOUNCEMENT FROM STAN, ROY, AND MARVEL COMICS

By the time this message appears in any of our mags, you'll already have noticed that all of our 36-page comic magazines are now 25¢— a nickel more than they were a few short weeks ago.

Maybe your first reaction to the price hike was the same as ours might be if we were in your shoes: "What's Marvel trying to do to us, anyway? Don't they know we've got enough troubles, what with inflation, shortages, and an energy crisis on our hands, without trying to clip us for 5¢ more every time we want a little fantasy-filled escape from it all? What is this— some kind of rip-off, so that Stan and Roy can vacation on the Riviera this year?"

If that was your reaction, it's an understandable one— and we'd just like to ask you to listen to our side of it for a minute before you decide:

This year, the widely-publicized paper shortage(in addition to various labor settlements among the companies that print, sell, and distribute Marvel Comics) caused additional expenses to Marvel of several hundred thousand dollars. That means that we had to make that much extra money just to stay even, despite the fact that our sales in 1973 were the best in the business.

So, we had no choice, really, but to increase the cover price of our magazines, the same way that just about everybody else has to.

And, just in case you think we're now getting rich off that new-found nickel: Believe it or not, that extra copper only covers about half the cost of the paper strike and other shortages.

What're we doing about the whole situation?

We think the answer's obvious, if you take a look at some of the titles we're now publishing besides our 36-pagers. There's our increasingly popular 75¢ line of full-scale magazines, first of all. Already, our four flagship 75-centers are being joined by THE DEADLY HANDS OF KUNG FU and the return (on March 26) of SAVAGE TALES— with two or three more much-requested types of mags already in the works.

Likewise, there's our spanking new, sensational 35¢ giant-size comics— a full 52 pages of colorful cavorting, and now a bigger bargain than ever!

Not only that, but the next few weeks will herald the coming of a brand new Marvel phenomenon: our swingin' SUPER-GIANTS, featuring one hundred big pages for just 60¢ including a feature-length new tale each and every issue. The Bullpen Bulletins Pages will give you the full scam, next time around— but rest assured that you're gonna be getting your money's worth!

Not only that— but we've got other plans we can't even hint at yet!

Well, that's about it. We've had our say.

About the only other thing we can do is to affirm once more that, just as we've been doing for over a decade now, every artist and writer in the Bullpen will be striving night and day, even harder than ever (if that's possible), to see to it that you consider— each precious coin spent on a Marvel mag to be one of the wisest investments you ever made.

Let's lick this thing together, okay?

Thanks for listening.

SUPER-SPECIAL ANNOUNCEMENT:

Looks like it's gonna be the Year of the Barbarian!

But not quite in the form we told it to you last month, as well as in the first great issue of a 35¢ thriller called GIANT-SIZE SUPER-STARS, featuring the Fantastic Four.

The way it's gonna be:

Conan has become so popular, with countless letters each and every week demanding more, more of our embattled Cimmerian — that we've finally had to yield to the hue and cry.

And so, in the future, in addition to twelve 36-page issues per year of CONAN THE BARBARIAN, we've brought back SAVAGE TALES— each issue of which will spotlight a novel-length epic of Conan, plus related stories, photos, and features— and all on a bi-monthly basis, this time! In short, it would seem that the two-issue trial run of SAVAGE TALES was a shining success— and the revived, revitalized 75¢ mag begins its new six-times-a-year run on March 26! (Like the man says: Look for it wherever magazines are sold. Mainly because sometimes SAVAGE TALES and its sister 75¢ mags are heaped in with our full-color comics, but most often not.)

And that's not all!

We also announced, a couple of months back, that every third issue of GIANT-SIZE SUPER-STARS would feature Conan, as well. Well, we've changed things just a bit on that one— and now, there'll be instead a 60¢, 100-page Cimmerian extravaganza called the SUPER-GIANT CONAN, four times a year (alternating with a SUPER-GIANT SPIDER-MAN Team-Up Mag, and a SUPER-GIANT AVENGERS, which Ye Editor is even now plotting and scripting, in answer to still another hue and cry).

The first issue of SUPER-GIANT CONAN will be on sale late this spring or early summer, and will star our brawling barbarian in an extra-long spectacular, as well as re-presenting a peerless pair of his most awe-inspiring adventures. And of course there'll be other, related stories and features tossed in— to make it worth any sword-and-sorcery fan's two quarters and a dime.

More details about Conan— his past, present, and most especially his future— in SAVAGE TALES # 4, on sale March 26th.

We'll return with our regular letters section next ish. Meanwhile, let us know how you've enjoyed John Buscema's penciling and inking these past two issues, okay? The Big Man really knocked himself out on them— and he'd like to know!

May Crom be with you— but not too close!

THIS IS IT! YOUR

MARVEL VALUE STAMP

FOR THIS ISSUE! CLIP 'EM AND COLLECT 'EM!

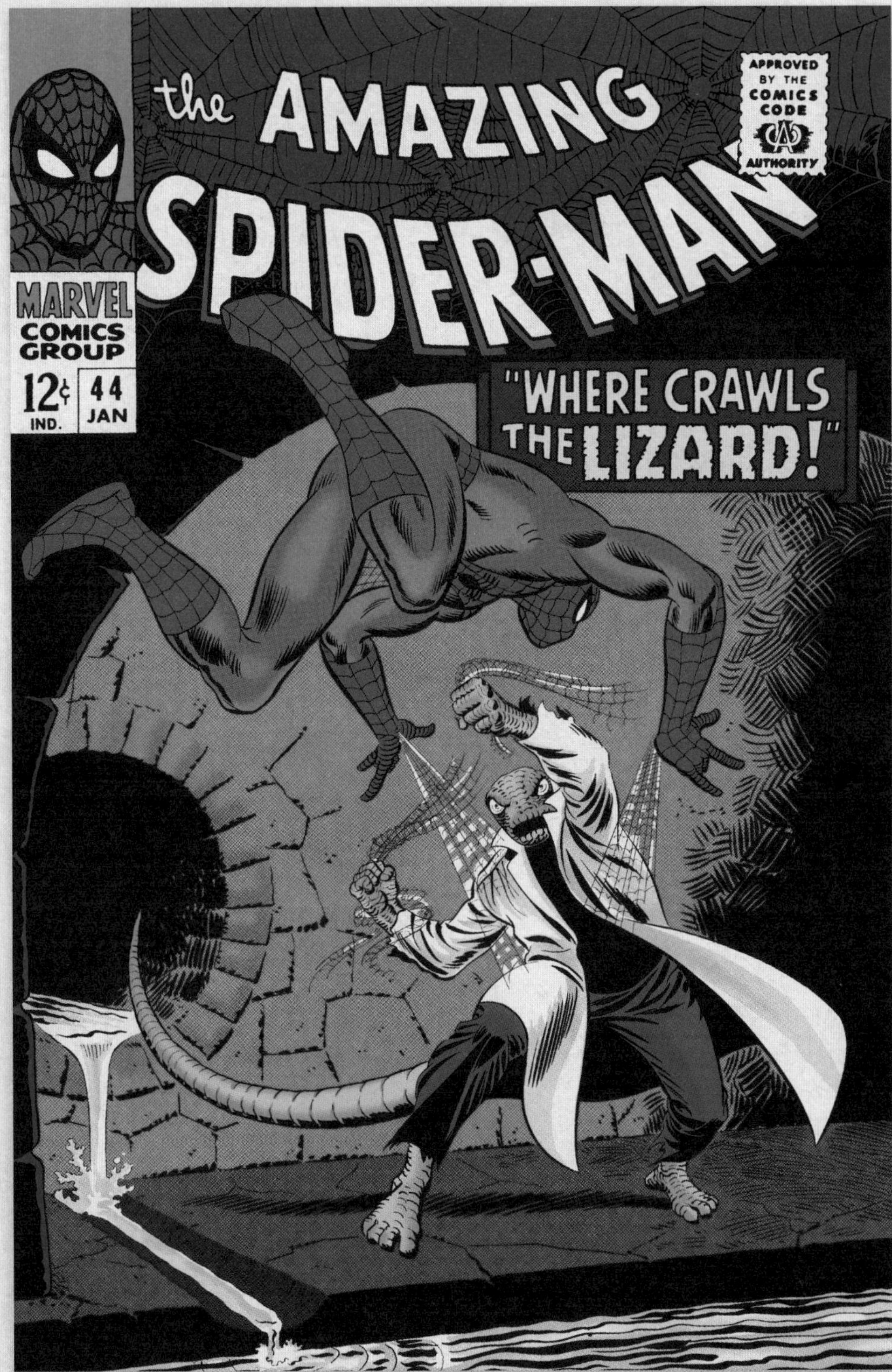

OPPOSITE **72: THE LIZARD** from *Conan the Barbarian* no. 39 (June 1974). Stamp also appears in *Werewolf by Night* no. 21 (September 1974) and *Ka-Zar* no. 10 (August 1975).

ABOVE *The Amazing Spider-Man* no. 44 (January 1967), art by John Romita Sr.

had nothing but action, which is okay for awhile, but I tended to lose interest towards the end of the mag.

Joel Kok
8107 N 41st Drive
Phoenix, AZ 85201

Joel, you raise several noteworthy points in your letter, first among them the contention that, because both Shang-Chi and Iron Fist are martial arts masters, they should share the same philosophy in common—which is a notion that might superficially sound valid until you stop to consider that they are, above all, individuals with distinctly different ways of responding to distinctly different sets of formative stimuli.

Who ever accused us of being long-winded?

As for the matter of excessively-extended sentences in the captions interfering with the story, that—believe it or don't—is a source of much consideration and discussion among the various writers around the Bullpen, all of whom have their own notions on the subject, which is why no hard-and-fast rule exists for it. Pretty much as in most matters, Marvel prefers to leave a certain amount of creative freedom for its people, and look how well it's paid off for you, the readers, in the long run. Still, we want you to know that we do value your comments and give them careful thought.

Finally, since the vengeance plotline has run its course, you'll be seeing new situations, new characters, new ideas in IRON FIST. Keep watchin'. And—thanks, Joel!

Dear Iron Ones,

MARVEL PREMIERE #17 was another great appearance of Iron Fist, the newest martial arts hero in Marveldom. Larry Hama does a fine job handling the art chores on this exciting character and anybody who has read a comic in recent years knows that Dick Giordano doesn't hurt the art a bit. His inks are necessary for Iron Fist, so keep him around, huh?

Doug Moench seems to be establishing himself as the scripter for the martial arts books—good. One caution, don't make Iron Fist too invincible. A little pain now and then might keep his thirst for revenge a bit more motivated and believable. A problem might exist after he catches up with Meachum, as you're going to have to invent a reason for him to continue. Keep up the outstanding work with Iron Fist and best wishes for continued success.

Chad Goyette
4401 Clark Avenue
Long Beach, CA 90808

Um, er, that's just it, Chad—Devil-May-Care Doug found himself buried under the martial arts books, what with the 75¢ DEADLY HANDS OF KUNG FU going monthly, the GIANT-SIZE MASTER OF KUNG FU, the two regular Iron Fist and Shang-Chi comics—and now the upcoming bi-monthly black-and-white IRON FIST magazine. And we may have forgotten some, if that's possible. Anyway, Doug decided—for the sake of his sanity—to stay with Shang-Chi, and Tony (the Tiger) Isabella opted to continue the steel-smashing exploits of the prodigy from K'un-Lun. And by all that's worthy, faithful one, don't dare miss the dazzling first issue of that aforementioned 75¢ IRON FIST magazine, lest the irate iron fist of vengenace descend on you!

Dear Stan, et al:

I am most impressed by the knowledge of comparative folklore demonstrated in the origin of Iron Fist as recounted in his adventure with Scythe. I refer specifically (as I am sure you are aware) to the episode of the dragon.

Iron Fist's killing the dragon and acquiring his full powers plunging his hands into its fiery heart immediately recall Siegfried's slaying of the dragon, Fafnir, and his acquisition of invulnerability (and other abilities) by bathing in the monster's blood.

In *your* story, the dragon's heart had been removed and was kept separate from the body. This situation, in which the heart, or some repository of vital essence, is kept apart from the body is a very widespread motif in world folklore, and is discussed by the late Prof. Tolkien in his beautiful and masterful essay, "On Fairy Stories." However, the Iron Fist episode differs from most other examples of this theme in that generally the being whose heart is out of his body is invulnerable and can only be killed by getting at the *heart.*

It is interesting and gratifying to see the variety of sources and genres which provide inspiration for *Marvel's* talented corps of writers.

Edmund S. Meltzer
165 E 19 Street, Apt. 2T
Brooklyn, NY 11226

People,

Strange.

I like MASTER OF KUNG FU, because it's philosophical. I don't want any more action in it. I like IRON FIST because it's action-packed, and I don't really want any more philosophy in it.

I just don't get it, but I *like* them both.

Dale A. Beash
1661 E Miller Road
Midland, MG 48640

Don't let it upset you, Dale—you're supposed to like them both. Where would we be if you didn't? Until next time, then, high-kicking honchos: *ciao.*

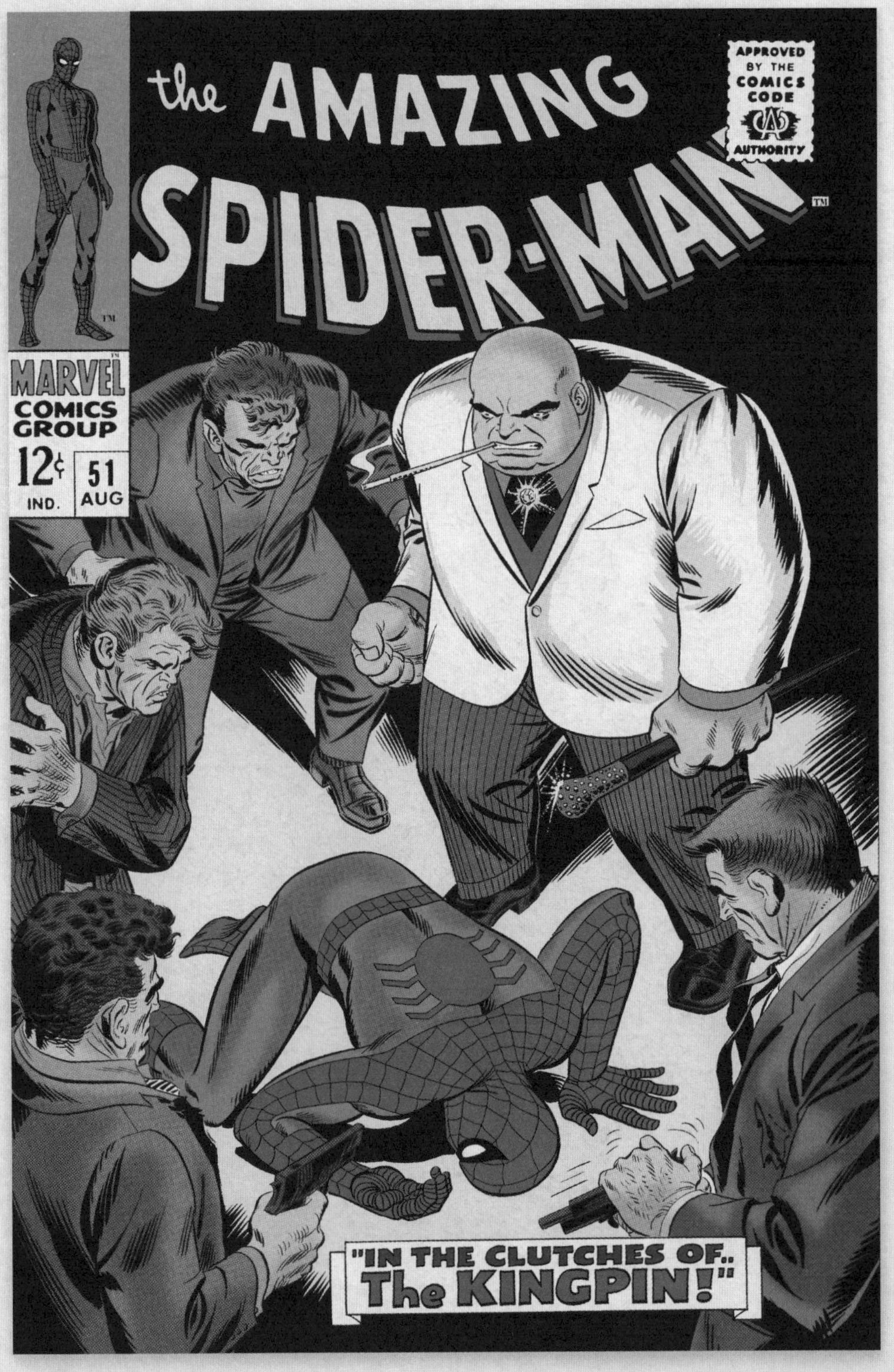

OPPOSITE 73: KINGPIN from *Marvel Premiere* no. 20 (January 1975). Stamp also appears in *Kull the Destroyer* no. 13 (April 1974), *Power Man* no. 21 (October 1974), and *Creatures on the Loose* no. 36 (July 1975).

ABOVE *The Amazing Spider-Man* no. 51 (August 1967), art by John Romita Sr.

a new comic brought forth such paeans of praise from its readers. As we mentioned earlier on this page, we're grateful.

We're glad you understood why we portrayed the fight scenes in that issue as brutally as we did. To have done otherwise would not only have made them somewhat less than credible, it would also have ignored one of Iron Fist's major strengths as a character: he is human; he can bleed; he can be hurt. Yes, he is stronger than most men, but his real strength lies in the way he uses the skills he has acquired. If his reflexes fail him, he can be wounded— or killed. Roy and Gil were simply trying to make that perfectly clear.

Dear Roy:

I loved it! IRON FIST has really got possibilities! It's neither a carbon copy of the TV show or the recent rash of kung fu movies. Marvel is always at its best when you are allowed to use your own creative geniuses rather than sticking to someone else's storyline. IRON FIST has got something that MASTER OF KUNG FU hasn't— namely, an immediate plot. It looks that feeling of unreality which pervades your other kung fu comic. Unlike MASTER OF KUNG FU, it doesn't give you the feeling you are sleep-walking, or viewing the events through a gauze curtain. Of course, this might have been due to the very powerful emotional scenes from Iron Fist's childhood. No other writer in comics can project such *real*, beautiful emotions as Roy Thomas can; of course, Gil Kane's fantastic artwork was a big help! Anyway, thank you very much for an excellent story.

Gail Teague
P.O. Box 218
Riverdale, Ca. 93656

You're very much welcome, Gail. But we feel obliged to say a word or two in defense of MASTER OF KUNG FU. It's true that IRON FIST is quite a bit different from that other mag; it was intended to be different, with more emphasis on action, more of a superhero feel, less orientation towards the philosophical side of the martial arts. But frankly, we think both mags are good. And most of our readers, fortunately for us, seem to agree. The two books complement rather than imitate one another. Which brings us to the following letter...!

Dear Marvel,

I am a steady reader of Marvel comics. I am also a kung fu fan, so when MASTER OF KUNG FU came out, I flipped. Then, IRON FIST came out, and the first idea that came to me was that these two should meet in battle. How about it?

Joe Rufe
349 Market St.
Brighton, Mass. 02135

We're planning something along these lines, Joe, for an upcoming special issue of one of our black-and-white martial arts mags— and if all goes as planned, it should be one of the single most exciting issues we've ever published! We can't reveal any details just yet, but we will say that what we have in mind is even *more* spectacular than the suggestion you've offered. Watch these pages for a near-future announcement.

THIS IS IT! YOUR
MARVEL VALUE STAMP
FOR THIS ISSUE!
CLIP 'EM AND
COLLECT 'EM!

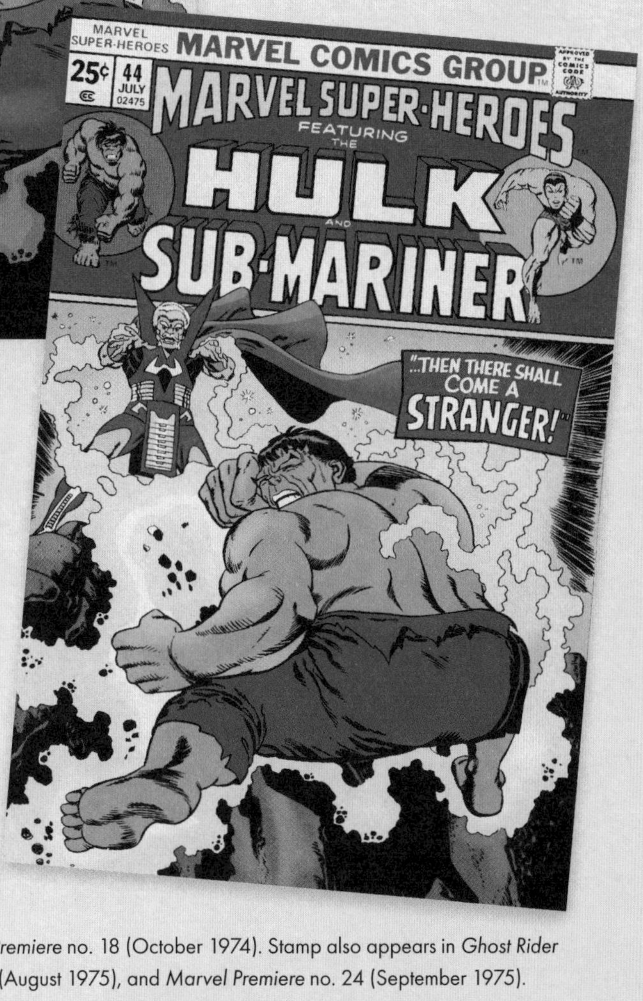

OPPOSITE **74: THE STRANGER** from *Marvel Premiere* no. 18 (October 1974). Stamp also appears in *Ghost Rider* no. 6 (June 1974), *Tomb of Dracula* no. 35 (August 1975), and *Marvel Premiere* no. 24 (September 1975).

ABOVE *Tales to Astonish* no. 89 (March 1967), art by Gil Kane. The artwork on the stamp is the original cover art before it was altered, and appears on the cover of *Marvel Super-Heroes* no. 44 (July 1974).

spent in high school and college are an important part of his character and will be reflected in the ways he will act and the attitudes that he will hold for the rest of his life.

If you allow Peter to remain the same age forever, he will be forced to become a product of all generations, a conglomeration of experiences and feelings that belong to several different ages, a college student in the year 2000 who remembers doing the Twist in high school.

Let Spider-man age.

Paul DeRogatis
Waban, Massachusetts

Dear Bullpen,

A few months back, in the FANTASTIC FOUR, you showed Wyatt Wingfoot graduating from college. Longtime Marvel readers will remember that Johnny Storm and Wyatt were roommates together during Johnny's one-and-only year of college.

What's all this got to do with Spider-man? Well, Johnny Storm and Peter Parker graduated from high school at the same time, and entered college the same year. Since Peter Parker and Wyatt Wingfoot both started college the same year, they should both graduate at the same time, right? And since Wyatt has graduated, Peter should be graduating too, right?

Incidentally, if Pete is a junior or senior in college, he should be about twenty-one be about twenty-one or twenty-two, so please stop referring to him as a "teenager."

Richard E. Robinson, B.S.
35 MMS - PSC Box 3036
George AFB, CA 92392.

Dear Spidey People:

To age or not to age. That is the question. Here is my answer: Let Parker stay in college a few more years.

He should, however—sooner or later—die.

The Lawgiver
Ape City, CA

Dear Friends,

Let Peter Parker graduate. Then you'll have a ball trying to decide what he can do—I mean, if it takes him nine years to graduate, it'll be 2001 before he gets a regular job!

Edward Rigdon
605 Florence Street
Dothan, AL 36301

Do we detect the tiniest trace of facetiousness in some of these letters, or is our widely-acclaimed imagination finally getting the best of us? Seriously, though, folks—while opinions are still pouring in—it looks as if the vast majority of you seem to prefer giving Petey a few more months in college, and then moving him on to graduate school or out into the stream of adult life. Of course, all the votes aren't in yet, so you still have time to join the debate.

Do we haveta tell you—the decision is yours!

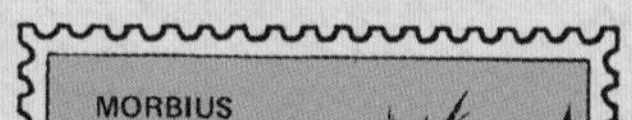

THIS IS IT! YOUR
MARVEL VALUE STAMP
FOR THIS ISSUE! CLIP 'EM AND COLLECT 'EM!

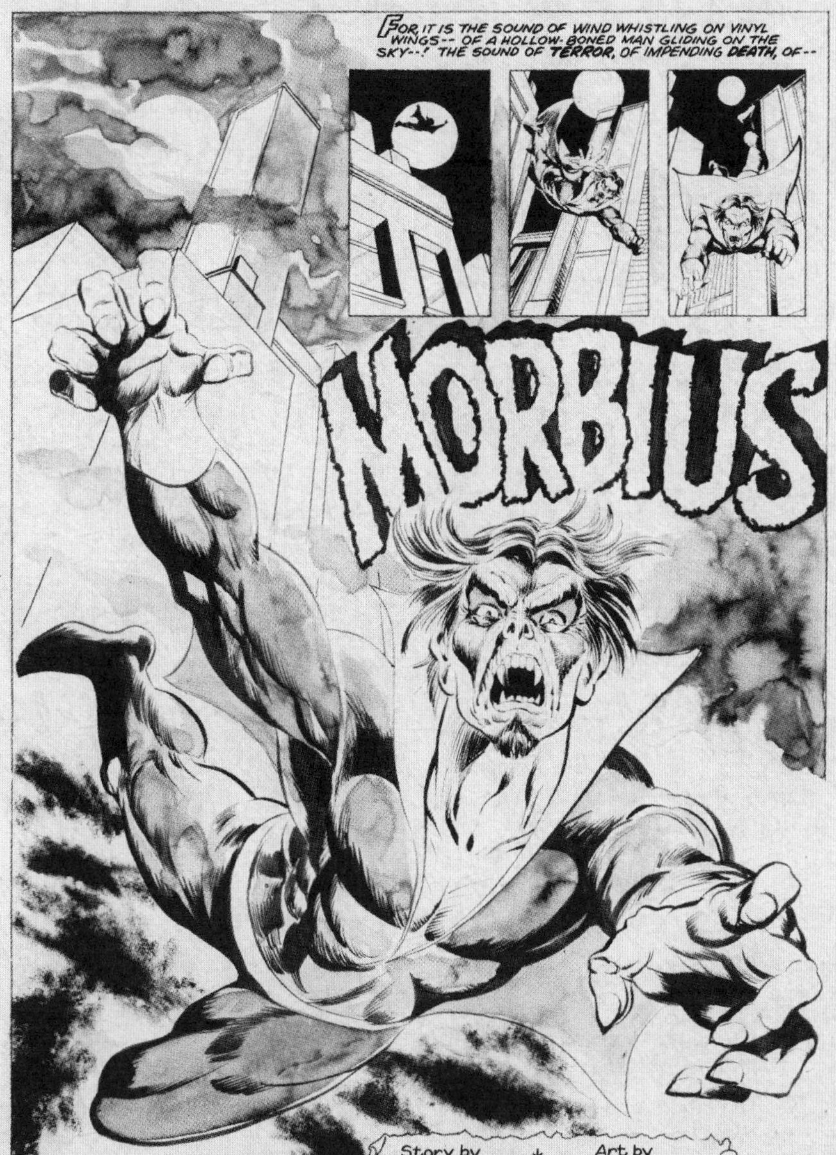

OPPOSITE **75: MORBIUS** from *The Amazing Spider-Man* no. 140 (January 1975). Stamp also appears in *Werewolf by Night* no. 15 (March 1974), *Worlds Unknown* no. 8 (August 1974), *Fear* no. 26 (February 1975), and *Fear* no. 31 (December 1975).

ABOVE *Vampire Tales* no. 1 (August 1973), art by Pablo Marcos.

Dear Bullpen,

I have always entertained the conception that there is *one*— and *only* one— realm of the damned which mortals call Hell. I may be right; then again, I may be right. Marvel displays three entirely different Hells, along with a different individual Lord of each Hell.

Hell Number one: *Hades.* Lord of Hell Number One: *Pluto.*

Hell Number Two: the hell visited in THOR #204 & 205. Lord of Hell Number Two: *Mephisto.*

Hell Number Three: the Hell with which SON OF SATAN and GHOST RIDER are involved. Lord of Hell Number Three: Satan (who has always reminded me of the Human Torch).

Could you please explain this matter?

Jeff Thompson
6807 Pennywell Dr.
Nashville, Tenn. 37205

We'll try, Jeff, but it's as confusing to us in some ways as it is to you. Still, here goes...!

The Hell ruled by Pluto, properly called the Underworld in mythology, by the way, is, we believe, something quite different from the realms of Mephisto and Satan. Just as Valhalla doesn't exactly correspond to the Judeo-Christian version of Heaven, Pluto's Underworld is something apart from what we mortals think of as Hell. (Perhaps the souls of the good of Asgard go to Valhalla?)

Mephisto and Satan, however, difficult as it may be for you to accept at first, are one and the same character. As we've shown in SON OF SATAN, the Devil is able to assume virtually any identity he wishes. He can appear to be a mortal...or a goat-headed demon with a corporeal shell...or a horned version of Johnny Storm...or Mephisto. Whatever visage best suits his purpose is the one he employs. He could even appear as a dancing troll or Howard the Duck if he really wanted to!

Hope that makes things a little clearer, anyway, Jeff. Yes? No? Other opinions, people?

Dear Marvel Madmen,

THOR #222, both story and letters section, set me thinking. In 1972, I picked up THOR # 197, my first comic purchase in four years. I was greeted by new creatures called Conway, Buscema, and Thomas. And I felt much like Steve Jetta did (in his letter in #222).

Stan Lee and Jack Kirby were (are) pioneers. They built a whole new concept in a field gone stale. One of their best creations, and still my favorite, is Thor, the embodiment of humanity's good intentions and fallible pride. We will never forget those beautiful years of discovery, but now both men have moved on to conquer new wildernesses; Kirby in his own books, Stan in new means of communication and entertainment. They could easily have rested on their laurels for another five years, but that's not what they were about, nor is Marvel now, in 1974.

For the past year, I have thrilled to the interpretations of my old favorites by Englehart, Gerber, Buckler, Starlin, Andru, and the aforementioned THOR crew. There were some queasy moments, true, but the movement has been ever upward, providing me with fulfillment not experienced since the original Avengers or the first full-length Thor epic. Marvel has indeed moved ahead, and its current crew deserves a better label than "Lee & Kirby stand-ins." Once again, we have superb stories and stellar artwork (ever noticed, Thorophiles, how Buscema/Sinnott make a sword *gleam?).*

By the way, monsters are nothing new at Marvel. I remember when THOR was just another eight-page feature in JOURNEY INTO MYSTERY, and stalwarts complained how it detracted from the "good fantasy stories."

For the next thousand years, Make Mine Marvel!

William C. Corse (MMMS #6662)
P.O Box 662
Beloit, Wis. 53511

We couldn't have said it better, Mr. Corse. Thanks. We mean that.

OPPOSITE **76: DORMAMMU** from *Thor* no. 227 (September 1974). Stamp also appears in *Doctor Strange* no. 5 (December 1974).

ABOVE *Strange Tales* no. 127 (December 1964), art by Steve Ditko.

Everything is coming to a head: Cap in the slammer, accused of murder? Harderman's operation explained? a truly unique new villain, don't kill off Moonstone too soon? Falc's new powers and costume; and finally, Leila's abduction by Stoneface. And all in nineteen pages. MARVEL is on the move again.

Last, but by no means least (to coin a phrase), let me say that Petra's coloring was better than ever this ish. Please keep her on CA&F, she's a real winner.

Well, what more can I say? Just that in Mike, Sal, Vinnie, and Petra you've got a winning team! Don't blow it, and (natch) MAKE MINE MARVEL!

David J. Belles, RFO, TTB, KOF
6010 Bell Avenue
Tumwater, Wash. 98501

P.S. Thanks for not having Cap use his super powers to escape from jail— the man is finally starting to act intelligently, I just hope he doesn't lope off with his "supporters" (who were probably sent by Harderman) and try to paste a legally innocent Moonstone. Nuff said!

That was our old friend J. Romita on the inks of #170's cover once again, Dave. And listen, we're glad you mentioned Sal and Vinnie's inside work as well. We were beginning to think everybody just bought the book and hung it on the wall without looking inside. Gosh, the accounting department was already making plans to publish the book with blank pages!

Dear Roy and Steve,

Giving Captain America extra strength is a move that's been needed for a number of years. His "superbly trained body" has been stretching our credibility for too long and too and too far. Besides, a living legend deserves some definite power to make him something special, to enable him to live up to his legend. Of course, this places the very sensitive, chip-on-his-shoulder Falcon in a very precarious position. For him, naturally, an inferior role in a partnership, or anything else, is intolerable, and for obvioussand excusable reasons. At least his physical inferiority is acknowledged, unlike that of a cowled member of another (world's finest????) team, and thus can lead to a lot of interesting conflicts and developments, especially as Falcon hasn't got the standby of being the world's greatest detective. On the other hand, perhaps you're considering dropping the Falcon from C.A., which wouldn't be a bad move since Cap doesn't really need a partner now, and it's not going to be very flattering for Falc when Cap keeps saying, "Okay Falcon, you take him, I'll take the other twelve!" It'll be interesting to see how you do resolve this, if it is resolvable.

Mike Cruden
8 Swinbourne Gr.,
Withington, Manchester 20 9PP,
England.

Your views parallel not only ours, but also the views of the vast majority of the people who commented on our (now long ago) change in Cap's strength. We wonder what the reaction will be to the changes to come. But more than that, we wonder what you, Mike, and our other non-American readers think about a character called Captain America. Every month, we get letters from England, Australia, and just about anywhere else where people speak English, commenting on our stories, but almost never on the concept of Cap itself. Is he just another character to you folks, or is he more—and if so, can you get behind it, or does it get in the way of your enjoyment?

Come to think of it, we're not entirely sure what Americans think about Cap. Why doesn't anybody with an opinion on the questions posed above send it to us. We're frankly curious about it all. And we'll feed the consensus— along with the most interesting missives— back to you on these very pages in he months to come. Deal?

Dear Marvel Idealists,

Thanks for telling us, in CAPTAIN AMERICA #169, that Steve Englehart is a conscientious objector. It makes me respect your fine writer even more.

Charles Boatner
2727 Midtown Court, Apt. 14
Palo Alto, Cal. 94303

THIS IS IT! YOUR

MARVEL VALUE STAMP

FOR THIS ISSUE! CLIP 'EM AND COLLECT 'EM!

MORE GIANT-SIZE DYNAMITE
FROM THE HOUSE OF IDEAS!
The DEFENDERS
NOW IN A FEATURE-LENGTH BLOCKBUSTER IN EACH ISSUE OF MARVEL'S NEWEST TRIUMPH!
ON SALE APRIL 23RD
GIANT-SIZE SUPER-TEAMS
1 JULY
02915
35¢
SPECIAL ISSUE
MARVEL COMICS GROUP
GIANT-SIZE SUPER-TEAMS
FEATURING:
THE DEFENDERS
LOOK FOR THE DEFENDERS IN THEIR OWN MAG, TOO--NOW ON SALE MONTHLY!!

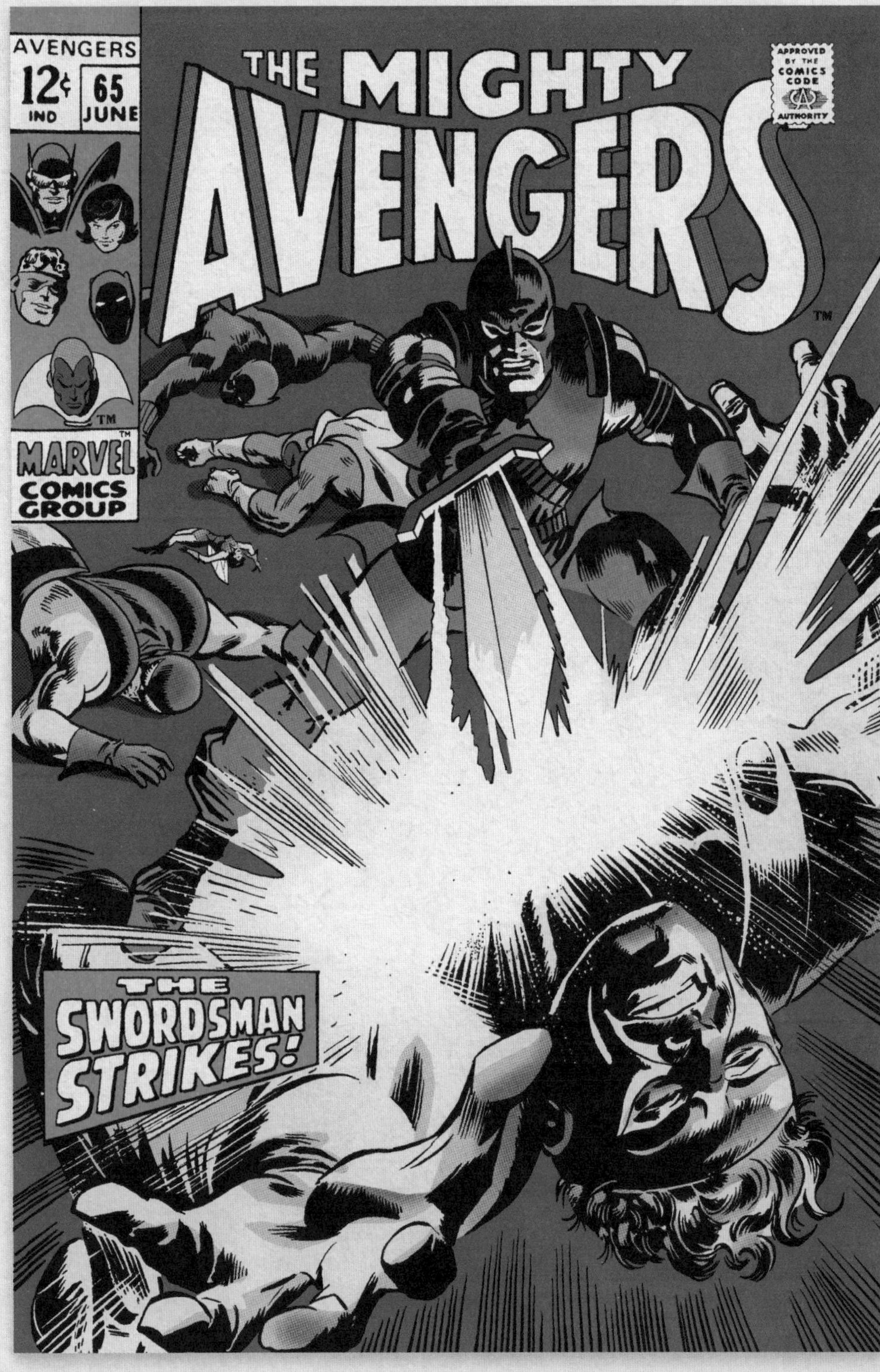

OPPOSITE **77: THE SWORDSMAN** from *Captain America* no. 175 (July 1974). Stamp also appears in *Fear* no. 21 (April 1974), *Giant-Size Man-Thing* no. 3 (February 1975), and *Tomb of Dracula* no. 39 (December 1975).

ABOVE *The Avengers* no. 65 (June 1969), art by Gene Colan and Frank Giacoia, with John Romita Sr.

DEFENDERS DIALOGUE

c/o MARVEL COMICS GROUP, 575 MADISON AVE. N.Y.C. 10022

Dear Marvel,

DEFENDERS #20, coupled with TWO-IN-ONE #7, comprised one of the best stories I've ever read. Since I've already written about the first part in TWO-IN-ONE, here goes about DEFENDERS #20.

The concept of destiny is a complicated subject matter to deal with, and it has been approached in many different ways. But, I must say, Steve, that your tying it in with the Nameless Ones was a stroke of near genius. The Nameless Ones tale from DR. STRANGE and the HULK was one of the classics of all time and their reappearance connected with Val/Barbara's identity search was sensational. The great thing about Marvel and the Marvel Universe is that it is one gigantic story. Every character has a past and as with any truly great characters, their past must have some bearing on their present and future lives. This is the major distinction between Marvel and the competition, namely that each character is complete, not merely a cardboard figure only going through the motions of the present. They have backgrounds and depth.

My mind is spinning with all the revelations of this ish. Not only are the Nameless Ones responsible for Val becoming Val, but they have influenced everything else's destiny by saving Celestia from the auto accident. The plan of theirs that Val and Stephen's powers would allow them to enter our world was something, and their defeat by not taking into account Ben's appearance instead of the Hulk's was not the usual cop-out denouement to such a grand plot.

My only complaint is that I felt this story should have been told over two issues. The pacing throughout was really great yet the ending seemed a bit rushed, hence my preference of a two-ish length. Val's dilemma is getting more and more fascinating and with next issues' developments (with her *and* Nighthawk), DEFENDERS is definitely one of the best superhero books around.

Sal's layouts were great as usual, but I was sorry that he couldn't finish it. Vince's finished art was OK but he is best as inker. Finally, since when does Stephen say "zapped" (page 16)?

Keep up the great work and as always, MAKE MINE MARVEL.

PMM Dean Mullaney
81 Delaware Street
Staten Is., NY 10304

P.S. Membership suggestions: Luke Cage & Sunfire

Gladly, Dean. And to answer your question, Stephen Strange says "zapped" only when he precedes it with "in your parlance" or words to that effect. It's true, his mystic training has made him more reserved, more formal than most men, but it's not as if he's an alien or even a product of another culture. He was born, and raised in the good ol' U.S. of A.

Regarding the destiny theme...the point of the story, which a good many readers failed to catch, unfortunately, was that the Nameless Ones in effect created the Defenders team! Add up all those captions on the last couple of pages, and that's what it says. (We've finally done it: created The Origin Nobody Noticed).

Dear Marvel,

So Barbara was married! You mentioned that her husband, Jack, was a member of the cult and induced Barbara to join.

But my emotional nature induces me to hope it was solely Celestia and Van Nyborg who approved of the marriage with the Nameless Ones. It would comfort Valkyrie to know that Barbara was not totally betrayed.

I can understand Val's identity problems, with no personal memory beyond a few months. And I can also understand her emotional attachment to the woman whose body she has acquired. But for all practical purposes, Barbara is dead. Instead of her body dying also, in it was born another woman. That woman is separate from Barbara, even though her body used to be Barbara's.

Valkyrie was born fully grown, with the general knowledge of an adult. Only her personal knowledge was completely lacking, as it is in some cases of amnesia. She has the choice of starting from where she is, with good friends and a purpose in life, or to continue groping for a past which is not here. I hope she is able to make the right decision.

Mary McGeehan
405 E. 5th Street
Santa Ana, CA 92701

Whoa, Mary— Barbara's personality isn't dead! It's submerged beneath (a) the facade of the Valkyrie and (b) Barbara's own insanity. And in fact, from time to time, Barbara actually manages to penetrate those barriers and "touch" Val's own identity. It's a complicated problem, and Val may never find a solution, but neither can she stop trying. And the "why" of all that will become more and more apparent as the months fly by. Watch and see.

Much as we hate to do it to her, our warrior-woman is in for the most trying time of either of her lives.

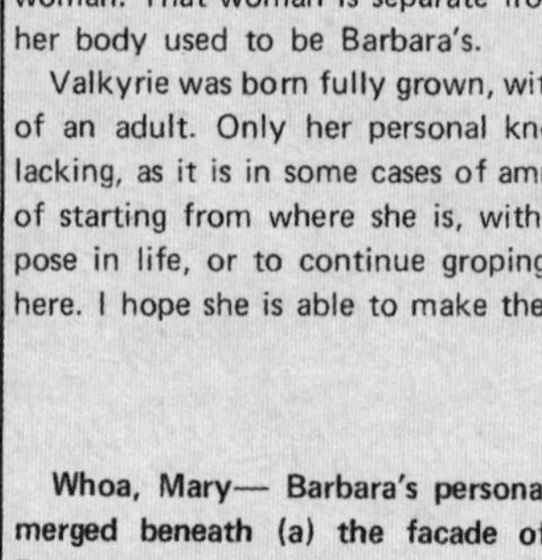

OPPOSITE **78: THE OWL** from *The Defenders* no. 23 (May 1975). Stamp also appears in *Fantastic Four* no. 149 (August 1974) and *The Avengers* no. 132 (February 1975).

ABOVE *Daredevil Annual* no. 1 (September 1967), art by Gene Colan and John Verpoorten.

panel) and, as a popular TV detective might say, "That's when it hit me." I looked up to the second panel on the same page and was positive of the resemblence. Obviously, this wasn't a coincidence. It was, rather, an excellent idea. What better way to stop people from comparing your character to the one on TV. And what a great way to teach Shang-Chi of life.

Meanwhile, I'd like to say that you handled the Man-Thing beautifully. The cover was great—by Gil Kane and Tom Palmer, right? Please have your artists sign their names on the covers they produce. Now I have to wait four months to see if my assumption is correct.

Two more requests—no, make that three. 1) Give the Silver Surfer his own mag. 2) Let's have nudity in your comics. And 3) Keep up the excellent work.

Eric Roland Martinez
21 Gray Street
Brentwood, N.Y. 11717

Dear Steve, Paul, etc.,

I was really impressed by MOKF #19. We see here the meeting of two vastly different yet somehow compatible beings, Shang-Chi and Man-Thing, those two who use opponents' fear to defeat them. An impressive guest appearance.

And now, No-prize time! I think I deserve my first for noticing how Lu Sun echoes Kwai Chang Caine. I cannot but notice this because of the controlled serenity in their exchange. It is fitting that Lu Sun's destiny not be combined with Shang Chi's. You guys effectively showed how Lu Sun was the Caine-like individual, not being oppressed by a situation like Shang-Chi's, able to look at life with the calmness shown in his face in the final frame. Here, I think, is comic artistry at its finest, when it can make the reader understand the underlying forces in the story, make the reader sit back afterwards and consider the natures of the protagonists, and understand their individual life-paths. A truly stunning achievement. Thank you.

Now, do I get my first, or not?

Timothy K. Johnson
P.O. BOX 5989
Sarosota, Fla. 33579

Unfortunately, Tim, there are those in this world (specifically, of the legal profession) who are not possessed of the serenity needed to allow us a direct reply to your conjectures, and so we'll have to hold up on that no-prize this time around.

We'll be frank to admit, however, that the Man-Thing's inclusion was a tribute to Steve Gerber's work on Manny's own book. There are some darn fine comics on the stands today, and that's one of 'em.

Finally, for the You-Heard-It-Here-First Department: sometime around the first of the year, the ubiquitous Mr. Englehart and Far-Out Frank Brunner will be teaming up to bring you a series devoted entirely to the devil doctor, Fu Manchu, in one of our black-and-white books. Set in the 1930's (pre-Shang-Chi), this will be a relentless pulp thriller completely beyond any pulp adaptation you've ever seen. Watch for it.

Bye!

THIS IS IT! YOUR
MARVEL VALUE STAMP
FOR THIS ISSUE! CLIP 'EM AND COLLECT 'EM!

OPPOSITE **79: KANG** from *Master of Kung Fu* no. 22 (November 1974). Stamp also appears in *Sgt. Fury* no. 119 (May 1974) and *Giant-Size Man-Thing* no. 5 (August 1975).

ABOVE *The Avengers* no. 23 (December 1975), art by Don Heck and John Romita Sr.

SOCK IT TO SHELL-HEAD

c/o MARVEL COMICS GROUP, 575 MADISON AVE. N.Y.C. 10022

First off this ish, a belated apology to the basketball partisans of Kansas City and Omaha: sorry we placed your Royals in their former Cincinnati home in issue #62. Scripter Mike Friedrich confesses to be too wrapped up in Raiders and 49ers, Giants and A's to keep up with everything else in sports.

Also, we firmly promise never again to spell "thought" as "thot"— nor mistake cubic centimeters for cubic inches (as in car engine size, folks).

All this is to clear enough space for as much comment as we can fit concerning the hottest topic ever to stack up the IRON MAN mail pile: the comics-breakthru "triangle" of Tony, Pepper and Happy.

Take it away, people . . .

Dear Marvel,

I have never before encountered such a relevant and mature page in any comic book as was the last page of IRON MAN #63. Personally, judging from Happy's character, any such incident in real life would spell total estrangement. Happy would never be convinced that the incident he walked in on was completely an isolated event; his mind would never accept that nothing even more serious had not taken place on other occasions. Or so I feel.

Nor would he ever again become reconciled with Mr. Stark. The rift between Happy and wife should as of now be unbridgeable. Happy is an insecure man. But of course one must remember that this event has taken place in a comic book; unrealistic possibilities are by rule probable.

For example, note Happy's closing observation: "My best friend—is in love with my wife!" Ridiculous. He might have said: "My wife—is in love with my best friend!" That would be more likely. But I do not believe any man would express either statement if he had been fearing infidelity on the part of his wife and friend. His choice of words would have been very much less kind, for his fear would not lie in the fact that Tony might be in love with Pepper. His fear more naturally would have been concerning the transgression of the Seventh Commandment; promiscuity is the name of the game. A man like Happy is too glandular to accept and/or forgive. I am hereby in advance dismissing the undoubtedly eventual happy ending for the Hogans (that I know will come about) as sheer nonsense.

Hector Randis Spartan
229-6th St.
New Westminister, B.C., Canada

Dear whoever is currently scripting Iron Man:

Must we have an instant replay of Peyton Place? I'm all in favor of quote: raw human emotion, unquote, in comics —but really! Iron Man is not the place to rehash used-up soap opera plots! Especially when the story is so predictable. Predictable plots make for dull stories, and dull stories make for loss of reader interest. Need I say more?

Gail Teague
P.O. Box 218
Riverdale, Ca. 93656

. . . I don't care about Tony's personal life! Unless some gamma-rays turn Hap into the Harpy's brother . . . get him and Pepper out! What is this? "Our Love Story"?

Steven Baeck
88-31 Elderts Lane
Woodhaven, N.Y. 11421

Dear Roy and Confreres,

. . . As for the Hogan dilemma, I am supporting Happy; though he is not conducting himself as one would expect of a selfless and concerned husband, his wife Pepper is even more inconsiderate and flagrant. She left Happy because he could not provide her with the social eminence Tony has to offer. Her references for a need to "grow . . . expand . . ." are merely misconceptions—though they do express a valid need; she really meant that she felt socially stagnant existing within Happy's lifestyle. Tony Stark, as well, still attracts her. Why else would she find it necessary to put such literal (i.e. geographical) distance between herself and her husband? She could easily have gotten a job in the relative neighborhood of their home, if an occupation was all she had in mind when referring to her need for personal cultivation. To be blunt, she is sick and tired of being nothing more than a homemaker. She wants the excitement and glamour of pre-marital days. This is perfectly understandable, and anyone with the ability to reason would sympathize with her. However, as far as the "successful marriage" is concerned, such actions will nigh invariably prove fatal. But why worry? This is, after all, a comic book. The outcome of this particular trial is predictable: either one or the other of the couple will be tragically killed—leaving the other partner to "bear up and carry on honorably"; or some super-menace will intervene whose advent will threaten the life of one of the Hogans (if not fulfilling the previous possibility), thereby uniting them firmer than ever, for ever and ever. Since when have major characters in a comic book ever undergone a divorce (or, digressing slightly, committed adultery —does this transcend murder as a sin?)? Common as rain in real life, perhaps; but, immature minds read these comics, and a divorce or act of adultery are not quite as simple and routine as general comic book murder and mayhem, and so much trauma is not good for them . . . etc. . . .

Dave Ammerman
217-27th Avenue
Altoona, Pa. 16601

Dear Mike,

. . . The scene on the fifth page of #63, between Tony and Roxie, was the highlight for me. I hope it develops into something good and wholesome and lasting. As with Spider-Man, IM's just beginning on a new romantic involvement; as with Spider-Man, he's had more than his share of hung-up relationships; and as with Spider-Man, he now has a chance to start from scratch, unencumbered by any hang-ups in the new relationship. And, as with Spider-Man, I hope he doesn't blow it and that this time no hang-ups ever interfere with his relationship. I really feel for the guy (even to the extent of forgiving him his "Tenderly, Tony, tenderly!"), and I really dig Roxie. Let this budding romance lead to a good, solid relationship soon, and spare Tony—and us—the usual heartbreak along the way. Roxie's just right for Tony. She's obviously better than him in one aspect, her uncompromising attitude toward the villains of history, the capitalists. Tony seems to recognize this. He calls it "a challenge." Well, maybe Roxie can show him the way. She can help him where he needs it, and he can learn and by doing that and providing his affection for her, show her that he's good enough for her. . .

. . . All along I've been hoping that Happy and Pepper could resolve their differences: Happy coming to accept his wife's role as a working woman, Pepper stopping her trips out of town so that she could at least come home to him every night, and possibly Pepper being let in on Tony's dual identity, a secret which Happy already shares, and Happy going back to work for Tony, too, along with Pepper. And when I saw Pepper in that tantrum I thought that surely it would come to that. But the dissapointment came on the last page, as did the rage. You're writing an adventure magazine, Mike, not a soap opera! The last development of the story was both unnecessary and bad. But as long as you threw it in, we're all going to suffer the consequences, including you.

. . . I hate Pepper Hogan. I think Happy should divorce her. Tony? He's just a victim of circumstances. If he can forget Pepper as a friend, he and Happy can still get along as before. Tony'll still have Roxie, and Happy can find someone to replace Pepper.

Lester Boutillier
2276 Castilione Street
New Orleans, Lc 70119

THIS IS IT! YOUR

MARVEL VALUE STAMP

FOR THIS ISSUE!

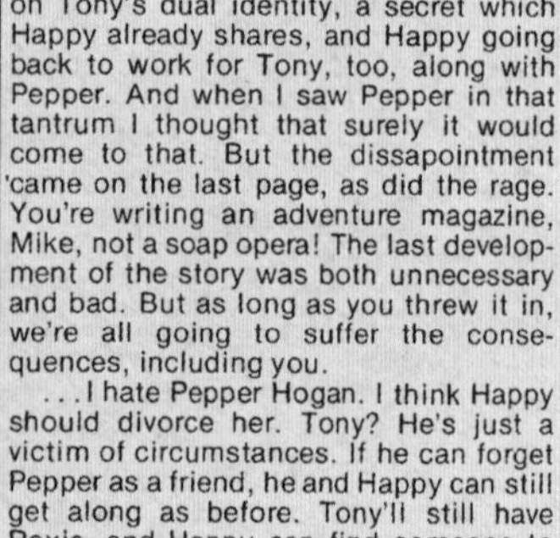

CLIP 'EM AND COLLECT 'EM!

OPPOSITE **80: THE GHOST RIDER** from *Iron Man* no. 67 (April 1974). Stamp also appears in *Thor* no. 229 (November 1974), *Tomb of Dracula* no. 26 (November 1974), *Tomb of Dracula* no. 29 (February 1975), *Conan the Barbarian* no. 49 (April 1975), and *Daredevil* no. 127 (November 1975).

ABOVE *Ghost Rider* no. 3 (December 1973), art by Jim Mooney and John Tartaglione.

doesn't have it and Iron Man does, Hawkeye always did remarkably well against Shellhead. I had hoped Clint would really smear Tony in DEFENDERS #9. Dr. Strange Vs. Mantis and the Panther was the best Dr. Strange that appeared in the entire Avengers-Defenders series. The Doc acted like the Master of the Mystic Arts instead of a super-hero.

AVENGERS # 117: I had hoped Val would show the Swordsman a thing or two, but I know it wouldn't have been logical if she had. (I would like to point out that Swordy handles that quintet remarkably well for one who's been an Avenger for such a short time.) Captain America vs. the Submariner should have happened long ago.

DEFENDERS #10: Thor vs. the Hulk appeared to have taken place only to prove, once and for all, that Goldilocks and Jade-jaws are exactly equal in strength. (I've always held that Purple-pants is a little stronger and sexier, whereas Winghead is smarter, cornier, has the advantage of Mjolnir and various other powers, and is slightly more of a male chauvinist pig.) The meeting of the Avengers and the Defenders in Chapter 10 was a real trip Super-heroes so seldom get together to talk things over, I always dig it when they do.

AVENGERS #118: Steve's attention to detail worked against him here: bringing in SHIELD to take care of the monsters and the expectable bickering within so large a group of heroes got the story off to an unfortunately slow start. As for the defeat of Dormammu, I wasn't sure how you were going to keep it from being an anticlimax, but you did it fairly well. The intervention of Loki was to be expected, but the final defeat of Dormammu at the hands of the Scarlet Witch was not. Wanda's been kept at a "zapping" level and never allowed to become as powerful she could be for all the years she's been around. The ending really made up for her "damsel in distress" role in AVENGERS #116.

Special congratulations from me to Bob Brown for apparently paying attention to how the Dark Dimension originally looked. Altho no one does those dimensions like Ditko did, Bob drew Ditko's Dark Dimension, Bob Brown style.

Jana C. Hollingsworth
474 Higginson Hall
Western Washington State College
Bollingham, Washington

Jana, in the Stainless One's file of AVENGERS plots, notes, and brainstorms is a complete psychological rundown and character analysis of every Avenger, both the ones he's solely responsible for and the ones who appear in their own books through other writers. Ofttimes, in the crush of moving eight heroes and assorted villains through a story, he can only touch upon the Avengers' deeper natures...and yet, you picked up on a lot of them. What more can a writer ask than a committed audience.

In the Stainless One's view, Iron Man is indeed too dynamic and technology-oriented to truly accept magic (no putdown intended in any of these observations. Tony Stark is simply different from Stephen Strange). The Surfer and the Vision were each logical in their opposing views; that's why they were chosen to lead off the Clash. And so on down the line.

Thank you, Jana. Readers like you make it all worthwhile.

Dear Friends,

What else can I call you guys ?

Whenever you seem to get too heavy on the relevance or symbolism in your books, along comes something like AVENGERS # 118 to remind us that Marvel still turns out the best illustrated fantasy around. Although there have been many high points in your various books, I haven't seen anything this monumental since the Avengers fought the Sentinels a year and a half ago.

Bob Brown's art was deceptively simple. It had just the right amount of excitement and suspense for this story. If a more spectacular artist like Adams or Brunner had done it, the results would have something—but they probably would have called more attention to themselves than the story. And what can I say about Steve Englehart? Every story that man writes astounds me, but this was the best yet. Even with fourteen heroes, things never seemed cluttered. The return of forgotten shapes like the Watcher and the Mindless Ones has become his trademark, and never has it seemed more appropriate. Practically the entire Marvel universe was in this book. From the F.F. to Thanos, all were united in fighting one menace. It was as epic a battle between good and evil as we'll ever see in the pages of a comic mag.

Perhaps the best statement to make about "To The Death" is that if, Heaven forbid, you stopped all publication tomorrow, it would stand as both a final summation and reaffirmation of all Marvel has been in the past thirty years. Thanks to everyone who's responsible for, as Steve calls it near the end,"...that bruised and battered dimension we've all come to know and love."

God bless you all.

Jerome Wilson
4524 Kinmount Road
Lanham, Maryland 20801

Dear People,

What has happened to the Avengers? Since Steve started writing for this book, we have seen the "retirements" of four Avengers: Hawkeye (# 109), Quicksilver (# 110), Black Widow (# 112), and Black Knight (DEFENDERS # 11). Which Avenger is next?

The Swordsman joins in # 114, but why him? Why not Hank and Jan or Hercules? They haven't been around for some time. I must say that Mantis, though not a full-fledged Avenger, is a welcome addition.

Steve, your stories continue to get better and better with each issue. So far you have brought Vision and Wanda together, you have shown some people's feelings against the idea of a mutant and android (or should I say two beings) in love (feelings not shared by all), and a somewhat different Wanda. You seem to have a talent for turning out such masterpieces as AVENGERS #108, #113, and #119. I would say that the AVENGERS are in good hands, just as long as you don't retire anymore of them.

So, until Thor decides to retire, MAKE MINE MARVEL.

R.F.O. K.O.F. Ronald Hayes

We've already tipped our hand a little in our answer to Ron, so let's just make two cryptic statements an take our leave.

(1) Nobody stays retired forever.

(2) This summer, the Avengers will join the Fabulous F.F. at the long-awaited wedding of Quicksilver and Crystal.

'Nuff said!

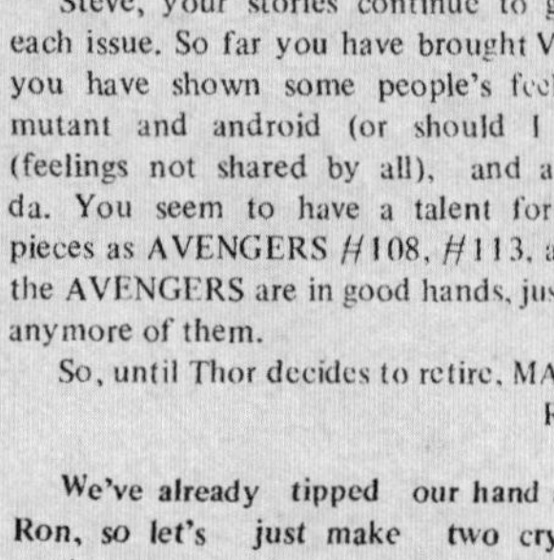

OPPOSITE **81: RHINO** from *The Avengers* no. 124 (June 1974). Stamp also appears in *Marvel Spotlight* no. 18 (October 1974) and *Ghost Rider* no. 9 (December 1974).

ABOVE *The Incredible Hulk* no. 171 (January 1974), art by Herb Trimpe and Jack Abel.

Fantastic Four ④ Fan Page

THE MARVEL COMICS GROUP, SIXTH FLOOR
575 MADISON AVE.,
NEW YORK, N. Y. 10022

A SPECIAL ANNOUNCEMENT FROM STAN, ROY, AND MARVEL COMICS

By the time this message appears in any of our mags, you'll already have noticed that all of our 36-page comic magazines are now 25¢— a nickel more than they were a few short weeks ago.

Maybe your first reaction to the price hike was the same as ours might be if we were in your shoes: "What's Marvel trying to do to us, anyway? Don't they know we've got enough troubles, what with inflation, shortages, and an energy crisis on our hands, without trying to clip us for 5¢ more every time we want a little fantasy-filled escape from it all? What is this— some kind of rip-off, so that Stan and Roy can vacation on the Riviera this year?"

If that was your reaction, it's an understandable one— and we'd just like to ask you to listen to our side of it for a minute before you decide:

This year, the widely-publicized paper shortage(in addition to various labor settlements among the companies that print, sell, and distribute Marvel Comics) caused additional expenses to Marvel of several hundred thousand dollars. That means that we had to make that much extra money just to stay even, despite the fact that our sales in 1973 were the best in the business.

So, we had no choice, really, but to increase the cover price of our magazines, the same way that just about everybody else has to.

And, just in case you think we're now getting rich off that new-found nickel: Believe it or not, that extra copper only covers about half the cost of the paper strike and other shortages.

What're we doing about the whole situation?

We think the answer's obvious, if you take a look at some of the titles we're now publishing besides our 36-pagers. There's our increasingly popular 75¢ line of full-scale magazines, first of all. Already, our four flagship 75-centers are being joined by THE DEADLY HANDS OF KUNG FU and the return (on March 26) of SAVAGE TALES— with two or three more much-requested types of mags already in the works.

Likewise, there's our spanking new, sensational 35¢ giant-size comics— a full 52 pages of colorful cavorting, and now a bigger bargain than ever!

Not only that, but the next few weeks will herald the coming of a brand new Marvel phenomenon: our swingin' SUPER-GIANTS, featuring one hundred big pages for just 60¢ including a feature-length new tale each and every issue. The Bullpen Bulletins Pages will give you the full scam, next time around— but rest assured that you're gonna be getting your money's worth!

Not only that— but we've got other plans we can't even hint at yet!

Well, that's about it. We've had our say.

About the only other thing we can do is to affirm once more that, just as we've been doing for over a decade now, every artist and writer in the Bullpen will be striving night and day, even harder than ever (if that's possible), to see to it that you consider— each precious coin spent on a Marvel mag to be one of the wisest investments you ever made.

Let's lick this thing together, okay?

Thanks for listening.

Dear Gerry, Rich, Joe, and Roy,

From the electrifying cover to the haunting concluding panel, the final segment of the F.F.'s tangle with Dr. Doom has erased several doubts I'd been having lately about this legendary feature. Unquestionably, the unleashing of Rich Buckler's monumental illustrative wizardry is responsible for returning this comic to the standards set during the Lee-Kirby era.

In disagreement with a policy that you have stated, I still stand firmly behind my belief that an artist can indeed make or break a strip. We need look no further than the legions of fans Rich has undoubtedly left spellbound for proof. The anticipation of classics yet to be born in what is truly "The World's Greatest Comic Magazine" is absolutely shattering.

This series also spawned Darkoth, a most fascinating and exciting being. If you had salvaged him, instead of sending him to his apparent doom (ouch!), you could easily have opened up a vast area of creative possibilities. He left as an enraged creature, seeking to right that which was evil and unjust. It was a perfect set-up that I think you threw away too hastily But then, when Dr. Doom returns from his apparent death, as he always does, hopefully Darkoth will have survived also.

Alan Rothman
151-12 24th Rd.
Whitestone, N.Y. 11357

Whether or not Darkoth will one day stalk the pages of FANTASTIC FOUR again is known only to Conway, Alan—and he's not telling. We'll all just have to wait and see.

Meanwhile, thanks for the good words on F.F. #144. And let the word go forth that the vast majority of Marveldom Assembled agreed with your evaluation of the issue, that it was a triumph.

However, we must dispute one statement in your letter, Mr. Rothman. (Notice how formal we get when we disagree? It's enough to send chills up your big toe!) We've never said that an artist can't "make or break a strip." In fact, it's obvious that that much is quite true. What we have said is that there's no one single "right" artist for any strip— that several artists can handle a strip equally well, though perhaps differently. There definitely is such a thing as the "wrong" artist for a strip; our contention is merely that there can be more than one "right" artist. Catch the distinction?

THIS IS IT! YOUR
MARVEL VALUE STAMP
FOR THIS ISSUE!
CLIP 'EM AND COLLECT 'EM!

OPPOSITE **82: MARY JANE WATSON** from *Fantastic Four* no. 147 (June 1974). Stamp also appears in *Man-Thing* no. 10 (October 1974).

ABOVE *The Amazing Spider-Man* no. 42 (November 1966), art by John Romita Sr.

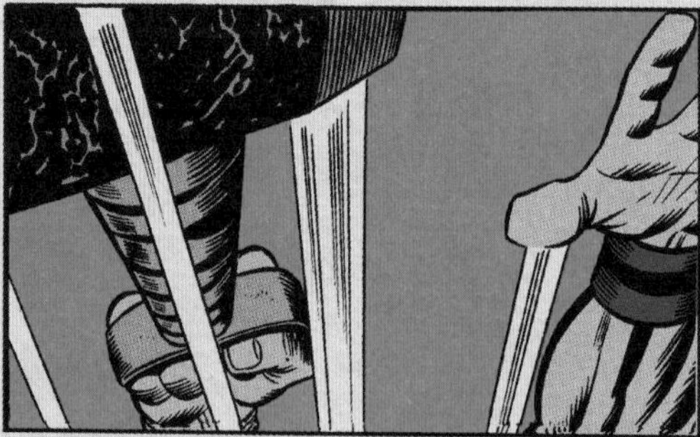

Fantastic Four and has done well in the years since his first appearance in JOURNEY INTO MYSTERY # 83. So how about bringing back the good old Earth adventures in which Balder comes down to Midgard in search of the God of Thunder to warn him that Surtur and Skagg have once again returned to Earth to create havoc for Loki?

Until Odin gets a crew cut. Make Mine Marvel!

Danny C. Ng
1211 Echo Avenue
Seaside, California

Rather than start the Earth/Asgard/outer space controversy all over again, allow us a moment to brief you on some of Gerry's plans for the next few months.

There's an epic in the works, people— a tale which will involve your favorite Asgardian heroes and villains, some long-unglimpsed earthbound characters, and one or two characters who hail from neither of those two domains. No kidding. We think Marveldom En Masse will be remembering for years to come the strange and unique storyline THOR will be following in the weeks and months ahead.

We won't say more, because we don't want to spoil any of the many surprises Gerry has planned, but we will say that the new and startling developments in the life of our golden-tressed god of thunder are guaranteed to move, shake, delight, and enthrall you, whether you support your local planet or yearn for the void beyond.

Enow spake!

Mr. Marvel,

THOR is great, fantastic, wonderful, and my favorite mag-half the time. The half when he's not on earth. The earth has Spidey, Daredevil, Cap and the Falc, Fantastic Four, on and on and on. Thor was meant for Asgard. Let the people who want to tie him down read those other thousands of mags. Let us keep Thor. I'm speaking for the whole gang down here in wolfpack country who want to put in our two cents. Marvel's the greatest!

Bob Bryan
Raleigh, N.C.

Dear Mr. Conway,

Aaaarrgh!!! Ye Gods! (No pun intended.) I've tolerated it for the last few months coming from Thor and Hercules, but now you have *Odin* saying Zounds! For your information, zounds is a distortion/contraction of the exclamation, "Christs' Wounds!" It really detracts from the story when I hear Odin wielding a Christian oath! Only a no-prize will appease mine Allfadur-wrath!

Jeff Westfall
Box 3815
Evansville, Ind. 47736

'Tis granted thee, Mr. Westfall, along with an honorary degree from Asgard State University in etymology.

Still, we don't think that'll stop Thor, Herc, and big-daddy Odin from exclaiming "Zounds!" upon occasion. We tried to convince them to loosen up a little, but they still preferred that more noble-sounding expression to the "zowie!" we suggested as an alternative.

Some days, ya just can't winneth.

THIS IS IT! YOUR

MARVEL VALUE STAMP

FOR THIS ISSUE! CLIP 'EM AND COLLECT 'EM!

OPPOSITE **83: DRAGON MAN** from *Thor* no. 231 (January 1975). Stamp also appears in *Man-Thing* no. 5 (May 1974) and *Marvel Spotlight* no. 16 (July 1974).

ABOVE *Fantastic Four* no. 44 (November 1965), art by Jack Kirby and Vince Colletta.

Fantastic Four Fan Page

Send letters to: STAN LEE
THE MARVEL COMICS GROUP
SIXTH FLOOR 575 MADISON AV.
NEW YORK 10022 N. Y.

Dear Armadillos,

Interesting. You've got the F.F. back on the right track. The Silver Surfer, Dr. Doom, and the classic brute humor of the Thing—all in one issue. What more could any F.F. addict want?

Well, for one thing you could restore the F.F.'s original costumes. That's right— give the Torch his own blue, baggy costume back and give the Invisible Girl (Woman?) *her* costume back, too (after bringing her back as an active member of the group, natch). Oh yeah, and get rid of Medusa!!!!

Desnek Rotifer
(in transit)

Why, Desnie, ol' buddy— how'd you *know*? In other words— see the last page of the very epic you hold in your hot little hands, and you'll think it's Christmas at springtime! And *no,* this isn't Rascally Roy Thomas and Rich (Swash) Buckler's idea of a joke: this is, like they say, the real thing! (Not to mention Torch, Reed, and Sue!)

With the surprise ending of this issue, we've pretty well restored things to where they were a couple of years ago— before Reed and Sue split up, before Johnny changed his threads, before Medusa came along. We say "almost" because nothing truly stands still; and during this time Johnny has lost his beloved Crystal forever to. Quicksilver (though the true-blue charms of voluptuous Valeria may just console him, in time— repeat, *may*) and, Sue has matured as a person (and maybe, just maybe, so has Reed).

As for the matter of the Torch's outfit, we figure that even a grade-C Junior Woodchuck can figure that one out: With the reappearance of the *original* Human Torch in addition to J. Storm, first in the pages of THE HUMAN TORCH and now, most magnificently, in the World War II wonderment of our new 50¢ GIANT-SIZE INVADERS mag (where he shares equal billing with Captain America and the Sub-Mariner, his sparring partners of those long-ago days), we figured there'd be even more confusion if both Torches were running around in red long-johns.

So we put Torch back in his *blue* overall undies. Some change, huh?

So everything's back to normal, right?

Wrong! Like we said, nothing stands still— so just wait'll you see what befalls our fabulous foursome *next* issue, in the offbeat saga we call "In One World— and Out the Other!"

Dear Stan Lee,

I'm going to make this short and fast. In FANTASTIC FOUR #155 you made a big mistake. You put Doctor Doom in the book, when he died in issue #144. In exchange for this scoop, I want a lifetime subscription to FANTASTIC FOUR. (P.S.: Stop making mistakes!)

Vincent Van Crouch
1309 Woodnell Ave.
Columbus, Ohio 43219

How can we, Vince? If we do, nobody'll be able to tell a madcap Marvel mag from all the other comics cavorting on the newsstand these days. Still, we keep *tryin'*— honest!

As for wanting a lifetime sub to F.F.—well, who doesn't? But alas, it behooves us to point out that (in our own sneaky fashion) we cleared up the little matter of the hairbreadth escape of Victor Von Doom in the first far-out issue of GIANT-SIZE SUPER-VILLAIN TEAM-UP, a few months back. Too bad if you were looking the other way, chum! Maybe somebody'll let you borrow his copy so you'll no longer be numbered among the Great Deprived?

Dear Marvel,

How can "The World's Greatest Comic Magazine" rise to even greater heights, as in #155? Simple: it's because of one character, and need I name him? The Silver Surfer is without a doubt the best character Marvel has. And where is he? In Marvel Limbo, striving for existence.

I say this: if Captain Marvel, Warlock, Dr. Strange, and even the X-Men can make a comeback, so can the Surfer! Even if you just gave him a new series that was a back-up for GIANT-SIZE F.F., that would be a step in the right direction. You've done this with Howard the Duck in the MAN-THING mag. Let Jim Starlin develop plotlines, Thomas do scripts, and Buckler or Cockrum do the art— and definitely get rid of the barrier! Let the Surfer become the Skyrider of the Spaceways once again.

J. Rosler
(no address given)

Can we level with you, J.R.? Thanks.

Frankly, each and every person in the entire Marvel Bullpen wants the Silver Surfer to return. However, there's a hang-up, and a quite understandable one: Stan (the Man) Lee has written all of the Surfer's epoch-making solo adventures to date, and is bound and determined that he, and he alone, shall script such a reincarnated mag. Only thing is, his publishing and editorial-directing duties keep him so busy that it'll probably be some months yet before he can devote himself to so much as a plot, let alone an actual script. And, frankly, we feel that the Smiling One has long since earned the right to determine if and when the Surfer makes that comeback you (and we) so devoutly wish to see.

But keep your fingers crossed, okay? May be *next* year...

THIS IS IT! YOUR

MARVEL VALUE STAMP

FOR THIS ISSUE!
CLIP 'EM AND
COLLECT 'EM!

OPPOSITE **84: DR. DOOM** from *Fantastic Four* no. 159 (June 1975). Stamp also appears in *The Avengers* no. 121 (March 1974), *Astonishing Tales* no. 28 (February 1975), and *Marvel Team-Up* no. 33 (May 1975).

ABOVE *Fantastic Four* no. 142 (January 1974), art by Rich Buckler and Joe Sinnott.

Uh-oh. Wait'll you see the last page of this issue, Bernie!

Anyway, to answer your question: where did you get the impression that blind persons can't enjoy plays? They can, after all, hear the dialogue. (And Candace was there to describe the action of the play to Matt.) We think, if you ask around, you'll be surprised at the number of sightless theatre goers.

As for the villains you'd like to see back...there's a new Jester story in the works, and you'll be seeing it after the wind-up of the Gladiator/Death-Stalker series. The others? As the old line goes, when you least expect it...!

Okay now,

DAREDEVIL #109 showed me that you plan to give Matt a new love interest, Candace Nelson, and ease the Black Widow out of the picture. Although I abhor this move for a variety of reasons, I guess your reasons for doing it will soon become clear. I can only say that I hope you will not plunge Natasha into oblivion as you did the Cat.

Bravo on Shanna's appearance!

Bonnie
(no surname or address given)

Candace Nelson as a new love-interest for Matt?

Maybe. Maybe not. We're not saying.

We will say this, though. The opinion seems equally divided at this point as to whether or not Natasha should remain a regular in the DAREDEVIL mag, and we're interested in hearing from as many of you as possible before we make a final decision. So, WRITE!! All of you! Right this minute! Grab whatever's at hand— stationery, post card, the envelope from your telephone bill, your baby brother— and jot down a line or two and send it our way!

Dear Roy, Steve, and Bob,

You're always asking us to write, no matter what, so that's what I'm doing.

The Gil Kane-Frank Giacoia cover on DAREDEVIL #109 wasn't too bad, but Horn-head looked— clumsy. As for the interiors, Bob Brown is a top artist in my book. However, Don Heck is the wrong inker for him. He gives dimension but is sketchy and tends to offset detail. I rather enjoyed, to say the least, the inks of Paul Gulacy over Mr. Brown's pencils and wouldn't mind seeing this pair as a regular team on D.D.

As for the scripting, I can only say this: this issue was the shot in the arm that D.D. has needed for quite some time. Combining the elements of mystery with the costumed villain/mystery organization concept fits especially well into the DAREDEVIL groove. D.D. is a man without fear, but most of us tend to forget that he is a man of mystery, too. (this ought to sound good to Steve, especially coming from a fellow St. Louisan.)

Dave Kalis
7570 Byron Place
Clayton, Mo. 63105

Praise always sounds good, Dave— to anybody!— no matter where it comes from!! But you were right: Steve enjoyed reading your letter.

This issue gets D.D. back solidly into the man-of-mystery role, we think. And you can expect to see this angle explored even more fully as time goes on.

As far as an inker for Bob Brown— we think we've found our man. And we're embarrassed to say he was under our noses all this time. We're speaking, of course, of valiant Vince Colletta, who inked this issue— one of Bob's best pencil jobs since taking over the strip, to our way of thinking— in grand style. If this one doesn't knock you out, we're gonna retire to Pago Pago and write funny animal comics for the rest of our lives. (Ooops! Sorry, Steve; we forgot about Howard the Duck!)

NEXT ISSUE: The wildest four-way battle you've ever seen, among Daredevil, the Gladiator, the Man-Thing, and the Death-Stalker! And wait 'til you see Stalky's macabre power! Plus: more on the Black Widow! Foggy Nelson! Richard Rory! And we may even find room for a plot! Don't miss DAREDEVIL #114! 'Nuff said?

THIS IS IT! YOUR
MARVEL VALUE STAMP
FOR THIS ISSUE!
CLIP 'EM AND COLLECT 'EM!

MARVEL BULLPEN BULLETINS • MARVEL BULLPEN BULLETINS • MARVEL BULLPEN BULLETINS

MONUMENTAL MEMOS OF CHILLERS, THRILLERS, AND FILLERS!

STAN LEE'S SOAPBOX

If you happened to miss the ol' Soapbox last ish, it's because I was in sunny Italy and didn't return in time to write it. But don't think I deserted you, O True Believer! I was there on your behalf, and now that I'm back I'm just bustin' to tell you about the fun and excitement of the biggest comic-book convention of them all. About 200 miles south of Milan, in the beautiful, ancient city of Lucca, they've been holding an annual comic-book congress for the past eight years. This year's Lucca 9 was the biggest yet. The whole town played host to writers and artists from all over the world. There were shows, panels, exhibits, and ceremonies lasting an entire week. Inside the main auditorium the seats were equipped with earphones through which you could hear translations of every speech in virtually every language. It was like being at the U.N., but lots more fun. And if those wild, warm, and wonderful Italians aren't the friendliest people around, then Thor bleaches his hair! But the thing that impressed me most—the thing I want you to know, is—in Europe comics are taken far more seriously by the adult population than in America. If you didn't know Lucca 9 was comic-book oriented you'd have thought it was a business convention. The adults, including the Mayor of Lucca himself, far outnumbered the youngsters in attendance. There were professors, businessmen, scientists, filmmakers, lawyers, and literally hundreds of other mature, serious fans deeply involved in one of the most popular art forms of all—the ubiquitous comic-strip! So here's to all of Marvel's fabulous friends in Lucca, and throughout the free world. So long as we strangers from different lands can come together in good will and mutual respect; so long as art can help to forge a lasting bond between people and nations; then so long shall there still be hope for an abiding peace upon this troubled earth.

Excelsior!

Stan

ITEM! We've lots of bombshells to explode this time around, so let's get rolling, shall we—?

ITEM! The big news this month — and we do mean *big* — is a fabulous pair of *new mags* sporting 52 great pages for just 35¢! That's right — our swingin' Summer-of-'73 Specials were such a rousing success, and so many of you requested more of the same, that we began work almost at once on a *regular line* of 35-centers. The only difference is, these new titles will contain mostly *new* stories and art, plus a whole passle of bonus features such as pin-ups, interviews, and more surprises than you can shake a Forbush at! The first of these mind-benders has already been on sale for a few weeks now: the *first* far-out issue of GIANT-SIZE SUPER-STARS, headlining the *Fantastic Four*, no less (with the ever-incredible Hulk as guest star)! As those of you who purchased this sell-out sensation already know, SUPER-STARS is a *monthly* mag, featuring no less than three rotating series, in the style of those Mystery Movies that've taken TV by storm. The F.F. led off the parade, of course, and this month's *second* slam-bang issue heralds the much-requested team-up of two of the most monstrous super-villains of all — Morbius, the Living Vampire, and the menacing Man-Wolf (alias John Jameson), against none other than your friendly neighborhood *Spider-Man!* While the third ish, on sale in April, will star still another of Marvel's mightiest: *Conan the Barbarian!* Then, the whole cycle will start all over again, with the F.F., Spidey, and Conan each appearing four times a year, in some of the most spectacular sagas ever recorded — we kid you not!

That's GIANT-SIZE SUPER-STARS, still on sale — if you're lucky!

Got it? Okay, then you're all set for our *next* scoop—!

ITEM! Our *second* magnificent new 35¢ mag has a title nearly as mind-boggling as the first: it's GIANT-SIZE CHILLERS, and it debuts March 12, starring (who else?) the one and only *Dracula* himself! But, this sinister series is called "The *Curse* of Dracula," and it'll be a wee bit different from the Lord of Vampires' other Marvel misadventures, for it'll deal mainly with those whose lives are touched by our blood-thirsting Count in some way, beginning with Dracula's very own *daughter*, as depicted on this self-same page! (Don't worry, though — our Transylvanian terror will appear prominently in each and every one of these tales!) And, since our new monthly CHILLERS mag has the same format as SUPER-STARS, Drac's new fear-fests will alternate with those of two other baneful new lights in the Marvel firmament: Werewolf by Night, and the macabre Man-Thing! All in GIANT-SIZE SUPER-CHILLERS!

Hope that's all clear, Flame-Keeper. 'Cause as of right now — you're on your own!

ITEM! And, sharing the limelight with these two blockbusters, have we got news for you! SAVAGE TALES is coming back for the third time — and *this* time, we're gonna go 'way out on a limb and predict that this most-honored Marvel mag is here to stay! In fact, we're so sure of it that we've already scheduled it for *bi-monthly* publications, like our other 75¢ titles, with the first of the new series going on sale March 26! There'll be brand-new, grand new Conan sagas by the likes of Barry Smith, John Buscema, Gil Kane, and Neal Adams — special items of interest to sword-and-sorcery swashbucklers the world over — plus a phantasmagorical new feature on the greatest fantasy films of all time! Now, if *that* isn't 'nuff said, we don't know what is!

ITEM! Whew! We've just room enough to tell you that a couple of other new series make their debut this month as well. One is *The Living Mummy*, who returns as the star of SUPERNATURAL THRILLERS, where he made his first foray a few months back. The other is *The Golem*, whose stomping grounds (and we mean just that!) will be STRANGE TALES. All this — plus an extra-special issue of WORLDS UNKNOWN, featuring an awesome adaptation of Columbia Pictures' new thriller, "The Golden Voyage of Sinbad!" Need we say it? It's the Marvel Age of Comics all over again!

ITEM! Due to a last-minute emergency, we had to forego our widely-acclaimed Bullpen Bonus Page this go-round. So, we'll have to wait till next month to tell you all about the brain-blasting bargains that'll be yours when you've amassed a complete set of MARVEL VALUE STAMPS — or about some of the hectic hijinx which the World's Weirdest Bullpen have been up to — not to mention the return of our capricious Checklist. Next time, though, we promise you two full pages of Marvel news and views! *Just wait and see!*

THE DAUGHTER OF
DRACULA
LURKS IN THE PAGES OF
GIANT-SIZE
CHILLERS
NUMBER ONE!
52 BIG PAGES --ONLY 35¢!
--AND SHE'S NOT ALONE!
ON SALE MARCH 12th!

OPPOSITE **85: LILITH, DRACULA'S DAUGHTER** from *Daredevil* no. 113 (September 1974). Stamp also appears in *The Incredible Hulk* no. 175 (May 1974), *Thor* no. 232 (February 1975), and *Master of Kung Fu* no. 31 (August 1975).

ABOVE Marvel Bullpen Bulletin from *The Amazing Spider-Man* no. 133 (June 1974), promotional art by unknown.

DEFENDERS DIALOGUE

c/o MARVEL COMICS GROUP, 575 MADISON AVE. N.Y.C. 10022

Dear Bullpen,

Sorry, Roy. Too bad, Denny. Tough luck, Gerry. Good try, Len. You're all great scripters, but remember this: STEVE ENGLEHART IS NUMBER ONE!

I have before me AVENGERS #115-118 and DEFENDERS #8-11, Steve Englehart's greatest work, otherwise known as the Avengers/Defenders Clash. This work, in my eyes, surpasses any superhero story written since the Fantastic Four/Inhumans stories many years ago by Lee and Kirby.

Congratulations are also in order for Sal Buscema (DEFENDERS) and Bob Brown (AVENGERS) for their splendid renderings. One question: who was the uncredited artist or inker on the Cap/Subby battle?

The Stainless One showed his genius by handling every character perfectly. Dr. Strange, the predominant character of the series, should be given back his own mag. This would leave a hole in MARVEL PREMIERE for a new Silver Surfer series (by Englehart, of course). Think about it, huh?

I hope the fate of the Black Knight in DEFENDERS #11 doesn't mean he will fade away into oblivion. You've got a chance for a brand new series set in the twelfth century.

Bring back the X-Men! KEEP ON FOOMIN'!

Mike Fanning
149 West Ave.
Ludlow, Mass. 01056

Gosh, Mike, if you like Steve's work, don't be shy— come right out and say so! We just hope you haven't deserted the dynamic Defenders, now that Len Wein is chronicling their adventures (and doing, we think, a fair-to-middling job of it, at least). Len's also the scripter on the macabre new BROTHER VOODOO mag, by the way, and you'll find him monthly in MARVEL TEAM-UP, too.

And for you, Mike, and your fellow Englehart fanatics— know ye that ol' Stainless is still hard at work on AVENGERS, on the mind-stunning MASTER OF KUNG FU, and on DR. STRANGE (in MARVEL PREMIERE), and that he'll soon be returning to CAPT. AMERICA & THE FALCON, as well as assuming the scripting chores on the Jim Starlin-plotted CAPT. MARVEL. (And we've just used up our quota of plugs for this answer.)

Incidentally, the uncredited (accidentally!) inker on the Cap/Subby segment of the Avengers/Defenders battle was Frank McLaughlin.

Dear Directors of the Defenders,

I started to write on how great the Avengers/Defenders saga was, but decided not to, since you'd be receiving those letters by the truckload. Instead, I'm writing to express a couple of my views on your greatest fighting group.

A couple of issues ago, it was mentioned that you are considering removing Dr. Strange from the group. To do so, I feel, would be as impossible as it was to drop Capt. America from the Avengers. The Defenders need Dr. Strange as much, if not more, than the Avengers needed Cap.

Being the loosely-knit non-group group that they are, the "members" must be led by someone strong enough to call them together and powerful enough to control them and keep them together until the job is done. Namor and the Hulk care very little about the Defenders, and their egos are such that only under rare situations would they attempt to call everyone together. Valkyrie has the team spirit, but not the power to hold the group in check. I don't know exactly how Silver Surfer feels about the team, but DEFENDERS #9 showed his lack of ability to control the Hulk.

Therefore, it seems that if the Defenders are going to exist, Dr. Strange must remain and retain the mantle of leadership that has fallen on his shoulders.

Which leads me to a second view of mine. In DEFENDERS #4, you (accidentally?) paralleled the AVENGERS by introducing the Valkyrie (AVENGERS #4 reintroduced Cap). Will this trend continue to issue sixteen? If so, after #15, Valkyrie will be the sole Defender left from the present group. I certainly hope you have bigger and better plans for the Defenders than that. Well, we'll see.

Finally, congratulations on not adding Black Knight and dropping Hawkeye. Neither would have fit in.

Hugh P. Simons, Jr.
308 Walker Hall
Normal, Ill. 61761

P.S.: I hope you do read all letters and consider them. I'd hate to feel this letter was a waste of time.

Obviously, Hugh, we read your letter— or it could never have appeared here — and we do consider all our readers' opinions and suggestions very carefully. (Including letters that are not typed, by the way. Hugh's wasn't. And if you don't happen to own or have access to a typewriter, reader, fear not. The notion that handwritten letters get tossed aside without being read is as mythical as Asgard. Maybe more so.)

But we're reluctant to say too much just yet about the ever-changing membership of the Defenders...at this point in time. You'll be seeing some rather dramatic developments, though, along those lines in future issues.

Meanwhile, other readers with other suggestions for other candidates for membership in the world's most exclusive non-club:

Dear Marvel,

So Hawkeye, Hulk, Subby, and the Silver Surfer have split, eh? Replacement time, folks! I hear that Nighthawk will be joining the gang... Well, that takes care of the magic, swordsmanship, and acrobatics. Now for the needed raw strength I've got it! Separate Rick Jones from Capt. Marvel, give him Hank Pym's growth serum, and presto! Goliath III. Also, bring Ant-Man and the Wasp out of retirement, as well as Red Wolf and Lobo, and the Cat. And let's not forget the Falcon or the Beast. There y'go, team, seven possibilites.

K. J. Robbins
1314 Cooper St.
Missoula, Mt. 59801

Dear Marvel,

In a recent Bullpen Bulletin you said that you were forced to cancel "secondary" features like the Cat, Warlock, and Red Wolf to concentrate on the big guns like Spidey and the Fantastic Four. But your "secondary" features are too good to remain in limbo. The Cat would be a great addition to the Defenders: she's simply too good a character to remain in Marvel limbo for years. Also, now that Hawkeye has left the ranks, you could bring in characters like Red Wolf (as good as Hawkeye any day), the Sub-Mariner's buddy Stingray (whatever happened to him?), and, since you have to end the Warlock story somewhere, why not let him go out in a burst of glory with Dr. Strange and the rest? Can't we have a return of the Marvel characters who deserve a second chance?

T. E. Pouncey
Douglass, Kansas

Interesting and provocative suggestions all! And while, as we mentioned, we don't want to give anything away— none of them are absolutely beyond the realm of possibility.

The WARLOCK saga, however, will be wrapped up (at least for a while) in an upcoming issue of THE HULK. And the Cat, we understand, will soon be returning in yet another magazine... but in wildly different form. More details when available, okay?

Now, though, let's close this letters page with a highly controversial, thought-provoking note on an entirely different subject.

Dear Steve and Sal,

The conclusion of the Avengers/Defenders epic left me a little disappointed. Leaving the Black Knight in the Crusades was a real letdown, and, overall, the battles between the Avengers and Defenders were nothing to speak of.

To me, the people involved in the Crusades were the biggest bunch of hypocrites around. There was no chivalry to it. It was a bunch of conceited fanatics who were sure they knew what made the world run. They wanted to advance Jesus' teachings of love, and they did it with a sword.

Let me quote some of your own words to you, Steve, from MARVEL SPECIAL EDITION (MASTER OF KUNG FU) #15: "...you speak with absolute assurance, completely convinced that your vision is the only proper way...and, like all men who speak thus...you are mad!" Sound familiar? Thought it would.

It seems only right that two religions, each convinced that its is the only way, and all others must die, should clash. They were made for each other.

That's all I have to say this time. Keep up the good work on the DEFENDERS, and pay attention to what you preach.

Ron Bain
2345 Neeley
Batesville, Ark. 72501

Comments, people?

OPPOSITE **86: ZEMO** from *The Defenders* no. 13 (May 1974). Stamp also appears in *Fear* no. 23 (August 1974) and *Supernatural Thrillers* no. 11 (February 1975).

ABOVE *Tales of Suspense* no. 99 (March 1968), art by Jack Kirby and Syd Shores.

Want to know why the merry men of Marvel tend to lose their minds on the average of once a week, Ralph? Read the next letter.

Dear Marvel,

Once you said that concerning all of your stories, you wanted the pan mail as much as the fan mail, because if you were doing anything wrong, you wanted to hear from us early. Well, maybe this isn't early, but I think it's well due. First of all, a resounding bravo for Harvey Phillips whose letter in THOR #219 brought up an ancient promise of yours that "a balance would be kept between Thor's adventures on earth and those in the lands and realms of...fantasy." Well?!

Don't get me wrong. I like the adventures, but, I mean, y' see one end of the world, you've seen them all! Get with it Even for a ten-year-old kid, a solid diet of nothin' but ice cream would soon grow nauseating.

Another thing. You've allowed Goldilocks to fall into a trap that another blue-clad, red-caped hero almost fell into a couple of years back. Now, Thor is too powerful to be believable, even in the realm of comicdom. How can a guy relate to someone who shatters planets, shrugs off ray-blasts that would decimate star-systems, battles whole armies (I think he talks them to death), etc.?

It's getting so almost every other issue begins with the earthshaking announcement that "THIS IS THE GREATEST THREAT THE UNIVERSE HAS EVER KNOWN!!" (Notice the faithful reproduction? all capitals.) After a while, it sorta loses some of its impact.

Don't make Thor so SUPER-super. Let's see some more "human" nature in him. A return to some of the style that gave Thor such a cult during the heyday of the Marvel Age of Comics— and I don't mean another falling out with Big Daddy Odin.

I remember a begoggled Thor using the mighty blast furnaces of our Nation to repair his damaged mallet...I remember Thor sipping a soda at a drugstore fountain and talking to some teenage kids...I remember Thor gently hugging a little girl whose father was serving in Vietnam and telling her she had a daddy she could be proud of...I remember Thor joking with a young kid who just souped up his new motorcycle and who offered to run a race with him that he'd never believe...

And y'know somethin'...? That's worth rememberin'.

Joe Cerniglia & Fred Lee Cain
c/o Kansas City Science Fiction & Fantasy Fan Club
2020 Olathe Blvd., Kansas City 66103

Okay, Marvelites, there you have it. Two very eloquent summings-up of the two different viewpoints on where Thor's adventures should take place and what sort of adventures they should be.

We're not sure this isn't an absolutely insolvable problem.

Gerry and John seem to like doing the far-out, super-cosmic, planet-rending, universe-shattering epics best. And thus far, most of our mail seems to be running in favor of those sagas, too.

But let's hear your ideas on the subject! Drop us a line— or two— or even a whole page, and tell us what you like and dislike about THOR...what you'd like to see in future issues... what your favorite THOR stories have been...and, of course, what you think of the very issue you're holding in your hands. We've got double the space now to print your letters; take advantage— now!

Let us and your fellow readers know what you're thinking. In other words, friends— WRITE!! (Is that subtle enough?)

Dear Gerry,

Okay, we all know that Thor has to have that hammer on him somewhere or he'll turn into Don Blake after sixty seconds. This has been shown to be true even in Asgard (issue #94). Does this mean he has to sleep with it, too, or wake up as Don Blake? What happens if he rolls over in the middle of the night?

Ann Nichols
11 Peach Tree Lane
Williamsport, Md. 21795

First of all, Ann, that early story was in error. In Asgard, whether he's carrying mighty Mjolnir or not, Thor remains Thor. On earth, if he wanted to maintain his Thor identity while asleep— yes, he would have to hold on to the hammer, or at least keep its leather thong about his wrist. If he rolls over in the middle of the night, though, a strange and wondrous phenomenon occurs: the big bum falls outta bed.

THIS IS IT! YOUR

MARVEL VALUE STAMP

FOR THIS ISSUE!
CLIP 'EM AND
COLLECT 'EM!

OPPOSITE **87: J. JONAH JAMESON** from *Thor* no. 224 (June 1974). Stamp also appears in *Marvel Team-Up* no. 25 (September 1974), *Tomb of Dracula* no. 34 (July 1975), and *Marvel Team-Up* no. 39 (November 1975).

ABOVE *The Amazing Spider-Man* no. 61 (June 1968), art by John Romita Sr., Don Heck, and Mike Esposito.

being born) I have seen a member of the Marvel Bullpen as a true, flesh-and-blood person. The feeling was food for thought.

It takes a lot for a person to admit that, maybe, he has not done a job equal to the expectations of others. It takes even more to say to all of us, "I blew it." Too often, it is easier to pass off criticism with flippancy, and I was impressed with the fact that you did not do so.

But, (I hear you say) its not the effort, its the result that counts. True, to an extent, but the effort does show through the finished work, and there was not a single issue between # 98 and the present that does not show this.

Sometimes, we fans grow to expect more than mortals can give. I'm sure William Shakespeare burned many pages of copy because he was dissatisfied with them, and I'm sure you have, also. I think part of the reason that you tried to do Gerry's DD, Roy's DD and Stan's DD is that you wished to follow an established "success formula."

Aesop demonstrates very aptly that we cannot satisfy every one. You must create your own conception of an idea, be it DAREDEVIL or MACBETH, and as your idea stands, so you will stand.

Remember, Steve, we may praise, and we may pan, but we're always on your side. Hang in there, baby. Don't feel you've "let us down." You Haven't.

Mark Spencer
(no address given)

Ah, well...we suppose this is as lousy a place as any to announce that as of this issue, scripted by Chris Claremont from Steve's plot, Steve is leaving DAREDEVIL to move on to other things. He does so reluctantly and with no little sadness, as he feels deeply about this book and, as he mentioned in DD #114, was just beginning to be satisfied with the direction of it.

Next month, Tony Isabella assumes the scripting on DAREDEVIL, and we'll be most anxious to know what you think of his efforts.

As for Steve, you'll find him this month in GIANT-SIZE DEFENDERS #3 and in every issue of the regular monthly DEFENDERS mag thereafter. As with DD, it's a mag he's always wanted to write, and when the opportunity arose, he felt he just couldn't pass it up. Here's hoping you agree. (Incidentally, if not coincidentally, Daredevil is the guest-star in that 32-page super-spectacular DEFENDERS tale. It's hard to let go...!)

A final word on this subject. Steve wants to thank each and every one of you who has taken the time and trouble to write to this magazine over the past several months. Your letters, as he's said often before, have been an invaluable aid in the reshaping of this magazine and an enormous source of support for his too-frail ego. To all of you— his undying appreciation. (And he says ya better write just as many DEFENDERS letters, or he'll be so mad—!)

Dear Marvel,

DAREDEVIL #114 was great, story-wise, art-wise and reading-wise...

But...

Face it, you blew it! There is one, and only one, three-fingered hero in the Marvel universe, the ever-lovin', blue eyed Thing!

So how come Man-Thing is shown throughout this entire issue with only three?

I really enoy Bob Brown's artwork, in some ways more than Colan, but hows about giving him some of Manny's books to read so that he can truly draw him as he is, OK? Thanks for listening! How's about a well earned no-prize?

Foomer James Farmer
63 Glenrich Avenue
Wilmington, Del. 19804

Bob had reference on Man-Thing, Foomer James, and shamefacedly admits he doesn't know how in the world he made that finger fumble. (And Steve, who's written the MAN-THING book for two years now is even more at a loss to explain how come he didn't catch it!)

So you get your no-prize. Manny gets his finger back. And all's right with the world.

THIS IS IT! YOUR
MARVEL VALUE STAMP
FOR THIS ISSUE!
CLIP 'EM AND COLLECT 'EM!

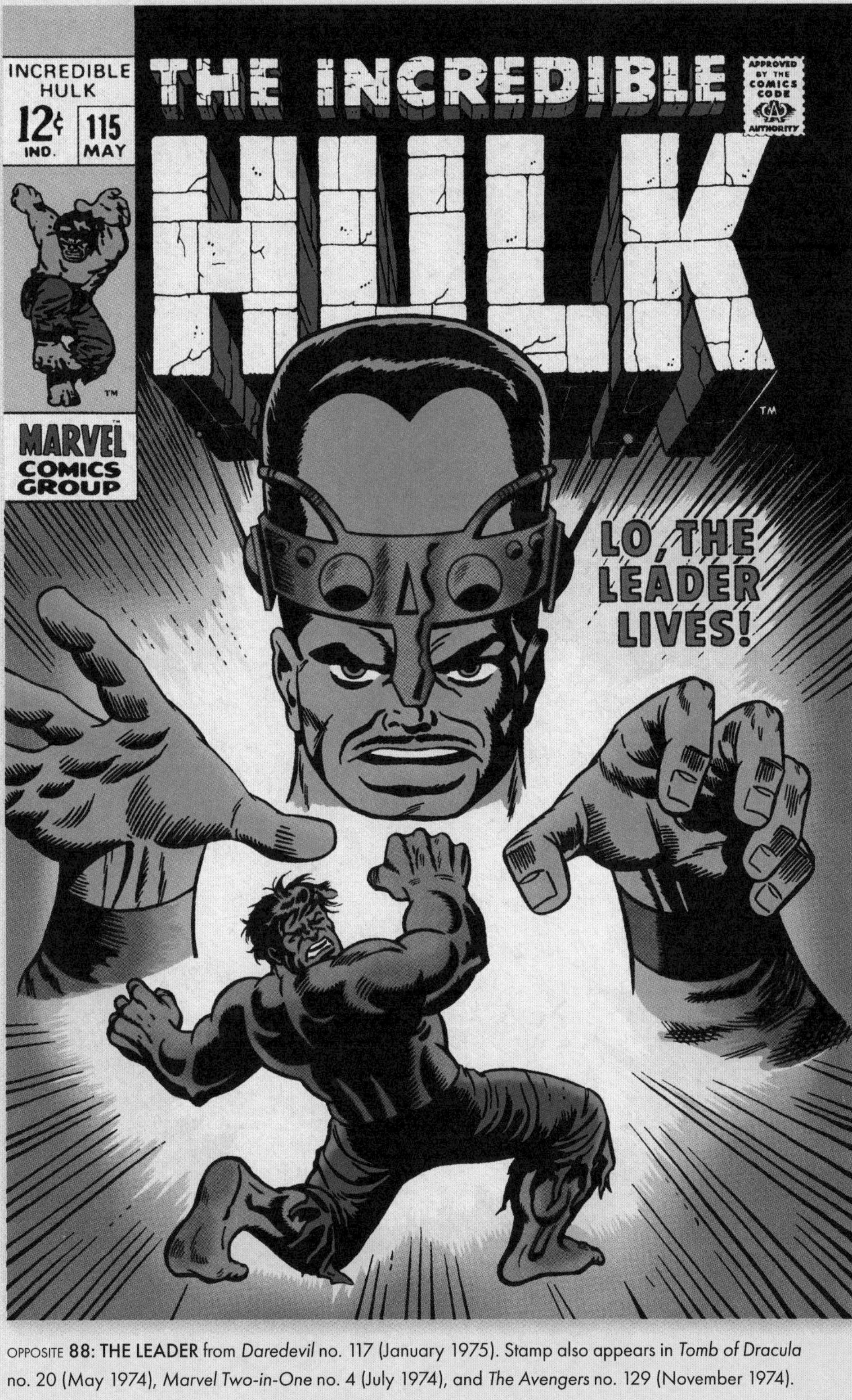

OPPOSITE **88: THE LEADER** from *Daredevil* no. 117 (January 1975). Stamp also appears in *Tomb of Dracula* no. 20 (May 1974), *Marvel Two-in-One* no. 4 (July 1974), and *The Avengers* no. 129 (November 1974).

ABOVE *The Incredible Hulk* no. 115 (May 1969), art by Herb Trimpe and Dan Adkins.

Dear Steve,

I enjoyed CAPTAIN AMERICA AND THE FALCON #174. This was one of the best books I've ever read. But:

Q: In C.A. #173, Linda Donaldson was unable to steal the electron-gyro, and so, Cap and the Falcon were brought in. But then we find out that Mr. Black is one of the Secret Empire. Wouldn't it have been easier for Mr. Black to steal the gyro than L. Donaldson, or two outsiders?

Q: How did Cap, Falcon, and the X-Men survive the Atomic Annihilator? Theory: I know little of Professor X... and it's my guess he had something to do with it!

Q: Why do your readers refer to other comic-book companies as competitors? As far as I'm concerned, Marvel has no rivals!

Tom York
4325 18th St.
Dorr, Michigan

A: The problem with either Linda or Mr. Black ripping off the electron-gyro was that both of them would immediately fall under suspicion because of their very access to the thing. Outside burglars were therefore required.

A: See Gabe Jones' explanation in #175.

A: Much as we'd like to gleefully go along with you, Tom, we feel obliged to say thee nay. Marvel may have finally made it from Number Two to Number One, but the other companies are still around, still prodding their people to turn out the best comics they can, and still doing their darnedest to make you buy those comics instead of ours. That's competition, amigo—and that's the way we like it! There can never be too many comic books in the world—at least, so say all true fans of our underrated, misunderstood little art form—and that includes each and every member of the Blushin', Blue-Eyed Bullpen! 'Nuff said?

Dear Steve and Sal,

I am just too fascinated with your Secret Empire series to say much. "It's Always Darkest" seemed so realistic, I was actually fearing for CA and F! I can't wait for the conclusion. You know, I walked over a mile to get #174 because the drugstore down the street from me didn't have it! That's how much I love Cap and Falc!

Happily,

Jesse Campbell

P.S. I hated the cover though. The Gil Kane art was ugly and it was blocked with too many word balloons.

Ah, yes...what was that old slogan? "I'd walk a mile for a Captain (America and the Falcon)."

Dear Marvel,

After waiting days for the climax of the "Secret Empire;" I went to my local drugstore and found CAPTAIN AMERICA #175 staring me in the face! I rushed home, read it, not once but four times! That is how much this issue affected me! To put it mildly, wow!

First off, I think Steve's story and message can be read many ways. Perhaps the man Cap unmasked was the President himself, or perhaps the man Cap unmasked was himself! What, you say? Let me explain. Cap himself is a symbol of our nation. He has the trust (and, once more) the respect of many —as did the leader of the Secret Empire. But the S.E. leader betrayed his trust and was evil. Perhaps Cap saw what could happen to a man who has too much trust!

I know I mixed you up, gang, but who says this isn't the Marvel Age of Mix-ups!

Robert S. Brodsky
2515 Hathaway
Alhambra, Ca. 91803

Mail reaction on #174 has already started to pour in, at the fastest rate since Steve and Sal's "Other Captain America" series ended, so we're presenting a sampling of it now just to wet your whistle, with much more to come on next month's letters page (and when we say "much more," we mean "MUCH MORE"). Enjoy, Cap-fan!

NEXT ISH: Well, we've had a respite from the crushing problems surrounding Steve Rogers these past two months, but CA&F #179 brings us back to the man who once was Captain America with a vengenace. It features a mvsterv villain called the Golden Archer, a desperate battle all across the city of New York, and even a heart-to-heart talk with Peggy Carter. You know you won't miss it, so what are we writing this blurb for? See you then!

Just a final reminder that our own Rascally Roy Thomas will be the major comic-book Guest of Honor at the star-studded San Diego (California) Comics Convention over the long weekend of July 31-August 5. A couple of others you might've heard of are gonna be Guests of Honor as well, including Charles ("Peanuts") Schulz, Milt ("Steve Canyon")Caniff, Gene ("Star Trek") Roddenberry, and fantasy author Ray Bradbury— just so you shouldn't get lonely.

Oh yes— and those of you with filled-up Marvel Value Stampbooks will receive a full dollar discount on con membership— as well as a pass to a private "Marvel 100" party where you'll meet Roy and such Marvel-type cohorts as Stainless Steve Englehart, Far-out Frank Brunner, Mike Friedrich and Royer, and MONSTERS OF THE MOVIES editor Jim Harmon. The whole shebang's being held at the El Cortez Hotel at 7th and Ash Streets in downtown San Diego, and advance full membership is $7.50, sent to San Diego Comics Convention, P.O. Box 17066, San Diego, Ca. 92117. (The price is slightly higher at the door— and of course you can pay less if you're merely going for one day, but the advance membership is your best bet.) See you there?

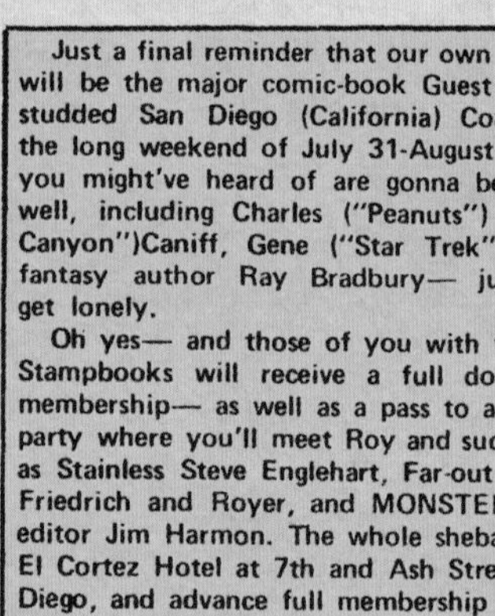

THIS IS IT! YOUR

MARVEL VALUE STAMP

FOR THIS ISSUE!
CLIP 'EM AND COLLECT 'EM!

OPPOSITE 89: HAMMERHEAD from *Captain America* no. 178 (October 1974). Stamp also appears in *Marvel Two-in-One* no. 3 (May 1974) and *Marvel Team-Up* no. 30 (February 1975).

ABOVE *The Amazing Spider-Man* no. 114 (November 1972), art by John Romita Sr.

of requests, Spidey teams up with everybody's favorite Man Without Fear— Daredevil! After that? We'll just have to wait and see. But we can promise more surprises than you can wiggle a web at!

Meanwhile, let's take a look at two letters of a more serious nature, both of which deserve the attention and thought of Marveldom Assembled.

Dear Bullpen,

What in the world is going on? Has the Comics Code gone out of business? Why are Marvel, D.C., and Charlton on this present trend toward near pornography and horror even in their superhero comics? Too many magazines are already on the market that feature nudity or semi-nudity, horror, and sadism, without comics doing so.

I like swords and sorcery fine, but the trend seems to be toward sex and savagery. If this spreads through the superhero comics of Marvel and D.C., I shall have to drop all of them, also.

Another trend I've observed in D.C. is using "God" as an exclamation. This is taking the Lord's name in vain and is not to be tolerated. I will buy no more Batman comics until this trend is reversed.

I've been reading Marvel since F.F. #1 and have been buying all your superhero mags, but I will drop them all if I have to start censoring them (because of nudity, horror, swearing, and so on) before allowing my children to read them. I am a friend of OLD Marvel, and I hope it speedily returns. Do you want a small hippy (*H*apless, *I*mpoverished mentally *P*ersons with *P*re-adolescent *Y*earnings) reading public, or will you publish comics children and normal adults can enjoy reading?

Jerry Hunter
Box 1511
Sitka, Alaska

Most of our mail, Mr. Hunter, tends to chide us for being too conservative on the points you've brought up, and we've published one or two of those letters. In an effort to present a balanced picture— and perhaps to entice other Marvelites who share your viewpoint to write and let us know— we're printing your comments as well.

Truthfully, though, we don't feel we've gone overboard on any of the elements you've mentioned. That doesn't mean that MARVEL TEAM-UP is suddenly going to begin featuring nude centerfolds, or that we're going to keep going farther in those directions as time goes by; it only means that, as far as our mail indicates, what we publish is not found offensive by the overwhelming majority of readers. Or by us.

Still, if there's some "silent majority" out there that does disapprove of what we've been doing, we hope they'll remain silent no more. In other words, people, whether you agree or disagree with Mr. Hunter's comments— WRITE! We can't make the changes you want— in whatever direction— unless you tell us they're needed.

Dear Marvel,

In regard to Robert Flake's letter in TEAM-UP #19:

He states he would like to see Spidey team up with the Zombie from your TALES OF THE ZOMBIE magazine. You tell him, "There is a Comics Code regulation prohibiting the use of the walking dead." But, in one of your competitors' magazines, *The Demon* #14 to be exact, there is a part of the story using the walking dead, and the cover bears the "Approved By The Comics Code Authority" stamp. If your answer to Rog's letter was a mistake, I myself wouldn't mind seeing Spidey and the Zombie together. But if your answer is not a mistake, WHAT GIVES?!

Stephen Read
3577 Herman St.
Fabreville, Laval
Quebec, Canada

The specific Comics Code provision we referred to, Stephen, states: "Scenes dealing with, or instruments associated with walking dead...shall not be used."

Which leaves us as baffled as you are.

THIS IS IT! YOUR
MARVEL VALUE STAMP
FOR THIS ISSUE!
CLIP 'EM AND COLLECT 'EM!

OPPOSITE **90: HERCULES** from *Marvel Team-Up* no. 24 (August 1974). Stamp also appears in *Marvel Team-Up* no. 19 (March 1974) and *Frankenstein* no. 14 (January 1975).

ABOVE Avengers model sheet (circa 1967), first published in *Alter Ego* no. 42 (November 2004), art by John Buscema.

Fantastic Four ④ Fan Page

Send letters to: STAN LEE
THE MARVEL COMICS GROUP
SIXTH FLOOR 575 MADISON AV.
NEW YORK 10022 N.Y.

Dear Gerry, Rich, Frank, Joe, and Roy,

Now that I've finally caught my breath after reading FANTASTIC FOUR #143, allow me to offer my reactions to it.

Right off the bat, Rich Buckler's illustration is purely astounding. His vibrant graphics boldly succeed in creating nerve-riveting tension, accelerated pacing, and gripping fear. In portraying Dr. Doom and his malevolent metallic machinations, he has captured and polished the very essence of this ultimate villain's evilness. Buckler is of the new generation of illustrators, and it is unquestionably evident that not only can he meet the F.F.'s demanding artistic standards, but that he will surpass and become the uncontestable master of them. This issue has given me stone-solid grounds for saying that.

Beginning with the cover, I unequivocally believe it was the finest that ever graced this feature. The Buckler-Sinnott team will enter the annals of comics history for this effort alone. Also, I strongly cast a "yes" vote for returning the old logo. In this case in particular, it would have been the ultimate capper to this otherwise magnificent cover.

The interiors were spellbinding, as I have already said. I realize that Frank Giacoia tried hard to sharpen up his often rough inking style, but the sparkle of Joe Sinnott's embellishment was sorely missed. I sincerely hope that Joe remains the F.F.'s permanent inker.

The story itself was a sheer delight. It is sagas such as this upon which the F.F. has built and still maintains its legendary excellence. I am going to reserve my complete judgment till after the final cataclysmic chapter next month. But by the bolts in Dr. Doom's armor, believe me, it's going to be a difficult task to wait until then!

Thanks.

Alan Rothman
151-12 24th Road
Whitestone, N.Y. 11357

You're welcome, Alan— and that's more than just a polite reply. Gerry and Rich both want to convey their deep appreciation for the enthusiastic reception you've given F.F. #143, because both of them feel it was one of their best efforts since entering comics.

Confidentially (in front of a zillion or so readers), it's been Rich's desire to draw the F.F. ever since he first laid eyes on the mag as a fan, lo those many years ago. The "vibrant graphics" that leap out at you from every Buckler F.F. page are born of sheer enthusiasm and love.

Likewise, Gerry's of the opinion that after months of experimenting he's finally captured exactly the right style for the FANTASTIC FOUR mag, and he's plugging away now at perfecting it.

In short, friends, you've got our stretching, flaming, long-haired, invisible, ever-lovin' blue-eyed pledge that the months upcoming are going to be some of the most fantastic in the long and hallowed history of this magazine.

And those of you who have been with the F.F. since its very first signal-flare billowed upon the already-smoggy New York sky will likely be among the most excited.

Dear Roy, Rich, and Gerry,

It's time for this bit again:

"Gee, I haven't written to a comic mag since my letter in SUB-MARINER #1, but I had to write about F.F. #143."

But it's true. When I cut my Marvel eyeteeth, Peter Parker was just beginning to show a spark of interest in one Gwen Stacy, and Victor Von Doom was looking green-eyed at the then-mysterious Silver Surfer's "power cosmic". Marvel was still a fresh, exciting movement. The only thing National had that came even close to your mags was a mag called Doom Patrol (may it rest in peace).

Then, Marvel seemed to lose its "house look." Kirby left, and Lee was less in evidence. A lot of hack work started coming out (Adams' and Steranko's X-MEN issues rising high above the morass).

But along came CONAN, the Kree-Skrull War, and— let's just say Roy was getting more feeling for his position.

But back to F.F. #143. Doc Doom, of course, was a sight for sore eyes (as has been one Mr. Wingfoot), and it would seem you've taken the proverbial step forward by moving backward. There was plenty of action. The reigning elements were those Lee employed in the 60's. A logical but mind-boggling plot, rich with subplots, continuity, and pathos. The art was like Kirby's best, but definitely Buckler, probably thanks to Frank Giacoia, and— aw, the heck with it! What I want to say is, I enjoyed it. Okay?

But the point is, I'd like to see the old logo back— for good. Sure, there's some nostalgia here. I loved that logo. But it's more than that. I mean, I prefer the new AVENGERS logo, but would you change Spidey's logo? I doubt it. It's too beautiful, too much a part of Spidey's mag.

So here's one longtime Marvelite's vote for the old logo...please? Thank you.

William M. Neville
6037 Freret, Apt. B
New Orleans, La. 70118

You're welcome, too, Bill— but this time it's more than a sincere reply. It's an exhausted reply! Yeesh! Reading your letter was a little like watching a ping pong tournament. We started out as the good guys, then we were the bad guys, then the good guys again, and now, finally, we're the guys with the new logo! Gee, Bill, that kind of back-and-forth-then-off-the-court-and-out-of-bounds letter really wrecks our nerves. Especially at five a.m. (or is it six already?), which is when this LP is getting typed. Anyway, we get the feeling we came out ahead, so we'll just take a deep breath, rub or rosy red eyeballs, try to remember what mag this is, and ask: what's a logo? (No, no, we're kidding! Honest!) (What's kidding?)

MARVEL
IS ON THE MOVE AGAIN!

MARVEL VALUE STAMP
FOR THIS ISSUE!

CLIP 'EM AND COLLECT 'EM!

STATEMENT OF OWNERSHIP, MANAGEMENT AND CIRCULATION ACT OF AUGUST 12, 1970: SECTION 3685, TITLE 39, UNITED STATES CODE

1. Title of Publication: FANTASTIC FOUR.
2. DATE OF FILING: September 25, 1973.
3. Frequency of Issue: Monthly.
4. Location of Known Office of Publication: 575 Madison Ave., New York, N.Y. 10022.
5. Location of the Headquarters or General Business Offices of the Publishers: Marvel Comics Group, 575 Madison Ave., New York, N.Y. 10022.
6. Names and addresses of the publisher, editor, and managing editor are: Publisher: Stan Lee, 575 Madison Ave., New York, N.Y. 10022; Editor: Roy Thomas, 575 Madison Ave., New York, N.Y. 10022; Managing Editor: John Verpoorten, 575 Madison Ave., New York, N.Y. 10022.
7. Owner (If owned by a corporation, its name and address must be stated and also immediately thereunder the names and addresses of stockholders owning or holding 1 percent or more of total amount of stock. If not owned by a corporation, the names and addresses of the individual owners must be given. If owned by a partnership or other unincorporated firm, its name and address, as well as that of each individual must be given.) Cadence Industries Corp., 21 Henderson Drive, West Caldwell, New Jersey; a public held company on the New York Stock Exchange.
8. Known bondholders, mortgagees, and other security holders owning or holding 1 percent or more of total amount of bonds, mortgages, or other securities (if there are none, so state) None.
9. For optional completion by publishers mailing at the regular rates (Section 132.121, Postal Service Manual) 39 U.S.C. 3626 provides in pertinent part: "No person who would have been entitled to mail matter under former section 4359 of this title shall mail such matter at the rates provided under this subsection unless he files annually with the Postal Service a written request for permission to mail matter at such rates."
In accordance with the provisions of this statute, I hereby request permission to mail the publication named in Item 1 at the reduced postage rates presently authorized by 39 U.S.C. 3626.
(signed) John S. Ryan, Vice President, Director of Circulation
10. For completion by nonprofit organizations authorized to mail at special rates. (Section 132.122, Postal Manual.) The purpose, function, and nonprofit status of this organization and the exempt status for Federal income tax purposes. (Check one.) ☐ Have not changed during preceding 12 months. ☐ Have changed during preceding 12 months. (If changed, publisher must submit explanation of change with this statement.)
11. EXTENT AND NATURE OF CIRCULATION.
A. Total No. Copies Printed (net press run): Average no. copies each issue during preceding 12 months: 463,315; single issue nearest to filing date: 474,698.
B. Paid Circulation: 1) Sales through dealers and carriers, street vendors and counter sales: Average no. copies each issue during preceding 12 months: 223,955; single issue nearest to filing date: 220,763. 2) Mail subscriptions. Average no. copies each issue during preceding 12 months: 1716; single issue nearest to filing date: 1624.
C. Total paid circulation: Average no. copies each issue during preceding 12 months: 225,671; single issue nearest to filing date: 222,387.
D. Free distribution by mail, carrier or other means. 1) Samples, complimentary, and other free copies: 150; single issue nearest to filing date: 150. 2) Copies distributed to news agents, but not sold: Average no. copies each issue during preceding 12 months: 237,333; single issue nearest to filing date: 252,000.
E. Total distribution (sum of C and D): Average no. copies each issue during preceding 12 months: 463,154; single issue nearest to filing date: 474,537.
F. Office use, left-over, unaccounted, spoiled after printing: Average no. copies each issue during preceding 12 months: 161; single issue nearest to filing date: 161.
G. Total (sum of E & F—should equal net press run shown in A): Average no. copies each issue during preceding 12 months: 463,315; single issue nearest to filing date: 474,698.
I certify that the statements made by me above are correct and complete.
(signed) John S. Ryan, Vice President, Director of Circulation

OPPOSITE **91: HELA, THE GODDESS OF DEATH** from *Fantastic Four* no. 146 (May 1974). Stamp also appears in *Conan the Barbarian* no. 41 (August 1974) and *Fear* no. 25 (December 1974).

ABOVE *Thor* no. 186 (March 1971), art by John Buscema and John Verpoorten.

And that's how the mail on our Hulk/Human Torch ish of MARVEL TEAM-UP came in— with an astounding eighty per cent of the comments favorable. And not just favorable: a remarkable number of those who praised M.T.U. #18 also requested that we do more stories like it, several every year, without Spidey. So we've decided to drop a bombshell on ya!

Unfortunately, we can't go into any great detail on the project just yet, but we'll say this much: although there will be a Spidey team-up every month, you'll also be treated to four M.T.U. issues a year featuring the more unusual team-ups you've requested! (But you'll just have to wait a month or so to find out how you can have your cake and eat it, too.)

Dear Marvel,

In the immortal words of Ben Grimm, "It's no-prizin' time!" I found an error in your correction of another error, which I feel should entitle me to an AUTOGRAPHED SUPER NO-PRIZE!!

In the letters page of M.T.U. #18, you state that there is no such thing as CAPTAIN AMERICA #58. Well, of course there is! In September of 1946, CAPTAIN AMERICA #58 was published by Timely Comics. If you want proof, look at page fifty-five of Steranko's History of Comics, Volume 1. There you will see a reproduction of the cover of C.A. #58. Now, don't try to squirm out of it by telling me about what you meant to say, or what it was you really meant to imply. Just speed my no-prize right along. How about it, guys?

Kevin Williams
16203 Oregon Avenue
Bellflower, Ca. 90706

Okay, Kevin, the no-prize is yours. Now are we allowed to squirm.. just a little?

While it's true that a CAPTAIN AMERICA #58 was published back in the halcyon days of the comics' alleged Golden Age by the Timely group (one of Marvel's previous incarnations, not a different company, for those of you who aren't students of the history of the medium), that issue was not the one alluded to in the footnote in TEAM-UP #13. The more so since that footnote mistakenly referred to ish #57, not 58, in the first place, all of which does not negate your original point, since if there was a #58 back in the 'forties, it's entirely reasonable to assume there was also a #57, and besides— WHAT ARE WE TALKING ABOUT?!?

Anyhow, the idea we were trying (and failing miserably) to get across is: there's been no such issue as CAPTAIN AMERICA #57 (or 58) in the Marvel Age (post-1961) of Comics. Okay?

Hello Bullpen,

It's really great to see an issue of MARVEL TEAM-UP like #18. I hope to see many more team-ups as unusual.

Len, would you please consider re-introducing some of Marvel's "Golden Age" heroes in M.T.U.? There are so many: the Patriot, Black Marvel, the Angel, Capt. Wonder, the Fin, Blazing Skull, the Destroyer, the Vision, the Whizzer...I could go on and on. But I think you get the idea.

In your occasional "non-Spidey" issues, I'd like to see the teams of: Human Torch & Iceman, Power Man & the Falcon, Dr. Strange & Shang-Chi, Silver Surfer & Capt. Marvel.

Well, by now you've got enough suggestions to last you 'til M.T.U. #100. Take care.

Wayne Santos
901-A Baker St.
San Francisco, Ca. 94115

Actually, Wayne, we never get enough suggestions— keep 'em coming! As for the revival of the Golden Age characters ...well, we already have new characters called Angel, Destroyer, Vision, and Whizzer. And as for the rest, we can't help thinking that today's crop of creations is far more interesting than the one that yielded the oldsters. But we're open to opinions, natch.

THIS IS IT! YOUR
MARVEL VALUE STAMP
FOR THIS ISSUE!
CLIP 'EM AND
COLLECT 'EM!

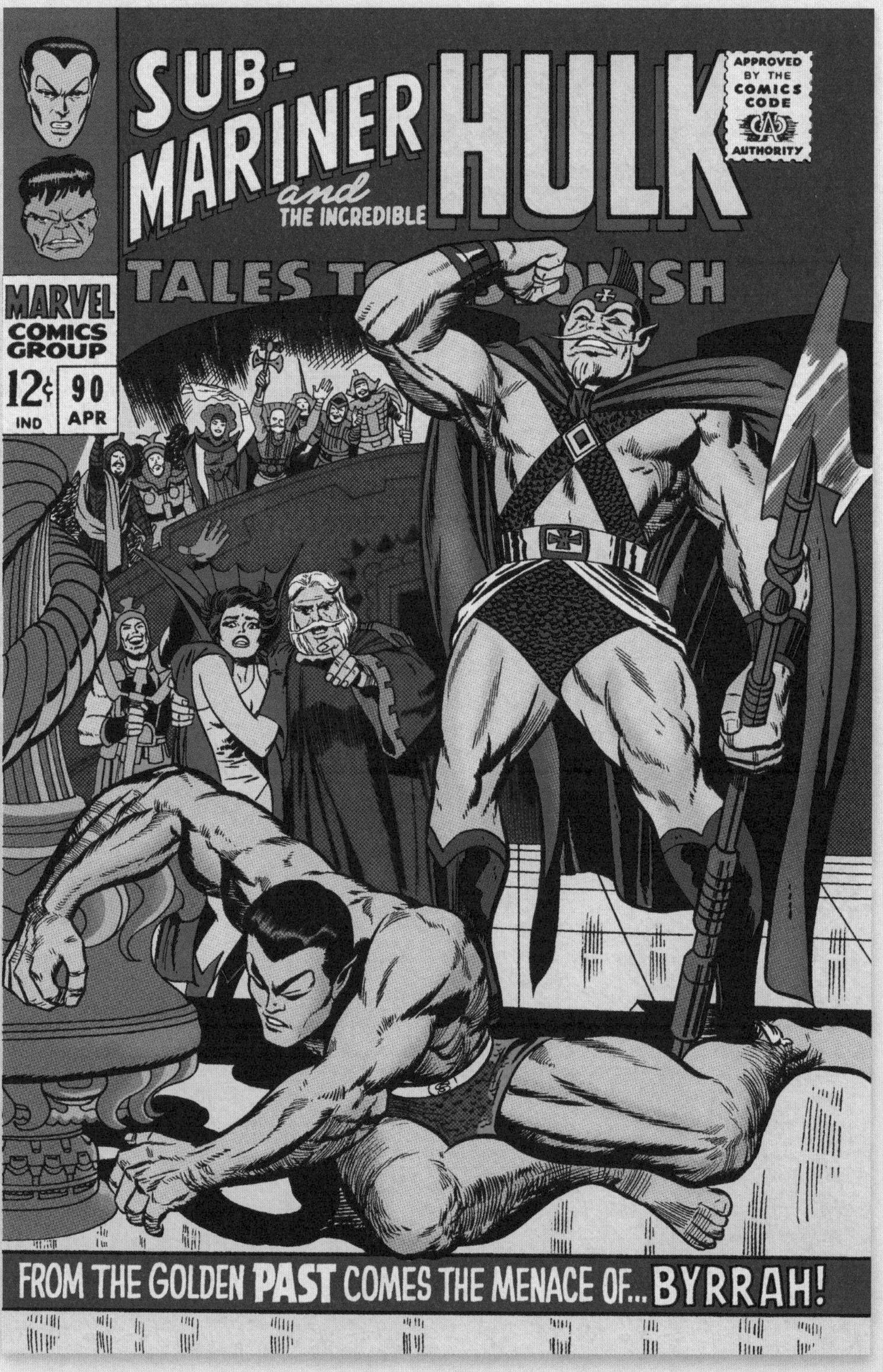

OPPOSITE **92: BYRRAH** from *Marvel Team-Up* no. 22 (June 1974). Byrrah is the only Marvel Value Stamp to appear in just one comic book.

ABOVE *Tales to Astonish* no. 90 (April 1967), art by Jack Kirby and Vince Colletta.

You guessed right, we're sad to say, about Sal's leaving the mag. Joe Sinnott returns as inker next issue, we think, but the penciller will be George Tuska, from whom we expect great Things. (Ouch!) And incidentally, let's have a hand for the two masters of pen and brush who have graced these pages in Joe's absence: Frank Giacoia (#4) and Mike Esposito (#5). We think they've turned in some magnificent work.

Steve is also tremendously pleased about the reaction to Wundarr's role in TWO-IN-ONE. (Do you get the feeling we should retitle this mag "FORTY-EIGHT-IN-ONE", what with the hordes of guest-stars who keep popping up?) Back when he and Val Mayerik created the character, they knew they had more on their hands than a mere parody, but it took a while to convince Marveldom Assembled.

Rob Sansing, you're correct about Steve's basis for his version of Ben. He went back to some of the earliest F.F. classics to get an idea of Ben's character, then turned to current masterpieces penned by Gerry Conway, added a touch of "whut I allus wanted Ben ta say," and the results seem to be making everybody very happy.

Finally, the common suggestion of these two letters: a reunion of Ben and D.D.? Yes! We can't say when, just yet. But this issue proved so popular that you can be certain of seeing the two of them together again reasonably soon.

More about future team-ups after the next letter...!

Dear Marvel,

Sal Buscema, as I've said time after time, is a great artist, and, man, he *proved* it in TWO-IN-ONE #3! The scenes of New York City, Daredevil, Reed, Wundarr, and of course the Thing were expertly drawn. I've always wanted to see Sal's work inked by Joe Sinnott. Needless to write, I wasn't disappointed.

Steve Gerber's Black Spectre storyline is working out quite well indeed. Some truly enjoyable parts of the story were Ben and Wundarr's experience (pages 11 and 14). Matt Murdock and Candace Nelson at the play, and the explanation of Wundarr's powers. This mag was well worth the quarter I paid for it.

Some future team-ups I would like to see are Ben and these characters: Silver Surfer, the Cat, Thor, the Demon Druid, Howard the Duck (?), Spider-Man, Black Bolt, and the X-Men.

Jackie Frost
Rt. 3, Box 176-C
W. Monroe, La.

Steve keeps insisting, Jackie, that Ben and Howard would make a great team...but somehow we just can't see it. They'd spend the whole mag fighting over whose cigars are whose.

As for the others you mentioned. Thor's coming next issue. And, except for the Cat and the Demon Druid, you can expect to see all the rest in due time. Steve also has stories in mind for Ben and Morbius, Ben and the Son of Satan, and several others. And he's eager to do a Thing/Luke Cage team-up, too, as soon as it's possible.

So, whatever else anyone tells you about this book, if they accuse it of being dull, you've got plenty of ammunition for eloquent rebuttal!

And that just about does it for this Ever-Lovin', Blue-eyed Letters Page, group. Don't forget— let us know what you thought of this issues tale — and, in particular, the GUARDIANS OF THE GALAXY. Do you want to see them again? Soon? We hope so. And let's hear your ideas for future Thing team-ups. And anything else you might have to say. Our ears are wide open for helpful suggestions, thoughtful criticism, and, of course, unrestrained praise. WRITE!!

See ya next ish! Which reminds us...

NEXT ISSUE: Bashful Benjy and the one and only god of Thunder get together for what we predict will be one of the most unusual sagas of the year. A different kind of menace. A different kind of action. And lots of that old Marvel magic. The Thing and Thor— in MARVEL TWO-IN-ONE #6:

THIS IS IT! YOUR
MARVEL VALUE STAMP
FOR THIS ISSUE!
CLIP 'EM AND
COLLECT 'EM!

OPPOSITE **93: SILVER SURFER** from *Marvel Two-in-One* no. 5 (September 1974). Stamp also appears in *Sgt. Fury* no. 118 (March 1974) and *Werewolf by Night* no. 23 (November 1974).

ABOVE *Silver Surfer* no. 16 (May 1970), art by John Buscema and Chic Stone.

LET'S RAP WITH CAP

SEND YOUR LETTERS TO: THE MARVEL COMICS GROUP SIXTH FLOOR 575 MADISON AV. NEW YORK 10022 N. Y.

Dear Steve:

CA&F #180 was another fine story, extending the string to an even greater length. There was so much in the issue it's hard to begin commenting but I feel mention should be made of the exceptionally realistic dialogue you are using. Rather than seeming as though you are putting words in the characters' mouths they just appear to be speaking of their own volition. The words flow from their mouths as they would from REAL people; they are down to earth emotional words instead of corny, hyped up ones. Without such, Steve (Rogers)'s current predicament wouldn't be as believable.

The unexpected (!), that's really what the book is about these days. Whenever I think I know exactly what's going to happen you spring another surprise on me. With Steve's soul-searching there is enough material to fill an entire issue alone but no, you take the unexpected route and include the return of Madame Hydra and Princess Python, not to mention the Serpent Squad, to boot. The whole way you're handling the situations is totally unpredictable and it's this unpredictability and mounting plots that's making the book better and better.

The Viper's death was handled extremely well because it was done quickly, quietly with no one knowing about it. What a change of pace from the usual in which a villain must die in full view while engaged in a battle with the hero. It was rather like a good mystery where people get knocked off in dark alleys or deserted places; very good. Also, instead of it being the climax it could have been, you've used it for building the rest of the tale. This marked another turn from the usual towards the unusual and in my opinion, more believable.

Next, Steve's discussion with Sharon was a dynamite little scene in that every word was packed with emotion and meaning; her wanting Steve all to herself is understandable, as was his realization that superheroing is in his blood. Sal's low angle in the third panel emphasized the tension between them very well.

The movie theatre scene was perhaps the best one in the whole book. The voice-over contrasting with Nomad's rejection of Cap sent those tingles through my body— the feeling usually reserved for deeply emotional happenings. It was enough to make ME want to become Captain America.

Thanks for a first-rate issue.

Dean Mullaney
81 Delaware Street
Staten Island, N.Y. 10304

Dear Steve and Sal,

Among other things, CA&F #180 was funny. There were lots of little jokes in it, similar to the mad tea party in DR. STRANGE #2 in that the super-hero was aware of the absurdities of being a super-hero. Without a doubt, the Nomad tripping over his own cape was the most unusual climax to a fight ever, and the Viper's comment added a lot.

The new Viper is an excellent character, better than the old Viper and also better than the old Madame Hydra. As far as I know, she is the first nihilist villain in comics; certainly the first at Marvel. She also seems to be a bit of a Marxist, but only on a theoretical level. The Lee/Steranko idea of having her hung up on her scarred face was just an imitation of Dr. Doom, but Englehart's characterization of her is both original and consistent with the earlier version. Her fatalism makes her far more dangerous than other villains with greater physical power.

Jana C. Hollingsworth
717 Mathes Hall
Western Washington State College
Bellingham, Washington

Dear Steve, Sal, Martha, et al.,

CAPTAIN AMERICA #179-180 opened up a whole new concept in comics, one which I've been awaiting for years. Just about my only reason for disliking Cap and other symbolic heroes is that they never change. I thought Cap always be that same super-strong, super-skilled Steve Rogers in that same red-white-and-blue costume. But you've turned him into a completely different hero!

I'd also like to mention Nomad's costume. Steve mentioned that it was similar to Cap's, as can be seen in the boots and gloves. But on page 17, it can be seen that the cowl was modeled after the Falcon's costume, as was the V-shaped opening in his shirt.

Michael Miller
158-15 79 Street
Howard Beach, N.Y. 11414

Dear People,

As for the empty costume of Captain America: I think 'twould be sort of heavy if it was filled out by one Sam Wilson, a.k.a. the Falcon. Sam was pretty upset about Cap leaving, and I think he might at least consider filling in until Steve comes back. Obviously, he doesn't *need* to do this, because he's just fine as his own man. Still, it's rather tempting to mind-play with the reactions of Americans (including Steve Rogers) should Sam one day come out of his office clad in red, white, and blue. Did I hear someone say potential?

Thank you for your time—not to mention a bit of fun and stimulation.

William Mills
440 Garfield Ave.
Eau Claire, Wisconsin 54701

NEXT MONTH: Frank Robbins returns, to illustrate a tale of fanaticism, fury—and the Falcon. To say more now would spoil the surprises in store, but rest assured that all 143 running plotlines will move onward and upward next time, culminating in a last-page lollapalooza that'll knock your socks off all over again. Remember this warning: read #185 without peeking ahead—and be firmly seated when you do!

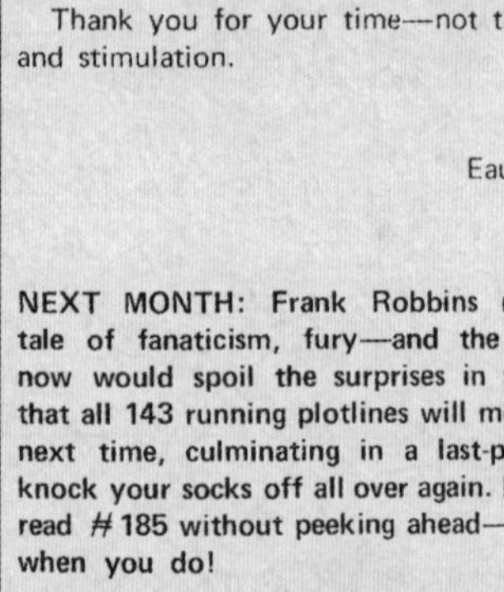

THIS IS IT! YOUR

MARVEL VALUE STAMP

FOR THIS ISSUE! CLIP 'EM AND COLLECT 'EM!

OPPOSITE **94: ELECTRO** from *Captain America* no. 184 (April 1975). Stamp also appears in *Marvel Premiere* no. 15 (May 1974), *Strange Tales* no. 176 (October 1974), and *Thor* no. 238 (August 1975).

ABOVE *The Amazing Spider-Man Annual* no. 1 (September 1964), art by Steve Ditko.

As for her costuming being evidence of sexism on our part, we can only say that none of our female readers has yet complained about it. We suspect that they admire her, as we do, for having the sheer nerve to dress however she pleases, no matter how outlandish.

Regarding the Black Widow, as we've mentioned before, Steve hasn't been trying to force her relationship with Daredevil in any particular direction: that relationship has taken on a life of its own, and as this very issue makes abundantly clear, it was never Steve's intention to write her out of the strip altogether.

Lastly, the secret of the Silver Samurai's sword— and the identity of the character himself— was left unrevealed on purpose! You'll be seeing him again in the not-too-distant future, and all will become clear at that time.

Incidentally, a funny aside with regard to ol' Silver Sam: the reason he didn't appear in ish #112 was a rather bizarre one. You see, Bob's drawings for DD #111 were being inked at the time Gene Colan had to start work on the next issue. And, as a result, we had no reference material on the Silver Samurai to send to Gene! After talking it all out, we decided that in view of the space limitations we were facing and the complexity of the scenes to follow, it was best just to strand the Samurai atop the Empire State Building and explain later how he made his escape. (Weird? You bet. But absolutely true.)

But we've dwelt long enough on the negative aspects— alleged negative aspects— of those issues. The fact is, DAREDEVIL #112 drew an unusual volume of mail, and nearly all of it was as favorable as Dean Mullaney, Jackie Frost, and Mark Gasper's letters. Indeed, there was even a clamor for a return of the Mandrill and Nekra to plague DD again, as well as a definite demand for more of Shanna's adventures, whether here or in one of our other magazines.

We couldn't be happier— or more grateful. All of us who worked on the Black Spectre series, including Steve Gerber, Bob Brown, Gene Colan, Sal Buscema (in MARVEL TWO-IN-ONE), Paul Gulacy, Jim Mooney, Don Heck, and Frank Chiaramonte, wish to extend their sincere thanks for the barrage of favorable mail, as well as their promise to keep on producing the kinds of stories we think you'll enjoy.

Now, to answer a few specific questions...

Although Gene Colan has been kind enough to handle the DAREDEVIL mag on those occasions when Bob Brown simply can't (as with this issue), his commitments on TOMB OF DRACULA prohibit his return on a regular basis. He will, however, shortly be assuming the artistic helm on another Marvel mag where he earned no small share of fame— DOCTOR STRANGE! Watch for his dramatic return soon! And don't miss this month's SON OF SATAN, on which he and Steve G. managed to get together on a decidedly different tale of demonic possession.

Meanwhile, though, we hardly think anyone will exactly mind Bob Brown remaining on the strip— particularly in view of the masterful jobs he turned in on the recent Death-Stalker series of stories. He'll be back next ish, natch, to conclude our Owl epic.

And, finally, on the matter of where and when you can see Shanna again: look for her in an upcoming issue of KA-ZAR, where she'll be co-starring with the Lord of the Savage Land. And, too, keep your eyes on SAVAGE TALES; we're considering a new series of Shanna solo adventures for that mag. What's more, we wouldn't be too surprised if she just happened to pop up in DAREDEVIL again before long, either. So have no fear— forgotten she ain't

And that's it. We've run out of time and space for this issue. Except, of course, for our omnipresent Yellow Box. . .

NEXT ISSUE: The Owl's plan revealed! Natasha on an errand of evil, with Daredevil's life in the balance! A surprise guest-star! And a climax you'll never forget! It's all in DAREDEVIL #117! Don't miss it! Or we'll clobber you with an exclamation point!!!

THIS IS IT! YOUR

MARVEL VALUE STAMP

FOR THIS ISSUE! CLIP 'EM AND COLLECT 'EM!

OPPOSITE **95: MOLEMAN** from *Daredevil* no. 116 (December 1974). Stamp also appears in *The Amazing Spider-Man* no. 136 (September 1974) and *Ka-Zar* no. 12 (November 1975).

ABOVE *Marvel Team-Up* no. 17 (January 1974), art by Gil Kane.

And I can side with her. I suspect this is why I refrain from any consideration of her manner.

Captain America, too, is undergoing an ugly mood; but since his condition is unassociated with amour and completely incidental to THE AVENGERS, I am going to withhold any comment.

I was pleased to find Solarr represented in this series. Not because I like the character, I must say, but because he offers grounds for believing that a couple regular villains of other series who I do have favourable feelings for may yet find representation in THE AVENGERS (or even THE DEFENDERS). In fact, I will end this letter with that specific request: offer more characters who erewhile have been confined to other series. Maybe my favourites may yet find the exposure I wish them.

(Did Bob Brown really provide *all* this issue's art? I cannot believe it.)

Hector Randis Spartan
c/o 12106-90th Ave.,
Surrey, B.C., Canada V3V 1B5

Thanks very much for your second paragraph, Hec—more specifically, for recognizing that although a character may do things of which you personally may not approve, the important thing is that she (or he) remain *in character.* We freely admit that Wanda's been hot-tempered of late, but as later events have shown, she had good reason to be.

And yes, Bob Brown *did* provide all the pencils for that particular ish. Look for more of his work in DAREDEVIL.

To the Marvel Madmen,

An allocution about the Avengers.

The Avengers

Never taken aback by abacus, accordion, abalone,
or any adversary,
they are adept at abating aberrant, aggresive advocates
of adverse activities.
All Avengers are ablaze with abundant, apparent, aliveness,
and are able, alert, agile, amazing, agents of
almighty alrightness.
They will not abort, abandon, or abbreviate their
alliance of above-average adventurers.
Ardently acclaimed as astonishing, astounding,
and appreciated,
they arrive at ambush or affray abruptly, and accurately,
and arrest or abolish abominable abusers of academic arts.
Avowed avoiders of attracting attention, they abhor
absurd acrobats
that run afoul of accelerating airplanes.
Assisted by an admirable, adroit Asgardian,
all with an alias,
they achieved an accomplishment they are acutely aware of.
They go, afire, to action,
with the axiom,
AVENGERS ASSEMBLE!

Does not such an eloquent allocution deserve a no-prize?

Denise Gilmer
503 Benicia Dr.
Santa Ross, Ca. 95405

THIS IS IT! YOUR
MARVEL VALUE STAMP
FOR THIS ISSUE!
CLIP 'EM AND COLLECT 'EM!

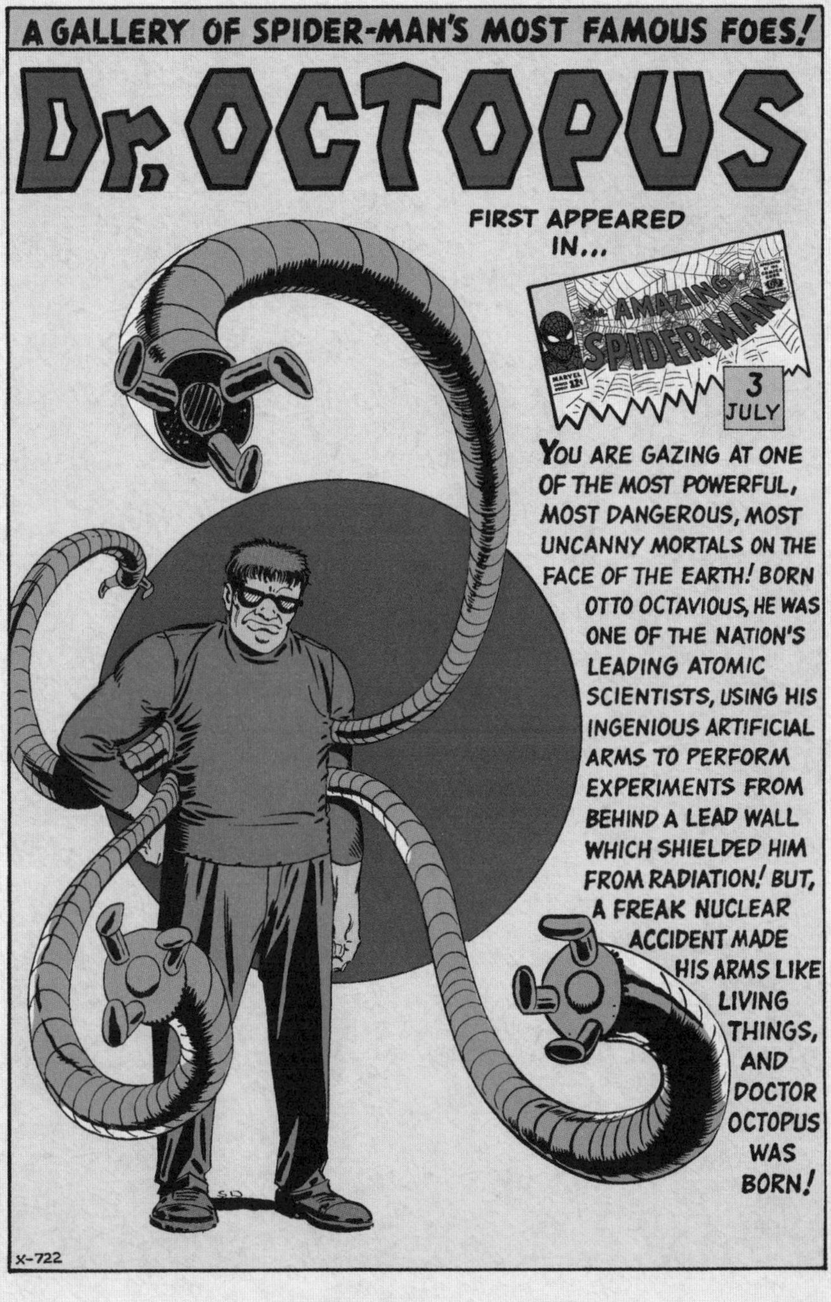

A GALLERY OF SPIDER-MAN'S MOST FAMOUS FOES!
Dr. OCTOPUS
FIRST APPEARED IN...
The AMAZING SPIDER-MAN
3 JULY
YOU ARE GAZING AT ONE OF THE MOST POWERFUL, MOST DANGEROUS, MOST UNCANNY MORTALS ON THE FACE OF THE EARTH! BORN OTTO OCTAVIOUS, HE WAS ONE OF THE NATION'S LEADING ATOMIC SCIENTISTS, USING HIS INGENIOUS ARTIFICIAL ARMS TO PERFORM EXPERIMENTS FROM BEHIND A LEAD WALL WHICH SHIELDED HIM FROM RADIATION! BUT, A FREAK NUCLEAR ACCIDENT MADE HIS ARMS LIKE LIVING THINGS, AND DOCTOR OCTOPUS WAS BORN!
X-722

OPPOSITE **96: DR. OCTOPUS** from *The Avengers* no. 130 (December 1974). Stamp also appears in *Tomb of Dracula* no. 21 (June 1974) and *Amazing Adventures* no. 26 (September 1974).

ABOVE *The Amazing Spider-Man Annual* no. 1 (September 1964), art by Steve Ditko.

Dear Gerry, Doug and Paul,

#20 was excellent and a fine addition to an already fine strip. The combination of caption and silent sequences are reminiscent of the cinema and are very good. The bits of the martial arts philosophy were well-handled—in short, the writing of this strip, even without the very-talented Steve Englehart, has not suffered.

To comment on the artwork, Paul Gulacy has a flair for storytelling. However, he must develop a style of his own; when one says that Gulacy is influenced by Jim Steranko and Jim Starlin, one is understating the point. At least he did have the courtesy to draw Mr. Steranko into the strip (re: Marston). Still, I did enjoy the art immensely and cannot help remembering how poor a certain bashful British artist was, just a few short years ago, so keep on trying.

May Shang-Chi live long and prosper.

Mark Gasper
(no address given)

Makers of Kung Fu:

There was no letters page in *Master of Kung Fu* #20. Why?

Ken Meyer, Jr.
3110B Revere Circle
Hill AFB, OT 84406

How about: *Because.* (No? Well, believe us, that's a lot easier than trying to explain the occasionally mildly mind-boggling miasmas we get ourselves into here at mighty Marvel; which is just another way of saying how in the heck do we know?)

Dear Stan, Doug, Gerry, Paul,

Shang-Chi is developing into one of Marvel's greatest superstars. Doug Moench and Gerry Conway did an excellent job with the script. I see, in Shang-Chi, a character that will soon rival Spider-Man and Silver Surfer in popularity. The son of Fu Manchu is the perfect or near-perfect example of the highest level a human being can reach, in terms of moral, spiritual, and mental development.

The art by Paul Gulacy was the *best* that he has done so far for Marvel. I find it hard to figure out Marvel's best artist. I've narrowed it down to a four-way tie: Buckler, Starlin, Brunner and Gulacy. I hope Moench, Gulacy and Milgrom stay with the mag—they are some talented, titanic trio. Congratulations for putting out such quality work. *Master of Kung Fu* is one of Marvel's very best.

Jackie Frost
RR 3- Box 176C,
West Monroe, La. 71291.

THIS IS IT! YOUR
MARVEL VALUE STAMP
FOR THIS ISSUE!
CLIP 'EM AND
COLLECT 'EM!

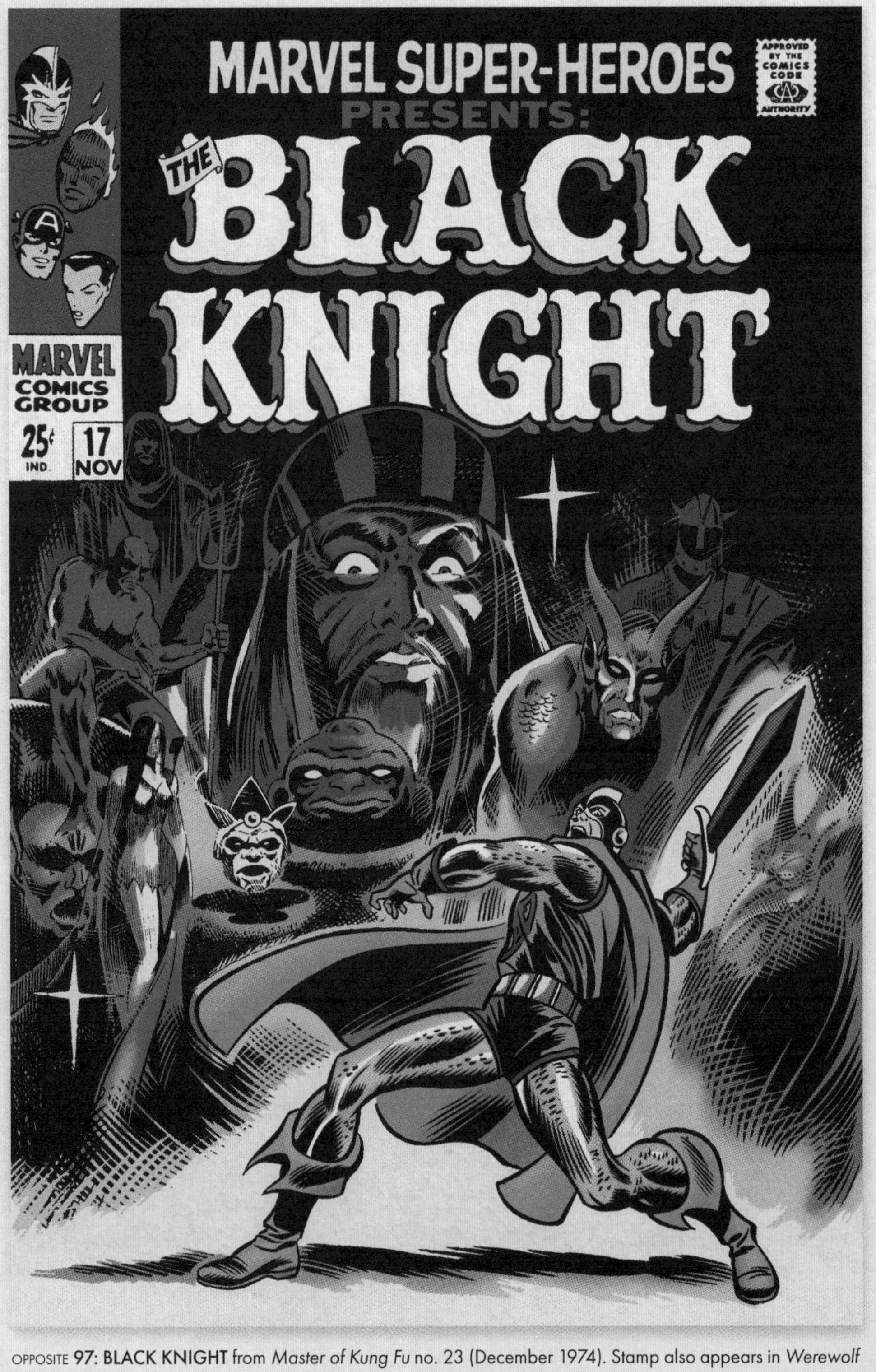

OPPOSITE **97: BLACK KNIGHT** from *Master of Kung Fu* no. 23 (December 1974). Stamp also appears in *Werewolf by Night* no. 20 (August 1974) and *The Invaders* no. 3 (November 1975).

ABOVE *Marvel Super-Heroes* no. 17 (November 1968), art by John Romita Sr. and Howard Purcell.

you find some way some issue to include Howard the Duck? I know it sounds goofy, but if the Defenders' adventures get any more offbeat, characters like Howard, or the Golem, or even Wundarr won't be too out of place!

T.E. Pouncey
Douglass, KS

Dear Marvel,

There seems to be some question as to what heroes should be permitted membership and who should be the leader. Dr. Strange makes a great leader, but his position should be rotated as it is in the Avengers. Hulk and Sub-Mariner don't belong in this group. Both are basically loners. My suggestion for new members: Falcon, to give him more exposure and a group to belong to, like Capt. America; Madame Masque, a great character with good potential; Sunfire, the Japanese mutant; and lastly, the Cat, because of the raw deal she got with her own mag.

Gary L. Guinn
1115 N. 8th St.
Nashville, Tenn. 37207

Dear Marvel,

Ever since the birth of the present Valkyrie in DEFENDERS #4, I have faithfully plunked my change down monthly, reveling in the fact that at *last* the Defenders had a "member" with whom I could identify. But now it seems that there are workings about to remove the blond Defender from the ranks of Marveldom. All I can say is, *how can you*?!?

This sword-swinging liberationist has provided a figure with whom your female readers can empathize. She has proven herself to be an integral part of the team. She represents the concept that super-strength need not be accompanied by massive muscles, and most importantly, her presence emphasizes the fact that women as well as men have a role in protecting the world from the sinister forces that would destroy our freedoms. You have great potential in this bold-hearted woman. Let's not waste it!

Barbara Golman
69 E. Cedar
Chicago, Ill.

Anybody wanna take a wild guess as to what burning issue has been occupying the thoughts of DEFENDERS readers lately? (Aw . . . you knew all along!)

Some answers, insofar as we are able to supply them:

For the present, at least, it looks as if Dr. Strange will continue as a regular non-member of the non-team. Sub-Mariner, however, aside from his appearance in GIANT-SIZE DEFENDERS #3 (in which Daredevil also guest-stars), will likely *not* be returning to the group. We've got big things in mind for Namor— and we guarantee, they'll thrill, stun, and delight you.

Nighthawk and Valkyrie? Yes. For the foreseeable future, both will be regulars in DEFENDERS.

New members? You bet. We're not sure yet exactly who they'll be, but we have some wild ideas in mind.

One thing, though . . . aside from guest-star appearances, all our instincts tell us not to let the group grow too big. Robbie Shive's suggestion of twenty members frankly scares us half to death. We prefer to think in terms of five or six regulars, maximum. Do you people agree? (Yes, that's a call for opinions.)

We could go on forever about all this, but we're just about out of room, so we'll close with one last note. Steve G., as Mr. Pouncey should be happy to hear, does plan to delve deeply into the personalities of *all* the Defenders in the months to come. And, again, you're going to be very surprised by the revelations that are in store.

But . . . that's for the future. For now, take care. We'll see you in thirty days!

THIS IS IT! YOUR
MARVEL VALUE STAMP
FOR THIS ISSUE!
CLIP 'EM AND
COLLECT 'EM!

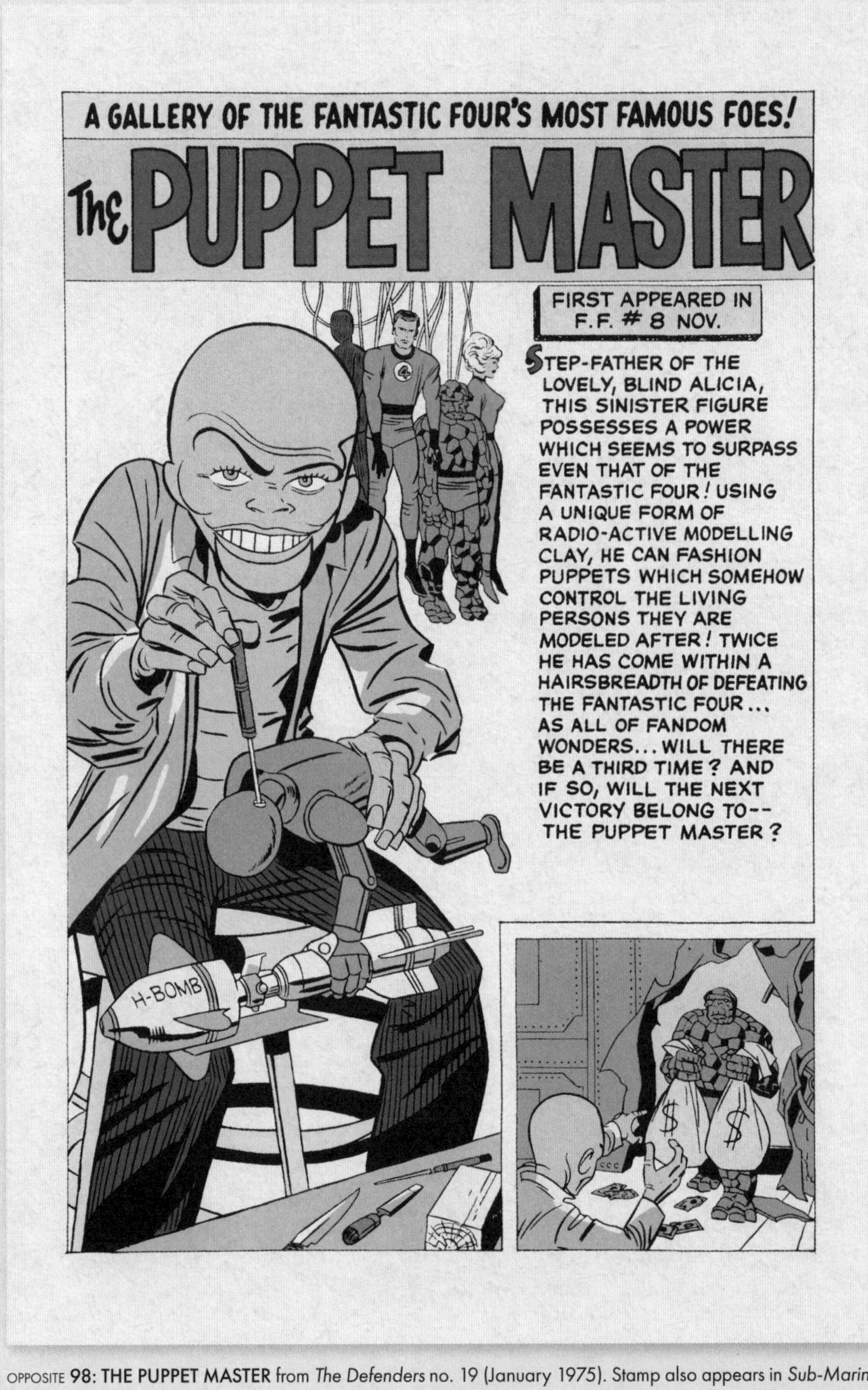

A GALLERY OF THE FANTASTIC FOUR'S MOST FAMOUS FOES!
The PUPPET MASTER
FIRST APPEARED IN F.F. # 8 NOV.
STEP-FATHER OF THE LOVELY, BLIND ALICIA, THIS SINISTER FIGURE POSSESSES A POWER WHICH SEEMS TO SURPASS EVEN THAT OF THE FANTASTIC FOUR! USING A UNIQUE FORM OF RADIO-ACTIVE MODELLING CLAY, HE CAN FASHION PUPPETS WHICH SOMEHOW CONTROL THE LIVING PERSONS THEY ARE MODELED AFTER! TWICE HE HAS COME WITHIN A HAIRSBREADTH OF DEFEATING THE FANTASTIC FOUR... AS ALL OF FANDOM WONDERS... WILL THERE BE A THIRD TIME? AND IF SO, WILL THE NEXT VICTORY BELONG TO-- THE PUPPET MASTER?
H-BOMB

OPPOSITE **98: THE PUPPET MASTER** from *The Defenders* no. 19 (January 1975). Stamp also appears in *Sub-Mariner* no. 70 (May 1974) and *Sgt. Fury* no. 120 (July 1974).

ABOVE *Fantastic Four Annual* no. 1 (September 1963), art by Jack Kirby.

we've been allowing the names of groups like Hydra and the X-Men, we think letting rocks onto the list is going just a tad too far.

Still. . .77 out of 78 ain't bad. Congratulations!

Dear Marvel,

Perhaps you can tell me (and the rest of Marveldom Assembled) exactly what Peter Parker has been doing in college for *NINE YEARS.*

Charles Hoffman
310 Morrow Avenue
Carnegie, Pa. 15106

Arithmetic, maybe??

His laundry? His own thing? The funky chicken? Penance for his sins?

Okay. Serious answer time, then, if none of these brilliant bits of repartee is sufficient to dazzle you.

We've sort of slowed down Pete's aging process because we felt the majority of our readers preferred to read about a college-age Spidey. Were we wrong? Would you rather see him graduate and move on? This is a pretty serious question, we think, and we'd like you to think long and hard before answering, folks. No snap judgments. But we'd like to hear from as many of you as we can on this matter. So, after you've considered all its implications, drop us a line. To age or not to age. . .that is the question. (And don'tcha wish you had a choice?!)

Just a final reminder that our own Rascally Roy Thomas will be the major comic-book Guest of Honor at the star-studded San Diego (California) Comics Convention over the long weekend of July 31-August 5. A couple of others you might've heard of are gonna be Guests of Honor as well, including Charles ("Peanuts") Schulz, Milt ("Steve Canyon")Caniff, Gene ("Star Trek") Roddenberry, and fantasy author Ray Bradbury— just so you shouldn't get lonely.

Oh yes— and those of you with filled-up Marvel Value Stampbooks will receive a full dollar discount on con membership— as well as a pass to a private "Marvel 100" party where you'll meet Roy and such Marvel-type cohorts as Stainless Steve Englehart, Far-out Frank Brunner, Mikes Friedrich and Royer, and MONSTERS OF THE MOVIES editor Jim Harmon. The whole shebang's being held at the El Cortez Hotel at 7th and Ash Streets in downtown San Diego, and advance full membership is $7.50, sent to San Diego Comics Convention, P.O. Box 17066, San Diego, Ca. 92117. (The price is slightly higher at the door— and of course you can pay less if you're merely going for one day, but the advance membership is your best bet.) See you there?

THIS IS IT! YOUR

MARVEL VALUE STAMP

FOR THIS ISSUE!
CLIP 'EM AND COLLECT 'EM!

OPPOSITE **99: SANDMAN** from *The Amazing Spider-Man* no. 137 (October 1974). Stamp also appears in *Werewolf by Night* no. 17 (May 1974) and *Daredevil* no. 120 (April 1975).

ABOVE *The Amazing Spider-Man Annual* no. 1 (September 1964), art by Steve Ditko.

THE SPIDER'S WEB

SEND YOUR LETTERS TO:
THE MARVEL COMICS GROUP, SIXTH FLOOR 575 MADISON AV., NEW YORK N. Y. 10022

Spidey chroniclers:

I opened #142 and there it was, the Spidermobile, in full color: I hate it. Fortunately, it did not play a part in the story itself, and for that I'm thankful. Please, Gerry, leave it right where it is—corroding into nothingness on the bottom of the Hudson River.

The nice touch in Spidey is knowing that he's human. Pete's sore, bandaged hands contributed nicely to that end. However, even this can be carried a step too far, as witness the last panel on page six; it robs the realism, not so much because of what happens, but rather because of the way it's drawn—cartoonishly. Despite his sojourn of lo these many months on SPIDER-MAN, Ross Andru still doesn't belong here.

It was also nice to see a bit different characterization on JJJ this time around, instead of solely the usual ranting and raving. The MAN-WOLF series has also been showing us some different sides of JJJ's personality—altogether, Jolly Jonah's one of Marvel's most interesting supporting characters. Keep him that way.

Y'know, now that I look at it, I think the problem is that there're too many black areas in this comic. For instance, the crosshatching on "Mysterio" is so thick that you almost can't see the green color applied over it. Remember—this is a *color* comic, not a black-and-white or a newspaper strip.

And that last page teaser with JJJ has got me *hooked.* I don't know what's coming down, but I sure intend to find out! Nice work, Gerry.

Phillip Grant
455 Cascade Drive
Lebanon, OR 97355

Interesting that you should bring up the MAN-WOLF series, Phil. since from time-to-time we like to mention here that JJJ's son—John Jameson—is the star of that aforementioned feature, and there are some very wild things going on in that book; *try it.* End of plug.

And *muchas gracias* for the run-down on SPIDEY #142. Gerry's beaming, Ross is smarting, and Joe Rosen wants to know why you didn't compliment him on his lettering!

Dear Marvel,

I never thought that you'd really hit home. In regard to Philip J. Atterberry's letter in #142, I whole-heartedly agree with him. I really wonder if you intend to change your covers for the better? Yes, Marvel, I am buying your comics IN SPITE OF YOUR COVERS! A cover should be a cover, not just another page.

Why not limit the word balloons to ZERO!? Do you remember NICK FURY, AGENT OF SHIELD #1, X-MEN #50, and CAPTAIN AMERICA #'s 111-112 just to name a few? Did you find those covers lacking because there were no word balloons? I doubt very much that when decision time comes every month at the newsstands, *word balloons* will sway a reader to buy your comics.

And you do have a tendency to clutter, rather than drawing simplistic yet eye-catching covers. A cover should be as complex as the subject demands! One important point that I learned at the Manhattan School of Music as a theory student is, "The most important tool a great composer and arranger can use is SIMPLICITY!" I would say the same goes for ART.

MARVEL, I love you, but you're sure makin' it difficult. Until next time, Make Mine Marvel (believe it or not!).

Ed Marchese
RR 1 Box 678-A
Hamburg, NJ 07419

Okay, Ed, we'll give *you* the same answer Lively Len Wein gave *us* when we asked him about those covers without word balloons: "Yeah, and look what *happened* to SHIELD and the X-MEN not long after!"

Meaning: Sales fell off drastically. Not that we're necessarily pontificating that it was because we didn't put word balloons on the covers—but ya never know. Anyway, we asked for your opinions, and we're glad you gave 'em to us.

How else are we to know if we're doing right or wrong?

Marveldom Central:

It's just plain high time Peter Parker realized he doesn't need that ol' sheepskin to be a webflingin' member of the human race; fact is, he doesn't even need it to make a decent living. With all his *Bugle* photo credits—you tell me—wouldn't a career in free lance photography make a lot of sense?

If nothing else, it might get him out of the Big Apple a little more frequently and that alone might do wonders for his mental health. But more than that, taking pix, even news pix, is, if not more fun, certainly more creative than reading textbooks, writing papers, and taking exams.

Oh yeah—and how 'bout letting Petey grow his hair a little bit? You know giving him a little more sex appeal? Making him a little less straight looking?

Mark Wurzbacher
Town Terrace Apts #7
Valley Park Drive
Chapel Hill, NC 27514

What would "The Spider's Web" be without at least one letter on the Petey-in-college controversy? And, more importantly, what would it be without an *end?* Too long, no doubt. So here we are, at the customary conclusion of this month's liltin' letters column, askin' y'all to be back here in four weeks for more of the same.

Only better.

OPPOSITE **100: GALACTUS** from *The Amazing Spider-Man* no. 145 (June 1975). Stamp also appears in *Sub-Mariner* no. 72 (September 1974) and *Fantastic Four* no. 154 (January 1975).

ABOVE *Fantastic Four* no. 49 (April 1966), art by Jack Kirby and Joe Sinnott.

THIS IS IT,
TRUE BELIEVER!

SERIES B

A PERSONAL MESSAGE FROM YOUR BENEFICENT BULLPEN

Betcha thought you'd never see it, didn't ya?

Well, you were wrong! Here it is. The Second Marvel Value Stamp–book has finally arrived–– and, boy, is it ever worth the wait! We've gone all out to make this the weirdest, wackiest, and most way-out little item you've ever laid your baby-blues on! (We don't care **what** *color your eyes are.)*

This time, though, we aren't letting you off as easy as we did in the first Stampbook. This time, not only do you have to cut the little buggers out of our Mighty Marvel Magazines and paste them up in this booklet, but you also have to figure out what each group of ten stamps forms a picture of. (We'll tell you this much: Each one of the first nine groups forms a memorable scene featuring the character talked about on each particular page.) And just wait till you see who the last group depicts! (No, effendi, it's not Galactus!)

Now, just what can you do with this little book? Well, after all 100 spaces are filled take this titanic tome around to any of the star-studded Comic Book Conventions, comic art dealers, or such which you should have seen mentioned in recent Marvel Mags; and you'll be able to collect the appropriate discount or goodie!

Keep this around–– it's sure to become a valuable collectors' item in years to come, just as the first one already has!

That's it for this time, group; keep your eyes glued to our terrific titles to collect the whole set. Enjoy!

THE AMAZING SPIDER-MAN™

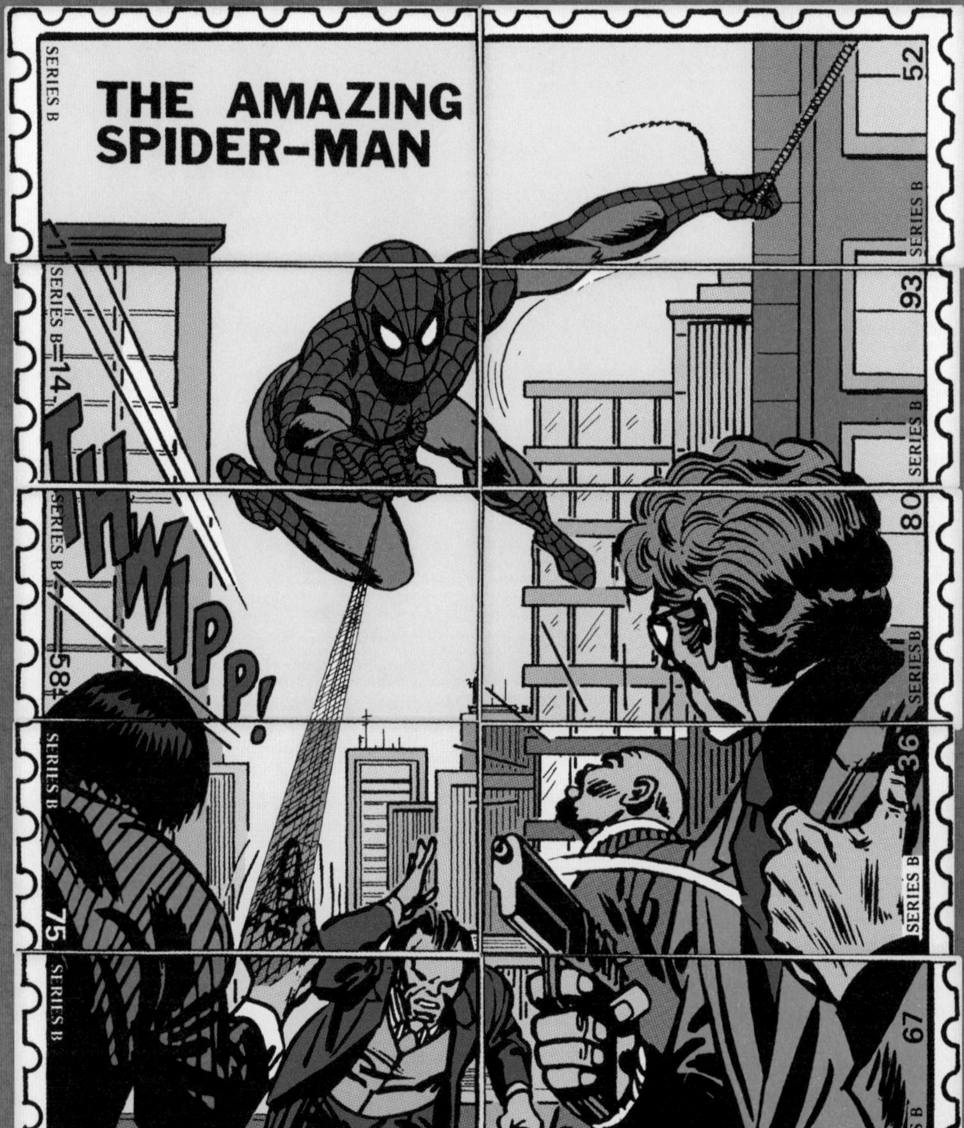

While attending a demonstration in radiology, high-school student PETER PARKER was bitten by a spider which had accidentally been exposed to RADIOACTIVE RAYS. Through a miracle of science, Peter soon found that he had GAINED the spider's powers...and had, in effect, become a human spider... Spider-man!

The Amazing Spider-Man no. 131 (April 1974), art by Gil Kane and Frank Giacoia; interior page from *The Amazing Spider-Man* no. 107 (April 1972), art by John Romita Sr. and Frank Giacoia. The composite of Spider-Man and the foreground figures was done in the bullpen, where the background was also added.

LET'S RAP WITH CAP

Dear Marvel,

To start it off, you have a great cover by Gil Kane and Dan Adkins, one of the best he's done this year. Then, I opened it up, eagerly awaiting Kirby. What? No Kirby?! Well, maybe it won't be too bad. Ya know what? It wasn't.

CAPTAIN AMERICA #190 was one of the best of my bunch of 18 that I'd bought at my neighborhood book store. 18 comics! And Cap really amazed me!

Concerning the art: Frank Robbins and Vince Colletta should get a pat on the back for this issue. Since Vinnie has left THE DEFENDERS, he can devote more time to a single mag, thus shooting his ink job up 90%!

The only thing that bugs me concerning the script is Nightshade referring to the werewolves as her "pretties," and this has *always* bothered me...in both comics and the movies, with the traditional scraggly witch chanting over her pot of boiling bat-wings. Otherwise, nice job, Tony.

Larry Dean
6362 Laurentian Ct.,
Flint, MI 48504

Sorry, Larry, but the cover of CAPTAIN AMERICA #190 was inked by none other than Joltin' Joe Sinnott himself!

As for Nightshade's calling the werewolves "pretties"—we sorta suspect that's just her way of letting us know she's not the "girl next door" type.

Dear Marv,

Tony Isabella turned in an excellent plot and script for CA & F #190. Two books in one month that I'd call first-rate jobs. He's finally becoming the good writer he was supposed to be (ah, the Ed Kranepool of the Bullpen!), and I look forward to his handling of THE CHAMPIONS.

Cap and the Falc haven't fought so much together in a while, helping each other out and working in tandem with specific maneuvers (Sam's instinctive knowledge of "maneuver 68" shows a lot of previous practice). And, this togetherness is more needed now than ever before, now that Sam must be constantly reminded that he IS a hero, working with CA. Teams, whether they be just duos or full rosters, are always more interesting when the members work hand in hand.

It was also very nice seeing Val back in action. She provided not a small bit of interest in the past, but was suddenly dropped from the strip. Hopefully, this will mark her return as a regular supporting SHIELD member. Too, Eric and Cochren added more depth; it was enjoyable seeing a SHIELD operation without Nick, Dum-Dum, and Gabe leading the fight.

Frank Robbins turned out another spectacular job. It's odd, how two completely different artists like Al Weiss and he both seem perfectly suited to illustrate Nightshade. She's a real fox, but also, a spoiled little kid (1957?). Al emphasized her foxy side, and Frank, the bratty side; each interpretation worked very well. Her pouting at the end of the issue, sighing "Oh Poo" was beautiful.

Frank's overall composition was also really nice, and I particularly enjoyed how he fit so many people into each of the fight panels—it really gave the impression of intensity.

However, I found my first example of a jarring cut in his usually flawless continuity. The last panel of page 18 sported Cap and the Falc apprehensively looking to the left of the panel, yet, the first panel of page 22 had the attackers appearing from the right, and not the left. However, it was a minor fluke in an otherwise beautiful ish.

Dean Mullaney
81 Delaware Street
Staten Is., NY 10304

Dear Tony, Frank, and Vince;

I planned to write and say how much better Frank's pencils look with Vinnie's inks but this month's bullpen announcement renders that obsolete.

I may be burned in effigy for saying this, but I regret to see Kirby take over drawing *and scripting* of Cap. For three years under Englehart and Buscema CA&F featured some of the greatest plots in comicdom: the other Cap, Cap's new strength, the Yellow Claw, the smear campaign culminating in the White House, Cap's resignation, the Nomad, and the Red Skull's return. The emphasis I've put on plot is not meant to slight Sal's equally fine action-packed art.

But Kirby is *all* art! What little plot exists serves only as an excuse to get to the action scenes. I'll stop here before all the King's loyal subjects take umbrage and plot against my continued wealth and well-being. Perhaps my fears will prove to be unfounded after a few issues. Thanks for listening.

UFO, KOR Steve Rogers
5427 43rd
Lubbock, TX 79414

Dear Jack Kirby,

I was glad to read of your return to Marvel and when I read you would be writing and drawing Cap I sent in for a subscription. I would like to see Captain America much as he was in TALES OF SUSPENSE and his early issues, minus the Falcon, Bucky, Rick Jones, etc., and working with S.H.I.E.L.D.

Is Sharon Carter still around? I haven't seen many of Cap's recent issues; if so, let's not have the on again-off again romance, or Cap mourning Bucky every issue. These were two small faults (in my opinion) of the classic issues of yesteryear. Anyway, glad you're back 'n looking forward to reading Cap.

Mike Underwood
6241 18th Ave. N
St. Petersburg, FL 33710

Well, Mike, now that you've read Jack (King) Kirby's first Cap story in so long, how'd ya like it? (We kinda enjoyed the issue!) Jack's plans will become evident as the months go by, but meanwhile, Marvelous Marv Wolfman assures us that Jack is thinking not of the *past* but of the *future*. Be here!

THIS IS IT! YOUR
MARVEL VALUE STAMP
FOR THIS ISSUE!

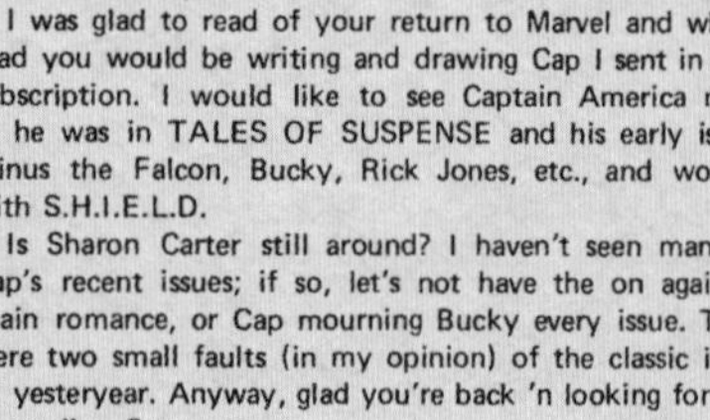

CLIP 'EM AND COLLECT 'EM!

1: THE AMAZING SPIDER-MAN from *Captain America* no. 193 (January 1976). Stamp also appears in *Power Man* no. 33 (July 1976).

GREEN SKIN'S GRAB-BAG

c/o MARVEL COMICS GROUP, 575 MADISON AVE. N.Y.C. 10022

Dear Bullpen,

Finally, the Incredible Hulk has lived up to his name. Others may not agree with me, but issue #196 was truly great. What really made it great was the art by Sal Buscema. The incredible variety of action poses and Hulk facial expressions especially pleased me. Look at the way the Hulk scatters the security force with one fell swoop of his arm; the way the Abomination and Wilbur Manners are drawn to show the power and size of the Abomination on panel 6 of page 11 (look at the size of that left hand!); the comic-horror face of the Hulk when the G-forces are playing games with his face; and the Kirbyesque brute face of the Hulk when he *kkrrumpp's* open the side of the space craft. These are the things I enjoy seeing in well-drawn stories.

You are probably going to receive a ton of letters on this, I know, but shouldn't the Hulk's pants have burned off on panel 5 of the last page? With "his skin sheathed in flame," I don't see how the pants survived. The only reason I bring this up is the past furor over Betty's dress, which when burst out of in her transformation into a harpy, miraculously reappeared in the following issue. It should be interesting to see the splash page of next issue's story.

No matter what, I genuinely enjoyed the magazine. So long as Sal Buscema continues to draw the Hulk's wanderings, there is no way I will miss an issue.

Lawrence J. Deyab
(No address given)

Truth to tell, Larry, our very own writer/editor has always had a theory about the Hulk's pants, and it goes something like this: While Bruce Banner doesn't wear specially-treated fabrics as do the Fantastic Four and others, the molecular composition of his pandemonious purple pants is nonetheless affected by those massive doses of gamma-radiation which he gives off, to the extent that they acquire certain added properties beyond those normally attributed to ordinary purple pants.

In other words, they didn't burst into flame during the Hulk's heated re-entry into our atmosphere. Nice try, Larry—but no cigar!

Dear Marvel,

I really enjoyed HULK # 196, which, in my opinion, is the best comic that you produce! There is only one thing that bothers me, though, and that is: why does the Incredible One have to repeat his name whenever he speaks? I know that his vocabulary is limited, but this is ridiculous. Also, I'm quite sure that by now everyone knows who the jade-skinned giant (notice, how I don't always mention his name) is!

And now for another question that's been on my mind for a while. Is HULK the best selling magazine that you produce?

Kerry Held
2913 Montgomery St.
Wantagh, NY 11793

Actually, Kerry, it's like this: Hulk doesn't *have* to repeat his name (we sincerely doubt whether anyone could force him to do so against his will), it just so happens that's his speech pattern, much the way each of us has our own particular method of verbal expression. Sheesh—Hulk talks like that because Hulk talks like that!

As for the sales status of this mag, it's among Marvel's top five. SPIDER-MAN takes the number one spot, natch, but the INCREDIBLE HULK is definitely a best seller, make no mistake about that!

Dear Marvel people—

In HULK # 196, page one, the men at Hulkbuster base are watching a tape supposedly from the Abomination's head. So here's my point—why do I see Abomination and the Hulk, if the camera is in the Abomination's head? I'll take my no-prize in bronze (since this is my first letter, I don't wanna be too pushy).

Barry Bedwell
Lynch, MD 21646

We had a reason for depicting the Hulk and the Abomination together, Barry, old boy, believe it or not. We felt it made for a much more dramatic splash page than just a shot of our Jade Giant punching at air, and so we availed ourselves of Artistic License.

And also, believe it or not, we really wanted to give ya that modest no-prize, Barry—but we reserve those for when you Marvelites catch us in genuine, bonafide boo-boos. Better luck next time, Bar!

Dear Hulkophiles—

I have for a long time been tempted to go back to Brand Echh, but HULK #196 has made those temptations a thing of the past (for now, anyway). Yet the one thing I would like to know is what would the Abomination do with $100,000,000 in uncut diamonds? Suppose he sold them for money—where is he going to spend it? He's not exactly the type to walk into a store unnoticed! I'd like to receive a no-prize for discerning this fact.

Paul Spataco
1835 E 29 St.
Brooklyn, NY 11229

Picky, picky, picky! Some people'll do *anything* to get a no-prize! In the mighty Marvel Universe, Paul, there's any number of things the always-astonishing Abomination could have done with his cool $100,000,000 — like buying an island and having his merchandise delivered! Or arranging for experiments to change him back to normal, if he was so inclined. Never underestimate the shifty intelligence of a supercilious super-villain (or of a letters-page answering armadillo!).

NEXT ISSUE: "The Sword & the Sorcerer!" — featuring the most unexpected barbarian of all...sort of. And if that sounds ambiguous, then you'll just have to be here for #201 to find out *why*. As for the future beyond that, be on the lookout for the return of somebody you've all been waiting for—and we don't mean the Boomerang! After that—pandemonium in New York! It's all here in 1976, gang—be sure you are, too!

MARVEL VALUE STAMP

CLIP 'EM AND COLLECT 'EM!

52: THE AMAZING SPIDER-MAN from *The Incredible Hulk* no. 200 (June 1976).

MAIL IT TO TEAM-UP

c/o MARVEL COMICS GROUP, 575 MADISON AVE. N.Y.C. 10022

People,

Emergency. The sound of ringing bells. Motions in whites. "Prepare this magazine for immediate revision. Orderly, contact Supervisor Wein and Dr. Conway. I want them in REVISION ROOM 38A. Nurse, prepare all tools...and I want those PENS sterilized. And bring erasers, hordes of them. You there! Are you a relative?"

"No sir, I'm a subscriber."

"Well, son, you have a sick friend."

"What's WRONG with him, doc? Please tell me that MTU won't FOLD!"

"That depends, son. Your friend is pretty bad off. He's suffering from a case of acute plot deficiency."

"But I thought..."

"Yes, you thought he was doing rather well, eh? Haven't you noticed that since issue #21, all the way through #37, his plot content has been dangerously LOW? And his character development is approaching CRITICAL!"

"But...but HOW?"

"He's caught in a syndrome, son, a type of SHOW syndrome. Much show and action, and little central THOUGHT. Hero meets villain, then destroys villain. It all takes place in one issue, a one nighter, with a weak plot draped over."

"Can we HELP him?"

"Only with an immediate transfusion of PLOT and CHARACTER! This will destroy future one-nighters and promote a growth of good, healthy, continuing stories...as well as provide him with BACKBONE, from which character development will almost certainly GROW. But for now, we can only WAIT!"

R. Hundertmark
Rockville, MD 20853

Dear 'R'...Well, by now MTU has, we hope, had its transfusion of ALL the prerequisites you feel it needed to become, once more, a strong and healthy addition to the Marvel Line-Up. Bill, Sal, Mike, et al., are putting their all into making it MORE than just a 'Team-Up' magazine...and they'd all like to hear what you think of it...doctor.

Dear Gerry, Sal, Vince and Marv,

MTU #'s 36 and 37. Well, uh...not bad, but (you've heard this a thousand times) the plot seems to be always the same. Meet 'em, chase 'em, catch 'em. For once, why don't you guys do something DIFFERENT?? Anything! PLEASE! It'll make your mag MUCH better.

Bill Caley
10944 Lawrie Cres.
Delta, B.C., Canada

Marv, Gerry, etc., etc.,

Let me say, here you have one schlep of a mag. MTU is monotonous. The plot hasn't changed for about two years.

Heroes team-up, go after villain. Villain captures heroes and sentences them to death by some fantastic means. Heroes escape by a miracle, thrash villain into ground. After a few issues of this one runs down to the newsstand and buys all the competition mags money can purchase to get away from such boring writing. They have it too, so we're left with the out of shooting ourselves and costing you readers.

Kirk O'Brien
1605 Concord Drive
Charlottesville, VA

I think we get the HINT, gang. But don't quit on MTU...as the last four issues have shown, CHANGE is the direction of the future, with continuing stories, heroes teamed-up for more than one issue, and more surprises than you're likely to find almost anywhere. Stay with us, friends.

THIS IS IT! YOUR
MARVEL VALUE STAMP
FOR THIS ISSUE!

CLIP 'EM AND COLLECT 'EM!

14: THE AMAZING SPIDER-MAN from *Marvel Team-Up* no. 41 (January 1976).

GHOST WRITERS!

c/o MARVEL COMICS GROUP, 575 MADISON AVE. N.Y.C. 10022

Startling revelation-time, people.

The Marvel Comics Group—from the publisher to the writers to the legendary Duffy Vohland—is fallible. Really. I wouldn't kid you. Stan once forgot the Hulk's name. I once forgot that a lead character was crippled and had him kick somebody. (In true Marvel tradition, of course, I then made the error the beginning of a new sub-plot.) And though I can't confirm it, the rumor is out that a certain befuddled editor has been turning in scripts for a book by the name of TOMB OF DAREDEVIL.

I know the above probably comes as a tremendous shock to you, but I figure the average Marvel reader is mature enough to recover from even the strongest blows to his belief in the historic entity that is Marvel. And this secret knowledge is necessary if you are to fully understand the reasons for this special edition of "Ghost Writers."

We have been lax, the armadillos and myself, in printing your views on recent issues of GHOST RIDER. Yea, we have allowed whole months to go by without a letters column appearing in these pages. And, yes, we have known the pangs of guilt for our failure in this area. But, hark, we stand ready to make amends for our wrongdoing by selecting the most representative letters on GHOST RIDER #13 to #16, and presenting them herein. Enjoy, folks!

Dear Tony, George, and the rest,

I want to thank you for GHOST RIDER #13's "You've Got a Second Chance, Johnny Blaze." Johnny is at last totally free of his curse, and can now use his powers to help those who need the sort of assistance that only a Ghost Rider can provide. He is leaving the rather limited (for him, at least) field of occult involvement for what should be a rewarding career as a superhero. He also seems to be getting his life to the point where it will provide him with steady employment, opportunities for action, and (by the important addition of supporting characters) interesting developments in his personal life. Just remember that no superhero may have his mind totally free of hassles, and you'll be fine.

The story itself was well-paced and well-planned, and fit letter perfect into the floor plan set up within the previous year of the Ghost Rider's adventures. The battle with the Trapster symbolizes that GR has left his days of fighting Satan far behind, though I suspect the Prince of Darkness will eventually show up again.

Finally, there was the artwork of George Tuska and Vince Colletta. This issue was their turning point as far as I'm concerned. I haven't a single complaint with Vinnie's inking of George's work this time, nor, I think, in the future.

Again, thanks.

Brian Jordan
53125 Oakton Drive
South Bend, IN 46635

Dear Flame Brains,

Unfortunately, I seem to have missed the first issue of THE CHAMPIONS, but I'll be darned if I'll miss the follow-up of the best Ghost Rider story since his run-in with the Phantom Eagle!

GHOST RIDER #14 ("A Specter Stalks the Soundstage") and this new change of pace for Johnny Blaze seem to be breathing new life into this once-dreary comic. If every issue can be like this one, I expect this mag to move up to monthly status soon. George Tuska's art was above par and Tony Isabella is definitely improving in the scripting department.

Until Johnny Blaze runs out of charcoal fluid...

Mark Dooley
105 Wehmeier Street
Columbus, IN 47201

As you can see, the mail on GHOST RIDER #13 and #14 was overwhelmingly favorable, but "Vengeance on the Ventura Freeway" (#15) and "Blood in the Water" (#16) split Marveldom right down the proverbial center...

Dear Marvel,

I can't say that GHOST RIDER #15 was a disappointment, but I can't say it was excellent, either. It was more of a...fair comic. The art could have been 100% better, but you could see that it was definitely a rush job, probably by inker Don Heck. I hope next issue is better...much better. On the story, I can't find any gripe. Tony Isabella wrote another winner, and that's all the praise that I need to give.

Larry Dean
6362 Laurentian Ct.
Flint, MI 48504

Dear Tony,

Well, you've done it again! You turned what could have been a pretty good issue into a pretty lousy issue! Issue #15 was just a redone GR #9. Redone very badly, I might add. Why, instead of GR's "friend" intervening, couldn't Johnny have just gone ahead and beaten the heck out of the Orb? Why?!? You're a fantastic writer, Tony, and I know you can do better than this.

Bob Brown's art wasn't too bad, but Klaus Janson is a better inker for him than Don Heck. Don did do a good job, though I'll be looking forward to Frank Robbins' mighty return in GR #17. The Son of Satan's gonna look awful good!

Ron Cartwright
5703 Cherry Ave., Apt. F-1
Long Beach, CA 90805

Dear Gang,

What can I say about GHOST RIDER #16, except that it was great? The cover was the best I've seen so far on the mag, maybe on any of your mags. I enjoyed the story itself because GR was fighting a true-to-life shark and not some supernatural foe. A welcome change.

Bruno Bertolini
135-49 115 Street
S. Ozone Park, NY 11420

Hey, you guys!

GHOST RIDER #16. You just hadda do it, didn't you? Everyone else in the industry has taken advantage of the "Jaws" craze. Why Marvel? The story was a bit too simplistic and contrived to really be interesting or even mildly entertaining. Sorry, people, but that's the way it goes. Better luck next time.

Mike Rutter
PO Box 130
Hampstead, MD 21074

Dear Marvel,

GHOST RIDER #16. The issue was pathetic.

Christy Marx
1811 Bellevue Avenue
Los Angeles, CA 90026

NEXT ISSUE: your comments on the first chapter of the trilogy that begun in GHOST RIDER #17, "A Private Armageddon." And remember: your letter on this ish will keep an armadillo off the street and on the job! Be good, troops.

MARVEL VALUE STAMP

FOR THIS ISSUE!

93: THE AMAZING SPIDER-MAN from *Ghost Rider* no. 18 (June 1976).

OMEGA MAIL

c/o MARVEL COMICS GROUP, 575 MADISON AVE. N.Y.C. 10022

It began as the simplest of ideas: a strip whose protagonist would be a twelve-year-old boy.

Why?

Because there weren't any such strips extant, for one thing. And for another, I'd always resented the lousy treatment kids had received in comics over the past three decades: either they had to be magically transformed into a full-grown man to be effectual, or they were saddled with an adult "mentor" and relegated to the duty of making bad puns during fight scenes.

I wanted to do a *real* twelve-year-old, a *human being* poised on the edge of puberty, facing all the enormous (and enormous-seeming) problems adolescence would bring— not one of the kid-sidekicks who have been a mainstay and a tired cliché of comics since that first trapeze broke, and the Flying Whoozits went plummeting to their sawdusty doom.

Yeah. That's what I wanted to do. So *there!*

The industry's initial reception to this novel concept might best be described as a raucous burst of unenthusiasm.

"Kids don't like to read about kids," I was told. "They want a hero they can look up to and identify with at the same time."

I interpreted that to mean an adult with the emotional maturity of an infant— yet another comic-book staple for the past three or four decades. The clown in longjohns who punches first and asks questions later.

My mature sophisticated reaction to these criticisms was: Blecch! *Yucch! WAAAUGH!!* (The latter with apologies to my duck friend Howard.)

But the critics had hit on one salient point: if the kid in this here hypothetical, non-existent strip were going to be real, he couldn't be the one to wear the leotards. And since magic words and Nega-Bands were out of the question, it was clear that this new feature would require the presence of both a protagonist— and a hero. One life-size, one slightly larger-than-life.

Now I was onto something, I felt— unfortunately, I hadn't any notion *what.*

Nevertheless, editors MARV WOLFMAN and LEN WEIN recognized the potential in this amorphous invention of mine. And I'd already developed a variation on the scene in which the kid— I was already calling him James-Michael by this time—discovers his "parents" are robots. So we took the whole pile of nebulous inspirations, none of them even on paper yet, to publisher STAN LEE, who, after hearing assurances that we did not have a "Bucky-Barnes-goes-it-alone"-type book in mind, not only liked the idea but gave it a name: OMEGA THE UNKNOWN.

Now all that remained was to fit the pieces of the jigsaw puzzle together. Not so easy when you don't know what the finished picture is supposed to look like.

Who was James-Michael? Why were his parents robots? What was his relation to Omega? Who was *Omega,* for cryin' out loud?!?

Enter: MARY SKRENES (pronounced SKREE-ness), writer of mystery, horror, romance, and funny-animal stories for virtually every comics publisher at one time or another over the past five years. You may have seen her byline in CRAZY or on movie reviews in THE DEADLY HANDS OF KUNG FU. You've surely seen her pseudonyms elsewhere.

Mary was munching on her Big Mac and I on my Quarter-Pounder (with cheese) when the subject of OMEGA entered the conversation. I poured out my tale of confusion and then

sat there, bun crumbs dropping from my lower lip into my lap, astounded as a dozen or so solutions to this problem I'd been wrestling with for weeks came rolling glibly off her tongue.

By the time dinner was over— two a.m. or so— we had the complete plot-outline for this issue and a firm direction in mind for the series. No question: she'd contributed as much to the creation of the strip as I had. I asked if she'd care to collaborate on the actual writing. (You've seen the credits.)

JIM MOONEY, with whom I'd worked on SON OF SATAN and MAN-THING, and whose fan I've been since those long-ago yesterdays when he drew "Tommy Tomorrow," was selected to illustrate OMEGA. I was elated. For, curiously, though Jim and I have never met, we seem to have an instinctive affinity for one another's styles.

The Omega costume was a product of three heads: mine, Len's, and that of art director JOHN ROMITA. (There's yet another guy whose stuff I admire. Wish I could remember the name of the strip he used to do...!)

And all the agony, all the ecstasy, all the labor, sweat, and cheap hamburgers suddenly came together as the magazine you're reading now.

Was it worth it?

There's only one way we'll ever know: WRITE!!

Better yet, go buy an extra copy and *then* write! And then join us again in sixty days.

Take care.

—STEVE GERBER

MARVEL VALUE STAMP

58: THE AMAZING SPIDER-MAN from *Omega the Unknown* no. 1 (March 1976).

Tomes to the Tomb!

c/o MARVEL COMICS GROUP, 575 MADISON AVE. N.Y.C. 10022

Since we inadvertantly covered TOMB OF DRACULA #39 in two separate letter cols (blame it on different Marvel Armadillos at work here, Dracophiles), we've got to cover both #40 and #41 this time, so this editorial-bold typeface will silence itself now until the *end* of the letter col. But we'll be back on the prowl next issue with answers all. Seeya then.

Dear Marv, Gene and Tom,

I've never read a comic as fast as I read TOMB OF DRACULA #40. The tension and suspense built steadily throughout the story and left me hanging to the last page. Any chance of TOD coming out bi-weekly? Seriously, TOD is consistently one of the best (if not the best) comics available. All of the characters and action are totally real and credible. Frank Drake has finally gotten a hold of himself and seems to know what he wants and how to get it for the first time. The flashbacks of Rachel and Quincy were terrific. They vividly portrayed not only the intensity of their involvement with Dracula but also the timelessness of Dracula himself.

I love Gene's artwork. He establishes an identity with characters as strong as the scripting. Beautiful coordination between script and art.

I can't end this letter without throwing in my 2¢ on Harold and Aurora. My first impression was "How corny!" Now, a few issues later, I still think they're corny, but, darn it all, I love 'em. How you made two such unlikelies fit so beautifully into this mag is beyond me. Plain old Marvel Magic!

The assault on Dr. Sun's house to retrieve Dracula's ashes was really good. When Rachel nailed Juno with the crossbow I almost stood up and cheered I was so excited, (even though I can't figure out where she got the darned thing—she wasn't carrying it with her—oh well.)

So—Dracula must live again and I can't wait!! Nuff Said!

Rook Jones
3053 Tremont Street
Allentown, PA 18014

Dear Marvel,

(With special regards to Marv Wolfman)

"It's not real." I said.

"Of course it ain't real, man; it's comic books," she said.

We seem to have a differing opinion on Harold H. Harold, the newest addition to Marvel's merry band of Vampire-busters.

On one hand, I find him repulsive. On the other hand, I think he may be one of the best characters to appear in Marvel Comics since Richard Rory himself.

You see, I can like Harold Harold because I can almost *identify* with him. A man pitted against the real odds of a very unreal world is a classic Marvel situation. Not all of us have radioactive blood, or collapsible armor, or mutant strength. My god, I gotta like poor Harold because he *is* me!!!

But then you gotta go and overdo it!!

As much as I can identify with Harold, I can't really "believe" (if that's the right word) all the stuff you make him do.

Observe page 26 of TOD #40.

Nobody, but nobody, with Harold's personality and obvious lack of macho is going to climb a rope 70 feet off the street. People aren't made that way. There are physical limitations to what a man can do, even in a panic.

Now check out page 11.

I realize that it's hard to draw the line between having Harold do nothing, and making him into the kind of character that Peter Sellers played in "Casino Royale," but come on, gang.

Vampires I can "believe." Talking brains I can "believe." A man with a silver stake on his hand I can "believe."

But Harold H. Harold becoming, even *accidentally*, a "hero" is stretching it.

If you are going to continue using Harold H. Harold in TOD, please ditch the gymnastics and the other stuff you have him do.

T. E. Pouncey
Douglass Kansas

Dear Marv,

It is sad that the first time I am moved by a story the way TOD moved me, it creates a feeling of sadness in me. TOD #41 was simply Fantastic!! But yet, it was degrading, disgusting, and revolting. I realize a Dracula-mag without Dracula won't sell very many copies. I realize Dracula is just one aspect of the villain-as-a-hero syndrome existing in comics today. I realize that Drac is just another expression of the Evil in our "Real" world. I realize that Marvel would have to be composed of complete and utter fools to allow the main man of "The Number 1 Fear Magazine" to stay killed off.

So I fully expected Drac to be restored in some way. And I must admit, Aurora's catalytical tears were an ingenious, even touching way of utilizing a supporting role. I was prepared for the old, well-known sneer of the high-born, the arrogance, the undying thirst...But Wow!!!! Drac's one issue of rest seemed to bring him a renewed vitality, an eviler-than-evil look in his eyes, a deeper thirst...Maybe he's a few decades younger or something, I don't know.

I was expecting *good,* but Gene, Tom, and John, as well as you Marv, gave me "excellence" that shocked me. On that complimentary note, I bring in my last point. Page 10, top; Drac's about to hit the airways in search of a meal-in-skirts. He gloats to Quincy and company: "I can exist with that knowledge—but can you?" I can't keep Drac dead. But I can stop buying. I know I'm reacting on impulse, but I would feel saner by not being a spectator at a blood-festival again.

Charles Kopecky
19419 Bockman Road
Marengo, IL 60152

Next: **the beginning of what may be the greatest Dracula epic ever—*we* don't want to say too much this time, but we guarantee you that Marv, Gene and Tom have some plans for everyone's favorite vampire to take place over the next year which will top anything we've ever done before. Stay with us and see for yourself why T.O.D. is *Comicdom's Number 1 Fear Magazine!***

MARVEL VALUE STAMP

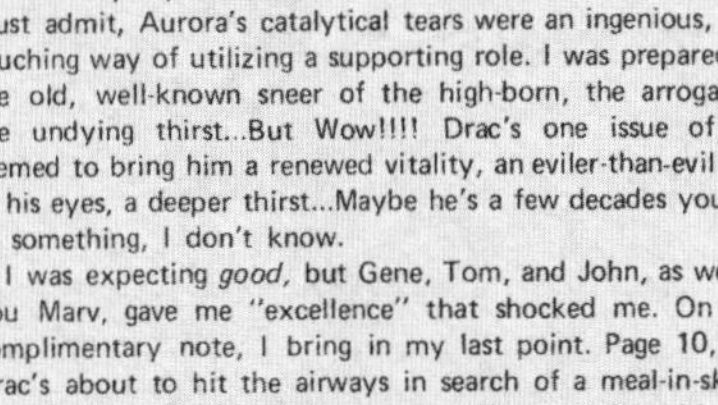

80: THE AMAZING SPIDER-MAN from *Tomb of Dracula* no. 44 (May 1976).

MAIL IT TO
TEAM-UP
% MARVEL COMICS GROUP, 575 MADISON AVE. N.Y.C. 10022

Dear Bill,

It seems that my assumption that being given a regular series to handle would show your good side was correct. Your first two-parter, though a little weak in the second segment, was nonetheless a big improvement for this mag. And this initial installment of the team-up with the Scarlet Witch was almost totally first rate. It's clearly evident that you are taking the book out of the catatonic state in which it was in. Congrats, and...thanks.

Over the past couple of years Wanda has developed into the complex type of personality which she should have had a long time ago. And for her first solo stint away from the Avengers, this story was an excellent one. Her remarkable displays of new found abilities were appreciated, as her being able to direct the focus of her hex powers is interesting to behold. No longer are her powers merely hit and miss; as was seen by her probe "ball" zipping around the world for help, she has great control of her powers. Too, her strength was shown well in that, despite Cotton Mather's attempts to subdue her, she still fought on. All in all, I am very pleased at your handling of the Scarlet Witch.

My only complaint is that I would have preferred not having the Vision come to the rescue as he did near the issue's end. Their relationship is a great one, but now that Wanda has become more like her namesake, she must also be able to stand on her own two feet, with *and* without the Vision. The old husband to the rescue routine, while admittedly appropriate considering their relationship, was not really needed (that is, unless the Visz plays a larger role in the story's conclusion But even if so, I'd still prefer Wanda being highlighted).

Spidey's involvement came about believably, as Wanda's plea was aimed for no one in particular, and that Spidey happened to be the one whom it contacted, was fine enough.

Also, Cotton Mather is a perfect adversary for the Scarlet Witch, and I look forward to the developments of next ish.

Equally first rate was the artwork. Sal B. and Mike E. did a little more than their usual, and it could be seen. The concentration on action oriented layouts provided a quick pace for the storv to follow.

Lastly, mention must be made of Ellen's coloring. Not because I feel like covering all aspects of the ish, but because she turned in an excellent job. Usually, due to the nature of her costume color, the Scarlet Witch has a hard time blending in with other characters, yet this ish, even in the scene with Spidey, the colors mixed well and I didn't need any sunglasses.

So, I guess you can say I liked it all. I did. Thanks Bill, and keep 'em coming.

Dean Mullaney
81 Delaware Street
Staten Is., NY

Dean, as always yours is the first letter to come in on an issue of MTU, and your criticisms are ever equally as important as your praise. As by now we hope you've seen, the Vision did participate in the totality of the story, and Wanda herself played probably the pivotal and most crucial role in defeating the Dark Rider. As an experiment, 95% of Marveldom seems to wildly approve of the new direction MTU has taken...and your letters have been in the vanguard of that approval. Thanks...from the heart.

Dear Marvel,

I just finished reading MTU #41 and I am writing to congratulate you on a wonderful job. Sal's artwork is perfect on MTU. He complements the pages of everything he draws. The story was great, too, although if Bill looks in his history books he will find that no witches were burned in Salem. Burning was a European tactic.

Despite that error, the book was *fantastic*!

Peter Harvey
51 Cedar Street
Salem, Mass.

Dear Marvel,

You've probably already received a hundred letters about this, but just in case you haven't, the Salem witches were not burned. *They were Hanged.*

Hang in there!

Richard Nathan
2002 Fourth Street
Santa Monica, Calif.

Ah *hem!* We must *protest!* We have been literally *flooded* with mail pointing out what reader's claim was our little oversight...and we plead NOT GUILTY! A) Wanda was presented to a crowd of scared, riotous, superstitious people whose first instinct was to follow the customs of Europe (from which most, if not all of them, had just recently come) and, indeed, "BURN THE WITCH!" B) They didn't, thanks to a timely interruption by MTU's star and the lady's husband, and C) all other witch-suspects were shown to have been hung in the issues following. So, while we admit that there was not a single "witch" burned at Salem...neither was there a single witch burned in the pages of MTU. So *there*!

Dear Falling Uniters,

MTU #38 stunk!

MTU #39 didn't... much.

MTU #40 had me saying *what the heck happened?*

MTU #41 had me applauding. There's continuation. There's a plot. There is a first hand, *first* exploration into this new look at Wanda's. It's everything a Marvel fan ever wanted out of this book. More! More! More! Or I'll team up with Alex Karras and there'll be one less publishing firm on Madison Avenue!

Until Spider-Man teams up with the Noisome Nebbish!

Mark Dooley
105 Wehmeier Street
Columbus, Ohio

You've got it, got it, *got it,* Mark! But you don't scare us a bit. After all, with Spidey, Wanda, the Vision, and—if necessary—a certain green-skinned giant, to protect us, we're ready to take on the entire lineup of the Miami Dolphins if we have to!

NEXT: DEATHLOK THE DEMOLISHER, and for all our web-slinger *knows*, the *end* of his entire way of life! Which makes us *wonder*...can even SPIDER-MAN alter the FUTURE?

THIS IS IT! YOUR
MARVEL VALUE STAMP
FOR THIS ISSUE!

CLIP 'EM AND COLLECT 'EM!

75: THE AMAZING SPIDER-MAN from *Marvel Team-Up* no. 45 (May 1976).

"Are they gonna let every one of Rich Buckler's drinking buddies work for Marvel whether they can draw or not?" Well, in less than a year George has become one of the best super-hero artists in the business, and promises to get even better. (You know, it's getting pretty embarrassing how many shots I've called wrong, artist-wise: Such "terrible" artists as Jim Steranko, Barry Smith, Craig Russell, and George Perez. I no do so good, hey?)

Although George would probably do a bang-up job on the Avengers, the F4, Super-Villain Team-Up and whatever else he puts his hand to, try to keep him on the INHUMANS since this is a strip which demands more skill than the average group strip. Instead of 8 or 9 super-heroes gallivanting around, here we have an entire race of strange-looking beings, each of them different. I can't imagine anyone who could do the job as well as George.

By the way, where were Crystal and Quicksilver?

Peter B. Gillis
18 Bayberry Road
Elmsford, NY 10523

Thanks for the ego-boosts, Pete, and we apologize for editing your epic-length letter down to manageable size; there's only so much room on these furshlugginer pages, you know...

As for Crystal and Quicksilver (né Pietro)...well, they *were* in the first issue. But they got cut out, unfortunately. And if that sounds like an intro to one of our notorious behind-the-scenes anecdotes, you heard it right the first time...

Here's the scoop: THE INHUMANS was originally slated to be a quarterly "Giant-Size" book, similar to THE X-MEN #1. Therefore, Doug plotted a mammoth 40-page story for the first issue — including a scene which featured Crystal and husband Pietro. However, he plotted the story some 14 hours before a meeting was held in which it was decided to cancel (at least temporarily) all Giant-Size books and convert THE INHUMANS to a normal-size bimonthly book.

Doug tore his hair out — all three feet of it, at the roots.

George then cried on Doug's shoulder while Doug cried on his.

And, together, they dried their eyes and set about the grim task of dividing the single 40-page story into two 18-page stories. It wasn't easy, especially since they had to add a flashback to the beginning of the second issue, recapping the first issue for those who may have missed it.

In other words, they hadda cut a whole bunch of stuff, The Crystal/Quicksilver sequence was included in that bunch. Sniff...

But take heart, Attilan-followers; both Crystal and Quicksilver — as well as Lockjaw — have found their way into THE INHUMANS #3! The Great Refuge is once again reunited — at least in between those periods of cataclysmic havoc constantly being wreaked by *some* odious villain or other...

NEXT ISSUE: The final battle with SHATTERSTAR! The awesome secret of FALZON! Lockjaw's flummoxed jaunt into the bizarre TWILIT DIMENSION! And more, of course.

Until then...be good.

MARVEL VALUE STAMP

36: THE AMAZING SPIDER-MAN from *The Inhumans* no. 3 (February 1976).

THE HAMMER STRIKES

c/o MARVEL COMICS GROUP, 575 MADISON AVE. N.Y.C. 10022

Dear Asgardian Chroniclers,

This is just a belated note to compliment you on the great 240th issue of THOR, and particularly on the reappearance of Fandral, Hogun, and Volstagg. Do you guys realize that these once-major characters had not appeared for some twenty-two issues?! As there has been hardly any response from letter writers on this subject, I was afraid that these old favorites were gone forever; but praise Odin they have returned and, hopefully will remain forever! It's good to see old Heimdall again also, along with the re-introduction of the Norse war-god Tyr. I'd like to see the latter developed into a regular character, and, eventually, confront his Olympian counterpart, Ares.

All in all, it's good to see Thor back in Asgard (it's been 17 issues guys!), and a greater use of mythological concepts. I refer to the use of the aforementioned characters, the head of Mimir, Bill Mantlo's assorted legendary references, and the introduction of the Egyptian gods. This is great stuff and I hope you keep it up.

Now, a few suggestions:

Delve deeper into the personalities, backgrounds, and non-fighting lives of your Asgardian characters: Fandral, Hogun, and Volstagg in particular. Bring back other forgotten folk such as Balder, Karnilla, Hela, Hildegarde, Krista, the "God Squad," and, last but not least, Sif. I think most of your readers would agree that following these suggestions might bring a new glory to the Thor saga. Before I depart, let me assure you that Roy's plot, Bill's script, Sal's pencils, and Klaus' inks were all excellent. Definitely keep the latter stalwart as permanent inker.

I leave you with the rousing immortal call . . . For Asgard! For Odin! For Irving Forbush!

Alan Stewart
1267 Greenbriar St.
Jackson, MS 39211

Dear Sirs:

How about some decent treatment for Thor's Asgardian companions? Surely they do not deserve to be condemned to prolonged and unnecessary inactivity!

Leonard Phillip Zenna
271 Etha Street
Brooklyn, NY 11208

Dear Marvel Asgardians,

It's good to see the old Asgardian buddies of Thor gobble between themselves again! How about a continued feature?

Pete Peterson
641 Church Road
Ann Arbor, MI 48103

A continuing feature, Pete?

Decent treatment, Lenny?

The reappearance of Fandral, Volstagg, and Hogun, Alan?

We're working on fulfilling all those wishes, fellows. We can take care of two out of three by ourselves, but there's one you'll have to help us on.

Y'see, gang, even as these immortal words are being typed, a super-saga starring Fandral, Hogun, and Volstagg entitled WARRIORS THREE is being prepared for MARVEL SPOTLIGHT #28! This peerless production, springing from the creative well of Lively Len Wein and Big John Buscema, will be on sale in the merry month of February. Watch for it!

We can guarantee that characters will be here and that they will have "decent treatment."

But now it's your turn.

In order to make the adventures of Hogun, Fandral, Balder, and the voluminous Volstagg a permanent series, you'll have to make the issue of MARVEL SPOTLIGHT in which they're presented sell well!

We'd like nothing better than to fulfill your every reading wish— but in order to do that it must be demonstrated that the book has a large enough audience.

Think of that issue of MARVEL SPOTLIGHT as as experiment.

Be there.

Dear Stan,

In the ORIGINS OF MARVEL COMICS, in Thor's Origin story, you said that Dr. Don Blake found the cane in a cave while running from aliens and hit it against a rock to turn into Thor.

Pleas tell me how he can be related to Odin and any other person from Asgard if he is a human from earth.

James Caccese
11 West Germantown Avenue
Maple Glade, NJ

That's a question the answer to which had been bothering us for quite a while, which is why we answered it ourselves in THOR #'s 158 and 159, where Stan and Jack revealed that Thor is not really Don Blake who was gifted with god-like powers, but rather a brash young Thor of centuries past, who, when Odin desired to teach him humility, was stripped of his godly abilities and shaped in the form of Don Blake, where he was destined to eventually discover his cane/hammer and regain his powers. Whew!

Comprende?

Good. Now if we could only get a certain Len Wein to understand the theory . . .

THIS IS IT! YOUR

MARVEL VALUE STAMP

FOR THIS ISSUE!

CLIP 'EM AND COLLECT 'EM!

24: THE AMAZING SPIDER-MAN from *Thor* no. 244 (February 1976).

BAD TIDINGS

c/o MARVEL COMICS GROUP, 575 MADISON AVE. N.Y.C. 10022

Dear Marvel,

All right gang, what's up, huh? In 5 issues of SUPER-VILLAIN TEAM-UP, two giant-sizes and three 25-centers, you've had no less than 4 writers, 5 artists, 5 inkers, 5 letterers, 5 colorists, and 3 editors! And now, as of SVTU #3, you say you got more coming. You call it a new direction; up to this point, I'm amazed at what direction you have been able to even attain. But don't get me wrong, folks, I am mighty pleased that Steve the Englehart is on his way. The guy just simply astounds and amazes my little mind. My only wish...NAY, not wish, DEMAND, is that he stick around for many months to come. Ya gotta admit, having a new publication with this hectic a production department ain't too good for first impressions. The story that just concluded this ish was never the less better than average. Doom was characterized rather nicely; the part at the end when he "murdered" Saru-San was a very nice touch. All of Doc's losses and stalemates are really starting to catch up with him, ain't they. Yep, the old doc looks like he's starting to develop a complex.

Doug Zimmerman
RFO, TTB, QNS, FOOMER
11322 Lafayette Street
Northglenn CO 80233

And so must you and all of Marveldom Assembled after last issue's fill-in—right, Doug? Unfortunately, when the Dreaded Deadline Doom or some other unforeseen catastrophe strikes, we have to do something—and we'd much rather give you an inventory fill-in story than a reprint. Even so, we know continuity suffers. Sorry, people—when we promised you a new direction for *last* time, we thought we meant it.

Dear Folks,

Every so often, I get a glimpse into the basic concepts and otherwise ideas behind stories and characters. Issue two was a dry bone, so I retrieved it from muh mandibles and sat down an' thought about it. Lo and behold, a vision didst appear. Why ever did I buy this crummy mag? It looked good at the time? I was remembering the very first issue with its fantastic artwork of so many months back? I like Doc Doom and... no, don't finish that. I like Doc Doom, period. Well, well—how about that?

Page 23, panel two, and Betty Dean Prentiss is speaking: "...If he (Namor) were to die, we'd all die a little."

Doom says nothing.

He has no alternative. He, and all of us, have just been told by a person that we had considered in no position to judge us that we're nothings if we don't follow the Sea King's example. It stops us—makes us think.

And for a second, we really *see* Doom. In a light undeniable.

His soul is our soul. His madness, his awe-inspiring power, his moods, they all belong to civilization: we have our tough armor, our insides vunerable to many touches, and a mantle to always stream in the winds in both victory and defeat.

Namor and Spider-Man are characters crafted from concepts. Doctor Doom is a mirror polished by our own hand.

He is a culture within his steel skin. When he desires to rule over all, isn't it really us who want to manage our own worlds and destinies? He is complete in all senses of the word.

Is a villain? Indeed. Are we?

"Well, well, well, would you carry a razor
In case, just in case of depression?"

—David Bowie, *Young Americans*

Coming full circle: It stops us—makes us think.

Bob Allen
1620 Fremont Street
Laredo, TX 78040

Your analysis of our characters is almost right on, in our opinion, Bob—but it seems to us you're taking an unnecessarily pessimistic view of things. Doom does indeed represent the basic power drive within us all—but Namor, based (as you say) on a concept, represents the ability to rise above self-centered arrogance—to become something more than simply human. Yes, Doom's attributes all belong to civilization in general—but so do Subby's. And it's the interplay, the never-ending give-and-take between the (literally) hard-nosed power-monger and the more complex man of inner freedom that keeps this old world running.

Before you conclude that we're all villains under the skin, Bob, you'd better think some more about how complete Doom *really* is.

Dear Marvel,

SUPER-VILLAIN TEAM-UP is one of Marvel's most colorful efforts to date. It is well written and drawn but I do have a question concerning its name.

Namor isn't a super-villain in the purest sense of the word. His portrayal as a noble "savage" in the first few DEFENDERS stories was the perfect characterization for the Sub-Mariner.

To be completely accurate, the title of the comic should be "Anti-Hero Team-up" since Namor is an "anti-hero" rather than a villain.

I feel that words like "villain" are misused when describing characters such as Namor, Sunfire, Moleman, and Galactus. These characters hover between being "villains" and being "guest stars," depending on the role they must fill. You can feel sorry for Moleman or hate him, depending on what the writer wants to use him for.

Would you consider making Doom and Namor "anti-heroes" instead of "Super-Villains"?

T. E. Pouncey
Douglass, KS

Here's a straight answer for you, T.E.: yes and no.

The main problem with the series so far, as we see it, is that we couldn't decide who the lead characters were. Dr. Doom was a bad guy acting almost like a good guy. Namor was a long-time good guy trying to act like a bad guy. And very few people that we've talked to could get themselves to buy it.

So, with this issue, we've put Doom back in his accustomed role of out-and-out villain, while Namor has gone back to being an out-and-out ...anti-hero. Naturally—because of our long-famous continuity—we're not forgetting what has gone before, or that Doom and Subby have plenty of facets to their characters, but we hope those characters will be easier to get a grip on now.

NEXT ISSUE: Okay, the team-up is underway, even if it's not like either of our super-stars ever expected—but a fighting-mad Fantastic Four is determined to break it up! In two short months, they'll invade the Balkan kingdom of Latveria, only to find...well, let's just say it's the last person they or you would think they'd find! And while all this is going on, the Shroud is hard at work on his mysterious scheme! In other words, SVTU #6 is gonna be one of the good ones! 'Nuff said!

MARVEL VALUE STAMP

67: THE AMAZING SPIDER-MAN from *Super-Villain Team-Up* no. 5 (April 1976).

FANTASTIC FOUR

A brilliant scientist—his best friend—the woman he loves—and her fiery-tempered kid brother! Together, they braved the unknown terrors of outer space, and were changed by cosmic rays into something more than merely human!

MR. FANTASTIC! THE THING! THE INVISIBLE GIRL! THE HUMAN TORCH! Now they are the FANTASTIC FOUR—and the world will never again be the same!

Fantastic Four no. 126 (September 1972), art by John Buscema and Joe Sinnott.

GHOST WRITERS!

c/o MARVEL COMICS GROUP, 575 MADISON AVE. N.Y.C. 10022

Dear Marvel,

With GHOST RIDER #14, Tony Isabella proves himself to be a storyteller extraordinary. The dialogue throughout the whole magazine was, in my own humble opinion, very realistic.

Although I'd never heard of The Orb before (mainly because I hadn't started collecting MARVEL TEAM-UP yet with #15), he seems to be a good villain for GR, considering the fact that Satan does get boring after some time. I guess my basic reason for liking "The Orb" is that he doesn't use the corny dialogue I still occasionally spot, such as "Release me at once, you mindless cretin!" or "You infidel! I shall destroy you yet!" So it's good to know he'll at least be around next issue.

On the art side: George Tuska isn't exactly my favorite artist, but I suppose I can tolerate him for one more issue. And, Vince Colletta is improving lately, proving so with his inking job this ish.

Larry Dean
6362 Laurentian Ct.
Flint, Michigan 48504

Dear Tony and Company,

GHOST RIDER #14 was another fine effort, as good as #13. It looks like Johnny Blaze in a Hollywood setting is going to work. Tony produced a very good script for "A Specter Stalks the Soundstage." I enjoyed the idea of Blaze and Stunt-Master slugging it out with the bewitched (be-Orbed?) mob and was almost sorry when Ghost Rider appeared. Why do all of the alter-egos have to be helpless imbeciles when trouble arises? It would be a refreshing change if they could sometimes solve their problems without going into a phone booth for the inevitable costume-change.

I like Blaze's cowboy act and dialect. It makes for interesting characterization. All of the supporting characters seem to be coming along well. The fight with the Towmotor was a lot of fun. I've been rubbing shoulders with fork-lift trucks for weeks at the factory where I'm spending my summer vacation and think they are fascinating engines of destruction.

I don't think the Orb is really dead. It's all a super-scientific put-on. I also don't think that Karen Page would blast G.R., regardless of what kind of hypnosis the Orb is using.

If I could think of something critical to say about the script I would, but it was a very good story. I wasn't quite as wild about the Tuska-Colletta art and I'm glad Frank Robbins is returning to become the regular (?) artist. Frank showed a good feel for the strip in #12. Any chance of Macabre Mike Ploog returning to his creation?

That's all for this issue. Keep Cruisin'.

Bob Hobart
7741 Dahlia Drive
Mentor, OH 44060

Dear Marvel Gang,

GHOST RIDER will probably never be my favorite mag. I guess I just don't like the character, but I will continue to buy and enjoy this book if it maintains the quality pesented in #14. The art by Mr. Tuska was really good—George and Vince make a very good team, although I'd rather see them on IRON MAN.

The main point of this letter is to congratulate Tony Isabella on finally getting rid of being a "silly" scripter and be-oming a good one. The characterization of Karen, Johnny, and the others was superb. I really liked Karen's "cold shoulder" to Johnny. I didn't think it was that "cold," but I suppose Johnny would. All I can say is, nice going.

Thank you for your time.

Steve Andrews
6827 Wentworth
Richfield, MN 55423

Dear Tony, George, Vince, Joe, Phil, Marv, etc, etc. . .

I'm happy to report that I have not found many No-Prizes in all my days of Marvel reading but this boo-boo stood out like a tomato in a pickle barrel. In the last frame on page 10, G.R. is wearing his Stunt Master costume, but then (here it comes!) in the first frame on page 11, G.R. is wearing his famous G.R. leathers! He doesn't change into his leathers when he is once more transformed into his devilish self at the end of the mag, and it's unlikely that he was wearing his leathers under his S.M. costume. First, he couldn't have shed his Stunt Master costume without being beaten to a pulp by the crowd, and second, any really good bike rider could tell you that two sets of clothes would be too confining.

So, if you fellows can wiggle out of this one, give yourselves a No-Prize—if not, I'm waiting for mine.

David Lynch
228 Cambridge Ave.
Kensington, CA 94708

Wouldn't ya know it! After coasting through this letters page on a cushion of complimentary comments, we'd have to end up with another greedy attempt to trick us out of one of our Uh-Uh Prizes. And what's worse, due to what we in the comics biz like to term "a big fat mistake," that aforementioned object of insubstantiality is actually yours, Dave!

Now pardon us, while we dry our tears and prepare for the next big blooper.

MARVEL VALUE STAMP

CLIP 'EM AND COLLECT 'EM!

30: FANTASTIC FOUR from *Ghost Rider* no. 16 (February 1976).

WISE QUACKS

c/o MARVEL COMICS GROUP, 575 MADISON AVE. N.Y.C. 10022

Gentlemen,

To those of you who might envision the demise of the redoubtable Howard the Duck, I say thee nay. And may Garko, the Man-Frog, sit on your face for even thinking so! I mean, what do Marvel comics stand for anyways? For alternate realities, that's what!. You reach out for the fantastic and shape it into a plausible, though bizarre, reality. And Howard the Duck is exactly that. Sure, it's a new direction for you, but that's what any creative venture needs to stay vital. I just hope there are enough good heads among you to keep Marvel from becoming too conservative and losing its imagination. Okay, so some people are going to argue that Howard is too fantastic and does not give you that anchor of reality. Or that Howard is just a rehash of the 'funny animals' theme of Walt Disney or the underground comix. But I say that Howard is a broader character than the stereotype, and therefore deserves a life. He is real, and we can identify with him because he is every-man, or rather, every duck. Too fantastic?

I can identify more with Howard than any other Marvel creation. His frustration, his reluctant courage, his humor in the face of his loneliness and utter isolation from his world, and the constant misunderstandings that plague him make him pretty darn real to me. Not only do I like the character of Howard, but also the premise of his being a strange duck in a strange world. It's believable enough, and it leads to interesting possibilities such as other aniples from Howard's world being shifted to Earth and giving Howard more opponents of his own kind, or having Howard hook up with some super hero like Spider-Man or the Hulk for a while. What I envision is a team-up of Howard with the Defenders, for Dr. Strange might be able to pass the dimensional barriers between the two universes, and they could journey to Howard's world to stop the strange forces there that are merging Howard's universe with our own.

Well, it's an idea to think about anyway. Just don't consign Howard to the musty dungeons of oblivion. Keep him alive, and keep Steve and Frank in control of his destiny, for their basic 'weirdness' is basically beautiful.

Jeff Avery
P.O. Box #891
Amherst, NH 03031

Dear Bullpen,

Cancel the Fantastic Four. Scratch Conan the Barbarian. Cross out the X-Men. Give Kull the axe. Do a hundred horrible things to the Marvel characters, but please don't let Howard the Duck fade away!

During times when I am not scrounging for food or reading comics I am majoring in journalism in a small mid-western college. For all the ridicule I receive for reading comics the only comic story that my fellow journalists will discuss is Howard the Duck. They talk about him at parties, they compare the story line with Orwell's "Animal Farm" and Walt Kelly's "Pogo." They laugh at characters like "Gordonski" a police commissioner who can accept a world of people dressed as spiders and bats and yellowjackets, but can't accept a duck in a sports coat, they love Howard and I dig Howard and hate to see it end before it really gets started.

Give Howard his own book. If that's economically impossible, then put him in a one-shot Marvel Premiere issue or let him guest star with the Fantastic Four.

Whatever you do, don't let Howard slide into limbo. He's too good to waste.

T. E. Pouncey
Douglass, Kansas

Dear Marvei,

The Howard the Duck story in GIANT-SIZE MAN-THING #5 was better than the story in G S M T #4, but it still wasn't as good as the two-part story in FEAR #19 and MAN-THING #1. The thing I liked best about that story was Howard's reality. Sure he was a talking duck with a jacket, a tie, a hat, and a cigar, but he was more like me than anyone else in the story. He wasn't noble and lofty and brave and pure. He was practical and a little bit cowardly. He didn't want to fight those demons at all, and when he saw that he didn't have any choice in the matter did he pick up a sword or fight hand to hand? No, he grabbed a gun and plugged the demons. Pow! Right in the heart!

Steve, you're a magnificent writer, but you are making Howard a bit too much of a hero for my tastes. He could be such a great satire on the Marvel super-heroes if he *isn't* heroic. For instance, you could do a great bit on the Silver Surfer by having Howard long for a girl he left behind in his own reality, but instead of it being lofty unphysical romance, Howard could remember her with a gleam in his eye and a leer on his bill. Hotcha!

I am not saying the strip shouldn't have any action, but Howard should be forced into the action. He should keep on fighting frogs and cows, but don't make it a matter of choice. I would rather identify with Howard than admire him.

Richard Nathan
2002 Fourth Street
Apt. #208
Santa Monica, CA 90405

And that, folks, is the way the comments went on Howard's two appearances in GIANT-SIZE MAN-THING. Until he saw these letters, Steve thought he knew what rave mail was all about (he'd seen all them other writers get it). The response to "Frog Death" and "Hellcow" all but bowled him over.

And as a result of your enthusiasm, O Marveldom Assembled, you're now holding second issue of a magazine called HOWARD THE DUCK in your hot little hands. And we're thrilled. We hope you are, too.

Steve and Frank know how special our wondrous waterfowl is to so many of you, and you can trust them to approach this strip with all the reverence it's due. We don't want to give away too much of what we have in mind for the duck's fear-fraught future, but we'll tell you that Steve has ideas for at least the next half-dozen stories already in his head, and that they'll be running the gamut from science fiction tales to kung fu to true-life romance. You're in for a good time, people.

As regards Richard Nathan's criticism: have no fear. Though our downy daredevil will fight if pushed too far, his definition of "too far" is still flexible enough to accommodate even the most desperate situation. If there's a way to avoid a confrontation honorably— or even dishonorably, if he can cut his losses— Howard will take it. He's a pragmatist and nobody's pigeon.

On the other hand, can even our feathered fury chicken out, so to speak, when the mysterious Kidney Lady plots his death at the legs and arms of the monstrous Chair-Thing? Unlikely. But we'll find out in sixty days. Join Howard, Bev, and Arthur then, huh?

MARVEL VALUE STAMP

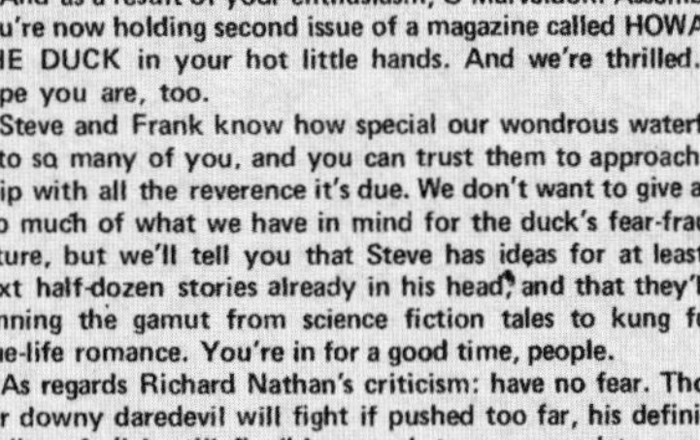

59: FANTASTIC FOUR from *Howard the Duck* no. 2 (March 1976).

SOCK IT TO SHELL-HEAD

c/o MARVEL COMICS GROUP, 575 MADISON AVE. N.Y.C. 10022

Before you have a fair chance to deluge us with mildly-reproachful missives about feeding you the same setting twice in one month (namely in SPIDER-MAN #151 and also in IRON MAN #84), we wanna do some quick explainin'!

It happened like this: While Lively Len Wein was here in New York plotting that aforementioned issue of Spidey, Happy Herb Trimpe was off in England choreographing a fantastic fight from Len's plot with the full measure of artistic license we allow our pulse-pounding pencillers—which means he altered the locale from the hospital to...the sewer. When the two jobs came in, it was too late to make major changes, thus the dual use of slimy sewers in the two tales. We think each of the stories still manages to pack in more than a smidgen of mighty Marvel magic despite the similarity of locales, and we just wanted to let you know that—no—we haven't run out of ideas. Not by a long shot. It was just one of those capricious coincidences that seem to happen to us here at mixed-up Marvel.

And now, we're gonna devote the rest of our lettercol to a final discussion of and tribute to the scintillatin' "Super-Villain War" that ran in these pages (off and on) for nine fantastic full issues.

So take it away, people!

Dear Bullpen,

Now that it's over, I think it fitting and proper that someone devote himself to a critical overview of the Black Lama's "War of the Super-Villains." Including the San Diego Affair, the war proper lasted from *IM* #69 to *IM* #81, with the last two issues of that series serving as an epilogue. The "war" was interrupted four times; for a reprint in *IM* #76; a fill-in in *IM* #79; and two forays into Vietnam, one in *IM* #74, the other in *IM* #78.

To truly appreciate the scope of the war, one should start with its cast of characters. First, the bad guys: Mandarin, Ultimo, Yellow Claw, the Mad Thinker, Modok, Whiplash, Man-Bull, the Melter, A.I.M., and Firebrand. In our intermediate category, we have the mastermind of this mess, the Black Lama. Finally, in the good-guy category, we have Iron Man, Sunfire, and, making a surprise cameo appearance, Marianne.

One of the most important and significant features of the "War" is that its scope allowed for the admission that several of the villains involved could (and did) beat Iron Man. Significantly, the Thinker did so when Iron Man was fresh, and only the Yellow Claw completely failed to do so. This factor gave the "War" an extra aura of realism, often lacking in stories involving villains of the first class.

Probably the best handled segment of the "War" was the Mandarin-Yellow Claw conflict. It effectively illustrated the differences in style and power between Mandarin and the Yellow Claw, as well as making excellent use of Sunfire and properly playing up the "man-in-the-middle" aspect of Iron Man's involvement. Involving, as it did, the certifiable, unalterable death of the Mandarin, the segment is important in the history of the Marvel Universe in its own right.

Moving on to the last phase of the "War," we come to the home planet period in which Stark and Firebrand go insane while the Black Lama supposeoly recovers his sanity. This segment is typified by half-explanations and sloppy, rushed reasoning and writing. No truly successful revolt could have been dispersed with so little effort and time. All in all, the conclusion to the Black Lama series, if indeed IM #15, 80-81 were the conclusion, was anticlimatic and altogether unsatisfactory.

Despite the poor quality of the ending, I must admit that the "War of the Super-Villains" is probably the best-ever Iron Man story. Mike Friedrich once again displayed the qualities that make him one of the best of the writers of Marvel's superheroes. Of the artists involved, I think Arvell Jones provided the best penciling, and Chic Stone the best inks on those pencils. Thank you for listening.

Ted Longstreth
4020 Seabridge Avenue
Orlando, FL 32809

Sorry to have cut your lengthy letter down to size, Ted—but it was the only way we could manage to fit it in this time! Even so, there's only room for one more mighty missive—

Dear Invincible Iron Man Innovators:

IRON MAN #81 was great storywise. You can tell that Mike really put a lot into this story. He undoubtably feels a sort of kinship and closeness with ol'Shellhead, and I, too, have grown to feel the same way about him since Mike took the book over quite some time ago. In past letters I've said that the super-villain war was for me just a big "fizzle," but after reviewing the whole thing, from the Lama's first appearance back in IM #53 (I think that was it, at this hour my feeble mind is starting to fade), to the conclusion of his story here in #81, I now see that it was truly brilliant. I hope that we never see the Black Lama again. He, like Mantis, should remain, part of Mighty Marvel's Magnificent History.

So, all in all I'd say that the Super-Villain war was a very deserving memorial to the plane of excellence Mike has kept in these pages over the years. In these hectic days, 30 issues is a heck of a long time for a Marvel scripter to stick on a title. My hat's off to ya Mike!

Then there's a fellow named Tuska. While his final stand on IM as the regular artist was several months ago, he did return for the two recent fill-in strips (both excellent), and he and Mike together produced some of the finest comics to come from Marvel. To him I also send my most sincere congratulations and respect. He has become one of the most powerful and dependable pencil pushers in comics.

Doug Zimmerman
11322 Lafayette St.
Northglenn, CO 80233

Thanks for the wondrous words, Doug—and we just wanna mention that with #88 Artful Archie Goodwin returns to script the adventures of his favorite Iron Man, while Gorgeous George Tuska is already back this ish.

So look to the future, Marvelites—for the reunion of the century (or at least the week!). Archie Goodwin and George Tuska, the Iron Man superteam supreme, are comin' at ya again in all their golden glory!

Who sez miracles don't happen at Marvel?

THIS IS IT! YOUR
MARVEL VALUE STAMP
FOR THIS ISSUE!

84: FANTASTIC FOUR from *Iron Man* no. 86 (May 1976).

APOLOGIA DEPT.

Due to circumstances for which no one is to blame (in other words, everyone in the blushin' bullpen keeps pointing an accusing finger at everyone *else*) you might have noticed a duplication of letter columns in IRON MAN #'s 81 & 82. Rest assured, pilgrim, you weren't suffering from double vision, t'was merely yet another example of your blunderous bullpen in action. We apologize, mellow one, and hope ya won't hold it against us.

Now, on to your letters...

Dear Iron-persons,

In the way of tying up a loose end, and since Marianne Rodgers is making another appearance, I thought I'd suggest why Tony Stark picked her of all people to call up 'way back in ish #36. If you think back all-l-l the way to TALES OF SUSPENSE #40, you may remember that it was a blonde named "Marion" who originally suggested painting the armor gold -- back when Shellhead was still scaring small children as well as evildoers. Wouldja believe that our Marvel reporter on the scene caught the name just a little wrong, and it was none other than...? Uh-huh.

Next it's Superhero Physics 102. Seeing the Copperhead get zapped by lightning over in DAREDEVIL, and then having I.M. mention his insulated tennis shoes all in *one* month is too much!

SIMPLE TRUTH: An object surrounded completely by a conductor (like Mr. C or our own Shellhead) is blocked off from radio waves, static, lightning bolts, etc. etc. Period. *Without* rubber shoes, teflon, cork lining, or seventeen herbs and spices. You're safe from lightning in a closed car NOT because it is rubber-tired, but because of the wrap-around metal that carries charges around. (So if you want to revive the Copperhead, feel free. Matt Murdock isn't a doctor or a physicist, after all...)

Other than that, so far, so good. When does GRANDSON OF ORIGINS come out?

Kevin Martin
Box 59187
Acton, IN 46259

Instead of saying a single word about your scientific mini-lecture, how about if we just let a No-Prize do the talking for us, Kev? As for GRANDSON OF ORIGINS, Smilin' Stan sez to keep watching his soapbox, cause ya just never know when SON will find a wife, and anyway it's all in the Marvel family, right?

(Ouch!!)

Dear Mike and Chic,

Seeing the gorgeous cover on IRON MAN #80, this occurred to me: after Kirby's finished with his special projects for you people, could you possibly put him to work on Iron Man? Cuz this strip can use some help. I don't know whether the loss of yer continuity is the major cause or not, but there are a lot of things in this issue that I don't like.

Foremost among them this month is this whole dimension the Black Lama is supposed to be from. The basic concept of futuristic city-states is interesting, but you handled it very poorly. It would have been far more interesting to let Shellhead and we readers jointly discover this new dimension, rather than to introduce it saying, "Awright, dere's whatcha been waitin' three months for, and we're only gonna explain it once, so pay attention." All right, I admit I paraphrased, but the effect is still the same. We are handed an *ad hoc* universe that is apparently intended to be grandiose. Yeech.

Even if this situation wasn't in effect, I'm not sure this pseudo SF bit is entirely appropriate to a mystical character like the Black Lama. I really doubt whether you had this origin in mind when you first introduced him, back in IRON MAN #53. The whole thing is kinda like having Doc Strange learn his magic at Stark Industries.

The "madstack" bits this ish were also kinda ridiculous, until I realized that this is your way of portraying the effects of dimension-madness on Tony. Not bad, but not too effectively communicated.

However, what's your justification for this dimension-madness? As readers of the Fantastic Four are all too familiar, lots of superheroes have switched dimensions without suffering adverse effects. What makes this dimension so different?

Well, next ish this whole shtick will be wrapped up, and we'll all be surprised by the return of Marianne Rodgers. Honestly, Mike, it's been pretty obvious that that's what you're leading up to.

If you're gonna bring back old characters, how about the Spymaster and Madame Masque? And how about Jasper Sitwell, who was last seen in a hospital bed in IRON MAN #42? Whatever happened to him? Personally, I have my own theory that Sitwell was kidnapped and brainwashed by the Spymaster, and that the two of them are now running an espionage organization to rival SHIELD itself! Wouldn't *that* be a story? Sitwell vs. SHIELD!! Oh, well, just an idea.

Anyway, back to this ish, it occurs to me that the super-villain war was originally supposed to be Marvel-wide! Nice try, Mike.

What this letter is trying to say is that while Iron Man is good, it's far from great. I know you can do better, Mike, just put a bit more into the story. Remember what the Chevrolet people say: "We did it before, we'll do it again."

Brian Nelson
4213 Great Oak Road
Rockville, MD 20853

You bring up some important points, Brian, and we hope you'll stay with us in the months to come 'cause we have a hunch that a lot of your questions will be answered (and if *we* don't know, who does?!).

MARVEL VALUE STAMP

56: FANTASTIC FOUR from *Iron Man* no. 84 (March 1976). Stamp also appears in *Marvel Presents* no. 5 (June 1976).

MAIL IT TO TEAM-UP

c/o MARVEL COMICS GROUP, 575 MADISON AVE. N.Y.C. 10022

Bill and Sal,

I must say, out of all the MARVEL TEAM-UPS, #38 had to be the best. The Beast and Spidey fit together like a puzzle, two heroes who take the agony out of fighting by coming out with cornball lines as if they were stand-ins for the Carson show.

The artwork, as usual, was fantastic but the plot...WOW! First at a slow, easy pace, then POW! Action Galore!

I definitely think the Beast is a powerful character, and I hope to see a lot of him in the pages of the Avengers. Besides all the above comments, the greatest scene in the book was when Spidey is related to as "hero," not villain.

Request: Howard the Duck and Spidey.—

Lonnie Wolf
Cherry Hill, NJ

Dear Marvel People,

I really enjoyed MTU # 38. With Spidey and the Beast's remarks put together, they make a great pair of comedians. One thing, though. On page 30; I thought Spidey was wanted for murder, yet the cops come to take the Griffin away, yet let Spidey go. What is this? Be kind to Spider-Man week? Please explain.

Kirk Carter
70 W. 35th St.
Eugene, OR 97405

O.K., Kirk. The explanation is easy (if somewhat shady). Spidey *is* wanted for murder...yet so is the Griffin. If you were a New York City policeman, having read the Bugle for years and having begun to *wonder,* perhaps, whether everything Jolly J. Jonah J. says about our hero is *true*...which of two evils would *you* be glad to see put away by the other, if you were given a choice?

Dear Bill and Sal,

I am proud to announce that MTU #38 and Dr. Strange #10 are this months co-nominees for the much-coveted MAX AWARDS. Ah, I can tell you're speechless over such joyous news, and you don't know quite what to say. Tut-tut. Say ye nothing. Instead, let *me* tell you why this issue deserved such recognition.

Bill, you have a rare talent that so few scripters possess. You make your characters so real it's as if I were really there with Spidey. Sometimes I get so engrossed in the story I actually start talking to the hero, encouraging him to do away with the villains.

However, I have a minor gripe about MTU. If you have a story about Spidey and eliminate Peter Parker and his hang-ups, well then, it's just not the same Spider-Man. See what I mean? In fact, why can't a single story be developed over two or three issues, creating a greater chance for character development? This is what you bring to most of the other heroes at Marvel.

As for the art—I felt Mike's inks are better with Sal's layouts than they are with Ross Andru's.

Well, till the day when Honest Irv's life story becomes a Movie of the Week, Make Mine MARVEL TEAM-UP!

Timothy Risuglia
3810 N. 65th Avenue
Omaha, NB 68104

Thank you Timothy...thank you MAX. As for continued stories...how's the one you're in the middle of right *now* suit you? Thou asketh, Tim...thou dost *receive!*

Dear Bill, Sal, Mike, Karen, Janice, Marv, Stan and anybody else who had anything to do with this story,

Some introduction, huh? Oh yeah, by the way...I loved MARVEL TEAM-UP #38.

Frank Alexander
Rte. 292
Holmes, ND 12531

Dear Marvel,

Whaaahoo! MTU #38 was an issue *supreme!* The setting, theme, plot, and everything else mixed like a caesar salad. The characterization of both our favorite wall-crawler and bouncing Beast resulted in the best issue of MTU in all of its history. Instead of two heroes fighting each other, Spidey gets a warm welcome from Beasty. And then the web-slinger cracks a joke that receives a fast reply from the furry X-Man. Indeed, these two made the Team-Up of the year.

Even in a single story for a single issue, the author, Bill Mantlo, receives a well-deserved squirt in the face from Spidey's web-shooter. No jive-talkin'! May Bill stay the regular writer of this mag.

The art turned out to be neatly drawn, for once. Sal Buscema's layouts were finished off beautifully by Mike Esposito. A powerful issue!

But now, to hasten my exit, may I suggest that this excellent comob join up again in some further, exciting adventures? Understand, friends?

(May the all-seeing Eye of Agamotto help this letter to be printed).

Michael Biegel
6 Valley Lane
Upper Saddle River, NJ 07458

Well, there it is...the first mail on the first issue by the team of Mantlo, Buscema, Esposito. By now it's common knowledge to Marveldom Assembled that our favorite Wall-Crawler *has* teamed-up with our favorite fowl, in the very first issue of Howard's own block-busting mag, HOWARD THE DUCK. It's also no news that, while not the rule, MTU will be trying out new areas in the way of multi-issue continued stories where the heroes *don't* begin by fighting each other, and the introduction of some new, and maybe surprising, team-ups. Stay tuned, friends...and Peace.

MARVEL VALUE STAMP

CLIP 'EM AND COLLECT 'EM!

34: FANTASTIC FOUR from *Marvel Team-Up* no. 42 (February 1976).

c/o MARVEL COMICS GROUP, 575 MADISON AVE. N.Y.C. 10022

Don, Craig and Fellow Conspirators,

I had thought of pulling out all my copies of AMAZING ADVENTURES and giving my summary on the progress of this series and of the development of the characters that comprise Killraven's Freemen, but this is not my "style" (though it seems to be the "style" of letter page writers).

I am basically "thought and word" motivated (having thought of myself as a poet and seeking poems in everything). Yet comics are visual and must ultimately appeal on this level.

Craig's work is very fine art. It is beautiful to look at. With the combination of Don's writing, I find that I am truly attracted to this strip. There are fewer (good, incredible, terrific, fantastic, super, etc.) writers than there are artists in the comic media. Don is the Robert Silverberg of comics (Jim Starlin being the Harlan Ellison) comparatively speaking.

Don's characterization of Hawk is (thus far) the only Indian that (from an Indian viewpoint) actually seems to be an Indian. Hawk *is* bitter, and this would be what most Anglos would think an Indian to be consumed by. Yet, this does not make Hawk an Indian to me.

Hawk does not ever actually reveal himself.

This, ultimately, is the Indian, within one's self, not being the silent, dark "red man."

Layer upon layer, within and within and perhaps, just perhaps, in the center of all spirits that whisper.

How do you respond?

With revenge?

As I have been taught you carry the dead with you. The only thing you own of yourself is your soul. When you die your body eventually crumbles within the earth. You cannot hold onto that. You only own your own spirit (and perhaps not that?). When Hawk appeared I was afraid he would be another Red Wolf. Thank you, Don. He wasn't.

The surprise of KILLRAVEN #32 was Hodiah Twist and Conrad Jeavons. Sherlock Holmes had been a safe retreat for me. It is always so easy to read him and feel so safe, so comfortable.

Sherlock knows all the answers, and therefore is so safe and comfortable. He will make everything "all right."

Yes, things are resolved there.

Don has made me rather ashamed of my passion for the passivity of knowing all.

Don has made me aware of something about myself I hadn't been before.

I wish to hide, and Holmes has been a good place to hide. Yes, things are resolved there, but is it not a pity something can't be resolved here?

Don, I look forward to the poetry that flows between you and Craig each issue.

Kathleen Shaw
4819 N. Brighton
K.C., MO 04119

It depends on what side of the Mural Phonics System you stand, Kathleen. Whether you take the position of Hawk's father, or the attitude that Hawk has toward this technological fantasy wonderland. Don't be so hard on yourself. You seem to be introspective and sensitive to what is happening around you, but, more importantly, about yourself.

And that's the important thing.

Both Don and Craig are moved by your letter and glad that their artistic efforts were able to move you, in turn. Better still, they are glad that their communication was considered and appraised and applied to your life.

You have paid us a very high compliment, Kathleen.

Thank you.

Mindbenders,

I wanted to write this LOC while "Only the Computer Shows Me Any Pespect" in AMAZING ADVENTURES #32 was still fresh in my mind, but I knew I'd have a hard time getting my thoughts down on paper.

I'll try.

It must be obvious to fandom that Don McGregor is the most exciting writer to come along since the beginning of comics. He experiments...and succeeds, with amazing consistency. T'challa's many battles over in JUNGLE ACTION, and Killraven's here prove that. Don's comics are for people that *think* when they read, not just look at the pictures (that's very easy to do with Craig Russell on the art chores—but more of him later). Many people, I'm sure, pass up those long balloonless meanderings to get to the evident action. I'm not one of them. Those many paragraphs may seem like babble to some, having little to do with the story at hand, but it doesn't read like that with me (and many other fans, of course). Don explores the characters...the minds of his typewriter stars/entering in/exposing all/excitement radiates...oops, sorry about that, guys. Don's style kinda grows on you. From the innocent simplicity of Old Skull to the many moods of K.R. I could go on and on, but you guys have only so much time. Don is an innovator, a master, and an artist. 'Nuff said.

Now for the other artist of the book, Craig Russell. When I saw his stuff in those Ant-Man shorts so long ago (was it that long?), I never would've thought he would come to be Marvel's most inventive artist, ranking alongside such greats as Steranko and Starlin. The ideas he must have! If you set him on anything, I'm sure he could make a classic of it in no time. Craig's figures sort of stand out of the page, radiating an aura of strength. If I can get to be one fourth the genius he is, I'll be happy.

I dunno—have I expressed myself adequately? Just lemme say that my admiration for these two guys is unending, because it's fresh, experimenting geniuses like Craig and Don that make comics great.

Ken Meyer Jr.
3110B Revere Circle
Hill AFB, UT 84406

NEXT ISSUE: "THE 24 HOUR MAN!" An astounding visual tour-de-force wherein Killraven and his Freemen encounter an incredible being living in a grotesque symbiotic relationship with one of the most awesome creatures that the artistic genius of Craig Russell can devise.

And for those of you who have been wondering what that mind sequence in "Only the Computer Shows Me Any Respect!" meant, we finally begin to delve into the question of why Killraven, curly red locks and all, is the focal point between the war of two planets. There's a reason, believe us!

THIS IS IT! YOUR

MARVEL VALUE STAMP

FOR THIS ISSUE!

CLIP 'EM AND COLLECT 'EM!

10: FANTASTIC FOUR from *Amazing Adventures* no. 34 (January 1976).

MAIL IT TO MAR-VELL

c/o MARVEL COMICS GROUP, 575 MADISON AVE. N.Y.C. 10022

SPECIAL NOTICE FROM BEHIND THE SCENES

Up until now, Messrs. Englehart and Milgrom have shared the plotting honors on this book, but this time, Atomic Al wanted to work one out all on his lonesome. Unfortunately, Steve had no call to mention that he was doing a super-hero western in THE AVENGERS right now, so Al's space western comes out looking kinda similar. The concept and tone of each tale are actually pretty far apart, but we do apologize for the foul-up.

Dear Everybody At 575 Madison Avenue,

CAPTAIN MARVEL has become one of those consistently great magazines—a far cry from the Good Captain's material of fifteen or twenty issues back. This magazine has really taken off! And the Watcher/Lunatic Legion story was but the tip of the iceberg of what I expect Steve and Al will be giving us in the months to come.

Al Milgrom and Klaus Janson are an artistic team who have at least rivaled Jim Starlin's work on this magazine. At least, I *hope* you've established Al and Klaus as the permanent team (some of your mags are *still* playing artist-inker musical chairs).

The story by Steve Englehart/Al Milgrom (Tony Isabella?) was also extremely fine this go-round, for myriad reasons.

The first being that we've finally established a DEFINITE pattern to Uatu, the Watcher. Who else but Steve Englehart (I assume he was responsible for this) would have shown us one of the mainstay guest stars of the Marvel Universe was, over all these years, suffering from a mental quirk? I think Steve sees the Watcher much as I see him: he should be aloof and detached from the affairs of Earth—keeping strictly to his pledge. I hope from now on that's the role you have planned for him. (Question: when we watched the many flashback scenes from the past on pages 18-22, why didn't any one bring up the Watcher's role in the creation of Galactus as we saw somewhere around THOR #169 or 170?)

Another reason was the split between Rick and Mar-Vell. The way I see it, two things could be done from this: return Rick to Earth to pursue his singing career and let Mar-Vell wander through space alone (which poses a problem—namely, who'll Mar-Vell talk to without a supporting character traveling with him?) or keep the pair together traveling together among the stars (you *do* intend to keep Mar-Vell back in space, don't you?).

A *third* reason #39 was a fine scripting job was the fact that Mar-Vell, in pleading Uatu's case, was saying in effect, "He [Uatu] is right; you're the ones who are all wrong!" In any other book, I have a feeling the story would have ended with the Watchers modifying their creed to at least occasional interventions. Not this one. The Creed of the Watcher remained intact; Mar-Vell was the one who was in the wrong, and he was mistaken to suggest the Watchers should modify their Creed.

I've a feeling this Watcher/Lunatic Legion story is one I'll remember for a long time and one I'll reread often.

Bruce Canwell
Meadows Rd. RFD #8
Bowdoin, MA 04008

We *had* established Al and Klaus as the permanent team here, Bruce, but Then Came DAREDEVIL, which gobbled up a lot of Klaus's time—so now we're back to square one on inkers. As we write this, we haven't the foggiest who'll be covering Al's pencils this time, but we're hoping to come up with a new regular soon.

Dear Steve and Al,

Interesting philosophy the Watchers have (I certainly hope it's not a reflection of the personal philosophy of the script writer). Unable to accept responsibility for acting, for deciding, they simply abdicate this responsibility by refusing to act. Teleport some of the works of the existentialist philosophers to the Watchers; they are in need of them. To avoid acting is to avoid *being!* The Watchers are also conceited enough to believe that they possess pure perception. "Everything that happens is true" (Emnu). This presumes that one can perceive exactly and objectively what happens, and that, to put it mildly, is highly unlikely.

Otherwise, CM #39 was well scripted and well drawn.

Ed O'Reilly
215 E. Lehr
Ada, OH 45810

Steve says it's *not* his personal philosophy, Ed, but he *does* take issue with the idea that it's not a viable one. Maybe *we* can't perceive everything exactly as it is, but a race that's done nothing but strive toward that goal for centuries is something else again. Remember, Rick Jones is now the only true human in this series; everyone else has to be taken in their own special contexts. And to quote the man who helped birth the first Watcher 'way back in FF #13, "'Nuff said!"

Dear Steve and Al and Klaus,

CAPTAIN MARVEL #39 was a cosmic masterpiece, and one aspect of it struck particularly close to home. This concerns the very reason why the Watchers *became* Watchers. Having given a race at an earlier stage of development than theirs the secret of atomic energy, and having seen that race use this gift for war, the Watchers were chastened, and made a drastic decision to prevent this from ever happening again. I can't help but see a correlation between this and the fact that both the U.S. and Russia have given nuclear reactors to other countries, to be used, it is hoped, for peaceful purposes. Yet, India has used the technology to become an atomic power, and Russia has just announced plans to supply Libya with similar information and equipment.

Who knows? One hundred years from now, we may be our own Watchers.

Ed Via
1648 Dean Rd.
Ronaoke, VA 24018

NEXT TIME: Mar-Vell and Rick come face to face in space with a driven Destroyer, as the malevolent machinations of the Supreme Intelligence begin to find a focus. But let us not forget that mysterious dance-hall girl, or the millenia-bloom, or anything else Steve and Al can come up with in the next sixty days. CAPTAIN MARVEL #43: Guaranteed to rock your socks!

THIS IS IT! YOUR
MARVEL VALUE STAMP
FOR THIS ISSUE!

CLIP 'EM AND COLLECT 'EM!

18: FANTASTIC FOUR from *Captain Marvel* no. 42 (January 1976).

THE HAMMER STRIKES

c/o MARVEL COMICS GROUP, 575 MADISON AVE. N.Y.C. 10022

Dear Marvel,

I simply loved Thor's time-spanning adventures with Zarko the Tomorrow Man and the Servitor in THOR #'s 242-245! I was very sad to see the Servitor ultimately destroyed. I liked him. He was an extremely interesting character, and I would rather have had him survive. But who knows, if reader response is favorable enough, you might be persuaded to recreate him in the near future.

What I liked even more was the fact that since Thor and his friends stopped the Time Twisters from coming into being, the 50th Century was restored, the events that sent Thor through time never occurred, and the day was pleasantly uneventful.

Keep up the quality, creative ones!

John Falteres
6509 E 96th
Salmon City, UT 84653

Salutations:

There is a striking parallel between Jane Foster/Sif and Don Blake/Thor. In both cases there is the fusion of god and mortal sharing a single "slot" in the universe. In the case of Don/Thor, the hammer effects the transition between god and mortal. In Jane/Sif's case, there is no such means—*but there could be*!!

It might be remembered that Don Blake spent several years (prior to the discovery of the hammer) totally unaware of the god within himself; nevertheless, Thor was there waiting for the hammer-blow that would bring him forth.

Can we then assume that Sif is forever gone? Isn't it more likely that she is lying dormant somewhere within Jane Foster, waiting to be called forth by some unrevealed stimulus?

I suspect that this is what you've had in mind all along, and that you're playing it cagey on your letters page.

William Allen
1012 Cannon #32
Helena, MT 59601

C'mon, Bill—*us*? Would *we* play cagey on a liltin' letters page? To even suggest such a thing is to imply that we actually know what's going on, and, truth to tell, us anonymous armadillo types are not privy to the darkest secrets of plotting until after the fact, lest we let slip with a calculated clue right here in cold type.

How's that for being evasive?

Dear Marvel,

I am desperately waiting for a subplot begun many issues ago to come to its conclusion. I am talking about THOR #235—specifically, Hercules' and Sif's battle with Kamo Tharnn. They battled him to obtain the runestaff to save Jane Foster's life, and Lady Sif said, "We must be gone before Kamo Tharnn doth awake. His wrath will be uncontrollable, and in his anger he will follow us to the very ends of the universe itself."

"So?" you say.

So, it's eleven issues later, and we've yet to see any trace of Kamo Tharnn. I know Hercules knocked him for a loop, but surely he's awakened by now! Granted, he would have a problem finding Sif, since she no longer (?) exists. But Hercules is still roaming around.

And moreover, what has happened to the runestaff? We last saw it shimmering upon the body of Jane Foster in THOR #236.

Well? Dost thou have the answers?

Rich Amarel
16 Rose Lane
North Grafton, MA 01536

Who, *us*? (Didn't we just go through this?)

Seriously, Rich, if you're at all familiar with Marvel, then you know that we take continuity seriously. We may not always tie things up as neatly or as quickly as we ourselves might like, but you can rest assured that everything will eventually be explained. It's a certainty.

However, exactly when (or even *where*) is indeed the most uncertain of all certainties. So bear with us, won't you? Thanks, Thorophile!

Dear Len, John and Joe,

The Time Twisters saga wound down superbly in THOR #245. It appears THOR will be heading ever-upward under your authorial hand, Len.

The THOR strip has always had some of the most potentially-powerful supporting characters to be found in the Marvel Universe—yet they have always been neglected by the strip's writers. I'm hoping you'll delve a bit into Fandral, Hogun, and Volstagg. I mean, they provide some snappy Asgardian dialogue and all, but so far they are the most one-dimensional supporting characters I've ever seen! Just what are they gods OF? What are their private lives like? Their hobbies? Do any of them have lovers or wives? The potential is there, but it's yet to be tapped.

And what of Balder? He's Thor's best buddy—yet he hasn't been seen (aside from that cameo in Asgard a couple issues back) for well over a year! And I seem to remember a Norn Queen named Karnilla who was in love with Balder. She hasn't popped up for a couple years, either. And no one's heard a peep from the God Squad that was created at the climax of the Ego Prime story those many moons ago.

Len, right now THOR could use a strong guiding hand behind ALL its characters. I just hope you're that man, because I'm really sick of seeing Balder return to Thor's side just as Fandral and Company decide to take a year's vacation.

Looking at the art, I have to admit I've never seen a Buscema/Sinnott collaboration that WASN'T great. John and Joe, all I can say is, "Keep it up."

Bruce Canwell
Meadows Rd. RFD #2
Bowdoin, ME 04008

Whew! Wotta lotta plot-weaving awaits writer Wein—but he's more than a match for the task, and we've got a feeling that you'll be seeing all kinds of wild-and-wonderful character and continuity bits coming together here in the not-so-distant future. In fact, next ish contains the culmination of the Odinsword story currently racing toward resolution, and you're really gonna be sorry if you miss *that* opus magnus!

See ya there, Marvelites!

MARVEL VALUE STAMP

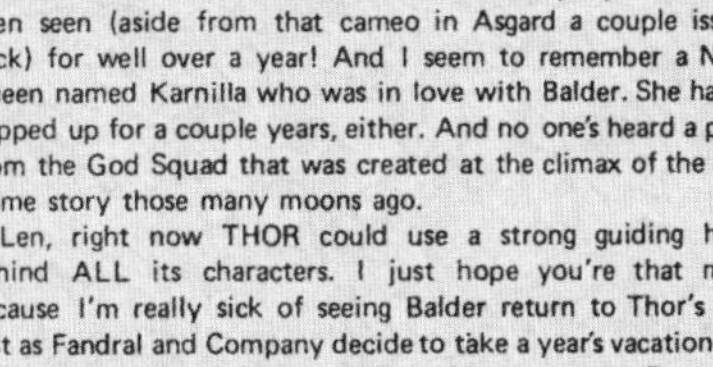

98: FANTASTIC FOUR from *Thor* no. 249 (July 1976).

THE SPIDER'S WEB

SEND YOUR LETTERS TO:
THE MARVEL COMICS GROUP, SIXTH FLOOR 575 MADISON AV., NEW YORK, N.Y. 10022

The substitution of our special text feature last issue in place of your letters means that we're truly swamped with mail, and most of it is hot and heavy and tremendously in favor of our special 150th issue. So we're gonna distill the representative essences to begin with, and then follow up with a couple full-blown letters and answers, just to make everyone happy. Ready? Here goes...

After reading SPIDER-MAN #150, I am happy to say that you've created another masterpiece. It kind of reminded me of some of Spidey's older issues. The combination of Archie Goodwin/Gil Kane was surprisingly good. Mr. Kane is one of my favorite artists, but I thought he did a good job on #150. Keep up the good work, Marvel.

Al Light
1134 Belmont Street
Albert Lea, MN 56007

SPIDER-MAN # 150 manages to be both quite a success and quite a disappointment. For one thing, as you virtually admit in the course of the story, it's a remake of SPIDER-MAN #100, in which Spidey dreams up fights with old enemies. The battles here are handled well, and I've always liked plots with a lot of old villains, but the feeling of *deja vu* is inescapable.

Peter Sanderson
27 Gov. Belcher Lane
Milton, MA 02186

Well SOMETHING was needed to clear the air after the Gwen thing, and before the Wein takeover, and Kane/Goodwin filler was a perfect choice. And a very nice treat also!

Dean Mullaney
81 Delaware Street
Staten Island, NY 10304

SPIDER-MAN#150 was probably one of the finest Spidey's in a long time. It was a fitting epilogue to the Jackal-Gwen Stacy-Clone affair. I'm glad you did not draw the thing out over several issues. This one resolution was sufficient. Archie Goodwin's one of the best in the business, and I'm sure that he and Gil will both be sadly departing after this issue, a hardy thanks for a job well done.

Steve Andrews
6827 Wentworth
Richfield, MN 55423

Dear Spider-Men:

After reading all of the outraged letters on the return of Gwen Stacy, I feel an important point is being ignored. The angry reactions are coming from folks who think realism is the most important factor in comics.

Yet comics are NOT realistic, including matters of life and death. All major characters who die, die in highly dramatic situations, not the senseless accidents which can happen in reality. In fact, comic characters are vulnerable to death only if their dying advances the plot. We all know that Spider-Man is invulnerable and immortal as long as he is popular.

I know how the Gwen fans feel. Marvel killed off my favorite character once, and Marvel became less vital for me; I read back issues and sent many boringly-repetitive "bring back" letters. Finally, Marvel did so. The explanation for the return was pretty thin, but I didn't care!

Realism is important, but only as it contributes to enjoyment. The main purpose of comics is to entertain. Gwen was apparently essential to some readers' enjoyment. That's why Gwen was and should have been brought back, despite any loss of believability.

Charlie Boatner
2727 Midtown Ct. Apt. 14
Palo Alto, CA 94303

You have made a very valid point, Charlie. We *do* strive for realism in the motivations and reactions of our characters—but in the context of *dramatic art.* Jade monosyllabic giants, wall-crawling web-slingers, golden-tressed thunder gods and the like are not inherently realistic; it is only the Marvel-style treatment of these characters that brings them to life with the sparkling verisimilitude that has made them near and dear to every Marvelite's heart. And we concur heartily with your conclusion: Our primary purpose has always been to entertain, and we hope above all never to lose sight of that goal.

And thanks for providing an alternate opinion on the Gwen controversy, Charlie—without taking sides here, we'd just like to add that differing viewpoints help to give us perspective. In comics, and in life. End of mini-moral!

Dear Marvel:

We've finally discovered how Peter Parker pays his rent and other bills, which seem insurmountable considering the pittance he gets from J.J.J. for his two-bit snapshots.

He's appearing in person at 7-11 stores across the country as a promotional gimmick to bolster sales of wonder lime, killer cola, and ka-pow orange slurpees with Spider-Man's image on the cups.

Are we to believe that Spidey is exploiting his own popularity in the Hollywood commercialist custom, and that his heroism is just publicity producing hoopla to implement his profit making scheme?

Or is he being blackmailed into this ploy by the conglomerate which holds some threat above his head? Maybe we saw a clone or something...

You owe it to your readers to unravel this mystery which has us all perplexed and bewildered.

Howard's Planet
c/o Bozo Manor 1847 Rogue Road
Yuba City, California

We'll try to be brief and straight with you, Planet person. There is a price to be paid for being the world's best-selling comics magazine or, to paraphrase, "With great fame there often comes wide exposure." As we've explained elsewhere, however, commercialism is not always the bogey it's made out to be. For instance, if our comics were non-commercial—i.e. unknown and unsaleable—we could not continue to exist, and there would be no SPIDER-MAN. Therefore, promotional tie-ins with places such as the 7-11 store benefit us by helping expose us to new audiences and, consequently, insure our own longevity.

And if they finally introduce the few straggling non-believers still lurking somewhere out there to this, the Magnificent Marvel Age of Comics, then they actually serve a very worthwhile purpose indeed, don't you agree?

Next ish—Marveldom Assembled reports on the authorial advent of Len Wein, so be here. Len will be waiting.

MARVEL VALUE STAMP

49: FANTASTIC FOUR from *The Amazing Spider-Man* no. 154 (March 1976).

COMMENTS TO KA-ZAR (AND ZABU)

c/o MARVEL COMICS GROUP, 575 MADISON AVE. N.Y.C. 10022

APOLOGIA: Regular readers of the KA-ZAR book will have probably noticed a number of minor discrepancies between our previous issue and the flashback presented near the beginning of this issue. Hey, people, we're sorry — honest — but even though we value continuity every bit as much as you readers do, the lack of it in this case was unavoidable.

Here's the story: As you know, last issue was pencilled by Larry Hama, while this issue was pencilled (and inked) by Val Mayerik. Now, whenever we make such artist-switches in the middle of a multi-issue story, problems *invariably* crop up — but they're problems which can usually be solved by a very simple expedient; namely, letting the follow-up artist study whatever the first artist has established in the way of overlapping visuals. This time, however, that very simple expedient suddenly turned extremely difficult — impossible, in fact. Due to variegated personal hassles, Larry Hama fell incredibly behind the deadline — necessitating a change in inkers on the last six pages and causing the book to be sent late to the printers. As an inevitable result, Val Mayerik was forced into pencilling this issue without benefit of seeing what Larry had done with last issue.

So it boils down to a case of two different artists' interpretations of the same plot. But don't get us wrong; the plot was far from sketchy or vague. In fact, Doug regularly turns in the longest and most detailed plots ever seen in the history of the bullpen. But he *does* like to give the artists certain options when it comes to matters specifically visual. For example, the total difference in design between Larry's version of Shauran, and Valiant Val's rambunctious rendition of the same.

And there were two or three other discrepancies also. Of his own volition (a procedure Marvel artists are encouraged to follow), Larry added a panel last issue in which Ka-Zar breaks off the top of Klaw's prosthetic sonic-blaster. Doug, knowing that Klaw would have *need* of that sonic blaster in the next issue (as Larry did not know), plotted that scene with Ka-Zar simply punching Klaw out — and Val adhered to that detail, resulting in instant discrepancy with Larry. And Mr. Hama also added the "long-distance-cable-rescue" of Klaw by Shauran, while Doug's plot called for Shauran's skycraft to zip right into the museum, whereupon Shauran would personally scoop Klaw right up off the floor. And you guessed it; Val stuck to Doug's idea and — bingo! — another disparity. You get the idea from there...

Again, we apologize. If there'd been time, it wouldn't have happened. But we must admit that we personally find the mix-up kinda intriguing. Think of it as an inside glimpse into the minds and methods of two different — but equally talented — artists.

And while we're being so long-winded, we'd like to thank Larry Hama for the fine work he turned in during his two-issue stint with Ka-Zar. Let us know what *you* thought of it — and while you're at it, why not dash off some comments on Val Mayerik's dynamic debut *this* issue...? We think it's Val's finest work to date (which kinda figures, since Ka-Zar is his favorite character and the Valiant One has been itching to draw the book for months now) and promises only to get better.

But *enough* on this issue already! Let's take a look at your comments on some of our *past* issues...

Dear Folks,

I would like to lodge a protest against the shortening of Zabu's tail. Why, you ask? Because the Ka-Zar series takes place not eons in the past, but in the present. I realize you have stated that the Savage Land is a place where evolution stands still; and I say that's ridiculous. I *will* concede that evolution is conservative, and that change will not occur unless necessary, but the sabertooth tiger, the wooly mammoth, and their ilk lived in a much colder habitat than the tropical climate now portrayed in the Savage Land. It is therefore probable that any mammals living within Ka-Zar's land would have thinner coats, larger ears, longer trunks, and longer tails — the latter three serving as "radiators" so the poor creatures can get rid of their excess heat.

Doug Scheffert
PO Box 30244
Lincoln, NB 68803

Your wish is our command, Doug. Take a peek at this very issue and you'll notice that Zabu is indeed sporting a longer tail than was his usual wont in the past. We're not sure, however, whether this development is attributable to your "radiator" theory or simply because artist Val Mayerik thinks Zabu looks more spiffy with a longer tail...

Either way, don't fight evolution, pal!

Dear Doug,

KA-ZAR #11's point is well-taken. Although Ka-Zar is irreverent to Illyana's and Tordon-Na's religious beliefs, the last panel of Doug Moench's script says it all. Religion is a social institution of the civilized world. Civilization, to Ka-Zar, has many times proven to be madness. Who's to say if religious worship *isn't?* Other social institutions have already shown the path to madness: Economy, knowledge, progress, you name it!

Don Heck and Frank Springer, I wish to thank you both for truly captivating artwork.

And now for a No-Prize. On page 10, panel 4, Sanda addresses Sylitha as "Sanda" — thus speaking to himself.

Marc P. Beauregard
181 Elm Street
New Bedford, MA 02740

Yeah, Marc, Doug admits the goof — or at least *assumes* it was his goof. Consider yourself No-Prized.

Now on to Decidedly Heavier Matters — namely, religion. (Strange how the very foundation of love so often opens a can of worms, isn't it?) In his script, Doug did not mean to condemn every religion extant. He merely meant to convey that a person like Ka-Zar (and like Doug himself, for that matter) does not easily take to INSTITUTIONALIZED religions, especially hypocritical ones, dogmatic ones, and — of course — ones which embrace ritual murder, like that practiced in the fictional city of Tordon-Na. But Ka-Zar (and Doug, again, for that matter) DOES practice a strict "religious" morality. And that's all that really counts, isn't it? If certain groups wish to split off and gather in private worship, that's fine — as long as they don't condemn or patronize any other group for doing the same. But above all, the Golden Rule — and Love — is where's it at to our way of thinking.

MARVEL VALUE STAMP

70: FANTASTIC FOUR from *Ka-Zar* no. 15 (April 1976).

THE INCREDIBLE HULK™

Dr. Bruce Banner was a scientist engaged in the study of radiation and its effects on man; until one fateful day, while attempting to save the life of a young trespasser, he was bombarded with energy from an exploding **Gamma Ray Bomb.** The tremendous force changed Dr. Banner from a mere man into the awesome green-skinned behemoth known as... **The Incredible Hulk!**

The Mighty World of Marvel Annual 1975 (1974), published in the UK by World Distributors, art by unknown. Hulk's face comes from the back cover of the annual and is by Herb Trimpe.

DEFENDERS DIALOGUE

c/o MARVEL COMICS GROUP, 575 MADISON AVE. N.Y.C. 10022

Dear Marv, Steve, & Sal:

Thirty days after having forgiven you for ish #30 (explain!!), I read #31's pulsating pages. Congrats for a job well done!

Steve Gerber is perhaps the best scripter this side of Smilin' Stan.

Sal Buscema is the *only* artist that does THE DEFENDERS any justice.

Jim Mooney is most probably the best inker for Sal's fine work (please keep the Madman's inky fingers on Sal's pounding pencils).

My only two (count them, one-two) complaints were: 1) *Pull-lleeze*, Steve G., tell us who that elf with the revolver is?!?!, and 2) Will you guys decide once and for all what color Kyle Richmond's hair is!??!!!??

'Till Bashful Benjy wears flowered shorts---

Kevin (The Thing) Urenda
(co-founder Highland High School ComiClub)
1309 Georgia St. NE
Albuquerque, NM 87110

Steve says the elf's identity is still a mystery to *him*. Kev—that some nameless, perhaps eternally unknowable outside force compels him to insert those one-page homicidal vignettes every few issues. But at least he's promised that we'll learn the who, what, and wherefore of it all as soon as he does.

As for Kyle's hair...well, we've just resigned ourselves to the notion that it varies in color depending upon how much sun he's had lately. (Sigh.)

Dear Steve,

It's been a long time since I last wrote to Marvel. (They never printed any of my hundreds of letters when I did write). But your recent work on the DEFENDERS has prompted me to write again.

Ever since I discovered MAN-THING, you have been my favorite writer. Your MAN-THING stories were what enabled me to see comics as a valid art form. I still see few other comics as truly artistic. THE DEFENDERS is definitely a consistent member of that few.

Other writers manage to tell a good story with plenty of action, and even manage to throw in interesting twists, tie up ten-year-old loose ends, and boggle the minds of the reading public. But only in your stories have I been able to find that special something which makes comics like the real world. Only your characters remind me of me. Other characters are fun to read about and easy to believe in the way I believe in real events I don't personally experience. But characters in your stories can be believed in the way I believe in myself and my closest friends. Other characters are real characters; yours are real people whom I actually know.

In MAN-THING, as Guy Lawley said in GIANT-SIZE #1, "every story has a moral, though not a Buster Brown-type 'I must not put soap under Granny's feet' kind of moral, but rather a philosophical point which the writer wants to get across." In the Man-Thing series, you created a work of art unequaled in the comic book medium. I knew that you weren't going to be writing MAN-THING before I knew it had actually been cancelled, and I was actually glad it was cancelled. For I could not, and cannot, bear the thought of anyone other than Steve Gerber writing about the Man-Thing, especially with Sallis's mind unclogged.

What you are doing in the DEFENDERS is different from what you did in MAN-THING. In MAN-THING, you could examine a different facet of human nature each issue. The framework of the comic was such that you could keep or throw away characters whenever you wished. But in DEFENDERS, you must deal with the same heroes each month. You have here investigated deeply the personalities of the Defenders. I believe that you have put more depth into the characters of the Defenders in a year or two than Stan and Roy have put into the Fantastic Four in fourteen years.

I think the artwork of Sal Buscema is just right for your inwardly-directed tales. His style, while far from being bad, does not draw attention to itself. Thus, one can more easily concentrate on the intellectual and psychological aspects of the story rather than the merely physical, although the physical is by no means shoddy.

But I've always enjoyed your mind stories more than your fight stories. I loved the Man-Thing stories, and I love the delvings into the pasts of Valkyrie and Nighthawk, which are still going on. Even my favorite villains of yours are the Headmen.

You use weirdness for a reason. Since your success with MAN-THING, it seems that everyone has tried his hand at a weird story or two. But your weird stories, besides being enjoyably weird, were also (I should say are also) intellectually stimulating and meaningful.

I started out to write about DEFENDERS #'s 31 & 32, and I've rambled off into ecstatic praise of my favorite writer and idol. (I suppose you never expected to get such praise until your funeral.) Just let me ask you to continue to uncover the personalities of Val and Kyle, and to strive to write all stories with guest appearances of the Man-Thing yourself. Good luck with HOWARD THE DUCK and OMEGA.

Chuck Ulrich
2160 Bryant St.
Palo Alto, CA 94301

Steve G. replies:

There are moments— and sometimes they last for months— in a writer's career when he looks back on all he's done, reflects on the meaning of it, the quality of it, the originality of it, and asks himself what he and his art are worth. Too often, the answer comes back a flashing red neon goose egg set against an interminable stretch of black sky.

Put less pretentiously, we all go through periods of doubt, frustration, self-evaluation, self-criticism, hopelessness I'd been deep into one of those periods when your letter arrived and told me in no uncertain terms that I was accomplishing with my writing all the things I was afraid I wasn't.

It felt good. Thanks.

THIS IS IT! YOUR
MARVEL VALUE STAMP
FOR THIS ISSUE!

CLIP 'EM AND COLLECT 'EM!

82: THE INCREDIBLE HULK from *The Defenders* no. 35 (May 1976).

AVENGERS ASSEMBLE!

c/o MARVEL COMICS GROUP, 575 MADISON AVE. N.Y.C. 10022

Dear Sirs,

Just finished reading AVENGERS #141 for the fifth time. I've been reading your books since the pre-superhero days, and rarely have I been so overwhelmed by a single issue as I was by this one. So much story in so few pages—!

George Perez! Wow! What a way to begin an issue! Although the coloring was a mite sloppy or faded in spots, the artwork was cinematic. Excellent action scenes, from the reintro of Cap on page 3 to the "Kramming" of the Beast on page 30. This is one artist who'll soon be at the top of the list.

As for the Avengers themselves, some suggestions: keep the Beast and Moondragon. Mr. McCoy, at least as portrayed by Steve, adds an extra-colorful flair to the mag. And besides, he ain't no slouch in a pinch. M.D.'s superiority complex is a nice touch which makes for a believable character, and her powers, tho not fully explained yet, seem to be of Avengers caliber.

As for Thor, Iron Man, and Cap, they should all be used, but not every issue. Mix 'em and match 'em. And good ol' Hawkeye, whom I've always liked, should leave the Avengers. He just doesn't fit.

You know, the characterization and the dialogue make all the assemblers seem like very real friends. What a task, considering the ever-shifting, ever-expanding roster.

Doug MacDonald
927-H Cherry Lane
East Lansing, MI 48823

The verdict, as we intimated last month, came in on George Perez's art, and it was resoundingly, overwhelmingly favorable. When you add that in with the long-suffering scripter's personal reaction, which was more of the same, you can understand why Steve called George and himself, who've only met face-to-face once, "dwellers in the same dream." If we may be permitted to go (not too far) out on a limb, we'd have to say that Perez is another of these guys like Smith and Starlin who's going to transform himself right before your eyes. Heck, these last few issues have shown that he already is. So thanks for the applause, folks; we like being on the right track!

Dear Marvel,

Greetings! I just read AVENGERS #141, and contrary to what I expected, it was a really superior issue. Why, you ask, did I ever think otherwise? Well, it appears that I was one of the few who were enjoying George Tuska's artwork, and when you announced that he would be put on another title, and that George Perez would take over the art chores, I was understandably depressed. But I was wrong! George has taken to the Avengers more easily than many of your better artists, and his style is easily one of the most visually interesting in the field today. Combined with the writing of Steve Englehart (who I don't praise as much simply because I think he is without peer as a writer), the result was fascinating reading.

Frank Smith
PO Box 407
Martinsville, VA 24112

Dear Steve and George,

Above all, apologies are *not* necessary. To Hades with "less complicated stories." A story as good as "The Phantom Empire *is* good because so much is going on, and is being handled so well. America is finally back. I couldn't be happier. Not only that, but he's brought his unresolved Englehart plot threads with him! Thank you for that, Steve. Here's hoping Cap stays awhile, although I have my suspicions that he'll go his separate way again at the conclusion of this adventure. By all means keep the Beast around for a good while. He is a fabulous character, and I don't even mind that you've been giving him more attention than the other members. Bringing back Patsy Walker and making Bruce Baxter a *bad* guy is muchly appreciated, too. The whole situation seems pretty mysterious at this point, but I'm sure it'll all come out in the wash. A nice touch was Hank and Jan recognizing Miss Walker, and all from a one panel cameo almost ten years ago! Phew, they've got memories that would put most true and tired comic fans to shame. All this, and the return of Kang. The Vision's comment, "Again? This is getting monotonous!" was wryly amusing—nicely done. Plus the Squadron Supreme, PLUS the Golden Archer! Boyoboy how I love this book, but I have trouble writing letters about it. All I can do is babble on and on, listing all the things I liked, which usually amounts to a lot. I can't help it, but my enthusiasm gets the best of me.

A word about the art. George Perez is super talented. With his layout style, I think Steve will be able to get more than ever before into each issue. George's artwork this issue was good, tho not his best. Vince Colletta does nothing for his pencils, and while he's not detracting from his work as he does on Robbins'pencils, I think you could do with a more dynamic inker for this series. Anyone from Giordano to Adkins would be good. I'm glad to see George aboard.

Fred G. Hembeck
280 Stockbridge
Buffalo,NY 14215

NEXT MONTH: The title of our thriller says it all. It's called "Twenty Thousand Leagues under Justice!" and it's a dull, heavy treatise on the mating habits of the Australian awk. No, wait a minute...there's a mistake here somewhere. Hmmm...it looks like you'll just have to be here to see what it's all about. Our lawyers have advised us to suffer a memory lapse.

But we can tell you something about what's coming up farther off in the future. Thanks to your continued good taste and patronage, we'll be offering an *all-new* AVENGERS GIANT this summer, featuring a 35-page excursion into depth. We promise to make it something special for ya (meaning—it won't guest star Kang). 'Nuff said!

76: THE INCREDIBLE HULK from *The Avengers* no. 147 (May 1976).

The revelation of the villain was not startling, but his new visual appearance was, and it made for a nice cliffhanger. The coloring was especially brilliant.

An extremely entertaining issue of IRON MAN. Congratulations to all involved, and see ya in thirty.

Kim Thompson
Gen Del Box 259
APO New York, NY 09184

Hey, that's *our* line, Kim! Now what're we gonna do for the end of this letters page?

As you know by now, Lively Len just couldn't keep up with four monthly titles, as well as the all-new annuals we're plannin' to spring on ya, and the special one-shots here and there like WARRIORS THREE (to appear soon in MARVEL SPOTLIGHT). So Iron Man has reverted to those revered raconteurs, Archie Goodwin and George Tuska.

And here's the inside lowdown on the art trio for #82. Herb penciled the book in England, mailing it directly to the Bullpen, where Marie was all ready to ink it. Unfortunately, after she'd already begun the job by (as you accurately observed) delineating a few faces here and there (and otherwise applying her bold brush), a conflict of time arose, and the job had to be given to Jack Abel for the finishes. Thus, the three-way collaboration on the art.

We're glad you and the majority of Marveldom enjoyed their efforts, Kim—it just goes to show that, even when we're "under the gun," we can still conjure up some of that good, old, four-color magic.

Dear People—

The artwork in IRON MAN #82 was beautiful, just beautiful, really beautiful!! When I read that Trimpe was going to take over this book a few months back, I wrote a "take Herb Trimpe off IRON MAN" letter and decided I'd send it to you after Herb drew his first issue. Well, #82 came along and I took that letter and destroyed it, because Herb's art wasn't ugly—it was beautiful! Some of the credit must also go to Jack Abel. I hope you plan on keeping him on Trimpe's pencils. I have been waiting and waiting for Jack to become a permanent inker on somebody's book, because every book he inks just comes out beautifully.

Before I close, I must thank you all for IRON MAN #82. Thanks, Len, for the fantastic story; thanks, Herb, for the beautiful art; and thanks, Jack and Marie, for the great inking. Until Iron Man becomes scrap metal—Make Mine Marvel.

Ricky Harrison
8006 Callison Drive
Glen Allen, VA 23060

Aw, heck, Ricky—we coulda told ya Herb would do all right by the art chores. He's one of the most misunderstood artists in our somewhat scintillatin' stable. And if you wanna keep a careful eye on his artistic career, then don't miss either SUPER-VILLAIN TEAM-UP or GHOST RIDER—cause Happy Herbie's doin' both of 'em, and he's doin' 'em with aplomb (not to mention with a pencil!).

Dear Stan,

I'd like to point out a mistake which has graced the pages of IRON MAN #'s 82 and 83, wherein I.M. fights the Red Ghost and his Super Apes. These are supposedly the same apes that the Fantastic Four fought, yet in IRON MAN #15, the Red Ghost says that his Super Apes were liquidated.

How could the apes fight Iron Man, if they were liquidated?

Steve Centonzo
(no address given)

Although Lively Len didn't have room to mention it, he really did have a good explanation for that seeming error. Y'see, while the Red Ghost had been informed that his former leaders had liquidated his apes, in reality the powers-that-be felt the Super Apes were far too valuable to be so casually destroyed. When ol' Reddy learned that they were still around, he "liberated" them, and they were united once again.

But just so there's no hard feelings, Steve, we'll send ya a no-prize anyway, just for being such a diligently meticulous True Believer. Stingy we ain't—at least, not this month!

Dear Marvel,

For once I am impelled to write you about an IRON MAN issue before I put the mag down. IRON MAN #83 showed the fruits of a new writer/artist combination with the climax to the Red Ghost series.

Here's a little poem my brother thought up:

The Human Torch has his fire,
Luke Cage's name was "Hero for Hire."
Conan has his primitive way,
Spider-Man has his old Aunt May.
Daredevil has a great hearing sense,
While Hulk without Banner is very dense.
Dracula has a very sharp fang,
Captain Marvel's adventures take off with a bang.
Insult Thanos, oh,would you dare?
Thor's the one with the golden hair.
Sub-Mariner has pointed ears,
Captain America has no fears.
The Fantastic Four is the greatest team,
Can't wait to see Doc Doom's next scheme.

Sheldon and Larry Gross
6528 N. Spaulding
Lincolnwood, IL 60645

Thanks for the kudos, brothers Gross,
Marvelites like you are really the most.
It's times like this when we all feel
That doin' comics beats makin' oatmeal!
(Huh?)

Well, now that we've spilled our poetic guts, it's time to come up with a snappy last line. See ya in—er, seems like somebody else already used that line on this letters page. How about a nice, succinct *au revoir*. No? Well then, maybe a "Be seein' ya around." Or a "You dare not miss next issue."

Or even a "Nuff said!"

And then there's...

MARVEL VALUE STAMP

97: THE INCREDIBLE HULK from *Iron Man* no. 87 (June 1976).

SEND YOUR LETTERS TO:
THE MARVEL COMICS GROUP
SIXTH FLOOR
575 MADISON AV.
NEW YORK 10022
N. Y.

Dear Marv, Bob, and Klaus,

If somebody had told me a year ago that DAREDEVIL would be made a better strip by getting rid of the Black Widow, or that Bob Brown would do an art job that would make me forget about Gene Colan. I would have laughed at him. Well, the kid's not laughing now. It's true. I enjoyed DD #125 as I haven't enjoyed DD in a long time.

Marv, I think you've hit on something with the direction you're taking the strip. (I was going to start this letter by saying "DD #125 was one of the best B*TM*N stories I ever read," but decided against it). Daredevil is, right now, Marvel's only masked crime-fighter (I'm excluding the Punisher from consideration, since he's a black-and-white (in more ways than one, ha, ha!)); Spidey is too much concerned with keeping his fragile sanity patched together to go out and catch crooks, and everybody else is more concerned with the end of the Universe and/or fighting super-villains who want to rule the world than to be concerned with the safety of our streets. DD is not a character who lends himself to fighting earth-shaking menaces; it is, then, odd that most of the writers have tried to put him into that mold. No, Daredevil's powers are ideally suited for combatting crime, crime as it affects us. And it's one reason why DD should have less of an identity crisis than most of Marvel's bunch: because both in his secret identity and out, he's applying himself to the same problem, crime. You know, there was something to the old, old cliche of a fighting DA becoming *The Muskrat, Avenger of Evil!* But here it's on a level a trifle deeper: the motivations are a little deeper as Matt seems to make clear in this issue. Daredevil as Crime-fighter is the type of tack that could make this strip different enough from the rest of the Marvel milieu to finally put it on its own legs after so long a time to make it more than "another superhero strip."

To Bob Brown and Klaus Janson, kudos; Bob Brown-Vince Colletta looked like everybody else-Vince Colletta, and was pretty dull. But whenever Bob gets a good inker, he turns in a stunning job. His Liliths were like that: so is this DAREDEVIL. If you hadn't put the credits on this issue, I, for one, would have sworn Gene Colan drew it. A great deal of the credit must go to Klaus's inking, and especially his coloring, which gave it that midnight mood that added so much to the story, but Bob's use of perspective and his pacing of shots were near-perfect. The difference between this issue and his work on the Hydra stories is just phenomenal. Of course, knowing Marvel, the Wolfman-Brown-Janson team will last for two issues at the longest, but you guys *do* do good work together.

Until DD gets a butler and a red telephone,

Peter B. Gillis
18 Bayberry Road
Elmsford, NY 10523

Well, Peter, Marv has been spending a lot of his time just trying to decide exactly who and what a Daredevil should be, and has even reread his entire collection a time or two to ensure that he had the proper feel for the character. And if you've read the last thirty-five or so issues of TOMB OF DRACULA, you already know that Marv is a writer who takes his work *seriously*. (Or at least that's what we've noticed ever since he began wearing garlic sprigs around his neck!)

As for Bob Brown, he's doing his darndest to get across the feel of the greatest acrobat *ever*— the one whose stage is not merely the Big Top— but the whole Big Apple! And with an inking assist from Klaus Janson, we know we'll all succeed every time!

Dear Marvel,

About Jay Zilber's letter complaining about becoming too wordy: I disagree. I don't think comics should be entirely a VISUAL medium or a SCRIPT medium—but rather, one where the art and story form a symbiotic bond, each one becoming stronger because of the other, complementing and improving each element (the X-MEN currently embody this concept, and DRACULA, DEATHLOK, and CAPTAIN MARVEL are other examples). To cut the word-count of a Don McGregor or a Tony Isabella would be a grave mistake. And as to eliminating "cuteness"—well, there are things a writer can do in the captions of a comic that can be done in no other medium—the one-to-one correspondence found in comics between writer and reader allows the usage of unique and humorous techniques in captions. If the humor becomes too corny—I think it's a mistake everyone should overlook, because the writer-reader relationship in comics is, to me, a precious one indeed.

Bruce Canwell
Meadows Rd. RFD #2
Bowdoin, ME 04008

We think so too, Bruce. The writer-reader relationship *is* a precious one. But so is the *artist*-reader relationship.

Comics, basically, is a visual medium. This does not mean that there should be little or no copy, only that the artwork must be colorful and enticing, in addition to the story being scintillating. A good comic only occurs when the proper artist-writer symbiosis occurs.

We'd like to think it happens more often at Marvel than anywhere else.

Dear Marvel,

As far as the Black Widow is concerned, I disagree with Bob Rodi's letter on mistreating the interesting lady. I have faith in Marvel and have always thought that she was treated right until you wrote her out of Matt Murdock's life entirely! Oh yes! She *belongs* in DAREDEVIL!

Marc P. Beauregard
181 Elm Street
New Bedford, MA 02740

You'll have to take that up with Tony Isabella and Don Heck, Mark, 'cause they've sent off that dynamic damsel to co-star with Hercules, Ghost Rider, Iceman and the Angel in Marvel's latest and greatest super-team sensation— THE CHAMPIONS!

(Of course, if enough letters are received demanding the Black Widow's return, Marv may just decide to steal her back. Come to think of it, we haven't had two writers fighting for the hand of a femme fatale in a long time!)

But always remember the famous words of Irving Forbush, who once said, "I was nowhere *near* Cleveland!"

See ya next month, effendi— we'll be watchin' for ya!

THIS IS IT! YOUR
MARVEL VALUE STAMP
FOR THIS ISSUE!

CLIP 'EM AND COLLECT 'EM!

4: THE INCREDIBLE HULK from *Daredevil* no. 129 (January 1976).

Dear Steve & Sal,

Bring back the "old" Nighthawk, huh? You know, the Nighthawk that would throw a left jab and a right hook or do some occasional acrobatics during a fight. Not the "new" Nighthawk who flys through a bunch of bad guys and they all go flying. C'mon Marvel! Captain America wasn't even able to do that until he got his new super-strength from the Viper. Bring back Nighthawk's "slam-banger" fights, like his one with Power Man back in ish #17.

How about the Falcon and Sting ray as future Defenders. I think the fans would like it.

John O'Neil
Stoneham, MA 02180

We're not ruling out Falc or Sting-y as possible candidates for DEFENDERS membership and/or guest-star appearances, John, but as you're aware if you've read the blurb at the end of this issue's tale, the next new character to appear on the scene will be coming from 'way out of left field. (Honestly, if anyone out there actually expected a ressurrection of the Red Guardian, we'd be astonished). Let's wait and see what the reaction to this utterly unexpected character revival will be, before we nominate any more costumed cavorters for Defender status.

As regards your suggestion about Nighthawk: frankly, we think you're right. Steve's been letting him rely far too much on the jet-pack and placing far too little emphasis on his pugilistic and acrobatic abilities. Once we get the poor guy reassembled (Nighthawk, not Steve: although...!), you have our word he'll be doing more with his fists and less with his flight plans.

In our defense, though, we should mention that 'twas not Kyle's strength so much as the sheer momentum he could build by dive-bombing an enemy from high-altitude that enabled him to bowl over a host of adversaries at one sweep. Clear?

Good. Then we'll close this month's Dialogue with another reminder not to miss our next landmark issue. All hype aside, you'll be seeing Val in her most savage struggle yet: you'll be meeting a new and controversial superdoer: and, so help us, you'll begin to see where the past several months of insanity have been leading. That's all in DEFENDERS #35, on sale in just thirty days. Be here!

MARVEL VALUE STAMP

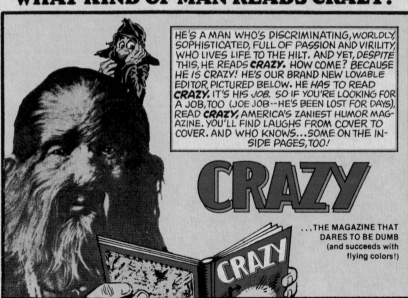

41: THE INCREDIBLE HULK from *The Defenders* no. 33 (March 1976).

SOCK IT TO SHELL-HEAD

c/o MARVEL COMICS GROUP, 575 MADISON AVE. N.Y.C. 10022

Marvelmen:

Thank you for IRON MAN #84. It was probably the best issue in a long time. The idea of a helpless Iron Man is just great. I never doubted that I.M. would beat the Black Lama or the Red Ghost in previous issues, but I was really surprised at seeing him lying helpless on a bridge!

The story was excellent, probably because of the fact that the Freak became more dangerous with the cobalt radiation in his body. Nice work, Len and Roger!

Herb Trimpe's work was a masterpiece. He's entered new dimensions in detail. But what, pray tell, happened to the yellow pullover Tony Stark wore under his shirt at the top of page 10? It somehow had disappeared by the time he changed to Iron Man at the bottom.

Hank Boehme
Grafelfingesh 84
8000 Munich 70
West Germany

All right, Hank, we give up—what *did* happen to that yellow pullover?

Seriously speaking, we find it uncomfortably incumbent upon ourselves to abashedly admit that, indeed, we erred. Therefore, in keeping with our policy of paying off Marvelites who embarrass us with these all-too-often bloopers, we're awarding you one mildly munificent and yet somewhat slightly dazed no-prize, in the new, improved, steel-mesh model (which comes complete with detachable accessory nosepiece).

Now, aren't you *glad* we forgot that furshluginer yellow pullover?

Dear Iron Persons:

I was reviewing the first part of the latest Freak story (#84), and found this direct quote: "And just in case any of you rollickin' readers are noticing any startling similarities between this situation and that of Spidey #152, see our letters section next issue-- ALL will be explained. --Len." I then turned eagerly to # 85, looking for the letters section, but it was gone! What gives?

Also, aren't you wearing out the Happy impersonates I.M./ gets hurt/enervator is only hope/enervator turns Hap into Freak/I.M. has to fight him without harming him storyline?!

Finally, you changed the letters page heading in #84, and there were two nose-less images of Iron Man incorporated in the new design. Careless!

Mike Cannon
2512 Cordova Lane
Rancho Cordova, CA 95670

By now, Mike, old man, you know that the explanation Len promised in that infamous footnote finally appeared in the letters section of ish #86, since the story in #85 ran an extra page, thus pre-empting said lettercol.

And speakin' of the new heading for this ever-lovin' letters page, you also know by now that our favorite Iron Individual has shed his proboscis—so ya had a clue an issue in advance, and ya misinterpreted it, Mike!

So it goes...

Dear Marvel:

I can barely relate to the fact that Tony Stark is a corporate, capitalist pig—but tell me, does he have to be a hypocrite, too?

In ish #82, page 7, panel 2, Stark contests to design projects to preserve the ecology, while on the previous page our hero flies through thick, black, polluting smoke...emitted from none other than Stark International!

the Ozone Kid
(no address given)

Believe it or don't, Oz, but we're way ahead of ya insofar as reducing Stark International's air pollution problem. Y'see, in true Ayn Randian fashion, Stark practices what he preaches; and you'll see that we're not just making excuses if you check out ish # 85, bottom of page 3, where the smog output of those selfsame smokestacks has been reduced to nil. And unless any of our absent-minded artists accidentally scribble in smoke in a future ish, just out of sheer habit, we can guarantee that ya won't be seein' anymore of it emitting from Stark International.

Dear Ferro-philes:

What've you guys got against Happy Hogan? Since his introduction in TALES OF SUSPENSE #45, he's been frozen by Jack Frost, mangled by the Mandarin, ruined by the Unicorn, socked by Shellhead, hacked by Hawkeye, pecked by Pepper, trounched by Titanium Man, "Freaked" out four times, and socked by rocks—and somehow survived a fall of well over 200 feet in Iron Man's suit.

And now, the Freak...*again*?

Gentlemen, I rest my case.

Tim Krenke
2730 N 46th Street
Milwaukee, WI 53210

Dear Marvel:

Just a short note to correct IRON MAN #84. Aside from TALES OF SUSPENSE #74 and I.M. #3, the far-out Freak also appeared in IRON MAN # 67. I will expect my no-prize shortly.

(By the way, ish #84 was fa-a-antastic!)

Randy Funk
154 Sumpwams Avenue
Babylon, NY 11702

Sorry, Randy! You're close, but no cigar this time! Ya see, the Freak from IRON MAN #67 was not *The* Freak, but rather an irradiated Eddie March. (Gee, it feels good to win one for a change!)

Well, that's it, ferro-philes—we're callin' it a column. That is, unless ya wanna see us sink further into a blue funk. (Sorry, Randy, we just *couldn't* resist!) But just give us a mere month, and we'll be back in fine form—we promise ya!

Ciao.

MARVEL VALUE STAMP

99: THE INCREDIBLE HULK from *Iron Man* no. 88 (July 1976).

the problems facing America today. I feel that you're helping to inform the younger readers of the current issues that face our American society.

Wendy Mayer
Box 50, Stambaugh Hall
Ada, OH 45810

Marvel has always managed to examine facets of American society and of the world at large, whether the problem is pollution, the Watergate affair, or just plain old lack of brotherhood. Our super-heroes don't live in a world all their own, Wendy. They live in the world occupied by you and we, and share all our problems and all our joys. And that's what Marvel is all about.

Comprende?

Dear Bullpen,

I thoroughly enjoyed Cap #191: Not only did it begin to tie up the Falcon double-identity problem but it was also just plain fun! The balance between the action and seriousness (i.e. both plot and character development) was done nicely. I'm glad to see it all ending. The Skull-Falcon bit was good while it lasted but enough is enough.

Frank did a great artistic job this issue. At first I didn't like his style but, as you said, he kind of grows on you. Stilty never looked better (except maybe on the magnificent cover) and Cap and Falc looked together!

On the writing side Mr. Mantlo really did a fine job. What is he? Some kind of workhorse? Practically every book I pick up today is written by him!

BRING BACK KULL!!

Garret Leffler
225 Dellwood Road
Buffalo, NY 14226

Boisterous Bill's problem seems to be that aside from the series he normally writes, he's also hard at work (as you may already know from reading some of our other lettercols) scripting a fill-in inventory story for every Marvel title. It just so happens that a number of them have been used in the same months, thus creating the impression of a backbreaking workload. See?

And as for Kull, hold onto your socks! He's a'comin', so just keep watchin', y'hear?

Dear Marvel,

HAPPINESS IS: Reading CAPTAIN AMERICA and finding out his creator is back.

LONG LIVE THE KING!!!

ROF David Baum
1709 N. 41 Avenue
Hollywood, FL 33021

HAPPINESS IS: Reading fan letters which wish us good luck in the future.

SADNESS IS: Approaching the end of a lettercolumn.

HAPPINESS IS: Knowing there'll be another one next month!

MARVEL VALUE STAMP

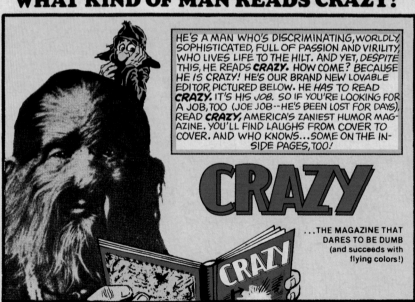

42: THE INCREDIBLE HULK from *Captain America* no. 195 (March 1976).

THE SPIDER'S WEB

SEND YOUR LETTERS TO:
THE MARVEL COMICS GROUP, SIXTH FLOOR 575 MADISON AV., NEW YORK ,N. Y. 10022

Not so long after getting Spidey involved in "Whodunit?", Lively Len and the rest of the Marvel Bullpen encountered their own behind-the-scenes whodunit—only this time no one's been able to come up with a solution. Y'see, the entire *file* of letters on issue #152 disappeared without a trace! As you may expect, there was considerable consternation and gnashing of teeth over this most unusual incident. But fortunately, we managed to scare up a few last-minute letters just under the proverbial wire, or "The Spider's Web" would be non-existent this month.

Okay, enough friendly chattering! On with the regularly-scheduled letters page!

Dear Peoples:

SPIDER-MAN #152 was hardly earth-shattering, but it was solid nevertheless. None of the scenes struck me as being the hyper-intense "How am I ever gonna get out of this one?!" kind. Spidey's opening fight-for-life sequence seemed somewhat commonplace, as comic death-traps go, though the escape was logical enough. Actually, the entire plot was more or less trivial. The Shocker wasn't that much of a menace, and he was defeated with comparatively little effort. (New York's financial situation being what it is, a grand-scale blackout might not be all that bad. At least we wouldn't have to pay our electric bills!)

This issue's interest, for me, lay in characterization and the interaction thereof. J.J.J. attempting to recover from his party in his own lovable fashion; Peter's ever-present secret identity/social problems; Spidey's battle repartee played against the Shocker's dead-serious (*dull*) super villain talk; the misunderstanding men in blue—yep, that's SPIDER-MAN all right.

Particularly interesting this time around were the supporting characters. So Flash Thompson has finally become a decent human being— it's about time! Harry's been cured and totally ennervated: he's kind of pathetic now, with his new–found wistfulness, but that's valid considering all he's been through. Just don't overdo it. Harry should go back to being a less uptight version of his old self, once he's readjusted to everything.

Mary Jane Watson. Oh no, don't tell me that MJ is going to pull a "Gwen" every time Peter cuts out to fight a baddie! That's going to get tiresome mighty fast, and I've always thought that Ms. Watson had a bit more depth. Why don't you let her figure out Petey's secret identity, and then spring the news on him when he tries to explain his next disappearance? This could be built up gradually, and it would give both characters a break.

This letter is way too long as it is, so I won't even venture a guess as to who the mystery man on page 7 is — how's that for restraint?

Naomi Basner
New York, NY

It's wog-boggling, Naomi, if ya wanna know the truth! Most of the letters on #152 hazarded guesses, and some of them were pretty far out, if memory serves us right. But the other outstanding topic of discussion in that mysterious, missing sheaf of missives was something else you mentioned briefly—namely, Ms. Mary Jane Watson—and the next letter deals with exclusively that topic.

Dear Len, Ross, et al,

Pardon me if I seem a bit confused, but have I missed an issue of SPIDER-MAN? The reason I ask is because of a number of rather disturbing incidents in #152, particularly those involving Mary Jane Watson. I mean, Mary Jane has known Peter Parker for quite a while, right? So why should she be angry about his sudden disappearance from the night—or rather, the issue—before? Worried or upset, yes! But angry?

Maybe I've gotten a wrong impression about M.J. over the last few years, but I thought Peter meant a great deal to her. It doesn't make sense that she should turn on him the way she did in issue #152.

Other than that, Len, I like the way you're keeping pace with Spidey's private life. Just watch out for Mary Jane, okay?

Janice Henry
Snow Low, AZ

Point taken, Jan! But we can't help drawing attention to the fact that, indeed, very few of us always react consistently, and that an accumulation of repressed feelings might well have caused M. J. to act as she did in #152. And now, before this discussion escalates into heavy psychology, let's squeeze in one last note...

Dear Marvel,

After carefully examing page seven of SPIDER-MAN #152, and page 10 of #154, I've come to the conclusion that the mysterious derelict is none other than Doctor Octopus.

Look carefully at page seven, panel 4 in #152—the man is holding a cup with two hands and pouring at the same time! This isn't possible, unless he has more than two arms. In #154, he trips a passerby without coming near him. That's the clincher!

(Hey, do I get a no-prize?)

Marc Blumberg
5435 Grove St.
Skokie, IL 60076

Well, by now you know that not only were your inferences astute, but they were also correct. Unfortunately, Marc, we can't hand out a no-prize, since your letter is one of the few to survive, and it just wouldn't be fair to the other Marvelites whose missives went astray. Now, if you could solve our very own letterical whodunit in the same fashion, *that* might well be worth a no-prize!

Meanwhile, it's time to exit stage left for another madcap month. See ya later, pilgrims!

THIS IS IT! YOUR
MARVEL VALUE STAMP
FOR THIS ISSUE!

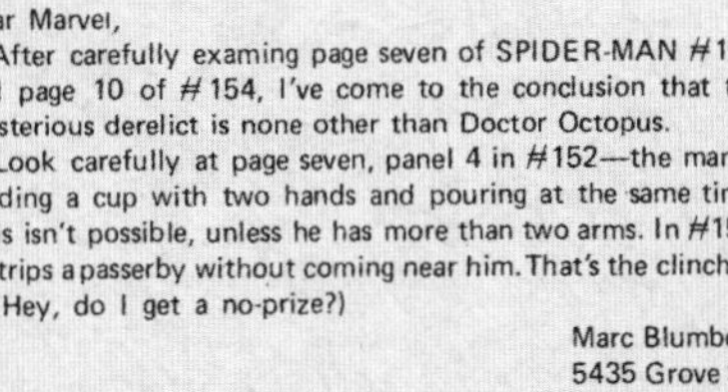

CLIP 'EM AND COLLECT 'EM!

83: THE INCREDIBLE HULK from *The Amazing Spider-Man* no. 156 (May 1976).

Tomes to the Tomb!

c/o MARVEL COMICS GROUP, 575 MADISON AVE. N.Y.C. 10022

Just a personal word or three from the Marvelous One before we dive into this issue's Tomb Tomes!

First of all, thanks to one and all for those great letters about the possible cancellation of T.O.D. For myself, Gene and Tom your outpouring of emotions was an incredible testimony to the hard sweat and tears that go into each issue. There still isn't any word about Drac's future, and for the moment, no news *is* good news, so let's just keep hoping. I'll keep you all posted.

Secondly, I'd like to give a personal thanks to everyone connected with both the San Diego Comic Convention and the Cleveland Comicon for making me feel right at home in a city so far from these shabby New York buildings. I had a great time visiting not only the convention, speaking with all of you out there, but seeing your cities as well. The only question I have is: Is it true that we really did fit 97 guests onto Tony Isabella's floor for sleeping?

And before I go, I also want to thank Marty Herzog of Toronto's Cosmicon for extending the invitaiton for this year's festivities, and if all goes well, I'll be trucking up there when the snows come down. Take care, peoples!

Dear Gentlemen,

I've only been reading Drac for the past fifteen months, but it's been love at first sight. I thought that it would be just a Chris Lee flick on paper; A simple case of him rising each night in search of blood, fighting off the fear crazed towns-people, getting a stake driven into his heart every three issues, only to have faithful Igor pull it out the next month. "Good evening. I bid you velcome. I bid you velcome!" This kind of trash kept running through my head. Another attempt at bandwagon jumping.

Boy, was I far off. #24 was my first crack at Drac and since then I've been hooked. Marv, you've taken this further than I thought it could be carried. Your Dracula is radically different from anything I have ever seen or read. I love it. Gene Colan wasn't my favorite artist, yet, on T.O.D. his work is just super. I'm glad he no longer uses all the weird shaped panels as he once did on D.D. Now I would rather have Gene on this book than any artist I can think of.

As for issue #38. Loved it. The art was, as always, perfect. The cover was nice. I think the interior artist should do his covers when it is possible. As for the story, well it was Wolfman all the way. I enjoy Harold H. Harold more than any other character except Hannibal King. Let him get his story with Drac putting the bite on him. Not too sure about Aurora. She is dumb, yet comes up with the needed idea. I'll have to wait and see. When I saw Doctor Sun I was shocked. I didn't know that he was a disembodied brain. Quincy and Frank will play a part in this somewhere.

Thank you for another enjoyable story. I await the next issue, and I hope there will be many more. I'm behind you all the way.

Mark Barsotti
Rt. One, Kowa, CO 80117

Dear Marvel,

You know what I've just realized? I've realized that TOMB OF DRACULA is one of my most favorite comic books ever to be put out on local newstands.

Without Marv Wolfman's analysis of Dracula, and the evil and terror that evolves around Drac, as well as the persistence of continuing and supporting characters, fans' heads will shatter with disbelief!

The illusions of sanity is something that Marv uses in his chores of authorism. We all undoubtedly know that when one writes personal opinions, relationships, and acquaintances of life are strong and tied into an improving story. Supposedly Marv is sane. Therefore his sanity is injected in plot, words, etc. Illusions are contained in all minds and Marv's shows in his work. The fantasy or horror is similar to illusions. It is all combined.

Constant rotation of characters also proves something. Indubitably, Marv enjoys people and their company. In his writing, the interlocking personal experiences between characters produces more information. Possibly Marv involves himself with many people and their private and surrounding problems. He knows how to relate to entities and their reactions. Marv understands hate-love-affection-sensitivity and other human emotions. His knowledge does not decline when an unknown, untackled factor shows up, it's fought and the characters also battle these elements in the sagas.

TOD is not only run by Dracula but half of the mag is dedicated to potential supporters. The accumulation of past, present, and future "parts" of certain human beings' lives is represented with the characterization of supporting and non-supporting persons. Angles are pushed more to the side of other peoples dealings in and on this planet. So Marv, we could say, writes of people and their dealings that are worded by what Marv sees, hears, and feels. Marv is the conductor and human beings are the players.

But he is not Dracula. Instead Drac is the total of evil and no more.

Gene Colan is the same. What one feels, one draws? Maybe, maybe not. The Daredevil strip appears to have the same type of art. But in D.D.'s mag the art is that of adventure and high swinging Evil lurks within the heart of Dracula...Gene knows! And it shows. The terror looms in his work and a softer shadow appears when man is about.

Shadows may be the main promise to this book. When a woman is shown there appears femininity...Drac shows and... Evil is drawn in. Gene is excellent for the comic and none other matches him.

One thing I've noticed though. Much of the artists' artwork is similar in someway to the artists' features. The similarity flows with the artist into the pencil and onto the Bristol board. This can add more proof to the theory of feelings shown in what one does.

TOMB OF DRACULA is nearing my No. 1 comic and I'll continue to support Drac. I never thought this man would be good...guess I was wrong...dead wrong! (Ooops).

Michael Biegel
6 Valley Lane, Upper Saddle River, NJ 07458

Marv and Gene say "Gawshhhh!"

Dear Marvel,

I would like to point out a little known (and probably little cared about) fact.

When you abbreviate "Tomb of Dracula" it reads "Tod," the German word for death, how appropriate!

For pointing this out I humbly request a bi-lingual no-prize.

Paul Reddin
326 St. Johns Place, Brooklyn, NY 11238

O.K.

MARVEL VALUE STAMP

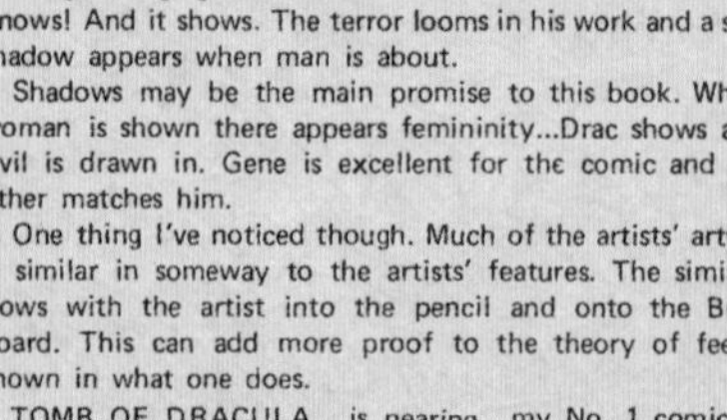

CLIP 'EM AND COLLECT 'EM!

19: THE INCREDIBLE HULK from *Tomb of Dracula* no. 41 (February 1976).

FIRST CLASS MAIL

c/o MARVEL COMICS GROUP, 575 MADISON AVE. N.Y.C. 10022

Dear Marvel,

I had just recently purchased a few of this month's comics, and while scanning the Bulletin I saw it: MARVEL PREMIERE #28, featuring The Legion of Monsters. Man-Thing, Werewolf, Ghost Rider, and Morbius! A one-issue spectacular!

I'm glad you were quick-witted enough to mention that this issue's characters didn't remotely resemble their former black-and-white mag counterparts.

And it may be a one-shot attempt, but who knows? The Legion of Monsters may show up later on, maybe in their own comic book. How's that for wishful thinking?

If you should decide to give The Legion of Monsters their own comic, try to rotate the membership. Be flexible in the types of characters featured. If what I'm saying sounds like I'm getting ahead of myself, it's only because the very idea is extremely appealing to me.

John Wayne Megala
9280 Wheeler Avenue
Fontana, CA

No plans are slated for LOM, John, but if enough letters like yours come in...who knows? Meanwhile, Ghost Rider can be seen in his own mag as well as in THE CHAMPIONS; Morbius will be popping up in MARVEL TWO-IN-ONE; Man-Thing's set for a guest-appearance alongside the ever-incredible HULK; and WEREWOLF BY NIGHT is still prowling your newsstands. Check 'em out, John...you'll be glad you *did*!

Dear Marvel,

I have finished reading MARVEL PREMIERE #28. The story was good and Steve's inks were fantastic. Robbins has improved since his recent work with Captain America.

I am a Manny Maniac. Since MAN-THING has been cancelled I have been going crazy to drown my sorrows. I'm still unsure as to why MAN-THING was cancelled. Was it because of bad sales, or because Gerber left? If it was because of the latter, then why couldn't Man-Thing get a new writer?

All right folks, it's time to send me a swamp-infested no-prize. Page 11, panel 2 stated that Man-Thing was amazed. How could this be when he's incapable of feelings?

Keep on trucking!

Ben Wong
374 Pearl Street
New York, NY

Sales and only sales, Ben. Nobody's ever really proven what makes or breaks a comic mag, but the one sure indicator is sales figures, and on MAN-THING they weren't good. But an upsurge of mail has come in pleading for a return of everybody's favorite swamp creature...and if we get enough positive reaction to Manny's guest-appearances in other books of the line, he may yet be reinstated to gladden hearts and soil carpets throughout Marveldom Assembled.

MARVEL VALUE STAMP

87: **THE INCREDIBLE HULK** from *Marvel Premiere* no. 30 (June 1976).

THE SILVER SURFER™

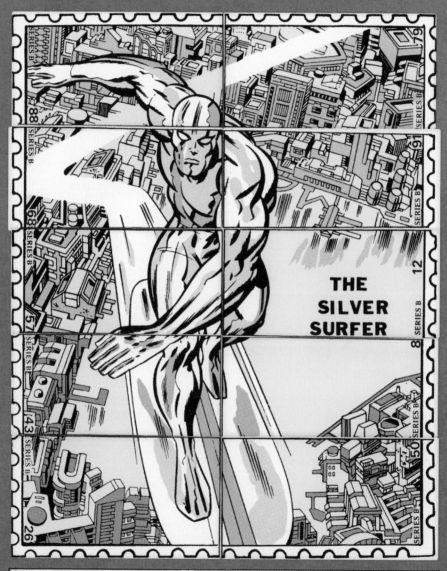

There was nothing left for the people of Zenn-La to discover. War, poverty, disease... all had long since been conquered on this wondrous world and **Norrin Radd** was bored! So, when he was offered the chance to take on the life of herald to the planet-devouring **Galactus** in exchange for the life of his homeworld, he accepted. Thus he became the sentinel of the spaceways... **the Silver Surfer!**

Fantastic Four no. 72 (March 1968), art by Jack Kirby and Joe Sinnott.

COMMENTS TO KA-ZAR (AND ZABU)

c/o MARVEL COMICS GROUP, 575 MADISON AVE. N.Y.C. 10022

Dear Doug & Gang,

KA-ZAR #'s 12 & 13 were delightfully replete with good plot twists and interesting symbolism. Especially neat was the way the Zebra-Men painted opposing stripes on their bodies to match the color of their brothers. If only men and women in this country could similarly feel less hostility toward their brothers and sisters of different races...and to see, through the eyes of God, that all people are beautiful.

Thanks also for the valuable insights into the effects of power and the human desire for same. Continue producing KA-ZAR on this level of intelligence and excitement, and I'll cheerfully continue reading.

James L. Bleeker
1131 Courtney St. N.W.
Grand Rapids, MI 49504

Dear Doug & Russ,

KA-ZAR # 12 was an all-around excellent issue. The interior art, like the cover, was fantastic. I believe you've finally found the artist best-suited for KA-ZAR; Russ Heath's gorgeous work in SAVAGE TALES # 10 was only a preview to the greatness here. The story was also great, with its nice balance of Ka-Zar, jungle action, dinosaurs, Sheesa, and weird menaces, but the conclusion leaves me hungry for more. I expect next issue to be filled with action; meanwhile, Doug Moench should get another pat on the back for this issue.

Larry Dean
6362 Laurentian Ct.
Flint, MI 48504

Dear Marvel,

Russ Heath is an excellent storyteller and marvelous illustrator, and I wish he'd appear more frequently. The KA-ZAR strip needs a definite artistic direction; my vote is cast for Russ.

Doug wrote a very nice story, too, with a wholly original concept for one of the Savage Land's tribes. The "zebra-men" was a brilliant stroke, as well as an ingenious way for so-called primitives to erase racial differences. An all-around enjoyable story, gang.

Kim Thompson
Gen Del Box 259
APO NY, NY 09184

Dear Folks,

KA-ZAR # 12 was a monumental step for comics — Russ Heath at Marvel!! Far-out!! My enthusiasm for this fantastic draftsman is based on concrete knowledge that Mr. Heath is one of the best all-around artists in comics! I've seen him do so many types of strips that I wonder if there's *anything* he can't draw — and draw expertly, every time.

Russ's mastery of the human anatomy (particularly the feminine gender) is already renowned, but now we see him tackle subjects a little more esoteric — things like dinosaurs, *very* pretty ladies, and striped men! I swear, that triceratops looked so realistic I thought it was going trample out all over my living room. Russ Heath has, in one issue, brought me (and many other art freaks, I'm sure) back to KA-ZAR with a vengeance!

Ken Meyer, Jr.
31110B Revere Circle
Hill AFB, UT 84406

Glad you dug the triceratops, Ken, but it wasn't the first such critter Russ Heath has drawn; check out the full-page dinosaur "pin-ups" in Joe Kubert's mid-fifties TOR comics.

Fellow Ka-Zarites,

Congratulations on another fine issue of everyone's favorite jungle lord. Mr. Moench, once again, has turned out a fascinating story. The "Zebra" people are simply fantastic — let's see more of these intriguing people.

And Mr. Heath's art...well, what can I say?? It was beautiful. Since I've always associated Russ with war comics, I couldn't believe I was actually seeing his talented pencils and inks on KA-ZAR. Russ is definitely the man to keep on this strip.

All in all, KA-ZAR # 12 was one of the top issues ever; you people have another classic on your hands.

Mark Kirkpatrick
1212 9th Avenue
Rockford, IL 61108

Dear Doug & Russ:

KA-ZAR # 12 was, quite literally, a joy to behold. Russ Heath's masterful artwork combined both elegance and power with compelling results. His panel layouts were imaginative, dynamic, and effective, and his command of human anatomy was among the best this long-time comics fan has ever seen. Russ's rendition of Sheesa — lush, yet malevolent — was particularly delightful. For the first time in many months, I've purchased multiple copies of KA-ZAR, and Russ Heath is responsible. Further KA-ZAR work by Russ is *definitely* indicated.

Ed O'Reilly
215 E. Lehr
Ada, OH 45810

Whew! Do you get the feeling, as we do, that Russ Heath did something right in issue # 12?

But, as good as that job was, we must answer the large number of requests for more Heath KA-ZAR work with a probable negative. Russ simply doesn't want to be tied to a regular stint on *any* mag. But it was nice while it lasted, and Devil-May-Care Doug especially enjoyed his latest collaboration with Russ — since he and the hedonistic Mr. Heath have been good buddies dating back to the days when the unlikely duo were the only two comics-type people (other than NARD 'N PAT biographer Jay Lynch) in Chicago. Indeed, Doug and Russ still fondly remember lying sprawled under a table, gorged and bloated on deep-pan pizza, at the My Pi on Sheridan Avenue. Or maybe it was the wine...

But even though Russ has departed the pages of KA-ZAR, we do have a regular artist now handling the strip — and we can't think of a more able artistic successor than Valiant Val Mayerik. Doug and Val are also good buddies — even if they haven't shared the same floor, bloated and gorged — and they've got some big plans for KA-ZAR up their collective sleeves, a hint of which is evidenced by this very issue.

But be here *next* issue when the Big Change *really* blasts wide open!

And until then...be good.

THIS IS IT! YOUR

MARVEL VALUE STAMP

FOR THIS ISSUE!

CLIP 'EM AND COLLECT 'EM!

88: THE SILVER SURFER from *Ka-Zar* no. 16 (June 1976).

THE EVER-LOVIN' BLUE-EYED
LETTERS PAGE!
c/o MARVEL COMICS GROUP, 575 MADISON AVE., NEW YORK, N.Y. 10022

Dear Roger, Len & Ron,

You're doing wonders with Ben Grimm's personality. MARVEL 2-in-1 #13 was really fun to read. I loved the humor in it, especially page 16. Even Cage himself was handled beautifully—his whole attitude was very well done. His coolness, logical thinking, and desire to aid his friend when in time of need. I notice he didn't stop to work out the financial arrangements before tearing off.

James L. Bleeker
1131 Courtney NW
Grand Rapids, MI 49504

D-d-dear Marvel,

I h-had w-w-waited f-f-for qu-quite a-a w-w-while t-to s-s-see the Th-Thing a-and P-P-Power Man t-teamed up, b-b-but, g-g- gentlemen, I w-was r-r-robbed! I h-had expected t-to s-see th-them t-teamed up against s-s-some worthy f-f-foe l-like a g-gangland c-c-criminal who w-was p-preying on f-folks in th-the g-g-ghetto; s-something out of the Th-Thing's n-natural element. Instead, w-we g-got an immense r-refugee f-from a G-G-Godzilla p-picture. E-e-euchh!

Th-the art w-w-was w-way b-below p-par, b-but the f-fights b-between B-Ben and C-Cage were g-good. As f-for th-the ch-character who t-talked l-like P-P-Porky P-P-Pig, well, what c-can I s-s-say? W-With T-T-Thomas t-taking over, I f-feel th-the Th-Thing is c-coming h-h-home at l-last.

Well, th-th-th-that's all, f-folks.

Paul Dini
San Francisco, CA

Dear Marvel,

TWO-IN-ONE #13 was excellent, and the art was superb. I just want to say, "Keep up the good work."

Wayne Ridge
Vermontville, MI

Dear Marv, Len, Roger, and Ron,

Re: MARVEL TWO-IN-ONE #13.

What, exactly, are you trying to prove—that you can pull a magazine down in one easy lesson? #13 was abominable, and downright DUMB! After all, aren't "My Son the Monster" stories just a little bit hackneyed, even when they are done right?

Really, guys, I love ya—but why did you put such a good team into such a monstrosity? And why the fight between Grimm and Cage? It was unnecessary, unless you wanted to impress the Thing and us with the strength of Power Man, and give us insight into his character.

#13 could have been a good magazine, comparable to other "monster-confrontation" mags (such as HULK #184) had you toned down the stuttering of Arnold Krank, which was very annoying, and given a more reasonable explanation of the origin of Braggadoom, it could have been very good.

I've thrown a lot of criticism your way, and I'm sorry I had to do it. Yet, hopefully, you see that I am trying to help. I have an interest in seeing better art, better stories, with some imagination in them; #13, sadly, flunked on most counts.

Steve Prince
5423 S., 1st Avenue
Phoenix, AZ 85041

Dear Roy,

MARVEL TWO-IN-ONE issue #13, the Thing and Power Man team up, in a story called: "I created BRAGGADOOM, the Mountain that Walked like a Man." Roy, start writing this book—FAST.

Ralph Macchio
188 Wilson Drive
Cresskill, NJ 07626

Dear Stan, Marv, Roger, Len, Ron, and Vince,

MARVEL TWO-IN-ONE #13 was a pretty competent, if not spectacular, issue. The monster itself was hardly original; in fact, it reminded me of the Chicken Heart that ate up New York City. But for some obscure reason, the issue was immensely readable, and quite entertaining. It was a potboiler, but a good potboiler. The wit and down-to-earthness of both Ben and Luke was fun, as were the pair's confrontations throughout the issue. Dr. Krank was a good one-shot character. The art was good, too. I'll be expecting a little more than this most of the time in this mag, but every once in a while, for a filler, this kind of thing is mucho fun!

Neal Meyer
Bickleton, WA 99322

The mail response to MARVEL TWO-IN-ONE #13 was—in a word—mixed, as indicated by the letters printed above. Indeed, opinions vary even among the trio of writers who worked on the story. Roger Slifer, who made his scripting debut with that outing, was not entirely satisfied with his dialoguing and agrees wholeheartedly with the readers who felt the stuttering of Arnold Krank was overdone—it was an experiment that didn't quite come off. You can fault us for failing, but you can't fault us for at least *trying* something a bit out of the ordinary.

Marv, on the other hand, still feels the story was successful as a light-hearted romp in the monster-hunting department, and is happy that so many readers enjoyed his rather offbeat terror-tale.

Len just waggles his finger in the direction of production potentate John Verpoorten's office, as he madly scribbles word balloons into place on those eternally-late Hulk pages that have to be downstairs for the mail pick-up in three more seconds. Judging from past experience, we guess that means he won't be ready to talk to us (or go out for coffee) until at least 7 p.m.

Finally, a last minute plug: If ya wanna check out the progress of the Wein/Slifer superteam, pick up IRON MAN #'s 84 and 85. And be sure an' let us know what ya think—after all, you know how insecure we are!

THIS IS IT! YOUR

MARVEL VALUE STAMP

FOR THIS ISSUE!

CLIP 'EM AND COLLECT 'EM!

79: THE SILVER SURFER from *Marvel Two-in-One* no. 15 (May 1976).

MAIL IT TO TEAM-UP

c/o MARVEL COMICS GROUP, 575 MADISON AVE. N.Y.C. 10022

Dear Team-up Team,

MTU #40 was yet another fine effort by Bill and Sal. The only thing I disliked about the whole book was the manner in which the Torch left. Didn't he have a few scores to settle with his captors? *You're darned right, he would!* It just seems so stupid: one minute he's trapped in a cage, and the next he's saying *So long! I don't care!* It seemed as if you just didn't want to keep him around because you were too lazy. Perhaps you thought that you would have too many characters in the book. After the hype on the cover all about *Spidey and the Human Torch together again,* having him split was rather cheap.

But enough of that. The rest of the story was *excellent!* Sal's illustrations were great as usual. The man is about the most consistently good artist in comics. I don't see how the guy can produce as much work as he does. He must not sleep, eat, or breathe. Then there's Bill Mantlo. On my list, he is among the top ten writers in comics today. I hope you keep him in the MTU corral for a long, long time. He's got Steve Gerber's emotional, corny touch, and Len Wein's great storytelling ability. When you mix them all together you get *Boisterous Bill!*

The last two pages of this book almost brought a tear to my right eye. All I can say is that it was truly moving. And weren't those fight scenes *super?* I've always liked those long, drawn-out sequences, one clobbering after another. I've got a few things to say about this new team. I seem to have missed their black and white appearance, so this was the first time I'd set eyes on them. For a Kung-Fu/Martial Arts group, they really please these weary old eyes (especially Lotus). I'm not a Kung-Fu fanatic, but I do occasionally pick up an issue of *Iron Fist.* These guys seem a bit different. I'll just say that I hope these dudes deal with more conventional fighters; the regular super-villain crowd. I'm not suggesting that you discontinue the other Martial Arts Format. It's just that it would be nice to see a different format within the Kung-Fu approach.

Anyway, it's time to say so long.

Doug Zimmerman
11322 Lafayette Street
Northglenn, Col.

Sorry if all that "hype" on the cover got to you, Doug, but, as the Torch was the featured *guest-star* of the previous issue, and as he *did* play a rather major role for at least *half* of the issue you refer to, we kinda feel that our cover blurb was, to say the least, justified. You also deal with a point that concerns us greatly here at Merry Marvel. A lot of readers who picked up on the *Spidey-Sons of the Tiger* team-up stated that they'd never seen the Sons...even though those worthies have seen at *least* twenty issues in our black-and-white *Deadly Hands of Kung Fu.* This is a distribution problem and, since we feel as strongly about our b&w line as we do about our color comics, all we can say is *subscribe,* effendi, and thou shalt not *miss*!

Dear Bill,

Congratulations on MTU #40. It was good to see the *Sons of the Tiger* in color. The characterizations remained clear and consistent, which doesn't always happen when too many known figures crowd into one story. To top it off, they played opposite Spider-Man very well. Spidey was his delightfully recognizable smartmouthed self.

Too bad the *Sons* don't have a color book. After all, they *are* (at least technically) three different colors.

William F. Wu
101 No. Ingalls #8
Ann Arbor, Michigan

Dear Marvel Mania,

MTU #40 was a real hit with me. The art was at it's normal *peak of greatness,* and I was *overjoyed* with the appearance of *Sons of the Tiger* along with *Spidey* and the *Torch.* But I noticed that you said it was their *first full color appearnace* anywhere. That's wrong! There was a *full color* appearance of *Sons of the Tiger* in *Savage Fists of Kung-Fu* #1. So, I'm asking for a no-prize for having sighted your mistake.

Jed Hotchkiss
Sherman Ct.
Box 42 Rt. 55
06784

Funny you should mention that, Jed. Y'see...okay, we admit it...we goofed. *Savage Fists* was *supposed* to have come out a little *after* MTU #40...but schedules being what they are in the Marvel Madhouse, something got switched, and the rest is history. Your no–prize is on the way.

Dear King People at Marvel,

MTU #40 was a good issue. I really liked the *Sons of the Tiger* and I think it was a fantastic idea to team them up with Spidey and the Torch. Mantlo's story and the art by Buscema and Esposito went together *perfectly.* The plot was just excellent. Making Big Man a woman was *fantastic.* Woman's Lib was probably shocked, but woman are equal in life *and* death, right?

I turned to pages two and three and found a big mess. The only thing missing from these two pages was the devil himself. The Torch throwing balls of flame, and Spidey dodging obstacles, knocking someone out with his webbing all at the time. *Wow!* Really great! Although I can't say it was very different. Spidey is always showing off.

In case you didn't know, I hardly ever write you without requesting a no-prize, and this letter's no exception. You gave the *Sons of the Tiger* the same costumes. The *Sons of the Tiger* have *never* worn the same costumes. Why should they now? They were just practicing, and since they never had the same outfits on when they were going to *show off* their Kung-Fu skills, why the change? I'll expect the no-prize soon.

Page 26, panel 6 and page 27, panel 1 were *ridiculous.* Even the Thing could never hit Sandman hard enough to knock him out. Why didn't Sandy just turn to sand? Huh, huh, why not? Why do the *Sons of the Tiger* wear red armbands and red belts? Wooldn't black be better for Kung-Fu experts?

All in all, MTU #40 was a very good issue. *Make Mine Marvel!*

Dan Munson
502 Westdale
Winona, Minn.

Okay, Dan...yours is Marvel. You too get a no-prize and the answer to all your questions (even the ones you didn't ask) is a resounding *Yes!* (Whew! Thought we'd *never* wriggle out of that one).

MARVEL VALUE STAMP

68: THE SILVER SURFER from *Marvel Team-Up* no. 44 (April 1976).

LET'S RAP WITH CAP

SEND YOUR LETTERS TO: THE MARVEL COMICS GROUP SIXTH FLOOR 575 MADISON AV NEW YORK 10022 N.Y.

Dear Marvel and Jack,

You bet your sweet association, Jack Kirby is back! Captain America lives again! While other artists draw, Jack Kirby paints. No one else can establish heroism as well as King Kirby. If he doesn't catapult Cap back to the top (where he deservedly belongs), I don't know if anyone can.

Tim Krenke
2730 North 46th Street
Milwaukee, WI 53201

We're sure that whatever the King does, he'll quickly bring Cap back into your favor, Tim, and we're sorry that you feel the Red, White, and Blue Avenger has stumbled in the past. But look out for the future— the best is yet to come!

Dear Gang,

After catching diabetes from the letter column in CAPTAIN AMERICA # 195, I decided some good old constructive criticism was needed. Of course, the issue itself helped me make that decision.

My main complaint is D. Bruce Berry. As inker, I suggest either Vince Colletta or Frank Giacoia.

This super-scientific plotline you've got going is fine, there is nothing wrong with it. But don't have these types of plots every issue, mix them up. Have Cap battle some super-science group for a few issues, then put him up against Batroc or Living Laser or some other superbaddie. However, if there is a steady diet of the super-science plots, Captain America will go the same route as (Devilish Competitor's books deleted) did. And that can't happen to Captain America.

Bill Kropfhauser
480 East Beck Street
Columbus, OH 43206

You should be glad to know (as your eyes have already told you if you've read this issue) that Frank Giacoia is here and plans to stay. And as for plots, well, we're not about to let the cat out of the bag about what happens in Cap's life *after* the completion of the current saga in ish #200. But keep watchin', Bill, we're sure to surprise ya!

Dear Jack,

I've got a few questions for you:

1) What else besides CAPTAIN AMERICA will you be doing for Marvel in the immediate future?

2) I'm dying to see you on the FANTASTIC FOUR again... any plans for that book?

3) Just because you've started doing CAP, are you going to stop doing cover work for Marvel?

4) Planning to unleash any new characters of your own for the Marvel line?

The Marveriter
Box 4112 S.R.A.
Anchorage, AL 99502

We've got a few answers for ya:

1&4) Jolly Jack has been awfully busy these past few months... busy whipping up a summer surprise which will be hitting the newsstands in June. It's an adaptation of a movie which you might have heard of— 2001: A SPACE ODYSSEY! In his spare time, Jack pencilled and scripted the CAPTAIN AMERICA ANNUAL, and created a new strip about a guy called Ikaris the Eternal which should be in your sweaty little palms next month. Look out for 'em, Marv— they shouldn't be missed!

2) Nope. Sorry.

3) Nay!! Perish forbid! And just to prove we're telling ya the honest-to-Aunt Petunia truth, just take a look at the cover of MARVEL PREMIERE #30, now on sale!

Dear Marvel,

I open to page one and there it is— Stan Lee/Writer; Jack Kirby/Artist; Frank Giacoia/Inker; Sam Rosen/Letterer. Then suddenly— POOF!! My dream was over.

Darn it!

Frank Alexander
Route 292
Holmes, NY 12531

Dreams can come true, Frank. They've come true in the past, and they can come true again in the future. So don't despair. Some day the super-team of Lee and Kirby may once again be joined. And what Marvelites have joined, let no Unbeliever put asunder, eh, Frankie?

Dear Jack,

Like any avid Marvel fan, I am really happy to see you back at Madcap Marvel.

Having you back on Captain America is, to say the least, great. Having read the latest three issues, it is easy to tell why you are heralded as "The Michelangelo of the comic book!"

Henry Marchand
799 Second Street
Secaucus, NJ 07094

Why, Hank?

Is it because Jack draws only while lying on his back? Is it because his astounding artwork is scrawled on pieces of plaster torn from his bathroom ceiling? Is it because he's five hundred years old?

"No!" comes the cry from the throngs of True Believers.

It's because they're both scared of heights.

We're only kidding. As every comics fan knows, it's because he's the one and only "King."

Nuff said.

THIS IS IT! YOUR

MARVEL VALUE STAMP

FOR THIS ISSUE!

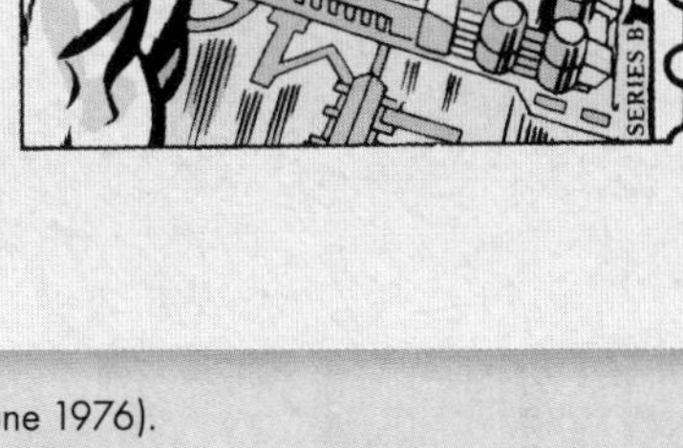

91: THE SILVER SURFER from *Captain America* no. 198 (June 1976).

CABLES OF CHAMPIONS

c/o MARVEL COMICS GROUP, 575 MADISON AVE. N.Y.C. 10022

Dear Marvel,

The Champions is a good name for the comic book. But I think that you have made a mistake! Why did you put the Iceman and Angel in the book?

The last time I saw them was in GIANT-SIZE X-MEN #1 when there were 12 (not counting the Beast) X-Men.

I think you should put in Black Goliath, Doc Samson or Star Hawk, because they don't have comic books of their own.

Make a new X-Men team! I know you can if you try!

Russell Jessie
755 Le Borune
La Puente, CA 91746

Have Black Goliath, Doc Samson, or Starhawk join the Champions because they don't have books of their own? Pooh!

Two of the three aforementioned heroes already have their own titles, although Starhawk will be sharing his with the Guardians of the Galaxy in MARVEL PRESENTS! And even Doc Samson is going to get a tryout all on his lonesome in a future issue of MARVEL SPOTLIGHT.

But what's this about a new X-MEN team? We already *have* a new X-MEN team, Russ, and author CHRIS CLAREMONT and artist DAVE COCKRUM are having enough heartache keeping tabs on their present heroes to want to start juggling team members again. But who knows *what* the future may bring, eh, Russ...?

Dear Stan and Co.,

Ten years ago a five-year old youth was introduced to the wonderful world of comic magazines via a book called THE FANTASTIC FOUR, written by Stan (the Man) Lee and drawn by Jack (King) Kirby.

Over the years the youth read suspenseful continued stories which progressed at a natural speed, stared at awesome art-work, had his morals shaped by the defeat of dastardly villains. Coped with a broken arm with the help of an injured web-slinger, enjoyed realistic dialogue and human problems, was shown the things wrong with the world and inspired to do something about them was voted "Most Intellectual" in school (with much credit ot MARVEL), and amassed a collection of over 1500 comics, including SPIDER-MAN #'s 1 and 2.

With CHAMPIONS #1, MARVEL's place in his life was strengthened even more. Some of Don Heck's best art ever, the suspenseful last page, the villains, the dialogue, etc. were all there.

Stan, Jack, Roy, etc...all the youth can say is—"Thanks for the memories... and the present... and the future."

Danny Tyree
1188 Verona Road
Lewisburg, TN 37091

And thank you, Danny, for such a touching letter—yes, verily (as Herc himself might have said), it hath brought a tear to our eyes! We're glad you've grown up with us, and what makes us even prouder is that our stories have progressed and changed and grown up along with you. Just thinking of it makes all the hard work worthwhile.

Pass us a handkerchief, Irv, before we drown!

Dear Tony and Don,

The first issue was a blockbuster. I have been collecting comics for only a year, so I didn't hear of the Angel or Iceman till Champions broke loose. The story took on an original form. (I had expected the superheroes to just get together and name themselves) and the end left me impatiently waiting for the 2nd issue. Don Heck's art was good as always. The combination was different. To think of it! The Angel and Ghost Rider as a part of a team! Oh well, until your next issue.

Stephen Ryan
11204 Farmland, DR.
Rockville, MD 20852

We're glad that we managed to shock you with an ending, Steve, but what's even better is that we've introduced you to two of our favorite heroes—Iceman and The Angel! Be sure to catch more of them in back issues of the X-MEN, and if it's still on sale somewhere, last summer's GIANT-SIZE X-MEN! Professor X will be X-pecting you!

Dear Marvel,

Today I picked up MARVEL CHILLERS #1, THE CHAMPIONS #1 and THE INHUMANS #1. All three were great but I would like to talk about THE CHAMPIONS. Tony Isabella's scripting, and Don Heck's art were far better than usual. Also I liked the angel's new costume. Who designed it?

Pluto, Ares & Hippolyta are good foes. In the future how about The Vanisher, Magneto and The Executioner and The Enchantress. All of these villains have fought at least one of The Champions. Good luck and here's to monthly publication.

Donald Wilson
1 N. Meadow L.
Richmond, VA 23230

Len Wein and Johnny Romita gladly accept your kudos for the Angel's new costume, since it was they who sat down on a sultry summer afternoon and thunk it up.

And your villains list will be greedily looked upon, Dan—it'll help save the Tiger from brain strain this Spring! Bless you m'boy! See ya in sixty!

MARVEL VALUE STAMP

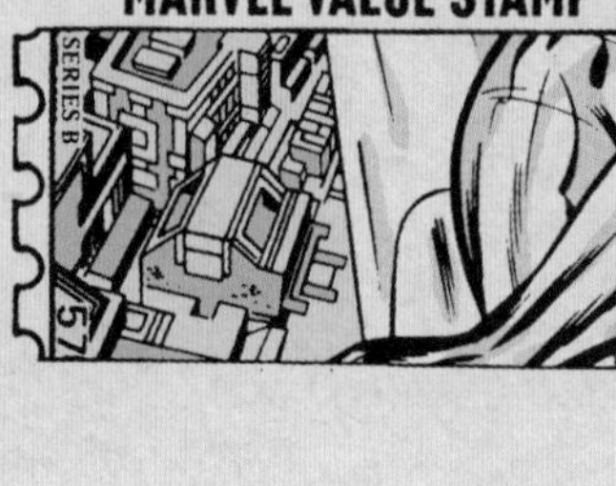

57: THE SILVER SURFER from *The Champions* no. 4 (March 1976).

DEFENDERS DIALOGUE

c/o MARVEL COMICS GROUP, 575 MADISON AVE. N.Y.C. 10022

Dear Defending Dynamoes,

I hate to tell you this, but the Defenders aren't going to work. The original idea of a group that is a non-team and doesn't really exist isn't going to last because as long as the four main Defenders (Hulk, Dr. Strange, Valkyrie, and Nighthawk) live and fight together, they will become a team in almost every sense of the word, and, not a non-team.

In FOOM #7 the Avengers' butler Jarvis states that there is no interdependency which binds the Avengers together as a team. But there is an interdependency which holds the Defenders together. There must be. All the Defenders are really "lost souls" (Dr. Strange might be the exception to the rule) who have found their places in life as Defenders.

Hulk and the Valkyrie are most obvious as "lost souls" because of their pasts. The Hulk has been tortured and persecuted his entire life, with only a few friendships, none of which have lasted. He has finally found friends and he realizes it, so why should he leave? Who would?

Valkyrie is really a lost soul. She was, as we all know, created by the Enchantress into the body of Barbara Denton Norriss. She has managed to scrape up Barbara's past, including an unwanted husband, but she has no real past of her own to build on. So she stays with the Defenders, where she belongs, and where she has friends who care about her. Let us not forget the relationships that she has built with the other Defenders. With Dr. Strange I see a sister and brother relationship. She is carrying on a troubled romance with Kyle. The most interesting of these relationships is that which I see has developed between herself and the Hulk. I would say that the Hulk almost has a crush, of sorts, on Val. And Val has grown quite fond of this greenskinned goliath with the mind of a small child. Nighthawk has gone from an aimless millionaire to an aimless villain. He has finally found his aim in life and his fulfillment as a Defender. What more can be said?

Dr. Strange is almost the exception. He has fulfillment and aim elsewhere. He has a past, he has a future. For all of these years he has been operating very well; he does not need steam.

Except, he is a loner of sorts. Even though he has saved humanity, he has remained apart from it. Very few humans even know of his existence. His relationship with Wong is strictly business. Clea is a loner. Other than those two, and besides the Defenders, he has no other human relations. Now perhaps, isn't he remaining with the Defenders because he needs other people? Because he can't exist as an island any longer? The others need their individual forms of fulfillment, he needs other people.

So there is an interdependency which holds the Defenders together. I say fine. Let their relationships grow and evolve as they must. It will be these relationships which decide who comes and who leaves the Defenders. But let it be natural. Don't foresee anything because you think so-and-so would look nice in this magazine.

I would like to see one or two new members though. Four isn't a very big group. Especially when two of the characters have their series and can't do much developing here. Let Steve Gerber create a new female character. I'm very much in favor of that.

Larry (the Fooman Torch) Twiss
227 Fox Run
King of Prussia, PA 19405

By way of insight, Larry, this new cohesiveness developing among the Defenders came as a surprise to Steve G., too. When he first assumed the writing duties on the book, Steve assumed the greatest challenge would be keeping four such completely "incompatible" personalities together in the same room for more than five minutes at a stretch.

In the space of just a few issues, however, it became clear that although Doc, Val, Kyle, and Greenie had virtually nothing in common, they complemented one another to a degree not seen since the advent of another fabulous foursome back in 1961.

The next several issues— which will comprise the weirdest "series" this magazine has ever seen— should provide ample evidence to support our thesis. And if you disagree, even if you hate every panel on every page, there's still one good reason to keep reading THE DEFENDERS:

Steve Gerber,

Please do something with the elf who appeared in DEFENDERS #25. You don't know mental agony and futility until you spend nights pondering a character who does not belong, does not fit in with what is happening, and who has apparently been forgotten about. I feel more paranoid and disturbed by the moment. I implore you to resolve his story before I go berserk and become a weather prophet.

Please?

Bill Burnworth
1821 Fletcher Street
Anderson, IN 46016

The elf appears again this issue. Wouldn't you like to know why?

See you in thirty days?

THIS IS IT! YOUR
MARVEL VALUE STAMP
FOR THIS ISSUE!

CLIP 'EM AND COLLECT 'EM!

12: THE SILVER SURFER from *The Defenders* no. 31 (January 1976).

Tomes to the Tomb!

c/o MARVEL COMICS GROUP, 575 MADISON AVE. N.Y.C. 10022

Dear Marv, Gene, Tom, and John:

For years now—three of four of them, precisely—I've watched the ever-continuing struggles of Drake, Harker, and Van Helsing against lord Dracula's cunning, all-convulsive pr de and bloodlust. I've watched and have been tensed to the slow, continuing, yet always *advancing* storylines as the characters first presented themselves, as their lives, loves and fears were unfolded, bit by bit I've watched as a host of other people, other thoughts, other ideas have entered into the web, not so much as flies to the spider than as honey-bees to the Venus fly-trap—equal creatures with inherent hopes and promises drawn to a natural beauty that cannot pretend to be, down deep, anything else, that must devour, like it or not and even so, to simply exist. I've seen death far too many times, enough to feel growing and growing within me a resentment that man feels the need to kill himself rather than band together as one human race against damnable parasites of any kind. And I've seen a world, no matter what, that is not my own, a world that offers no facades, no glossed-over veneers of con-man deceit, an omnipotent, omnipresent viewpoint that, if t'were reality, would give more insights in a day than an organized religion could do in a hundred hundred years.

That's how I see TOMB OF DRACULA: that's how I've been seeing it for unaccountable months since Marv Wolfman first took to scripting it. Perhaps I see it as one long novel, as a single story carried out chapter by chapter, nothing rushed, nothing hurried, nothing left to a questionable quality. Everything about the strip has proclaimed its high standards to its audience without being showy or flashy about it. Maybe Gene Colan *is* often forgotten, grouped less with the Kirbys and the Sterankos than with others—but he consistently puts his soul and heart's desire into every page, panel, line, every tone, every shadow, every single expression of fear, happiness, disbelief, shock, pain and satiated lust. Tom Palmer knows how to bring every nuance of Gene's details out into clarity, out into dark, moody openness. Totally and without any restrictions or exceptions, Gene Colan and Tom Palmer are the greatest and most versatile *art team* of this decade. Placed together with Marv Wolfman's fluid writing style, escalating climaxes, and sheer imaginative expertise, you have made TOMB OF DRACULA a book I have always looked to for consistently excellent entertainment. It's a quality product put together with love and a craftsman's skill.

In finality, I'd like to state belatedly the purpose of this perhaps enthusiastic missive. I don't want to see TOD cancelled at all—and if this single person can help in anyway to keep that from happening, my zealous aid will always be ready. There are a lot of others, too, who feel precisely the same way. Good luck.

Frank S. Lovece
947 Maple Drive
Morgantown, WV 26505

Which, Franky, is maybe the best time to tell you that, at least for the present, TOD will not be cut in frequency. No, Faithful Ones, unfortunately the reason is *not* because of a sudden upsurge in sale., but because TOD is one of Marvel's best selling British titles, and, consequently, we must keep it going here to help out our mother-country. Well, for the present, Marvelous Marv, Gentleman Gene, and Terrific Tom will be content with that; however, we'd like to think we can sell America's number one fear magazine in this country as well. And, of course, if sales really do dip beneath a somewhat respectable percentage margin, TOD will be cut back. The war is not over, Dracophiles—there's just a temporary truce.

Dear Marv, Gene, and Tom,

With all the awe-inspiring events occurring in TOMB OF DRACULA over the last few issues, a letter of comment is definitely in order. As much as I'm aware that Dracula is perhaps the most despicable villain to stalk the earth, I have to admit my sympathies have been with him to some extent as he finds his powers slowly draining away. Most especially, I felt a certain empathy towards him this issue, #39, as the Prince of Darkness fought against overwhelming odds in what was a battle with a foregone conclusion; Dracula was going to die. Perhaps it's the sense of warped nobility he exudes, or the fact that Dr. Sun is an even more reprehensible personage than Dracula, whatever, I was really rooting for Vlad in his desperate conflict with Sun's lackey, Juno. There was a certain unconquerable majesty in the way Dracula fought back against such a massive adversary, though his own powers had been halved. His fighting "spirit" refused to accept defeat, and I can think of no other term to accurately describe it, though I know how repulsive that term sounds when it's suggested as an attribute of Dracula. It's quite a tribute to you as an author, Marv, to bring about this reaction in a member of your audience, for this character has become so real we even feel for him when intellectually we're aware that a perverse human parasite has just been executed. What's more, I thought only Shakespeare capable of injecting a healthy dose of humor through several outrageous characters in a dire circumstance, but with Harold H. Harold and Aurora Rabinowitz stumbling somewhat flat-footedly into a den of evil, and not muffling my enjoyment of the story a single bit, in fact, enhancing it, you've got yourself one heck of a literary talent Mr. Wolfman.

Of course I was exceedingly let down to read last issue that sales of DRACULA have fallen lately. I'm certain it had to do with the glutting of the market with far too many horror titles, and in a short time, sales will have risen again. We both know this book deserves far better than cancellation.

The Colan-Palmer art team just staggers my imagination with their pencil-ink virtuosity, and they have indubitably established Marvel's Dracula as the definitive, visual version.

Marv, let me offer my sincerest hopes for the continuance of TOMB OF DRACULA for many, many years to come. One final thing. Are we ever going to see the Thomas-Giordano adaptation of Stoker's DRACULA continued, or is the project dead for good? And will we ever see that fascinating vampiress, Lilith, in these pages or elsewhere? Her series was still in its formative stages when DRACULA LIVES was cancelled, and left her without a home.

Ralph Macchio
188 Wilson Drive
Cresskill, NJ 07626

Ralph, we thank you for your comments, and, Marv, Gene, and Tom also wish to thank the *thousands* of you out there who have expressed their heartfelt hopes that Drac survives its current fight.

Believe us when we say this—we really *want* Drac to continue—even more than you do (after all, besides enjoying writing and drawing the blamed things, we actually get *paid* for the job—if doing this book can be called a job, when we all really dig it so much).

MARVEL VALUE STAMP

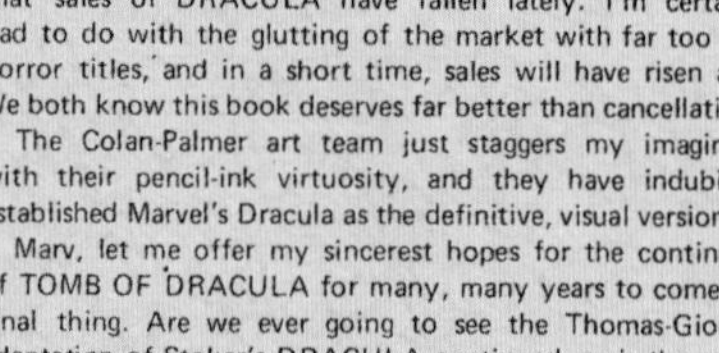

43: THE SILVER SURFER from *Tomb of Dracula* no. 42 (March 1976).

Tomes to the Tomb!

c/o MARVEL COMICS GROUP, 575 MADISON AVE. N.Y.C. 10022

Dear Marv, Gene, and Tom,

Interesting, very interesting. That is what I have to say about T.O.D. #37. I loved the whole story. The art, everything. The two things that I really liked most were the characters. Harold H. Harold. What a name, but this guy proves to be a most unique person. He is someone I can relate to totally; his personality and mine are almost identical; frustrated, yet he still seems to hold his sense of humor even at the very worst of times. I hope you don't intend to write him off with next issue. True, he has no definite purpose as to the doing away of Dracula like Van Helsing or Drake, but I think that if somehow you could fit him in permanently that it would do the book one better. True, this is a "horror" book but like any other book it needs its humor somewhere along the lines as a relief.

Now for something completely different....Frank Drake. Ever since the first issue he has been sitting there and hardly anything has been done with him. Unlike Quincy, who over the past couple of issues we have found out more than anybody else with maybe the exception of Taj. That talk that Brother Voodoo gave him was just what the doctor ordered. Frank Drake is the only relative of Dracula that must account for something, surely now he doesn't want to stop his crusade to kill the ancestor that brought disgrace to its name!! After all the name was so bad that Frank changed it.

I'll have to end now because this letter is entirely too long, so I'll leave you guys with the only words I can find fit at this time to describe this issue........... WELL DONE.

John J. Lewandowski
182 Griffith Street
Jersey City, NJ 07307

Dear Marvel,

What have you done? You've taken a classic horror comic and turned it into a copy of AARGH! I'm referring to TOMB OF DRACULA #37, which was possibly one of the biggest wastes of my money! Personally, I like AARGH! But I don't buy T.O.D. for a humor story. Harold H. Harold—sigh!

C'mon, Marv! Stick to the serious side of Dracula.

On a lighter side: I'm glad to see that Frank Drake has finally "got it together," and found out that his place is indeed with Rachel and Quincy.

As shown to us on pages 11 ,14 & 15: It is Dr. Sun behind the power drain of Dracula. But Juno looks like a carbon-copy of Razor Fist, in a past issue of MOKF. Anyway, he does look like an interesting character.

And now I leave on this short note:

Yea, Colan n' Palmer.

Larry Dean
6362 Laurentian Ct.
Flint, MI 48504

Harold and Aurora brought forth more comments than virtually any other TOMB OF DRACULA characters, with readers either loving or hating our dubious duo. As for the reason for the characters, well, as Marvelous Marv put it—"Drac's been such a downer for so long, we needed something up just so you'd know where down is!" We've been kinda wondering about our wild Wolfman ever since he ascended to the editorial throne. But then, we always heard that when one became an erudite editor, one had to go through a frontal lobotomy.

Dear Transylvanian Armadillos:

The Boston area is a fine place to live, but it's so quiet. Nothing much ever happens. Oh, last month there was all that noise at the airport as if they were firing all these guns at somebody, but that was unusual.

Anyway, I was walking through Boston Common last night analyzing TOMB OF DRACULA #37 for one of my many fans (actually I was talking to myself but I'm using poetic license) and, incidentally, describing my plans for graduate study. "Yes, fan," said I, "soon you will be able to call me Doctor Sanderson."

A guy with big teeth and a cape whipped about. "Sun?" he muttered, "Doctor Sun? It can't be. He's neither Oriental nor disembodied. But I can't afford to ignore him, for even now my powers are waning, and I must never die again!"

"Who's the cliche expert?" my fan asked.

"Oh, probably a foreigner here for the Bicentennial. Hear the accent? Probably took a crash course in English and didn't get beyond learning stilted constructions. We'd sound the same speaking high school French to Frenchmen.Anyway,T.O.D.#37 is a departure for the series. It's the mag's first comedy and a good one, too. Harold H. Harold (undoubtedly named after *Catch-22's* Major Major Major) is a likable incompetent we can still identify with. He's sort of a Woody Allen type, and Wolfman gives him good witty dialogue.

At that precise moment, the guy in the cape leapt out of a tree towards us. Unfortunately, he didn't make it all the way. He got caught in the branches and just dangled there, mumbling Rumanian curses.

"Ignore him," I told my fan. "He's just looking for attention. It might not be so funny next issue if Dracula bites Harold. Wolfman may be trying for an abrupt shift of mood from farce to terror. We'll see. I'm very pleased with the Boston setting, of course, but I wish Gene Colan had drawn in some identifiable locations. Wolfman's references to Beacon Hill and Harvard are good, and I suppose the opening scene took place right here on the Common. Specific references to places give readers the sense they really are in Boston, so the more there are, the better, as long as it doesn't get excessive and self-conscious."

"Do you suppose Wolfman went to Harvard?"

"If he's having Drac murder Harvard students? He probably went to Yale."

We saw the guy in the cape leap again, so we ducked and he went right over our heads and down the staircase to the underground trolley. He sure made a racket falling down those stairs. I hope he had a token.

Then this other clown runs up to me. "Hey, mister, do you know any vampires I can interview?"

"Vampires! In Boston? Are you crazy? Get out of here before I call the cops!" The nerve of some people.

Next month I'll find someplace quiet to do my critique of T.O.D. Harvard Yard, maybe?

Peter Sanderson
27 Gov. Belcher Lane
Milton, MA 02186

THIS IS IT! YOUR
MARVEL VALUE STAMP
FOR THIS ISSUE!

CLIP 'EM AND COLLECT 'EM!

8: THE SILVER SURFER from *Tomb of Dracula* no. 40 (January 1976).

DEFENDERS DIALOGUE

c/o MARVEL COMICS GROUP, 575 MADISON AVE. N.Y.C. 10022

Dear Marvel,

The last five issues (GIANT-SIZE DEFENDERS #5 and DEFENDERS #26-29) have given the Guardians of the Galaxy a good point of embarkment. I'm not too crazy about the solar sails or cranial aelerons of Starhawk's costume, but that is my biggest criticism. I can hardly wait to see the Guardians' first issue, and I hope that a really good artist has been chosen for them.

As for the Defenders, they were their usual excellent selves, which poses a problem. People, I'm getting bored. Sure, I buy them, I read them, I love them, but the excitement is gone. Maybe there's too much character study. I'm not sure. I do think, in any case, that the Defenders need someone new for permanent membership. There should be a variety of characters to explore, not just the Valkyrie, who is all we've seen of late. (Granted, Nighthawk had his bit with the Sons of the Serpent, but Val had her share, too.)

In #29, I suffered one disappointment: the involvement of Jack Norriss. His role was of dubious importance. He stunned a guard and watched Doc make fences vanish and Badoon legions fall asleep. No wonder he believed that he wasn't needed. He wasn't! But had Doc just said that so major an undertaking would require all his attention, Jack would have been a necessary advantage. After all, how could the Vishanti help Doc dissolve fences if a Badoon is shooting him in the back?

Small deals like this make the Doc more fallibly human, with perhaps a smattering of limitation, as well as the wisdom to exercise caution while casting spells. Also, it gives Jack more of a place hanging around the Defenders. However, I don't want Norriss to be an "everyman": Steve used that angle when the crowds saw Jack attack the Sons of the Serpent to save Val. Steve wisely avoided having the slave hordes inspired by "what one man can do" at the Badoon camps.

The Defenders are good, and I hope they will be better. In the end, you'll always have me for a reader: how enthusiastic I'll be is another story.

Rich Hango
83 Hazel Street
Clifton, NJ 07011

Point-by-point, Rich:

Al Milgrom will be illustrating the GUARDIANS strip. We think he qualifies as a "really good artist," don't you? (Steve G., natch, will be doing the writing on that book, too.)

We've been exploring Nighthawk a little more thoroughly recently, and there's more to come. We promise.

Also, very soon, in yet another complete reversal of our position on the issue, Steve and Sal *will* be introducing a "new" character for potential permanent membership in the Defenders. And, believe us, it's just about the *last* character you ever expected to see again, anywhere!

Regarding Jack Norriss' role as aide to Doc in the liberation campaign: it *was* necessary, for exactly the reasons you stated. Steve omitted mention of the fact because (a) he felt it seemed obvious, and (b) there wasn't a whole heck of a lot of space to go into details. Dr. Strange does have limitations...even though every time we try to illustrate them a couple hundred letters pour in telling us Doc can do anything. (He can't, folks. Sorry.) And the need to summon up concentration in order to cast a perfect spell is one of those. Further (and we think Steve Englehart would agree with this), the more complex the spell, the greater the concentration required. The Sorcerer Supreme, he is; God, he ain't. It's that simple, really.

Dear Marvel,

It took a very long time (and several rereadings) for me to figure out why I didn't like DEFENDERS #29. I think it was the ending, because when it was all over, I sat there muttering, "What? What?! What was that?"

At first, I thought the concept you were trying to get across was too complex, or perhaps too simplistic, or at least badly explained. Actually, taken in itself (and yes, it could've stood a more complete explanation), it was a rather neat idea. It was the idea's mouthpiece that jarred. Jack Norriss is not (or in the past was not) a very good person or a very good husband, and now we are being asked to believe in his insight and courage and untutored wisdom. Further, if I read you aright, we are now playing poor misunderstood Jack against the big bad old Defenders. We pity him, because his wife doesn't think of him. Nighthawk resents him.

The conclusion that Jack made may have been a valid one, but he came out sounding a little too much like a Rick Jones, plain old human among the superfolks type. At a guess, Steve, you're beginning to pour a little too much of yourself into this character, as you did in other ways with Richard Rory in MAN-THING. This is the wrong mag for that, because it's one where the characters are capable of seeing and voicing things for themselves. Norriss' role in THE DEFENDERS is too crucial at present for even the smallest bit of ego-tripping to be harmless.

For one thing, it's a mistake to have him trailing along on their missions. We all know the members have their personal lives, but that doesn't give them the right to drag groupies along. Kyle and Trish thrashed out their hassles during off-duty hours: let Val and Jack do the same. It gives the story more depth, anyway.

By the way, he's got to stop calling her "Barbara."

Jo Duffy
311 Davis Hall
Wellesley College, Wellesley, MA 02181

• Surprise, Jo— he has! Which may just be an indication of how harshly you've judged him. The facts are, we don't know how good a person or how good a husband he was to Val/Barbara. We only know that he got mixed up, as did she, with a cult that sent Mrs. Norriss hurtling into the dimension of the Nameless Ones. Whether Jack was in favor of that— whether *Barbara* was, for that matter— is still open to question. We do know that he left the cult after Barbara's sacrifice and that he spent the several years thereafter in seclusion. So maybe Jack really wasn't overly thrilled with the way things worked out for himself and his new bride.

Think about it. His behavior since re-entering Val's life hasn't been so much malicious as it's been utterly bewildered! Now, as time passes, he's beginning to work things through. And the results, we guarantee, are going to take all of Marveldom by surprise...and not necessarily *pleasantly*.

That's it for this issue's Dialogue, folks. Join us again in thirty days. Until then, don't let the sun catch you crying, and patronize your friendly neighborhood Ludberdite.

THIS IS IT! YOUR

MARVEL VALUE STAMP

FOR THIS ISSUE!

CLIP 'EM AND COLLECT 'EM!

26: THE SILVER SURFER from *The Defenders* no. 32 (February 1976).

THE HAMMER STRIKES

c/o MARVEL COMICS GROUP, 575 MADISON AVE. N.Y.C. 10022

Marv,

THOR #241—ah, such a comic! I had wondered how the Egyptian gods series was going to end. I was very glad to see that Horus and company ended as friends to the god of thunder and hope to see more of them quite soon.

I was also very pleased to see that you took no liberties with the name "Nut." It might strike the modern reader as a bit strange, but anything good enough for the pyramid builders is good enough for me, and should be good enough for Marvel. Realism, and all that.

Bill Mantlo, probably the finest writer you have corralled since Steve Gerber, turned out a script that was neither overly action-packed nor overly cerebral. It was not Shazam! material, but solid nonetheless.

Can we assume that Buscema and Sinnott worked on this comic as they did on a couple of FANTASTIC FOUR's a while ago? Whatever style they used, I want to see more of it. The art turned out so dark and moody that it fit the strip perfectly. Encore!

David B. Kirby
2816 Monument Avenue, Apt. 1-B
Richmond, VA 23221

Dear Marvel,

I hate to be picky since I really enjoy THOR. However, I think I found a mistake in the artwork of #241. On page 23 in the last panel Seth is holding a sword in his right hand ready to anihilate Thor. But as we returned to this confrontation four pages later, Seth is suddenly holding his sword in his left hand. Now unless Seth is ambidextrous and did a quick sword switch, you guys goofed. No offense John and Joe, but I think I deserve a No-Prize.

Eric Nelson
Hinman Box 3525
Dartmouth College
Hanover, NJ 03755

Oh, all right, Eric, your No-Prize is on the way—but *handle* it with care, willya, you know how fragile the little devils are!

But now, on to the responses to the letter from a Ms. Polly Goodnough published in THOR #241...

Dear Marvel,

In a democracy, we usually hear both sides of an important issue. On the matter of the Sif/Jane/Thor triangle, Marveldom has heard Ms. Goodnough's point of view; I request that Marveldom now hear mine.

Although Sif is a lovely, strong and self-sacrificing Goddess, Thor obviously needs more than this in a woman. I speak in avid defense of the "scorned" Jane Foster. I am an old fan of Thor's. I have seen the love and loyalty that Thor has given to Jane and, after many years, feel that she is the true mate, the *only* mate for Thor. After all, Thor is not always a God, right? And does Sif love the mortal Don Blake?

Jane does. It is Jane who can love and relate to him as a Sif *never* could—Jane loves the man and the God and understands them both. Thor was not being a cad when he left Sif for Jane. Not even the threat of losing his powers could make Thor lose the memory of the true love of his life—Jane Foster. I realize that I fight for the underdog in this battle, but I am moved to speak. Sif was not forced into giving her life for Jane's. She gave it because she wanted to, because she loved Thor and knew he loved another. From the time Thor held Jane's weak hand, Sif knew what she had to do. Sif gave Thor his beloved because she knew that was what he wanted more than anything—even above her love.

Thor is no cad; he deserves to have his Jane and Sif deserves the right to stick to her choice. If Ms. Goodnough and Marveldom really love Sif, they'll stand by her and welcome Jane back to the world of the living and Thor's arms. For Sif knew what Ms. Goodnough does not— Jane is Thor's true love, he finds love in her arms and in Sif's he found solace. I pray that Marveldom lets Thor have his love, for it will burn brighter than *any* hopefully lit candle.

Patricia McCoy
9864 Stearns Ave
Oakland, CA 94605

Sirs:

I have just finished reading the letter-essay from Polly Goodnough in the November issue of Thor, and I must echo the general sentiment behind it, if not its somewhat mawkish expression.

It is the first issue of Thor I have purchased since the July issue, wherein my wild, unfounded hopes led me to believe you might rectify your error by killing off Jane Foster and somehow reinstating Sif as a flesh-and-blood immortal...

I've seen too many of the touchingly vulnerable female foils the Marvel heroes take such delight in rescuing from the results of their own helpless feminine stupidity. I'm tired of the sweet young things who serve as bound and gagged props in a drama where their only notable contribution is a bravely quivering chin and a shouted warning to the delivering hero.

There is a genuine psychological need for such as Sif—a woman who stands beside instead of behind her male consort. Sif conducts herself with a dignity and pride alien to the extremely ordinary, uninteresting, and weak-minded Jane Foster, whose simpering dialogue seems pirated from the pages of "True Romance"—it's positively peppered with copious "darlings" and "beloveds." Sif does not indulge in exhibitionistic weeping; it seems to be one of Jane Foster's natural states. I can readily envision Jane Foster drowning as she wallows in her own tears while begging for her life—and/or Thor's—at the foot of Loki's throne; Sif, I can only picutre rallying the troops for rescue operations, bless her.

In short, gentlemen, I believe you've mistakenly killed the wrong woman. I strongly suggest that you deliver Sif to her own reincarnated body, and let Jane Foster expire touchingly, tearfully, graciously in a final scene that just MIGHT possibly redeem her memory. If not, I, too, see no alternative but washing my hands entirely of what is beginning to be the disgustingly maudlin Thor series.

J. Philipps
4587 Alps Drive
Mehlville, MO 63129

Now do you understand, dear peoples, why comic book editors go mad? For every letter requesting...nay, *demanding* that we return Sif to Thor's side, there was an equally emotional missive threatening us with the fires of Geirrodur's furnace if we do anything to upset the recent reuniting of Thor with Jane Foster.

MARVEL VALUE STAMP

50: THE SILVER SURFER from *Thor* no. 245 (March 1976).

CONAN THE BARBARIAN™

"Know, O prince, that between the years when the oceans drank Atlantis and the gleaming cities, and the rise of the sons of Aryas, there was an Age undreamed of.

Hither came Conan, the Cimmerian, black-haired, sullen-eyed, sword in hand, a thief, a reaver, a slayer, with gigantic melancholies and gigantic mirth, to tread the jeweled thrones of the Earth under his sandaled feet."

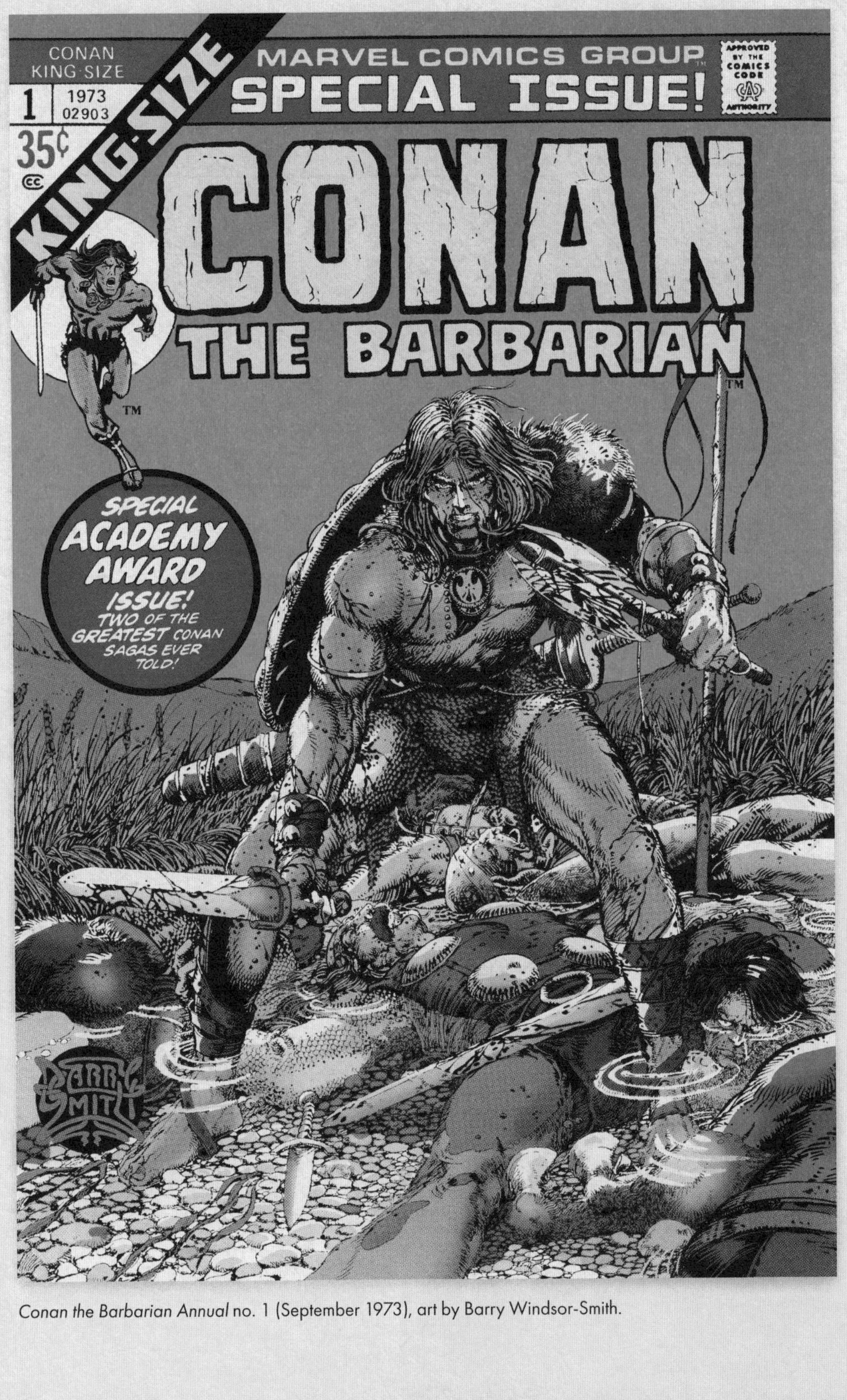

Conan the Barbarian Annual no. 1 (September 1973), art by Barry Windsor-Smith.

THE EVER-LOVIN' BLUE-EYED

LETTERS PAGE!

c/o MARVEL COMICS GROUP, 575 MADISON AVE., NEW YORK, N.Y. 10022

Roy, Bill and Bob,

My compliments on Two-In-One # 11. I think it was excellent. It had the kind of plot that is considered a classic. Now there are only two problems: (1) Why, on the cover, is the golem talking? (2) On page 28, panel 2, the Thing says, "....after tacklin' the Golem, you guys are Jello." Now I ask – how the heck does he know that the monster is the Golem when throughout the beginning he just talks of him as a "statue-faced monster." Please give me a no-prize. Please. It would be my first one. Have a heart.

Michael J. Vassallo
31-25 58th Street
Woodside, NY 11377

Give this man a no-prize... ***but,*** **if you'll just open to page 22, and begin reading from the second panel, all will be made clear to you.**

And now for the gamma ray controversy...

Dear Bullpen:

You guys produce the best comics in the business!! However, lest you get swelled heads, you make some of the worst mistakes. On page 6, panel 6, Ol' Benjy is feeling sorry for himself, and in his mind asks, "I wonder why them gamma rays picked orange?" If gamma rays made him the Thing, he would be a "walking pile of *green* rocks!" Cosmic rays, not gamma rays are what turned Ben Grimm into the Thing! Remember?

Foomer Jim McNamara
1610 Metropolitan Avenue
Bronx, NY 10462

Dear Gang:

Ben says that gamma rays made him the Thing. Any true Marvelite knows that it was cosmic rays that made him that way (gamma rays picked on Bruce Banner, remember?).

Besides the goof-up, it was a very good story with fine art work.

Mark Blair
Austin, TX

Len,

Correct me if I am wrong, but wasn't it *cosmic* rays which changed Ben Grimm into that orange pile of rocks? Anyway, gamma rays change you green! (See the Hulk, the Leader, the Abomination.)

David Burd
95 Brookwood Road
Clifton, NJ 07012

Dear Marvel,

...Two in One #11 was pretty good except for one Boo-Boo! Any Marvelite knows that the Thing was not hit by gamma rays. The *Hulk* was.

Alex Porter
341 West Gate
St. Louis, MO 63130

Dear Roy, Bill, Bob & Jack:

...You guys said that the Thing was created by gamma rays. Now am I wrong, or was it supposed to be cosmic rays, or maybe you've just made a slight mistake...?

Raymond Talogy
28-28 35th Street
Long Island City, NY 11103

Bill and Len were just made aware of the catastrophy — they seem to be turning green in a poorly lit corner of the room and can't comment at this time. Anyway, wouldn't life be rather dull (and this page empty) without a few harmless mistakes?

Dear Marvel,

Marvel Two-In-One #11 was welcome, since it contained the long-awaited conclusion to the Golem series. One thing about Marvel is that even if a series is cancelled, you find some way to tie up the loose ends somehow, somewhere. It is this fetish for continuity that makes Marvel unique. I must take issue, however, with Roy and Bill's handling of the Thing on those first few pages. The action starts with the Thing running around, knocking people over, because he's late for a train. We then find out that he stiffed a cab driver for his fare (by hanging him up on a stop sign yet) because *he* couldn't be bothered carrying change because the trunks he likes to wear won't hold them. He then knocks down the gate keeper (along with the gate) and then proceeds to wreck the entire train platform in an effort to stop the train that he was late for. I understand that Marvel wants to get away from the goody-good type hero, but isn't this a bit much? Then, when the Thing gets on the train, he wonders why the people still think of him as a monster. After the things he did, I'd be afraid to go near him even if he looked like the Black Widow! I know that Reed Richards will supposedly pay for it, but he ran up damages that must have totaled thousands of dollars. So take it easy on this kind of stuff in the future, huh? It's this kind of stuff that makes a fella agree with J.J. Jameson's outlook on super-heroes.

Larry Feldman
1445 E. 102 St.
Brooklyn, NY 11236

Actually, Bashful Benjamin was a bit overzealous and Roy and Bill have decided that it was just another case of repressed anxiety. They simply allowed Ben to wreck a considerable portion of Grand Central Station, while attempting to catch the train to Disney World, thereby releasing dangerous "bottled-up" frustrations resulting from their own daily commuter shuffle.....yep, it's just amazing how we tie all those loose ends.

THIS IS IT! YOUR

MARVEL VALUE STAMP

FOR THIS ISSUE!

CLIP 'EM AND COLLECT 'EM!

11: CONAN THE BARBARIAN from *Marvel Two-in-One* no. 13 (January 1976).

not only the Human Torch but also Reed and Sue about to enter Hyper-Space was deliberate. After all, the name of the mag is FANTASTIC FOUR, and it's always been our policy (at least, we *think* it has) to take a little dramatic license (see letter from Rich Hango, above) in order to present a more intriguing cover. It's not that we have any vested interest in *lying* to you or anything: rather, it's that we feel the cover of F.F. # 163 was, as we say, "symbolically true," and that's all we ask. Ah, but if you had mentioned in your letter that Gaard has six fingers on his left toe— now *that's* the way to win a no-prize, for sure!

Dear Marvel,

I've been reading, enjoying, and collecting your comics for many a year. FANTASTIC FOUR, Starlin's WARLOCK, and anything that Doug Moench writes are my favorites.

Two things have prompted me to write, however. First is your policy of continued stories. I know it's hard to start and finish a story in one issue, but when it takes three or four issues to end a tale, this (to me, at least) is ridiculous!

Second is the credits. Now, I know what an author is, and what an editor is, and a letterer, too. But in the name of bashful Benjy's Aunt Pětunla, what is the difference between an artist, a colorer, an inker, and an embellisher?

Glen Held
2913 Montgomery Street, Wantaugh, NY 11793

Ah, your second paragraph really takes us back, Glen— to those halcyon days in the middle 1960's when Smilin' Stan Lee and Jack (King) Kirby first introduced the continued-story concept, which had gone unused in the comics medium for some years. The battle of the letters-pages raged for a long time, but in the end it seemed that the mass of Marveldom Assembled was quite content, nay, *eager* to give the Bullpen all the room it needed to tell the kind of story its artists and writers wanted to tell— be it one issue, or a dozen. We thought the matter was pretty well settled by now; but, if some of the rest of you want to join Glen in re-opening it— well, we can't fill these lavish letters-pages with love-notes to Jovial Joe Rosen, can we?

As to your second point: It may vary a bit, but generally we've been using the term "artist" to refer mainly to the man who pencils the story, or to that occasional illustrator who both pencils and inks the work. The inker, of course, is the man who goes over the pencils with India ink so that they'll show up nice and black (God and our printer willing!).

Lately, we've started using the admittedly-imprecise term "embellisher" to refer either to an inker who adds quite a bit to the penciled art in going over it— or, more often, to one who works over rough, unfinished pencils (called "layouts" in the trade) so that he is doing nearly as much actual drawing as he is inking. This is the way Joltin' Joe Sinnott works with Rich "Swash" Buckler on F.F., and the way nearly everybody works with the Buscema Siblings. It's not that we feel "embellisher" is necessarily the best and only word in the world for what Joe and others do; it's just that, rack our enfeebled brains as we might, we've never been able to come up with a better word!

Any suggestions?

MARVEL VALUE STAMP

38: CONAN THE BARBARIAN from *Fantastic Four* no. 167 (February 1976).

MAIL IT TO MAR-VELL

c/o MARVEL COMICS GROUP, 575 MADISON AVE. N.Y.C. 10022

Before we get into the letters this month, we'd like to cover an aspect of issue #40 that's aroused a lot of controversy—namely, those glitter people Rick was so abashed at seeing outside his concert. Many, many people wrote to say that if that was what Al thought current fashions look like, he's as out of touch as Rick. Well, to set the record straight, let it be known that Al didn't pencil those people the way they finally appeared. It seems that that issue's *inker* decided to fix the outfits, and so reworked what Al had put down.

Believe us, people—Al Milgrom can boogie with the best of 'em!

Dear Steve, Al, Orz, and Inking Staff,

Well, here it is at last! What, you ask. The return of Mar-Vell to the Kree homeworld, is what! You know, if I really had to choose the greatest idea to come from Ol' Marvel, I think I'd have to choose the Kree and that great ruler of theirs, the Supreme Intelligence. That's why CM # 16 has been my most prized possession; I've read and reread that mag so much I have the thing memorized. That's why when I picked up CM #41 I almost cried tears of joy. Mar-Vell was back amongst the stars, back on Hala, homeworld of the Kree. Those scenes in the Hall of Judgment even beat those in CM #16! All I can say is thank you, each and every lovin' one of ya!

OK, down to business. This is Al Milgrom's finest work yet. Every panel was perfect—well, except for one. Page 22, panel 4: Rick's only supposed to have one wrist-band (he's even saying so), but lo and behold! he has two! So send me a no-prize already! Anyway, Al used a more cramped style of paneling this time around, and I, for one, am a sucker for that. It's something so few artists have used since Kirby—Buckler being one of the few to come to mind. I hope Al continues to do this. The inks were beautiful, too, so send my congratulations to all the people involved.

Scripting you want? Scripting we got this ish. Steve, you've reached a new plane of excellence with this issue. It's all the little things you throw in, down to the casual mention of Warlock's Universal Church of Truth. Starlin's WARLOCK and your MAR-VELL are two of the finest comics on the market. On the question of Rick's staying with Mar-Vell, my vote is YES! With this issue's wonderful realization that both of them are in almost every way one and the same, the possibilities have become endless. Now all you must do is get Rick a costume, maybe one along the lines of Marv's old one.

Doug Zimmerman
11322 Lafayette Street
Northglenn, CO 80233

And as you saw in #42, Doug, Rick did get his costume. As you can probably tell, Steve and Al are having a ball with our boys' continuing evolution, and that touch gladdened their hearts as much, we hope, as yours. Don't worry, though—as this issue's contents have hinted, Rick remains the same guy he always was. In fact, we'd like to emphasize that here, because to our eyes, Rick and Marv are not, have not been, and never will be "one and the same." It's their contrasting views of their cosmic adventures that *really* grab us, and as the French are so fond of murmuring, "vive la difference!"

Dear Steve and Al,

Congratulations! When Jim Starlin left, I figured Captain Marvel had had it. The magazine had taken on quite a distinctive look, one that suited it beautifully, and it looked like when the master of the cosmic and metaphysical left for other pages, there would be a Starlin-shaped hole in the Kreeman's life. No one is ever quite as boggling as Starlin when exploring those lines, and they seemed to be the only areas of exploration open to Mar-Vell that were uniquely his.

For a few issues, it looked like the worst was true...there was one month when the Captain Marvel pastry ad had the most authentic-looking artwork in the magazine, and Rick and Marv both seemed to have undergone personality changes for the worse. Now, Milgrom and Mar-Vell mesh beautifully. You've taken the work of Kirby and the work of Starlin, and instead of looking like cheapo copies of the styles of other men, you've made everything on Hala look like you designed it, Steve. I apologize for doubting you, even in the privacy of my own mind. I should never forget the subtlety that is your stock-in-trade. The personality clashes were just leading up to the divorce, and you've neatly removed one of the mag's biggest potential pitfalls. It's all right for Ben Grimm to hate being the Thing, and it is fine for the Silver Surfer to lament being trapped on Earth, but there are enough of these problems in Marveldom already, and I lived in hourly dread of the day that some heavy-handed writer was really going to go at the idea that Rick and Captain Marvel resented their forced space-sharing.

In so doing, you've also given yourself quite a few brand new areas to explore. The possibilites are endless in the discovery of new consequences of the Rick/Marv joining. They have sort of a symbiotic empathy that's fascinating. To those who want Rick to move on, I say thee nay! Can't you see that he has moved on into a whole new phase of his life, without leaving the pages of this mag? What interests me about Rick is that unlike say, Johnny Storm or Peter Parker, he's so totally ordinary. He has no inherent nobility or heroism, and despite all of his experience with supertypes, he almost invariably reacts to mind-blowing experiences by getting his mind blown, just like your man in the street. With Rick, you always get the feeling of "What am I doing involved in *this?"* at the most crucial or incongruous moments.

You've also freed yourself from Starlin's shadow by exploring a story that is totally along Englehartesque lines. This tale wouldn't mean half so much if you hadn't already provided deep insight into the origins of the Kree mentality in the Celestial madonna series in the Avengers. That last page confused me beyond belief, although I'll hazard a guess that the gem is related to the Alpha and Omega stones from Marvel Team-Up (#16?).

Jo Duffy
311 Davis Hall
Wellesley College, Wellesley MA 02181

We're not saying, Jo...yet!

Dear Steve and Al—

You know, I've the impression that I have absolutely NO IDEA what's going on in CAPTAIN MARVEL any more. Stranger still, my enjoyment of the magazine is, if anything, augmented by this unfortunately-not-unique phenomenon.

Richie Howell
Jordan J-36
Harvard/Radcliffe, Cambridge, MA 02138

MARVEL VALUE STAMP

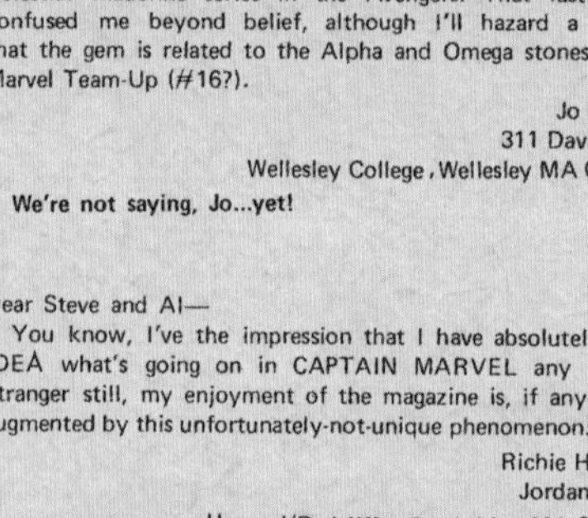

60: CONAN THE BARBARIAN from *Captain Marvel* no. 43 (March 1976).

GREEN SKIN'S GRAB-BAG

c/o MARVEL COMICS GROUP, 575 MADISON AVE N.Y.C. 10022

Bear with us for a moment in our uneasy amazement, but as we sit—becalmed and bewildered—preparing this letters page, there are absolutely no wild and reactionary or controversial letters at hand (usually there are at least a few on each of our titles). So we're going to have a nice, calm, normal, friendly, chatty column this time...and please, don't anyone accuse us of being old-fashioned. Y'know how we hate to blush...

Dear Stan, Sal, Len, etc.,

I would like you to know that—in all the time I have collected Marvel Comics—I have never run across such a delightful masterpiece as HULK # 195. It really provided entertainment and enjoyment. If you ask me, it was one of the gamma-rayed goliath's most fantastic and promising adventures. I really loved the way you brought little Ricky Bower into the Hulk's life, although I wish he could have stayed longer than two days.

Also, I am trying for a no-prize. Y'know, the Abomination is only s'pose to have two toes (one big toe and the other flat one), but on the cover he has three—count 'em, three—toes!

James Arbuckle
701 Konnick Place
Honolulu, HI 96818

If we ever entertained any intentions of slipping out of awarding a non-denominational no-prize, Jim, it was never after getting such kind words on the issue in question. Yeah, you're right (two toes hath the Abomination)—and, yeah, the no-prize is yours!

Dear Len and Len,

HULK # 195 proved one important thing. And that is, given creative writing (which you *definitely* give), the ol' "puny human" routine can still work. No matter how used a basic concept becomes, no matter how formularized, interesting twists can make it new and fresh once again.

And that was exactly the case with HULK # 195. How many times has the Hulk become involved with a "friend" such as little Ricky, and how many times has the Hulk decided that this "friend" isn't true? And, how many times has the bad guy talked the Hulk into joining him with "just you and me against the world?" I wouldn't even attempt to count how many times—and yet this story worked extremely well.

The new twist that made it work was the Abomination's personality, and the situation in which he was placed. The Abomination is a great character—a true villain—but instead of being the intense egomaniac crybaby, he will roll with the punches and bide his time. His reaction to the news that a bomb was planted in his head failed to make him explode in a fit of lunacy, and while obviously perturbed (who wouldn't be!) he played along with Ross until he was able to break out. Yet his annoyance at Ross' plan was understandable enough to believe that he could talk the Hulk into being his ally through sheer emotion.

Which leads me to another great twist, Ross' fake-out. I was all set to lambast you for allowing the new, more liberal Ross to stoop to such tactics, and then you come out stating that the entire episode was a ruse. Nice going, Len.

All I can say about the art is that I'm surprised how easily I've made the transition from Trimpe to Buscema. While not slighting Sal's talents, a lot of credit also goes to Joe Staton and his incredibly smooth and soft inks. Too, Glynis was great.

Dean Mullaney
81 Delaware Street
Staten Island, NY 10304

Dear Len and the gang,

HULK # 195 was fabulous. Sal, your art work was great; and who can forget Len with his superb writing?

Now let's talk about Greenskin and the Abomination. It was a great idea to bring the Abomination back. You know why? Because he's pure evil. And what an outstanding fight! But boy, that Abomination is a rat! Pretending to be the Hulk's friend. Hah!

Brian McCall
1578 Clifton St.
Baldwin, NY 11510

Dear Len, Sal and Joe;

I have just read HULK #195 and let me tell you, I am quite impressed with the story. I thought that the script was great, Len—but I really think that this Hulkbusting business is for the birds. Why don't you start Hulk out in a new life? 'Nuff said!

Patrick Bachand
East Greenwich, RI

Not quite, Pat. Y'see, Len himself agrees with you that the Hulk series has settled a little too comfortably into a pattern of late, thus he's already made pandemonious plans that will go into effect in stages over the next year. The result will be more action, excitement and sheer surprises than you can shake a slightly-vexed jade behemoth at!

And if you don't wanna hate yourself forever and ever, then dpn't miss our stupendous, colossal, wog-boggling 200th issue. That's in a scant 720 hours, give or take a minute or two.

See you there, Hulkophiles!

THIS IS IT! YOUR
MARVEL VALUE STAMP
FOR THIS ISSUE!

CLIP 'EM AND COLLECT 'EM!

86: CONAN THE BARBARIAN from *The Incredible Hulk* no. 199 (May 1976).

DEFENDERS DIALOGUE

c/o MARVEL COMICS GROUP, 575 MADISON AVE. N.Y.C. 10022

Dear Defending 'Dillos:

I'm enjoying the present Headmen series more than any other DEFENDERS story, because every issue Steve Gerber comes up with such wonderful weirdness. It might take the form of a sinister deer, the unique and amusing personalities of Nagan and Ruby, Chondu's new body, Nighthawk's fantasy about his past, or Nebulon's bozo show. For that matter, it might even be the nefarious elf himself. Whatever form the weirdness takes, it's marvelously entertaining. There are so many books about super-hero groups on the market that each one will have to make itself unique to survive the inevitable end of the fad. It's DEFENDERS' sheer unconventionality that will assure its continuance, I think.

I'm relieved to see that you didn't resurrect Black Widow's husband, and that the new Red Guardian is instead a most attractive woman. I don't believe that Dr. Strange could have sent for her without revealing why he needed her, but maybe he put a few spells on some officials. I suspect that you may be trying her out as a possible new Defender. I like her, but she is rather similar to Black Widow, and I suspect she's needed more in Russia to assist victims of political oppression. The idea of a super-hero existing in the USSR *against* the authorities' will is very interesting, and Reddy may fare best not as a regular Defender but as a guest star in any Marvel stories set in Russia (like the Hulk's recent sojourn there).

You really messed one thing up this issue. Long ago Eternity altered reality so that Dr. Strange's name in his civilian identity became Dr. Sanders. This is a nearly perfect name and demonstrates Eternity's good taste. For years I've admired the way that Marvel has evaded having anyone address the "normal" Dr. Strange by his last name. But this issue, someone did, and called him by his old name, Stephen Strange. I protest. If you don't go back to calling him "Dr. Sanders" I'll have to change my name to Strangerson. But I don't want to! After all, Hoggoth knows I'm already Strange enough.

Peter Sanderson
Room 921 Johnson Hall
Columbia University
New York, NY 10027

A few clarifications (and/or further obfuscations), Pete, since a number of the points you've raised also troubled other readers:

One of these days, the two Steves—Gerber and Englehart—are going to have to get together with neo-editor Gerry Conway and decide just what Dr. Strange's civilian appellation really is. As Gerber understood it, the "Sanders" name went up in smoke with Doc's very transitory super-hero phase a number of years back. Steve G. just kinda likes the idea that Dr. Strange's "secret identity" is Dr. Strange.

Doc, by the way, did disclose to certain authorities the reason he required Tania's aid—but not the *whole* reason. He simply explained that Kyle Richmond would die if he (Kyle) failed to undergo an extremely delicate neurosurgical operation, one only Tania could perform. All clear?

Now then, as for whether the Red Guardian will remain with the Defenders permanently—only you Marvelite types can decide. We plan to keep her around for a while, long enough for you to get a good look at her in action, and then we'll just have to wait for your verdict.

Dear Totally-warped Ones,

Re: DEFENDERS #34.

You're right, you *are* all bozos in this book!

Has anybody ever suggested a nice, long rest in the local mental ward to you, Mr. Gerber?

Doug Zimmerman
11322 Lafayette St.
Northglenn, CO 80233

Dear Steve,

Cut out that "crazy" talk. DEFENDERS #34 proves you are most definitely a genius.

David Fink
3713 Merridan Dr.
Concord, CA 94518

Well, you're both wrong! Steve is a ploddingly dull, somniferously average reg'lar guy and solid citizen. He told us so himself, at the top of his lungs, from his hiding place under the basement stairs.

Dear Steve,

When Barbara Norriss went insane, Dr. Strange assumed it was because she had been happy being mated to her captors. With what we now know about Barbara, I think I can offer another explanation.

Barbara had mated with the Weird Brothers knowing that she was already married to Jack Norriss. She had "re-married" only to escape the unbearable loneliness of her prison, and did so thinking she would never return to Earth and Jack.

When Dr. Strange released her, she must have realized she would eventually have to face Jack with the crime on her conscience, as it may well have been all during the time of her mating with the monsters.

I think her guilt drove her mad. What do you think?

Ann Nichols
P.O. Box 2368
Sierra Vista, AZ 85635

We think this is one of the wildest story suggestions we've heard in some time, Ann—and we thank you for it.

Now it's up to you to decide whether you've been complimented by a genius or a lunatic. (Cf. previous two letters.)

Anyway, we'll be back in thirty days with "Riot in a Women's Prison"—the searing saga of a lonely lady warrior in solitary confinement. Don't miss it.

THIS IS IT! YOUR
MARVEL VALUE STAMP
FOR THIS ISSUE!

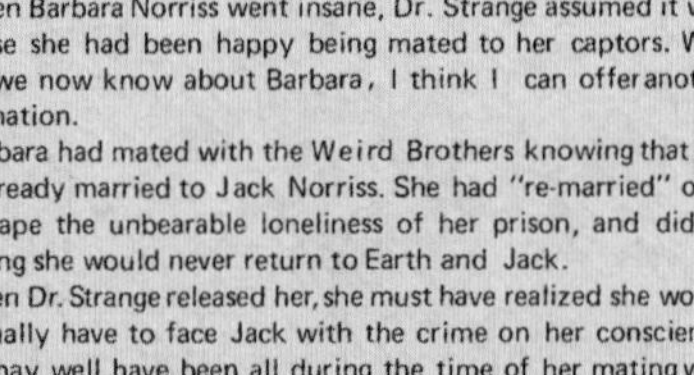

6: CONAN THE BARBARIAN from *The Defenders* no. 38 (August 1976). Stamp also appears in *The Amazing Spider-Man* no. 152 (January 1976).

LET'S RAP WITH CAP

SEND YOUR LETTERS TO: THE MARVEL COMICS GROUP SIXTH FLOOR 575 MADISON AV NEW YORK 10022 N.Y.

Dear Marvel,

I've uncrossed my fingers long enough to whip off this letter of comment on Jack Kirby's second issue of the mammoth bicentennial saga he's got running in CAPTAIN AMERICA. The nightmares I've had about what this book would become under Jack's handling made the one experienced by Cap on pages two and three look positively idyllic by contrast. I've had visions of this title being changed to include pages of uselessly large panels masquerading under the euphemismistic heading of "chapters, "as well as shallow plotting, and virtually no characterization. But in all honesty, and without trying to sound too optimistic, Jack has started concentrating on doing what to all intents and purposes he has been neglecting sorely for the past several years, and that is telling a STORY. Jack has pleasantly surprised me and that's no hype. Instead of handing us the above stated horrors, he has begun a story with numerous connecting plot threads, interesting new characters, and a hefty dose of characterization.

Specifically, Jack did not sacrifice plot to visuals, because right after that dynamite double-page spread, he went right to business cramming dialogue and captions with all the fervor of Dauntless Don McGregor. I find the introduction of General Heshin and the aristocratic Taurey, intriguing, most especially because of the unexpected link Taurey has with Steve Rogers. I can sense the gradual drawing together of things as the nation's bicentennial approaches, and it should make for a startling conclusion. What shocked me most of all was Jack's superb handling of the Cap/Falcon relationship. Contrary to the "black Bucky" I felt Sam Wilson would become, with all the emphasis Steve Englehart placed on him being removed, just the opposite has occurred, with Jack managing to very nicely graft the new/old personality of Snap Wilson with the social worker/good guy we've known for so many years and coming up with a more pugnacious, volatile personality who doesn't mind taking independent action if and when he thinks it's necessary. I was pleased with the argument Steve and Sam had about how far America has grown up in two hundred years, for it brings into the light the fact that things weren't all rosy when this country was in its nascent stages, and perhaps there was more prejudice and ignorance rampant than there is today. Nicely done, Jack. The street-wise instincts of Snap Wilson have also been in evidence, something I hope will be continuing. The Falcon is definitely his own man, and it's to Jack's credit he's handled it so well.

Perusing the last two issues and prognosticating on what is to come, I find my apprehensions slowly fading as Jack gets back into the Marvel Manner and shakes off the last vestiges of dust from the creative crypt he's been in for the past couple of years. I had really grown bored with his work at National and was preparing to give up any hope that he'd return to Marvel and explode with a fresh burst of imagination. Dreams do come true, sometimes, so once again, welcome home, Jack, you've been missed.

Ralph Macchio
188 Wilson Drive
Cresskill, NJ 07626

Dear Marvel,

"The Trojan Horde" wasn't unlike many of the other Kirby stories, except that it was flavored with the spirit of Captain America and Marvel! Jack's usual storyline consists of a great deal of science-fiction that is sometimes hardly agreeable or understandable. But "Trojan Horde" somehow seemed...different, that's it! Perhaps it was because of the presence of two of my favorite characters—Cap & Falc, who else?

Cap was, of course, his usual talkative and thoughtful self, which he has remained for 30 years, as Jack knows well, having handled him for some 20 years, I'd estimate. But Falcon became a highly different character than the one other artists and writers have handled! He was more like a mixture of Leila, as she used to be, and Flip Wilson!

Well, Kirby's second Cap issue was better than his first, but I shall expect better as we go runnin' along.

Gregg Stamey
21 Hampton Heights
Canton, NC 28716

Dear Mr. Kirby,

It's been quite a while since you've worked for Marvel Comics, and by now, I believe I can safely say you've noticed the changes. And you may have wondered if your style still fits. It does.

But I feel that comics have matured since you've left. They, or rather WE (as I feel that the fans are as much a valid part of the industry) have grown beyond the usual boundries, to explore the potential that the world of the comic book can achieve. There will be no turning back.

You have been in comics far longer than I would care to consider. Your work has been unique and outstanding, when compared to the scribblers of that day. But that was yesterday. I'm talking about TODAY!

What are YOU, compared to:

JOHN & SAL BUSCEMA?
NEAL ADAMS?
JIM STARLIN?
AL MILGROM?
RICH BUCKLER?
GENE COLAN?
DAVE COCKRUM?

Still one heck of an artist!
Best of Luck!

the Marveriter,
Box 4112 S. R. A.
Anchorage, Alaska 99502

Thanks, Ralph, Gregg, and Marveriter (may we call you Marv?) for your overwhelming support of the King's return to the fold. We're glad to hear that you all affirm your faith in the man who created Cap, lo, these many years ago.

After all these years in one of the nuttiest and most bombastic businesses ever, Jack's happy to know that his fans are still for him—although neither of the Buscema brothers, nor any of the other talented artists whom you've mentioned —should be slighted! As we've always said, the best in the business have always worked for Marvel, and now that Jack's back, we've completed the set.

See ya next month, effendi, as we present Captain America's "Love Story!" Ciao!

THIS IS IT! YOUR
MARVEL VALUE STAMP
FOR THIS ISSUE!

CLIP 'EM AND COLLECT 'EM!

78: CONAN THE BARBARIAN from *Captain America* no. 197 (May 1976).

THE SPIDER'S WEB

c/o MARVEL COMICS GROUP, 575 MADISON AVE., N.Y.C. 10022

Dear Len, Ross, and the rest—

Congratulations!!! You finally did it! SPIDER-MAN #153 was the best story since Smiley left the web-head's book, way back when. As a matter of fact, SPIDEY has been sharply increasing in quality with each issue since #150. This latest was easily the best one-shot story I've read this month. First, a fantastically good cover portraying innocence, aggression, competition, heroism and color. (The taxi-cab sequence reminded me of a vintage FF saga wherein the Thing accidentally demolished an antique car while trying to fix it.) Then, MJ making up with Pete. Far out!

The story was touching and true-to-life, and the comparison between Bolton's running for his daughter and his football game of the past was a stroke of genius! Further, Spidey's changing his mind about the bother of hitting the murderer was also very good and conveyed the perfect feeling. In short, I enjoyed every aspect of this issue, from Ross's intricate detail of the church on page one, to the story's many twists and ironies. I hope I have conveyed my feelings adequately, because for once Spider-Man has so many good things going for him that I can't name them all.

Thanks again. Touchdown.

Jeff Silva
Box 36
Lakeview, WA 98491

Hey, Jeff—the blushin' Bullpen thanks you for the kindly kudos! That issue went over in a big way, and your letter is representative of the majority of mail. In fact, to prove we aren't whistlin' "Dixie" when we say that ish really made a smash, we were unsuspectingly ambling down Manhattan's Seventh Avenue just the other day, when we suddenly came upon a record store window display featuring at least five copies! We don't know what they were doing there, gang—but we ain't about to complain! Not us! In fact, we're waitin' to see what they do when the new Spidey rock album comes out, since they're gonna have to go some to top the display they gave ish #153!!

Dear Gentlemen,

In my humble opinion, SPIDER-MAN #153 was the finest work by Marvel, in terms of emotional impact and character developments, that I have seen in a long time. The idea of using a non-regular character for the story focus was a welcome change of pace. Much is said of superheroes' courage and endurance — but Dr. Bolton proved it is not their exclusive property. For me, the whole story consisted of Bolton's race against death on page 26. I applaud you loudly for the tasteful, low-key epithet by Spider-Man on the last page.

Mark Kreighbaum
Great Lakes, IL

People,

You guys goofed. On the cover of SPIDER-MAN #153, your goalposts are not consistent with the interior art. As you carefully pointed out in the story, goalposts did once look like the ones on the cover. Now, I know you always have an answer—I just want to hear it.

Mark Scott
Fridley, MN

With perfect candor and a certain amount of satisfaction, we can say that for once, Mark, we didn't goof. Not at all. Y'see, when Lively Len Wein and Jazzy John Romita got together for a cover conference, they discussed just which depiction of the goalposts they should go with, and after some cogitation they opted to avail themselves of artistic license and use the classical version for easier identification. There you are, Mark—we may not *always* have an answer, but we sure did this time!

Dear Marvel,

I have just finished reading Roger Slifer's somewhat wordy "explanation" of your fantastic Jackal series. Now, I really hate to make trouble, but you blew it again! To see what I mean, check out issue #137, page 26, panels 5 & 6. I ask you, gentlemen, just what is Spidey doing? Right on! He's with his spare costume and is taking the cartridges from it (obviously he took them, and probably his costume as well). Yet, Mr. Slifer plainly states that Prof. Warren furnished his clone with them. Case closed. Sentence will now be served: Mr. Slifer and all his Marvel cohorts shall make apologies to all Marvelites and send me one honest-to-gosh no-prize. Marvel Forever!!!

Robert Kaleel
P.O. Box 723
Clinton, NC 28328

You assume too much, Bob, old bean. Although Spidey did stop to get some cartridges from his spare costume, it's never stated that he took them *all*—and since he was on his way to a battle, it would have been pointless to pick up his extra costume at that point. Therefore, the costume in question *and* at least some webbing cartridges remained behind for the clone to utilize. Fair 'nuff? We're not handing out any no-prizes this month, Bob—Roguish Roger is vindicated!

Dear Guys—and Lady,

SPIDER-MAN #153, was hokey, clichéd, and obviously over-sentimental. It was implausible and extremely overdone.

So why are there tears in my eyes?

There are so many things wrong with this story that I'd normally not even want to know about it. For example, the up and down scene between Peter and M.J. Yeesh. Talk about manufactured problems. You expect us to really believe that? And how about the old *deja vu* trick? Flashbacks Anonymous strikes again.

Maybe I'm just a sentimental slob, but even though it was poorly expressed, the idea of loving someone enough to die for her/him, gets to me. So, in spite of a few large faults, "The Deadliest Hundred Yards" still came up a winner.

Thank you, and would someone pass me some kleenex? I've got something in both eyes.

Sheldon Wiebe
1090-1330 8 St. S.W.
Calgary, Alberta, Canada T2R 1B6

We've only just got room to sneak in a few frantic words about next ish, so we'll leave you with these to ponder over: "Hammerhead is Out!" If you like action, if you like adventure, if you like to be amazed—be here for SPIDER-MAN #158. 'Til then, 'nuff said!

MARVEL VALUE STAMP

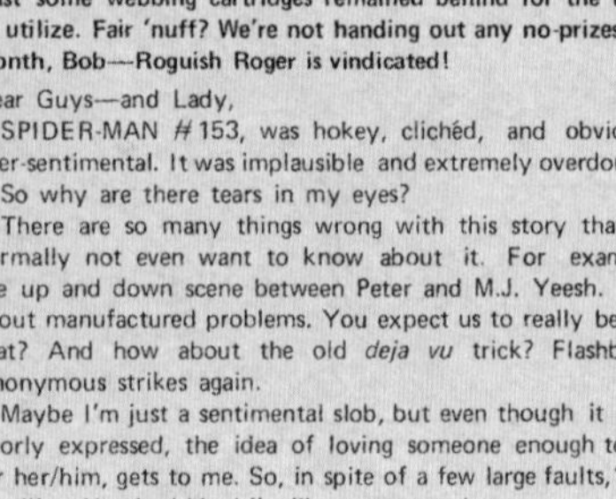

94: CONAN THE BARBARIAN from *The Amazing Spider-Man* no. 157 (June 1976). Note that the stamp is printed upside down on the letters page.

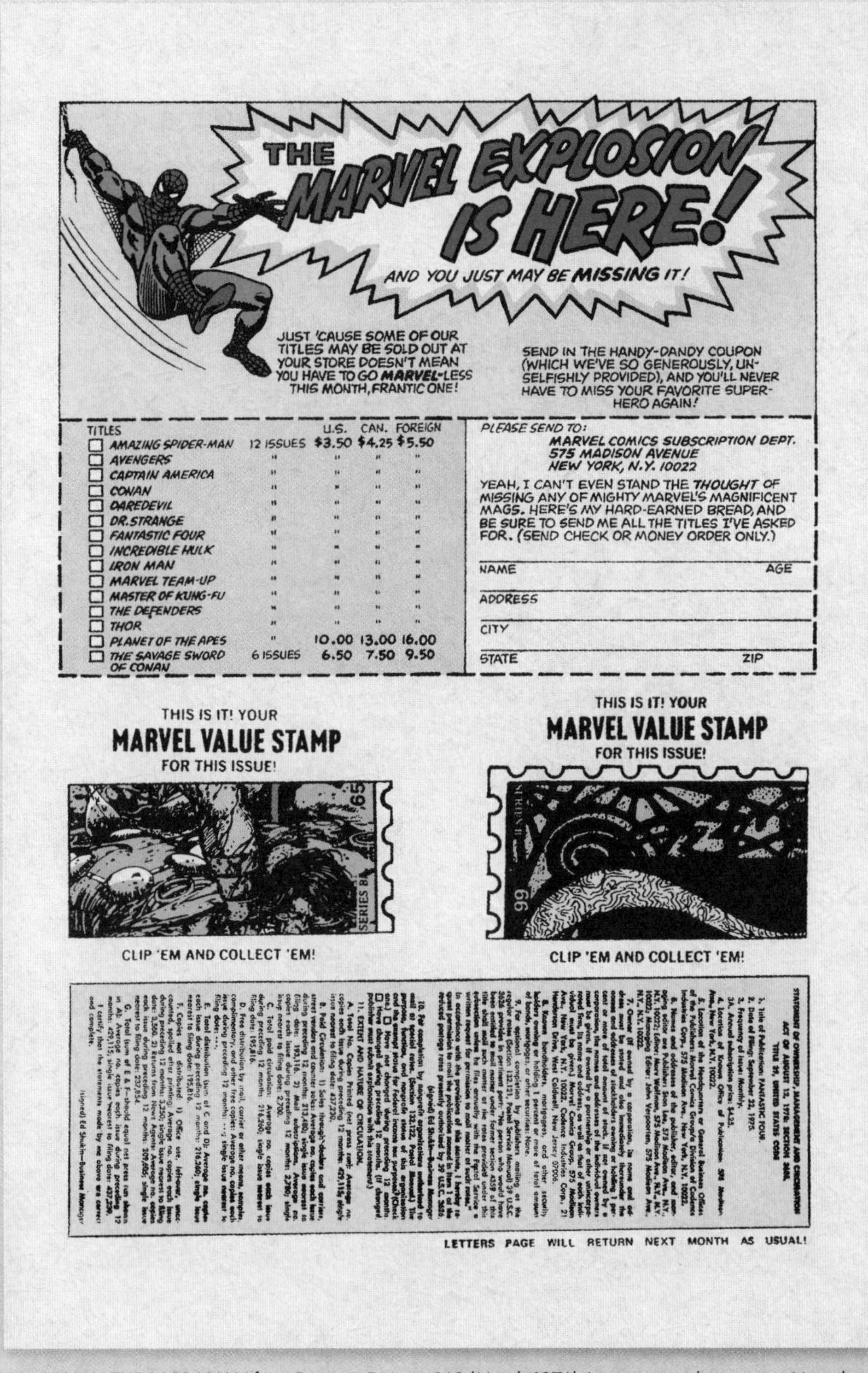
THE MARVEL EXPLOSION IS HERE!
AND YOU JUST MAY BE MISSING IT!
JUST 'CAUSE SOME OF OUR TITLES MAY BE SOLD OUT AT YOUR STORE DOESN'T MEAN YOU HAVE TO GO MARVEL-LESS THIS MONTH, FRANTIC ONE!
SEND IN THE HANDY-DANDY COUPON (WHICH WE'VE SO GENEROUSLY, UN-SELFISHLY PROVIDED), AND YOU'LL NEVER HAVE TO MISS YOUR FAVORITE SUPER-HERO AGAIN!
TITLES U.S. CAN. FOREIGN
AMAZING SPIDER-MAN 12 ISSUES $3.50 $4.25 $5.50
AVENGERS
CAPTAIN AMERICA
CONAN
DAREDEVIL
DR. STRANGE
FANTASTIC FOUR
INCREDIBLE HULK
IRON MAN
MARVEL TEAM-UP
MASTER OF KUNG-FU
THE DEFENDERS
THOR
PLANET OF THE APES 10.00 13.00 16.00
THE SAVAGE SWORD OF CONAN 6 ISSUES 6.50 7.50 9.50
PLEASE SEND TO:
MARVEL COMICS SUBSCRIPTION DEPT.
575 MADISON AVENUE
NEW YORK, N.Y. 10022
YEAH, I CAN'T EVEN STAND THE THOUGHT OF MISSING ANY OF MIGHTY MARVEL'S MAGNIFICENT MAGS. HERE'S MY HARD-EARNED BREAD, AND BE SURE TO SEND ME ALL THE TITLES I'VE ASKED FOR. (SEND CHECK OR MONEY ORDER ONLY.)
NAME AGE
ADDRESS
CITY
STATE ZIP
THIS IS IT! YOUR
MARVEL VALUE STAMP
FOR THIS ISSUE!
65
SERIES B
CLIP 'EM AND COLLECT 'EM!
THIS IS IT! YOUR
MARVEL VALUE STAMP
FOR THIS ISSUE!
66
CLIP 'EM AND COLLECT 'EM!
STATEMENT OF OWNERSHIP, MANAGEMENT AND CIRCULATION
LETTERS PAGE WILL RETURN NEXT MONTH AS USUAL!

65: CONAN THE BARBARIAN from *Fantastic Four* no. 168 (March 1976). Letters page also contains Marvel Value Stamp no. 66 (right) for DR. STRANGE: MASTER OF THE MYSTIC ARTS.

GREEN SKIN'S GRAB-BAG

c/o MARVEL COMICS GROUP, 575 MADISON AVE. N.Y.C. 10022

Dear Len,

I'm sorry, but your story in HULK #192 failed to impress in any way; it seemed overlong in coming to the battle between the monsters, a rather uninteresting battle at that. Aside from some nice Scottish accents, Mactavish and Macawber contributed very little to the plot; the monster itself was sketchily delineated; since it was the basis of the plot and of the conflict, I found that annoying. Just why was Angus so obsessed with killing the creature? If it was a Moby Dick fixation (something that was handled in this selfsame magazine five years ago, and considerably better to boot), the Scottish fisher was much too calm about the whole thing; if it wasn't, I found my sympathies on Macawber's and the monster's side. Apart from that, the ending was awfully contrived.

The two "sub-plot" pages enthused me even less. The Talbot affair is getting so boring it's incredible. As a regular in a series, he didn't seem to have much of a mind anyway, so what's all the fuss about? And Samson was a good one-shot character. One-shot, Len, get it?

The art was typically nice Trimpe storytelling with excellent Staton inking, but I wish you'd reunite Joe with Sal Buscema, or even let him do some solos. He seems a bit wasted on Herb to me.

Kim Thompson
Gen Del Box 259
APO NY NY 09184

Sorry you were less than pleased with that particular issue of the HULK, Kim. For an in-depth answer to some of the more negative feelings of your letter, see our reply to Ed Via elsewhere on this page.

The sub-plot with Glenn Talbot is slowly but surely growing to a climax and his final fate will be revealed in our 200th issue coming up in a few short months. Hang in there just a handful of issues longer, Kim, we're sure you'll agree that it was worth the wait!

As for a re-integration of the Buscema/Staton team, *that* little request was fulfilled with our last issue. So whaddaya think, pilgrim? Did Sal and Joe live up to your expectations? We're really agog with the combination, but we won't rest easy until you give us *your* verdict. Let us know.

Dear Marvel,

Hulk #192 was ridiculous. I say this for several reasons. The artwork was poor; I know the Hulk didn't win any beauty contests before, but he's never looked worse. Is this the Hulk everyone used to know and fear? Although the layouts were good, the faces, human figures, etc., were noticeably bad.

The dialogue and certain incidents in the story were unbelievable. I am tired of scenes specifically designed to show Hulk's strength (that also make no sense). An example of this is on page 2; after being caught in a fisherman's net, the Hulk "warns" the man to free him. Why not just burst out of the net, instead of threatening a helpless fisherman: And do you really believe that Angus Mactavish would mistake the Hulk for the sea monster? When on page 6 you said "To coin a cliche, the Hulk is 'dead to the world'," I stared disbelievingly. Surely you realize how often you've used Hulkliches throughout the issue ("puny humans," "Hulk will smash," or "Hulk will smash puny humans"). The (totally implausable) changing of the Loch Fear monster and Jamie Macawber into stone was no doubt inspired by old comic book stories in which an evil (?) gets retribution for his evil doings. This "retribution on earth" idea is an old, bad one, but that's exactly the type of meaning this ending conveys.

The Hulk used to be a character whose uniqueness combined with the usual Marvel Comic's high quality made it an exceptionally good magazine. I hope it will be again, someday.

(Unsigned)

Dear Len,

The Hulk versus the Loch Ness Monster? Why not.

Anyway, "The Lurker Beneath Loch Fear" was first rate entertainment. Its points about greed and the things it drives men to were well taken, though I can't help but wonder why Angus Mactavish was so adamant about killing the monster. He said a lot about the Serpent's Moon and so on, but how much of a threat was it, really?

I think you're going to get a lot of letters criticizing the ending of "Lurker." Some people won't like the fact that the monster, whom there are even pet names for—like Nessie, was destroyed. Others will think the turning man and beast(ie) to stone bit was hokey. I **liked** that touch; maybe it **was** hokey, but I still liked it. So tell whoever complains to go lick a carp.

Ed Via
1648 Dean Road
Roanoke, VA. 24018

Ed, as indicated by the two letters above, there *were* some complaints about HULK #192 and—as much as we hate to admit it— not all of them were ill-founded; Lively Len Wein himself wasn't as pleased with the final result of that particular issue as he would have liked.

"The Lurker Beneath Lock Fear!" suffered from a problem that manifests itself from time to time in comic book stories —the plotline called for a few additional pages in order to come across with its full impact. When Len originally plotted the "Lurker" story, he had very carefully taken into account the various motivations of the characters and carefuly plotted several scenes building up to the ultimate confrontation between Mactavish and Macawber. Unfortunately, Happy Herbie discovered that by the time he had illustrated all of the scenes essential to the storytelling of the saga, there was not enough space to devote to all of the character bits called for in the plot, and a couple of these were dropped resulting in what appeared to be a lack of development in the characters. The motivation was there in the *plot*, it just didn't make the transition to the printed page as well as we would have liked.

All which goes to prove that although we occasionally fumble and drop the ball, we're always in there trying for the touchdown. And the cheers, as well as the well-meaning cat-calls, of you fans rooting us on are what keep us on top once the final scores are tallied!

MARVEL VALUE STAMP

CLIP 'EM AND COLLECT 'EM!

28: CONAN THE BARBARIAN from *The Incredible Hulk* no. 196 (February 1976).

JUNGLE RE-ACTIONS!

c/o MARVEL COMICS GROUP · 575 MADISON AVENUE · NEW YORK NY 10022

Seeing as this will be one of the last letters pages dealing with "Panther's Rage," we feel that it is fitting to include an in-depth analysis by that in-depth critic who has analyzed the Panther novel since its beginnings. So without further fanfare, let's let Rambunctious Ralph Macchio, letter correspondent supreme, take over.

Go ahead, Ralph. The stage is yours.

Dear Don and Billy,

Assessing "Panther's Rage" up to and including its penultimate chapter, issue #17, is an enormous temptation for one to become lost in the mire of extended metaphor. If art is the shorthand of reality, as I've so often thought, then perhaps the best way any artistic endeavor can be "summed up" is through simply allowing that work to react on you, and let the perceptions flow effortlessly, without the stinting straitjacket of searching for meanings or messages; for if the artist has been successful in his prime function, which is communication, then the observing participant, if he has opened his mind, need not worry that he has missed the figurative boat somewhere along the way.

There are several mutually operative antagonisms extant in "Panther's Rage" which are really at the core of the struggle in Wakanda. We have three major figures in the drama, two of whom, Killmonger and T'Challa, are present throughout most of the series prominently, and the final, Kantu, who emerges as a vital link in the climax, though is not seen with the constant regularity of the previous two. Perhaps the most important relationship in the series is between Erik Killmonger and the Black Panther. Killmonger has stated clearly on several occasions that he cares almost nothing for what the Panther has done or will be doing to extinguish his revolutionary flame. He has a zealous, single-minded determination that will allow no obstacle to stand in his way. As a counterpoint to this, is T'Challa, a man beseiged by doubts and fears which have whittled away his motivations even as we are viewing him. He has doubts about his own identity, not only as a chieftan and ruler, but as a man as well. He is a man attempting to come to intellectual grips with the basic questions of existence, only to find his emotional makeup reacting to situations with almost inexplicable passions. T'Challa is the perfect counterbalance to the awesome, monolithic determination of his human adversary, Erik Killmonger. While attempting to stem the tide of an impending revolution, T'Challa is also embarking on an odyssey of self-discovery which will ultimately lead toward an acceptance of his fears, though not necessarily a conquering of them. The age-old struggle between those who are immovable juggernauts, trampling all in their desires for power, and those who question every move they make, thus giving the appearance of weakness on the surface, while actually strengthening their internal fiber for conflict, has been played out upon the Wakandan stage under the expert choreography of Don McGregor.

We now have all the important figures, save one, aligned on the scale of conflict for figurative measurement. The missing figure is the child, Kantu. When Erik Killmonger is pushed off the precipice in the climax, he is not pushed by either the Black Panther or Kantu. He is forced over the edge by the basic id portion of the Wakanda chieftan, T'Challa, for in truth, that is what Kantu really is. T'Challa has essentially come full circle, and his final conflict with Killmonger will indeed "give our battle a sense of symmetry." T'Challa the man, has come to an understanding of things he did not possess two years ago, and this fortifies him. And it is the "Panther of old" who makes the attack upon Killmonger, still, this is not enough to defeat his adversary, something beyond confidence and retribution itself—hate, is necessary. And the ideal vessel for such a pure, primal emotion, is the very antithesis of intellectual probing and moral uncertainty, a nine-year-old child, reacting very much as T'Challa himself did when he had been given the opportunity of revenge upon the man who had killed his own father. Hate cannot be intellectualized or conceptualized, it merely exists and can only be dealt with on a primal level beyond the reach of the mind. T'Challa and Kantu are inexplicably entwined, for each is but a different side of the same coin, with each emerging dominant in response to a given situation. The Panther's rage achieved its consummation through a circular journey which took the protagonist from ignorance and adversity to recognition and response. Perhaps it could have been equally well titled: "Panther's Progress."

So many people have worked so long and hard to make this a truly memorable serial that will long stand as one of the finest achievements of the Marvel Age. But heartfelt and personal thanks must go to long-suffering Don McGregor, who had the confidence in this medium as well as his audience to attempt such an ambitious project. We all love you Don, and wish you nothing but the best as you continue to set precedents in the furthering of your illustrated novel. The "Panther's Rage" series has done more than take us into the inner workings of an African society or a royal chieftan's head, it has allowed us to follow the evolution of a rather remarkable and unique contribution to the small list of people who help ensure that popular culture will have its share of timeless achievements. Don, thanks—for everything.

Ralph Macchio
188 Wilson Drive
Cresskill, NJ 07626

Don thanks you, Ralph, for taking the time to evaluate and write your incisive conclusions. And Don claims that he's only been long-suffering since 1975, which he says hasn't been the best century he's ever lived through.

On the serious side, Don was astounded at your insight into the progression of the Panther novel from its initial stages on through its final chapters. You detail many of the transitions in the characters, especially the Panther, and obviously understand the interactions among them.

NEXT ISSUE: "A Cross Burning Darkly, Blackening the Night!" Some of the finest Billy Graham graphics yet. And it might be a good thing they haven't yet changed our title from JUNGLE ACTION to the BLACK PANTHER, because no one is sure if our Jungle King can get himself out of this trap.

And stay with us, People, because 1976 is going to be the Panther's year. Just wait'll we introduce the merely magnificent character called Wind Eagle. And for the Bicentennial, you'll actually witness the Panther in the Reconstruction Period, fighting in the aftermath of the Civil War. How do we pull that one off? Be with us for our upcoming issues and find out.

MARVEL VALUE STAMP

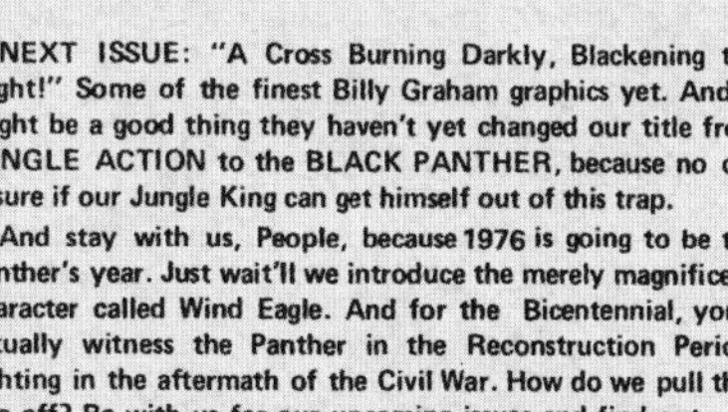

44: CONAN THE BARBARIAN from *Jungle Action* no. 20 (March 1976).

DRACULA™

Hidden in the shadows where legend and reality merge, there are tales of a being who has lived more than five hundred years! They say he is a creature born not on Earth, but in the deepest bowels of hell itself. They say he thrives upon the blood of innocents, that he is the King of Darkness... the *Prince of Evil,* and that even the bravest man quakes in fear at the meerest mention of his name... COUNT DRACULA!

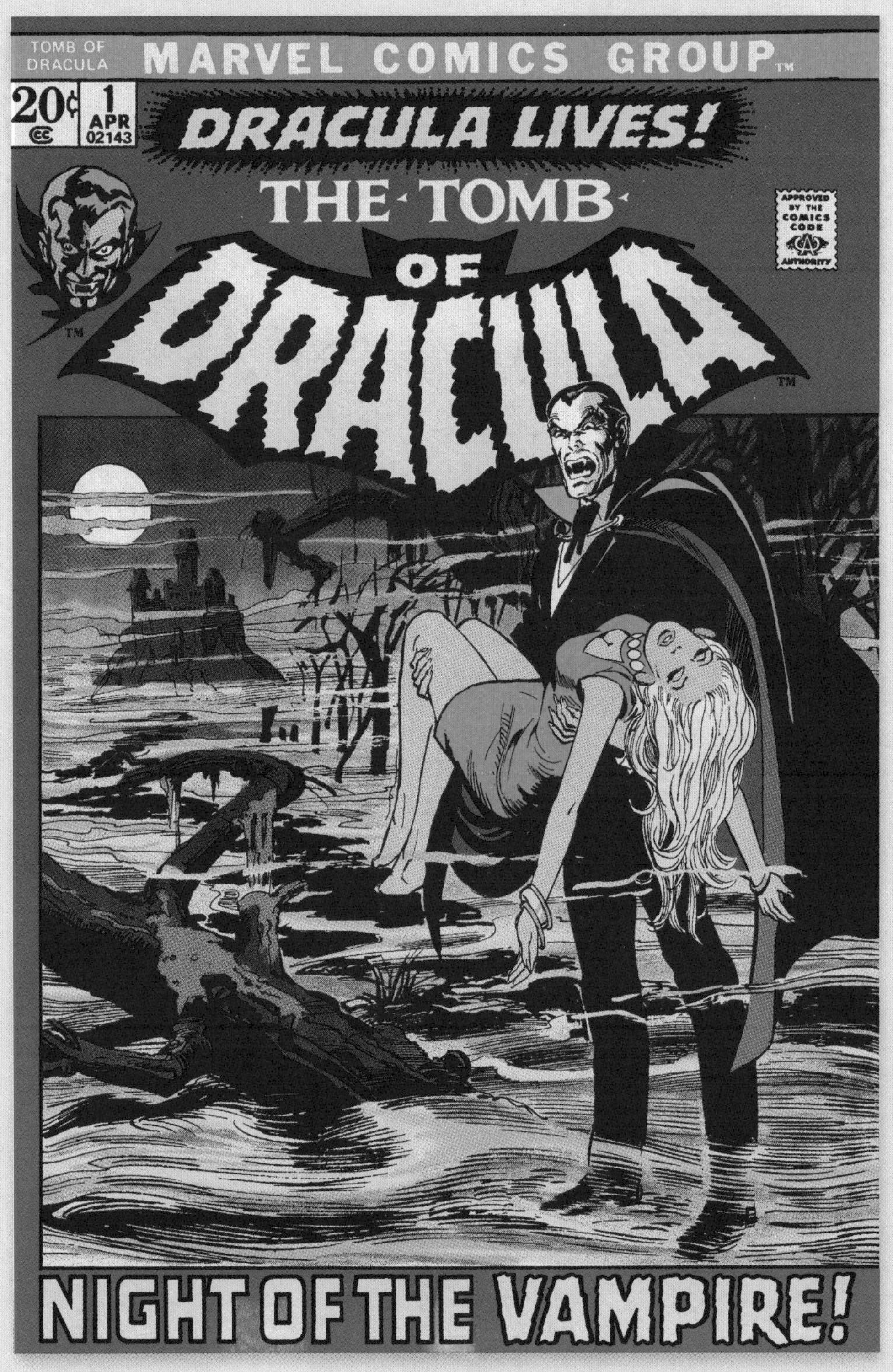

Tomb of Dracula no. 1 (April 1972), art by Neal Adams. In creating this stamp, the production department at Marvel took the cover image that Neal created and flopped it, then redrew the image for some reason. Most notable changes can be seen on the characters' faces, Dracula's cape, and the background.

LET'S RAP WITH CAP

SEND YOUR LETTERS TO:
THE MARVEL COMICS GROUP
SIXTH FLOOR
575 MADISON AV.
NEW YORK 10022
N. Y.

It'll be awhile until your letters catch up with Kirby's cataclysmic return to CAPTAIN AMERICA, so in the meanwhile here's a smattering of opinions on issue #190—

Dear Ladies and Gentlemen:

Wow. Nightshade is SOME villainess. She's an enigma, really, since we know very little about her, except that she's a fox, and that she's 18 years old (having the hold over men that SHE does at 18 is another enigma in itself).

Her battle with Cap was quite a change from her werewolf adventure. Actually, when I heard that Nightshade was returning, I was a little perturbed. . . CAP #164 is a modern-day classic, and adding a sequel to it ruins it (somehow, knowing that Nightshade in fact DID not die ruins the beauty of the ending), but she's being handled so nicely that I really don't think I'll complain.

Of course, at Nightshade's tender age, there's always the possibility that she isn't evil at all. . . just screwed up. Look at her performance in this issue. She's hardly Madame Hydra. In fact, as Cap noted in #164, she seems to be playing around, posing, etc., not realizing that this is the Big Time. Conversely, her distrust of the Yellow Claw belies wordliness and a jaded maturity.

Whatever, I get the distinct feeling that Nightshade could very well turn out to be a heroine. It's tradition at Marvel, you know. Look at the record of villainesses-turned-heroines: Black Widow, Medusa, Thundra, Zephyr, Scarlet Witch, Moon Dragon, Valkyrie, and undoubtedly some I've forgotten.

As I noted before, Nightshade isn't out-and-out bloodthirsty, like Nekra and the others; real villainesses do not, after being defeated, give in with a whimper of "Oh, poo." But I'd like to see as much of Nightshade as possible. . . keep that in mind as far as her future goes. I'd rather have a popular villainess in a good number of magazines than a heroine who doesn't appear in any; but I DO feel that Nightshade has the makings of a heroine.

I'll bet it's strange to get a letter on CAP #190 that doesn't say anything about the Falcon situation. . . but I have nothing to say. This issue's development was interesting, but I'd much rather wait until #191 when it all comes together. I only hope you're not trying to fade out Falc.

Looking forward to the King's return. . .

Bob Rodi
515 South Fifth Street
Columbia, MO 65201

Dear Marv,

Though CAPTAIN AMERICA AND THE FALCON has lost some of the drive it had under Steve Englehart, the book is still marvelously readable and entertaining.

But I have a plea: Please, please don't let Jack Kirby edit/write **Cap.** Plot and illustrate, yes, but anybody who's suffered through his destruction of one superb concept after the other has got to admit that he can't develop or script a series.

Kim Thompson
Gen Del Box 259
APO NY, NY 09184

Kim, we have no quarrel with your right to your own opinions—we only ask one thing, and that's fairness. Even the most notorious and hard-hitting East Coast film critics customarily wait until they've seen the subject they're criticizing before they condemn it. Can we ask any less of you? Please, in all fairness to Jack and his return work on the character which he created, give the book a fair chance. *Then* let us know what you think, okay?

Dear Marv and Tony,

CAPTAIN AMERICA #190 could have been an excellent issue, but it was ruined by the footnotes and captions. I read Marvel mags for both the action and the "revelance" that are found on most of your pages—not for your clever "in" remarks that turn up in your all-to-frequent footnotes. Marv, for no reason you interrupt this mag's action at several points by joking about whether we've bought past issues of different comics. Tony, you take all the realism out of the magazine when you say things like, "Would you believe inventor Tony Stark called it 'The Wild Bill Robot' when he. . .?" and, "What would you call a robot built to be the fastest draw in the west, east, etc?"* *"And the first clown who says Kid Bolt is gonna get such a shot in the chops." Finally, the funny (?) captions gave way to a few good pages of CA. The worst atrocity of all comes toward the end, however, when you mention that Cap and Falcon are still alive here on page 30. Again, this destroyed the realism. Fellows, please cut the cute stuff. Tony, it bothered me a little in DAREDEVIL (the Hydropillars), but here in my favorite mag it really upset me!

Actually, since Jack Kirby is taking over Captain America, we'll be seeing the end of the horrible captions, anyway. But just so this letter wasn't a total waste, guys, think about what I'm saying every now and then as you work on your other strips.

Kenneth A. Jones
RD 2 Box 18
Tamaqua, PA 18252

Your letter's not a waste, Ken; you made some valid points and you can be sure we appreciate your concern. After all, it's our avowed aim to entertain you, and you can be sure we're always experimenting with new and better ways to do so. Sometimes we fail, but it ain't cause we're not tryin'!

Til next issue— stay mellow!

MARVEL VALUE STAMP

CLIP 'EM AND COLLECT 'EM!

27: DRACULA from *Captain America* no. 194 (February 1976).

SOCK IT TO SHELL-HEAD

MARVEL COMICS GROUP, 575 MADISON AVE. N.Y.C. 10022

As was forseen, IM #78 drew a barrage of mail, both pro and con, on what was purposefully MEANT to be a controversial subject for *any* comic magazine...the serious treatment of a serious subject, the war in VIET NAM. We've chosen two representative letters which, because of their length, are all limited space will allow...but the comments were varied and intelligent throughout, a response all responsible appreciate and are grateful for.

Dear Stan, George, Bill, et al.:

For once I am moved to begin typing a letter to you before I even put down the issue. I refer to issue #78 of IRON MAN. My GOD, gentlemen, what have you DONE? Do you REALLY think that the world is ready for an intelligent, literate COMIC BOOK?

This issue crystallizes the character of the "new" Iron Man even better than issue #49, entitled "Must There Be an Iron Man?". You have finally struck the perfect motivation to explain to the world Iron Man's continued existence, and have depicted the most believable, uplifting, inspiring maturation of a comic book character that lives in recent memory. The script, with Tony's musings...from the piercing "not an evil man...just ignorant, God help us ALL," to the final, touching, "...the metal man was CRYING"—Bill Mantlo not just told a GOOD story... Darn it, this is the stuff of LITERATURE!

Iron Man is rapidly becoming the best-written, best-plotted and most mature character in your whole stable. Keep it up. As Iron Man finds his place in the world by avenging his OWN actions, let us hope that America grows up too, and instead of pinning the blame from Viet Nam on others, just simply LEARNS from its mistakes.

Keep us thinking, Bullpen.

Dave Osterman
QNS RFO
4518 Chadwick Rd.
Evansville, IN

Dear Marvel,

Untold stories and their like are the kind we readers generally expect from the competition, but not from Marvel. This small quirk didn't ruin the beautiful art job done on IM # 78 by Tuska and Colletta. Storywise, however, it was a horse of a different color.

Bill Mantlo's story was too one-sided and it reeked of liberal-defeatist do-nothing propaganda. The story was NOT about Iron Man at all, but about Viet Nam and our involvement there. Mr. Mantlo showed that war is a HORRIBLE thing (pages 6, 7 and 15). He also showed a man in anguish because his creation (the laser-cannon) took the lives of innocents who had nothing to DO with the Viet Cong or the war. This is all very NICE, all very TRUE and it probably really happened in Nam and in real life.

But the reason I say Bill's story reeks of propaganda is because he portrays us (Iron Man IS an American, isn't he) again as VILLAINS, even though he says in the story that we were MISGUIDED villains, by way of copping out. This is the kind of propaganda the liberal-defeatists would LIKE the world and the American public to believe. War IS horrible I agree, and I realize that it's the innocents, the little people who die and suffer, but why blame the Americans? What about the mass murders committed in Hue during the 1968 Tet offensive? The world knows about our withdrawal from Indochina...but why doesn't North Vietnam withdraw from Cambodia? Why doesn't the North explain the killing of village head-men throughout the war? I could go on and on!

Hec Rambla
712 W. 176 St.
NYC, NY

Conclusion:

There was MORE, marvelites, MUCH more...and though we had to cut Hec's letter short a bit, the gist of it remains. So, was IM #78 a meaningful SUCCESS, or did it FAIL to convey the horror, the sheer USELESSNESS of war as Bill saw it when he penned the issue? Most letters seemed to be favorable, and most expressed the same sense of outrage and, at the same time, approbation of the way the subject and the character was handled. We're listening, friends to ALL the currents awash out there in the land...and we'll try to respond as feelingly as we can to them in our books...always.

THIS IS IT! YOUR
MARVEL VALUE STAMP
FOR THIS ISSUE!

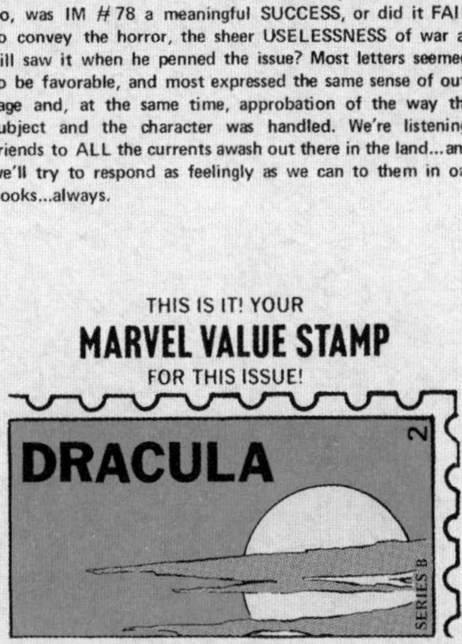

CLIP 'EM AND COLLECT 'EM!

2: **DRACULA** from *Iron Man* no. 81 (December 1975). Stamp also appears in *Iron Man* no. 82 (January 1976) and *Son of Satan* no. 5 (August 1976).

OMEGA MAIL

c/o MARVEL COMICS GROUP, 575 MADISON AVE. N.Y.C. 10022

I've been working for Marvel for a couple years now, and I know just about everybody up here, at least by their first names. However, the other day, as I sauntered past the mailroom to John Warner's office for a cup of his famous coffee, I was accosted by a Marvel employee I'd never seen before. I didn't catch the guy's name, but he came vaulting over the mailroom's half-door snarling, "Hey—you that Skrenes broad?"

Luckily, I happened to be carrying Steve Gerber's cassette recorder. I figured, whatever the ensuing events, I might as well get them on tape, so I clicked the thing on as I held it out in front of me to ward off the possible attack. What follows is a transcript of that...interview.

* * *

GUY: I just read OMEGA #2, an' I wanna know what's goin' on!

MS: What do you mean?

GUY: I mean, James-Michael's a 12-year-old kid, right?

MS: That's correct.

GUY: He's one o' them brainy types, used to thinkin' alla time, an' he comes from the mountains, where they don't teach the facts o' life, right?

MS: We've indicated that he's been raised in near-isolation...

GUY: Right! He hasn't had hardly no dealin's with people. Are you outta your mind puttin' a kid like that down in Hell's Kitchen?! Do you know what kinda people hang out down there?

MS: Yes...

GUY: I don't believe you! Let me tell you just what it's like down there. It's right near 42nd Street and the Times Square district. Sure, you got them Broadway theatres, but mostly you got sleazy bookstores and movie houses. Degenerates cruise the streets 24 hours a day. Floozies, hypsters, con artists, addicts, winos, bums, shopping-bag ladies! Everywhere you look there's an eye missing, an arm, a leg, twisted bodies with oozing sores sleeping in doorways. People don't talk down there, they scream.

Ninth Avenue leads downtown, right into the Lincoln Tunnel. The traffic is constant, and the noise level is ear-splitting. Exhaust fumes mix with the odor of human waste, rotting fruit, soggy cardboard, cow blood dripping from the meat market deliveries, booze on every breath, and cooking fumes from Mexican, Chinese, Italian, Greek, Indian restaurants, and as many different bakeries.

The kids there would curl your hair. You don't see many of 'em, and the ones you do see are off the leash and tough. They got concrete postage stamps for playgrounds, but they'd rather play chicken with the crosstown traffic or get their yoks from tippin' over blind cripples. Who's James-Michael gonna be friends with—the kid down the block with the switchblade in every pocket who plays mumbley-peg with his two-year-old sister when he has to babysit her?

I'm tellin' ya, James-Michael will be eaten alive in that neighborhood!

MS: That's conjecture on your part.

GUY: Con...what?

MS: If James-Michael gets eaten up by the neighborhood, the series won't have much future...

GUY: Well, you'd still have Omega. What's with that turkey, anyhow? He's always gettin' zapped an' he don't say nothin'!

MS: Maybe he hasn't had anything to say yet...

GUY: Oh, jeez! Look, who are you, anyway? Just what do you do on OMEGA, huh? I mean, Gerber's a big-name writer. I never heard of you!

MS: Gosh, what can I say?

GUY: Just spill, sister. How do you an' Gerber work together, if you really do?

MS: Listen, if I tell you, will you get off my toe, huh, please?

GUY: Okay, sure, an' you don't have to cower like that, neither.

MS: Gee thanks. All right, this is how it works...about six o'clock of an evening, SG and I go to the McDonald's at 34th Street and Eighth Avenue. One of us gets the food while the other grabs a table in the back, away from the crowd. We review the continuity of the book while we eat. Afterwards, over coffee, we plot this issue.

GUY: Yeah, an' then what?

MS: We work in what has come to be called the "Skeates Style." That is, I divide up the script page into panels with pen lines and type in the panel descriptions. Since we plot this book very tightly, we already have much of the dialogue by then, and I type that, too. I do whatever more I feel like handling and then turn the script over to Gerber to finish.

GUY: Hah! So then it's really up to Gerber!

MS: Would it make you happy if he did the panel descriptions on the next one, and I finished it up?

GUY: Gerber would never allow that. He wants control on his books.

MS: So do I, pal.

A bit of indelicate verbiage followed, whereupon I realized I'd better get to my cup of coffee or I'd blow a gasket right there in Marvel's ever-hallowed hallway. I turned on my heels and stormed toward J.D.W.'s haven of refuge. Behind me all the way, his voice hissed, "I'm gonna tell Gerber on you! He won't let you get away with it!"

As the guy said, jeez!

-----MARY SKRENES

* * *

Uh, Mary...I'd been meaning to tell you about Sanchez of the mailroom...listen, don't take him too seriously, see...he only picked on you 'cause Don McGregor wasn't around...

----MARV WOLFMAN

THIS IS IT! YOUR

MARVEL VALUE STAMP

FOR THIS ISSUE!

CLIP 'EM AND COLLECT 'EM!

85: DRACULA from *Omega the Unknown* no. 2 (May 1976).

Dear John and Roy:

On page 11 of issue #54, the giant says that the price for entrance to the oracle's cave is "Your right arm—sheared off at the elbow!" Flash now to page 15, panel 5. As any astute-minded university major with two degrees in anatomy (or, in this case, a 15-year-old grade niner like me) can see, the skeleton hand there is from a *left* arm, severed just slightly above the wrist. When will my no-prize arrive? Otherwise, the story and artwork were superb.

Fernando Pereira
345 Rimilton Ave.
Toronto, Ont., Canada
M8W 2E7

Actually, of course, the giant really meant that it was the *sword-arm* that would be cut off, and it was obvious from where Conan wore his sword that he was right-handed. As for that skeletal hand, its attached forearm was meant to be buried partly in dirt, but perhaps the pic didn't make that as clear as it should. So, we'll give you your no-prize on a technicality, just show you that our heart (if not necessarily our hand) is in the right place.

Dear Roy and John,

CONAN #54 was an issue which was at once disturbing and magnificently rendered. I don't think I really need to explain what disturbed me about it—just think how you'd react if a mirror image of yourself came at you with a broadsword, and in order to defeat it, you had to raise a dead man.

There was also a glimpse of Peter Lorre in old Renquis; I can just hear Lorre delivering lines like, "Yes, I know, I know...though sometimes I confess...I forget." After saying that, he'd laugh evilly and slip around a corner. Great stuff, Roy!

Now for the "magnificently rendered" part. John Buscema has gotten so good at drawing Conan that I think his version of the Cimmerian during this period of his life will probably become the definitive one, just as Barry Smith unquestionably captured the barbarian-thief Conan so perfectly.

Finally, I was somewhat surprised by Detsugsid's letter in CONAN #54. Can it actually be that someone's getting tired of the countless coined names that keep popping up in fantasy? Will Lupalina, Stefanya, and Murilo be replaced by Harvey, Marvin, and George? By Crom, let it not be so!

Edward Via
1648 Dean Rd.
Roanoke, Va. 24018

In all fairness, Ed, we think that letter-writer's point was rather that there were just a few too *many* characters running around in our multi-part "Conjurer's Curse" tale, and we're almost inclined to agree. Now, wait'll we start getting letters from people who get N'Yaga and M'Gora mixed up, even after our writer/editor altered the latter's name somewhat to try to clarify things!

Dear Conan Cohorts:

My first reaction to CONAN #55 came the minute I read the caption "Were ever a less likely trio charged with the fate of a world?"Since when is Conan a "world-beater"? Maybe he *has* saved the world umpteen times since CONAN #1, but he always did it in his own sullen, reluctant, bored, and superstitious manner. He usually did it for some deceitful, sloe-eyed wench, or at best for a mindless, fickle princess with as much brains as the camels in her caravan. Or for just plain ol' Hyborian cash. "World-beating" should be left to the superheroes....

Even more serious is the sequence in this story in which Conan duels with Vanni. Come on, Roy. That was plain murder. The Conan in story form would *never* kill such an unworthy foe in such an uneven match. Conan would have just slapped Vanni's princely posterior with the flat of his sword, or something similar. And this poor fool Vanni even turned his head!? What is Conan becoming?

Marvin Sander
2065 Rockaway Parkway
Brooklyn, NY 11236

What he always *was*, we think, Marv: namely, a guy who kills them as needs killin'! Surely you remember "God in the Bowl," the original REH tale in which Conan grabbed a sword and beheaded the treacherous Aztrias, who was merely trying to get the Cimmerian to take a murder rap for him. Or the scene in "Shadows in the Moonlight" in which Conan's Turanian foe was wounded, but the barbarian kept hacking away at him until he resembled nothing human. REH's quote: "This was no longer battle, but butchery." We could go on and on, but we think you get our point; we disagree almost entirely with your interpretation of what Conan would do in some given situations. Any other comments, people?

As for Conan being a world-beater...well, we never said that he and his friends *knew* they held the fate of the world in their hands; they were just trying to save Murilo and company from a grisly fate, and if a few million other people benefited, then so be it. Sorry if we confused you, ol' buddy.

Dear Roy,

After the semi-failure of the Kothar adaptation, I was getting a bit leary about multi-part epics in CONAN. Thanks for setting my head straight, Roy. CONAN #52-55 made up one of the most entertaining Conan stories I've ever read.

Actually, much of my enthusiasm is due to the introduction (and re-ditto) of some supporting characters to go with Conan. I loved Murilo, and Tara-and-Yusef are an interesting pair. I just hope you give Tara's youthful suitor a little more character than he has now, or I'll lose all my respect for the ravishing acrobat's taste in boyfriends.

Kim Thompson
Gen. Del. Box 259
APO NY NY 09184

You'll have to wait a while to see if and when Tara and Yusef (together or separately) return to the Conan mag. In fact, we asked Roy, and he said, "Well, I've got plans for them, but not till issue #120 or so." As to whether he was kidding or serious—we'll have to leave it to you to judge. We *do* know that the Rascally One had been planning certain aspects of Bêlit's origin for *several years now*. He's got a lot of patience, that lad.

Oh yes, and just for the record—if you don't count the Conan/Bêlit saga itself as a "multi-parter," then we've got another one coming up, starting next issue. Hope you and a few zillion other Hyboriophiles can dig it...

MARVEL VALUE STAMP

CLIP 'EM AND COLLECT 'EM!

33: **DRACULA** from *Conan the Barbarian* no. 59 (February 1976).

CABLES OF CHAMPIONS

c/o MARVEL COMICS GROUP, 575 MADISON AVE. N.Y.C. 10022

Dear Tony, Bill, George, and Vince:

You have five fantastic characters who work well together, and so far you have given them one great story to kick off the series. The only problem is that you haven't made a team out of them yet. There has been no mention that there will be a team after the one-night stand that got things rolling. How will they finance themselves? Why will they band together? Why do they call themselves the Champions? What will make them different from the herd of other super teams that are flocking together on the newstand? All of these details have to be ironed out. The only thing that has become clear is that the Black Widow is and *MUST* (get that?) remain the team leader. But there was no reason for Natasha to go with the Iceman and the Angel to where we found them at the beginning of this story. And how did Ghost Rider know where to find them? The only reason I can think of is that they formed the team between issues, which would be a sin, as I'm very eager to see how the team is formed.

George and Vince are turning out some of the best art that they've ever done, lately, in all of the various strips that they've done. This issue was great! Let's keep it up.

As you may have guessed, I'm very enthusiastic about the prospects. Just explain some of the details and keep up the excellence.

Larry Twiss
227 Fox Run
King of Prussia, PA 19406

Dear Tony, Bill, George, Vince, Karen, George, and Marv,

Let me talk about The Champions as a group. Good choices, except for one person— The Black Widow. She doesn't seem to fit in with all the others in that group. She has no strength like Hercules or Angel...just her widow stings and agility. I think she should be replaced by Tigra, the Were-Woman.

Brett Slack
195 Oak Street
Amityville, NY 11701

All adventurous afficionados of our latest superteam effort will be perplexed to learn of the difference of opinion as to the Black Widow's role in THE CHAMPIONS. Missives are coming in demanding that this beauteous former Russian spy should either rule or be ruled, and to tell ya the truth, our sympathies have already swung to one side. But d'ya think we're gonna tell ya here? Nah! Be sure to check out our next issue.

Tony's glad that you like Tigra enough to recommend her for membership in The Champions, Brett. Why? He writes that feature every other month in MARVEL CHILLERS, and is pleased to know that *you're* pleased. End of unabashed plug.

As for the art of George Tuska, Larry, you'll be glad to hear that the Gorgeous One is now permanent artist on this bi-monthly bonanza!

And as for the group's *raison d'etre,* take a gander at the answer to the next letter.

Dear Marvel,

As for the CHAMPIONS #3 well..I think maybe you're trying. Maybe. At least the pacing was good, the characterization and artwork genuinely mediocre. It still isn't Marvel quality by a long shot. Okay. I trust you'll try harder still. But I still can't see the "why" of the Champions. Why should they stay together? Bobby and Warren were never really close, not like Bobby was with Hank. And will they ever find happiness on *Search For Purpose*? There seems to be no real attraction between the rest of the group, and no real leader to keep them together. Doc & The Defenders have just been too busy to try and split, and we don't want the Champions to be imitation Defenders, do we boys? Might I suggest that unless the Champs are a *gigantic* financial success we have them all pack their bags, have a last drink of Tequila, and go their separate ways never to re-form. Don't drag out this nth rate comic book until it meets a slow economic and critical death.

Joseph Noke
Apartment #3
5204 South Kimbark
Chicago, IL 60615

Well, Joe, Tony and Don hope that the contents of this issue have helped clear up for you some of the conceptualization of THE CHAMPIONS. If you save your sheckels 'till next time around (that's sixty days, sport), you'll not only get to see Rampage riot on, but you'll also learn more about the only superteam that's in it for the money.

Dear Stan and the gang,

What's this? Complaints about the CHAMPIONS!? I think it is the best supergroup ever. One suggestion, though. How about adding Spider-Man? If you did, The Champs would truly be a superteam supreme.

Martin Greene
27 Willis Street
Boston, MA 02125

We'd love to comply with your wish, Marty—only the wall-crawling wonder's schedule has been entirely filled as of late, and will most likely remain so in the near future. What with his titanic tales in MARVEL TEAM-UP, SPIDER-MAN ANNUAL, SPIDEY SUPER-STORIES, and the reprint MARVEL TALES, we're surprised that he has enough time even to appear in his own bombastic book, THE AMAZING SPIDER-MAN.

However, if a free spot ever comes up in your friendly neighborhood Spider-Man's time, we'll see if we can squeeze in a surprise visit to the Champions.

So stick close, Marty. You never know what may happen when your batty Bullpen is in charge!

THIS IS IT! YOUR
MARVEL VALUE STAMP
FOR THIS ISSUE!

CLIP 'EM AND COLLECT 'EM!

77: **DRACULA** from *The Champions* no. 5 (April 1976).

THE HYBORIAN PAGE
c/o MARVEL COMICS GROUP, 575 MADISON AVE., NEW YORK, N.Y. 10022

Messrs. Thomas, Buscema, and Marcos:

At last he is back! He lost his way somewhere, became apathetic and sluggish, throughout his service in the Crimson Company; he seemed subordinate and soft, almost civilized. I feared he was lost forever. But, with number 56, he is returned, the savage barbarian of impulse and suspicion.

"The Strange High Tower in the Mist" was the Conan story I have missed for over half a year, and feared I would never see again. And, like a reunion with an old friend, reading it excited and satisfied me. Mr. Thomas has finally recaptured the mystery, the horror, and the flow of the Hyborian atmosphere, and presented a tight, fascinating Conan adventure. Mr. Buscema contributed one of his most expressive works, and Mr. Marcos' inks outlined the issue's mood splendidly.

Now that he is back, please do not let him wander again. Send him on to Argos, on to the sea, and into the savagery of Bêlit's piracy.

I'm with you till Thoth-Amon's ring rusts.

Lonson Armstrong
Box 496
Burton, OH 44021

That'll be a while, Lonny. (By the way, we hope we got your first name right; it was a bit hard to tell the "a's" from the "o's" in your signature.) However, we might as well mention here and now that Thoth-Amon will be appearing ere long in these very pages— and also in the pages of an upcoming 50¢ CONAN ANNUAL, on sale this coming summer, when Roy and artist Vicente Alcazar at last adapt the very first King Conan story of all, "The Phoenix on the Sword."

But, what's with all this "Mister" stuff? You trying to make our beleaguered Bullpenners feel old or something? Next thing you know, you'll be trying to get one of 'em into a necktie!

Dear Marvel,

CONAN #56 was just great— the cover fantastic, the story incredible. As for the gorgeous woman introduced on p. 7, all I can say is that it's too bad she wasn't real. In the future, I hope you'll have another woman appear in Conan's life— one who looks just like this one, but is real. It's about time Conan found himself a girl to love and protect and to have his children. Keep up the great work on CONAN.

Wilson Rivera
89 Maujer Street
Brooklyn, NY 11206

We'll try, Wilson. Alas for your stated wishes, it's pretty well established in Conan's life, as recorded from the 1930's to the present, that he never married till he was in his forties and was king of the civilized nation of Aquilonia. Still, in a way, you can get at least one of your wishes just by picking up the latest issue of our $1 companion title, THE SAVAGE SWORD OF CONAN, which is now on sale—and which should be displayed wherever other black-and-white comics (such as DEADLY HANDS OF KUNG FU, PLANET OF THE APES, *et al.*) are found. For, it's there that Roy and John have completed Marvel's serialization of Robert E. Howard's one-and-only Conan novel, *Conan the Conqueror,* which was previously begun in our late lamented GIANT-SIZE CONAN. It's 58 pages of action from start to finish—and, like they say on TV, you're gonna like it a lot!

Dear Roy, John, Pablo, and Stan,

My reaction to CONAN #56 is mostly positive. Roy has scripted another nice sword-and-sorcery story. Actually, though, I do get tired of seeing all this magic-and-monsters stuff, which is prevalent every issue. Just gets monotonous. Know what I mean, Roy? It's not the quality of the stories I'm attacking; it's the lack of variety in them. Next issue, however, it looks like it'll be just what the doctor ordered. In fact, I know it will be. As always, make mine Marvel, folks.

PMM Jack Frost
Rt. 3, Box 176-C
West Monroe, LA 71291

You were right as rain there, Jack. There was virtually *no* touch of sorcery at all (except a little image-casting by a little old lady) in ish #57— ditto in #58, "Queen of the Black Coast." And the current series, while it has sizable alligators who might be considered monsters, is more of a jungle adventure than a sword-vs.-sorcery tale *per se.* Now the question is, how long before everybody starts writing in and asking us whatever happened to all the magicians and wizards! Personally, we just write 'em the way we think 'em up— and, most of the time, it seems to us that the Conan stories just write themselves. (Oh, yeah, Thomas? So then how come you can't get 'em to write themselves during the daytime, instead of at 3 A.M.? Riddle us *that!*)

Dear Roy, John, Pablo, Phil, and John C.:

Just read CONAN #56. Saw Conan ride off "on the road to sea-washed Messantia" with a very tattered red cloak. Can't wait for #57. Bet he arrives in sea-washed Messantia already bedecked in a new cloak, instead of buying a new one once he gets there. What do you think?

Vicky Peyton-Roberts
217-15 Nimitz Drive
W. Lafayette, IN 47906

We think you're dead right, Vicky gal. Y'see, it's like this: in between issues #56 and #57, Conan and company ran into a bunch of road-brigands whom they defeated and, lo and behold, one of 'em was sporting a shiny red cloak which our raggedy Cimmerian appropriated for his own, so that he could start out the next issue all shiny and new. And if you believe that one, we've got some swampland in New Jersey we'd like to sell you....

MARVEL VALUE STAMP

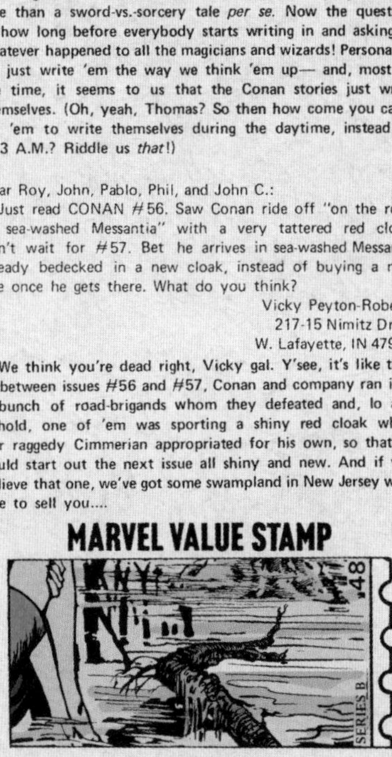

48: DRACULA from *Conan the Barbarian* no. 60 (March 1976).

THE HAMMER STRIKES

c/o MARVEL COMICS GROUP, 575 MADISON AVE. N.Y.C. 10022

Dear Marvel,

Is this the Len whose latest issue of SPIDER-MAN I criticized?

Couldn't be!

The author of the 244th issue of THOR did a great job, whoever he is. We have some excellent characterization, some close to excellent plotting, the threatening spectre of a dark beauty from Thor's past—who, although she is somewhere in Jane, will *stay* in the past (hint, hint). And Odin has finally proven that he's off his nut. That really is great. But it will probably turn out to be someone other than Odin. He has all the luck; he always ends up smelling like a rose. But what are All-Fathers for?

A good ish, whoever wrote it.

Lester Baptiste
120-31 Benchley Pl.
Bronx, NY 10475

Gee, what a nice letter from—Les Baptiste? Naw, it *couldn't* be! Well, whoever scribbled that sensational scroll, it seems he's become a reluctant recruit to the ever-swelling ranks of the legion of Len likers—even if he *does* hate to admit it!

As for the All-Father, just pick up our very next issue when our scintillating sub-plot comes to a climax. Take our word for it, pilgrim, it's a wowser!

Dear Len,

I just finished THOR #244. Wow, what a downer of an ish. There was only one bright moment in the whole mag, and that's when Thor thought he saw Sif for that one second. It wasn't much, but it was enough to give me a clue as to what is going to happen.

Jane Foster is going to find an umbrella or something, tap it on the ground, and, lo and behold—Sif is back.

In the future, please go deeper into Thor's personality (like with Spidey) and put a happy moment or two in, huh?

Eric Robinson
Box 41 Pet 9
1141 USAF SAS
APO New York 09221

Only *one* bright moment in the whole mag? We just got done looking back over that issue, Eric, and we found at least 3.6 bright moments! Len and John always labor to include an absolute minimum of no less than two bright moments in every single story, and in this case we just don't see how you could have missed all those dazzling extra-radiant moments—unless, of course, you were wearing shades while you read that ish.

Have a care, friend Eric—at Marvel we're meticulous about our multitude of bright moments!

Len, John, Joe, Glynis, and Joe,

I have to admit that I wasn't too pleased with Len's debut issues of THOR. They seemed to consist mainly of fight scenes which seemed overly familiar. But lately, I'm pleased to say things appear to be on the upswing. Len seems to have gotten a feel for our Asgardian friends and the future looks promising. Some of the reasons for my change of heart are the return of Fandral, Hogun, Volstagg, and (at long last) Balder; the Servitor's loyalty to Zarrko; and the return of Firelord. Now just bring back Sif (Jane Foster's dialogue is soooo corny), Karnilla, and don't bring back Loki! Then I will be truly happy.

Dennis Sellers
Rte. 4
Huntingdon, TN 38344

How *dare* you not be truly happy right *now*, Denny?! After all, we figure that fully four more issues have appeared since you wrote your missive, and that should be enough to make even *you*—hard to please Thorophile that you are—enormously ecstatic.

And if you *aren't*...er...well, we can't win 'em all. Right?

Dear Sirs,

I have always ranked Thor as one of the best Marvel characters, and your recent Time-Twisters series has done a great deal to enforce that belief. The Servitor, while he lasted, was an able addition to the Marvel Universe, and I was sorry to see him go.

Len, if these few issues were a preview of things to come, I hope you stay with this mag for a long, long time. Nuff said.

Henry Marchand
799 Second St.
Secaucus, NJ 07044

Len has no present plans to abandon the scripting of THOR for a long, long while to come—so he's more than grateful for the kudos that have been coming his way, since he was just a mite apprehensive about mastering all that archaic Asgardian grammar.

But lest ye think all our mail is complimentary or semi-complimentary, let us hereby dispel that illusion—

Dear Marvel,

I never thought much of Thor from the beginning. I still don't!

Jeff Martin
991 N.W. 201 St.
Miami, FL 33169

But you never know what you'll think of Thor in the future, Jeff—unless you pick up next issue! That goes for the rest of you loyal Marvelites, too (hint, hint).

THIS IS IT! YOUR
MARVEL VALUE STAMP
FOR THIS ISSUE!

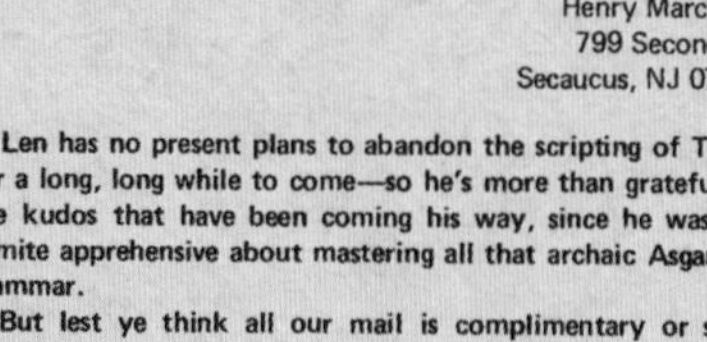

CLIP 'EM AND COLLECT 'EM!

96: DRACULA from *Thor* no. 248 (June 1976).

SKULLDUGGERY

c/o MARVEL COMICS GROUP, 575 MADISON AVE. N.Y.C. 10022

Nothing changes faster than permanence in the Mighty Marvel Magilla, and here's the latest proof: despite everybody's best intentions, this issue turns out to be Steve Englehart's one and only outing with SKULL THE SLAYER. See, DR. STRANGE just went monthly, and.... Oh well, who cares about reasons. What you care about is who's gonna be here next time, and all we can say is that any one of the current possibilities should blow your boundaries all over again. Check us out in sixty days see who won— in addition to yourself, of course.

Dear Marvel,

Again, you've come out with another great title! SKULL THE SLAYER has, with its second issue, turned into one of my favorite titles. I thought #1 was fantastic, but # 2 was stupendous!

Marv Wolfman's (I still don't believe that's his real name) script was great, and the narration style reminded me of Doug Moench's WEREWOLF BY NIGHT (which I really hope isn't cancelled). The idea of the alien and his power belt was, in my opinion, a good addition to Skull and to the strip. The only thing that seemed a little bit fakey was the skull on the belt. Another thing I enjoy is the Bermuda Triangle idea, which leaves a lot to be explained. With this in the strip, there's always the possibility of others (advanced humans) wandering around somewhere.

The art was, shall I say, simply unmentionable. Steve Gan is really doing a great job on the strip, and hopefully will be around for some time to come. Each panel is a sheer work of art. The thing that makes his style stand out is, he really has no other artist's technique. Like Smith, he has a style totally his, and that is basically why I like it!

About the coloring, which I usually (that means never) don't mention... Michele Wolfman is doing a great job, so I suggest you keep her on SKULL also. After all, this is her only comic so far.

So, 'til Deathlok gets his 1,000 mile tune-up, MAKE MINE MARVEL!

Larry Dean
6362 Laurentian Ct.
Flint, MI 48504

Dear Marv,

Well, Marv, after four years of perseverance you finally got SKULL published, but not for the better. The things that always put MARVEL on top are lacking: reality, and the human personality. Individual characters who not only face super-villains, but taxes, recessions, divorce, politics, prejudices and the Ultra-Brite "How's your love life?" syndrome.

Skull just doesn't have personality and neither do his supporting characters. Ann has potential, but only if you don't take the strong will of a liberated woman and make her the constant reason for SKULL to risk his neck because she fell down running away from a stampede.

I also feel that (war-hero or not) Skull is just too fearless. Please, Marv, don't give him super powers (which you touched the surface of in Issue 2). This would withdraw from the original ideal you had of SKULL being a different sort of mag.

Even with all this criticism I do think the Viet Nam scenes, and the vets trying to readjust, was expertly done, as was Steve Gan's fine artwork.

One last thing, please don't make SKULL similar to a treeswinger from, as you aptly put it, MARVEL's Declining Competition.

Brian Lowry
13832 Erwin Street
Van Nuys, CA 91401

Origin issues (and SKULL #1 and 2 were conceived as one long story) always have to skim over a few factors just to get the entire situation set up, Brian. In this case, characterization *wasn't* hit all that hard, but since characters are Steve's forte, we trust those loose ends have been gathered up by now, and SKULL's continuing epic has earned your wholehearted approval. Marv and Steve sure hope so, anyway!

Dear SKULL-people,

No-prize time, fellas. In SKULL THE SLAYER #2, page 27, Corey yells "Brontosaurus," as he looks at a creature break the surface of the water. The so-called Brontosaurus is an Elasmosaurus. This FOOMer rests his case.

Vinny Lombardi Jr.
183 Olive Street
Piscataway, NJ 08854

PS. What flavors do your no-prizes come in?

You know, Vinny, every one of us Bullpenners (even us Armadillos) was a Marvel FAN before he was a Marvel PRO, so we all have pretty long memories concerning our books—and do you know, it sure seems as if *any* time *any* scripter has used a dinosaur in a story, he's gotten its name wrong. Really—it's like a rule. Name a 'saur and get a load of letters. In fact, not one of these turkeys knows that *I'm* not really an armadillo...but don't tell 'em, or their egos will really be shot to shreds.

Anyway, Vin, you can have your no-prize in any flavor you want—if you can get it out from under the Pterodactyl standing guard in our storeroom. Don't worry...he ain't heavy. He's my brother.

MARVEL VALUE STAMP

54: DRACULA from *Skull the Slayer* no. 4 (March 1976).

IRON-FIST FULS

c/o MARVEL COMICS GROUP, 575 MADISON AVE. N.Y.C. 10022

Dear Chris, John and Co., ,

In all truthfulness, I've never enjoyed voraciously much of Chris Claremont's work. Oh, the "War is Hell" series I enjoyed, and there are certain aspects of the new X-MEN book that strike me well, but there was quite little else of Chris' that impressed this humble personage. IRON FIST, under his tutelage, didn't sit well with me at all.

However, IRON FIST #2's "Valley of the Damned" not only struck me as a tender and beautiful tale, but a scathing display of what envy and jealousy can do to a man, even in "paradise." At last, we see Chris Claremont become at one with the art, quite a step upward from the muddling we've been treated to for too long. Part of the reason, I suspect, comes from the very excellent (and still growing) talents of John Byrne. When that husky Canadian first started his stint at Marvel I was, though, somewhat disappointed—where was deft draftsman and envisionist extraordinaire I'd known from Charlton? All this one saw was a ghost of John's more-than-considerable artistry (trying to play a "straight" artist rather than retaining his deceptively light normal style was, I suspect, at least part of the reason). Ah, but here in IF #2! Now *that's* John Byrne like we've seen for the last couple of years in fanzines and other pro comics work! His storytelling style is improving with gigantic strides, and his use of angles for expression and effect is getting to be marvelous—perhaps with just a touch of Paul Gulacy inherent, but still very much his own man. And finding a point to this ramble, if Chris improves his own understanding of the character and concept as he's been doing, running side by side with John Byrne, IRON FIST will continue and continue to reach for certain what the cliche calls, "a pinnacle of greatness."

Still, some specifics to "Valley of the Damned" are in order. Plotwise, the flashback sequences—and the point they most certainly made—did not appear to me to be just a writing gimmick . . . they fitted so naturally within the framework of the story I nodded to myself, "Of course." The dialogue, forced to be clear and concise by John's masterful expressions (page 30, # 3, I'll always recall fondly) worked exquisitely (the sequence with Miranda's uncovering sticks particularly in my mind, but it went well throughout). And while I don't care for Frank Chiaramonte's clear (though simplistic) inking on such sketchy artists as Don Heck or Sal Buscema, I found he complemented John's strong, linear style as well as anyone else I've yet seen. If you're looking for a permanent art team on IF (enough with the ring-around-the-writer!), I humbly suggest Byrne and Chiarmonte in tandem.

Final notes: Misty Knight is great—great potential, great charisma. Keep up what you've been doing, Chris—Misty is as un-stereotyped a "Black-female-detective" as a blond-haired, blue-eyed Italian (we do exist, y'know!) is of that race. Keep it up, I say! 'Cause if every issue of IRON FIST is as enjoyable as #2, you've got me in your corner—construe *that* one any way you can. . . !

Frank Lovece
947 Maple Drive, No. 15
Morgantown, WV 26505

What can we say, Frank, other than thank you.

As to the whys of your letter, we agree that Jocular John Byrne is one dynamic artist—and, more importantly, that he's been getting better with each succeeding issue of IRON FIST. Put succinctly, if you thought issue #2 was something, wait 'till you see what our Crazy Canadian has done with issues three, four and five! To say that we here at Marvel were impressed by his work would be an understatement akin to saying the sun is hot; and we're hoping that all you out there in Marveldom Assembled end up feeling the same.

Dear Marvel,

After reading all my Iron Fist issues once more, in addition to IRON FIST #2, (which by the way brightened the afternoon for me as well as occupying all of it), I ask: *"Iron Fist has a Sister?!"* Apparently so, by name of "Miranda" who died before Danny Rand ever left the city of Kun-Lun for revenge on Meachum. Let's see lots more on where she was when Wendell Rand and his wife were killed and Danny was alone. Also, did she enter Kun-Lun later with Conal? In any event, let's learn more.

By matter of curiosity, why have Ward and Joy Meachum been written out? Recent letters pages have told Marveldom, also, that more background will be presented on Lei King the Thunderer and Yu-Ti, I, personally, am intrigued by Yu-Ti. He revealed to Iron Fist (before refusing immortality) that he understood Danny's feelings for loss of loved ones, for he was Wendell Rand's brother. So why didn't the pangs of revenge affect him at all? How did *he* first come upon K'un-L'un to *become* Yu-Ti, "the august personage in jade"? How did he convince Wendell (his brother) that it existed and to bring his wife and child over? How, specifically, did he attain "dragon-king" status?

But now for a definite "no-squirming-out-of-this-mess" no-prize!

Interlude! Page 14, panel one, *September 11*, 1975, *Wednesday!* Page 16 and 17, flashback, page 18, panel one, *September 12*, 1975, *Friday*????

Conclusion: Huh?? I've heard of the difference between our time (reality) and so-called "Marvel-time" but—this is ridiculous!

(PMM) Marc P. Beauregard
181 Elm Street
New Bedford, MA 02740

Caught that, didja, Marc? Sneaky fella, ain'tcha—to catch that the K'un-Lun Kid has a sister. Well, you're right—in a way. But she didn't immigrate to K'un-Lun, as Danny Rand did; Miranda was born there. In fact, Danny was the first outsider to be admitted to the Immortal City—on any sort of permanent basis—in almost a *million years*.

As for Joy Meachum, dear old Uncle Ward, and the mysterious stranger from issue #1, you might already have noticed, if you're reading this issue—and we assume you are—that they have made a suitably ominous reappearance. More on that in upcoming issues. Also, much more on all the delightful people Danny left back in K'un-Lun, including some revelations we think will surprise the pants off you (in private, of course; we wouldn't want you should be embarrassed).

In closing, though, we have to admit that you got us good, Marc ol' buddy. We did indeed foul-up on issue #2's interludes. The copy should have read, "September 10, 1975, Wednesday" instead of the September 11th that was printed. Which only goes to show that even a well-trained armadillo can make a mistake. Which means you'll get your no-prize in the mail. *Grrrrr!!*

See ya in sixty, folks!

MARVEL VALUE STAMP

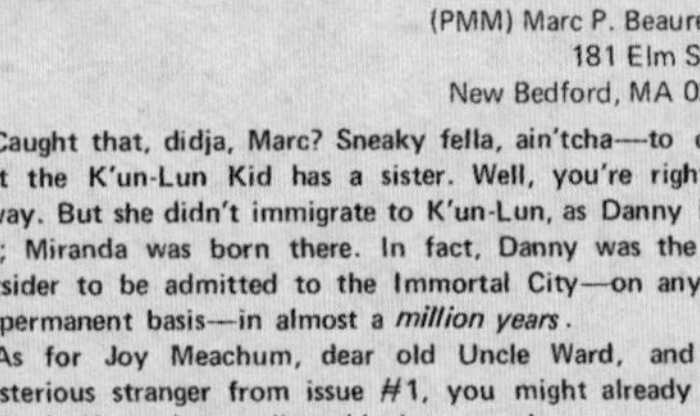

61: DRACULA from *Iron Fist* no. 4 (April 1976).

SKULLDUGGERY

c/o MARVEL COMICS GROUP, 575 MADISON AVE. N.Y.C. 10022

Four years of waiting. Four years of wondering. Four years of SKULL THE SLAYER sitting in Marv Wolfman's mind, raging to be unleashed. And then, Marv took the plunge. Would Marveldom Assembled accept this latest offering from the House of Ideas? Were those four years worth it?

***Were* they—!**

Dear Marv and Steve,

Congratulations! SKULL THE SLAYER #1 was an unqualified success, and no one is more surprised than I. You see, comics with cavemen put me to sleep. Somehow, cavemen are some sorta trend among the comics being put out today, and your competitor's entries into the field have bored me. Oh, of course I expected more from Marvel; I always do. I knew SKULL would be readable. What I didn't know was that it would be darn near perfect.

I'll start by complimenting the art. I hadn't been overly impressed by Steve Gan's artwork in the black and whites, and I believe that his fine line style is ill-suited for the medium. However, that same fine line style is eminently suited for color comics, and the art was absolutely beautiful. Gan's artwork resemble's Al Williamson's work very much, but it never looks like swipes, just influence. Marv, as much as I loved Steve's art, I think your coloring of this issue was the single most impressive coloring job I've seen in years, *really*. It fit the artwork *perfectly*. It reminded me very much of the coloring and art on the first issue of King Comics Flash Gordon, which came out maybe 10 years or so ago. Whew, what a job! Please keep Gan on the art, and if all possible, try to continue coloring the book, huh Marv?

But good art does not make a book, which is something that took me years to realize. A great script can carry poor art, but great art usually can't do a *thing* for a rotten script, except make the reader wonder why the artist went to so much trouble. What I'm trying to say is that Marv's script was as important as Steve's art for making the book work. In fact, SKULL THE SLAYER #1 was one of those rare books that was perfectly balanced between superb art and superb script; usually one element outweighs the other, but not in this case. What I liked about SKULL were the concepts. Using the Bermuda Triangle was an excellent, if obvious, idea. Scully's background was well presented, and quite suited for the series. The aspect of using a varied time scheme in the upcoming issues sounds downright exciting. You'll be able to present people, and even THINGS, from all time periods, even the future, and that should be downright enthralling. And Marv, your narration was as good, if not better, than in your excellent TOMB OF DRACULA series, and that's heady praise indeed. Especially well done was your constant juxtaposition of references to media and media related items with tne stark contrast of a primitive world.

Well, I don't know what else to say, really, except that I can hardly wait for the next issue. I'm glad you've had four years to play with SKULL in your head, because, if issue one is any indication (and I'm betting it is) you know *exactly* where you want to go with it, and what you want to say with it. It's gonna be lots a fun seeing it all develop.

Reading a comic like SKULL THE SLAYER #1 makes wading through all the mediocrity worthwhile. Marvel puts out the best comics that there are, and this is one of the best ones. Bravo!

Fred G. Hembeck
280 Stockbridge
Buffalo, NY 14215

Dear Marv and Marvel,

I don't know how you do it, but you Marvel madmen never seem to stop coming up with exciting, original new mags. SKULL THE SLAYER #1 was merely the latest in a long progression of new concept masterpieces.

Not only is the concept of SKULL new, but the scripting style is, also. Marv, you write all your strips in decidedly unconventional styles, but this was the wildest yet. I liked it. I also liked Steve Gan's artwork, which was (as you mentioned, Marv) perfect for this book. Other good points were the well-defined characterizations, the surprising Wolfman-produced coloring, and the idea that a time warp is the secret of the Bermuda Triangle.

I think that I'll refrain from further comment until I see what happens when Skull meets his fellow survivors and until the role of the cave man (?) is made clear. I have some speculations about these things, but I could be all wrong.

Anyway, I liked #1, and you can be sure I'll keep reading.

Mark Caldwell
Box 184
Cedar Crest, NM 87008

But four years are four years, and a lot can happen in that time. One of the things that happened was Smilin' Stan picking Marv to become our editor, and—as with Rascally Roy and Lively Len before him—Wolfman Marv has discovered that editing can eat into your time. So, with loads of regret, we must announce that this is Marv's last outing with his brain-child...and with him goes Steve Gan, who's gotten caught up with CONAN.

But fear not, front-facer! SKULL yet lives, in the hands of two more of Marvel's mightiest! Next time around, we've reunited Steve Englehart and Sal Buscema, who certainly need no further hype, to carry Scully onward...and believe you us (since we've seen Steve's plot), he's going *'way* onward! Marv wanted a series that continually evolved, and that's what you'll get...in SKULL THE SLAYER #4!

(P.S. Englehart's also picking up SUPER-VILLAIN TEAM-UP with *its* fourth issue, out next month, and you're bound to dig the new things he's scheduled over there...while Marv keeps right on creating classics for TOMB OF DRACULA and DAREDEVIL. Like the man said—how can you lose?)

Bye!

THIS IS IT! YOUR

MARVEL VALUE STAMP

FOR THIS ISSUE!

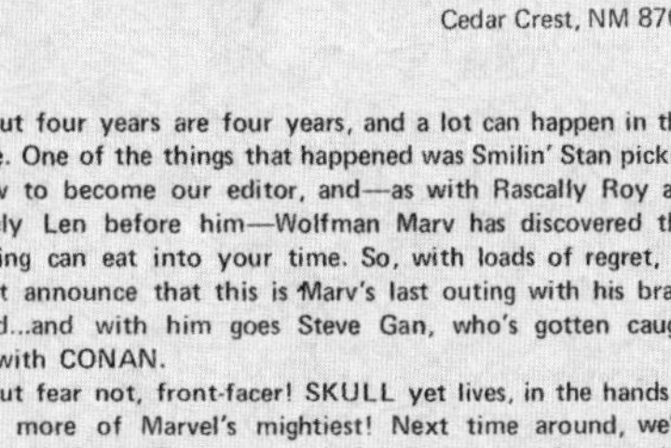

CLIP 'EM AND COLLECT 'EM!

22: DRACULA from *Skull the Slayer* no. 3 (January 1976).

THE MIGHTY THOR™

Until a vacation in Norway, **Dr. Donald Blake** was no more than an average, mortal man... or so he thought. While exploring the Norwegian backwoods, Dr. Blake accidentally stumbled upon a gnarled stick which in reality was the mystical **Mjolnir**, the powerful "Uru Hammer" of Norse Mythology. From the moment the lame doctor first tapped the stick on the ground, he was restored forever and always to his true identity as the master of nature and the elements, the *God of Thunder*— **The Mighty Thor!**

Tales of Asgard no. 1 (October 1968), art by Jack Kirby and Frank Giacoia.

SOCK IT TO SHELL-HEAD

c/o MARVEL COMICS GROUP, 575 MADISON AVE. N.Y.C. 10022

Dear Mike and George,

Comment, IRON MAN #79: Good.

Am I correct in understanding that this story was written with the intent of using it as a sort of "reserve" in case Mike or George got bogged down with the deadline doom? If so then my hat is indeed off to you dear-hearted chaps, you've unknowingly saved me from the terrible anguish of ripping my hair out when I discovered that I had paid good money for a sub-standard reprint.

Thanks amigos.

I hope this sort of practice is made standard procedure in all of your mags in the future.

MARVERITER!

Marveriter
Box 4112 S.R.A.
Anchorage, AK 99502

The practice has *already* been made standard procedure, Marv, 'cause Mighty Marvel wants to make sure that no rapacious reprints, as good as they may be, find a place in our awesome original titles. The bulk of the scripting has gone to Boisterous Bill Mantlo, who has become so overwhelmed with work that he's been forced to leave his position as Jumbo John Verpoorten's Assistant Production Manager to handle the staggering amount of work.

Fill-ins, held in reserve until the dreaded deadline doom demands that they absolutely must be used, have already been done (or are, in fact, in the drawer) for most of our merely magnificent titles.

Mighty Marvel is Number One—! And we *still* try harder!

Dear Marvel, Mike, and Many other Madmen:

As a writer, the overall greatness of Mike Friedrich's work is second only to Steve Englehart. Among his all-time classic series are Ant Man, and Iron Man. A former fan himself, he innately knows how to write the way a fan would want a comic to be written.

But every now and then, Mike outdoes himself. He writes an almost perfect comic masterpiece. Indeed IM #79, "Midnight on Murder Mountain," was just short of absolute perfection.

"Midnight" used cliches, it is true. But where would the story have been without them? Can you imagine the sight of the Lodge on a sunny day? It would be like the Pittsburgh Steelers playing baseball: Interesting and nice to look at, but not very awesome.

Right from the beginning the reader knows that something bizarre is going to happen. But in fact that which does happen, however bizarre, is the single flaw in the story. By engaging in the typical super-hero fight scene, the mood which has been so painstakingly and masterfully built is detracted from. There is no law that every comic must contain a physical conflict; as proof read Denny O'Neil or Bob Haney or even Steve Englehart.

But as Aries like Mike (and my girl-friend) don't like criticism, and also because I have just sailed M & M's into my typewriter and it is getting hard to type, I will close.

Mark M. Thomase
2615 E. 46th Avenue
Denver, CO 80216

Mike thanks you, George thanks you, Vinnie thanks you, and even old Irv Forbush thanks you. But we've never considered the fact that "things" happened in our stories to be a flaw.

Just as you say that there is no law that every comic must contain a physical conflict, there is also no law that all stories must go without one. Marvel has had stories in the past without fight scenes when relatively feasible, but remember that there is nothing inherently wrong with action or fight scenes.

In fact, we happen to think they're best at mighty Marvel!

Dear Marvel,

I'm going to make this short and very sweet! IRON MAN is without a doubt one of Marvel's greatest mags! IRON MAN #79 was great. A fitting end for Dr. Kurakill! George Tuska did his normal super job. One last thing— get rid of IRON MAN's nose! It doesn't make his mask look like a helmet.

John Cate
902 Helix Drive
Concord, CA 94518

Well, John, Tony Stark's newest scripter, Lilting Len Wein, has been thinking along those lines himself! We're not going to tell you any hows or whens— We'll just tell ya to be on the lookout for the latest change in IRON MAN's life. It'll knock you outta your tree!

THIS IS IT! YOUR
MARVEL VALUE STAMP
FOR THIS ISSUE!

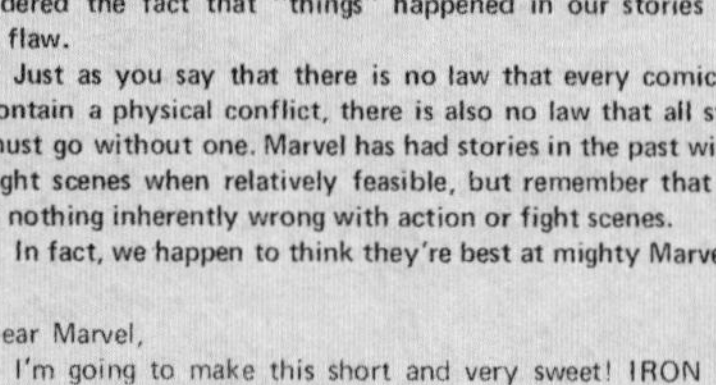

CLIP 'EM AND COLLECT 'EM!

16: THE MIGHTY THOR from *Iron Man* no. 83 (February 1976).

THE HAMMER STRIKES

c/o MARVEL COMICS GROUP, 575 MADISON AVE. N.Y.C. 10022

Dear Marvel,

I went into my favorite comic mag store the other day and couldn't find any of my regulars from Marvel, so I decided to buy my first THOR.

I took it home rather skeptically but WOW, this is a great mag. If you people wanted to hook me on THOR then #239 was great bait...I'm hooked.

I would have liked to know a little more about the events leading up to #239 but I can't expect Good ol' Marvel to stop and tell me everything. Anyway, the art was superb and the story even better.

Steve Will
404 Pearl St.
Decorah, IN 52101

It's always great to find a new reader, Steve, and we're especially proud that you've already been enjoying *other* super-spectacular Marvel series. It couldn't have happened to a nicer guy! And if there are any more of our bombastic books that you haven't tried yet, or have somehow missed catching in the glut of newsstand nonsense, be sure to keep your eyes glued to the pages of any Marvel comic, 'cause in just a few months we'll be returning the Mighty Marvel Checklist to these hallowed pages Watch for it!

And if you don't really understand the shape of things at present, try to pick up past issues at comic cons throughout the country, or else just keep following THOR... and all shall be revealed.

Dear Messrs. Thomas, Buscema, et. al.,

It matters not; this letter is about THOR. I always liked THOR, but I had never really given much thought to collecting him. Every time I had looked at his book, it seemed he was fighting Loki again. I was sick of Loki, ever since I had tried to draw him, Thor, and Odin for a school project and he was the only lousy one..Then the THOR TREASURY EDITION came out, and I was interested again. But I didn't like the stories Gerry Conway was cranking out. 3ut then I looked at THOR #239 when it came out and I bought it for two reasons—or maybe three:

(1) Sal Buscema. One of the best pencillers in the field, I had never seen him do THOR. That's because Brother John had been doing it, and his work on Conan, to my eyes, had spoiled him for the superhero biz. This was the first time EVER that it looked as though Sal's work surpassed John's, and the next reason I bought the issue tells why:

(2) Joe Sinnott inking Sal Buscema! Wow! I don't believe this had ever happened before, and it was about time! The art job was one of the best I've seen anywhere in years (except for Jane Foster), and though I love Jim Starlin, Rich Buckler, and Dave Cockrum, Sal and Joe equaled them in one swell foop (as the Human Torch has been known to say). That being the critique of the art, reason next is the biggest reason I bought the book:

(3) Roy Thomas. Roy is still my favorite fantasy writer, Steve Englehart having gone down a bit (sorry, Steve, but that's the way you is)—and I don't remember ever having seen Roy doing THOR. Boy, the changes that had been wrought since I last actively read an issue! Jane Foster is back (all right!!), Thor is speaking more normally every day, Odin in exile, and a lousy cover. (Sorry, Gil, but that's the way *you* is). Roy's script and plot were superb. I'm really sorry Roy has to leave the strip, but Bill Mantlo in ish #240 did an excellent job with dialogue.

Len Wein is coming on the strip! Okay! I guess if anybody but Roy has to do it, Len's the man. HULK and THOR are now on my must buy list, and Roy, Len, Sal, Joe, etc., go to it!

Mark Zutkoff
2302 Chetwood Circle
Timonium, MD 21093

So you like our power-packed writer/penciller/inker combination, eh, Mark? We're sure Sal would be one of the first to thank you himself, if he wasn't off busy receiving his Irving Forbush Award as Best Penciller.

And Len Wein, who gets to work with Sal on both Hulk and Thor, is simply very, very happy.

Dear Marvel,

I really thought THOR #239 was terrific although I wished the battle between Thor and Ulik had been a few pages longer! I liked it mainly because Jane Foster had really played a part in the story. She is one of my very favorite supporting characters and I hope you will be using her as a regular in THOR. I also hope that you'll be keeping Hercules and maybe Firelord as regulars.

Gee, I never really noticed that Sal Buscema drew this issue until I finished it. I really dig that artist! His style is so unique. I hope he'll be doing more of THOR and I do wish he would come back and draw Captain America.

Before I sign off I would like to ask these questions:

(1) In what issue of FOOM will the winners of the second Annual Irving Forbush Awards be announced?

(2) Will Xorr or the 4-D Man be returning?

(3) I would like to see Thor meet up with the Mad Viking who was featured in MAN-THING #16, #17 and #18. Is there any chance that they might?

Well, I guess that's about all I have to say. Until the Silver Surfer goes to a beach party, MAKE MINE MARVEL!!!!!!!!

Dallas Young
Route #1
Dike, TX 75437

If you really like Hercules, Dallas, perhaps you should hurry down to your newsdealer to see if you can still pick up a copy of MARVEL PREMIERE #26, featuring Hercules, Prince of Power! But if you can't make it down to the store for awhile— relax! You'll still be able to catch Firelord in a try-out issue of MARVEL SPOTLIGHT. Who says Marvel doesn't aim to please!

We are glad you like Sal (for the same reason as those in the previous letter) because he's been named Best Penciller by FOOMdom Assembled. And the entire results for those awards will be printed (or already have been by the time you read this) in FOOM #11, the special Jack Kirby issue. Send for it!

As for your second and third questions, we'll have to answer with a definite "We're not sure." Neither of the events of which you speak have been planned for the near future, but who knows— we just may change our minds.

See ya in thirty!

THIS IS IT! YOUR

MARVEL VALUE STAMP

FOR THIS ISSUE!

CLIP 'EM AND COLLECT 'EM!

7: THE MIGHTY THOR from *Thor* no. 243 (January 1976). Stamp also appears in *The Inhumans* no. 6 (August 1976).

and recognizable as the males, instead of suiting some one-character-fits-all rule. Jan's apparent flightiness and actual maturity make good foils for Wanda's hot and cold flashes of emotion, and could be well-played in terms of helping the latter adjust to married life. Also, the fact that the one "available" woman in the group is so enigmatic and standoffish can make for some interesting conflicts.

I love the way you're handling the Beast. Despite his different speech patterns and appearance, he *feels* right, as though this were the man that the X-Man of the Thomas/Roth days was bound to grow to be.

Good luck. Brand new artist, whoever you are. You've got a hard act to follow.

Mary Jo Duffy
81 Kensington Road
Garden City, NY 11530

Okay, Mary Jo — what do you think of this issue?

Dear Marvel,

I guess the Vision is still having problems of some sort (like amnesia). In AVENGERS #140, on page 26, he says (referring to taking the Beast's serum into Hank Pym), "But not while I can control the density of myself, my costume, and all within it," and pours the serum into a fold of his cape. Then, on page 27, he says, "For I know not how the Beast has caused the serum to become as phantasmal as myself."

You do still give out no-prizes, I assume.

Benjamin M. Yalow
3242 Tibbett Avenue
Bronx, NY 10463

We do, Ben—but to get yours, you'll have to ride the subway into Manhattan and catch the bleary-eyed proofreader who apparently missed the first line before adding the second. Be warned! He may be bleary-eyed, but he's fast—and he's got a few vicious armadillos to back him up!

Still want to try...?

Dear Marv and Steve,

You guys are going to have an irate SUPER-VILLAINS UNION picketing 575 Madison Avenue! Sheesh! AVENGERS #140 didn't even have one villain! The worst part was that the story was so smoothly written, the reader hardly noticed that until the last page!

Personally, the in-between-cosmic-epic tales you've been running since the resolution of the Mantis-Swordsman-Vision series have been refreshing. The disappearance of Hawkeye, the Moondragon conflicts, the not-so-mysterious redhead, and Jan's struggle for her life (I actually feared for her life...rare indeed in a comic mag)...all are keeping me in suspense without each sub-plot foolishly trying to outdo the other.

Danny Tyres
1188 Verona Road
Lewisburg, TN 37091

You're one of many readers (and the second on this page) to tell us you thought Jan Pym might snuff it, Danny, and we take such sentiment as a fine compliment indeed. Thank you (and you, too, Mary Jo— and all you others).

MARVEL VALUE STAMP

39: THE MIGHTY THOR from *The Avengers* no. 144 (February 1976).

IRON-FIST FULS

c/o MARVEL COMICS GROUP, 575 MADISON AVE. N.Y.C. 10022

Dear Parties Concerned:

John Byrne is an artist with a vengeance. I've admired his stunning artwork eleswhere, and seeing his work on Iron Fist in MARVEL PREMIERE #25 was a big kick for me. Inker McWilliams was a big help to the overall lustre of Byrne's work. . . what a fabulous art job!

Now that Iron Fist has the first really good art he's had since Larry Hama left the strip, I've become excited about the whole deal again. I'm glad you'll finally be giving us IRON FIST. . . and the fact that it will be a four-color book instead of the original b&w doesn't bother me a bit. Unlike Shang-Chi, Iron Fist is a super-hero, or at least, his strip has a super-hero flavor. As MARVEL PREMIERE #25 has shown us, the four-color genre is the only one for Danny Rand. I liked the solo issue of DEADLY HANDS OF KUNG FU. . . but compared to what John Byrne and a splash of color can do for Iron Fist. . . well! Let's just say there is no comparison.

The book's direction has taken a turn toward super-heroics, too. Pitting Danny against villains like Angar the Screamer (a villain I find intriguing, and one with much potential) and other Marvel bad guys suits me fine. Martial arts is nothing if not an adaptable concept, and pouring it into the super-hero mold is an extremely fascinating experiment. . . one, I think that is working out well.

A note to scripter Claremont: Now, more than ever, with Iron Fist appearing in his own comic, it will be necessary to bring the "iron fist" transformation into every issue. I knew, of course, that this was necessary from the beginning. . . but I haven't been complaining, since the scripters of this comic have done just this very thing without making the power seem dull and repetitious, or by playing down the power. Please don't change that. The new IRON FIST comic may give you opportunities to play it up or down, but I think it's just jim-dandy as it sits.

Thanks for a really good comic book, MARVEL PREMIERE #25 makes me tingle when I think of the new IRON FIST going monthly, at this, the time of it's greatest quality. But, tell me, will PREMIERE, with it's tryouts, still continue to come out seven times annually?

Robert E. Rodi
515 South Fifth Street
Columbia, Missouri 65201

Thanks for your letter, Bob; if there's anything we need here in the Bankrupt Big Apple these days, it's a good word or three to take our minds of the ever-increasing cost of living. And we have to agree with you all the way, Jocular John Byrne *is* an artist with a vengeance, one we think well-suited to carry on the high standards established by Gil Kane back in MARVEL PREMIERE #15 (By the way, if you thought Al McWilliams did a dynamite inking job on MARVEL PREMIERE #25 & IRON FIST #1, what do you think of Frank Chiaramonte's embellishment on IRON FIST #'s 2 & 3? We were impressed and we think you will be, too. Let us know, huh?)

As for the book's direction, the emphasis from now on *will* be that of a super-hero strip—which is what we think IRON FIST is—rather than a Martial Arts series, which is pretty much what *Shang-Chi* is all about. Iron Fist, essentially, is a super-hero whose powers just happen to be those of the Martial Arts, whereas Shang-Chi is a Martial Artist who just happens to get involved in super-hero situations. What all this comes down to, in the end, is a difference in attitude—IRON FIST being the more traditionally constructed of the two books, wherein our hero will have a secret identity and all the attendant hassles, what-have-you. The goals of the two characters are somewhat similar—both men are striving to realize their fullest potential as human beings; it's just that the paths they take to reach that goal are different. As you say, this *is* an 'extremely fascinating experiment,' one we hope will work out just fine in the months and years ahead.

Dear Chris and Marv Wolfman,

Congratulations to Iron Fist (and his creators) for finally being featured in a magazine all his own. Pairing him off with Iron Man was something that had to occur someday with the similarity of names. It was well handled and not at all contrived as some of your team-ups seem to be. Best of all, the fight didn't continue on until a predictable tie had occurred. Iron Man is without question the most powerful of the two and he proved it. Lets see more team-ups of this type. How about an Iron Fist-Karnak fight?

David A. Lofvers
66 Crestfield Drive, Rochester, NY 14617

This must be our lucky week, tons of letters pouring in from all sides and almost all of it favorable; a body'd almost be tempted to think we were doing something right around here for a change. But seriously, folks, glad to see you liked our Living Weapon's premiere appearance in his own mag, Dave; we hope you like the succeeding issues just as much. About an Iron Fist-Karnak team-up/fight, we can't say much at the moment, save that we passed the idea along to Cheerful Chris and Devil-May-Care Doug Moench (who—as all of you are no doubt aware of by now—handles the scripting chores on the brand-spanking new INHUMANS book). What may come of it, Yu-Ti only knows, but if anything does, Marveldom Assembled will be the first to find out (after the armadillo, of course).

But now to answer some general comments—the first of which harkens back to one Bob Rodi made in his letter—that is, the continual last-resort use of Iron Fist's *iron fist* to punch out the villain and save the day. True, Iron Fist's power has been used a trifle excessively in that fashion in the past, but in the next few issues, we think you'll see that change. Indeed, Chris promises that you'll start to see Iron Fist use his power in ways never-before dreamed of. Or something like that anyway. In fact, you'll see it starting next issue, with the conclusion of Iron Fist's epic two-part battle with the Ravager. And when you do see Chris's ideas, let us know what you think about them, huh? (After all, it does get lonely around here without any letters to read.)

Concerning Iron Fist's battle with Khumbala Bey: we're afraid we have to agree with some of you, Iron Fist could have beaten the tar out of the big oaf with no problem at all—except that Khumbala was bigger, as fast, as strong and as agile as Iron Fist, and was a Martial Arts champion in his own right, to boot. Admittedly, the fight wasn't all it could have been—and for those lacks, Chris accepts a lion's share of the responsibility—but neither was Iron Fist facing a pushover. Not an excuse—but, hopefully, an explanation. (By the by, if it's interestingly choreographed fights you want, check out the roundhouse brohouhas in this and next issue; if that ain't what the doctor ordered, we don't know what is.)

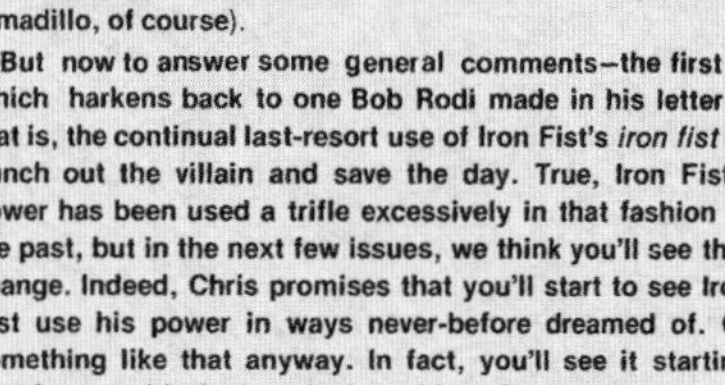

CLIP 'EM AND COLLECT 'EM!

32: THE MIGHTY THOR from *Iron Fist* no. 3 (February 1976).

LET'S LEVEL WITH
DAREDEVIL
SEND YOUR LETTERS TO: THE MARVEL COMICS GROUP SIXTH FLOOR 575 MADISON AV. NEW YORK 10022 N.Y.

Dear Red Underwear Types,

Re: DAREDEVIL #127.

Outside of the ridiculous title, "You Killed that Man, Torpedo...And Now You're going to Pay!", the latest DD was a fantastic study in terror. You actually become entangled in a death battle between DD and the Torpedo. *Earthquake* on a smaller scale. The only thing that can really be commented on was the overly burdened dialogue during the big fight. "I'll tell you...but I'm not gonna stop fighting 'cause, frankly, I don't trust you." That was dumb. If the dialogue had been spread out over a few panels, I could buy it. But it came off just a little silly and unbelievable.

However, it was a neat beginning to another subplot on Matt Murdock's violent nature and what it can do. The only thing I ask is that we don't have a repeat of the Captain America/Nomad conflict a few months ago. Okay? Neato, Marv.

Until Matt trips over his billy club...

Mark Dooley
105 Wehmeier St.
Columbus, IN 47201

Dear Gang,

I really liked DAREDEVIL #127. It continued the upswing movement we've been having in this mag for the past few months. Having DD alone is just the way he should be, and the Torpedo is the type of villain he should be fighting, either non-superpowered, or unperfected in the usage of superpowers.

No doubt about it; Marv Wolfman is the master of supporting characters. I have the feeling that he creates them, lets them run around in his head with a tape-recorder, and then transcribes what comes out. Either that, or he actually knows people like them, which seems reasonable, since, if a guy like Steve Gerber exists I don't see why Heather couldn't.

The art this time was near perfect. Bob and Klaus belong together on this mag. Keep 'em.

Steve Andrews
6827 Wentworth
Richfield, NM 5542

And what, Mr. Andrews, ever gave you the bizarre notion that Steve Gerber actually *does* exist? We here in the bullpen always thought that he was a product of the tortured mind of Howard the Duck!

We were gonna ask Marv about your theory on how he comes up with the supporting characters of his cast, but when we approached him he was furiously pounding out the next issue of DAREDEVIL, his head tilted slightly to one side—almost as if he were listening to something. You don't think...?

To Who(m) ever is writing Daredevil these days:

You know, you really ought to hand out scorecards! Anyway, Marv, you've done a good job, and #127 is a classic.

Up until now, all of Marvel's battle royals have either been held in the villain's lair or in a deserted area. Finally, a battle in a populated area that actually intrudes (and how!) into the lives of innocent people, and nearly *kills* them! DD's reaction is perfect —self-fear. This is probably the first time he has realized just what could happen if he loses control of himself. A sobering thought, to be sure.

I'm not too thrilled with the introduction of Heather. She seems like too much of a consolation prize to me. If you're planning on having 'Tasha come back and find them together, forget it! Far too cliché. Which leads to my second gripe, Marvel's treatment of love. Starting with FF #4, Marvel has blazed a trail of broken hearts all through the Marvel Universe. Consider the following: Thor and Sif, Thor and Jane Foster, Sub-Mariner and Lady Dorma, Torch and Crystal, Peter Parker and Gwen Stacy, Hawkeye and 'Tasha, DD and Karen Page, and now DD and 'Tasha. All in love, yet none together (with the possible exception of Thor and Jane Sif). I mean, really, people do get along in the real world, you know, so how about a few happy relationships, OK?

Third, I disagree with Jay Zilber's letter in #125 berating Marvel for its use of captions. First, while comics are a visual medium, without captions and word balloons the story would be somewhat harder to follow, no? Second, while some captions may seem frivolous, they probably are the writer's way of letting loose. Writing comics isn't easy, y'know!

RFO James J. Murray
3009 W. 7th St.
Lawrence, KS 66044

We know, Jimmy, *believe* us, we know!

Thanks for your comments, especially for coming to our defense, concerning our use of captions. The general consensus of Marveldom en masse on that particular subject seems to indicate the majority of you feel that our writers' use of captions really heightens the effect of the story rather that detracts from it—an enhancement we are always striving towards.

And in reply to another one of your comments: no, Heather is *not* any sort of a consolation prize. And, as we delve a bit more into her character and background in the months to come we're looking forward to your impressions as we discover other aspects of her character that have, as of now, hardly even touched the surface.

And speaking of Heather, what say we take a look at another reader's questions regarding her previous appearance...

Dear Marvel,

DAREDEVIL's #126 & 127 were pretty good considering all the boo-boos you people made in them. Like in issue #126, page 14, in the last panel Heather called her boyfriend "Franky," but in panel two, page 15 she calls him "Frankly." *And*, to top it all off, in issue #127, page six, she says he got married. But he's not "Franky" anymore, he's "Freddy"!

What is this? He gets married and already she forgets his name, or what? I just hope you guys give me a no-prize for this.

As always, Make Mine Marvel.

Frank Gabriel
(address unknown)

We *would* have sent you a no-prize if you had only remembered to type your *address* on your letter (It's so nice to realize that your beleaguered bullpen aren't the *only* ones to mess up from time to time. We just seem to bungle more *frequently* than anyone else we know). But we humbly promise never to forget anyone's name again. Okay Fred...uh, we mean, *Franky?*

'Til we meet again; aficionado, be good to yourself.

MARVEL VALUE STAMP

47: THE MIGHTY THOR from *Daredevil* no. 131 (March 1976).

COMMENTS TO CAGE

c/o MARVEL COMICS GROUP, 575 MADISON AVE. N.Y.C. 10022

Dear Marv,

Don McGregor on LUKE CAGE has obviously changed the slant of the book. CAGE has always been a very action orientated strip, and it works that way. He's a street fighter, and there's no other book in which we can see such raw punching out. I mean, if you want that kind of stuff, Cage is your man.

Yet from the beginning, a sort of relevancy has been tried, an attempt to maintain Cage's streetwise individuality. But this aspect has not always succeeded. And here's where Don comes in. Cage's links with his surroundings and fight for justice against "the establishment" is given more accent. Oh, the action is still there, even to a heightened degree such as Wentworth's being blown to bits with the shotgun, yet the additional text asides complete the social comments as well.

In short, the action and street attitudes are still there, but both are more intense, more shocking, and more believable. McGregor on CAGE? Right on, brother; play on, drummer.

The team of Tuska and Colletta worked well this ish also. Quickly, I might credit Don for the very good breakdowns in a few spots, but Tuska has proven his ability in action sequences... though not as often as he should. The layouts on pages 3, 6, and 7 were especially good. And for the first time in many months, Vince Colletta has interpreted Tuska's pencils well. The scratchy lines of late were absent, and that fine Colletta detail is back. Nice goin'.

Well, in the hope that CAGE will finally fulfill the promise originally laid down, good luck.

Dean Mullaney
81 Delaware Street
Staten Is., NY 10304

Don thanks you for the hearty welcome to his efforts, Dean. No one wants to take odds on whether or not Don is really going to manage writing a monthly book (that is, and do it on time), but the Dauntless One is entering the fray in his inevitable, dauntless fashion (which means that even he's not sure) and has Fearless (Does that mean the same as Dauntless?) Frank Robbins scouting the William Cullen Bryant Park for our opening sequence next month.

And John David Warner has promised to get together with Don for a photo-taking spree which will cover the entire network of Manhattan. If all that really does come about, we're just wondering where Don is going to get all the money to develop those pictures.

After such a venture as that, Don, you'd better make that monthly deadline.

Why is it that everything Don McGregor touches turns to gold?

He took control of KILLRAVEN and made that series superb. He had control of the BLACK PANTHER, and where a lesser writer would have made T'Challa's series a mediocre one, Don McGregor gave us "Panther's Rage," a story that is perhaps the greatest tale ever told in the comics medium, when one considers all the philosophical, moral, and religious angles of the tale.

We have Cage in jeopardy—fine. But we also have Cage being dogged by Detective Chase; we have Cage faced with eviction from his office, or at very least squeezed for money when the rent is raised; and we have Cage in a run-in with Big Businessmen (pages 22 through 26 made this entire issue GREAT!).

It's strange. . .as I read through the first three or four pages, I was thinking, "Hmmph—this almost appears to be a Shaft story." Yeah, I was drawing all sorts of comparisons between Shaft and Cage at the start of this issue. I finally decided that, with Don McGregor at the helm, Cage will easily be better than the Shaft series of movies.

Bruce Canwell
RFD # 2
Bowdoin, ME 04008

Bruce, we're glad you got a kick out of the book and Luke's multitude of crises, but we've got this apprehensive feeling that Cage is not quite so enthusiastic about his personal catastrophes.

No way.

Still, Cage will consider the encounters you mention as the "good old days" in the future, since the I.R.S. (that paternal, resurrected over-seer who rises each April with its hand outstretched) is due to contact him. If these harassments and others continue, Cage might have to miss the next episode of "Mary Hartman, Mary Hartman," which he keeps watching in hopes that it will tell him how to get out of these messes.

NEXT ISSUE: Remember the old children's rhyme (or is it new to you?) "Sticks and Stones Can Break Your Bones"? Well, next issue, add a "But Spears Can Kill You!" to the saying.

A new villain appears to put the point home, and his name is Spear.

Spear — if he misses his target...he missed on purpose.

And his target is...Noah Burstein!

We need you with us, People, and Cage needs all the moral support he can get. Believe it! Be with us as we tear up 41st Street, as Charlton Grundge and Grassy Moss return with a nefarious scheme to get our very own Power Man, as Claire and Luke try to enjoy a quiet dinner...but most of all, to see the soda machine go berserk.

Which it does. Go berserk, that is.

It's all here next issue, Gang. Until then, be kind to each other. Be kind to yourselves.

And hang in there!

MARVEL VALUE STAMP

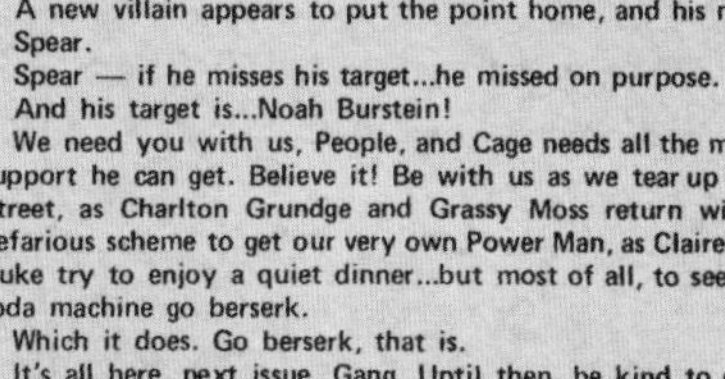

55: THE MIGHTY THOR from *Power Man* no. 32 (June 1976).

COMMENTS TO KA-ZAR (AND ZABU)

c/o MARVEL COMICS GROUP, 575 MADISON AVE. N.Y.C. 10022

Well, people, we *asked* for your reactions to Valiant Val Mayerik's artistic debut on the KA-ZAR strip...and, man, did we *get* 'em! Herewith, a brief sampling of same...

Friends,

For the first time, I am enthusiastic about an issue of KA-ZAR. Not just interested or amused, but downright excited and gripped with suspense. Why? Because of Val Mayerik. His work suits KA-ZAR as neatly as a fur loincloth. Loved the way he did every character, including the grotesque winged creature and Zabu's tail—and especially the green conquistadors, Shauran and Traikar, who must be the best nasty villains to appear since the Kree.

For the first time ever, I anticipate the next issue of KA-ZAR with impatience and delight.

Elizabeth Holden
211 Sunnyside Ave.
Ottawa, Ontario, Canada

Hallelujah—!

Enter the Michelangelo of comics, Valiant Val Mayerik! This chap has penciled and inked one of the finest stories in Marvel's long history. Although the inking is a bit blurry in some panels (deadlines, unfortunately, must be met), art of this caliber cannot go unheralded.

Gentlemen, you have started the new year on the right foot, so watch your step.

J. Cabell Sale
(no address given)

We'll try, J. Cabell; however, one point should be noted. The "fuzziness" in #15 is attributable to the printing—not to Val's inking style.

Dear Doug and Val,

KA-ZAR has become artistically interesting again. I speak; of course, of Val Mayerik's auspicious debut in KA-ZAR #15. Val's rapid development at Marvel has been most intriguing, and with the truly fine work to which he has treated us in "When Shatters the Gateway to Hell," it becomes clear that Val Mayerik is an artist of masterful abilities. By all means, keep this guy around. Chain him to the drawing board if need be!

Ed O'Reilly
215 E. Lehr
Ada, OH 45810

Dear Marvel,

Val Mayerik is the best thing that could have possibly happened to KA-ZAR. After employing a different artist on almost every issue in the strip's recent history, I hope you decide to stop here—because you've got a winner on your hands.

Doug's story was also good—and I like the way things are progressing. At one time I was convinced that Doug and Val were suited only for horror stories; glad to be proven wrong, and I hope this is one team which will *continue* to do KA-ZAR.

Robert Abrams
6450 N. Sacramento
Chicago, IL 60645

You'd better believe it, Rob! Doug and Val are having a gas with the KA-ZAR strip—and since they've only *begun* to get into it, there's *no way* they're gonna quit *now*.

(And by the way, Doug himself hails from Chicago—and once lived up in Rogers Park not so very far from your address, Rob. So how's the old neighborhood doing, pal...?)

Dear Doug and Val,

I love Val's art this issue—some of his finest work to date, with many panels suggesting a strong resemblance to the styles of Frank Frazetta and Boris Vallejo. Keep it up.

I also liked the story very much. However, even though I fully understand and forgive the issue-to-issue discrepancies which you kindly explained in the letter column, there is one particularly horrendous mistake you cannot explain away. On page 17 Tandy states that her paper has been receiving reports of "UFO sightings, proceeding *north* to the *Arctic* where your Savage Land is located." Now, any long-time KA-ZAR fan knows that the Savage Land is actually located far *south* in the *Antarctic*. Accordingly, I shall expect a forest green, vibranium no-prize, forwarded post-haste to—

James L. Bleeker
1131 Courtney N.W.
Grand Rapids, MI 49504

You've got it, Jim. Doug fully admits the error—possibly the worst one he's ever made. In fact, he *still* can't believe he did it. But thanks to you (and a kazillion *other* sharp-eyed readers), the record is hereby set straight: the Savage Land is located in the Antarctic—*not* the Arctic. And after we've so humbly apologized, what more can we say...?

Dear Sirs:

I've been following the actions of KA-ZAR ever since issue #1, and now I must admit that it has evolved from "just another comic" to one which is a delight to read. The art is well up to par with the rest of your books, and the plotline seems to have a strong sense of continuity from one issue to the next—finally. Please keep up the good work.

Paul Brown
Paradise, RR #1
Annapolis County
Nova Scotia, Canada

And there we have it, people. KA-ZAR's new collaborative team has sought and apparently found your approbation. Val Mayerik is a hit—and so is Doug Moench, despite his colossal blunder. But most importantly, every single letter has been enthusiastically positive about the "Big Change" developing in the strip—and Val and Doug obviously couldn't be happier. But the trip is far from over, people—so stick around for the ride, and leave the driving to Moench and Mayerik; we promise you a journey through the mist-shrouded realms of the imagination that you won't soon forget!

And in the meantime...be good.

THIS IS IT! YOUR

MARVEL VALUE STAMP

FOR THIS ISSUE!

21: THE MIGHTY THOR from *Ka-Zar* no. 17 (August 1976)

c/o MARVEL COMICS GROUP, 575 MADISON AVE. N.Y.C. 10022

SOME STRAIGHT TALK FROM STAINLESS STEVE

With this issue, DR. STRANGE goes monthly. Yeah, I know—last time we said such an occurrence was somewhere out on the horizon—but when the Powers That Be make up their corporate minds, they always seem to want to start yesterday.

When we heard the word from on high, our first thoughts were of heading for the hills. Gene was set just right drawing one and a half books a month (the monthly DRACULA and the bi-monthly DOC), Tom was satisfied with his schedule, and I...well, each issue of DR. STRANGE that I've been involved with has been a true labor of love, with the accent on labor, and two months seemed just about the right amount of time to spend on each one.

However...

(1) Two years ago, Jim Starlin and I conceived a character called Shang-Chi. That was another labor of love, and I intended, within the book's bi-monthly format, to trace the rising and advancing of a spirit. MASTER OF KUNG FU was to have been a second DR. STRANGE. But after five issues, it was decided that Shang-Chi appear, not *just* monthly, but twice a month, in two unrelated story-lines. I followed my conscience and told them they'd have to get another scripter, which they did—and Doug Moench has done a great job with the character.

(2) Nine months ago, I voluntarily dropped off CAPTAIN AMERICA to pursue two exciting new projects: an epic galactic series, called STARLORD and an odyssey of the gods called THOR THE MIGHTY—unfortunately, both of them were shot down in flames before I'd hardly begun.

In other words, folk: you can't always get what you want. But even at that, I might still have cut out, if it hadn't been for two other factors.

(3) When Dr. Strange had his own book in the late '60's, it failed. The insider's official explanation has always laid it off on Gene's panel layout ("you couldn't follow the story"). But it's been my conviction for some time that the real reason is far more basic: in the late '60's, despite all the hue and cry over mind expansion, there just weren't enough spacy people reading comics to support a mystic—while today there are. In fact, as I say, there are so many spacers around that this book is not just supported. This book is a certified hit.

That means there are a lot of people out there who dig Dr. Strange as he now is, and they deserve consideration. Then, finally—

(4) I just flat out love this series myself.

So...Gene and Tom and I thought about this series...and here we still are. I don't know what went through each of their heads while they made up their minds, but I'd guess it was something similar. It may be tough—heck, it *will* be—but the three of us are determined to keep at it, and to keep the quality high. May we, and you, all prosper in the days ahead.

Okay—let me cover a few more bits of business before I get into what's coming up in the next few issues. First, as briefly noted last issue, Frank Brunner and I are working up a three-part story to take some of the strain off Gene. We don't know whether Gene will need that relief, but who can complain at having *both* of the "only artists for DR. STRANGE" appearing in the next year. Besides, if Gene doesn't need the respite, it'll just give him more time for...the GIANT-SIZE DR. STRANGE!

Yes, we've taken another look at those oversized books of last year, and come up with what we hope is a viable solution this time. Starting soon, we'll be releasing one or two giant books a month, each concentrating on a different series...and as things stand now, next October should see the once-yearly appearance of a special tale of sorcery. This will be an all-new, 35 page extravaganza—and after the fun I had with the extra-length AVENGERS epics, this one should be a real ball. (Yes, Virginia, there'll be a similar GS AVENGERS, in July).

Didn't we tell you DR. STRANGE was a hit?

Now then—what's happening in the near future? Well, next month, a story Frank and I wanted to do 'way back when will finally come to pass: the first encounter between the master of the mystic arts and the lord of evil, Dracula! This one's going to be even weirder than you might expect, because it'll be a two-parter, beginning in next month's DRACULA #44, and ending a week later in DR. STRANGE #14. But even stranger than that, though Marv Wolfman will be writing his book and I'll be writing mine, the art on both books will be by Gene and Tom! Nifty, huh?

Then, in March, DR. STRANGE #15 will begin a new multi-parter, leading out of the ending to this issue's madness. We don't want to say anything specific about it, since you may not have gotten to that ending yet, but we ask you this: how would *you* feel, if you learned the secret Stephen Strange learns this month?

Well, thanks for listening, and don't forget, *next month* the story takes you to DRACULA as well as DR. STRANGE.

Bye!

MARVEL VALUE STAMP

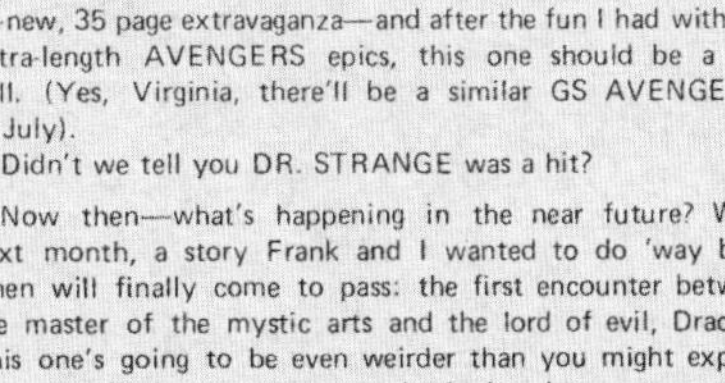

72: THE MIGHTY THOR from *Doctor Strange* no. 13 (April 1976).

GIVE ME LIBERTY— OR GIVE ME THE LEGION!

An Historical Footnote by ROY THOMAS

Necessity, they say, is the mother of invention.

Most times, she is a stern parent— but occasionally, a most welcome one as well. This was one of those times.

You see, when I conceived some months back the idea of a comic-mag to be called THE INVADERS— a title which would co-star Captain America, Sub-Mariner, and the original Human Torch in World War Two action against the Axis Powers— I immediately realized that the very *name* of the group was going to present problems of sorts.

THE INVADERS is, in *our* opinion anyway, a heckuva fine title for a mag. Only thing is, *what* do our super-stars of yesteryear *invade?* Why, obviously, nothing less than Hitler's Fortress Europa, of course— Nazi-occupied Europe which in early 1942 stretched from the Russian front to the English Channel, where German stood facing Briton across a few miles of water and a whole lot of guns.

Somehow, though, this seemed to me to miss a lot of story possibilities for one of the most interesting wartime areas of all: the United States herself, in those days of V-mail and Victory Gardens, of Bogart and Rosie the Riveter, of rationing and the black market and the ever-present threat of Nazi saboteurs.

And so, even before GIANT-SIZE INVADERS #1-and-only went on sale, I was already hard at work on a couple of try-out issues of a second WWII title, to be composed of some of the lesser superheroes from the Timely Comics of the period, which preceded the Marvel Age by a couple of decades.

The name of the group came first— *also* by about twenty years, in fact.

For, as a junior-high student back in the early 50's, I had created, written, and drawn (in pencil, on typing paper, mostly without benefit of a ruler) a 68-page super-group comic-book I called THE LIBERTY LEGION. (Ta ta ta *ta* ta ta!) It was composed of such deathless characters as the Flame Man, the Tornado, the Acrobat, the Catman, and some half-a-dozen others, and reflected my continuing love-affair with superhero groups.

(Footnote within a footnote: In the early 1960's, by sheer coincidence, a Texas-based trio of talented comics fans published their *own* Liberty Legion group in a fanzine— and I hope they don't take offense that I've staked out a claim in Marvel's name. But honest, fellas— I was there first.)

Anyway, once the name was chosen, the group itself began to form in my mind. Some of the choices came easy. First off, there'd be the Red Raven, who had appeared in only one story in the 1940's but whom I had resurrected in a story I'd plotted for THE X-MEN several years back.

The Patriot and Miss America, of course, were obvious choices to be the Home Front equivalents of Captain America— something sorely needed by any group calling itself the Liberty Legion, the more so since virtually every comics company in the early 40's had at least *one* red-white-and-blue-clad do-gooder. The Whizzer had been popular, too, when he and Miss America had appeared in a story I wrote for GIANT-SIZE AVENGERS #1 (and besides, they'd been members of Timely's ill-fated All-Winners Squad in the late 40's), so I figured I'd show how they had met in the first place— though they're obviously still a few years and a number of kisses away from connubial bliss.

The Thin Man was fun, too, both because of his powers and his name (obviously derived from the Dashiell Hammett detective novel and the movies based thereon); I chose Jack Frost both for his Iceman-like power *and* because he was one of the earliest creations of a scripter named Stan Lee, who has since gone on to bigger things (and better names).

I was wrestling with the *seventh* member (for, I'd decided mystically that the Liberty Legion just *had* to have seven members) and had discarded such characters as the original Vision, Defender, Falcon, Hercules, Black Widow, and others because there'd be confusion with their modern-day counterparts— heroes such as the Fin, Father Time, the Challenger, Major Liberty, and others for a variety of reasons— and such worthies as the Blazing Skull and the original Destroyer mainly (in fact, *solely*) because, like the Invaders themselves, they fought mostly abroad.

(That doesn't mean that at any time any and all of the above might not pop up in THE INVADERS or some future incarnation of THE LIBERTY LEGION, of course. I burn as few bridges behind me as I can.)

At any rate, just then, my friend and fellow longtime comics-fan Bobby Vann (no relation to movie actors or dancers, he vows) suggested an obscure entity called the Blue Diamond. I decided to use him, mostly because he added a certain element of sheer physical power which I felt the Legion could use.

As to whether these seven will be a permanent alignment in case of a regular LIBERTY LEGION book at a later date— well, only the future itself will tell. Even I don't know.

Meanwhile, we hope you've enjoyed the first several dozen pages of this tale, which began in THE INVADERS #5 and continues in this issue of MARVEL PREMIERE— and that you'll follow it thru its action-packed climax in INVADERS #6 and its ultimate, frenzied conclusion in the next ish of PREMIERE itself.

After that— well, how about bombarding us with cards, letters, and candygrams, and maybe— just maybe— the Home Front superheroes will live again, in still another mighty Marvel super-group mag called— THE LIBERTY LEGION.

One thing's for certain: if I can't get away with using a name like that in the halcyon, star-spangled days of World War Two —it sure ain't likely I'll ever get the chance anywhere else!

MARVEL VALUE STAMP

62: THE MIGHTY THOR from *Marvel Premiere* no. 29 (April 1976).

Mutant Mail-Box

ADDRESS YOUR LETTERS TO THE MARVEL COMICS GROUP, SIXTH FLOOR, 575 MADISON AVE, NEW YORK, N.Y. 10022

Chris, Len, Dave, Sam, Karen, Petra and Marv—I congratulate you! "Warhunt" was everything a comic (for that matter, ANY dramatic) story should be. The pace moves rapidly, characterizations are continually improving as the saga of the new X-Men unfolds, the plot works well—a very successful issue.

Artwise, this issue is every bit as good as its predecessors. Gil Kane's X-MEN covers have been really great, and this one was no exception. Dave Cockrum works well with every inker you give him, it seems. It should be interesting to see exactly what inker becomes "permanent" on this strip (if, indeed, any one does). In my humble opinion, the X-MEN is one of Marvel's best magazines—and Dave Cockrum's art is no small factor in that opinion.

Colossus's concern for the other X-Men, and his obvious confidence in his own abilities ··· Nightcrawler's further demonstration of his fascinating powers and his fast-developing friendship with Cyclops, which has been demonstrated over the past couple issues. . .the Banshee, in this issue, proves himself to be able to think on his feet and only confirms my thoughts as to seeing the Banshee eventually become Cyclops's second-in-command. The Wolverine was pretty much ignored this go-round, but I have no doubts that he'll eventually get some time in the limelight.

Professor Xavier was obviously distraught by Thunderbird's suicide (you have to call it that—Banshee could have stopped Nefaria). He was also pretty sharp with Cyclops on page 27. I'm wondering if Xavier will blame Cyke for Thunderbird's death—if so, it would be incredibly great story material, and also something of an X-Men first. Prof. Xavier has always been pretty much a sidelight character—he was never shown as having much emotional output, and was trapped pretty much in the role of regulating X-Men activities. I think things are beginning to change.

Whew—sorry to get so long winded, folks. But I think X-MEN is the best new magazine of this year. So, I leave with two questions—

Why did you spell Storm's real name "Orro" when in GS X-MEN 1-and-only her name is "Ororo"?

Bruce Canwell
Meadows Rd. RFD #2
Bowdoin, MA 04008

Whew, ourselves, Bruce—but don't feel bad about being long-winded; it's letters like yours that make all the stresses and strains and hassles and occasional disasters involved in putting out these bi-monthly epics well-worth the effort.

As to Professor X remaining in the background, you'll see as of this issue that that's no longer the case. The good professor is as much a part of the X-Men as any of his students; and we can assure you that whatever minor holocausts come down on their collective heads in days to come, they'll come down on Charles Xavier's head as well. And vice versa. Or something like that, anyway.

But you had to mention "Orro," didn't you? You had to go and do that? You had to go spoil a near-perfect letter. Well, to clear up any nascent controversy, the lady's name is *Ororo*. Okay? Okay. (Just goes to show that even our Pulse-Pounding Proofreaders are as human as the next guy.)

Dear Marvel,

After reading X-MEN #95 I found myself astounded that such an issue could be assembled. Every aspect of the issue was a masterpiece. First the story by Chris Claremont was great, with snappy dialogue, and just enough action. The Ani-Men are interesting villains and make a good team.

Dave Cockrum's art was beautiful, especially pages 3, 18 and 26. I really like Dave's rendition of Cyclops and the Wolverine, not to mention the fact that I love Nightcrawler's costume.

On the matter of Thunderbird's death, when I first realized Thunderbird was dead I was disappointed and angry, but then something hit me. I remembered that you guys at Marvel strive to put reality into your comics. And then I realized that in real life the good guys don't always come out of everything unhurt or, as is the case with Thunderbird, alive. And now I'm not so angry. Peace People.

Steve Pauwels
41 Clifton Drive
Simsbury, CT 06070

Len & Dave,

After reading GIANT-SIZE X-MEN #1, I was proud to see one of my people, an American Indian—America's First Citizens—become a member. But to my dissatisfaction, in X-MEN #94, you started to oppress him. The story and art were good, but I was angry to see Thunderbird treated harshly.

But the clincher was in X-MEN #95. You killed him. Why was he chosen? Why Thunderbird?

Tom Runningmouth
2523 Kimball Street
Philadelphia, PA 19146

A serious question, Tom; and one which deserves an equally serious answer.

As Steve Pauwels' letter states, we here at Marvel strive to put a semblance of reality into our comic books. And, like it or not, Death—the fact of dying, of being killed—is a part of that reality, just as it is a part of 'real' life. People live, people die; you may not want them to, it may hurt a lot; but they die just the same. Just as, in comics, Captain Stacy died, the Swordsman died, Junior Juniper died. And Thunderbird died. It happens.

Why Thunderbird? Because he was the weakest potential character in the X-Men. He had no powers which weren't duplicated by other members of the team—Colossus, or Nightcrawler, or Wolverine—and, harsh as it sounds, duplicated better. But worst of all, his character—as a character—had nowhere to go. All he was, all he really ever could be, was a wise-cracking, insolent, younger, not-as-interesting copy of Hawkeye the Marksman in the Avengers—and if you have any questions as to the problems Hawkeye's been having as a character, just look at all the roles he's taken in the past ten years. Proudstar deserved a better deal than that, and he could never get it, which is why he had to die. Because, when you think about it, it was better that he die with honor rather than spend the rest of his comic-book life trying to force himself into a persona he wasn't.

We're sorry Thunderbird had to die, too, Tom, but we also think it was for the best.

THIS IS IT! YOUR
MARVEL VALUE STAMP
FOR THIS ISSUE!

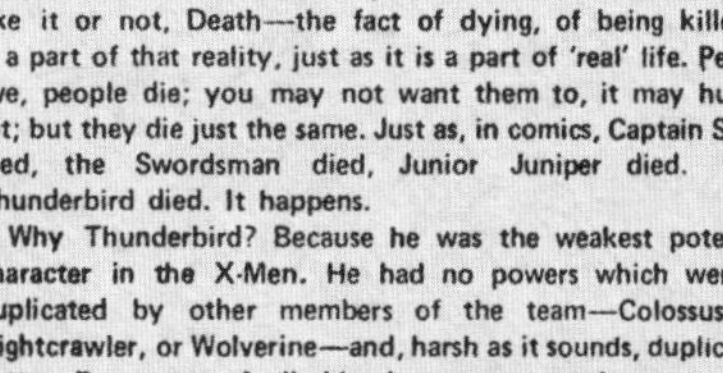

CLIP 'EM AND COLLECT 'EM!

20: THE MIGHTY THOR from *The X-Men* no. 97 (February 1976).

DR. STRANGE
MASTER OF THE MYSTIC ARTS

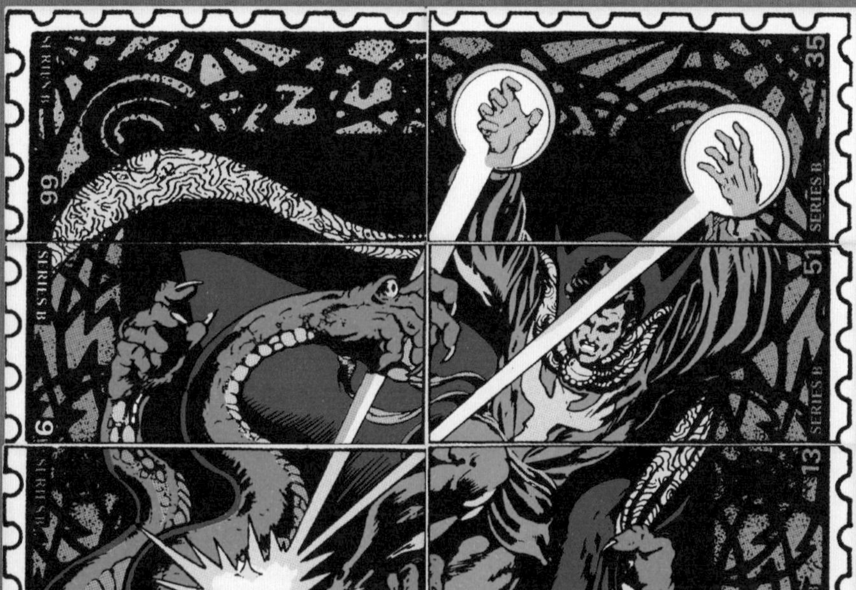

Once he was a man like most others—— a worldly man, seduced and jaded by material things. But then he discovered the separate reality, where sorcery and men's souls shaped the forces that shape our lives. In that instant, he was born again, to become a man like no other—— a man who had left us behind, as he strove to stand against the unseen subtle perils hovering thick and black around our fragile existence...and so began the mystic majesty of... DR. STRANGE!

Doctor Strange no. 1 (June 1974), art by Frank Brunner.

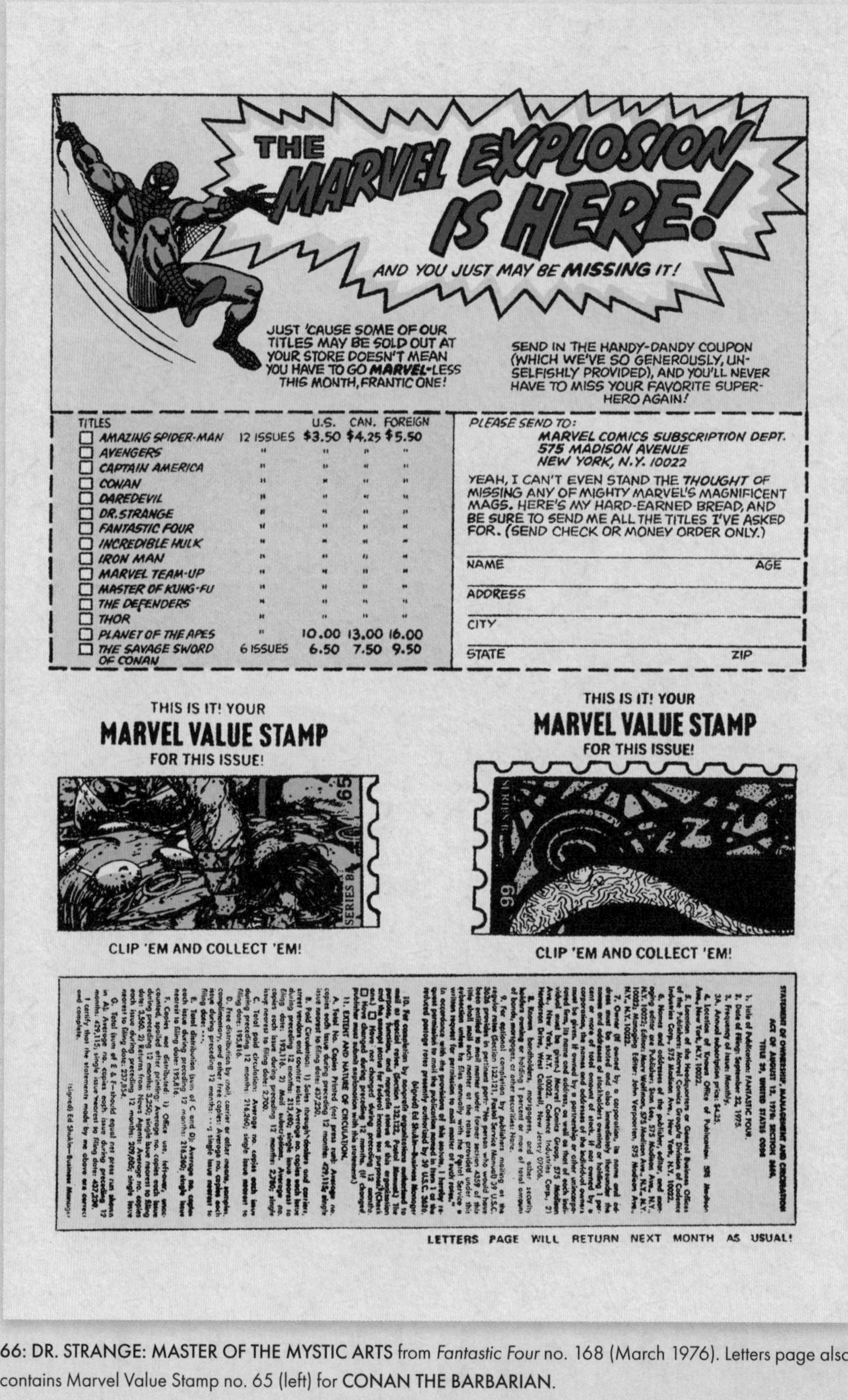

THE MARVEL EXPLOSION IS HERE!
AND YOU JUST MAY BE MISSING IT!
JUST 'CAUSE SOME OF OUR TITLES MAY BE SOLD OUT AT YOUR STORE DOESN'T MEAN YOU HAVE TO GO MARVEL-LESS THIS MONTH, FRANTIC ONE!
SEND IN THE HANDY-DANDY COUPON (WHICH WE'VE SO GENEROUSLY, UN-SELFISHLY PROVIDED), AND YOU'LL NEVER HAVE TO MISS YOUR FAVORITE SUPER-HERO AGAIN!
TITLES U.S. CAN. FOREIGN
AMAZING SPIDER-MAN 12 ISSUES $3.50 $4.25 $5.50
AVENGERS
CAPTAIN AMERICA
CONAN
DAREDEVIL
DR. STRANGE
FANTASTIC FOUR
INCREDIBLE HULK
IRON MAN
MARVEL TEAM-UP
MASTER OF KUNG-FU
THE DEFENDERS
THOR
PLANET OF THE APES 10.00 13.00 16.00
THE SAVAGE SWORD OF CONAN 6 ISSUES 6.50 7.50 9.50
PLEASE SEND TO:
MARVEL COMICS SUBSCRIPTION DEPT.
575 MADISON AVENUE
NEW YORK, N.Y. 10022
YEAH, I CAN'T EVEN STAND THE THOUGHT OF MISSING ANY OF MIGHTY MARVEL'S MAGNIFICENT MAGS. HERE'S MY HARD-EARNED BREAD, AND BE SURE TO SEND ME ALL THE TITLES I'VE ASKED FOR. (SEND CHECK OR MONEY ORDER ONLY.)
NAME AGE
ADDRESS
CITY
STATE ZIP
THIS IS IT! YOUR MARVEL VALUE STAMP FOR THIS ISSUE!
65
SERIES B
CLIP 'EM AND COLLECT 'EM!
THIS IS IT! YOUR MARVEL VALUE STAMP FOR THIS ISSUE!
SERIES B
66
CLIP 'EM AND COLLECT 'EM!
LETTERS PAGE WILL RETURN NEXT MONTH AS USUAL!

66: DR. STRANGE: MASTER OF THE MYSTIC ARTS from *Fantastic Four* no. 168 (March 1976). Letters page also contains Marvel Value Stamp no. 65 (left) for CONAN THE BARBARIAN.

READERS' SPACE

Beginning with our third issue, this sector of magazine space will be reserved for your comments, questions, and criticisms regarding the GUARDIANS OF THE GALAXY. It thus behooves us to recall at this juncture one of the immutable laws of physics: for every action, there is an equal and opposite reaction.

Translation: you have to act (by writing letters) before we can react (by making nasty replies in bold type). Otherwise, we won't have a letters page. So take a hint, huh, space-pilgrim? Hitch your typewriter or ballpoint— no crayons, please— to a starship, shift into Harkovian creative drive, and WRITE!!

(Or, so help us, we'll get even more sickeningly cutesy the next time we're forced to remind you. And that's no idle threat. You've no idea the linguistic atrocities we're capable of committing.)

Okay, now *that* we've got that out of our propulsion systems...!

A word or two is in order about the earth of 3015 A.D., the far-future era in which our GUARDIANS tales are set.

As you've no doubt noticed, it's a very different world from our own. There are no food shortages, no gas shortages, no inflation or unemployment. Primarily because there's also no problem with overpopulation: the only resource in short supply, thanks to the Badoon, is *people*.

Fifty-million human beings are left alive— more than enough for a softball game, true, but a mere *one-sixtieth* of earth's present population.

But before the coming of the Badoon, not only was earth itself teeming with life— earth *colonies* had been established on three of our nine planets and on the fourth planet in orbit about the nearest star, Alpha Centauri.

Mercury, the smallest planet in our solar system and the nearest to the sun, became a mining colony, inhabited by genetically-altered humans able to withstand the enormous heat of the Mercurian day (temperatures approaching 400 degrees centigrade) and the brittle cold of its month-long nights. Tiny though the planet is, its importance to humanity's progress in that future era was tremendous: here was found in sufficient quantities the fuel that made the Harkovian hyperdrive work. Its discovery on Mercury made faster-than-light space travel a reality and set man on his course to the stars.

So far as is known, every member of the Mercurian colony met his death during the Badoon invasion.

Neither Venus nor Mars was ever colonized. Venus, with its enormous atmospheric pressure and its surface temperatures approaching 800 degrees centigrade, proved too great a challenge even for the genetic engineers. Mars, as terrans learned to their sorrow back in 2001, was already inhabited. (Check out any issue of KILLRAVEN if you doubt us.)

The surface of Jupiter, too, proved too difficult an environment to colonize. But "floating cities" contained in plastiglass bubbles were constructed in the planet's atmosphere, and from this vantage point the scientists of Charlie-27's race were able to study Jupiter itself and the other giant planets, Saturn, Uranus, and Neptune.

Perhaps the greatest feat of earth's geneticians was the creation of the silicon-based humanoids who inhabited earth's colony on Pluto, the solar system's last outpost. These crystalline men and women, though created in man's own image, had virtually nothing in common with their earthborn ancestors. Their method of reproduction, their patterns of growth were vastly different from those of earthmen— and just *how* different will become clear when we delve into Martinex's "youth" in issues to come.

Centauri-IV, as luck would have it, was an earthlike world, inhabited by a race of blue-skinned primitives whose lifestyle resembled, though hardly duplicated, that of the American Indian before the arrival of the Europeans. That culture survives now only in Yondu, the weapons master, the natural hunter of the Guardians. The rest of his people were wiped out, along with the terran colonists, by the Badoon.

Which brings us back to the Homeworld, an earth which has known scientific advances far beyond our imagination, which has savored the thrill of interplanetary exploration...and which, for eight years, has worn the yoke of slavery. It's an embittered planet now, in 3015 A.D. Its people are weary. And whether it can rise up from the ashes of its conquest and liberation is an open question.

The future, it seems, even 1040 years from now, is only beginning.

MARVEL VALUE STAMP

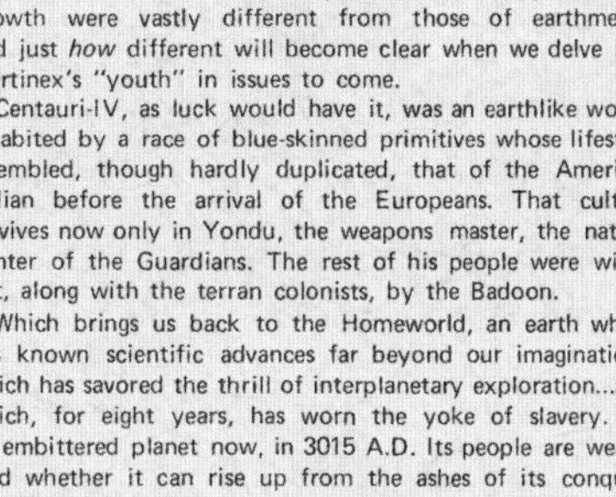

35: DR. STRANGE: MASTER OF THE MYSTIC ARTS from *Marvel Presents* no. 3 (February 1976).

GREEN SKIN'S GRAB-BAG

c/o MARVEL COMICS GROUP, 575 MADISON AVE. N.Y.C. 10022

Dear Len and Herb,

HULK #191 brought to a close one of the most interesting stories to feature the Green Goliath in some time. For the Hulk, a creature who can hardly think straight, who remembers very little of what happens to him, to find himself led "over the rainbow" by a golden man and deposited in a world where everything is sweetness and light; well, let's just say that I never thought the word "paradise" would be inadequate to describe personal bliss.

The fact that I don't like the Shaper of Worlds did not cause me to dislike the story itself, any more than the fact that the Hulk's paradise was too good to last lessened the effect when the Toad Men came and took it away from him. I hope you'll use the Shaper sparingly in the future; his powers are such that overuse would make him all the more obnoxious.

You didn't really dwell on this point, but I think I'll mention it. Do you realize how *ironic* the last few issues of the Hulk have been? He's met a girl who sees him not as a monster but as a beautiful person, and he can't accept it. He's visited a place where the people he loves are with him all the time, only to have it turn out that they were never there to begin with. In issue #191, he allowed himself to be used as a Judas Goat to save Jarella and "Crackajack," who were in reality two antennaed alien animals. And, most ironic of all, the sole casualty that was depicted was Glorian; unselfish, generous, Glorian. It makes you stop and think.

Thanks for listening, guys, and keep up the good work. 'Cause with stories like "Mind over Mayhem" and "Triumph of the Toad," the Hulk is looking very, very good.

Ed Via
1648 Dean Road
Roanoke, VA 24018

Dear People,

I am extremely sorry to see Herb Trimpe leave the Hulk's magazine after so many years. I am one who goes for consistency in series, and in these days when it seems like that is a thing of the past, I really appreciate a writer or artist who sticks around for any length of time. And Herb has been around for so long that I don't know of any other Hulk.

Herb's devotion really showed through in his work. No matter who he worked with, it was always beautiful. Although sometimes he might have appeared stiff, he was a master storyteller.

And the stories that he was involved with. No matter whether he was working with Thomas, Englehart, Wein, or others, I always loved it. Looking back over all of these years is truly a pleasurable task. Who can forget the Beast, the Abomination, the Wendigo, and many others?

The past years, not months, have been the best and each issue got better and better. So sad that he has to leave now.

Good-bye, Herb; Greenskin and I are going to miss you.

Larry Twiss
227 Fox Run
King of Prussia, PA 19406

We couldn't have put it better ourselves, Larry. Happy Herb's stint on the HULK has been a long and enjoyable one. Thanks to all of you who expressed your sadness at his departure from this series.

But the past aside, we're anxiously awaiting Marveldom's verdict on ol' Greenskin's *newest* penciller—our pal Sal Buscema! (Although he's not all *that* new; after all, he has been illustrating our Green Goliath in a comic mag entitled the Dynamic Defenders for well over two years!) *We* think Sal is doing a fantastic job, but you know how insecure we get if we're not constantly reassured by the *real* editors of these books. So let's hear what you think, Marvelites—we're countin' on you.

Dear Marvel,

In HULK #191, pg. 19, I quote: "Greenskin shares Banner's knowledge," then goes on to explain that the Hulk acquired his knowledge of Russian through that process as was used in #189.

In HULK #163, page 14, panel one: "the Hulk doesn't understand Russian."

Yours truly apprehensive of no-prize delivery,

Mark Wierman
809 Annabelle St.
Vestal, NY 13856

Okay, you've got us. Len Wein was so set on wiggling out of that little language barrier problem a few months back that he had forgotten that Stainless Steve Englehart had already established, as you pointed out, that the Hulk could *not* comprehend Russian. So no-prizes are on the way to both you and Michael Galiatsator who also spotted that same discrepancy.

Dear Bullpen,

I've got it! Every single person in the MARVEL TREASURY EDITION #5 centerfold!

Here goes! From left to right: The Hulk, Jim Wilson, Bruce Banner, Talia, Rick Jones, the Leader, the Glob, Kang, Crackajack Jackson, Hulk, Bruce Banner, Armbruster, Betty Ross Talbot, Hammer, Anvil, Glenn Talbot, General Ross, Subterraneans, Moleman, Wendigo, Xeron, Jarella, Doc Samson, and, last but not least—Happy Herbie! Right? Right!

Rush me my green, Gamma-radiated no-prize soon!

Mark Berman
605 Race St.
Denver, CO 80206

Indeed you *do* have it, Mark. And you can pride yourself on being the *only* Hulkophile who identified the little guy peeking out from that rock as Happy Herb Trimpe himself—who couldn't resist sketching himself into that collection of the Hulk's friends and foes! But treat your green, Gamma-radiated no-prize with care, True Believer, you never can tell what would happen if it ever fell into the wrong hands!

THIS IS IT! YOUR
MARVEL VALUE STAMP
FOR THIS ISSUE!

CLIP 'EM AND COLLECT 'EM!

9: DR. STRANGE: MASTER OF THE MYSTIC ARTS from *The Incredible Hulk* no. 195 (January 1976).

GREEN SKIN'S GRAB-BAG

c/o MARVEL COMICS GROUP, 575 MADISON AVE. N.Y.C. 10022

Dear Len, Herb, Joe, and Stan,

Gil Kane's blockbusting cover on HULK #193 was great. As long as Gil keeps turning 'em out like this, you can be sure I will congratulate him. The inks by John Romita were fine, too.

Len Wein's script this ish was above fair. Doc Samson is an extremely fascinating superhero. He'd make it pretty well in a series of his own wouldn't you think? Greenskin is in excellent hands with "Wonder Wein" at the controls. The thing that Len does best, as Bill Blyberg pointed out in this issue's letter column, is dialogue. You seldom find a writer who can come up with great lines like Len can write. Stan and Roy are exceptions.

The graphics were eye-pleasing. So this was Happy Herb's last issue of the Hulk, huh? Sob. Sal Buscema will do a great job with the art chores, but we're all gonna miss titantic Trimpe. Herb and Joe Staton's art this issue was superior. I mean, wow, I enjoyed everything the art had to offer! Joe's inks, as we all can testify, are a joy to behold. I hope he continues to stay on, so he can give Sal a hand with the pictures when Sal takes over next issue. I thought the Trimpe/Staton splash this ish was super-duper, especially the way Joe carefully utilized the zip-a-tone on the Hulk. Wonderful touch. Green forever, and Marvel, too!

Jack Frost
Route 3, Box 176-C
West Monroe, LA 71921

It's always enjoyable to start out a GRAB-BAG with a rave review of a previous issue—especially when the letter is indicative of almost 100% of this issue's total mail response. Thanks, folks, we appreciate it.

As you can see, Jack, Joe Staton has not departed from ol' Greenskin's adventures. In fact, Joe seems to be having as much fun with this strip as everyone else.

You think that Doc Samson would do pretty well in a series of his own, do you? Well, keep an eye out in the upcoming months for our emerald-maned adventurer's appearance in our recently revamped try-out title, MARVEL SPOTLIGHT. If enough of our readership agrees with your appraisal of the Darlin' Doc's appeal, then there's a chance he could be awarded a series of his very own! It's up to *you*. True Believers!

Dear Marvel,

HULK #193 was a pretty good issue. Herb Trimpe's art was excellent throughout, and Len wrote a creative, unpredictable script.

I think the most creative and unpredictable part was during the final battle scene, where the Hulk is leaping across the World Trade Center. Just when we expect him to clobber Doc Samson, wham! the Hulk finds himself in a forest, fighting Triton and Xemnu (nice job on these two, Herb).

These ironic, bizarre, plot twists always keep the book fresh and exciting, Len. "Weird" Gerber's got nothing on you!

Beppe Sabatini
10501 Birnham Road
Great Falls, VA 22066

P.S. I don't like to be picky, but actually there are no forests on top of the World Trade Center. This is only a minor mistake, though.

Uh...Beppe, are you *sure* you read the same issue of our emerald giant's mag that we produced? We could be wrong (Forbush knows, we are often enough), but we certainly can't find *any* trace of a forest fire atop the World Trade Center in our copies of Hulk #193. We can't even find a mention of Triton and Xemnu (although the titanic teddy bear *is* scheduled to make a return appearance in this mag soon—free plug!).

Y'see, it's not that we mind you fabricating a few plot twists of your own, it's just that the Lively One thinks your particular idea is so bizarre that he's threatened to use it in next month's SPIDER-MAN! See what you've started?

Hulk People:

In HULK #193 was Herb Trimpe aided in the drawings of Doc Samson? And, if so, was it Jazzy Johnny Romita who assisted?

RON FRITZ
173 Gass Road
Pittsburgh, PA 15229

Yep, ya hit the nail on the proverbial head, Ronnie. Johnny did indeed lend his artistic talents to a couple of the Doc Samson figures. Sometimes it's difficult, when working in the unique Marvel style of having the artwork drawn before the comic is actually scripted, to get precisely the expression or stance that the writer has in mind. When that occasionally happens, as in this particular instance, Jazzy Johnny is always around to put his skills to use in making such alterations. And it's always a real kick to us when you perceptive fans notice the extra effort we put into a particular scene.

Take care till we meet again, Marvelites, and have a Hulky New Year.

MARVEL VALUE STAMP

51: DR. STRANGE: MASTER OF THE MYSTIC ARTS from *The Incredible Hulk* no. 197 (March 1976). Stamp also appears in *The Invaders* no. 7 (July 1976).

SCAREMAILS

c/o MARVEL COMICS GROUP, 575 MADISON AVE. N.Y.C. 10022

And now, a few words on The Scarecrow's first fantabulous appearance!

Dear Marvel,

No. 1 shock-star is right! I was wondering when someone was gonna hammer and chisel a story starring a grotesque scarecrow as a new defier of crime, so you can imagine how dumb-struck I was when my baby blues viewed the misshapen Scarecrow's first tale upon the racks.

He (?), she (?), it (?) is neither of the B*tm*n, Sh*d*w, or Sp*ctr* creed, so what then is The Scarecrow? He, she, it appears to be a wretched-looking he, she, or it who sends human garbage to the bowels of heck. About all I know for fact is that this . . . whatever comes from an old oil painting (refreshingly different), is terribly (I mean it) fascinating.

Tom Scott
844 South First Street
DeKalb, IL 60115

The letters on that premiere performance were overwhelmingly favorable and, unfortunately, there's really no space to print them all. Why, we've now enough letters for a *dozen* Scarecrow lettercols.

But we would like to thank Ralph Macchio, Ralph Del Vecchio, Dean Mullaney, Fred Hembeck, Roger Klorese and the dozens of others who took time out to send their comments and criticisms on that first feature, and hope that they'll take time out to comment on *this* one-shot. Who knows, if enough fans hit the mails, The Scarecrow may finally get his own title!

Sirs,

Had I been asked for my personal and professional opinion regarding *comic books* and their social value merely one hour before I picked up and began to casually browse through my ten-year-old's copy of DEAD OF NIGHT's "Scarecrow," I would have (I am now almost ashamed to admit) scoffed at the very thought. How wrong I was indeed!

Whether *Scarecrow* is innovation or exemplory of current trends in comics I wouldn't know, for my knowledge in this area is meager and my experience is limited to swapping Sub-Mariners back in the 40's. Regardless, hats off to Scott Edelman, the author of this profound psychological essay. Obviously Mr. Edelman has an extensive background in psycho-analytic theory. The exemplification of the prototypical authoritarian father-figure in the guise of a scarecrow, the frustrated cathexsis of libidinal energy toward the "Kalumai" (ingenious!), and the subtle Freudian overtones, all are but too apparent to the trained reader.

Fearing that I was perhaps "reading too much" into the story, I took the liberty of forwarding a copy to a colleague, Professor Charles Epstein at the Western Behavioral Sciences Institute, and his comments very nearly mirrored mine.

In closing, I would like to congratulate Marvel Comics and especially Mr. Edelman on a job well done. Perhaps some day we will all be relieved of the stigma attached to comic books as I was. By Scarecrow.

Richard Rudnitsky Ph. D
Professor of Clinical Psychology
(no address given)

And if you *really* want to see more of this sinister super-hero, we can do no more than reiterate your final two words and hope that *all* fear fans will follow your advice.

Buy Scarecrow.

Dear Scott,

I don't know where to begin. You really caught me off guard. I thought DEAD OF NIGHT was a reprint magazine. I thank my lucky stars that I at least looked to see where this story had originally been presented, and found out this was it! I've been with Marvel for over 10 years and I always appreciate new writers and artists coming into the fold. The art and the story were both great.

There are a lot of things I want to know but I assume many of them will be handled in the next few issues. Don't tell us too much about the Scarecrow. Keep him a mystery for as long as possible. I like Jess, Dave, and Harmony, and I think a lot of this magazine could go into the development of their individualities.

Let me close by saying that I am really excited and anticipate great things for this series. I'm giving you plenty of slack because I want to see where you're going. And don't ever worry about hanging yourself. Marveldom assembled will come to the rescue if and when needed.

Rook Jones
3053 Tremont St.
Allentown, PA 18104

Rook, you're right when you say that there are many things to be handled in the next few issues of THE SCARECROW in the way of plot development, characterization, etc. The only problem is that at this point in time there *is* no book by that name.

The second story of our straw man's adventures (the first being, for those of you who missed it, in the pages of DEAD OF NIGHT #11) was originally supposed to be THE SCARECROW #1, but a few months back, when we underwent a slight cut-back of our mystery line, we decided to play it safe with *this* shock star and slowly test for sales before thrusting him forth in his own title.

If the sales figures of DEAD OF NIGHT #11 and, of course, this issue of MARVEL SPOTLIGHT warrant it, The Scarecrow may get his own title in the not-too-distant future. All it takes is a little patience and a lot of sales.

So just wait a few months, Mr. Jones, and mayhap you'll see a new title on your local newsstand— and to tell you the truth, no one would be happier than us!

THIS IS IT! YOUR

MARVEL VALUE STAMP

FOR THIS ISSUE!

CLIP 'EM AND COLLECT 'EM!

23: DR. STRANGE: MASTER OF THE MYSTIC ARTS from *Marvel Spotlight* no. 26 (February 1976).

Dear Roy,

No-prize time is here! In #162 I spotted two possible goofs. Number one: Arkon put the alternate Reed in Adamantium chains, from which Reed later broke loose. All Marvelites know that Adamantium can't be broken by Thor, and Thor is far stronger than the alternate Reed-Thing.

Number two: You had a caveman, a Greek hoplite, and an Indian with a tomahawk (no less) attacking the HQ of the F.F., when they were supposed to be attacking the New York of the alternate earth.

Anyway, it was a complicated but good installment. Rich, I haven't forgotten you. You and Roy make a terrific team; keep it up!

Dan Morris
165-10-26th Ave. N.
Wayzata, MN 55391

We'll have to put your no-prize nomination before our Honorary Committee, Dan (said committee consisting roughly of Sanchez of the Mailroom, Howard the Duck, Honest Irv Forbush, and anybody within ten feet of home base at the time). For, we figure that Arkon could have (and we figure that he did) borrowed a few of the warriors-out-of-time especially to attack the Baxter Building: at least, that's what Roy and Rich had in mind at the time, for better and/or for worse. Likewise, while Adamantium would hold either Thor *or* the Thing, it was the combination of *two* Things, somehow managing to mentally combine their powers across the dimensions for a split second, that enabled the Reed-Thing to break free!

Oh well, what the hey— we've already dispensed one no-prize this page, so we might as well turn loose of one more! But, if anybody tells Smilin' Stan Lee that we're giving'em away so hot and heavy, the next issue of FANTASTIC FOUR will probably be written and edited by the aforementioned Sanchez or Irv! Sheesh— the perils of the comic-book biz!

Dear Roy, Rich, and Joe,

I've been waiting a long time for someone to realize the full potential that these three worlds— earth, alternate earth, and the fifth dimension— could have if all three were used in one epic story. Wouldn't you know it'd be Marvel's top writer, Roy Thomas! And what better mag to use the worlds in than "The World's Greatest Comic Magazine"? And what better artists for that mag than the fabulous team of Rich Buckler and Joe Sinnott? (And if you get the idea that I love the present F.F. mags, give yourself a chromium-plated no-prize!)

Carl Dennison
Rt. 3, Box 160
Hendersonville, NC

Now *there's* a guy we can appreciate— somebody who wants to give the blushin' Bullpen a no-prize for a change! You're all heart, C.D.—or, to quote Benjamin J. Grimm 'way back in F.F. #4: "That and a dime'll get me a cup of coffee!" Only thing is— now it won't even do that! Oh well, thanks anyway, guy.

Dear Roy,

In case you do not realize it, you should be sending me a no-prize! Would you like to know why? Okay.

It all started on page 23, panel 4. Ben says, "Watch it, Big Brain!" To which Reed "Thing" Richards replies, "I know who it is, Ben. He's your world's version of Sue Grimm's brother Johnny."

Now, no one told me there was a Sue Grimm! Sue Richards I've heard of, but Sue Grimm? Really, Roy! Send no-prize to—

Bob Bonner
Box 382
Smithers, B.C., Canada
VOJ-2ND

Sorry, Bob, but we've long since given away our quotas of no-prizes for this issue, and after all, we can't just give away no-prizes like they were executive vice-presidencies or something. It's been clearly stated, in virtually every story in which the Reed Richards version of the Thing appeared, that in his dimension (or continuum, as we've been told we should more properly call it) Ben Grimm is married to the former Sue Storm— making her Sue Grimm! We wouldn't bring it up, but one or two other Marvel buffs also took us to task as if we'd goofed in referring to "Sue Grimm"— but for once, we were right as rain! (Maybe *righter,* considering how polluted the rain is these days!) Better luck next time, good neighbor!

THIS IS IT! YOUR
MARVEL VALUE STAMP
FOR THIS ISSUE!

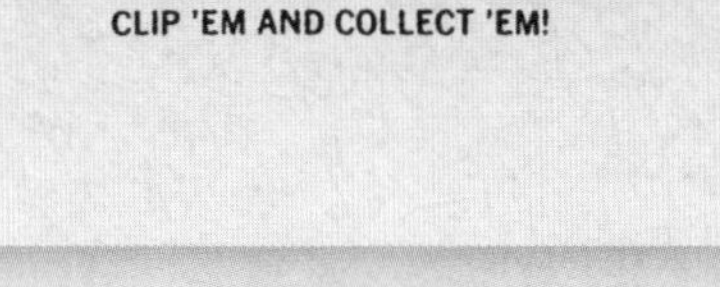

CLIP 'EM AND COLLECT 'EM!

13: DR. STRANGE: MASTER OF THE MYSTIC ARTS from *Fantastic Four* no. 166 (January 1976).

Since we usurped this space last ish for a special feature on Uri Geller, and an intimate insight into the mighty Marvel Bullpen itself, that means we have two issues of The Man Without Fear to cover this month. Ah, the wages of sin!

Hence, without further ado, we're gonna hop, skip and jump right into your colorful, cavortin', and occasionally critical comments. Here we go—

Dear Marvel,

There was something terribly sardonic in the latest appearance of the Man-Bull, in DAREDEVIL #129. I've never liked Man-Bull—I still don't. But I certainly see the irony of his being manipulated by the Matador into stealing the Golden Bull of China. Having him walk away from his fight with Daredevil so that he could go back and deal with the man who used him, who gave him false hope, was another ironic touch. All in all, it was far superior to the "smash-em-up" stories which usually accompany the Man-Bull wherever he goes.

Ed Via
1648 Dean Rd.
Roanoke, VA 24018

Dear Marvel,

I just got through reading DD #129 and I am requesting a no-prize on the grounds of:

1) In THOR #146 the golden bull had no ears, but in DD #129 the bull had ears.

2) In THOR #146 the golden bull was much larger than in DD #129.

3) In THOR #146 the tail points away from the bull's body, in THOR #147 the bull's tail points up, but in DD #129 the tail points straight down. Since the bull is an inanimate object, it cannot wag its tail.

But overlooking these tacky mistakes (which I'm not), the story and art were pretty good. Please send my no-prize to the address listed below. DAREDEVIL is a good magazine, so don't spoil it by being careless.

Larry Will
231 S. Cuyler Ave.
Oak Park, IL 60302

Actually, Larry, while most of your erudite observations are accurate, they hearken back to another title and another time; but we've decided to give you a no-prize anyway, just on the sheer determination of your argument and the exceptional amount of evidence you've assembled. Fair enough, friend Will?

Dear Marv,

Re: DAREDEVIL #130:

Let's start with the cover. It was beautiful! It brought back memories of some of the great issues of the late 60's featuring Gene Colan artwork and such outstanding bad nasties as the Jester, Mr. Fear and Death's-Head (remember him?).

Now, what about the story? After stepping in the right direction with the past four or five issues, "Here Comes the Death-Man" seemed to pause and take a breath before resuming that forward movement. After all, Daredevil started out as a costumed crime-fighter who was right at home battling colorful super-baddies like the Matador, the Stilt-man and Electro. It was good to see him returning in this direction with characters like Copperhead and the Torpedo. But Death-Man didn't come off the same way. The character was colorless and predictable, the voodoo theme is overused, and the moralizing was not very subtle. Involving Daredevil with political conspiracies, supernatural overtones, and "heavy" moral lessons takes the fun out of the strip. Hopefully, issue #130 was just a short break from the return to the masked super-villain.

Finally, the inside artwork! It, too, was beautiful. With Bob Brown you've found the next best thing to Gene Colan. Bob Brown is breathing that familiar excitement into Daredevil, and much congratulations should be extended his way.

All in all, issue #130 was a fair time-out from super-bad guys. I am eagerly awaiting a return to the costumed criminal. I hope I won't be disappointed!

Mike Christiansen
704 S. 3rd Street
Rockford, IL

Dear Marvel,

A close look at DAREDEVIL #130 reveals a clearly racist main plot. Why is Simi's mother the only person besides Daredevil who wants to challenge Brother Zed's death sentence? Why do her "friends" stand by and even help Brother Zed try to murder an innocent child? True, Zed could easily stop any *one* of them with his hypnotic power, but certainly not all of them, and that no one at all even tried to stop him implies they lack humanity.

While I've got your attention, catch this dialogue (page 23, panel 3): "Human sacrifice went OUT when human INTELLIGENCE came in. Or am I giving you more CREDIT than you deserve?" It reeks of the dumb, superstitious savage routine. Any self-respecting Haitian would've been insulted by the whole story.

Karen Chapdelaine
121 King Ave. – Apt. #1
Columbus, OH 43201

Okay, Karen, since the point of our story seems to have slipped you by, we'll elucidate it here to allay your misapprehensions. The offbeat tale wasn't biased against Haitians, either intentionally or unintentionally, but rather against the blind superstitions of voodoo. It was such superstition that kept the others from interfering when Brother Zed tried to murder the child, and it was also superstition and unquestioning obedience to ritual at the expense of human life that Marv condemned with the quote you found objectionable. We appreciate your concern, Karen, but in this instance we think it was unfounded, and we hope you'll give the story in question another reading in light of the facts we've pointed out.

NEXT ISSUE: A city goes stark raving mad under the sinister spell of—*The Jester*! Be here, faithful ones, or forever be filled with regret at the wonder that has gone unwitnessed!

THIS IS IT! YOUR
MARVEL VALUE STAMP
FOR THIS ISSUE!

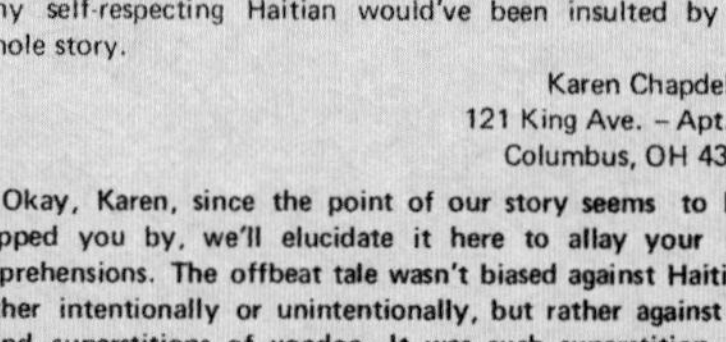

CLIP 'EM AND COLLECT 'EM!

95: DR. STRANGE: MASTER OF THE MYSTIC ARTS from *Daredevil* no. 134 (June 1976).

BAXTER BUILDING BULLETINS

c/o MARVEL COMICS GROUP, 575 MADISON AVE. N.Y.C. 10022

Dear Roy,

I was sitting around thinking, after having read F.F. #166, that all too often in our business the very people who work on the various magazines don't get around to telling their fellow writers (and artists) how *good* they feel a strip or character or direction is... how well they feel the book is being treated, how fine a development they see taking place in a companion title. I guess the word is *feedback*; we get precious little of it.

So that's what *this* is, a letter to a fine magazine I've been reading for 166 consecutive issues, through good and bad, thick and thin. And what prompted me to sit down and write *now* is what you've managed to achieve in a few short issues, and how well you've managed to get "The World's Greatest Comic Magazine" back to the heights it *should* have occupied, lo, these past few years, but somehow never did.

So keep on truckin', Roy. From one writer to another, my deepest congratulations. Peace.

Bill Mantlo
New York, NY

Roy's reply:

"What can I say to a guy who took time off from scripting MARVEL TWO-IN-ONE and several other Marvel mags to drop me an encouraging word? Just one thing: Thanks, buddy."

Dear Friends,

Question. Why, in F.F. #166, is BRIGADIER GENERAL Sellers always referred to as "Colonel"? Is it possible that he just made his first star and still isn't used to being addressed as "General" yet? If so, then why didn't the F.F. notice it? Well, to help you out in the future, I submit the following list of U.S. Military officers' insignia of rank:

Second Lieutenant— Gold Bar
First Lieutenant— Silver Bar
Captain— Two Silver Bars
Major— Gold Oak Leaf
Lieutenant Col.— Silver Oak Leaf
Colonel— Silver Eagle
Brigadier General— 1 Silver Star
Major General— 2 Silver Stars
Lieutenant General— 3 Silver Stars
General— 4 Silver Stars

I hope the above list will help you avoid any future confusion in military insignia of rank. That will keep you from getting several thousand letters like this one in the future, too, most likely. Aside from that minor error, F.F. #166 looks like the beginning of a very interesting tale. So, the Fantastic Four is down to the Fantastic Three again. This should get very weird.

SSgt. Michael L. Kuhne
573-64-5357
602 DASC Box 222
APO New York 09107

It did, Sarge; at least, we *meant* for it to. And thanks a million for the above listing, since, as you guessed, we were bombarded by letters (and not just from guys in the service, either) spotting our grievous goof. It seems Roy's story synopsis called for a colonel, and he didn't realize until too late that Gorgeous George Perez was as shaky as *he* is on anything higher than an Eagle Scout.

So why are we printing your list in this issue instead of simply tacking it up on the Bullpen wall? Why, because if we did that, it'd just get lost again— but this way, from now to doomsay, if anybody asks a question about U.S. Military insignia, we'll just arch an eyebrow and refer 'em to F.F. #170. 'Preciate it, soldier.

Dear Roy,

You goofed on F.F. #166. On page 23, it says, "Sue! Throw a force field around his head, to shut off his air supply! Even the Hulk can't hold out for long if he can't breathe!"

And in 1974 CHRISTMAS TREASURY EDITION, in "The Avengers Take Over," Rick says, "The Hulk is going to drown if you don't go after him." And Captain America says, "No, he won't— because he's got the strongest lungs in the world. He can hold his breath for at least twelve hours."

Everything except that was "right on."

Ricky Lell
102 Cypress Ave.
Greenwood, SC 29646

Maybe you'll even forgive us that supposed goof, Rick, when we clue you in that (assuming Captain America was familiar enough with the Hulk's physiology to comment accurately about his 12-hour lungs) Sue's secret is that she managed to surround the Hulk with a force field just as he had finished *expelling* a breath. Nobody, not even ol' Greenskin, can *hold* a breath he hasn't *taken*. Awfully clever, that Susan!

Dear Marvel,

The other day I was browsing around the dimestore, and: "F.F. # 166. Ah, another Thing-Hulk battle. Might as well buy it; what have I got to lose?"

Then, at home: "Hey, the plane's wing is breaking. Well, waddaya know, Reed and Johnny saved the plane! Beautiful! Even Sue took a part! But Ben didn't do anything. Well, what the hey? He's saved them a hundred other times, anyway, like Reed said. Well, here they go after the Hulk. Ta, ta, da! Hey, they've captured him. Terrific! (For them.) Hey! Reed's changed him back to Dr. Banner! What in... Ben's freed him. 'The Thing and the Hulk...Side by Side!' "

Great job, art, and story!

Gregg Stamey, Jr.
21 Hampton Heights
Canton, NC 28716

Glad you liked it, Gregg. We probably get more requests for annual (or even semi-annual) slug-fests between the Thing and the Hulk than anything this side of the return of the Silver Surfer. So the challenge each time is to figure out a way to do something with that battle which has never been done before, to make it a worthy successor in a long line which stretches back to F.F. #12 and then the immortal two-issue clash in F.F. #25-26. If our mountain of mail can be believed, most Marvelites seem to feel that F.F. #166-167 fared 'way above average in the Thing/Hulk sweepstakes— and, when we consider the competition, that makes Roy, George, Vinnie, and Joe quietly humble. (Well, *humble*, anyway. They're very seldom *quiet*.)

90: DR. STRANGE: MASTER OF THE MYSTIC ARTS from *Fantastic Four* no. 170 (May 1976).

THE EVER-LOVIN' BLUE-EYED

LETTERS PAGE!

c/o MARVEL COMICS GROUP, 575 MADISON AVE., NEW YORK, N.Y. 10022

Marv,

Bill Mantlo may very well be one of the finest new writers in the Marvel Bullpen, but he is not above carelessness. Witness TWO-IN-ONE #12, featuring the Thing and Iron Man.

In the synopsis Bill gave of Prester John's adventures, he completely left out the fact that the evil eye was the instrument used to cause the great Avengers-Defenders serial of a couple of summers ago. Since I consider this one of the best epics in the Marvel Age of Comics (surpassed only by the Avengers Celestial Madonna series and, possibly, the 1950's Captain America sequence that heralded Englehart's first efforts at scripting Cap), I think this was a very obvious mistake. However, in my kindness, I offer not ONE, but TWO explanations for the omission.

First of all, the easy out: In DEFENDERS #11, the end of the aforementioned epic, Dr. Strange wiped out all knowledge of the fight from the earth-dwellers. Thus Bill himself couldn't possibly have realized how the evil eye was used because he'd been made to FORGET that it ever WAS used. (I, of course, being a part-time GOD, was not affected by Strange's spell.)

Explanation the second: When John appeared in DEFENDERS #11, he said he was HIDING the eye for the second time BEFORE he gained in the FIRST time, indicating that he'd done a little time-hopping. Also, probably due to a colorist's error, he was white-headed this issue instead of his normal red hair. We could assume, however, that the white hair was due to age, not a mistake, and that he travelled into the past many years AFTER he fought the Thing and Iron Man. Consequently, he could not have related that eons-old incident to the two heroes as he himself was not aware that the eye had been re-formed after it's explosion in FF #54. Iron Man was, but didn't mention it because the urgency of the battle and a desire to keep the Defenders a still-secret organization motivated him.

No thanks are needed, Bill. Just accept my wishes for luck in the future...and don't let it happen again.

David B. Kirby
2816 Monument Avenue
Richmond, VA 23221

But thanks are offered anyway, David...and it WON'T happen again. Meanwhile, although we unquestionably accept YOUR explanation, our own research seems to suggest that if we extend the radius of pi by 3.7 meters to the left and add an arc of about three degrees, we'd...Nope. Looks like we can't wiggle out of THIS one.

Dear People (?),

I am ENRAGED! In TWO-IN-ONE #12, Blue-eyed Benjamin Grimm remarked that a Big Mac was not NOURISHING! Balderdash! A Big Mac may have about the same amount of nourishment as that of an empty cereal box...but it has SOME nourishment, at least. Do NOT make this mistake again.

Kurt Busiek
41 Somerset Rd.
Lexington, MA 02173

Okay, Kurt. We won't. But what's to stop Bashful Benjamin? The Hulk, maybe?

Dear Bill and Len Wein,

Just now I finished issue #12, and I can't help but feel that something is missing. That something is the addition of a sub-plot featuring Wundarr and Namorita. Apparently these two left with Steve Gerber. They're too GOOD to fade away into limbo. How about an entire issue featuring the Thing and these two?

By the way, does anyone on your staff read the letters page? How about that monster-duck team-up we're all waiting for?

David A. Lovfers
66 Crestfield Drive
Rochester, NY 14617

David, in one heckuva brief letter, you've raised some important questions. Questions that deserve ANSWERS. Yes, someone in the Bullpen DOES read the letters page, as well as all the thousands of letters that don't make it onto that page. That someone is usually the WRITER of that particular issue the fans are commenting on...or someone who reads them and passes comments, criticisms and suggestions on to him...so your pleas and praises do NOT go unheard. As to Wundarr and Namorita...for the time they DO seem to be in limbo. But the former is slated for a future solo-issue of MARVEL PREMIERE and neither the present writer, Boisterous Bill, or the scheduled future writer of TWO-IN-ONE, Rascally Roy himself, have said anything about using them, so it's anyone's guess at this point. As to that "monster-duck team-up"...yes, well, that's something we'd ALL like to see...but Howard is Steve's duck, and he ought to be given the chance to do it, now that our fearless fowl has his very own mag. So, David, as we said...we are listening. Peace.

As we've said, starting in a few issues, Rascally Roy Thomas will be picking up the scripting chores on MARVEL TWO-IN-ONE, and both he and Embattled Bill Mantlo would like to thank Marvelous Marv, Lively Len and Rockin' Roger for pinch-hitting with last issue's Thing-Power Man team-up, giving Bill a chance to plot ahead a few issues with what promises to be something you've all been asking for...a CONTINUED STORY. Rampaging Ron Wilson is sharpening more pencils than have ever been seen since Jack Kirby came back, and all concerned are getting ready to tackle one of the most block-busting tales in what somebody somewhere has dubbed..."The Marvel RENAISSANCE of Comics"! Be here!

MARVEL VALUE STAMP

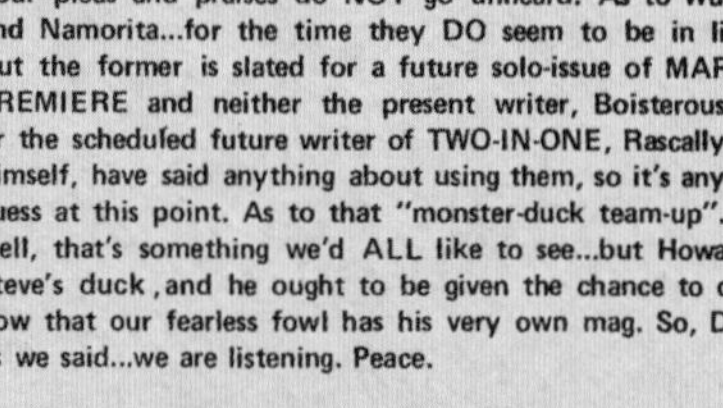

45: DR. STRANGE: MASTER OF THE MYSTIC ARTS from *Marvel Two-in-One* no. 14 (March 1976).

THE HAMMER STRIKES

c/o MARVEL COMICS GROUP, 575 MADISON AVE. N.Y.C. 10022

Dear Marvel,

THOR #241 brought the god of thunder's encounter with the gods of ancient Egypt to a very successful conclusion. It was majestically illustrated by John Buscema and Joe Sinnott, whose spectacular depiction of the gods' savage confrontation with the skeletal minions of Seth against the backdrop of space was absolutely fantastic. Roy Thomas, who started all this back in #239, should've hung around. But let's not take anything away from Bill Mantlo, who stepped right in and delivered a dramatic, imaginative script.

Regarding Polly Goodnough's beautiful letter: she's right. Sif's sacrifice *was* rather callously brushed aside by Thor. When I see Jane Foster holding a spear on the Troll King, or joining Thor in mortal combat with an evil god, I get the feeling you're saying to us that Sif's spirit is still in there fightin'.

But that's not good enough, people! You know and I know that Odin could separate Sif from Jane without harming her. He could wave his sceptre and mumble something godly, and that would be it.

So do it. Do it now. If for no other reason, do it because it's what Thor fans want. After all, we *have* had something to do with the book's success these past thirteen years, haven't we?

Edward B. Via
1648 Dean Road
Roanoke, VA 24018

Yea, verily, friend Via! Marveldom has had *everything* to do with our success. However, we must gently remind you that no one reader can possibly represent the vast and varied tastes of all Thor-ophiles. Witness Patricia McCoy's letter here last ish, if ye doubt; every Marvelite has a vote to cast, and it is the aggregate of those votes that determines the will of Marveldom Assembled. Thus has it always been and thus shall it ever be!

Dear Stan, Len, John and Joe:

THOR #242 once again proved that Thor and his friends are the noblest Asgardians, while his father has a lot to learn. First, Odin goes through his self-induced exile, then he learns of the part of Sif that is now a part of Jane Foster, and finally he fights alongside Jane Foster; but he still refuses to allow Thor and Jane to go together. What an arrogant, egotistical, pompous fool!

I never had a very high opinion of the All-Father in the first place. I wouldn't be surprised if he started the long battle between the Trolls and the Asgardians. He has certainly not learned humanity from his attempt.

Other than that this issue was pretty good.

Larry Twiss
227 Fox Run
King of Prussia, PA 19406

Dear Marvel,

Come on, people! Don't pull Thor down into that same worn out, stale routine of Pop Odin disowning his son because his son insists on loving the mortal Jane Foster. It even sounds boring! Much as I liked Jane before she was more-or-less taken out of the series, even then I was getting sick and tired of the old angry dad routine. So please don't let this theme drag on. You can do much better.

Cheryl Klepper
Box 2, Sadler Curtilage
Dickinson School of Law
Carlisle, PA 17013

Your letters, Larry and Cheryl, are representative of a surprising amount of mail this month. But—without giving away anything of import—we think it imperative to mention that while the basic situation may resemble the earlier Odin-Thor-Jane Foster problem at first glance, the resolution will be far-and-away entirely that of current editor-*cum*-author Len Wein. *He* asks but one thing—patience. And *we* guarantee it's worth the wait.

If you doubt, come back next month and check us out!

MARVEL VALUE STAMP

STATEMENT OF OWNERSHIP, MANAGEMENT AND CIRCULATION ACT OF AUGUST 12, 1970: SECTION 3685, TITLE 39, UNITED STATES CODE

1. Title of Publication: THOR.

2. Date of Filing: September 22, 1975.

3. Frequency of Issue: Monthly.

3A. Annual subscription price: $4.25.

4. Location of Known Office of Publication: 575 Madison Ave., New York, N.Y. 10022.

5. Location of the Headquarters or General Business Offices of the Publishers: Marvel Comics Group/a Division of Cadence Industries Corp., 575 Madison Ave., New York, N.Y. 10022.

6. Names and addresses of the publisher, editor, and managing editor are Publisher: Stan Lee, 575 Madison Ave., N.Y., N.Y. 10022; Editor: Marv Wolfman, 575 Madison Ave., N.Y., N.Y. 10022; Managing Editor: John Verpoorten, 575 Madison Ave., N.Y., N.Y. 10022.

7. Owner (If owned by a corporation, its name and address must be stated and also immediately thereunder the names and addresses of stockholders owning or holding 1 percent or more of total amount of stock. If not owned by a corporation, the names and addresses of the individual owners must be given. If owned by a partnership or other unincorporated firm, its name and address, as well as that of each individual must be given.) Marvel Comics Group, 575 Madison Ave., New York, N.Y. 10022. Cadence Industries Corp., 21 Henderson Drive, West Caldwell, New Jersey 07006.

8. Known bondholders, mortgagees, and other security holders owning or holding 1 percent or more of total amount of bonds, mortgages, or other securities: None.

9. For optional completion by publishers mailing at the regular rates (Section 132.121, Postal Service Manual) 39 U.S.C. 3626 provides in pertinent part: "No person who would have been entitled to mail matter under former section 4359 of this title shall mail such matter at the rates provided under this subsection unless he files annually with the Postal Service a written request for permission to mail matter at such rates."
In accordance with the provisions of this statute, I hereby request permission to mail the publication named in Item 1 at the reduced postage rates presently authorized by 39 U.S.C. 3626.

(signed) Ed Shukin—Business Manager

10. For completion by nonprofit organizations authorized to mail at special rates. (Section 132.122, Postal Manual.) The purpose, function, and nonprofit status of this organization and the exempt status for Federal income tax purposes. (Check one.) ☐ Have not changed during preceding 12 months. ☐ Have changed during preceding 12 months. (If changed, publisher must submit explanation with this statement.)

11. EXTENT AND NATURE OF CIRCULATION.

A. Total No. Copies Printed (net press run): Average no. copies each issue during preceding 12 months: 388,446; single issue nearest to filing date: 396,639.

B. Paid Circulation: 1) Sales through dealers and carriers, street vendors and counter sales: Average no. copies each issue during preceding 12 months: 195,606; single issue nearest to filing date: 186,097. 2) Mail subscriptions. Average no. copies each issue during preceding 12 months: 1,610; single issue nearest to filing date: 1,534.

C. Total paid circulation: Average no. copies each issue during preceding 12 months: 197,216; single issue nearest to filing date: 187,631.

D. Free distribution by mail, carrier or other means, samples, complimentary, and other free copies: Average no. copies each issue during preceding 12 months: ---; single issue nearest to filing date: ---.

E. Total distribution (sum of C and D): Average no. copies each issue during preceding 12 months: 197,216; single issue nearest to filing date: 187,631.

F. Copies not distributed: 1) Office use, left-over, unaccounted, spoiled after printing: Average no. copies each issue during preceding 12 months: 3,081; single issue nearest to filing date: 3,451. 2) Returns from News Agents. Average no. copies each issue during preceding 12 months: 188,149; single issue nearest to filing date: 205,557.

G. Total (sum of E & F—should equal net press run shown in A): Average no. copies each issue during preceding 12 months: 388,446; single issue nearest to filing date: 396,639.

I certify that the statements made by me above are correct and complete.

(signed) Ed Shukin—Business Manager

73: DR. STRANGE: MASTER OF THE MYSTIC ARTS from *Thor* no. 246 (April 1976). Note that the stamp is printed upside down on the letters page.

CAPTAIN AMERICA™

1941! The world at war! And in a full-security laboratory, frail *Steve Rogers* became **CAPTAIN AMERICA**, the American super-soldier! For four thrilling years, he struck back at the Axis' treacherous attack–– until a freak stroke of fate threw him into suspended animation... to awaken in the mid-1960's, a man *twenty years* out of his time. Since that day, **CAPTAIN AMERICA** has sought his destiny in this brave new world!

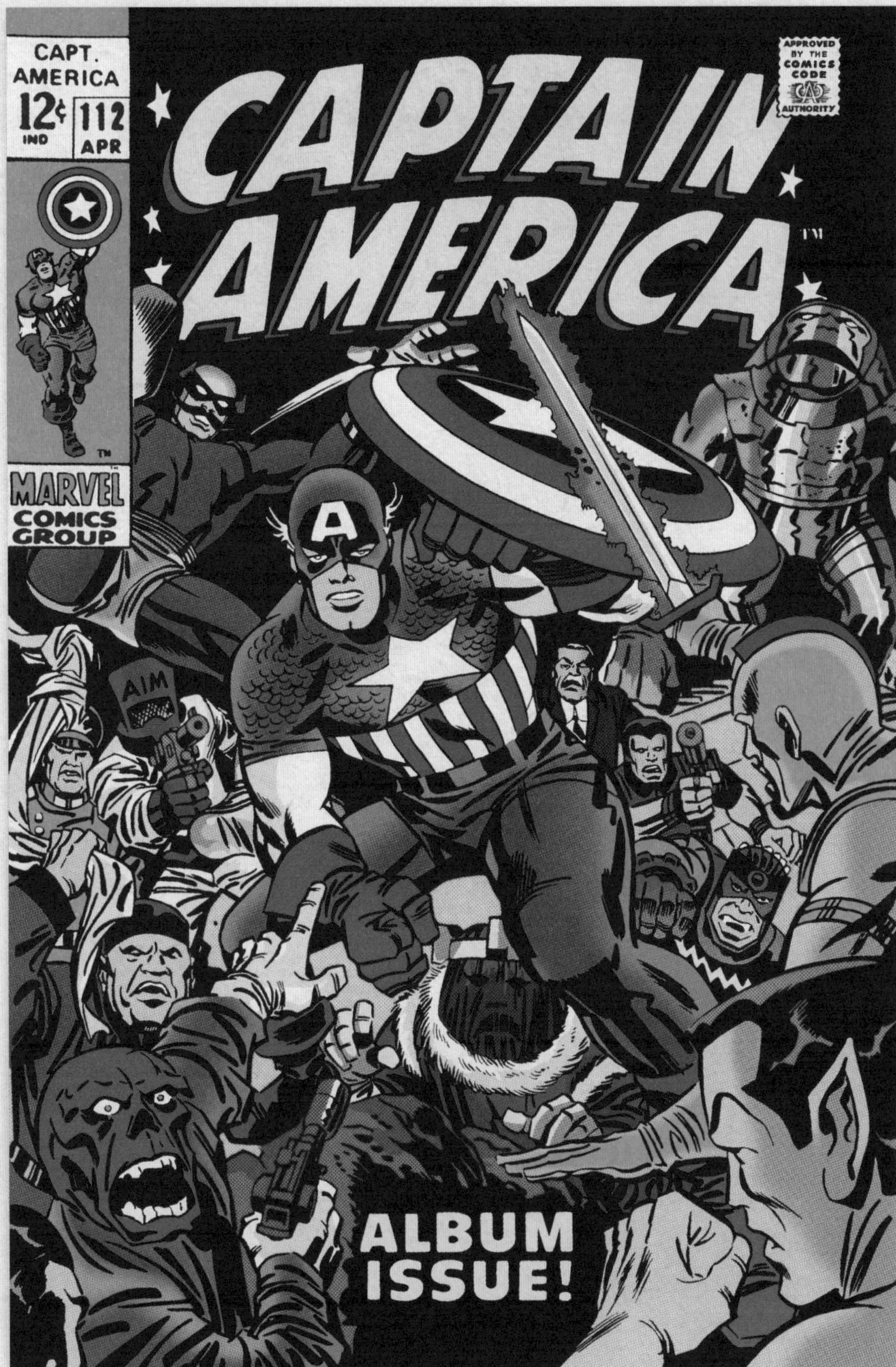

Captain America no. 112 (April 1969), art by Jack Kirby and Frank Giacoia.

AVENGERS ASSEMBLE!

c/o MARVEL COMICS GROUP, 575 MADISON AVE. N.Y.C. 10022

Dear Marvel,

In issue #136, Terry Kay Martin says that Wanda is being "knocked for loving a being who can't ever return her love by giving her children." I want you guys to clear up something for me and all of Marveldom.

In ish #57, Goliath states that "he's [Vison] every inch a human being except that all his bodily organs are constructed of synthetic materials."

I assume that he is more or less human because of that statement, and most likely, if he has a heart, he is going to have blood and so on.

It is even more likely that if Ultron-5 created the Vision as a son, he would provide him with the ability to be a father.

If Wanda and Vizh really want children and assuming that Ultron-5 didn't provide Vizh with that ability, you can: (1) have them adopt a child, (2) have Vision pretend to go wild, recreate Ultron-8 and have him give Vision his missing ability.

Michael Blake
6207 Capella Avenue
Burke, VA 22015

Mike, this is a question that's raged ever since Wanda and the Vizh first took notice of each other. To settle it once and for all, it's Steve's opinion that Goliath was telling the literal truth in that long-ago line...as far as he knew it. But we really doubt if even Ultron-5's science could come up with a *synthetic* gland capable of producing *human* life. (Moreover, we don't think he'd have wanted to. His aim was to create a son and a slave, not a full-fledged man.) So the newlyweds' only option, as we see it, would be adoption—*if* they wanted a child. Frankly, that was Steve's original idea for them, but Paty convinced him that Wanda's not looking to become a mother. Thus, we come right back to where we started: no kids, for whatever reason you like. Remember, as Wanda herself said in GSA #4, "Love is for souls, not bodies."

Now, that should clear everything up, but somehow, we have the feeling we've just unleashed a whole new floodtide!

Dear Steve,

This letter is being written to benefit one Jan Pym and maybe even a Marvel writer. I've been reading Marvel comics for seven years now, and, although you may not realize it, you now have the chance to do something which I don't believe has been seriously attempted by any writer for Marvel.

There are several super-hero groups around, and no matter what their differences, they all have one thing in common (besides being composed of super-heroes)—each has only one or at the most, two, female members. I am really beginning to believe that comic writers can't handle more than one heroine at a time on a regular basis. Take the F.F.—they gain a new female only when the original one bows out. I was going to admit that the X-Men had three, but two have left. Now the Avengers have a chance to have three women (and two of them married which is very unusual) regulars, something new—and after 7 years that's hard to find—and what happens? It looks as if you intend to kill one off. Don't do it! Accept the challenge! Break down the new frontier! After all, why write about something as trite as the hero mourning loss of wife, when you have something fresh to try?

Ann Nichols
P.O. BOX 125
Williamsport, MD 21795

Why indeed?

We don't want to tip our hand too early, Ann, but as you know by now, Jan Pym did not die—and as you know from the answer to Larry Twiss elsewhere on this page, the final roster of our little group is yet to be determined. Reaction to Steve's handling of women has been very favorable thus far, and we have no plans to foul up now.

Dear Steve, George, and Vinnie,

I can see that the sub-plots are moving right along. We have some fine examples of the comradeship between Iron Man and Thor, as well as a look at how Moondragon and the Beast are reacting to the other Avengers. Right now, Yellowjacket seems to be driven by the simple need of revenge, which is getting kind of stale. The Wasp better not die, or else.... I fear that in your drive for new members you have overloaded the ranks. True, there were only five active members in this issue, but once the Vision and Wanda return from their honeymoon and the Wasp recovers (which better happen for all three of them), the Avengers will start their crowd act again. Then Hawkeye will return from the 12th century, with or without the Black Knight. If you must drop somebody from the roster, let it be Moondragon, the Black Knight, or the Beast.

On page 19, Iron Man says that the Quinjet was built by Stark Industries. As we all know, Stark Industries has changed its name a long time ago to Stark International. Do you have an excuse for this error, or have I finally caught myself a no-prize?

Larry (the Fooman Torch) Twiss
227 Fox Run
King of Purssia, PA

You have, Lar. The stainless scripter forgot all about the name change, so the no-prize is on its way.

As for the "crowd act" ...well, if you'll remember, this whole sequence, beginning with #137, has concerned the search for a new permanent team, and you can take it for granted that some of that crowd is destined not to make the final cut. In other words, we've deliberately brought in more people than we ever intended to keep—and it's not just the newcomers whose fates are on the line. *Nobody* should be counted either in or out as yet.

Heck, as far as that goes....

NEXT ISSUE: This one takes us back to the Brand Corporation, where more deviltry than you thought possible is afoot, and where a forgotten room holds the key to an incredible transformation. Meanwhile, back out west, *two* startling decisions are reached—and it all comes together in an ending (or a beginning) you won't want to miss! Cryptic,

THIS IS IT! YOUR
MARVEL VALUE STAMP
FOR THIS ISSUE!

CLIP 'EM AND COLLECT 'EM!

17: CAPTAIN AMERICA from *The Avengers* no. 143 (January 1976).

COMMENTS TO CAGE

c/o MARVEL COMICS GROUP, 575 MADISON AVE. N.Y.C. 10022

Bill, George, Mac, and Marv:

We have here a particularly characteristic issue of Luke Cage, of late. At least, in terms of direction and interest-appeal. Both script and art-wise. LUKE CAGE #27 was far superior to its two predecessors. Bill Mantlo had proven to be a new shining star in the ranks of Bullpen writers. And—surprise!— George Perez has done some of the finest artwork since the Tuska-Graham episodes of Cage.

Still, there is a definite feeling of vagueness about this book. Like the Surfer mag, the hero seems to be getting into needless conflicts for the sake of having a fight to make an issue around. In the Lee stories the battle was always justified, however late, and had a meaning for the surfer and the readers. The same cannot be said here. The book has turned into almost a hack product, passing from writer to writer, almost regularly. Sad, sad...

All these 'almosts' herein are here because there is still a chance to rescue the book. The Cottonmouth stories were closest to what the book should be: glimpses into a black, city-based super-hero, the types he sees everyday (like Englehart's Flea), etc. Or else, why do a black super-hero comic at all?

Before you ask, Mac, is for McWilliams — whose inks were superb.

Les Baptiste
120-31 Benchley Pl.
Bronx, NY 10475

Bill and George thank you for your approval of their efforts, Les. It's often a difficult task for a fill-in writer and/or artist to do only one issue of a series. And we think Bill and George did a great job.

Cage won't be playing such musical scripting and art chores in the future, Les. Dauntless Don M. is committed to giving this series a definitive direction in plot, character and theme; and we think much of that is all ready apparent with these opening issues.

But stay with us, Les. Because these guys are just beginning to show the kind of excitement they've got up their sleeves.

Dear Power Man:

Well, after that scraggly, banal tale in POWER MAN #25 (I think Cage would've stayed home if he knew the outcome of this cross country trip would be so bleah), Steve Englehart finally gives us a fine mystery tale that Dan Curtis would be proud of. Coupled with the best Tuska and Colletta artwork for this mag, it was a nice farewell for Steve. We'll miss you, Kid.

And don't forget the housewarming party for Don McGregor in LUKE CAGE, POWER MAN #27. You're catering.

Psst! How about making this mag monthly?

Mark Dooley
105 Wehmeier St.
Columbus, IN 47201

Are you kidding, Mark?

You might have noticed that housewarming party came an issue late, and that Bill Mantlo and George Perez covered beautifully while Jumbo John Verpoorten (our peerless production chief over whom no one can peer) singed Don with a verbal blasting that is still heard in the far corners of the Bullpen.

Monthly, you ask.

Sheesh!

And Don's not even out of traction yet.

Dear Marvel,

POWER MAN #27 was o.k. The art was o.k. But o.k. is not good enough. I want to be able to say that Luke Cage was fantastic. But the only way I am going to call it fantastic is if you make the proper changes. For instance change his name back to Hero for Hire. It sounds more like a black man making a living through the toils of Harlem. Power Man sounds as if he's got it made. But that's not as important as what is on the inside. I wish that somehow, someway you would get Billy Graham back behind the pencils. When I look back to my old LUKE CAGE mags I marvel at his art. He draws expressions that are "out of sight" and he can draw muscles that are realistic. I think Billy Graham would be able to come back with a little effort. If not I think I will stop buying LUKE CAGE. The main reason I buy comics is to marvel at the artwork. If I see a comic's art that is not good, I do not buy it. I hope to see Billy return. I think your sales will go up and you'll be able to put him back to monthly. My friends agree.

Robert Dugan
Sag, MI 48601

Don't stop buying CAGE now, Robert, or Rich and Don will be left wondering how you feel about their collaborative effort on this very issue of POWER MAN.

Not only that, but do you really mean to tell us that you wouldn't buy a book that had your letter in it? We can't promise that will happen every time you write, but if you stick with us, we think you'll be more than pleasantly surprised.

NEXT ISSUE: "And Over the Years, They Murdered the Stars!" The conclusion to our contemporary trilogy featuring Piranha Jones and Cockroach Hamilton. And it's a conclusion that you can't afford to miss!

If Cage survives the three-way death trap that ends this issue, Man, have we got some way-out wonderment in store for you. That is...*if* Cage survives.

And *if* Manhattan survives!

And *if* Don can figure a way to get Cage and Manhattan out of this.

Anyhow, even if Cage *doesn't* make it, even if Manhattan should fall (and some people say it all ready has), you'll see more of D. W. Griffith's young lady friend, more of Quentin Chase and his detective work on our very own endangered Power Man, more of the mysterious figure that haunts Noah Burstein at his store front clinic (we had to pass that by this time around), and a few other surprises that we want to hit you when you're least prepared.

And until -- not if -- all this comes to pass, we know we've left you waiting on tenterhooks for POWER MAN #30, so we won't end with our usual catchphrase, "Hang in there!" This time around, we just don't think it's needed.

THIS IS IT! YOUR

MARVEL VALUE STAMP

FOR THIS ISSUE!

CLIP 'EM AND COLLECT 'EM!

25: CAPTAIN AMERICA from *Power Man* no. 29 (February 1976).

c/o MARVEL COMICS GROUP, 575 MADISON AVE. N.Y.C. 10022

Dear Steve, Gene and Frank,

DOCTOR STRANGE #9, while not as much a hot-needle-between-the-eyes issue as, say, the Death issue (#4), gave me a peculiar lift, an elation that was a bit hard to define, but was a feeling that, indeed, I had participated in something special.

The story was, to be simplistic, the triumph of good over evil, something which is supposedly treated in 90% of all the comics produced. What was different was not that the evil was especially nasty this time around, but that the force which triumphed was not simply a Hero employing "one last desperate chance, uhh!" It was love, sharing, the union of being that defeated the force of evil. It is not easy to portray such a triumph (Denny O'Neil and Neal Adams tried, and to my mind, failed, in X-MEN #65), but Steve and Gene, you managed it with elegance.

Reading, not just reading a comic book, but most any work of fiction, is a process of "getting into" the story, of getting "caught up" in it. We participate. (That's one reason why one feels abused when reading a story about a "hero" who does something very immoral, like murdering many people. We feel as if we've participated in something against our principles.) And this participation is a form of love. When someone says that they love the comics, it's no metaphor: getting wrapped up in a comics story is a form of love. The thing that was so special about DOCTOR STRANGE #9, was that it was one of the few stories that loved us back.

What I mean by that is that this commitment, this involvement that we feel toward what's going on in the pages of the magazine, we are told on pages 27 and 31, is linked to the same commonality and participation that beat mack the elemental evil of Dormammu. How can that be? On first glance, it seems absurd: we have no amazing powers to make bolts of light come from our fingertips (at least, some of us don't;) how can there be a relationship between reading a comic and defeating evil? (a pretty fundamental question, once you think about it.)

Comic books are escape literature, right? Sure. Only what do you escape into? In Doctor Strange, the thing we participate in is Truth, and as Keats said, Beauty. Steve has managed to make this strip a very spiritual, very elevated strip. It would be presumptuous to say that Englehart has The Proper Conception Of The Way Things Are; but his Dr. Strange is definitely a real spiritual man. And Gene Colan (probably my all-time favorite artist) portrays Dr. Strange with an elegance that is unsurpassed by anyone. What we enter into here is a participation in the best thing about life, that Truth and Beauty. Those are the things that beat Dormammu: those are the things that we as readers, thanks to Steve and Gene, possess.

There may have been more meticulously done books (Chiaramonte's inks, which I on the whole dug, were a bit sketchy in places); there may have been more erudite scripts done; but I have rarely read a book which had as much to give. Thanks.

Peter B. Gillis
18 Bayberry Road
Elmsford, NY 10523

Dear Marv,

What words to describe DOC # 10? All I know is that again I am compelled to state that this was one of the finest issues. Steve Englehart's story was beyond comparison. Yet, by far the finest aspect of the issue was Gene Colan's contribution. Even with the not-so-good Chiaramonte inks, Gene's artwork was simply awesome.

Steve Englehart continues to develop the Doc, creating a more widely knowledgable—both in the mystic arts, and in human understanding—personality. The entire opening monologue, as the Doc speculates on the many doorways of life's existance, was a beautiful piece of writing. Too, Eternity (ever one for thoughtful philosophy) introduced a very fine point pertaining to man's understanding of himself and his universe. This latest psychological challenge for the Doc looks to be another interesting growth.

And, somehow, Steve managed to write the story, including Eternity, Mordo, and Nightmare, and nothing was crowded.

Dean Mullaney
81 Delaware Street
Staten Island, NY 10304

Dear Steve and Gene,

Your description of "Alone Against Eternity" on page 1 was wonderfully accurate. "A saga of the strange...unlike all others"...how true. It took me two readings to discover that there was no physical conflict in this issue. None at all, except for Doc's mental struggle with Eternity to try to stop the end of the world.

Steve, your handling of the supporting characters continues to improve. I believe that this is the first time since his inception that Baron Mordo has been treated differently. It's about time we saw something fresh concerning him. However, please find something to do with his and the aged Genghis' mental difficulties. They are both rather disturbing in their new state of mind (lessness).

Gene, your art has improved greatly since even the past excellent issues. Your stuff begins to better Brunner himself, in your own way. Page 15 fascinates me; the coloring job was beautiful.

I'll end with a few suggestions. First, keep Kane off your covers. His work is so poor, especially on Doc and Clea, that it defies comparison. At least he isn't showing everyone's nostrils like he usually does. Keep Tom Orzechowski doing your lettering. There is no one better. And lastly, add my vote to Bob Rodi's. Clea deserves much more space than she got this issue. Perhaps it would help if you thought of her as Doc when he first appeared, and Stephen as the Ancient One.

Keep it going,

Bill Burnworth
1821 Fletcher Street
Anderson, IN 46016

NEXT ISSUE: Still two months away, DR. STRANGE #13 promises to be all that its number indicates. In short, we'll see what happens when the world is naught but ashes...*and* why the Ancient One is back...*and* who Eternity may be...*and* why reality is exactly what it used to be, even if it's not.

Bye!

MARVEL VALUE STAMP

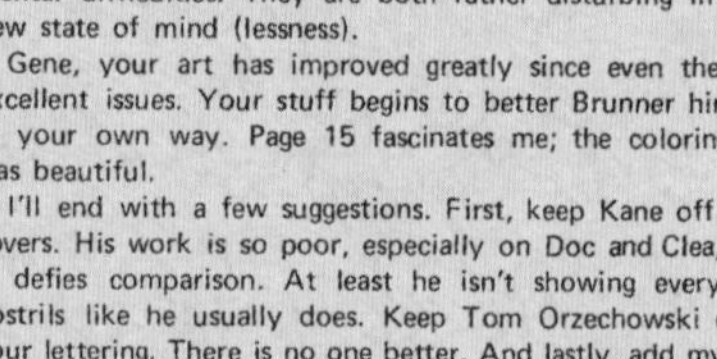

37: CAPTAIN AMERICA from *Doctor Strange* no. 12 (February 1976).

DEFENDERS DIALOGUE

c/o MARVEL COMICS GROUP, 575 MADISON AVE. N.Y.C. 10022

Dear Bozos,

Yep, that's right. The title of #34 summed it up. Since Gerber's first psychotic playground was cancelled, he seems to have transferred all his fears and phobias to DEFENDERS. Can you imagine Steranko's confusion in about fifteen years as he describes the current DEFENDERS episode in volume ten of his *History of Comics?*

"Jack Norris, husband of Barbara Norris whose body is currently occupied by the Valkyrie, is trapped in the brain of Chondu the Mystic, while his body lies near death in the sanctum of Dr. Strange. Chondu's brain has been transplanted into the body of Kyle Richmond (a.k.a. Nighthawk). Jack/Chondu/Kyle holds the Nighthawk's brain in a bowl (a bowl? not a glass capsule or steel vault?) of life-preserving chemicals as he faces Nebulon, a handsome, golden-skinned, celestial man, who showed his true form in #14 as a pink, slimy, tentacled slug-thing. Chondu's consciousness is rendered harmless in the body of a baby deer (that's right, a baby deer). Meanwhile, three confused Defenders are running around, not really knowing who they're chasing."

Confusing? You betcha! But all this certainly makes for easy distinction between the Defenders and the hordes of other super-groups popping up these days. By the way, you might as well drop the non-team label. This bunch is firmly established as a group.

Steve Rogers
5427 43rd
Lubbock, TX 79414

Dear Marv, Sal, Jim, and Steve:

Quite a book you've got there! I refer specifically to DEFENDERS #34. You guys have really done an all-around good job. And the weird thing is that the general goodness of the DEFENDERS sort of sneaked up on me.

My favorite comics are WARLOCK, HOWARD THE DUCK, DOCTOR STRANGE, CAPTAIN MARVEL, KILLRAVEN, and DEATHLOK. And all of them have something spectacular to offer. You know, it seems to me that any half-decent artist can throw together a passable story. The Marvel artists, however, obviously use their imaginations to figure out just what the writer was mentally seeing when he wrote the piece.

But what, you ask, does this have to do with the DEFENDERS? Well, everything and nothing. You see, there's nothing really tremendous about the DEFENDERS, but everything's so very good—and, I think, getting better with each issue.

For instance, take Steve Gerber's writing...*please*!! (I don't really mean that; it just slipped out.) He's not trying to do the rise and fall of the entire universe like Starlin and Englehart. He's just writing the down-to-earth, everyday adventures of a bunch of people who just happen to have super-powers–with some very interesting new ideas; namely Ruby...and the Elf!

(Please don't tell the Elf story straight out. If there's a pattern to his killings, please let it reveal itself slowly...a page at a time.)

And the art! I've liked Sal Buscema's work ever since he did that CAPTAIN AMERICA series about the two Caps. He draws muscles fuller and more realistically than 95% of all comic artists. As for Jim Mooney...his inks tend to smooth out rough figures very well. And, since Sal is a pretty fine (in the sense of "not bold") penciler to begin with, they complement each other well. In fact, the thing that really inspired this letter was Nighthawk's somewhat-sheepish grin on the splash of issue #34.

Anyway, I think I'll just close this letter quick...without mentioning the Bozos...

Naw, I will. They're great!!

Mark H. Kernes
3900 Chestnut, Apt. 714
Philadelphia, PA 19104

You people keep astonishing us.

Poor Steve Gerber, who's built a career on providing fans with copious cause for outraged letters of comment, moaned and sulked around the office for days when he learned that the overwhelming majority of Marvelites dug the bejabbers out of DEFENDERS #34. When pressed for *his* view on *your* views, he mumbled, somewhat sullenly: "A remarkable capacity for adaptation to unfamiliar environments...they're the fittest... they'll survive." You figure it out. It's too metaphysical for us.

Meanwhile, we'd like to explain away a few alleged blunders for which several readers called us—make that "hauled us"—onto the carpet. To wit:

We had hoped the Whole World would infer from the survival of Nighthawk's brain in an open dish of "life-preserving chemicals" that the Headmen truly are Geniuses Extraordinaire and not just pretenders to their respective thrones. Honest, it was planned that way to give you a subtle glimpse of just how far their scientific expertise extends. Of course, it's impossible for a human brain to stay alive under those conditions—except *they made it work!*

Next up, the absence of emerald hue from Greenskin's skin in the "Bozo" sequence: intentional again. You'll note that the Hulk did turn as verdant as a fresh-picked stringbean again once Dr. Strange removed the spell of concealment from...ah, hah! Now you've got it! Good!

All of which brings us to a final, slightly querulous query.

Dear Steve,

Will you at least tell us if you intend to reveal who that dwarf is before 1980?

Ann Nichols
P.O. Box 125
Williamsport, MD 21795

There are no dwarves in this magazine, Ann. The only short person in sight is that apparently homicidally-inclined elf. Is that who you mean?

See you in thirty days, folks!

THIS IS IT! YOUR
MARVEL VALUE STAMP
FOR THIS ISSUE!

53: **CAPTAIN AMERICA** from *The Defenders* no. 37 (July 1976). Stamp also appears in *Marvel Feature* no. 3 (March 1976).

GREEN SKIN'S GRAB-BAG

c/o MARVEL COMICS GROUP, 575 MADISON AVE. N.Y.C. 10022

Dear Hulk Folk,

The last Hulk ish I read was # 173, when Herb Trimpe was artist and Hulk was truly his ever lovin' self. But when I bought and read # 194 I nearly had a heart attack! Who's this Sal Buscema and what's happened to the Emerald One and all the main characters? It looks like someone took a live eggbeater and shoved it into Hulk's face!

What has happened to Herb Trimpe? Bring 'em back!

RFO Randy Peters
484 N. Wiltenbang Avenue
Springfield, OH 45503

Dear Marvel,

For the past few years HULK has been my very favorite magazine, and the artwork from Happy Herb is what made it so great (of course, the stories were tops, too, but that's irrelevant right now).

I've tried to take a positive attitude towards the strip without Herb, but there is definitely something wrong. The script in # 194 was as great as ever, but I couldn't shake the feeling that Hulk wasn't the same Hulk I've known for so long. Like it was an imposter trying to play the part of ol' Greenskin.

Look, I'm not putting down Sal Buscema's work at all. He is certainly a very talented guy, but when it comes to the Jade Giant, he just can't achieve what Herb did. So I hope you guys show this letter to Herb, seriously, cause Hulk is no longer Hulk without him.

Bob Steel
34 Washington Road
Scotia, NY 12302

Y'know, folks, it's really strange how opinions change. When Herb first started on the Hulk, and during his lengthy tenure here, right up to his last issue, there were minor gripes about his work. Now that he's gone—and just in case we might have gotten the mistaken impression that those lone voices represented the majority of our readers—virtually all of Hulkdom Assembled has turned out to lament his leaving.

Unfortunately, there's nothing we can do about Herb's own decision—and it's indeed a fitting tribute to his years here that his departure is so sorely protested.

However, things have a way of smoothing out, as is already witnessed by the incoming accolades for Our Pal Sal, and unless we're *way* off base, it won't be long until *all* of Hulkdom Assembled settles down in awesome appreciation.

Dear Len, Sal and Joe,

As with many others, I'm a Staton fan all over. Whoever he inks he succeeds in truly embellishing. I commend the discretion of whoever had Sal Buscema supersede Herb Trimpe. Sal is, as was Herb before him, adept at adroitly conciliating anyone who might not at first like his work. Sal's strong point is his bellicose action scenes—in fact, he's so proficient at them that he may well be comicdom's #1 action illustrator. With Joe backing him, you can't miss.

PMM Jack Frost
RR 3 Box 176-C
West Monroe, LA 71291

Dear Emerald Ones:

Wrote to tell you HULK # 194 was great, especially the guest artist! Now, it's no-prize time, so listen carefully. On the letters page of that same issue, the fourth letter asks, "How much does the Hulk weigh and how tall is he?" And you refer them to the typed intro copy on page one. I looked and the information wasn't there—but it *was* on the intro copy of #193.

Nuff said.

Cary Bradlogue
(no address given)

Aw heck, Cary, it was just a teensy-tiny mistake that we thought no one would notice (after all, we didn't)—until you and every other cottin-pickin' letter writer in the Marvel Universe advised us otherwise, that is! Since we can't no-prize each and every one of ya individually, consider yourselves no-prized collectively. And don't mention a word of this to Stan!

Meanwhile, Lively Len informs us things are gettin' hot here, beginning next ish with the Hulk vs. S.H.I.E.L.D.—and then continuing in our celebrated 200th issue, where the Talbot sub-plot will finally culminate!

There's action ahead, Marvelites. Be here!

MARVEL VALUE STAMP

FOR THIS ISSUE!

STATEMENT OF OWNERSHIP, MANAGEMENT AND CIRCULATION ACT OF AUGUST 12, 1970: SECTION 3685, TITLE 39, UNITED STATES CODE

1. Title of Publication: INCREDIBLE HULK.

2. Date of Filing: September 22, 1975.

3. Frequency of Issue: Monthly.

3A. Annual subscription price: $4.25.

4. Location of Known Office of Publication: 575 Madison Ave., New York, N.Y. 10022.

5. Location of the Headquarters or General Business Offices of the Publishers: Marvel Comics Group/a Division of Cadence Industries Corp., 575 Madison Ave., New York, N.Y. 10022.

6. Names and addresses of the publisher, editor, and managing editor are Publisher: Stan Lee, 575 Madison Ave., N.Y., N.Y. 10022; Editor: Marv Wolfman, 575 Madison Ave., N.Y., N.Y. 10022; Managing Editor: John Verpoorten, 575 Madison Ave., N.Y., N.Y. 10022.

7. Owner (If owned by a corporation, its name and address must be stated and also immediately thereunder the names and addresses of stockholders owning or holding 1 percent or more of total amount of stock. If not owned by a corporation, the names and addresses of the individual owners must be given. If owned by a partnership or other unincorporated firm, its name and address, as well as that of each individual must be given.) Marvel Comics Group, 575 Madison Ave., New York, N.Y. 10022. Cadence Industries Corp., 21 Henderson Drive, West Caldwell, New Jersey 07006.

8. Known bondholders, mortgagees, and other security holders owning or holding 1 percent or more of total amount of bonds, mortgages, or other securities: None.

9. For optional completion by publishers mailing at the regular rates (Section 132.121, Postal Service Manual) 39 U.S.C. 3626 provides in pertinent part: "No person who would have been entitled to mail matter under former section 4359 of this title shall mail such matter at the rates provided under this subsection unless he files annually with the Postal Service a written request for permission to mail matter at such rates."

In accordance with the provisions of this statute, I hereby request permission to mail the publication named in Item 1 at the reduced postage rates presently authorized by 39 U.S.C. 3626.

(signed) Ed Shukin—Business Manager

10. For completion by nonprofit organizations authorized to mail at special rates. (Section 132.122, Postal Manual.) The purpose, function, and nonprofit status of this organization and the exempt status for Federal income tax purposes. (Check one.) ☐ Have not changed during preceding 12 months. ☐ Have changed during preceding 12 months. (If changed, publisher must submit explanation with this statement.)

11. EXTENT AND NATURE OF CIRCULATION.

A. Total No. Copies Printed (net press run): Average no. copies each issue during preceding 12 months: 367,199; single issue nearest to filing date: 371,458.

B. Paid Circulation: 1) Sales through dealers and carriers, street vendors and counter sales: Average no. copies each issue during preceding 12 months: 194,832; single issue nearest to filing date: 186,703. 2) Mail subscriptions. Average no. copies each issue during preceding 12 months: 1,667; single issue nearest to filing date: 1,560.

C. Total paid circulation: Average no. copies each issue during preceding 12 months: 196,499; single issue nearest to filing date: 188,263.

D. Free distribution by mail, carrier or other means, samples, complimentary, and other free copies: Average no. copies each issue during preceding 12 months: ---; single issue nearest to filing date: ---.

E. Total distribution (sum of C and D): Average no. copies each issue during preceding 12 months: 196,499; single issue nearest to filing date: 188,263.

F. Copies not distributed: 1) Office use, left-over, unaccounted, spoiled after printing: Average no. copies each issue during preceding 12 months: 426; single issue nearest to filing date: 380. 2) Returns from News Agents: Average no. copies each issue during preceding 12 months: 170,274; single issue nearest to filing date: 182,815.

G. Total (sum of E & F—should equal net press run shown in A): Average no. copies each issue during preceding 12 months: 367,199; single issue nearest to filing date: 371,458.

I certify that the statements made by me above are correct and complete.

(signed) Ed Shukin—Business Manager

74: CAPTAIN AMERICA from *The Incredible Hulk* no. 198 (April 1976).

CABLES OF CHAMPIONS

c/o MARVEL COMICS GROUP, 575 MADISON AVE. N.Y.C. 10022

We're pretty much going to let your letters speak for themselves this time, peerless people, except for one rather important exception—so let's get on with it, shall we?

Dear Editor,

Given time THE CHAMPIONS looks like it can turn into one great book. In the beginning, though, as I imagine befalls more than a few origin stories, there are rough spots. I like the heroes you've chosen for this new super-group. Ghost Rider's needed a place to fit in for a long time, and it's nice to see the Black Widow doing something—even if it isn't with the Avengers, who by rights have prior claim on her. Two X-Men are more than I could hope for, and Hercules as the big headliner is nice to see, since it'll give him a place in the sun that won't be shared by Thor; he still needs to get out of the lecture circuit, however, because it really doesn't suit him.

The plot started weakly, albeit full of action. The tying thread was the pursuit of Venus, and every hero came together only at the end of this first episode. The art dismayed me somewhat. I've liked Don Heck ever since his days with the competition; sadly, his work at Marvel has simply not been as good. Maybe he needs a new inker and I suggest Vince Colletta, since the Defenders spot they worked on is definitely the highpoint of his recent work.

That last panel simply does not stun me, as the script almost seems to want it to. Having Ares and Hippolyta in armor would, I think, have had more shock value.

Rich Hango
83 Hazel Street
Clifton, NJ 07011

Lost Champions—

I know I myself suggested a new supergroup, but I'm shocked at this piece of trash. When Bob McLeod or any inker of his caliber embellishes Don Heck's pencils they can almost look fine. But this crude job by the very simple/sloppy Mike Esposito just did it in. The finest part is the cover by Kane. This kind of an issue convinces me that making $ is more important than time and quality.

Shame!!

Marnin Rosenberg
17 Schenck Ave., Apt 2H
Great Neck, NY 11021

Dear People,

Why another super-group? Methinks you are overloading the market. With the Avengers, Defenders, X-Men, Invaders, Fantastic Four, Inhumans, and now the Champions, we're about to either witness a grand renaissance of super-hero groups, or a grand short-circuit of the same.

CHAMPIONS #1 was a very good issue, though there are a few points I'd like to raise. What is this group's distinction? Borrowing critic Jana C. Hollingsworth's super-group theory, we have a democratic group (Avengers), a formless group (Defenders), a school (X-Men), a militia (Invaders), a family (the FF), a race/society (the Inhumans), and . . . and what? The Champions have no distinction at this point.

The Black Widow is possibly the most dynamic heroine at Marvel, and to reduce her from star-status in DAREDEVIL to the "token female" is unforgivable (especially in THIS day and age). I'm hoping you add Venus as a regular member, to take the "tokenism" off Natasha's shoulders. Don't disappoint me! There are plenty of heroines you could use in this group . . . Zephyr, Tigra, Shanna . . .

THE CHAMPIONS is never going to get off the ground unless you get your act together fast. As it is, your group lacks the "Marvel magic"—the quality in Marvel books—that implies that commercialism was an afterthought, not the basis for the whole project.

Bob Rodi
515 South Fifth Street
Columbia, MO 65201

While we agree with your observation that the Champions must be developed into a separate and unique super group, and understand your use of the term "commercialism" to denote your displeasure with our first issue, it is important to understand that, while it has become fashionable to decry commercialism, our economic system is based precisely on that theme and in order for publishers or record producers or film-makers to remain in business their products must appeal to a fairly wide audience. Otherwise, there would be no comics or records or movies—so, in that sense, most projects are wisely conceived to be commercial and there is nothing inherently wrong with that. Most people in media, ourselves included, would like to reach as wide an audience as possible.

This doesn't necessarily excuse us from your criticisms, Bob. We just wanted to do our bit for clearing up a commonly held misconception; if we weren't commercial, we wouldn't be here now for you to criticize—or to enjoy. End of lecture and end of letters column. We'll go easier on our rap next issue, folks.

Honest!

MARVEL VALUE STAMP

CLIP 'EM AND COLLECT 'EM!

29: CAPTAIN AMERICA from *The Champions* no. 3 (February 1976).

SPOTLIGHT MAIL

c/o MARVEL COMICS GROUP, 575 MADISON AVE. N.Y.C. 10022

Dear Marvel,

I just thought I'd drop you a brief note to let you know how much I enjoyed your MARVEL SPOTLIGHT edition of THE SEVENTH VOYAGE OF SINBAD. I have long been a Ray Harryhausen fan and, of all his films, this one is my favorite.

It happens that I have a copy of the original 1958 comic book adaptation of this film. However, this early version is much less faithful to the film in plotting, dialogue and the drawn monsters.

Your new version is much more satisfying! John Warner's script quotes generous dialogue excerpts from the film, and so, it is a much better souvenir of this great fantasy classic! Also, the monsters are magnificently drawn—particularly, the Cyclops and the Dragon!

Thank you for this fine adaptation! I can't wait to see what your writers and artists do with the new Harryhausen film, SINBAD AT THE WORLD'S END (or whatever it's finally called)! I'm looking forward to this film turning up either as a color comic or in the pages of MARVEL MOVIE PREMIERE.

I also hope that MONSTERS OF THE MOVIES and UNKNOWN WORLDS OF SCIENCE FICTION someday return. Good luck to all your publications!

(Mr.) Carmen Minchella
15321 Veronica
East Detroit, MI 48021

Thanks, Car. With support like yours, we don't really see how we could go wrong! By the by, did'ja know that the other adaptation you mentioned, done by another company, featured the artistic wizardry of none other then John Buscema? Historians take note!

Dear Marv,

Somehow, I just can't understand the reasoning behind the adaptation of the SINBAD movie. The only possible explanation for this editorial nonsense is that the adaptation of GOLDEN VOYAGE somehow made a lot of money (something I tend to doubt), or that SEVENTH came with it as a package deal. Because adapting the movie in one issue of an 18-page comic has got to be the most ludicrous thing ever attempted.

I'll have to admit that Warner and Trinidad did a pretty good job with what they had, but they just had so *little*; even the expediency of the Gerber-style narrational pages couldn't prevent the story from being excessively rushed, not in the sense of not being soignée, but rather that of stuffing the tomatoes into the itty-bitty can. Forty pages is an *absolute* minimum for the adaptation of a full-length movie, and I personally don't feel comfortable 'til the 50-page mark has been reached.

So, I hope you'll keep from doing such things in the future. By all means, please use the book for solo-starring Marvel super-heroes and leave such experiments to PREMIERE; also, how about one-shots by heroes who've had their books cancelled and might be able to work well in a new format, but don't have enough immediate sales potential to warrant a try-out *series?* For example, the Silver Surfer, Ant-Man, Sub-Mariner, Beast, Man-Thing, Black Widow, Brother Voodoo. I realize most of these are in groups now, with many guest-starring occasionally, but if suddenly you find a plot that would work perfectly with one of these characters, there's no reason to shoehorn it into some other magazine where he can guest star.

Of course, the prime function of MS should be to put the Spotlight on heroes who have never had their own series and who seem to warrant a tryout; how about a Mr. Fantastic solo where he really can do some spectacular stretch-stunts without any one-upmanship from the rest of the group ? A Vision and Scarlet Witch feature ? solos from some of the new X-Men ? Some of the old ones ? like the Ms. Marvel strip you've been rapping about for some time now, not to mention the Iceman ditto promised five years ago...The Squadron Supreme ? Clea, Mistress of the Mys — that doesn't sound quite right, does it ? Mantis, Falcon, Valkyrie, Blade—I think you can figure out enough by yourselves. If not, we readers sure are going to provide you with suggestions.

I was about to rage about the absence of a lettercol, but then I remembered that SON OF SATAN had inherited the next two, so there's nothing to do but wait 'til the reactions to SINBAD come pouring in, two issues from now. Or at least trickling. Well, at least, this was one (or didn't you notice ?)

Kim Thompson
Gen Del Box 259
APO NY,NY 09184

Kim, you've pretty well summed up the attitude of the Bullpen in general concerning the future of MARVEL SPOTLIGHT. Keep your eye on this mag, 'cause we think you're gonna be (pleasantly) surprised in the months to come. And as you can see, the letters page is indeed back!

We're sorry you were disappointed by the adaptation of THE SEVENTH VOYAGE OF SINBAD. We kinda enjoyed it ourselves—as, seemingly, did the majority of Marveldom assembled—but we do agree that it would have been nice to have more space. Unfortunately, due to a number of technicalities we had to keep it down to one issue. The length for the new adaptation has yet to be determined.

Dear Marvel,

This episode of Sinbad so far surpassed his first appearance in WORLDS UNKNOWN that there are no comparisons to make. Sonny Trinidad has executed his finest color effort to date and the story by John Warner was crisp and exciting. I would welcome a Sinbad series if it could be maintained in this fashion.

Marnin Rosenberg
17 Schenck Avenue, Apt. 2-H
Great Neck, NY 11021

MARVEL VALUE STAMP

69: CAPTAIN AMERICA from *Marvel Spotlight* no. 27 (April 1976).

Tomes to the Tomb!

c/o MARVEL COMICS GROUP, 575 MADISON AVE. N.Y.C. 10022

The mail continues to pour in on Dracula's death in issue #19, and despite a few criticisms here and there, the consensus is an overwhelming lettercol ovation. Witness...

Dear Marv, Gene, and Tom:

Dracula is dead.

A momentous occasion? True. He has finally been beaten.

But we know that Marv will resurrect him in some way or another. Just as we know that Harker and company still have to face Dr. Sun and his evil; until he is abolished, the fight isn't over. So this issue was rather anti-climatic. No suspense was really built up to the point in the story where Juno sinks the stake into Drac; it came too early in the story to be a climax.

And although Harold H. Harold and Aurora were quite nice the last couple of times that they appeared, their appearance here seemed to destroy whatever suspense there was. But despite what I've said, the issue was a good one. By comparison to other comics, it was superb.

The cover was nice, perhaps a little weak. I noticed the way that you've blended the trademark picture of Drac back up into the price and issue number, like the old Marvel comics where everything was in a box in the upper left corner. Keep it that way and do it with the other magazines. It creates a nice blend of the nostalgic and the modern. The new logo is all right.

Glad to see this issue had a letters page. So many of them don't, it seems—and a comic without a letters page is like a day without orange juice, sort of. Except I can make it through a day without orange juice. But we need those letters pages.

Larry Twiss
227 Fox Run
King of Prussia, PA 19406

Thanks for your comments, Larry.

About the corner box on the cover, an old Marvel trademark, it seems that most fans and Bullpenners were in agreement for a change—so Marv's in the process of gradually switching back to them. Who says Merry Marvel doesn't listen to its vast legions? But let's give credit where it's due: Marv's the man who made the decision.

And we're glad he did.

Dear Vampiric Armadillos:

TOMB OF DRACULA #39 looked a bit rushed in places. The fight scene dialogue was hackneyed and the participants spent too much time standing around making long redundant speeches instead of having at each other.

But Dracula's death scene was superb. The amount of blood and decay shown provided the right amount of shock without becoming offensively lurid. Drac's speech exemplified his best qualities: courage, nobility, honor and respect for worthy opponents. It's a bit odd that he thinks so highly of Van Helsing since she couldn't bring herself to kill him that time in the Transylvanian Alps, but presumably he regards that as an uncharacteristic blunder. I see that he doesn't commend Drake; I suspect it's because he's so offended that one of his descendants would dare take up arms against him. I can't see Dracula's point in referring to Dr. Sun as a machine, since Sun's lust for power seems all too human to me.

Sun's plan is a good one, but I keep wondering why Dracula never thought of trying something similar. That's one of a number of holes in your story logic. Shouldn't Sun's glass case be hooked up to all sorts of machinery to supply him with food and oxygen and to allow him to speak and sense things by mechanical means? Certainly, the present Boston multi-parter is the best written series in this mag's history. No wonder they named Marvel after you, Marv.

Peter Sanderson
Rm. 921 Johnson Hall
Columbia University
New York, NY 10027

Actually, Pete, after that last line it's kinda difficult for us to contradict you, but we think that if you look back at the Dr. Sun issues you'll see that the old boy *is* connected to an ubiquitious assortment of unidentified equipment of the sort you suggest. But we promise not to hold this minor oversight against you, Pete, as long as you keep dishin' out those compliments and criticisms!

Dear Marv,

The economics of comics puzzle me. Here we have superbly crafted stories, fine artwork—a high-quality mag all around—fighting for its very life. It gets so going to the newsstands every month to see if DRACULA survives is as exciting as the stories themselves!

"Issue #39 shows the magazine's bids to improve itself. The new logo, the stamp COMICDOM'S NUMBER ONE MAGAZINE OF FEAR, and the new representation of the title character in the upper left are all indications of the book's fight for life (by the way, I notice several of your covers have eliminated the "character circle" and gone back to the enclosed rectangle: A great idea).

Inside, there is very little that you can do to improve. Everything is perfect. Mood, mystery, suspense—there's even humor and satire in this issue. And all the elements of the story blend and merge until they become as one with the Colan/Palmer artwork (is it true the Louvre intends to hang some of these works for public display?).

The prose is magnificent: Dracula's dying speech is alone worth the quarter (fifty cents, actually—I bought two copies).

My fingers are still crossed for TOD's survival. Good luck to you all.

Bruce Canwell
Meadows Rd. RFD #2

Now wait just a minute, Bruce! *Nothing* is as exciting as what we've got planned for next issue—not even our continuing battle for survival. Beginning here, in one mere month, is the storyline all Marveldom's gonna be talkin' about: A Dr. Strange/Dracula crossover that will continue into the Master of the Mystic Arts' own book! You dare not miss it, fear fans; truly, you dare not.

Until then... *sleep well!*

MARVEL VALUE STAMP

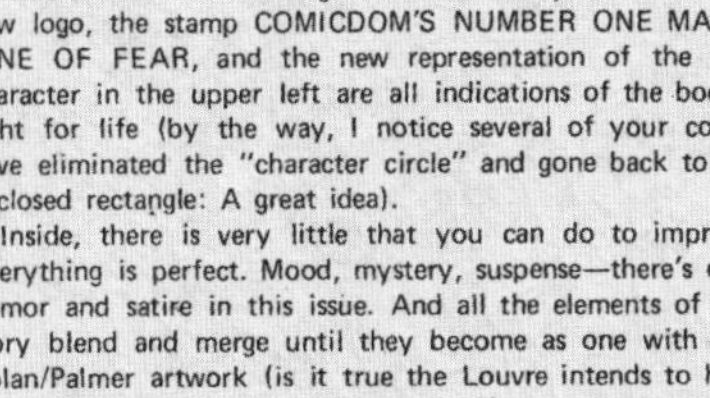

64: CAPTAIN AMERICA from *Tomb of Dracula* no. 43 (April 1976).

MINDLOCKS

c/o MARVEL COMICS GROUP, 575 MADISON AVE. N.Y.C. 10022

Dear Cyborgs,

Well... ASTONISHING TALES #31 answered the burning question, "Can one shove an unabashed cyborg called Deathlok into a ten-page story, add action and suspense, but still have room for a plot?"

Yep.

I was dismal about the page count, but after reading it and that Watcher reprint, I felt I spent my two bits well. But let's not do this often, Okay?

'Nuff said!

Mark Dooley
105 Wehmeier Street
Columbus, IN 47201

Dear Len, Doug, Rich, and Stan,

Today I went out and spent over ten dollars on comics and have just finished reading the new ASTONISHING TALES featuring Deathlok. Excellent! Except... you know, somehow I feel shortchanged. I spend my hardearned sheckels on your comics and I wind up with half a demolisher.

Do me a favor and get it together. Please?

J. C. Leroy
P.O. Box 1628 375 CES.
Scott AFB, IL 62225

Well, you know what they say——

You can please some of the people all of the time and all of the people some of the time... so why the heck can't Marvel please *all* of the people *all* of the time!?

At least we try!

Dear Marvel,

It seems to me that the Deathlok series is wandering aimlessly. I don't know if Doug Moench is going out of his way to avoid comparisons to a certain multi-million dollar guy or not, but I get that impression. This is a very promising mag and at times Doug has shown flashes of brillance on the script.

The cover was beautiful, but very misleading. I don't think I would call this "The most savage... shocker of all!!" Please avoid this. It only heightens the disappointment on this issue, what with only ten pages of story. How can you expect to get a series going by doing this? Deathlok wasn't in ish #29, so that means only one full story in six months!

Whatever happened to the concept of "Death machine for hire!" as presented in ish #26? It seems that that got lost in the shuffle. So far *nothing* has been shown of this "alternate world." Nothing. We still have no idea whether a war still rages, between whom, and what of the rest of the world.

Get rid of Ryker. He has "Thunderbolt" Ross all over him. He even resembles him. Deathlok should be hunted by *both* sides (ours and the baddies he was created to destory), plus OTHERS who hope to gain, thru him.

Lets have more destruction and action. Since he was built to kill and destroy, so be it. Even tho' Luther Manning sometimes has Michael Morbius type revulsion at himself and his actions, don't stop. After all, he is more machine than human being, so his humanity should lose.

Leave Deathlok a loner. Now that his wife is out of the way he has nothing to tie himself to his past. Leave it that way!

The interplay between Luther and the computer works very well, as does the artwork. Rich Buckler does a fine job no matter who he teams with. Let's try to keep him around awhile, OK?

I have great expectations (good name for a book, huh?) for Doug and this strip and it really kills me that its going nowhere. Here you have a conglomeration of Luke Cage, the Silver Surfer, Morbius, and Iron Man, among others, and with a little direction and thought Deathlok could be one of Marvel's most popular characters. I really believe this. I only hope I get to see it.

Steven Rohosky
111 Dorothy Avenue
Edison, NJ 08817

In accordance with popular rumor, Steve, Doug Moench is no longer scripting Deathlok the Demolisher. The writing reins have passed to Boisterous Bill Mantlo, who's taken what you've said to heart, and who has begun showing some of the background to Deathlok's world this very issue!

Who says Mighty Marvel isn't eager to please?

Dear Mr. Letter Column Man,

Where has the lettercolumn been? I haven't seen it in the last three issues. Have you been on a trip or were you fired?

Dave Singer
Minneapolis, MN

To tell ya the truth, Dave, the particular armadillo who writes the ASTONISHING TALES lettercol has spent a few months in armadillo heaven— Canarsie. But he's back now, ready to inflict Marveldom Assembled with the weighty wit of his bombastic brain.

And if you're real good, and promise to brush after every letter, he'll sing a few refrains from "As Time Goes By."

Steve... this could be the start of a beautiful friendship.

THIS IS IT! YOUR

MARVEL VALUE STAMP

FOR THIS ISSUE!

CLIP 'EM AND COLLECT 'EM!

3: CAPTAIN AMERICA from *Astonishing Tales* no. 33 (January 1976). Stamp also appears in *Marvel Two-in-One* no. 18 (August 1976).

MAIL IT TO TEAM-UP

c/o MARVEL COMICS GROUP, 575 MADISON AVE. N.Y.C. 10022

Dear Marvel,

MTU #39 was one of the best team-ups I've read. First, the cover was *sensational.* The pigeon incident was good. The coffin with the air holes caught my eye right away. I thought, however, that they would have heard Spidey come in. Still, it was great!

In MTU #34, Roger Conner wrote in his letter that MTU was one of Marvel's top ten best-sellers. It's probably because the kids that buy it like Spidey.

I do agree with team-ups from the 60's, and of having team-ups without the Torch, or Spidey. Anyway, MTU #39 was great and I can't wait for next ish.

Make Mine Marvel!

Mark Drewes
3217 Carlson Road
Garden Prairie, Illinois

the reason MTU is one of Marvel's best-sellers *is* that red and blue person with the webbing who pops up every issue, so that sort of negates having an issue, at least in the forseeable future, without him. But, as always, things like that depend on the reaction of you, the reader, and the all-powerful indication of sales figures...which drop dramatically when our ever-lovin' wall crawler *isn't* on the cover of MTU.

Dear Marv,

Bill Mantlo's *Shades of Stan Lee* imitations have been some of the low points in the Marvel Universe of late. And here he comes again with another one in MTU #39. But it worked! It really worked! Maybe it's because I'm an old Crime Master and Big Man fan, but this current plotline is enthralling.

The last two pages were probably the finest part of the ish. From MTU's past record, I was all set for a rushed wrap-up of the story, and was I fooled. Not only by the story continuing and being expanded to include the Crime Master and Sandman (in his original Spidey #4 costume). How nice it is to have a good story in MTU for a change.

It was also nice seeing Montana and Fancy Dan once more; obviously, the Crime Master and Big Man aren't the originals (that is, unless you've gone clone crazy), but the mystery and old style plotting surrounding them was certainly enough to generate some excitement. This is the one time Bill Mantlo has brought back the Stan Lee flavor effectively.

To which I just add.... *Onward.*

Dean Mullaney
81 Delaware Street
Staten Island, NY

Bill pleads guilty to being a great admirer of the old Stan Lee style, Dean...but emphatically denies that he is imitating it, any more than is any other writer at Marvel who has inherited his character and parameters from the Man. But your enthusiasm for the plot-line of MTU #39 (the conclusion of which is already out by the time you're reading this) more than made up for your opening line...and Bill forgives you...from up on that cloud your raves have put him on.

Dear Bill, Sal and Mike,

I've been with Marvel right from the start, yet this is the first letter I've sent you guys. That should give you an idea of what I thought of MTU #39. It was really fantastic and a lot of fun to read. I would never have thought that so many surprises could fit into 18 pages. It was an all around *fantastic* piece of work. It brought me back to the Spider-Man of the 60's. Definitely the *best* MTU to date.

Bill, may you live forever so you can stay on MTU. I can't wait to see who you put as the Big Man and Crime Master. I hope it's somebody we know as a character. The Big Man could be the clone of Foswell (only kidding). My only regret was that the story wasn't in SPIDER-MAN. It would have made a *Fantastic* 150th issue.

By the way, is there any chance that Steve Ditko could be working at Marvel in the near future?

Rick Hazeldine
62 Cumberland Street
Springfield, Mass.

Steve has gone on to other things, Rick, and though, like all early Spidey fans, we miss him, we feel that both Ross and Sal are doing some of the finest Spidey work to date. (But even *we* keep a sneaking hope that a gentleman named Romita will try his hand at pencilling the old web-spinner again...just for old times sake).

Dear Bill and Sal,

MTU #39 is about the best issue I have read yet. Spidey's encounter with Mosquito was touching, and his rescue of the Torch on page 24 was both funny and original.

The Sons of the Tiger next issue, eh? That is a brilliant move on Bill's part. It's about time the Tiger Sons broke into comics. Bill, if they get their own comic I'd rather see you script it than anybody else.

I do agree with Mark Barsotti. You should present team-ups of the 60's. There were a lot of chances for team-ups then. I'd like to see one every three issues. MTU shouldn't team Spidey up with somebody every month, either. You've had a lot of requests for non-Spidey team-ups, use 'em.

Waiting for MTU #40 with eagerness, I am yours sincerely....

Mark Long
2928 117 Street
Toledo, Ohio

Dear Fiery Arachnids,

When I picked up MTU #39 I was certain it would be a turkey like the Spidey-Beast team-up. Two is twice the fun, or in this case, twice the flop.

It was after midnight, in between Joey Bishop filling in for Johnny and Tom talking to several political cartoonists, that I finally got to it. I saved MTU and WEREWOLF BY NIGHT for last with the theory that you always save the worst for the wrap-up of this week's comic buying.

I read it and was astonished! Instead of finding *This month's Flunky,* I found a very cool team-up tale with more than just the action first, nad to hell with the plot. The return of the Crime Master was a fantastic surprise, along with his usurper, the Big Man, the last of the Enforcers and the promise that The Sons of the Tiger would be here next issue. Why can't every MTU be as good as this?

Until Spidey teams up with Aunt May....

Mark Dooley
105 Wehmeier Street
Columbus, Indiana

The reason every issue of MTU can't be as good as issue 39 is simple, Mark.–each succeeding one has got to be *better!* As for Aunt May...

MARVEL VALUE STAMP

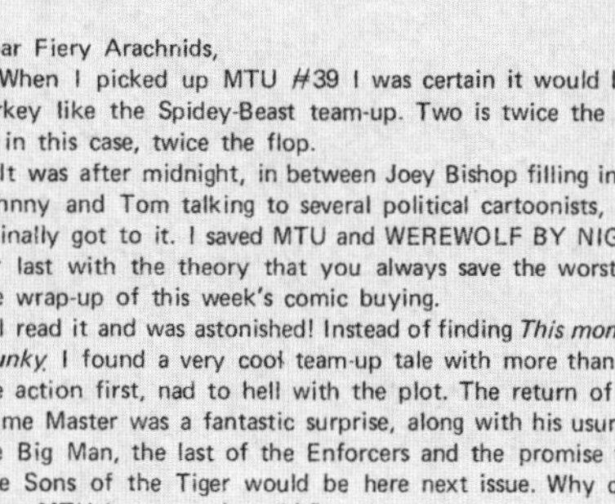

46: CAPTAIN AMERICA from *Marvel Team-Up* no. 43 (March 1976).

WARNING: This most powerful of all beings in the Merry Marvel universe holds the life and death of every capricious character in his mighty hands. Is it Galactus? Is it Ego, the Living Planet? Is it Irving Forbush? We say this— there's but one way to find out, Faithful One! So get out your scissors and glue and start pasting this pin-up into position— how **else** can you discover the true maniacal mind behind the Mighty Marvel Madness?

Marvel house ad for *Spider-Man: Rock Reflections of a Superhero* by Lifesong Records (1975), art by Marie Severin.

LET'S LEVEL WITH
DAREDEVIL
SEND YOUR LETTERS TO: THE MARVEL COMICS GROUP SIXTH FLOOR 575 MADISON AV. NEW YORK 10022 N.Y.

Dear Marvel,

DAREDEVIL #126 was outstanding! I enjoyed every panel and was much pleased with the artwork. The Torpedo is certainly an interesting if not unusual villain (?). However I was very much puzzled over the actions and reactions of DD throughout the entire story. For instance, his reactions to the attempt of Brock Jones to save the child from the car on page six. Not only was our favorite Man Without Fear a bit sarcastic to Jones, he was positively pompous and overbearing in attitude and appraisals of himself and his prowess. This is not the Daredevil we all know from the past, the calm hardworking hero dedicated to his cause, and not merely in just bettering his own image. Be that as it may, DD further continues his haughty demeanor when he rushes to the aid of the policemen recently upset by the Torpedo's attack. The new attitude continues on when later DD tackles the Torpedo and loses. Not only does he not give the Torpedo a chance to speak his piece, but actually attacks the Torpedo from behind when the Torpedo spares his life and wants only to continue his "mission." WOW, a different DD entirely! I can only think that the changes in Daredevil must be part of the whole new look that's going to be popping up soon in these pages, as foreshadowed on the letters page of DD #126.

I'd like to devote some time to the Torpedo. He could easily be one of the most exciting co-stars to ever appear (certainly one of the most dramatic) in a DD story. However please don't ruin him with the old cliche line of a good-guy turned bad because of being misunderstood. Let Brock Jones continue on as the Torpedo and not as a villain. I was upset by the death of the first Torpedo, especially because DD himself was responsible for it. If Daredevil had not forced Torpedo to fight he would not have even attempted to K.O. DD with his power punch. It was only the Torpedo's sense of decency and unwillingness to kill that saved Jones, but due to certain red-garbed interference the Torpedo himself had to suffer. I think in a future issue he should be made aware of his error and some searching of his conscience done. It would most probably result in some interesting and very personal subplots as well as maybe some new character evaluation of DD.

That's it for now, except thanks again for a new outlook for the DAREDEVIL series and here's to the exciting changes to come.

John Slepetz Jr.
Acton, MA

Thanks for your comments, John, we appreciate them.

However, we feel we must take issue with some of the conclusions you have drawn concerning Daredevil's behavior. First of all, we disagree with your statement that DD was "pompous and overbearing in attitude" in the sequence with Brock Jones. Take a look at similar situations in some of our other books over the years, and we think you'll have to agree that Daredevil's comments in this instance are no more offensive than those in the past. Daredevil is a man who has spent years honing his mind and body to the peak of perfection. He naturally feels himself more capable of handling a rescue situation than your average pedestrian, and has an ample amount of concern for everyone involved. After all, DD himself was robbed of his eyesight in a similar incident years before.

It was simply the sympathy, we believe, that you felt towards Brock from the earlier sequence that made DD's comments seem a bit more caustic than usual—proving only that Marv succeeded in accomplishing his objective in writing that episode.

You must also take into consideration Daredevil's past development when analyzing his confrontation with the Torpedo. Daredevil has faced a multitude of dangerous adversaries, and, consequently, our Man Without Fear is rather like a policeman who, after years on the force, develops a rather reflexive action toward lawbreakers. DD's first impression of the Torpedo was the sound of the Torpedo smashing thorugh a police car. From Daredevil's viewpoint, the Torpedo had already established himself as an offender—and DD has had enough experiences with super-foes in the past, who have sturck the moment he lowered his guard, to take any chances with the Torpedo.

Dear Marv and Bob,

Cute plot. Ambitious citizen takes on the costumed identity of a nameless "man with a mission," swearing to fulfill that mission, the nature of which we do not know. A particularly good touch was designing the Torpedo's headpiece so that his hair showed. Any other super-hero would have noticed the hair-color discrepancy between the two "Torpedoes," but not Daredevil, the man without sight. Of course there's his famous heartbeat-hearing faculty, but the noisiness of a bludgeoning foe like the Torpedo might negate that.

New romantic interest? Not really; I can't quite see DD and BW going separate ways for keeps, and besides, I like their contrasting characters. But Matt Murdock lives not in a cocoon, and all that.

Now as to direction for DD, I strongly recommend that you emphasize Matt Murdock's profession. Perhaps you have seen some trace of the much-neglected mini-series "The Law," which represents television's only real attempt at portraying real-life courtroom circumstances. DAREDEVIL is Marvel's most humanistic effort—people are, for the most part, people. In such a mag, I can easily visualize an alliance between courtroom suspense with super-heroic antics.

'Nuff said.

Harvey Phillips
10222 Kiekhill
Houston, TX 77034

How does it feel to have your thought processes in tune with the minds of the Marvel madmen, Harvey? Last issue you were able to thrill to courtroom drama as Matt defended the Man-Bull and this issue you're witness to the grand opening of The Storefront. And with this newest development in the life of Marveldom's favorite swashbuckling Man Without Fear there promises to be courtroom action aplenty in the future!

Keep those cards and letters coming folks! And until next month—be gentle to yourself.

THIS IS IT! YOUR
MARVEL VALUE STAMP
FOR THIS ISSUE!

CLIP 'EM AND COLLECT 'EM!

15: STAN (THE MAN) LEE from *Daredevil* no. 130 (February 1976).

OMEGA MAIL

c/o MARVEL COMICS GROUP, 575 MADISON AVE. N.Y.C. 10022

Dear Steve and Mary,

After reading the first issue of OMEGA THE UNKNOWN, I could see why he started in his own mag...instead of in MARVEL PREMIERE or some other such book. The storyline was so perplexing that it had to be a new Marvel milestone. I mean, the title character doesn't even utter one lousy monosyllable throughout the entire book. And that's not to mention the enigmatic young lad who has robots for parents! And since the befuddled Marvelite who reads it knows next to nothing about what these two people have to do with each other, he quietly resigns himself to the fact that he will inevitably purchase the next ish. So, till Iron Man puts ears on his helmet, make mine Marvel!

Jeff Johnson
358 Jefferson Ave.
Elgin, IL 60120

Dear Steve,

I was not in the least surprised at the first issue of OMEGA THE UNKNOWN. Marvel has a habit of putting out the best—in story as well as art. Your latest addition to the long line of classics was no exception. The idea of a young boy playing a major role in a series—and not being just another kid-sidekick, spouting corny phrases—is both fascinating and long overdue. I can see immediately that the character of Omega is going to be an intriguing one, soon to take his place alongside the other great heroes. I have faith in your ability; and I truly enjoyed this, the first of many issues to come.

Keep up the excellent work.

Alisa A. Johnson
P.O. Box 184
Yanceyville, NC 27379

Dear Stan,

I deplore the direction you Marvel Manipulators are twisting the lives of certain characters under the guise of realism. Why the psychological dramas? Where are your PhD's in psychoanalysis? Do you think this sells comic mags these days, or is it your own ego trip?

OMEGA is a *sick* comic book. No kid of mine will ever read an issue of it, if the first issue is any indication of what Steve and Mary are trying to do. Their style of writing is choppy, trite, melodramatic, and shallow. They've lifted the nervous-breakdown/hospital thing and the character of Amber (Mary Jane) from SPIDER-MAN; the dual-universe thing from CAPTAIN MARVEL...but maybe I'm getting ahead of myself on this first issue.

Please save us from comic book writers with delusions of grandeur! We don't want you to take the medium in this direction. And *please*, no cop-outs about giving your characters depth, or making it easier for your readership to relate. I'm having a heck of a time even caring any more, I'm so burned out on the little psychological ploys you've injected into a medium which should contain only a minimum...with a maximum of graphic happenings. I'm bored. Let me read "Rose Garden" or "David and Lisa" for the psychological studies, and Marvel for escapism!

Len Chamberlain
Fort Collins, CO

Dear Steve, Mary, and Jim:

OMEGA THE UNKNOWN is one of the most interesting books your fertile minds have dreamed up. As I often do—especially with new comics—I read the letter page first, and frankly i' sounded a bit too much like SHAZAM! That's okay, but it really wasn't what I wanted. Then I read the story, and like recent issues of the DEFENDERS, it left me confused.

But, folks, *that* is good.

Other writers would have given us a pat explanation of all that's coming down. I've been pondering the relationship between the boy and Omega. Do they have some common origin, what with James-Michael's parents being robots? Is Omega some sort of guardian angel? Or do they merely share the same destiny?

I hope OMEGA succeeds. It has great potential!

James L. Bleeker
1131 Courtney NW
Grand Rapids, MI 49504

This letters page, unfortunately, does not reflect the true proportion of positive-to-negative reaction on OMEGA THE UNKNOWN #1. Truth is, we scored more like twelve-to-one on the plus side. But we haven't the space to print thirteen letters—only to thank the many, many readers who understood what Steve, Mary and Jim were hoping to accomplish, and who found it stimulating as well as entertaining. That was their goal.

And the nightmare—or is it a slapstick farce?—is only just beginning. As if the Hulk, Electro, and the most depressing neighborhood in New York City weren't enough to contend with, next issue presents Omega with a far more sinister foe, the mysterious El Gato, while James-Michael struggles to survive in an environment decidedly unconducive to education. And in the months to come, you'll be meeting more additions to our supporting cast, getting reacquainted with some old Gerber standbys, and, yes, even learning the origin of Marvel's most enigmatic duo.

Meanwhile, your duty—remember—is to write: long letters, short letters, typed letters, belles lettres, capital and lower-case letters in your favorite alphabet from Arabic to Roman (sorry, no Sanskrit), apprising us of your appraisal of OMEGA THE UNKNOWN. Got that? As Nick would say, "Talk, ya creeps!" We're listening.

Take care. See you in sixty!

THIS IS IT! YOUR
MARVEL VALUE STAMP
FOR THIS ISSUE!

CLIP 'EM AND COLLECT 'EM!

100: STAN (THE MAN) LEE from *Omega the Unknown* no. 3 (July 1976).

Dear Daredevil-ers,

Wish I could say that DAREDEVIL is getting better. In recent issues I find more realistic supporting characters, villains with unusual abilities instead of stereotyped gimmicks, plenty of action and acrobatics, well-paced storylines, interest-catching covers, and so on and so forth. But all this fails to keep me from being disappointed in the last half-dozen issues. The glue that should be holding the whole magilla together just isn't there. What I'm talking about is the artwork.

Bob Brown's stint on AVENGERS produced some of the most exhilarating, action-filled art I've ever seen in that magazine. I can't believe that the same person—the man who did those final fantastic issues of the pre-Starlin WARLOCK—is now working on DD. Even going back a year or so to the Hydra and the Copperhead stories, one can see the difference between the splendid artwork then and the artistic meandering now. What has happened to Bob Brown in the past few months? I know he's capable of doing a better job. Perhaps Bob is no longer inspired by the possibilities of the strip. If so, I can understand that; an artist can become bored by what he has to do, and simply grind out the figures and backgrounds. Maybe Bob would become inspired by working on another strip. Whatever the case, please find an artist who's willing to give DAREDEVIL the splendid art it deserves.

Glenn Rowsam
2818 23rd Ave.
Oakland, CA 94606

Glenn, in all the world of comics there are few artists who have devoted as many years and as much effort to their work as Urbane Bob Brown, for whom we have a tremendous regard here in the Bullpen. Unfortunately—and you couldn't have known this—Bob has been seriously ill in recent months, and it is to his credit that he's consistently managed to meet deadline after deadline.

However, he is now recuperating and taking a well-deserved rest, which means that we have a few fill-in artists lined up for the next several issues, starting with the one you're holding in your hands. Next month's action epic will also be limned by Big John Buscema, while the penciler for #138 is, as yet, uncertain. Issue #139 will feature the far-out art of Our Pal Sal Buscema, and, hopefully, Bob Brown will be back with #140.

So let's all get together in wishing him well, and in eagerly looking forward to his flashy and fabulous return to the artistic helm of DAREDEVIL!

Dear Marvel,

DAREDEVIL #132 ended well—Bullseye deserved everything he got. I do wish DD would make as many wisecracks during battle as he used to, way back when.

Also, a suggestion: Can you contrive a way to get DD back into his original black-and-yellow suit, just once, for old time's sake? It would be a real gas!

Jesse Carpenter
2485 Bryant Street
Palo Alto, CA 94301

Funny you should mention DD's old duds, Jesse! It just so happens that Marvelous Marv is even now making plans to have said outfit pop up in the not-too-distant future. As to just when and how...well, you know what they say. "Even a man who is pure at heart, and says his prayers at night, can become a Wolfman..."

What's that you say, Marv? The wrong quote? Oh, well...

Dear Marvel:

This deals with a matter that began when Daredevil battled Hydra and cropped up again when DD tangled with Torpedo.

Confused? I don't blame you. What I'm talking about is Hornhead's ability—or lack of same—to detect color. If Daredevil could tell that Hydra's hordes were wearing green uniforms, then he could tell the difference between blonde and gray hair...the theory being that his radar sense could tell the difference between the minute, varying amounts of radiation reflected by each color.

Now, just to show that I'm not a self-centered person—the type who believes that only he is right—here are a few other possibilities:

1. DD cannot have a radar sense, since all the radiation that would be constantly bombarding him would blank it out.
2. When DD gained his radar sense so many years ago, the radiation broke his mind, and he has been living in a mental institution ever since...dreaming up everything that has supposedly happened to him.
3. The amount of radiation created by color is too minute for DD to notice.
4. The radiation blends together, nullifying its own effects.
5. Matt Murdock has a mental block—created by guilty feelings about his father's death—that keeps him from sensing colors.
6. Ignore this letter.
7. DD doesn't feel it's worth his time to sit up nights with a box of crayons, memorizing radiation levels.

Well...?

Bill Keim
552 Douglas St.
Chula Vista, CA 92010

Okay, Bill, we pick #6.

Seriously, Mr. K, we all know now that DD can not sense colors...except when someone in your abashed Bullpen errs. And we promise not to let that happen again! Ya see, we've got this new, color-blind armadillo...

Marv:

You must think we readers are a bunch of mongoloid idiots, or else you have an overdeveloped sense of dramatics. What I'm talking about is the way Daredevil and the other characters talk to themselves during a fight—constantly. I say nuts to all that!

Rene Blansette
R. I. Notch Lick Road
Carrollton, KY 41008

Yeesh! We're gonna beg off on this one, Rene, and refer you instead to Jesse Carpenter's letter on this selfsame page. Once again, Marvelites, we'll leave it up to you to battle it out amongst yourselves—and we'll report the majority opinion right here on a future letters page. Go to it, gang!

And while you're doin' that, we'll be doin' diligent duty in the never-ending battle against the Dreaded Deadline Doom, to bring you da best-ever DAREDEVIL sagas in months to come. You can count on it!

So stay tuned, ya hear?

THIS IS IT! YOUR
MARVEL VALUE STAMP
FOR THIS ISSUE!

5: STAN (THE MAN) LEE from *Daredevil* no. 136 (August 1976). Stamp also appears in *The Invaders* no. 4 (January 1976).

Tomes to the Tomb!

c/o MARVEL COMICS GROUP, 575 MADISON AVE. N.Y.C. 10022

Dear Transylvanian Friends,

I enjoy TOD very much, and I feel like such a creep for not having started sooner! I'd been a Dracula fan for two years, and thought I knew everything (well, almost everything) about him. Then I discovered TOD, and I flipped over it! My writing teacher likes it, too, although she doesn't flip over my constant interest in our handsome blood addict. Mind you, I have only read two issues, but I'm hooked. Harold H. Harold is a lot like me, and it would be nice if Drac put the bite on him. I can't blame Aurora for loving Drac, I do myself, but I'd guard my throat if I were her. Rachel is torn between love and hate. Harker, on the other hand, is torn apart in all directions due to all the losses he has faced, but he brings Dracula back because he knows that Doctor Sun will win if Drac remains a pile of ashes. Blade is something else; he has to watch out, for once Doctor Sun is done in, Drac is sure to turn on him. Drac truly deserves all that dialogue you give him, and his creative way of thinking is amazing. No one else could do better than the great Marvel Bullpen. You guys deserve a Pulitzer for Most Creative Literary Geniuses of the Year. Congrats on a masterpiece of power and terror, as only you can do it. And "fangs" for the memory.

Susan Pitcher
1106 Belmont Ave.
Collingswood, NJ 08108

Dear Marvel,

The conclusion of the Doctor Sun story was great. DRACULA is probably one of Marvel's harder mags to write, but Marv Wolfman has been doing a consistently excellent job. No other writer has captured Dracula's character so perfectly.

TOMB OF DRACULA #42 also contained one of the best art jobs that Colan and Palmer have done in the series. Gene Colan and Tom Palmer are one of the best art teams in comics history. I hope they remain on TOMB OF DRACULA, and also on DOCTOR STRANGE, for a long time.

I also hope the adaptations of Dracula will eventually continue. Roy Thomas and Dick Giordano had done an excellent job so far.

Keep up the good work.

Joe Castelli
1543 Evanston Street
Pittsburgh, PA 15204

Unfortunately, Joe, there are no plans to continue the Stoker adaptations at present, and since we don't want to condense it, we'll have to wait until there's an opening someplace. But knowing Mighty Marvel, where nothing stays dead for long, we're sure the adaptation will be popping up someplace, somewhere.

By the way, Marv (along with a few other Bullpen buddies) will be hopping down to Pittsburgh in March to attend the Pittsburgh Comix Club Pitt Con (Thanx, Ben!)

Dear Creators,

DRACULA is the definitive Marvel example of an excellent comic.

I say this with a memory of the very first issue, in its fledgling attempt to avoid clichés and give new meaning to the tales of man versus the supernatural. From the beginning, DRACULA succeeded—and more than succeeded. The oft-questioned word quality may be applied to this effort. Quality not contained in the script, nor in the artwork nor the inks nor at the printer's. Quality that is a feel— a tangible sensation of satisfaction both subjective and omni-present because it is a comic that reaches on all levels; its writing describes, its artwork portrays, and the overall effort is not so much a "reading" of a comic as it is an *experience* of that successful collaboration— when one can hear the leathery slap of batwings on the wet night air's smokey grayness — when the trembling rage of a frustrated vampire reaches us because we know his motivations so well— or even when a moral decision cannot be completely right nor completely wrong, but must be realistically gray: *for the best,* as when Dracula was revived to battle Dr. Sun.

Messrs. Wolfman, Colan, and Palmer can be proud of themselves. The sales figures do not reflect on their success. Hopefully, they can continue bridging the gap from reading to experiencing their work on Dracula, Lord of Vampires.

Les Baptiste
120-31 Benchley Pl.
Bronx, NY 10475

Les, what can a quartet of overworked creators say, but thanks. Marv, Gene, Tom and John work as hard as they can to produce each issue, and we kinda think their love for the book shows through. Comics are essentially an entertainment media, but when we can give something just a wee-bit *more* than a half-hour's entertainment, we feel that the extra effort is worth it.

Next month: THE MARRIAGE OF DRACULA, and the most bizarre monster that you've ever seen anywhere. Look for the story, "Let Us Be Wed In Unholy Matrimony!" It's the beginning of a brand-new Dracula epic that no True-Believer will want to miss!

92: STAN (THE MAN) LEE from *Tomb of Dracula* no. 45 (June 1976).

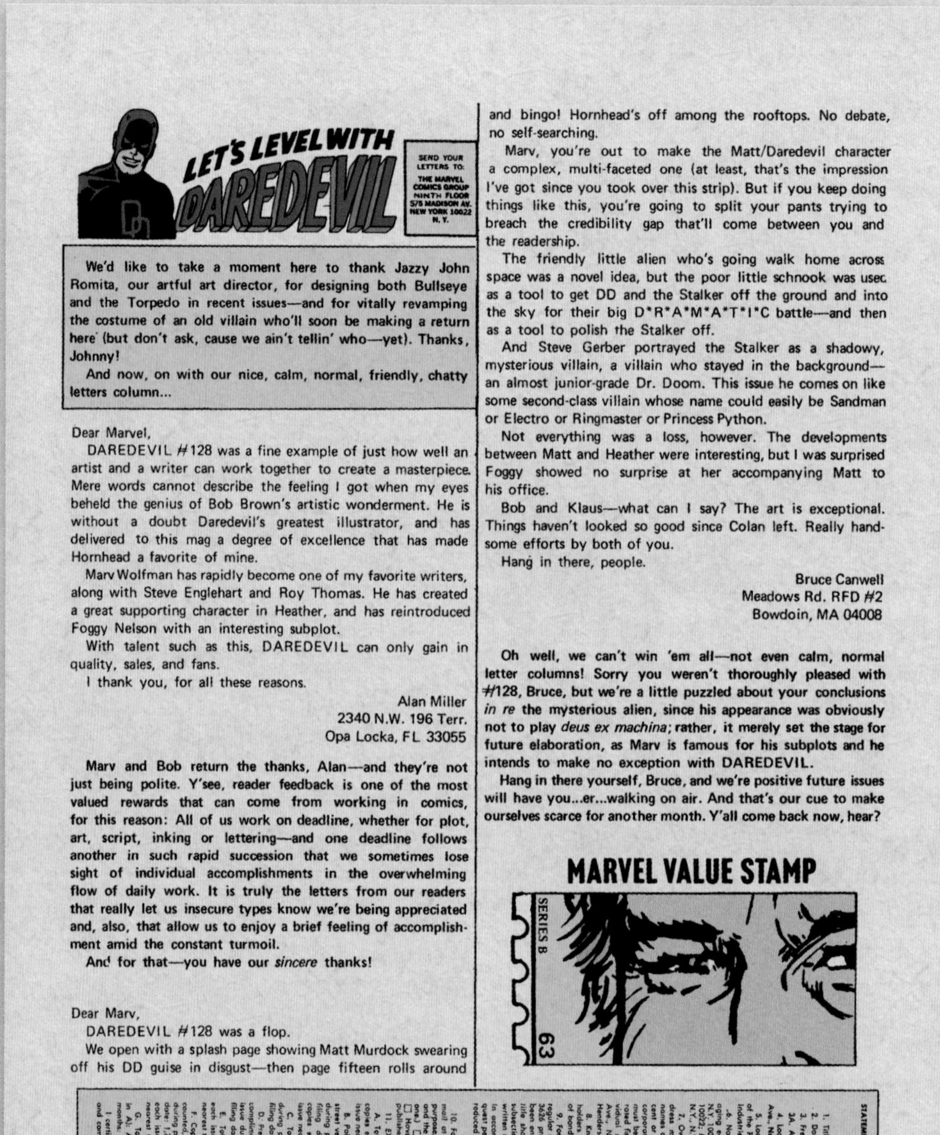

LET'S LEVEL WITH DAREDEVIL

SEND YOUR LETTERS TO: THE MARVEL COMICS GROUP NINTH FLOOR 575 MADISON AV. NEW YORK 10022 N.Y.

We'd like to take a moment here to thank Jazzy John Romita, our artful art director, for designing both Bullseye and the Torpedo in recent issues—and for vitally revamping the costume of an old villain who'll soon be making a return here (but don't ask, cause we ain't tellin' who—yet). Thanks, Johnny!

And now, on with our nice, calm, normal, friendly, chatty letters column...

Dear Marvel,

DAREDEVIL #128 was a fine example of just how well an artist and a writer can work together to create a masterpiece. Mere words cannot describe the feeling I got when my eyes beheld the genius of Bob Brown's artistic wonderment. He is without a doubt Daredevil's greatest illustrator, and has delivered to this mag a degree of excellence that has made Hornhead a favorite of mine.

Marv Wolfman has rapidly become one of my favorite writers, along with Steve Englehart and Roy Thomas. He has created a great supporting character in Heather, and has reintroduced Foggy Nelson with an interesting subplot.

With talent such as this, DAREDEVIL can only gain in quality, sales, and fans.

I thank you, for all these reasons.

Alan Miller
2340 N.W. 196 Terr.
Opa Locka, FL 33055

Marv and Bob return the thanks, Alan—and they're not just being polite. Y'see, reader feedback is one of the most valued rewards that can come from working in comics, for this reason: All of us work on deadline, whether for plot, art, script, inking or lettering—and one deadline follows another in such rapid succession that we sometimes lose sight of individual accomplishments in the overwhelming flow of daily work. It is truly the letters from our readers that really let us insecure types know we're being appreciated and, also, that allow us to enjoy a brief feeling of accomplishment amid the constant turmoil.

And for that—you have our *sincere* thanks!

Dear Marv,

DAREDEVIL #128 was a flop.

We open with a splash page showing Matt Murdock swearing off his DD guise in disgust—then page fifteen rolls around and bingo! Hornhead's off among the rooftops. No debate, no self-searching.

Marv, you're out to make the Matt/Daredevil character a complex, multi-faceted one (at least, that's the impression I've got since you took over this strip). But if you keep doing things like this, you're going to split your pants trying to breach the credibility gap that'll come between you and the readership.

The friendly little alien who's going walk home across space was a novel idea, but the poor little schnook was used as a tool to get DD and the Stalker off the ground and into the sky for their big D*R*A*M*A*T*I*C battle—and then as a tool to polish the Stalker off.

And Steve Gerber portrayed the Stalker as a shadowy, mysterious villain, a villain who stayed in the background—an almost junior-grade Dr. Doom. This issue he comes on like some second-class villain whose name could easily be Sandman or Electro or Ringmaster or Princess Python.

Not everything was a loss, however. The developments between Matt and Heather were interesting, but I was surprised Foggy showed no surprise at her accompanying Matt to his office.

Bob and Klaus—what can I say? The art is exceptional. Things haven't looked so good since Colan left. Really handsome efforts by both of you.

Hang in there, people.

Bruce Canwell
Meadows Rd. RFD #2
Bowdoin, MA 04008

Oh well, we can't win 'em all—not even calm, normal letter columns! Sorry you weren't thoroughly pleased with #128, Bruce, but we're a little puzzled about your conclusions *in re* the mysterious alien, since his appearance was obviously not to play *deus ex machina*; rather, it merely set the stage for future elaboration, as Marv is famous for his subplots and he intends to make no exception with DAREDEVIL.

Hang in there yourself, Bruce, and we're positive future issues will have you...er...walking on air. And that's our cue to make ourselves scarce for another month. Y'all come back now, hear?

MARVEL VALUE STAMP

SERIES B

63

STATEMENT OF OWNERSHIP, MANAGEMENT AND CIRCULATION ACT OF AUGUST 12, 1970: SECTION 3685, TITLE 39, UNITED STATES CODE

1. Title of Publication: DAREDEVIL.
2. Date of Filing: September 22, 1975.
3. Frequency of Issue: Monthly.
3A. Annual subscription price: $4.25.
4. Location of Known Office of Publication: 575 Madison Ave., New York, N.Y. 10022.
5. Location of the Headquarters or General Business Offices of the Publishers: Marvel Comics Group/a Division of Cadence Industries Corp., 575 Madison Ave., New York, N.Y. 10022.
6. Names and addresses of the publisher, editor, and managing editor are Publisher: Stan Lee, 575 Madison Ave., N.Y., N.Y. 10022; Editor: Marv Wolfman, 575 Madison Ave., N.Y., N.Y. 10022; Managing Editor: John Verpoorten, 575 Madison Ave., N.Y., N.Y. 10022.
7. Owner (If owned by a corporation, its name and address must be stated and also immediately thereunder the names and addresses of stockholders owning or holding 1 percent or more of total amount of stock. If not owned by a corporation, the names and addresses of the individual owners must be given. If owned by a partnership or other unincorporated firm, its name and address, as well as that of each individual must be given.) Marvel Comics Group, 575 Madison Ave., New York, N.Y. 10022. Cadence Industries Corp., 21 Henderson Drive, West Coldwell, New Jersey 07006.
8. Known bondholders, mortgagees, and other security holders owning or holding 1 percent or more of total amount of bonds, mortgages, or other securities: None.
9. For optional completion by publishers mailing at the regular rates (Section 132.121, Postal Service Manual) 39 U.S.C. 3626 provides in pertinent part: "No person who would have been entitled to mail matter under former section 4359 of this title shall mail such matter at the rates provided under this subsection unless he files annually with the Postal Service a written request for permission to mail matter at such rates." In accordance with the provisions of this statute, I hereby request permission to mail the publication named in Item 1 at the reduced postage rates presently authorized by 39 U.S.C. 3626.

(signed) Ed Shukin—Business Manager

10. For completion by nonprofit organizations authorized to mail at special rates. (Section 132.122, Postal Manual.) The purpose, function, and nonprofit status of this organization and the exempt status for Federal income tax purposes. (Check one.) ☐ Have not changed during preceding 12 months. ☐ Have changed during preceding 12 months. (If changed, publisher must submit explanation with this statement.)

11. EXTENT AND NATURE OF CIRCULATION.

A. Total No. Copies Printed (net press run): Average no. copies each issue during preceding 12 months: 311,247; single issue nearest to filing date: 313,957.

B. Paid Circulation: 1) Sales through dealers and carriers, street vendors and counter sales: Average no. copies each issue during preceding 12 months: 158,364; single issue nearest to filing date: 138,968. 2) Mail subscriptions. Average no. copies each issue during preceding 12 months: 1,227; single issue nearest to filing date: 1,340.

C. Total paid circulation: Average no. copies each issue during preceding 12 months: 159,591; single issue nearest to filing date: 140,308.

D. Free distribution by mail, carrier or other means, samples, complimentary, and other free copies: Average no. copies each issue during preceding 12 months: - - -; single issue nearest to filing date: - - -.

E. Total distribution (sum of C and D): Average no. copies each issue during preceding 12 months: 159,591; single issue nearest to filing date: 140,308.

F. Copies not distributed: 1) Office use, left-over, unaccounted, spoiled after printing: Average no. copies each issue during preceding 12 months: 1,832; single issue nearest to filing date: 1,790. 2) Returns from News Agents: Average no. copies each issue during preceding 12 months: 149,824; single issue nearest to filing date: 171,859.

G. Total (sum of E & F—should equal net press run shown in A): Average no. copies each issue during preceding 12 months: 311,247; single issue nearest to filing date: 313,957.

I certify that the statements made by me above are correct and complete.

(signed) Ed Shukin—Business Manager

63: STAN (THE MAN) LEE from *Daredevil* no. 132 (April 1976).

THE HYBORIAN PAGE

c/o MARVEL COMICS GROUP, 575 MADISON AVE. NEW YORK, N.Y. 10022

Dear Hyborian Armadillos:

CONAN #58 contains an exciting chase sequence, well-done fight scenes, and the fine art and dialogue we've come to expect from this magazine. Yet, there's something very disturbing about the issue.

Although the best of the REH Conan stories Marvel has done are quite superior to most of the Thomas Conan scripts it is nonetheless true that in style and spirit the new tales are indistinguishable from the originals. Or, rather, this is *usually* the case. We've come to look upon the comic book Conan as a man with a strong commitment to his own code of honor; and so it comes as a shock when he becomes Bêlit's partner and lover at the close of this issue.

After all, she was responsible for the brutal slaughter of the helpless Argossean sailors, a massacre committed solely for the sake of material gain. Quite rightly, you encourage us to side with Conan in his battle against the pirates, but by doing so you leave us appalled by his later defection to them.

I haven't read the original REH story, but it looks as if Conan will become as merciless and bloodthirsty as Bêlit, now that he's accepted her cause. If indeed Howard meant Conan to be still so amoral at this stage of his life, the Conan of your previous issues should have been less noble than he was. But that would have made him much less sympathetic as a hero. You're really in a bind here, and I don't see how you can resolve it.

Peter Sanderson
Rm. 921, Johnson Hall
Columbia University
New York, NY 10027

Actually, Peter, we've always found it quite *impossible* to resolve certain aspects of the Cimmerian's turbulent life, mostly because Robert E. Howard, by skipping about willy-nilly in whatever period of that life which he chose to, managed to leave out many details which might have reflected poorly on his hero's rough-hewn nobility.

On the other hand, to us, that's always been part of the charm of Conan. Rather than feel we're in a bind, we prefer to think that the Marvel version of Conan is at least as consistent in his actions as the original Howardian version. Yes, Conan is basically a soldier of fortune, not a moral philospher— but that occupation hardly prevents him from still feeling basic decent human emotions. He fights on the side of the Argossean sailors despite the fact that the battle is all but hopeless and that he might fare better by surrendering at an early stage. But then, when he's done all he can to stave off slaughter— and when, indeed, he's even avenged the death of the shipmaster Tito (nearly the only element of importance which Roy and John added to the original story), his practical side takes over and he figures, "If you can't lick 'em, join 'em." Can't say as we blame 'im.

We're glad to report, though, that you're far from correct in guessing that Conan will now become as savage as Belit herself. In fact, we see that as one of the most interesting aspects of the strip as it goes forward now—for instance, Conan stopping his over-zealous lady love (who will let nothing stand in the way of her eventual revenge on the slayers of her father, as shown in issue #59) from massacring a village of blacks whose only sin is that their ivory was stolen by the Dragon-Riders.

Out of just such contrasts (both internal and external) are some of the best stories, in comics and in other literature, born.

One final word in Roy and John's defense; if you'll take the time to read the prose "Queen of the Black Coast," you'll find that (contrary to what you suggest in your second paragraph above) CONAN #58 was indeed yet another of the issues in which both the "style and spirit" of REH's tales were kept— or at least, that's what our award-winning artisans had in mind. Read the original; then see if you don't have to modify your judgment. Meanwhile, keep watching— to see how we resolve the very dilemma you pointed out in your thought-provoking letter.

And thanks for writing it!

Dear Roy,

This simpering jellyfish is "the she-devil Bêlit"— "Conan's fiercest foe?" Who are you trying to kid?

Michael Zaloudek
389 Garner URH
Champaign, IL 61820

Nobody, honest! Roy and John were fully aware that everybody has his own idea of the Shemitish she-pirate is his own mind— so we were bound to fall short in the eyes of some people. Personally, they're just happy that only the barest smattering of letters protested their portrayal of Bêlit— and, since the predictable complaint of some of *those* letters was that Bêlit was not as nearly nude as in the original story, it's just one of those cases where you can't make everybody happy. We hope Conan's amorous captain'll grow on you, Mike; we know she already has on us!

Dear Roy and John,

CONAN #58's "Queen of the Black Coast" was the first I had read of your adapted comic-book versions of Robert E. Howard's epic tales. I was not disappointed. As a faithful reader of Conan paperbacks for many years, I was cynical when I saw you were going to try an adaptation of my all-time favorite among the Cimmerian's endeavors. But John Buscema sold me, with some almost incredible artistry that was simply out of this Hyborian world! Fantastic!

However, I do seem to have found a small ambiguity in overworked Roy's script, for which I will be anxiously awaiting a genuine Marvel no-prize. On page 27, panel 5, the she-devil Bêlit addresses our hero as "Conan," although she apparently had not yet discovered his name (correct me if I'm wrong). Furthermore, in panel 7, Bêlit seems strangely overfamiliar with the barbarian's background and origin. Or, to quote: "You are cold, man of the north— as cold as the snowy mountains that bred you."

Ruling out "women's intuition," you should have a rough time worming your way out of that one, so you may send the no-prize to:

William Marshall
11211 Carver Ct.
Burnsville, MD 55337

The no-prize is yours, Bill. In Howard's original story, when Bêlit observes that Conan is "no soft Hyborian," he replies, "I am Conan, a Cimmerian." Somehow, our otherwise erudite writer/editor forgot to include that line in his final script (it *was* in the rough draft, but somehow got left out by mistake) and, in our usual rush to get the book to our pandemonious printers, he neglected to edit it back in when he proofread the issue. Hope it didn't spoil the issue for you, lad— but, judging from the enthusiasm you expressed above, we rather suspect it didn't! Always glad to welcome a new CONAN reader aboard the sea-roving *Tigress*!

MARVEL VALUE STAMP

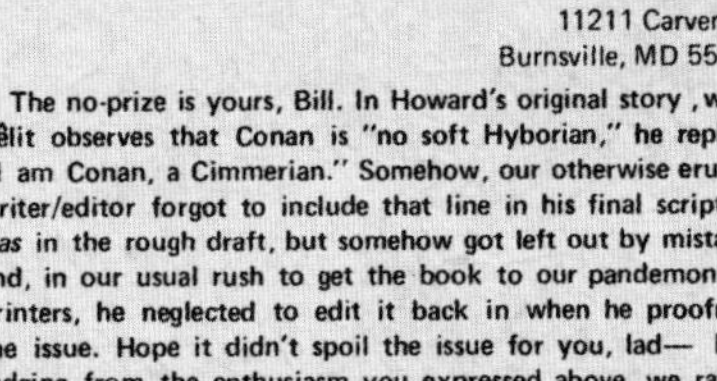

89: STAN (THE MAN) LEE from *Conan the Barbarian* no. 62 (May 1976).

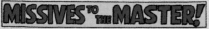

MISSIVES TO THE MASTER!

c/o MARVEL COMICS GROUP, 575 MADISON AVE. N.Y.C. 10022

Dear Doug:

I have great feelings about Shang-Chi's new role, from the Bond-like adventures to his new outfit to Leiko. I immensely enjoy reading lively action and strong characterization without the old stereotypes like father Fu still lurking beyond the latticework. The "new series" is thoroughly enjoyable so far in all respects. (However, I *was* a little surprised to see Leiko Wu with red hair in # 34...another half-Asian, half-Caucasian? Or did Mordillo supply a hairdresser?)

One heavier point: I think it's well established that Black Jack is a good guy, a professional agent, and an ally of Shang-Chi. While his use of the term "Chinaman" may be more out of orneriness than hostility, I find it unlikely that Shang-Chi would give him tacit toleration indefinitely. In addition, to the extent that any media figure can be a role model for younger readers, it's not advisable that people pick up this particular habit practiced by Black Jack. Not every recipient has Shang-Chi's training in patience.

Cheers,

Bill Wu
316 E. Madison #15
Ann Arbor, MI 48104

Good to hear from you again, Bill.

No; Leiko (whose last name is also Wu, by the way) is not another product of "miscegenation," nor did Mordillo forcibly dunk her head in a vat of Clairol. In fact, no one was more surprised than Doug (can't shake that ole third-person) to see his new character's hair colored so blatantly wrong — especially since the very same colorist had correctly colored Leiko's hair black in the previous issue. The mix-up still hasn't been entirely explained (as few things are in the hallowed halls of Marvel Madness), but the situation has been rectified with #35 onward.

As for Black Jack's proclivity for the use of the term "Chinaman," I'm afraid this is where we differ, Bill. As we see it, Black Jack uses the term as a form of reverse-affection. The big lug is too stubborn and cantankerous and embarrassed to concede that he actually likes— and respects — Shang-Chi. He'd probably give his life for Chi, but we doubt that he'll ever use Chi's proper name.

And over on Shang-Chi's side of the looking glass, we don't think it's a matter of tolerance or patience. Assuming Chi even realizes that "Chinaman" is often intended as a slur (after all, what's in a name? and "Chinaman" snarled by a bad guy carries a completely different connotation than "Chinaman" spoken by a grinning Black Jack Tarr), we have a hunch our Master of the Martial Arts is sort of above taking insult from something which is rather insignificant in its proper perspective. Remember, Shang-Chi is portrayed as being more "noble" and "philosophical" than the average person — someone who is able to grasp the heart of a matter without being swayed by a superficial facade. In fact, Doug has always meant to infer that Shang-Chi *humors* Black Jack's somewhat obnoxious idiosyncracies.

But we must admit, Bill, that your last point — that of Black Jack serving as a model for younger readers — has given us pause for thought. We've assumed that most — if not all — readers were astute enough to grasp that which we've explained above. If not, we'll change...but let us know, people; every vote counts, and in matters like this it doesn't take many votes to sway us...

Dear Doug and Paul,

You know how I can go on and on about an artist when I adore his work. Well, this time (MOKF #34), I'll just say that Paul Gulacy turned in another classic in his long line of the same.

However (and you thought you were off the hook, didn't ya?), I *will* go on about the story, something I seldom do. Doug Moench seems to be constantly trying to prove that he's the best writer at Marvel — and he's constantly succeeding!! "Cyclone at the Center of a Madman's Crown" was extremely exciting from page one to the end. I especially loved all the little things that were running around Mordillo's island — things like the talking train and Brynocki which spiced the story up considerably, adding a bit of humor to an otherwise chilling tale. Doug seems to have an amazing knack for portraying the inside of a madman's mind. Where were you before comics, Doug?

A last note: I hope you keep Shang-Chi's new, skin-tight "gi," as I (and I suspect many other Marvelites) like it tremendously.

Ken Meyer, Jr.
3110B Revere Circle
Hill AFB, Utah 84406

Doug wasn't even *born* before comics, Ken. They started somewhere around 1938 or 1939, and he didn't start until his mother lost some nine pounds on February 23, 1948.

But seriously, Doug was in his own private looney-bin of the mind prior to beginning his career as a comics writer — busily and hectically pounding out men's magazine fiction, Sunday supplement newspaper feature-articles, and even two novels (one of which was sold but never published: the publisher went bankrupt). Then, at the ripe old age of twenty-two (ripe, at least, to spring-chicken Gerry Conway), Doug turned to comics and made his insanity public.

As for Shang-Chi's erstwhile superheroish-jump suit "gi," we're afraid it's a thing of the past — at least for the forseeable future. Both Doug and Paul have received orders from Up-Front: Get Shang-Chi back in his pajamas and keep him there! So, unless enough of a clamor to the contrary is raised, there the matter — and Shang-Chi's bod — rests.

Dear Paul & Doug,

I'm growing tired of trying to write a letter which adequately praises MASTER OF KUNG FU. My wastepaper basket is filled to the brim with crumpled wads which failed to express my appreciation for the beautiful job you two are doing. If you don't start making some mistakes, I'll start thinking you aren't human. You *are* humans, aren't you?

Wayne Vincenzi
24 Fredric St.
Wawuet, NY 10954

Dear Wayne: Yeah.

MARVEL VALUE STAMP

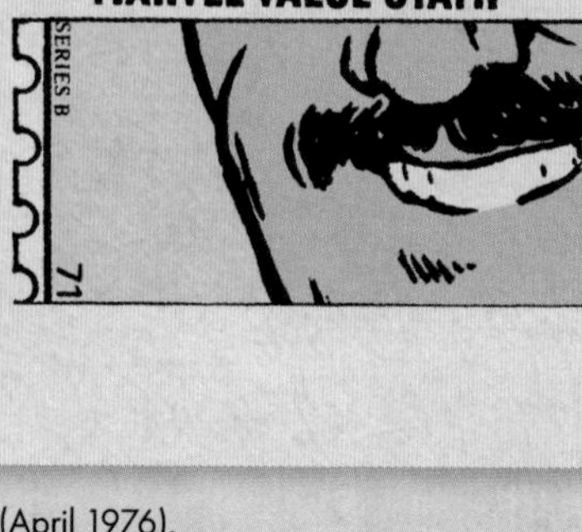

71: STAN (THE MAN) LEE from *Master of Kung Fu* no. 39 (April 1976).

MISSIVES TO THE MASTER!

c/o MARVEL COMICS GROUP, 575 MADISON AVE. N.Y.C. 10022

APOLOGIA: There really is a good reason why this letters page is three issues late. Honest! Fact is, the two-parter presented in issues #36 & 37 ("Cages of Myth, Menagerie of Mirrors" and "Web of Dark Death") was originally intended as a single 40-page story for the fifth issue of the now-defunct GIANT-SIZE version of MOKF. When the GIANT was regrettably cancelled, it was decided to present the epic story in Shang-Chi's monthly book. Now, when you try to squeeze a 40-page story into two 18-page issues, something's gotta give — namely, the letters pages. (However, even a bona fide PAID AD was dropped from #37 — in addition to the letters page.) But take heart, people; the letters page is back to stay — and, in fact, doubles to TWO pages beginning next issue. Now for the letters...

Dear Doug and Paul,

Please excuse my silence during the past three months, but I felt it best to wait until the "Crystal Connection" trilogy was concluded. Now that the wait is over, I must express my view on the "new direction" to which MOKF has detoured — something which should stir controversy among your readers, since the thematic change seems to violate the basic premise of the Shang-Chi book.

However, Shang-Chi's choice to follow the path of "direct action" rather than continuing along the road of pacifism is a more realistic way of dealing with the world. Waiting around to be provoked while your fellow man is attacked or in danger of future attack is a rather apathetic and non-humanitarian philosophy. Besides, as the adage says: "An ounce of prevention is worth a pound of cure."

One of the most difficult tasks facing today's entertainment media is the problem of producing action-packed dramas, populated by believable characters in a dramatic situation, and which say something meaningful to society. The "Crystal Connection" trilogy solved this perplexity for the graphic story medium. The poetic genius of Doug Moench has proved fundamental in construction what may prove to be the definitive espionage thriller of the seventies, Marvel-style. Through the late sixties and early seventies, Marvelites were first tormented by poorly written tales of this genre in the Steranko-less SHIELD stories, and then left without *any* espionage tales at all. But in the new MOKF, Mr. Moench seems destined to rekindle the suspense thriller flame at Marvel, and few things could be done better than with the phenomenal aid of Paul Gulacy. His artwork is the perfect complement for Doug's powerful scripts. Paul truly shines through with a clear, distinct style all his own — and one which I'm proud to say is housed at Marvel.

Doug and Paul have created literary milestones in the further structuring of characterization for Chi, Tarr, Smith, and Petrie — as well as the development of the headstrong Clive Reston, who is rumored to be the son of James Bond and the great-nephew of Sherlock Holmes.

And these two gentlemen have also produced some of the best antagonists this side of "Panther's Rage." The ruthless mastermind Velcro, his deadly aide Razor-Fist, the seductively dangerous Pavane, and the countless henchmen with true characterizations of their own.

I'm waiting for more (especially on this mysterious Mordillo) but frankly, after these past three issues, I truly wonder where the new wonderment mentioned on #31's letters page is going to come from — though it's obvious that the capabilties of Misters Moench and Gulacy know no limits.

Clyde Talley
14700 Blythe St. #18
Van Nuys, CA 94102

Dear Marvel,

Boy, am I glad Paul Gulacy is back.

MOKF #33 was great. As usual, Doug penned a real winner of a script. The new villain Mordillo is an extremely exciting concept, and I really hope he stays around for a few issues.

Boy, am I glad Paul Gulacy is back!

Larry Dean
6362 Laurentian Ct.
Flint, MI 48504

Seems to be an echo around here. We've heard the same sentiment expressed in virtually every one of the kazillion letters MOKF has been receiving.

Boy, are *we* glad Paul Gulacy is back!

Dear Marvel,

I see Doug's been taking his Gerber pills again.

Jerry Lazar
4 Bly Ct.
Great Neck, NY 11023

Nope, but we've heard nasty rumors that Gerber has been dipping into the Doug pills lately...

Dear Masters of Kung Fu,

I have been silent too long. If none stand in awe and admiration of Paul Gulacy's artwork, I shall admit that I do. If those who see are too stunned to honor his skill, then humbly I will. Perceptual pen poised with the sensitive vibrations of inner vision focusing with poetic intensity, he endows his art with the soul of subtlety and kinetic communication. Actions flow, pictures impact, shocking the unprepared senses. Like the strokes of a master surgeon, Paul Gulacy's images relieve the pain within one's mind. A classical stream of motion amidst a landscape of delicate drama, art transcending the moment. Here lies sheer bliss. One must study his powerful pages with much more than a student's delight. How may one thank you for letting us view the life of a man's gifted craft?

A few thoughts of equal feeling rise in behalf of the poetic sense of Doug Moench. His chosen words ring flawlessly in tune with Gulacy's artwork. One appreciates the detail in his words. Gulacy and Moench: Two poetic artists who portray in harmony not only drama and a theme of events, but humor in understatement.

In a letter you published in DAREDEVIL #56, I was fortunate to be among the first to voice admiration for Barry Smith, then an up-and-coming neophyte. For what it's worth, from a now 21-year-old student of film, Gulacy and Moench have that same admiration.

Rick Werft
314 Harford Place
Upland, CA 91786

Whew! That's all we can say to you, Rick — that and thanks.

And to the rest of our readers, all we can say is: Wouldja believe we actually *boned down* Rick's letter? Tickled and ego-blown as we were, even *we* can be embarrassed. Gawrsh...

MARVEL VALUE STAMP

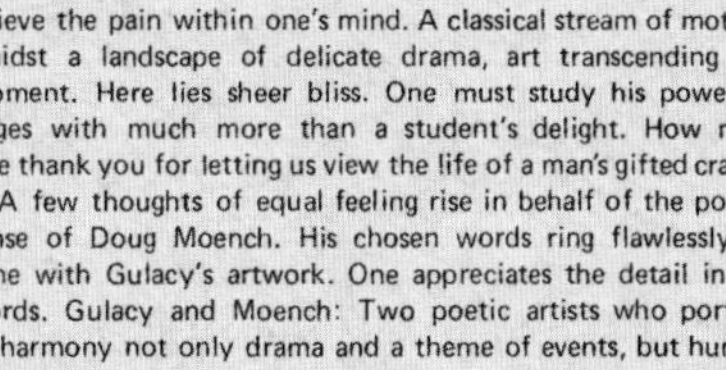

40: STAN (THE MAN) LEE from *Master of Kung Fu* no. 38 (March 1976).

BAD TIDINGS

c/o MARVEL COMICS GROUP, 575 MADISON AVE. N.Y.C. 10022

Dear Marvel:

SUPER-VILLAIN TEAM-UP has proven to be less of a team-up magazine than was originally expected. Instead of following the usual pattern of revolving guest stars with a permanent star, it is more on the order of a partnership mag like CAPTAIN AMERICA and the Falcon. In some ways this is good. I enjoy being able to look into the character of Dr. Doom; he has always been an enigma (as much as Namor). Sometimes I see him as a protagonist (SUPER-VILLAIN TEAM-UP and FF #116) and more often in his other role as the World's #1 Menace. The writing of this mag has been masterful. I find myself rooting for a Doom-Subby victory over the world, though this plot has only been mentioned and not realized. It is amazing that the continuity has not been totally demolished, since there've been three different writers and now will be a fourth. Settle down with a regular scripter already! The Stainless one is as good as any.

Nuff Said?

Russ Pass
6723 N. Drake
Lincolnwood, IL

Dear Bullpen,

Although I do enjoy seeing Namor again in print somewhere, I do not like the fact that he has to be part of a villain team-up. I concur with Peter Sanderson's letter on Subby's character in S-VT-U #3 that stated the "pro-peace" Namor of the 60's has forever supplanted the hawkish '40's Subby.

Sure Namor has quite a savage temper, but I still don't think that qualifies him as a villain. I'd say get him out of this mag and put him somewhere more suitable, but at this point you don't have any other mags where he'd fit.

I thought the story was well done, especially where Namor decided to take his revenge personally on page 19. I do think some of the action frames on Namor were a bit awkward, especially shots of him running or walking.

Next I'd like to claim a No-prize. Namor was still wearing the metal rings around his wrists from where he broke free of his shackles in issue #2. However, on page 6, panel 3, the left arm has no such ring; whereas one panel down, there it is again.

Finally one last comment. Even though Namor's new costume doesn't look bad and is supposed to serve an important function, I don't like it.

Somehow he seems less mighty, less savage, and less regal than when he was just adorned by his ol' scaly green trunks. I would like to see them return. I hope that the coming of Stainless Steve Englehart and your mystery artist will mean some favorable changes for our favorite amphibious monarch (And I don't mean Howard the Duck!!).

John M. Slepetz, Jr.
20 Henley Rd.
Acton, Mass. 01720

All right, John, after sentencing our put-upon proofreaders to a month of reading Brand Ecch, we gracefully (hah!) bestow upon you one handy-dandy No-Prize (not to be confused with a similar item available in the Negative Zone and known as a Yes-Prize). Happy hooligans and all that!

LOOKS LIKE YOU GOT YERSELF THE NUMBER ONE SPOT ON POINTY EARS HATE LIST, DOC--
--AN' HE'S MAD!

Dear Marvel,

SUPER-VILLAIN TEAM-UP #3 was great. As for the Sub-Mariner, he was great as a super-hero. I always enjoyed him in his own mag, battling *against* villains. He was just fantastic! As for the death of Betty Dean, it was a tragedy. First, it was the beautiful Lady Dorma, who I was a fan of, and now Betty Dean.

Attuma, Tiger Shark, and Dr. Dorcas are all great villains, but have Dr. Doom and Namor meet other baddies who want to rule the world. Like Diablo, Crimson Dynamo, Titanium Man, Radioactive Man, Fu Manchu, Loki, The Enchantress, and The Frightful Four.

Keep up the great work on this mag, and have it become monthly if possible. Return the Liberators in their own mag. Please think about it.

Wilson Rivera
89 Maujer Street
Brooklyn, NY 11206

Sure, Wil, sure—we'll think about it. But the way mags have been comin' and goin' here lately, don't ask us to actually *do* anything about it until we have a solid concensus of opinions from the much-beleagured but ever-buoyant Marveldom Assembled (and if you think that's a none-too-subtle hint for more feedback from you fans, take one collective step forward).

Tally ho!

MARVEL VALUE STAMP

CLIP 'EM AND COLLECT 'EM!

31: STAN (THE MAN) LEE from *Super-Villain Team-Up* no. 4 (February 1976).

JUNGLE RE-ACTIONS!

c/o MARVEL COMICS GROUP · 575 MADISON AVENUE · NEW YORK NY 10022

AN INITIAL REACTION TO INITIAL REACTIONS OF THE PANTHER VS. THE KLAN.

The first deluge of letters have come into our humble offices, concerning the new direction of our BLACK PANTHER series, and we feel many of them have been as stimulating as the story itself. We hope you won't shy away from us, people, 'cause your reactions and opinions are valued highly, and we'd like to see where many of you stand on our decidedly different format.

Dear People,

In JUNGLE ACTION #19 we begin a second Black Panther novel, entitled, "The Panther vs. The Klan." "Panther's Rage" was a novel about revolution—its motivations, its causes, its vehicles, its misuse and its effects on individuals, on a people and on a society. But now the setting has been changed and the very mood of the story has been altered noticeably. Gone is the lyricism, the romanticism of the lush, verdant, primitive (yet also modern) hidden world that is Wakanda. It has been replaced by the more contemporary setting of a small Georgian town. Yet there is a sort of romanticism pervading the story, that of a way of life which, as the story tells us, is slowly passing away. The lifestyle is one on which this nation was based and—to some degree, at least—as this lifestyle passes away, so do the ideals which form the foundation for this country.

Because of the change in setting a new cast of characters is needed. Tayette, Kazibe, Taku and Chandra would be out of place in this new setting.

Yet all that has transpired before has not been forgotten, the events have had an important effect on the people that participated in them.

The new characters introduced in "Blood and Sacrifices" are people striving to survive.

Kevin Trublood (an unlikely name, that) appears to be someone who believes in the dream that founded this country. But he not only believes, he acts! He fights for the ideals that he believes to be sacred, in the face of massive pressure and overwhelming force. Yet, in the mythic sense of the word, he is not a hero, for he is only a common man. When he punches someone, his hand hurts like any normal person's hand would.

Monica's parents are the last remnants of a form of life which will soon pass from the American scene. They are anachronisms, out of touch with the modern world. Yeah, but man, they're charming, they're kind, they're generous, they're sincere and they're the sort of people who are a pleasure to talk to.

Jessica Lynne is a woman who has taken care of people her entire life. Her sacrifices to her children and her husband have been bloodless for they have been sacrifices out of love.

Monica's father in his own way is also a beautiful person. He escapes into a fantasy of solitaire; yet, is solitaire so different from life? There are many ways to play both, but no matter which game you choose, you lose much more often than you win.

The setting, the characters, the tone and the mood of the series may have been changed, but the effort put into the book has not. One can almost sense the sacrifices made for this book. Oh yeah, maybe Billy's storytelling did fall down in a couple of places, but overall the artwork is enchanting. The dialogue sequence between Kevin, Monica and T'Challa on page 14 was incredibly well handled visually. Billy's interpetation of Monica's parents—and the entire sequence taking place in Monica's house, for that matter—really showed that Billy has a unique flair for portraying real people not often found in comic book art.

As you can see from the letter, I'm committed to this strip. Judging by the opening segment, "The Panther vs. the Klan" might be even more important than "Panther's Rage."

But, I just wanted to let you know that at least someone appreciates what you people are trying to do. So no matter what the obstacles, hang loose, and let your minds wander free, OK? Cause out here we really dig the journeys you take us on.

Mark Gasper
32-25 167 Street
Flushing, NY 11358

Well, this journey has just begun, and we think we have merely begun to define the perimeters of our new epic, Mark, so we're glad you're along for the ride.

By the way, if the *next* plotline for "The Panther Vs. The Klan" seems a bit weird even for Don, you can blame it on Dick Summer of WNBC radio. The Dauntless One studiously spread his research material out before him at about two in the a.m., and with all good intentions turned on the afore-mentioned Mr. Summer's nighttime show. A bit of quiet musical and lyrical insights wouldn't have been intrusive, while Don and the Panther sweated out the creative hours of that upcoming epic. But, instead of such tranquil fare, the sincere Mr. Summer had the Penthouse Pet of the Year on his show, answering phone calls from the audience at large. Don claims her voice was extremely sultry and seductive, and lured him from his diligent perusal of tomes concerning the Reconstruction Period of American History.

Don admits he was more than a bit daunted as he considered Miss Anneka's request for written profiles from her fans, and he claims he held a lengthy debate with himself (that would make Kevin Trublood appear terse) as to whether or not he should call Mr. Summer and tell him how distracting this was. We think he really wanted to talk to Anneka.

Anyhow, Don requested we print the above answer so that Peerless Production Chief John Verpoorten will understand if Don blows next issue's deadline.

You've got to admit, Big John, he keeps those excuses original.

But we don't buy it at all, Mr. Summer, since we feel the Dauntless One could have turned off the radio at any time.

And as Don replies, "Can a moth fly away from the flame? Huh? Can he?"

We don't think the question requires an answer.

NEXT ISSUE: "DEATH RIDERS ON THE HORIZON!" A new villain. His name? The SOUL-STRANGLER! And he rides a mission of death during the Reconstruction Period (which is 1867, or thereabouts, if Don has done his research correctly), but he is quickly due to cross paths with our Panther-Devil. That's it, Pantherites, the King of the Wakandas faces another diabolical death-trap, this time in the most bizarre place and time ever. And hang in there, gang, because Wind-Eagle is due to take flight...and it's a trip you aren't going to want to miss.

MARVEL VALUE STAMP

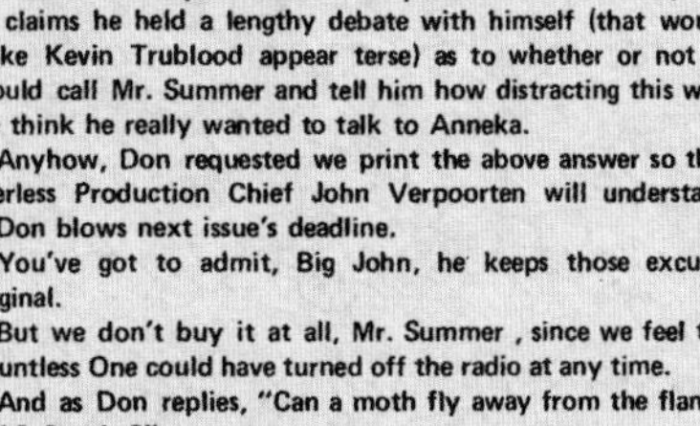

81: **STAN (THE MAN) LEE** from *Jungle Action* no. 21 (May 1976).

MIGHTY MARVEL ON THE MOVE !

MARVEL MARCHES ON!

MIGHTY MARVEL VALUE STAMP
POSTER EMPORIUM!
TO COMMEMORATE OUR SENSES-SHATTERING SECOND STAMP ALBUM, WE ARE OFFERING YOU SUPER-SPECIAL SAVINGS ON OUR ASTONISHINGLY ARTFUL POSTERS.
ONLY 50¢ EACH!
YOU HEARD US RIGHT, O FEARLESS FRONT FACER! IN APPRECIATION FOR ALL THE SUPPORT YOU'VE GIVEN US OVER, LO, THESE COUNTLESS YEARS, YOUR BULLPEN BUDDIES ARE GOING WILD WITH THE MOST SENSATIONAL SALE IN THE HISTORY OF POSTERDOM! IF YOU WANNA TALK ABOUT UNBELIEVABLE BARGAINS, HOW ABOUT THESE?
YOU CAN GET SPIDER-MAN BY JOHN ROMITA, CONAN THE BARBARIAN BY NEAL ADAMS, DRACULA BY NEAL ADAMS, THE INCREDIBLE HULK BY HERB TRIMPE, CAPTAIN AMERICA BY JOHN ROMITA, AND BRUCE LEE BY NEAL ADAMS. ADD WONDERMENT TO YOUR WALLS AND SOME EXCITEMENT TO YOUR EXISTENCE. BUT TAKE ADVANTAGE OF THIS SALE RIGHT NOW, PILGRIM--'CAUSE AT THESE PRICES, THEY'RE SURE TO SELL OUT!
THE INCREDIBLE HULK
THE AMAZING SPIDER-MAN
DEADLY HANDS KUNG FU
CAPTAIN AMERICA
THE SAVAGE SWORD CONAN
DRACULA
SEND ALL ORDERS TO: MIGHTY MARVEL POSTER SALE
MARVEL COMICS GROUP
575 MADISON AVENUE
NYC, N.Y. 10022
HOW CAN I PASS ON A DEAL LIKE THIS? I ENCLOSE* ____ IN CHECK OR MONEY ORDER FOR THE POSTERS CHECKED BELOW.
___ SPIDER-MAN ___ CONAN ___ DRACULA
___ THE HULK ___ CAPT. AMERICA ___ KUNG FU
NAME ___ AGE ___
ADDRESS ___
CITY ___ STATE ___ ZIP ___
*NEW YORK AND NEW JERSEY RESIDENTS PLEASE ADD SALES TAX.
A BULLPEN BARGAIN BONUS!
DON'T DELAY! ORDER TODAY!
SPECIAL STAMP BOOK BONUS
SEND IN YOUR FILLED STAMP BOOK AND GET ANY OF THE ABOVE POSTERS FOR ONLY 50¢ EACH (PLUS 25¢ FOR POSTAGE AND HANDLING).
P.S. YES, TRUE BELIEVER, WE'LL SEND YOUR BOOK BACK SO YOU CAN USE IT FOR OTHER STAMP BOOK SPECIALS!

Now, here's a specially-reserved space for some Marvel-boosting comic-art conventions to do their thing--!

NEW YORK COMIC ART CONVENTION	**SAN DIEGO COMIC BOOK CONVENTION**	**CONVENTION (OTHER)**

MVS BARGAINS OTHER THAN CONVENTIONS:

MVS DISCOUNT "A"	**MVS DISCOUNT "B"**	**MVS DISCOUNT "C"**
MVS DISCOUNT "D"	**MVS DISCOUNT "E"**	**MVS DISCOUNT "F"**

Time to start saving the NEXT nifty series of MV Stamps? To get another stampbook, send 50¢ to: MARVEL VALUE STAMPBOOK, c/o MARVEL COMICS, 575 Madison Avenue, NYC, 10022. 'Nuff Said!

MAGAZINE MGT. CO.
MERCHANDISING 9th FLOOR
575 MADISON AVENUE
NEW YORK, N. Y. 10022

THIRD CLASS MAIL

THE AMAZING SPIDER-MAN™

While attending a demonstration in radiology, high-school student PETER PARKER was bitten by a spider which had accidentally been exposed to RADIOACTIVE RAYS. Through a miracle of science, Peter soon found that he had GAINED the spider's powers...and had, in effect, become a human spider... Spider-man!

FANTASTIC FOUR

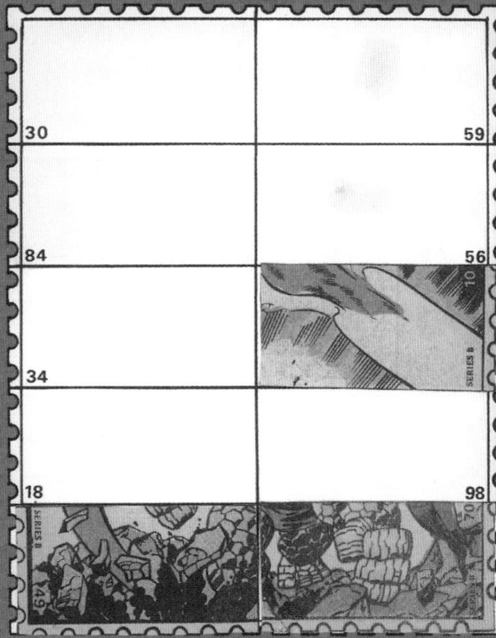

A brilliant scientist— his best friend— the woman he loves— and her fiery-tempered kid brother! Together, they braved the unknown terrors of outer space, and were changed by cosmic rays into something more than merely human!

MR. FANTASTIC! THE THING! THE INVISIBLE GIRL! THE HUMAN TORCH! Now they are the FANTASTIC FOUR—and the world will never again be the same!

THE INCREDIBLE HULK™

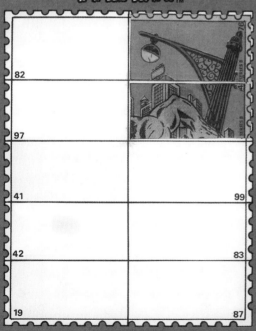

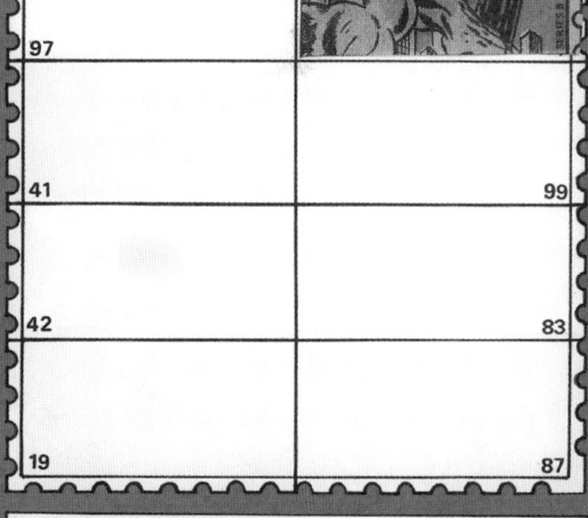

Dr. Bruce Banner was a scientist engaged in the study of radiation and its effects on man; until one fateful day, while attempting to save the life of a young trespasser, he was bombarded with energy from an exploding **Gamma Ray Bomb**. The tremendous force changed Dr. Banner from a mere man into the awesome green-skinned behemoth known as... **The Incredible Hulk!**

THE SILVER SURFER™

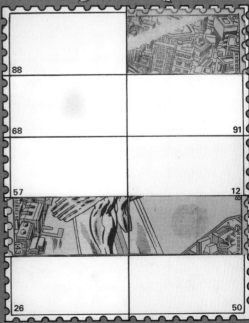

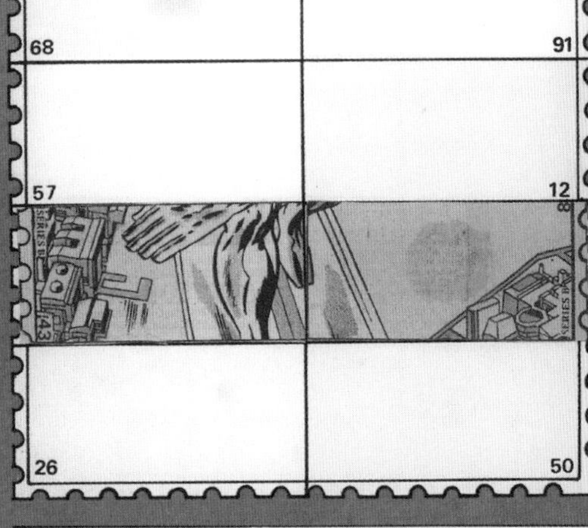

There was nothing left for the people of Zenn-La to discover. War, poverty, disease... all had long since been conquered on this wondrous world and **Norrin Radd** was bored! So, when he was offered the chance to take on the life of herald to the planet-devouring **Galactus** in exchange for the life of his homeworld, he accepted. Thus he became the sentinel of the spaceways... **the Silver Surfer!**

CONAN THE BARBARIAN™

60 86

78 65 44

"Know, O prince, that between the years when the oceans drank Atlantis and the gleaming cities, and the rise of the sons of Aryas, there was an Age undreamed of.

Hither came Conan, the Cimmerian, black-haired, sullen-eyed, sword in hand, a thief, a reaver, a slayer, with gigantic melancholies and gigantic mirth, to tread the jeweled thrones of the Earth under his sandaled feet."

DRACULA™

27

85 33

77 48

96 54

61

Hidden in the shadows where legend and reality merge, there are tales of a being who has lived more than five hundred years! They say he is a creature born not on Earth, but in the deepest bowels of hell itself. They say he thrives upon the blood of innocents, that he is the King of Darkness... the *Prince of Evil*, and that even the bravest man quakes in fear at the meerest mention of his name... COUNT DRACULA!

THE MIGHTY THOR™

16

39 32

47 55

21 72

62 20

Until a vacation in Norway, Dr. Donald Blake was no more than an average, mortal man... or so he thought. While exploring the Norwegian backwoods, Dr. Blake accidentally stumbled upon a gnarled stick which in reality was the mystical Mjolnir, the powerful "Uru Hammer" of Norse Mythology. From the moment the lame doctor first tapped the stick on the ground, he was restored forever and always to his true identity as the master of nature and the elements, the *God of Thunder*— The Mighty Thor!

DR. STRANGE
MASTER OF THE MYSTIC ARTS

66 35

23

95

45 73

Once he was a man like most others–– a worldly man, seduced and jaded by material things. But then he discovered the separate reality, where sorcery and men's souls shaped the forces that shape our lives. In that instant, he was born again, to become a man like no other–– a man who had left us behind, as he strove to stand against the unseen subtle perils hovering thick and black around our fragile existence...and so began the mystic majesty of... DR. STRANGE!